THE INTELLIGENT INVESTOR
Revised Edition

Through chances various, through all
vicissitudes, we make our way. . . .

Aeneid

THE INTELLIGENT INVESTOR

A BOOK OF PRACTICAL COUNSEL

REVISED EDITION

BENJAMIN GRAHAM

Updated with New Commentary by Jason Zweig

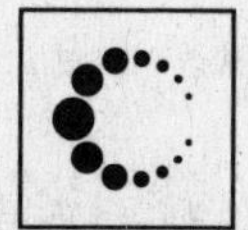

COLLINS BUSINESS

An Imprint of HarperCollins*Publishers*

To E.M.G.

Grateful acknowledgment is made for permission to reprint:

"The Superinvestors of Graham-and-Doddsville," by Warren E. Buffett, from the Fall 1984 issue of *Hermes,* Magazine of Columbia Business School. Reprinted by permission of *Hermes,* Magazines of Columbia Business School, copyright © 1984 The Trustees of Columbia University and Warren E. Buffett.

"Benjamin Graham," by Warren E. Buffett, from the November/December 1976 issue of *Financial Analyst Journal.* Reprinted by permission of Financial Analysts Federation.

First Collins Business Essentials edition 2006.

HarperCollins books may be purchased for educational, business, or sales promotional use. For information, please write to: Special Markets Department, HarperCollins Publishers, 10 East 53rd Street, New York, New York 10022.

Designed by Nancy Singer Olaguera

Library of Congress Cataloging-in-Publication Data

Graham, Benjamin, 1894–1976
The intelligent investor / Benjamin Graham.—Rev. ed./updated with new commentary by Jason Zweig.
p. cm.
Includes bibliographical references and index.
ISBN-10: 0-06-055566-1 (pbk.)
ISBN-13: 978-0-06-055566-5 (pbk.)
1. Securities. 2. Investments. I. Zweig, Jason. II. Title.
HG4521.G665 2003
332.67'8—dc21 2003047894

09 ❖/RRD 40 39 38 37

Contents

The text reproduced here is the Fourth Revised Edition, updated by Graham in 1971–1972 and initially published in 1973. Please be advised that the text of Graham's original footnotes (designated in his chapters with superscript numerals) can be found in the Endnotes section beginning on p. 579. The new footnotes that Jason Zweig has introduced appear at the bottom of Graham's pages (and, in the typeface used here, as occasional additions to Graham's endnotes).

Preface to the Fourth Edition, by Warren E. Buffett

I read the first edition of this book early in 1950, when I was nineteen. I thought then that it was by far the best book about investing ever written. I still think it is.

To invest successfully over a lifetime does not require a stratospheric IQ, unusual business insights, or inside information. What's needed is a sound intellectual framework for making decisions and the ability to keep emotions from corroding that framework. This book precisely and clearly prescribes the proper framework. You must supply the emotional discipline.

If you follow the behavioral and business principles that Graham advocates—and if you pay special attention to the invaluable advice in Chapters 8 and 20—you will not get a poor result from your investments. (That represents more of an accomplishment than you might think.) Whether you achieve outstanding results will depend on the effort and intellect you apply to your investments, as well as on the amplitudes of stock-market folly that prevail during your investing career. The sillier the market's behavior, the greater the opportunity for the business-like investor. Follow Graham and you will profit from folly rather than participate in it.

To me, Ben Graham was far more than an author or a teacher. More than any other man except my father, he influenced my life. Shortly after Ben's death in 1976, I wrote the following short remembrance about him in the *Financial Analysts Journal*. As you read the book, I believe you'll perceive some of the qualities I mentioned in this tribute.

BENJAMIN GRAHAM
1894–1976

Several years ago Ben Graham, then almost eighty, expressed to a friend the thought that he hoped every day to do "something foolish, something creative and something generous."

The inclusion of that first whimsical goal reflected his knack for packaging ideas in a form that avoided any overtones of sermonizing or self-importance. Although his ideas were powerful, their delivery was unfailingly gentle.

Readers of this magazine need no elaboration of his achievements as measured by the standard of creativity. It is rare that the founder of a discipline does not find his work eclipsed in rather short order by successors. But over forty years after publication of the book that brought structure and logic to a disorderly and confused activity, it is difficult to think of possible candidates for even the runner-up position in the field of security analysis. In an area where much looks foolish within weeks or months after publication, Ben's principles have remained sound—their value often enhanced and better understood in the wake of financial storms that demolished flimsier intellectual structures. His counsel of soundness brought unfailing rewards to his followers—even to those with natural abilities inferior to more gifted practitioners who stumbled while following counsels of brilliance or fashion.

A remarkable aspect of Ben's dominance of his professional field was that he achieved it without that narrowness of mental activity that concentrates all effort on a single end. It was, rather, the incidental by-product of an intellect whose breadth almost exceeded definition. Certainly I have never met anyone with a mind of similar scope. Virtually total recall, unending fascination with new knowledge, and an ability to recast it in a form applicable to seemingly unrelated problems made exposure to his thinking in any field a delight.

But his third imperative—generosity—was where he succeeded beyond all others. I knew Ben as my teacher, my employer, and my friend. In each relationship—just as with all his students, employees, and friends—there was an absolutely open-ended, no-scores-kept generosity of ideas, time, and spirit. If clarity of thinking was required, there was no better place to go. And if encouragement or counsel was needed, Ben was there.

Walter Lippmann spoke of men who plant trees that other men will sit under. Ben Graham was such a man.

Reprinted from the *Financial Analysts Journal*, November/December 1976.

A Note About Benjamin Graham by Jason Zweig

Who was Benjamin Graham, and why should you listen to him?

Graham was not only one of the best investors who ever lived; he was also the greatest practical investment thinker of all time. Before Graham, money managers behaved much like a medieval guild, guided largely by superstition, guesswork, and arcane rituals. Graham's *Security Analysis* was the textbook that transformed this musty circle into a modern profession.[1]

And *The Intelligent Investor* is the first book ever to describe, for individual investors, the emotional framework and analytical tools that are essential to financial success. It remains the single best book on investing ever written for the general public. *The Intelligent Investor* was the first book I read when I joined *Forbes* Magazine as a cub reporter in 1987, and I was struck by Graham's certainty that, sooner or later, all bull markets must end badly. That October, U.S. stocks suffered their worst one-day crash in history, and I was hooked. (Today, after the wild bull market of the late 1990s and the brutal bear market that began in early 2000, *The Intelligent Investor* reads more prophetically than ever.)

Graham came by his insights the hard way: by feeling firsthand the anguish of financial loss and by studying for decades the history and psychology of the markets. He was born Benjamin Grossbaum on May 9, 1894, in London; his father was a dealer in china dishes and figurines.[2] The family moved to New York when Ben was a year old. At first they lived the good life–with a maid, a cook, and a French gov-

---

[1] Coauthored with David Dodd and first published in 1934.

[2] The Grossbaums changed their name to Graham during World War I, when German-sounding names were regarded with suspicion.

erness–on upper Fifth Avenue. But Ben's father died in 1903, the porcelain business faltered, and the family slid haltingly into poverty. Ben's mother turned their home into a boardinghouse; then, borrowing money to trade stocks "on margin," she was wiped out in the crash of 1907. For the rest of his life, Ben would recall the humiliation of cashing a check for his mother and hearing the bank teller ask, "Is Dorothy Grossbaum good for five dollars?"

Fortunately, Graham won a scholarship at Columbia, where his brilliance burst into full flower. He graduated in 1914, second in his class. Before the end of Graham's final semester, three departments–English, philosophy, and mathematics–asked him to join the faculty. He was all of 20 years old.

Instead of academia, Graham decided to give Wall Street a shot. He started as a clerk at a bond-trading firm, soon became an analyst, then a partner, and before long was running his own investment partnership.

The Internet boom and bust would not have surprised Graham. In April 1919, he earned a 250% return on the first day of trading for Savold Tire, a new offering in the booming automotive business; by October, the company had been exposed as a fraud and the stock was worthless.

Graham became a master at researching stocks in microscopic, almost molecular, detail. In 1925, plowing through the obscure reports filed by oil pipelines with the U.S. Interstate Commerce Commission, he learned that Northern Pipe Line Co.–then trading at $65 per share–held at least $80 per share in high-quality bonds. (He bought the stock, pestered its managers into raising the dividend, and came away with $110 per share three years later.)

Despite a harrowing loss of nearly 70% during the Great Crash of 1929–1932, Graham survived and thrived in its aftermath, harvesting bargains from the wreckage of the bull market. There is no exact record of Graham's earliest returns, but from 1936 until he retired in 1956, his Graham-Newman Corp. gained at least 14.7% annually, versus 12.2% for the stock market as a whole–one of the best long-term track records on Wall Street history.[3]

---

[3] Graham-Newman Corp. was an open-end mutual fund (see Chapter 9) that Graham ran in partnership with Jerome Newman, a skilled investor in his own right. For much of its history, the fund was closed to new investors. I am

How did Graham do it? Combining his extraordinary intellectual powers with profound common sense and vast experience, Graham developed his core principles, which are at least as valid today as they were during his lifetime:

- A stock is not just a ticker symbol or an electronic blip; it is an ownership interest in an actual business, with an underlying value that does not depend on its share price.
- The market is a pendulum that forever swings between unsustainable optimism (which makes stocks too expensive) and unjustified pessimism (which makes them too cheap). The intelligent investor is a realist who sells to optimists and buys from pessimists.
- The future value of every investment is a function of its present price. The higher the price you pay, the lower your return will be.
- No matter how careful you are, the one risk no investor can ever eliminate is the risk of being wrong. Only by insisting on what Graham called the "margin of safety"—never overpaying, no matter how exciting an investment seems to be—can you minimize your odds of error.
- The secret to your financial success is inside yourself. If you become a critical thinker who takes no Wall Street "fact" on faith, and you invest with patient confidence, you can take steady advantage of even the worst bear markets. By developing your discipline and courage, you can refuse to let other people's mood swings govern your financial destiny. In the end, how your investments behave is much less important than how you behave.

The goal of this revised edition of *The Intelligent Investor* is to apply Graham's ideas to today's financial markets while leaving his text entirely intact (with the exception of footnotes for clarification).[4] After each of Graham's chapters you'll find a new commentary. In these reader's guides, I've added recent examples that should show you just how relevant—and how liberating—Graham's principles remain today.

---

grateful to Walter Schloss for providing data essential to estimating Graham-Newman's returns. The 20% annual average return that Graham cites in his Postscript (p. 532) appears not to take management fees into account.

[4] The text reproduced here is the Fourth Revised Edition, updated by Graham in 1971–1972 and initially published in 1973.

I envy you the excitement and enlightenment of reading Graham's masterpiece for the first time—or even the third or fourth time. Like all classics, it alters how we view the world and renews itself by educating us. And the more you read it, the better it gets. With Graham as your guide, you are guaranteed to become a vastly more intelligent investor.

INTRODUCTION:

What This Book Expects to Accomplish

The purpose of this book is to supply, in a form suitable for laymen, guidance in the adoption and execution of an investment policy. Comparatively little will be said here about the technique of analyzing securities; attention will be paid chiefly to investment principles and investors' attitudes. We shall, however, provide a number of condensed comparisons of specific securities—chiefly in pairs appearing side by side in the New York Stock Exchange list—in order to bring home in concrete fashion the important elements involved in specific choices of common stocks.

But much of our space will be devoted to the historical patterns of financial markets, in some cases running back over many decades. To invest intelligently in securities one should be forearmed with an adequate knowledge of how the various types of bonds and stocks have actually behaved under varying conditions—some of which, at least, one is likely to meet again in one's own experience. No statement is more true and better applicable to Wall Street than the famous warning of Santayana: "Those who do not remember the past are condemned to repeat it."

Our text is directed to investors as distinguished from speculators, and our first task will be to clarify and emphasize this now all but forgotten distinction. We may say at the outset that this is not a "how to make a million" book. There are no sure and easy paths to riches on Wall Street or anywhere else. It may be well to point up what we have just said by a bit of financial history—especially since there is more than one moral to be drawn from it. In the climactic year 1929 John J. Raskob, a most important figure nationally as well as on Wall Street, extolled the blessings of capitalism in an article in the *Ladies' Home Journal*, entitled "Everybody Ought to Be

Rich."* His thesis was that savings of only $15 per month invested in good common stocks—with dividends reinvested—would produce an estate of $80,000 in twenty years against total contributions of only $3,600. If the General Motors tycoon was right, this was indeed a simple road to riches. How nearly right was he? Our rough calculation—based on assumed investment in the 30 stocks making up the Dow Jones Industrial Average (DJIA)—indicates that if Raskob's prescription had been followed during 1929–1948, the investor's holdings at the beginning of 1949 would have been worth about $8,500. This is a far cry from the great man's promise of $80,000, and it shows how little reliance can be placed on such optimistic forecasts and assurances. But, as an aside, we should remark that the return actually realized by the 20-year operation would have been better than 8% compounded annually—and this despite the fact that the investor would have begun his purchases with the DJIA at 300 and ended with a valuation based on the 1948 closing level of 177. This record may be regarded as a persuasive argument for the principle of regular monthly purchases of strong common stocks through thick and thin—a program known as "dollar-cost averaging."

Since our book is not addressed to speculators, it is not meant for those who trade in the market. Most of these people are guided by charts or other largely mechanical means of determining the right moments to buy and sell. The one principle that applies to nearly all these so-called "technical approaches" is that one should buy *because* a stock or the market has gone up and one should sell *because* it has declined. This is the exact opposite of sound business sense everywhere else, and it is most unlikely that it can lead to

---

* Raskob (1879–1950) was a director of Du Pont, the giant chemical company, and chairman of the finance committee at General Motors. He also served as national chairman of the Democratic Party and was the driving force behind the construction of the Empire State Building. Calculations by finance professor Jeremy Siegel confirm that Raskob's plan would have grown to just under $9,000 after 20 years, although inflation would have eaten away much of that gain. For the best recent look at Raskob's views on long-term stock investing, see the essay by financial adviser William Bernstein at www.efficientfrontier.com/ef/197/raskob.htm.

lasting success on Wall Street. In our own stock-market experience and observation, extending over 50 years, we have not known a single person who has consistently or lastingly made money by thus "following the market." We do not hesitate to declare that this approach is as fallacious as it is popular. We shall illustrate what we have just said—though, of course this should not be taken as proof—by a later brief discussion of the famous Dow theory for trading in the stock market.*

Since its first publication in 1949, revisions of *The Intelligent Investor* have appeared at intervals of approximately five years. In updating the current version we shall have to deal with quite a number of new developments since the 1965 edition was written. These include:

1. An unprecedented advance in the interest rate on high-grade bonds.
2. A fall of about 35% in the price level of leading common stocks, ending in May 1970. This was the highest percentage decline in some 30 years. (Countless issues of lower quality had a much larger shrinkage.)
3. A persistent inflation of wholesale and consumer's prices, which gained momentum even in the face of a decline of general business in 1970.
4. The rapid development of "conglomerate" companies, franchise operations, and other relative novelties in business and finance. (These include a number of tricky devices such as "letter stock,"[1] proliferation of stock-option warrants, misleading names, use of foreign banks, and others.)†

---

* Graham's "brief discussion" is in two parts, on p. 33 and pp. 191–192. For more detail on the Dow Theory, see http://viking.som.yale.edu/will/dow/dowpage.html.

† Mutual funds bought "letter stock" in private transactions, then immediately revalued these shares at a higher public price (see Graham's definition on p. 579). That enabled these "go-go" funds to report unsustainably high returns in the mid-1960s. The U.S. Securities and Exchange Commission cracked down on this abuse in 1969, and it is no longer a concern for fund investors. Stock-option warrants are explained in Chapter 16.

5. Bankruptcy of our largest railroad, excessive short- and long-term debt of many formerly strongly entrenched companies, and even a disturbing problem of solvency among Wall Street houses.*
6. The advent of the "performance" vogue in the management of investment funds, including some bank-operated trust funds, with disquieting results.

These phenomena will have our careful consideration, and some will require changes in conclusions and emphasis from our previous edition. The underlying principles of sound investment should not alter from decade to decade, but the application of these principles must be adapted to significant changes in the financial mechanisms and climate.

The last statement was put to the test during the writing of the present edition, the first draft of which was finished in January 1971. At that time the DJIA was in a strong recovery from its 1970 low of 632 and was advancing toward a 1971 high of 951, with attendant general optimism. As the last draft was finished, in November 1971, the market was in the throes of a new decline, carrying it down to 797 with a renewed general uneasiness about its future. We have not allowed these fluctuations to affect our general attitude toward sound investment policy, which remains substantially unchanged since the first edition of this book in 1949.

The extent of the market's shrinkage in 1969–70 should have served to dispel an illusion that had been gaining ground during the past two decades. This was that leading common stocks could be bought at any time and at any price, with the assurance not only of ultimate profit but also that any intervening loss would soon be recouped by a renewed advance of the market to new high lev-

* The Penn Central Transportation Co., then the biggest railroad in the United States, sought bankruptcy protection on June 21, 1970–shocking investors, who had never expected such a giant company to go under (see p. 423). Among the companies with "excessive" debt Graham had in mind were Ling-Temco-Vought and National General Corp. (see pp. 425 and 463). The "problem of solvency" on Wall Street emerged between 1968 and 1971, when several prestigious brokerages suddenly went bust.

els. That was too good to be true. At long last the stock market has "returned to normal," in the sense that both speculators and stock investors must again be prepared to experience significant and perhaps protracted falls as well as rises in the value of their holdings.

In the area of many secondary and third-line common stocks, especially recently floated enterprises, the havoc wrought by the last market break was catastrophic. This was nothing new in itself—it had happened to a similar degree in 1961–62—but there was now a novel element in the fact that some of the investment funds had large commitments in highly speculative and obviously overvalued issues of this type. Evidently it is not only the tyro who needs to be warned that while enthusiasm may be necessary for great accomplishments elsewhere, on Wall Street it almost invariably leads to disaster.

The major question we shall have to deal with grows out of the huge rise in the rate of interest on first-quality bonds. Since late 1967 the investor has been able to obtain more than twice as much income from such bonds as he could from dividends on representative common stocks. At the beginning of 1972 the return was 7.19% on highest-grade bonds versus only 2.76% on industrial stocks. (This compares with 4.40% and 2.92% respectively at the end of 1964.) It is hard to realize that when we first wrote this book in 1949 the figures were almost the exact opposite: the bonds returned only 2.66% and the stocks yielded 6.82%.[2] In previous editions we have consistently urged that at least 25% of the conservative investor's portfolio be held in common stocks, and we have favored in general a 50–50 division between the two media. We must now consider whether the current great advantage of bond yields over stock yields would justify an all-bond policy until a more sensible relationship returns, as we expect it will. Naturally the question of continued inflation will be of great importance in reaching our decision here. A chapter will be devoted to this discussion.*

---

* See Chapter 2. As of the beginning of 2003, U.S. Treasury bonds maturing in 10 years yielded 3.8%, while stocks (as measured by the Dow Jones Industrial Average) yielded 1.9%. (Note that this relationship is not all that different from the 1964 figures that Graham cites.) The income generated by top-quality bonds has been falling steadily since 1981.

In the past we have made a basic distinction between two kinds of investors to whom this book was addressed—the "defensive" and the "enterprising." The defensive (or passive) investor will place his chief emphasis on the avoidance of serious mistakes or losses. His second aim will be freedom from effort, annoyance, and the need for making frequent decisions. The determining trait of the enterprising (or active, or aggressive) investor is his willingness to devote time and care to the selection of securities that are both sound and more attractive than the average. Over many decades an enterprising investor of this sort could expect a worthwhile reward for his extra skill and effort, in the form of a better average return than that realized by the passive investor. We have some doubt whether a really substantial extra recompense is promised to the active investor under today's conditions. But next year or the years after may well be different. We shall accordingly continue to devote attention to the possibilities for enterprising investment, as they existed in former periods and may return.

It has long been the prevalent view that the art of successful investment lies first in the choice of those industries that are most likely to grow in the future and then in identifying the most promising companies in these industries. For example, smart investors—or their smart advisers—would long ago have recognized the great growth possibilities of the computer industry as a whole and of International Business Machines in particular. And similarly for a number of other growth industries and growth companies. But this is not as easy as it always looks in retrospect. To bring this point home at the outset let us add here a paragraph that we included first in the 1949 edition of this book.

> Such an investor may for example be a buyer of air-transport stocks because he believes their future is even more brilliant than the trend the market already reflects. For this class of investor the value of our book will lie more in its warnings against the pitfalls lurking in this favorite investment approach than in any positive technique that will help him along his path.*

---

* "Air-transport stocks," of course, generated as much excitement in the late 1940s and early 1950s as Internet stocks did a half century later. Among the hottest mutual funds of that era were Aeronautical Securities and the

The pitfalls have proved particularly dangerous in the industry we mentioned. It was, of course, easy to forecast that the volume of air traffic would grow spectacularly over the years. Because of this factor their shares became a favorite choice of the investment funds. But despite the expansion of revenues—at a pace even greater than in the computer industry—a combination of technological problems and overexpansion of capacity made for fluctuating and even disastrous profit figures. In the year 1970, despite a new high in traffic figures, the airlines sustained a loss of some $200 million for their shareholders. (They had shown losses also in 1945 and 1961.) The stocks of these companies once again showed a greater decline in 1969–70 than did the general market. The record shows that even the highly paid full-time experts of the mutual funds were completely wrong about the fairly short-term future of a major and nonesoteric industry.

On the other hand, while the investment funds had substantial investments and substantial gains in IBM, the combination of its apparently high price and the impossibility of being *certain* about its rate of growth prevented them from having more than, say, 3% of their funds in this wonderful performer. Hence the effect of this excellent choice on their overall results was by no means decisive. Furthermore, many—if not most—of their investments in computer-industry companies other than IBM appear to have been unprofitable. From these two broad examples we draw two morals for our readers:

1. Obvious prospects for physical growth in a business do not translate into obvious profits for investors.
2. The experts do not have dependable ways of selecting and concentrating on the most promising companies in the most promising industries.

Missiles-Rockets-Jets & Automation Fund. They, like the stocks they owned, turned out to be an investing disaster. It is commonly accepted today that the cumulative earnings of the airline industry over its entire history have been negative. The lesson Graham is driving at is not that you should avoid buying airline stocks, but that you should never succumb to the "certainty" that any industry will outperform all others in the future.

The author did not follow this approach in his financial career as fund manager, and he cannot offer either specific counsel or much encouragement to those who may wish to try it.

What then will we aim to accomplish in this book? Our main objective will be to guide the reader against the areas of possible substantial error and to develop policies with which he will be comfortable. We shall say quite a bit about the psychology of investors. For indeed, the investor's chief problem—and even his worst enemy—is likely to be himself. ("The fault, dear investor, is not in our stars—and not in our stocks—but in ourselves. . . .") This has proved the more true over recent decades as it has become more necessary for conservative investors to acquire common stocks and thus to expose themselves, willy-nilly, to the excitement and the temptations of the stock market. By arguments, examples, and exhortation, we hope to aid our readers to establish the proper mental and emotional attitudes toward their investment decisions. We have seen much more money made and *kept* by "ordinary people" who were temperamentally well suited for the investment process than by those who lacked this quality, even though they had an extensive knowledge of finance, accounting, and stock-market lore.

Additionally, we hope to implant in the reader a tendency to measure or quantify. For 99 issues out of 100 we could say that at some price they are cheap enough to buy and at some other price they would be so dear that they should be sold. The habit of relating what is paid to what is being offered is an invaluable trait in investment. In an article in a women's magazine many years ago we advised the readers to buy their stocks as they bought their groceries, not as they bought their perfume. The really dreadful losses of the past few years (and on many similar occasions before) were realized in those common-stock issues where the buyer forgot to ask "How much?"

In June 1970 the question "How much?" could be answered by the magic figure 9.40%—the yield obtainable on new offerings of high-grade public-utility bonds. This has now dropped to about 7.3%, but even that return tempts us to ask, "Why give any other answer?" But there are other possible answers, and these must be carefully considered. Besides which, we repeat that both we and our readers must be prepared in advance for the possibly quite different conditions of, say, 1973–1977.

We shall therefore present in some detail a positive program for common-stock investment, part of which is within the purview of both classes of investors and part is intended mainly for the enterprising group. Strangely enough, we shall suggest as one of our chief requirements here that our readers limit themselves to issues selling not far above their tangible-asset value.* The reason for this seemingly outmoded counsel is both practical and psychological. Experience has taught us that, while there are many good growth companies worth several times net assets, the buyer of such shares will be too dependent on the vagaries and fluctuations of the stock market. By contrast, the investor in shares, say, of public-utility companies at about their net-asset value can always consider himself the owner of an interest in sound and expanding businesses, acquired at a rational price—regardless of what the stock market might say to the contrary. The ultimate result of such a conservative policy is likely to work out better than exciting adventures into the glamorous and dangerous fields of anticipated growth.

The art of investment has one characteristic that is not generally appreciated. A creditable, if unspectacular, result can be achieved by the lay investor with a minimum of effort and capability; but to improve this easily attainable standard requires much application and more than a trace of wisdom. If you merely try to bring *just a little* extra knowledge and cleverness to bear upon your investment program, instead of realizing a little better than normal results, you may well find that you have done worse.

Since anyone—by just buying and holding a representative list—can equal the performance of the market averages, it would seem a comparatively simple matter to "beat the averages"; but as a matter of fact the proportion of smart people who try this and fail is surprisingly large. Even the majority of the investment funds, with all their experienced personnel, have not performed so well

---

* Tangible assets include a company's physical property (like real estate, factories, equipment, and inventories) as well as its financial balances (such as cash, short-term investments, and accounts receivable). Among the elements not included in tangible assets are brands, copyrights, patents, franchises, goodwill, and trademarks. To see how to calculate tangible-asset value, see footnote † on p. 198.

over the years as has the general market. Allied to the foregoing is the record of the published stock-market predictions of the brokerage houses, for there is strong evidence that their calculated forecasts have been somewhat less reliable than the simple tossing of a coin.

In writing this book we have tried to keep this basic pitfall of investment in mind. The virtues of a simple portfolio policy have been emphasized—the purchase of high-grade bonds plus a diversified list of leading common stocks—which any investor can carry out with a little expert assistance. The adventure beyond this safe and sound territory has been presented as fraught with challenging difficulties, especially in the area of temperament. Before attempting such a venture the investor should feel sure of himself and of his advisers—particularly as to whether they have a clear concept of the differences between investment and speculation and between market price and underlying value.

A strong-minded approach to investment, firmly based on the margin-of-safety principle, can yield handsome rewards. But a decision to try for these emoluments rather than for the assured fruits of defensive investment should not be made without much self-examination.

A final retrospective thought. When the young author entered Wall Street in June 1914 no one had any inkling of what the next half-century had in store. (The stock market did not even suspect that a World War was to break out in two months, and close down the New York Stock Exchange.) Now, in 1972, we find ourselves the richest and most powerful country on earth, but beset by all sorts of major problems and more apprehensive than confident of the future. Yet if we confine our attention to American investment experience, there is some comfort to be gleaned from the last 57 years. Through all their vicissitudes and casualties, as earth-shaking as they were unforeseen, it remained true that sound investment principles produced generally sound results. We must act on the assumption that they will continue to do so.

Note to the Reader: This book does not address itself to the *overall* financial policy of savers and investors; it deals only with that portion of their funds which they are prepared to place in marketable (or redeemable) securities, that is, in bonds and stocks.

Consequently we do not discuss such important media as savings and time desposits, savings-and-loan-association accounts, life insurance, annuities, and real-estate mortgages or equity ownership. The reader should bear in mind that when he finds the word "now," or the equivalent, in the text, it refers to late 1971 or early 1972.

COMMENTARY ON THE INTRODUCTION

If you have built castles in the air, your work need not be lost; that is where they should be. Now put the foundations under them.

–*Henry David Thoreau,* Walden

Notice that Graham announces from the start that this book will not tell you how to beat the market. No truthful book can.

Instead, this book will teach you three powerful lessons:

- how you can minimize the odds of suffering irreversible losses;
- how you can maximize the chances of achieving sustainable gains;
- how you can control the self-defeating behavior that keeps most investors from reaching their full potential.

Back in the boom years of the late 1990s, when technology stocks seemed to be doubling in value every day, the notion that you could lose almost all your money seemed absurd. But, by the end of 2002, many of the dot-com and telecom stocks had lost 95% of their value or more. Once you lose 95% of your money, you have to gain 1,900% *just to get back to where you started.*[1] Taking a foolish risk can put you so deep in the hole that it's virtually impossible to get out. That's why Graham constantly emphasizes the importance of avoiding losses–not just in Chapters 6, 14, and 20, but in the threads of warning that he has woven throughout his entire text.

But no matter how careful you are, the price of your investments *will* go down from time to time. While no one can eliminate that risk,

[1] To put this statement in perspective, consider how often you are likely to buy a stock at $30 and be able to sell it at $600.

Graham will show you how to manage it—and how to get your fears under control.

ARE YOU AN INTELLIGENT INVESTOR?

Now let's answer a vitally important question. What exactly does Graham mean by an "intelligent" investor? Back in the first edition of this book, Graham defines the term—and he makes it clear that this kind of intelligence has nothing to do with IQ or SAT scores. It simply means being patient, disciplined, and eager to learn; you must also be able to harness your emotions and think for yourself. This kind of intelligence, explains Graham, "is a trait more of the character than of the brain."[2]

There's proof that high IQ and higher education are not enough to make an investor intelligent. In 1998, Long-Term Capital Management L.P., a hedge fund run by a battalion of mathematicians, computer scientists, and two Nobel Prize–winning economists, lost more than $2 billion in a matter of weeks on a huge bet that the bond market would return to "normal." But the bond market kept right on becoming more and more abnormal—and LTCM had borrowed so much money that its collapse nearly capsized the global financial system.[3]

And back in the spring of 1720, Sir Isaac Newton owned shares in the South Sea Company, the hottest stock in England. Sensing that the market was getting out of hand, the great physicist muttered that he "could calculate the motions of the heavenly bodies, but not the madness of the people." Newton dumped his South Sea shares, pocketing a 100% profit totaling £7,000. But just months later, swept up in the wild enthusiasm of the market, Newton jumped back in at a much higher price—and lost £20,000 (or more than $3 million in today's money). For the rest of his life, he forbade anyone to speak the words "South Sea" in his presence.[4]

---

[2] Benjamin Graham, *The Intelligent Investor* (Harper & Row, 1949), p. 4.

[3] A "hedge fund" is a pool of money, largely unregulated by the government, invested aggressively for wealthy clients. For a superb telling of the LTCM story, see Roger Lowenstein, *When Genius Failed* (Random House, 2000).

[4] John Carswell, *The South Sea Bubble* (Cresset Press, London, 1960), pp. 131, 199. Also see www.harvard-magazine.com/issues/mj99/damnd.html.

Sir Isaac Newton was one of the most intelligent people who ever lived, as most of us would define intelligence. But, in Graham's terms, Newton was far from an intelligent investor. By letting the roar of the crowd override his own judgment, the world's greatest scientist acted like a fool.

In short, if you've failed at investing so far, it's not because you're stupid. It's because, like Sir Isaac Newton, you haven't developed the emotional discipline that successful investing requires. In Chapter 8, Graham describes how to enhance your intelligence by harnessing your emotions and refusing to stoop to the market's level of irrationality. There you can master his lesson that being an intelligent investor is more a matter of "character" than "brain."

A CHRONICLE OF CALAMITY

Now let's take a moment to look at some of the major financial developments of the past few years:

1. The worst market crash since the Great Depression, with U.S. stocks losing 50.2% of their value–or *$7.4 trillion*–between March 2000 and October 2002.
2. Far deeper drops in the share prices of the hottest companies of the 1990s, including AOL, Cisco, JDS Uniphase, Lucent, and Qualcomm–plus the utter destruction of hundreds of Internet stocks.
3. Accusations of massive financial fraud at some of the largest and most respected corporations in America, including Enron, Tyco, and Xerox.
4. The bankruptcies of such once-glistening companies as Conseco, Global Crossing, and WorldCom.
5. Allegations that accounting firms cooked the books, and even destroyed records, to help their clients mislead the investing public.
6. Charges that top executives at leading companies siphoned off hundreds of millions of dollars for their own personal gain.
7. Proof that security analysts on Wall Street praised stocks publicly but admitted privately that they were garbage.
8. A stock market that, even after its bloodcurdling decline, seems overvalued by historical measures, suggesting to many experts that stocks have further yet to fall.

9. A relentless decline in interest rates that has left investors with no attractive alternative to stocks.
10. An investing environment bristling with the unpredictable menace of global terrorism and war in the Middle East.

Much of this damage could have been (and was!) avoided by investors who learned and lived by Graham's principles. As Graham puts it, "while enthusiasm may be necessary for great accomplishments elsewhere, on Wall Street it almost invariably leads to disaster." By letting themselves get carried away–on Internet stocks, on big "growth" stocks, on stocks as a whole–many people made the same stupid mistakes as Sir Isaac Newton. They let other investors' judgments determine their own. They ignored Graham's warning that "the really dreadful losses" always occur after "the buyer forgot to ask 'How much?' " Most painfully of all, by losing their self-control just when they needed it the most, these people proved Graham's assertion that "the investor's chief problem–and even his worst enemy–is likely to be himself."

THE SURE THING THAT WASN'T

Many of those people got especially carried away on technology and Internet stocks, believing the high-tech hype that this industry would keep outgrowing every other for years to come, if not forever:

- In mid-1999, after earning a 117.3% return in just the first five months of the year, Monument Internet Fund portfolio manager Alexander Cheung predicted that his fund would gain 50% a year over the next three to five years and an annual average of 35% "over the next 20 years."[5]

---

[5] Constance Loizos, "Q&A: Alex Cheung," *InvestmentNews,* May 17, 1999, p. 38. The highest 20-year return in mutual fund history was 25.8% per year, achieved by the legendary Peter Lynch of Fidelity Magellan over the two decades ending December 31, 1994. Lynch's performance turned $10,000 into more than $982,000 in 20 years. Cheung was predicting that his fund would turn $10,000 into more than $4 million over the same length of time. Instead of regarding Cheung as ridiculously overoptimistic, investors threw

- After his Amerindo Technology Fund rose an incredible 248.9% in 1999, portfolio manager Alberto Vilar ridiculed anyone who dared to doubt that the Internet was a perpetual moneymaking machine: "If you're out of this sector, you're going to underperform. You're in a horse and buggy, and I'm in a Porsche. You don't like tenfold growth opportunities? Then go with someone else."[6]
- In February 2000, hedge-fund manager James J. Cramer proclaimed that Internet-related companies "are the only ones worth owning right now." These "winners of the new world," as he called them, "are the only ones that are going higher consistently in good days and bad." Cramer even took a potshot at Graham: "You have to throw out all of the matrices and formulas and texts that existed before the Web. . . . If we used any of what Graham and Dodd teach us, we wouldn't have a dime under management."[7]

All these so-called experts ignored Graham's sober words of warning: "Obvious prospects for physical growth in a business do not translate into obvious profits for investors." While it seems easy to foresee which industry will grow the fastest, that foresight has no real value if most other investors are already expecting the same thing. By the time everyone decides that a given industry is "obviously" the best

---

money at him, flinging more than $100 million into his fund over the next year. A $10,000 investment in the Monument Internet Fund in May 1999 would have shrunk to roughly $2,000 by year-end 2002. (The Monument fund no longer exists in its original form and is now known as Orbitex Emerging Technology Fund.)

[6] Lisa Reilly Cullen, "The Triple Digit Club," *Money,* December, 1999, p. 170. If you had invested $10,000 in Vilar's fund at the end of 1999, you would have finished 2002 with just $1,195 left–one of the worst destructions of wealth in the history of the mutual-fund industry.

[7] See www.thestreet.com/funds/smarter/891820.html. Cramer's favorite stocks did not go "higher consistently in good days and bad." By year-end 2002, one of the 10 had already gone bankrupt, and a $10,000 investment spread equally across Cramer's picks would have lost 94%, leaving you with a grand total of $597.44. Perhaps Cramer meant that his stocks would be "winners" not in "the new world," but in the world to come.

one to invest in, the prices of its stocks have been bid up so high that its future returns have nowhere to go but down.

For now at least, no one has the gall to try claiming that technology will still be the world's greatest growth industry. But make sure you remember this: The people who now claim that the next "sure thing" will be health care, or energy, or real estate, or gold, are no more likely to be right in the end than the hypesters of high tech turned out to be.

THE SILVER LINING

If no price seemed too high for stocks in the 1990s, in 2003 we've reached the point at which no price appears to be low enough. The pendulum has swung, as Graham knew it always does, from irrational exuberance to unjustifiable pessimism. In 2002, investors yanked $27 billion out of stock mutual funds, and a survey conducted by the Securities Industry Association found that one out of 10 investors had cut back on stocks by at least 25%. The same people who were eager to buy stocks in the late 1990s–when they were going up in price and, therefore, becoming expensive–sold stocks as they went down in price and, by definition, became cheaper.

As Graham shows so brilliantly in Chapter 8, this is exactly backwards. The intelligent investor realizes that stocks become more risky, not less, as their prices rise–and less risky, not more, as their prices fall. The intelligent investor dreads a bull market, since it makes stocks more costly to buy. And conversely (so long as you keep enough cash on hand to meet your spending needs), you should welcome a bear market, since it puts stocks back on sale.[8]

So take heart: The death of the bull market is not the bad news everyone believes it to be. Thanks to the decline in stock prices, now is a considerably safer–and saner–time to be building wealth. Read on, and let Graham show you how.

---

[8] The only exception to this rule is an investor in the advanced stage of retirement, who may not be able to outlast a long bear market. Yet even an elderly investor should not sell her stocks merely because they have gone down in price; that approach not only turns her paper losses into real ones but deprives her heirs of the potential to inherit those stocks at lower costs for tax purposes.

CHAPTER 1
Investment versus Speculation: Results to Be Expected by the Intelligent Investor

This chapter will outline the viewpoints that will be set forth in the remainder of the book. In particular we wish to develop at the outset our concept of appropriate portfolio policy for the individual, nonprofessional investor.

Investment versus Speculation

What do we mean by "investor"? Throughout this book the term will be used in contradistinction to "speculator." As far back as 1934, in our textbook *Security Analysis,*[1] we attempted a precise formulation of the difference between the two, as follows: "An investment operation is one which, upon thorough analysis promises safety of principal and an adequate return. Operations not meeting these requirements are speculative."

While we have clung tenaciously to this definition over the ensuing 38 years, it is worthwhile noting the radical changes that have occurred in the use of the term "investor" during this period. After the great market decline of 1929–1932 *all* common stocks were widely regarded as speculative by nature. (A leading authority stated flatly that only bonds could be bought for investment.[2]) Thus we had then to defend our definition against the charge that it gave too wide scope to the concept of investment.

Now our concern is of the opposite sort. We must prevent our readers from accepting the common jargon which applies the term "investor" to anybody and everybody in the stock market. In our last edition we cited the following headline of a front-page article of our leading financial journal in June 1962:

SMALL INVESTORS BEARISH, THEY ARE SELLING ODD-LOTS SHORT

In October 1970 the same journal had an editorial critical of what it called "reckless investors," who this time were rushing in on the buying side.

These quotations well illustrate the confusion that has been dominant for many years in the use of the words investment and speculation. Think of our suggested definition of investment given above, and compare it with the sale of a few shares of stock by an inexperienced member of the public, who does not even own what he is selling, and has some largely emotional conviction that he will be able to buy them back at a much lower price. (It is not irrelevant to point out that when the 1962 article appeared the market had already experienced a decline of major size, and was now getting ready for an even greater upswing. It was about as poor a time as possible for selling short.) In a more general sense, the later-used phrase "reckless investors" could be regarded as a laughable contradiction in terms—something like "spendthrift misers"—were this misuse of language not so mischievous.

The newspaper employed the word "investor" in these instances because, in the easy language of Wall Street, everyone who buys or sells a security has become an investor, regardless of what he buys, or for what purpose, or at what price, or whether for cash or on margin. Compare this with the attitude of the public toward common stocks in 1948, when over 90% of those queried expressed themselves as opposed to the purchase of common stocks.[3] About half gave as their reason "not safe, a gamble," and about half, the reason "not familiar with."* It is indeed ironical

---

* The survey Graham cites was conducted for the Fed by the University of Michigan and was published in the *Federal Reserve Bulletin*, July, 1948. People were asked, "Suppose a man decides not to spend his money. He can either put it in a bank or in bonds or he can invest it. What do you think would be the wisest thing for him to do with the money nowadays–put it in the bank, buy savings bonds with it, invest it in real estate, or buy common stock with it?" Only 4% thought common stock would offer a "satisfactory" return; 26% considered it "not safe" or a "gamble." From 1949 through 1958, the stock market earned one of its highest 10-year returns in history,

(though not surprising) that common-stock purchases of all kinds were quite generally regarded as highly speculative or risky at a time when they were selling on a most attractive basis, and due soon to begin their greatest advance in history; conversely the very fact they had advanced to what were undoubtedly dangerous levels as judged by *past experience* later transformed them into "investments," and the entire stock-buying public into "investors."

The distinction between investment and speculation in common stocks has always been a useful one and its disappearance is a cause for concern. We have often said that Wall Street as an institution would be well advised to reinstate this distinction and to emphasize it in all its dealings with the public. Otherwise the stock exchanges may some day be blamed for heavy speculative losses, which those who suffered them had not been properly warned against. Ironically, once more, much of the recent financial embarrassment of some stock-exchange firms seems to have come from the inclusion of speculative common stocks in their own capital funds. We trust that the reader of this book will gain a reasonably clear idea of the risks that are inherent in common-stock commitments—risks which are inseparable from the opportunities of profit that they offer, and both of which must be allowed for in the investor's calculations.

What we have just said indicates that there may no longer be such a thing as a simon-pure investment policy comprising representative common stocks—in the sense that one can always wait to buy them at a price that involves no risk of a market or "quotational" loss large enough to be disquieting. In most periods the investor must recognize the existence of a *speculative factor* in his common-stock holdings. It is his task to keep this component within minor limits, and to be prepared financially and psychologically for adverse results that may be of short or long duration.

Two paragraphs should be added about stock speculation per se, as distinguished from the speculative component now inherent

---

averaging 18.7% annually. In a fascinating echo of that early Fed survey, a poll conducted by *BusinessWeek* at year-end 2002 found that only 24% of investors were willing to invest more in their mutual funds or stock portfolios, down from 47% just three years earlier.

in most representative common stocks. Outright speculation is neither illegal, immoral, nor (for most people) fattening to the pocketbook. More than that, some speculation is necessary and unavoidable, for in many common-stock situations there are substantial possibilities of both profit and loss, and the risks therein must be assumed by someone.* There is intelligent speculation as there is intelligent investing. But there are many ways in which speculation may be unintelligent. Of these the foremost are: (1) speculating when you think you are investing; (2) speculating seriously instead of as a pastime, when you lack proper knowledge and skill for it; and (3) risking more money in speculation than you can afford to lose.

In our conservative view every nonprofessional who operates *on margin*† should recognize that he is *ipso facto* speculating, and it is his broker's duty so to advise him. And everyone who buys a so-called "hot" common-stock issue, or makes a purchase in any way similar thereto, is either speculating or gambling. Speculation is always fascinating, and it can be a lot of fun while you are ahead of the game. If you want to try your luck at it, put aside a portion—the smaller the better—of your capital in a separate fund for this purpose. Never add more money to this account just because the

---

* Speculation is beneficial on two levels: First, without speculation, untested new companies (like Amazon.com or, in earlier times, the Edison Electric Light Co.) would never be able to raise the necessary capital for expansion. The alluring, long-shot chance of a huge gain is the grease that lubricates the machinery of innovation. Secondly, risk is exchanged (but never eliminated) every time a stock is bought or sold. The buyer purchases the primary risk that this stock may go down. Meanwhile, the seller still retains a residual risk–the chance that the stock he just sold may go up!

† A margin account enables you to buy stocks using money you borrow from the brokerage firm. By investing with borrowed money, you make more when your stocks go up–but you can be wiped out when they go down. The collateral for the loan is the value of the investments in your account–so you must put up more money if that value falls below the amount you borrowed. For more information about margin accounts, see www.sec.gov/investor/pubs/margin.htm, www.sia.com/publications/pdf/MarginsA.pdf, and www.nyse.com/pdfs/2001_factbook_09.pdf.

market has gone up and profits are rolling in. (That's the time to think of taking money *out* of your speculative fund.) Never mingle your speculative and investment operations in the same account, nor in any part of your thinking.

Results to Be Expected by the Defensive Investor

We have already defined the defensive investor as one interested chiefly in safety plus freedom from bother. In general what course should he follow and what return can he expect under "average normal conditions"—if such conditions really exist? To answer these questions we shall consider first what we wrote on the subject seven years ago, next what significant changes have occurred since then in the underlying factors governing the investor's expectable return, and finally what he should do and what he should expect under present-day (early 1972) conditions.

1. What We Said Six Years Ago

We recommended that the investor divide his holdings between high-grade bonds and leading common stocks; that the proportion held in bonds be never less than 25% or more than 75%, with the converse being necessarily true for the common-stock component; that his simplest choice would be to maintain a 50–50 proportion between the two, with adjustments to restore the equality when market developments had disturbed it by as much as, say, 5%. As an alternative policy he might choose to reduce his common-stock component to 25% "if he felt the market was dangerously high," and conversely to advance it toward the maximum of 75% "if he felt that a decline in stock prices was making them increasingly attractive."

In 1965 the investor could obtain about 4½% on high-grade taxable bonds and 3¼% on good tax-free bonds. The dividend return on leading common stocks (with the DJIA at 892) was only about 3.2%. This fact, and others, suggested caution. We implied that "at normal levels of the market" the investor should be able to obtain an initial dividend return of between 3½% and 4½% on his stock purchases, to which should be added a steady increase in underlying value (and in the "normal market price") of a representative stock list of about the same amount, giving a return from dividends and appreciation combined of about 7½% per year. The half and half division between bonds and stocks would yield about 6% before income tax. We added that the stock component should carry a fair degree of protection against a loss of purchasing power caused by large-scale inflation.

It should be pointed out that the above arithmetic indicated expectation of a much lower rate of advance in the stock market than had been realized between 1949 and 1964. That rate had averaged a good deal better than 10% for listed stocks as a whole, and it was quite generally regarded as a sort of guarantee that similarly satisfactory results could be counted on in the future. Few people were willing to consider seriously the possibility that the high rate of advance in the past means that stock prices are "now too high," and hence that "the wonderful results since 1949 would imply not very good but *bad* results for the future."[4]

2. *What Has Happened Since 1964*

The major change since 1964 has been the rise in interest rates on first-grade bonds to record high levels, although there has since been a considerable recovery from the lowest prices of 1970. The obtainable return on good corporate issues is now about 7½% and even more against 4½% in 1964. In the meantime the dividend return on DJIA-type stocks had a fair advance also during the market decline of 1969–70, but as we write (with "the Dow" at 900) it is less than 3.5% against 3.2% at the end of 1964. The change in going interest rates produced a maximum decline of about 38% in the market price of medium-term (say 20-year) bonds during this period.

There is a paradoxical aspect to these developments. In 1964 we discussed at length the possibility that the price of stocks might be too high and subject ultimately to a serious decline; but we did not consider specifically the possibility that the same might happen to the price of high-grade bonds. (Neither did anyone else that we know of.) We did warn (on p. 90) that "a long-term bond may vary widely in price in response to changes in interest rates." In the light of what has since happened we think that this warning—with attendant examples—was insufficiently stressed. For the fact is that if the investor had a given sum in the DJIA at its closing price of 874 in 1964 he would have had a small profit thereon in late 1971; even at the lowest level (631) in 1970 his indicated loss would have been less than that shown on good long-term bonds. On the other hand, if he had confined his bond-type investments to U.S. savings bonds, short-term corporate issues, or savings accounts, he would have had no loss in market value of his principal during this period and he would have enjoyed a higher income return than was offered by good stocks. It turned out, therefore, that true "cash equivalents" proved to be better investments in 1964 than common stocks—in spite of the inflation experience that in theory should have favored stocks over cash. The decline in quoted principal value of good longer-term bonds was due to developments in the money market, an abstruse area which ordinarily does not have an important bearing on the investment policy of individuals.

This is just another of an endless series of experiences over time that have demonstrated that the future of security prices is never predictable.* Almost always bonds have fluctuated much less than stock prices, and investors generally could buy good bonds of any maturity without having to worry about changes in their market value. There were a few exceptions to this rule, and the period after 1964 proved to be one of them. We shall have more to say about change in bond prices in a later chapter.

3. Expectations and Policy in Late 1971 and Early 1972

Toward the end of 1971 it was possible to obtain 8% taxable interest on good medium-term corporate bonds, and 5.7% tax-free on good state or municipal securities. In the shorter-term field the investor could realize about 6% on U.S. government issues due in five years. In the latter case the buyer need not be concerned about

---

* Read Graham's sentence again, and note what this greatest of investing experts is saying: The future of security prices is never predictable. And as you read ahead in the book, notice how everything else Graham tells you is designed to help you grapple with that truth. Since you cannot predict the behavior of the markets, you must learn how to predict and control your own behavior.

a possible loss in market value, since he is sure of full repayment, including the 6% interest return, at the end of a comparatively short holding period. The DJIA at its recurrent price level of 900 in 1971 yields only 3.5%.

Let us assume that now, as in the past, the basic policy decision to be made is how to divide the fund between high-grade bonds (or other so-called "cash equivalents") and leading DJIA-type stocks. What course should the investor follow under present conditions, if we have no strong reason to predict either a significant upward or a significant downward movement for some time in the future? First let us point out that if there is no serious adverse change, the defensive investor should be able to count on the current 3.5% dividend return on his stocks and also on an *average* annual appreciation of about 4%. As we shall explain later this appreciation is based essentially on the reinvestment by the various companies of a corresponding amount annually out of undistributed profits. On a before-tax basis the combined return of his stocks would then average, say, 7.5%, somewhat less than his interest on high-grade bonds.* On an after-tax basis the average return on stocks would work out at some 5.3%.[5] This would be about the same as is now obtainable on good tax-free medium-term bonds.

These expectations are much less favorable for stocks against bonds than they were in our 1964 analysis. (That conclusion follows inevitably from the basic fact that bond yields have gone up much more than stock yields since 1964.) We must never lose sight

* How well did Graham's forecast pan out? At first blush, it seems, very well: From the beginning of 1972 through the end of 1981, stocks earned an annual average return of 6.5%. (Graham did not specify the time period for his forecast, but it's plausible to assume that he was thinking of a 10-year time horizon.) However, inflation raged at 8.6% annually over this period, eating up the entire gain that stocks produced. In this section of his chapter, Graham is summarizing what is known as the "Gordon equation," which essentially holds that the stock market's future return is the sum of the current dividend yield plus expected earnings growth. With a dividend yield of just under 2% in early 2003, and long-term earnings growth of around 2%, plus inflation at a bit over 2%, a future average annual return of roughly 6% is plausible. (See the commentary on Chapter 3.)

of the fact that the interest and principal payments on good bonds are much better protected and therefore more certain than the dividends and price appreciation on stocks. Consequently we are forced to the conclusion that now, toward the end of 1971, bond investment appears clearly preferable to stock investment. If we could be sure that this conclusion is right we would have to advise the defensive investor to put *all* his money in bonds and *none* in common stocks until the current yield relationship changes significantly in favor of stocks.

But of course we cannot be certain that bonds will work out better than stocks from today's levels. The reader will immediately think of the inflation factor as a potent reason on the other side. In the next chapter we shall argue that our considerable experience with inflation in the United States during this century would not support the choice of stocks against bonds at present differentials in yield. But there is always the possibility—though we consider it remote—of an accelerating inflation, which in one way or another would have to make stock equities preferable to bonds payable in a fixed amount of dollars.* There is the alternative possibility—which we also consider highly unlikely—that American business will become so profitable, without stepped-up inflation, as to justify a large increase in common-stock values in the next few years. Finally, there is the more familiar possibility that we shall witness another great speculative rise in the stock market without a real justification in the underlying values. Any of these reasons, and perhaps others we haven't thought of, *might* cause the investor to regret a 100% concentration on bonds even at their more favorable yield levels.

Hence, after this foreshortened discussion of the major considerations, we once again enunciate the same basic compromise policy

---

* Since 1997, when Treasury Inflation-Protected Securities (or TIPS) were introduced, stocks have no longer been the automatically superior choice for investors who expect inflation to increase. TIPS, unlike other bonds, rise in value if the Consumer Price Index goes up, effectively immunizing the investor against losing money after inflation. Stocks carry no such guarantee and, in fact, are a relatively poor hedge against high rates of inflation. (For more details, see the commentary to Chapter 2.)

for defensive investors—namely that at all times they have a significant part of their funds in bond-type holdings and a significant part also in equities. It is still true that they may choose between maintaining a simple 50–50 division between the two components or a ratio, dependent on their judgment, varying between a minimum of 25% and a maximum of 75% of either. We shall give our more detailed view of these alternative policies in a later chapter.

Since at present the overall return envisaged from common stocks is nearly the same as that from bonds, the presently expectable return (including growth of stock values) for the investor would change little regardless of how he divides his fund between the two components. As calculated above, the aggregate return from both parts should be about 7.8% before taxes or 5.5% on a tax-free (or estimated tax-paid) basis. A return of this order is appreciably higher than that realized by the typical conservative investor over most of the long-term past. It may not seem attractive in relation to the 14%, or so, return shown by common stocks during the 20 years of the predominantly bull market after 1949. But it should be remembered that between 1949 and 1969 the price of the DJIA had advanced more than fivefold while its earnings and dividends had about doubled. Hence the greater part of the impressive market record for that period was based on a change in investors' and speculators' attitudes rather than in underlying corporate values. To that extent it might well be called a "bootstrap operation."

In discussing the common-stock portfolio of the defensive investor, we have spoken only of leading issues of the type included in the 30 components of the Dow Jones Industrial Average. We have done this for convenience, and not to imply that these 30 issues alone are suitable for purchase by him. Actually, there are many other companies of quality equal to or excelling the average of the Dow Jones list; these would include a host of public utilities (which have a separate Dow Jones average to represent them).* But

---

* Today, the most widely available alternatives to the Dow Jones Industrial Average are the Standard & Poor's 500-stock index (the "S & P") and the Wilshire 5000 index. The S & P focuses on 500 large, well-known companies that make up roughly 70% of the total value of the U.S. equity market. The Wilshire 5000 follows the returns of nearly every significant, publicly

the major point here is that the defensive investor's overall results are not likely to be decisively different from one diversified or representative list than from another, or—more accurately—that neither he nor his advisers could predict with certainty whatever differences would ultimately develop. It is true that the art of skillful or shrewd investment is supposed to lie particularly in the selection of issues that will give better results than the general market. For reasons to be developed elsewhere we are skeptical of the ability of defensive investors generally to get better than average results—which in fact would mean to beat their own overall performance.* (Our skepticism extends to the management of large funds by experts.)

Let us illustrate our point by an example that at first may seem to prove the opposite. Between December 1960 and December 1970 the DJIA advanced from 616 to 839, or 36%. But in the same period the much larger Standard & Poor's weighted index of 500 stocks rose from 58.11 to 92.15, or 58%. Obviously the second group had proved a better "buy" than the first. But who would have been so rash as to predict in 1960 that what seemed like a miscellaneous assortment of all sorts of common stocks would definitely outperform the aristocratic "thirty tyrants" of the Dow? All this proves, we insist, that only rarely can one make dependable predictions about price changes, absolute or relative.

We shall repeat here without apology—for the warning cannot be given too often—that the investor cannot hope for better than average results by buying new offerings, or "hot" issues of any sort, meaning thereby those recommended for a quick profit.† The contrary is almost certain to be true in the long run. The defensive investor must confine himself to the shares of important companies with a long record of profitable operations and in strong financial condition. (Any security analyst worth his salt could make up such

---

traded stock in America, roughly 6,700 in all; but, since the largest companies account for most of the total value of the index, the return of the Wilshire 5000 is usually quite similar to that of the S & P 500. Several low-cost mutual funds enable investors to hold the stocks in these indexes as a single, convenient portfolio. (See Chapter 9.)

* See pp. 363–366 and pp. 376–380.

† For greater detail, see Chapter 6.

a list.) Aggressive investors may buy other types of common stocks, but they should be on a definitely attractive basis as established by intelligent analysis.

To conclude this section, let us mention briefly three supplementary concepts or practices for the defensive investor. The first is the purchase of the shares of well-established investment funds as an alternative to creating his own common-stock portfolio. He might also utilize one of the "common trust funds," or "commingled funds," operated by trust companies and banks in many states; or, if his funds are substantial, use the services of a recognized investment-counsel firm. This will give him professional administration of his investment program along standard lines. The third is the device of "dollar-cost averaging," which means simply that the practitioner invests in common stocks the same number of dollars each month or each quarter. In this way he buys more shares when the market is low than when it is high, and he is likely to end up with a satisfactory overall price for all his holdings. Strictly speaking, this method is an application of a broader approach known as "formula investing." The latter was already alluded to in our suggestion that the investor may vary his holdings of common stocks between the 25% minimum and the 75% maximum, in inverse relationship to the action of the market. These ideas have merit for the defensive investor, and they will be discussed more amply in later chapters.*

Results to Be Expected by the Aggressive Investor

Our enterprising security buyer, of course, will desire and expect to attain better overall results than his defensive or passive companion. But first he must make sure that his results will not be worse. It is no difficult trick to bring a great deal of energy, study, and native ability into Wall Street and to end up with losses instead of profits. These virtues, if channeled in the wrong directions, become indistinguishable from handicaps. Thus it is most essential that the enterprising investor start with a clear conception as to

---

* For more advice on "well-established investment funds," see Chapter 9. "Professional administration" by "a recognized investment-counsel firm" is discussed in Chapter 10. "Dollar-cost averaging" is explained in Chapter 5.

which courses of action offer reasonable chances of success and which do not.

First let us consider several ways in which investors and speculators generally have endeavored to obtain better than average results. These include:

1. Trading in the market. This usually means buying stocks when the market has been advancing and selling them after it has turned downward. The stocks selected are likely to be among those which have been "behaving" better than the market average. A small number of professionals frequently engage in short selling. Here they will sell issues they do not own but borrow through the established mechanism of the stock exchanges. Their object is to benefit from a subsequent decline in the price of these issues, by buying them back at a price lower than they sold them for. (As our quotation from the *Wall Street Journal* on p. 19 indicates, even "small investors"—perish the term!—sometimes try their unskilled hand at short selling.)

2. Short-term selectivity. This means buying stocks of companies which are reporting or expected to report increased earnings, or for which some other favorable development is anticipated.

3. Long-term selectivity. Here the usual emphasis is on an excellent record of past growth, which is considered likely to continue in the future. In some cases also the "investor" may choose companies which have not yet shown impressive results, but are expected to establish a high earning power later. (Such companies belong frequently in some technological area—e.g., computers, drugs, electronics—and they often are developing new processes or products that are deemed to be especially promising.)

We have already expressed a negative view about the investor's overall chances of success in these areas of activity. The first we have ruled out, on both theoretical and realistic grounds, from the domain of investment. Stock trading is not an operation "which, on thorough analysis, offers safety of principal and a satisfactory return." More will be said on stock trading in a later chapter.*

* See Chapter 8.

In his endeavor to select the most promising stocks either for the near term or the longer future, the investor faces obstacles of two kinds—the first stemming from human fallibility and the second from the nature of his competition. He may be wrong in his estimate of the future; or even if he is right, the current market price may already fully reflect what he is anticipating. In the area of near-term selectivity, the current year's results of the company are generally common property on Wall Street; next year's results, to the extent they are predictable, are already being carefully considered. Hence the investor who selects issues chiefly on the basis of this year's superior results, or on what he is told he may expect for next year, is likely to find that others have done the same thing for the same reason.

In choosing stocks for their *long-term* prospects, the investor's handicaps are basically the same. The possibility of outright error in the prediction—which we illustrated by our airlines example on p. 6—is no doubt greater than when dealing with near-term earnings. Because the experts frequently go astray in such forecasts, it is theoretically possible for an investor to benefit greatly by making correct predictions when Wall Street as a whole is making incorrect ones. But that is only theoretical. How many enterprising investors could count on having the acumen or prophetic gift to beat the professional analysts at their favorite game of estimating long-term future earnings?

We are thus led to the following logical if disconcerting conclusion: To enjoy a reasonable chance for continued better than average results, the investor must follow policies which are (1) inherently sound and promising, and (2) not popular on Wall Street.

Are there any such policies available for the enterprising investor? In theory once again, the answer should be yes; and there are broad reasons to think that the answer should be affirmative in practice as well. Everyone knows that speculative stock movements are carried too far in both directions, frequently in the general market and at all times in at least some of the individual issues. Furthermore, a common stock may be undervalued because of lack of interest or unjustified popular prejudice. We can go further and assert that in an astonishingly large proportion of the trading in common stocks, those engaged therein don't appear to know—in polite terms—one part of their anatomy from another. In this book we shall point out numerous examples of (past) discrepancies between price and value. Thus it seems that any intelligent person, with a good head for figures, should have a veritable picnic on Wall Street, battening off other people's foolishness. So it seems, but somehow it doesn't work out that simply. Buying a neglected and therefore undervalued issue for profit generally proves a protracted and patience-trying experience. And selling short a too popular and therefore overvalued issue is apt to be a test not only of one's courage and stamina but also of the depth of one's pocketbook.* The principle is sound, its successful application is not impossible, but it is distinctly not an easy art to master.

There is also a fairly wide group of "special situations," which over many years could be counted on to bring a nice annual return of 20% or better, with a minimum of overall risk to those who knew their way around in this field. They include intersecurity arbitrages, payouts or workouts in liquidations, protected hedges of certain kinds. The most typical case is a projected merger or acquisition which offers a substantially higher value for certain shares than their price on the date of the announcement. The number of such deals increased greatly in recent years, and it should have been a highly profitable period for the cognoscenti. But with the multiplication of merger announcements came a multiplication of obstacles to mergers and of deals that didn't go through; quite a few individual losses were thus realized in these once-reliable operations. Perhaps, too, the overall rate of profit was diminished by too much competition.†

---

* In "selling short" (or "shorting") a stock, you make a bet that its share price will go down, not up. Shorting is a three-step process: First, you borrow shares from someone who owns them; then you immediately sell the borrowed shares; finally, you replace them with shares you buy later. If the stock drops, you will be able to buy your replacement shares at a lower price. The difference between the price at which you sold your borrowed shares and the price you paid for the replacement shares is your gross profit (reduced by dividend or interest charges, along with brokerage costs). However, if the stock goes up in price instead of down, your potential loss is unlimited–making short sales unacceptably speculative for most individual investors.

† In the late 1980s, as hostile corporate takeovers and leveraged buyouts multiplied, Wall Street set up institutional arbitrage desks to profit from any

The lessened profitability of these special situations appears one manifestation of a kind of self-destructive process—akin to the law of diminishing returns—which has developed during the lifetime of this book. In 1949 we could present a study of stock-market fluctuations over the preceding 75 years, which supported a formula—based on earnings and current interest rates—for determining a level to buy the DJIA below its "central" or "intrinsic" value, and to sell out above such value. It was an application of the governing maxim of the Rothschilds: "Buy cheap and sell dear."* And it had the advantage of running directly counter to the ingrained and pernicious maxim of Wall Street that stocks should be bought because they have gone up and sold because they have gone down. Alas, after 1949 this formula no longer worked. A second illustration is provided by the famous "Dow Theory" of stock-market movements, in a comparison of its indicated splendid results for 1897–1933 and its much more questionable performance since 1934.

A third and final example of the golden opportunities not recently available: A good part of our own operations on Wall Street had been concentrated on the purchase of *bargain issues* easily identified as such by the fact that they were selling at less than their share in the net current assets (working capital) alone, not counting the plant account and other assets, and after deducting all liabilities ahead of the stock. It is clear that these issues were selling at a price well below the value of the enterprise as a private business. No proprietor or majority holder would think of selling what he owned at so ridiculously low a figure. Strangely enough, such

---

errors in pricing these complex deals. They became so good at it that the easy profits disappeared and many of these desks have been closed down. Although Graham does discuss it again (see pp. 174–175), this sort of trading is no longer feasible or appropriate for most people, since only multimillion-dollar trades are large enough to generate worthwhile profits. Wealthy individuals and institutions can utilize this strategy through hedge funds that specialize in merger or "event" arbitrage.

* The Rothschild family, led by Nathan Mayer Rothschild, was the dominant power in European investment banking and brokerage in the nineteenth century. For a brilliant history, see Niall Ferguson, *The House of Rothschild: Money's Prophets, 1798–1848* (Viking, 1998).

anomalies were not hard to find. In 1957 a list was published showing nearly 200 issues of this type available in the market. In various ways practically all these bargain issues turned out to be profitable, and the average annual result proved much more remunerative than most other investments. But they too virtually disappeared from the stock market in the next decade, and with them a dependable area for shrewd and successful operation by the enterprising investor. However, at the low prices of 1970 there again appeared a considerable number of such "sub-working-capital" issues, and despite the strong recovery of the market, enough of them remained at the end of the year to make up a full-sized portfolio.

The enterprising investor under today's conditions still has various possibilities of achieving better than average results. The huge list of marketable securities must include a fair number that can be identified as undervalued by logical and reasonably dependable standards. These should yield more satisfactory results on the average than will the DJIA or any similarly representative list. In our view the search for these would not be worth the investor's effort unless he could hope to add, say, 5% before taxes to the average annual return from the stock portion of his portfolio. We shall try to develop one or more such approaches to stock selection for use by the active investor.

COMMENTARY ON CHAPTER 1

All of human unhappiness comes from one single thing: not knowing how to remain at rest in a room.

–Blaise Pascal

Why do you suppose the brokers on the floor of the New York Stock Exchange always cheer at the sound of the closing bell–no matter what the market did that day? Because whenever you trade, *they* make money–whether you did or not. By speculating instead of investing, you lower your own odds of building wealth and raise someone else's.

Graham's definition of investing could not be clearer: "An investment operation is one which, upon thorough analysis, promises safety of principal and an adequate return."[1] Note that investing, according to Graham, consists equally of three elements:

- you must thoroughly analyze a company, and the soundness of its underlying businesses, before you buy its stock;
- you must deliberately protect yourself against serious losses;
- you must aspire to "adequate," not extraordinary, performance.

---

[1] Graham goes even further, fleshing out each of the key terms in his definition: "thorough analysis" means "the study of the facts in the light of established standards of safety and value" while "safety of principal" signifies "protection against loss under all normal or reasonably likely conditions or variations" and "adequate" (or "satisfactory") return refers to "any rate or amount of return, however low, which the investor is willing to accept, provided he acts with reasonable intelligence." (*Security Analysis,* 1934 ed., pp. 55–56).

An investor calculates what a stock is worth, based on the value of its businesses. A speculator gambles that a stock will go up in price because somebody else will pay even more for it. As Graham once put it, investors judge "the market price by established standards of value," while speculators "base [their] standards of value upon the market price."[2] For a speculator, the incessant stream of stock quotes is like oxygen; cut it off and he dies. For an investor, what Graham called "quotational" values matter much less. Graham urges you to invest only if you would be comfortable owning a stock even if you had no way of knowing its daily share price.[3]

Like casino gambling or betting on the horses, speculating in the market can be exciting or even rewarding (if you happen to get lucky). But it's the worst imaginable way to build your wealth. That's because Wall Street, like Las Vegas or the racetrack, has calibrated the odds so that the house always prevails, in the end, against everyone who tries to beat the house at its own speculative game.

On the other hand, *investing* is a unique kind of casino—one where you cannot lose in the end, so long as you play only by the rules that put the odds squarely in your favor. People who *invest* make money for themselves; people who *speculate* make money for their brokers. And that, in turn, is why Wall Street perennially downplays the durable virtues of investing and hypes the gaudy appeal of speculation.

UNSAFE AT HIGH SPEED

Confusing speculation with investment, Graham warns, is always a mistake. In the 1990s, that confusion led to mass destruction. Almost everyone, it seems, ran out of patience at once, and America became the Speculation Nation, populated with traders who went shooting from stock to stock like grasshoppers whizzing around in an August hay field.

People began believing that the test of an investment technique was simply whether it "worked." If they beat the market over any

---

[2] *Security Analysis,* 1934 ed., p. 310.

[3] As Graham advised in an interview, "Ask yourself: If there was no market for these shares, would I be willing to have an investment in this company on these terms?" (*Forbes,* January 1, 1972, p. 90.)

period, no matter how dangerous or dumb their tactics, people boasted that they were "right." But the intelligent investor has no interest in being temporarily right. To reach your long-term financial goals, you must be sustainably and reliably right. The techniques that became so trendy in the 1990s—day trading, ignoring diversification, flipping hot mutual funds, following stock-picking "systems"—seemed to work. But they had no chance of prevailing in the long run, because they failed to meet all three of Graham's criteria for investing.

To see why temporarily high returns don't prove anything, imagine that two places are 130 miles apart. If I observe the 65-mph speed limit, I can drive that distance in two hours. But if I drive 130 mph, I can get there in one hour. If I try this and survive, am I "right"? Should you be tempted to try it, too, because you hear me bragging that it "worked"? Flashy gimmicks for beating the market are much the same: In short streaks, so long as your luck holds out, they work. Over time, they will get you killed.

In 1973, when Graham last revised *The Intelligent Investor,* the annual turnover rate on the New York Stock Exchange was 20%, meaning that the typical shareholder held a stock for five years before selling it. By 2002, the turnover rate had hit 105%—a holding period of only 11.4 months. Back in 1973, the average mutual fund held on to a stock for nearly three years; by 2002, that ownership period had shrunk to just 10.9 months. It's as if mutual-fund managers were studying their stocks just long enough to learn they shouldn't have bought them in the first place, then promptly dumping them and starting all over.

Even the most respected money-management firms got antsy. In early 1995, Jeffrey Vinik, manager of Fidelity Magellan (then the world's largest mutual fund), had 42.5% of its assets in technology stocks. Vinik proclaimed that most of his shareholders "have invested in the fund for goals that are years away. . . . I think their objectives are the same as mine, and that they believe, as I do, that a long-term approach is best." But six months after he wrote those high-minded words, Vinik sold off almost all his technology shares, unloading nearly $19 billion worth in eight frenzied weeks. So much for the "long term"! And by 1999, Fidelity's discount brokerage division was egging on its clients to trade anywhere, anytime, using a Palm handheld computer—which was perfectly in tune with the firm's new slogan, "Every second counts."

FIGURE 1-1

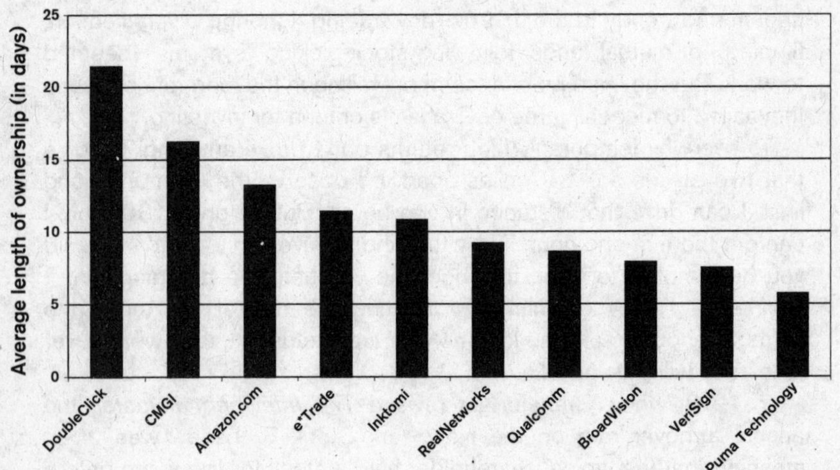

And on the NASDAQ exchange, turnover hit warp speed, as Figure 1-1 shows.[4]

In 1999, shares in Puma Technology, for instance, changed hands an average of once every 5.7 days. Despite NASDAQ's grandiose motto—"The Stock Market for the Next Hundred Years"—many of its customers could barely hold on to a stock for a hundred hours.

THE FINANCIAL VIDEO GAME

Wall Street made online trading sound like an instant way to mint money: Discover Brokerage, the online arm of the venerable firm of

[4] Source: Steve Galbraith, Sanford C. Bernstein & Co. research report, January 10, 2000. The stocks in this table had an average return of 1196.4% in 1999. They lost an average of 79.1% in 2000, 35.5% in 2001, and 44.5% in 2002—destroying all the gains of 1999, and then some.

Morgan Stanley, ran a TV commercial in which a scruffy tow-truck driver picks up a prosperous-looking executive. Spotting a photo of a tropical beachfront posted on the dashboard, the executive asks, "Vacation?" "Actually," replies the driver, "that's my home." Taken aback, the suit says, "Looks like an island." With quiet triumph, the driver answers, "Technically, it's a country."

The propaganda went further. Online trading would take no work and require no thought. A television ad from Ameritrade, the online broker, showed two housewives just back from jogging; one logs on to her computer, clicks the mouse a few times, and exults, "I think I just made about $1,700!" In a TV commercial for the Waterhouse brokerage firm, someone asked basketball coach Phil Jackson, "You know anything about the trade?" His answer: "I'm going to make it right now." (How many games would Jackson's NBA teams have won if he had brought that philosophy to courtside? Somehow, knowing nothing about the other team, but saying, "I'm ready to play them right now," doesn't sound like a championship formula.)

By 1999 at least six million people were trading online—and roughly a tenth of them were "day trading," using the Internet to buy and sell stocks at lightning speed. Everyone from showbiz diva Barbra Streisand to Nicholas Birbas, a 25-year-old former waiter in Queens, New York, was flinging stocks around like live coals. "Before," scoffed Birbas, "I was investing for the long term and I found out that it was not smart." Now, Birbas traded stocks up to 10 times a day and expected to earn $100,000 in a year. "I can't stand to see red in my profit-or-loss column," Streisand shuddered in an interview with *Fortune*. "I'm Taurus the bull, so I react to red. If I see red, I sell my stocks quickly."[5]

By pouring continuous data about stocks into bars and barbershops, kitchens and cafés, taxicabs and truck stops, financial websites and financial TV turned the stock market into a nonstop national video game. The public felt more knowledgeable about the markets than ever before. Unfortunately, while people were drowning in data, knowledge was nowhere to be found. Stocks became entirely decou-

---

[5] Instead of stargazing, Streisand should have been channeling Graham. The intelligent investor never dumps a stock purely because its share price has fallen; she always asks first whether the value of the company's underlying businesses has changed.

pled from the companies that had issued them—pure abstractions, just blips moving across a TV or computer screen. If the blips were moving up, nothing else mattered.

On December 20, 1999, Juno Online Services unveiled a trailblazing business plan: to lose as much money as possible, on purpose. Juno announced that it would henceforth offer all its retail services for free—no charge for e-mail, no charge for Internet access—and that it would spend millions of dollars more on advertising over the next year. On this declaration of corporate hara-kiri, Juno's stock roared up from \$16.375 to \$66.75 in two days.[6]

Why bother learning whether a business was profitable, or what goods or services a company produced, or who its management was, or even what the company's name was? All you needed to know about stocks was the catchy code of their ticker symbols: CBLT, INKT, PCLN, TGLO, VRSN, WBVN.[7] That way you could buy them even faster, without the pesky two-second delay of looking them up on an Internet search engine. In late 1998, the stock of a tiny, rarely traded building-maintenance company, Temco Services, nearly tripled in a matter of minutes on record-high volume. Why? In a bizarre form of financial dyslexia, thousands of traders bought Temco after mistaking its ticker symbol, TMCO, for that of Ticketmaster Online (TMCS), an Internet darling whose stock began trading publicly for the first time that day.[8]

Oscar Wilde joked that a cynic "knows the price of everything, and the value of nothing." Under that definition, the stock market is always cynical, but by the late 1990s it would have shocked Oscar himself. A single half-baked opinion on *price* could double a company's stock even as its *value* went entirely unexamined. In late 1998, Henry Blodget, an analyst at CIBC Oppenheimer, warned that "as with all Internet stocks, a valuation is clearly more art than science." Then, citing only the possibility of future growth, he jacked up his "price target" on

[6] Just 12 months later, Juno's shares had shriveled to \$1.093.

[7] A ticker symbol is an abbreviation, usually one to four letters long, of a company's name used as shorthand to identify a stock for trading purposes.

[8] This was not an isolated incident; on at least three other occasions in the late 1990s, day traders sent the wrong stock soaring when they mistook its ticker symbol for that of a newly minted Internet company.

Amazon.com from $150 to $400 in one fell swoop. Amazon.com shot up 19% that day and—despite Blodget's protest that his price target was a one-year forecast—soared past $400 in just three weeks. A year later, PaineWebber analyst Walter Piecyk predicted that Qualcomm stock would hit $1,000 a share over the next 12 months. The stock—already up 1,842% that year—soared another 31% that day, hitting $659 a share.[9]

FROM FORMULA TO FIASCO

But trading as if your underpants are on fire is not the only form of speculation. Throughout the past decade or so, one speculative formula after another was promoted, popularized, and then thrown aside. All of them shared a few traits—This is quick! This is easy! And it won't hurt a bit!—and all of them violated at least one of Graham's distinctions between investing and speculating. Here are a few of the trendy formulas that fell flat:

- **Cash in on the calendar.** The "January effect"—the tendency of small stocks to produce big gains around the turn of the year—was widely promoted in scholarly articles and popular books published in the 1980s. These studies showed that if you piled into small stocks in the second half of December and held them into January, you would beat the market by five to 10 percentage points. That amazed many experts. After all, if it were this easy, surely everyone would hear about it, lots of people would do it, and the opportunity would wither away.

  What caused the January jolt? First of all, many investors sell their crummiest stocks late in the year to lock in losses that can cut their tax bills. Second, professional money managers grow more cautious as the year draws to a close, seeking to preserve their outperformance (or minimize their underperformance). That makes them reluctant to buy (or even hang on to) a falling stock. And if an underperforming stock is also small and obscure, a money manager will be even less eager to show it in his year-end

[9] In 2000 and 2001, Amazon.com and Qualcomm lost a cumulative total of 85.8% and 71.3% of their value, respectively.

list of holdings. All these factors turn small stocks into momentary bargains; when the tax-driven selling ceases in January, they typically bounce back, producing a robust and rapid gain.

The January effect has not withered away, but it has weakened. According to finance professor William Schwert of the University of Rochester, if you had bought small stocks in late December and sold them in early January, you would have beaten the market by 8.5 percentage points from 1962 through 1979, by 4.4 points from 1980 through 1989, and by 5.8 points from 1990 through 2001.[10]

As more people learned about the January effect, more traders bought small stocks in December, making them less of a bargain and thus reducing their returns. Also, the January effect is biggest among the smallest stocks–but according to Plexus Group, the leading authority on brokerage expenses, the total cost of buying and selling such tiny stocks can run up to 8% of your investment.[11] Sadly, by the time you're done paying your broker, all your gains on the January effect will melt away.

- **Just do "what works."** In 1996, an obscure money manager named James O'Shaughnessy published a book called *What Works on Wall Street.* In it, he argued that "investors can do *much better* than the market." O'Shaughnessy made a stunning claim: From 1954 through 1994, you could have turned $10,000 into $8,074,504, beating the market by more than 10-fold–a towering 18.2% average annual return. How? By buying a basket of 50 stocks with the highest one-year returns, five straight years of rising earnings, and share prices less than 1.5 times their corporate revenues.[12] As if he were the Edison of Wall Street, O'Shaughnessy obtained U.S. Patent No. 5,978,778 for his "automated strategies" and launched a group of four mutual funds based on his findings. By late 1999 the funds had sucked in more than $175 million from the public–and, in his annual letter to shareholders, O'Shaughnessy stated grandly: "As always, I hope

---

[10] Schwert discusses these findings in a brilliant research paper, "Anomalies and Market Efficiency," available at http://schwert.ssb.rochester.edu/papers.htm.

[11] See Plexus Group Commentary 54, "The Official Icebergs of Transaction Costs," January, 1998, at www.plexusgroup.com/fs_research.html.

[12] James O'Shaughnessy, *What Works on Wall Street* (McGraw-Hill, 1996), pp. xvi, 273–295.

that together, we can reach our long-term goals by staying the course and sticking with our time-tested investment strategies."

But "what works on Wall Street" stopped working right after O'Shaughnessy publicized it. As Figure 1-2 shows, two of his funds stank so badly that they shut down in early 2000, and the

FIGURE 1-2

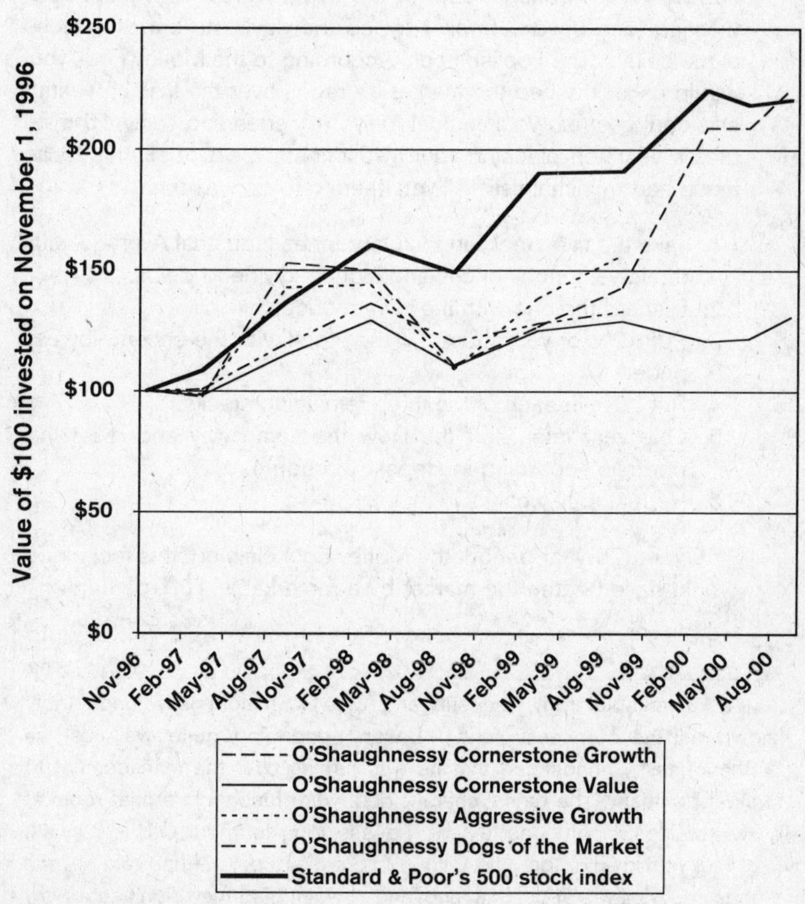

Source: Morningstar, Inc.

overall stock market (as measured by the S & P 500 index) walloped every O'Shaughnessy fund almost nonstop for nearly four years running.

In June 2000, O'Shaughnessy moved closer to his own "long-term goals" by turning the funds over to a new manager, leaving his customers to fend for themselves with those "time-tested investment strategies."[13] O'Shaughnessy's shareholders might have been less upset if he had given his book a more precise title–for instance, *What Used to Work on Wall Street . . . Until I Wrote This Book.*

- **Follow "The Foolish Four."** In the mid-1990s, the Motley Fool website (and several books) hyped the daylights out of a technique called "The Foolish Four." According to the Motley Fool, you would have "trashed the market averages over the last 25 years" and could "crush your mutual funds" by spending "only 15 minutes a year" on planning your investments. Best of all, this technique had "minimal risk." All you needed to do was this:

  1. Take the five stocks in the Dow Jones Industrial Average with the lowest stock prices and highest dividend yields.
  2. Discard the one with the lowest price.
  3. Put 40% of your money in the stock with the second-lowest price.
  4. Put 20% in each of the three remaining stocks.
  5. One year later, sort the Dow the same way and reset the portfolio according to steps 1 through 4.
  6. Repeat until wealthy.

  Over a 25-year period, the Motley Fool claimed, this technique would have beaten the market by a remarkable 10.1 percentage

---

[13] In a remarkable irony, the surviving two O'Shaughnessy funds (now known as the Hennessy funds) began performing quite well just as O'Shaughnessy announced that he was turning over the management to another company. The funds' shareholders were furious. In a chat room at www.morningstar.com, one fumed: "I guess 'long term' for O'S is 3 years. . . . I feel your pain. I, too, had faith in O'S's method. . . . I had told several friends and relatives about this fund, and now am glad they didn't act on my advice."

points annually. Over the next two decades, they suggested, $20,000 invested in The Foolish Four should flower into $1,791,000. (And, they claimed, you could do still better by picking the five Dow stocks with the highest ratio of dividend yield to the square root of stock price, dropping the one that scored the highest, and buying the next four.)

Let's consider whether this "strategy" could meet Graham's definitions of an investment:

- What kind of "thorough analysis" could justify discarding the stock with the single most attractive price and dividend–but keeping the four that score lower for those desirable qualities?
- How could putting 40% of your money into only one stock be a "minimal risk"?
- And how could a portfolio of only four stocks be diversified enough to provide "safety of principal"?

The Foolish Four, in short, was one of the most cockamamie stock-picking formulas ever concocted. The Fools made the same mistake as O'Shaughnessy: If you look at a large quantity of data long enough, a huge number of patterns will emerge–if only by chance. By random luck alone, the companies that produce above-average stock returns will have plenty of things in common. But unless those factors *cause* the stocks to outperform, they can't be used to predict future returns.

None of the factors that the Motley Fools "discovered" with such fanfare–dropping the stock with the best score, doubling up on the one with the second-highest score, dividing the dividend yield by the square root of stock price–could possibly cause or explain the future performance of a stock. *Money* Magazine found that a portfolio made up of stocks whose names contained no repeating letters would have performed nearly as well as The Foolish Four–and for the same reason: luck alone.[14] As Graham never stops reminding us, stocks do well or poorly in the future because the businesses behind them do well or poorly–nothing more, and nothing less.

---

[14] See Jason Zweig, "False Profits," *Money,* August, 1999, pp. 55–57. A thorough discussion of The Foolish Four can also be found at www.investorhome.com/fool.htm.

> Sure enough, instead of crushing the market, The Foolish Four crushed the thousands of people who were fooled into believing that it was a form of investing. In 2000 alone, the four Foolish stocks–Caterpillar, Eastman Kodak, SBC, and General Motors–lost 14% while the Dow dropped by just 4.7%.

As these examples show, there's only one thing that never suffers a bear market on Wall Street: dopey ideas. Each of these so-called investing approaches fell prey to Graham's Law. All mechanical formulas for earning higher stock performance are "a kind of self-destructive process–akin to the law of diminishing returns." There are two reasons the returns fade away. If the formula was just based on random statistical flukes (like The Foolish Four), the mere passage of time will expose that it made no sense in the first place. On the other hand, if the formula actually did work in the past (like the January effect), then by publicizing it, market pundits always erode–and usually eliminate–its ability to do so in the future.

All this reinforces Graham's warning that you must treat speculation as veteran gamblers treat their trips to the casino:

- You must never delude yourself into thinking that you're investing when you're speculating.
- Speculating becomes mortally dangerous the moment you begin to take it seriously.
- You must put strict limits on the amount you are willing to wager.

Just as sensible gamblers take, say, $100 down to the casino floor and leave the rest of their money locked in the safe in their hotel room, the intelligent investor designates a tiny portion of her total portfolio as a "mad money" account. For most of us, 10% of our overall wealth is the maximum permissible amount to put at speculative risk. *Never* mingle the money in your speculative account with what's in your investment accounts; *never* allow your speculative thinking to spill over into your investing activities; and *never* put more than 10% of your assets into your mad money account, no matter what happens.

For better or worse, the gambling instinct is part of human nature–so it's futile for most people even to try suppressing it. But you must confine and restrain it. That's the single best way to make sure you will never fool yourself into confusing speculation with investment.

CHAPTER 2

The Investor and Inflation

Inflation, and the fight against it, has been very much in the public's mind in recent years. The shrinkage in the purchasing power of the dollar in the past, and particularly the fear (or hope by speculators) of a serious further decline in the future, has greatly influenced the thinking of Wall Street. It is clear that those with a fixed dollar income will suffer when the cost of living advances, and the same applies to a fixed amount of dollar principal. Holders of stocks, on the other hand, have the possibility that a loss of the dollar's purchasing power may be offset by advances in their dividends and the prices of their shares.

On the basis of these undeniable facts many financial authorities have concluded that (1) bonds are an inherently undesirable form of investment, and (2) consequently, common stocks are by their very nature more desirable investments than bonds. We have heard of charitable institutions being advised that their portfolios should consist 100% of stocks and zero percent of bonds.* This is quite a reversal from the earlier days when trust investments were

---

* By the late 1990s, this advice—which can be appropriate for a foundation or endowment with an infinitely long investment horizon—had spread to individual investors, whose life spans are finite. In the 1994 edition of his influential book, *Stocks for the Long Run,* finance professor Jeremy Siegel of the Wharton School recommended that "risk-taking" investors should buy on margin, borrowing more than a third of their net worth to sink 135% of their assets into stocks. Even government officials got in on the act: In February 1999, the Honorable Richard Dixon, state treasurer of Maryland, told the audience at an investment conference: "It doesn't make any sense for anyone to have any money in a bond fund."

restricted by law to high-grade bonds (and a few choice preferred stocks).

Our readers must have enough intelligence to recognize that even high-quality stocks cannot be a better purchase than bonds *under all conditions*—i.e., regardless of how high the stock market may be and how low the current dividend return compared with the rates available on bonds. A statement of this kind would be as absurd as was the contrary one—too often heard years ago—that any bond is safer than any stock. In this chapter we shall try to apply various measurements to the inflation factor, in order to reach some conclusions as to the extent to which the investor may wisely be influenced by expectations regarding future rises in the price level.

In this matter, as in so many others in finance, we must base our views of future policy on a knowledge of past experience. Is inflation something new for this country, at least in the serious form it has taken since 1965? If we have seen comparable (or worse) inflations in living experience, what lessons can be learned from them in confronting the inflation of today? Let us start with Table 2-1, a condensed historical tabulation that contains much information about changes in the general price level and concomitant changes in the earnings and market value of common stocks. Our figures will begin with 1915, and thus cover 55 years, presented at five-year intervals. (We use 1946 instead of 1945 to avoid the last year of wartime price controls.)

The first thing we notice is that we have had inflation in the past—lots of it. The largest five-year dose was between 1915 and 1920, when the cost of living nearly doubled. This compares with the advance of 15% between 1965 and 1970. In between, we have had three periods of declining prices and then six of advances at varying rates, some rather small. On this showing, the investor should clearly allow for the probability of continuing or recurrent inflation to come.

Can we tell what the rate of inflation is likely to be? No clear answer is suggested by our table; it shows variations of all sorts. It would seem sensible, however, to take our cue from the rather consistent record of the past 20 years. The average annual rise in the consumer price level for this period has been 2.5%; that for 1965–1970 was 4.5%; that for 1970 alone was 5.4%. Official govern-

TABLE 2-1 The General Price Level, Stock Earnings, and Stock Prices at Five-Year Intervals, 1915–1970

	Price Level[a]		*S & P 500-Stock Index*[b]		*Percent Change from Previous Level*			
Year	Wholesale	Consumer	Earnings	Price	Wholesale Prices	Consumer Prices	Stock Earnings	Stock Prices
1915	38.0	35.4		8.31				
1920	84.5	69.8		7.98	+96.0%	+96.8%		– 4.0%
1925	56.6	61.1	1.24	11.15	–33.4	–12.4		+ 41.5
1930	47.3	58.2	.97	21.63	–16.5	– 4.7	– 21.9%	+ 88.0
1935	43.8	47.8	.76	15.47	– 7.4	–18.0	– 21.6	– 26.0
1940	43.0	48.8	1.05	11.02	– 0.2	+ 2.1	+ 33.1	– 28.8
1946[c]	66.1	68.0	1.06	17.08	+53.7	+40.0	+ 1.0	+ 55.0
1950	86.8	83.8	2.84	18.40	+31.5	+23.1	+168.0	+ 21.4
1955	97.2	93.3	3.62	40.49	+ 6.2	+11.4	+ 27.4	+121.0
1960	100.7	103.1	3.27	55.85	+ 9.2	+10.5	– 9.7	+ 38.0
1965	102.5	109.9	5.19	88.17	+ 1.8	+ 6.6	+ 58.8	+ 57.0
1970	117.5	134.0	5.36	92.15	+14.6	+21.9	+ 3.3	+ 4.4

[a] Annual averages. For price level 1957 = 100 in table; but using new base, 1967 = 100, the average for 1970 is 116.3 for consumers' prices and 110.4 for wholesale prices for the stock index.

[b] 1941–1943 average = 10.

[c] 1946 used, to avoid price controls.

ment policy has been strongly against large-scale inflation, and there are some reasons to believe that Federal policies will be more effective in the future than in recent years.* We think it would be reasonable for an investor at this point to base his thinking and decisions on a *probable* (far from certain) rate of future inflation of, say, 3% per annum. (This would compare with an annual rate of about 2½% for the entire period 1915–1970.)[1]

What would be the implications of such an advance? It would eat up, in higher living costs, about one-half the income now obtainable on good medium-term tax-free bonds (or our assumed after-tax equivalent from high-grade corporate bonds). This would be a serious shrinkage, but it should not be exaggerated. It would not mean that the true value, or the purchasing power, of the investor's fortune need be reduced over the years. If he spent half his interest income after taxes he would maintain this buying power intact, even against a 3% annual inflation.

But the next question, naturally, is, "Can the investor be reasonably sure of doing better by buying and holding other things than high-grade bonds, even at the unprecedented rate of return offered in 1970–1971?" Would not, for example, an all-stock program be preferable to a part-bond, part-stock program? Do not common stocks have a built-in protection against inflation, and are they not almost certain to give a better return over the years than will bonds? Have not in fact stocks treated the investor far better than have bonds over the 55-year period of our study?

The answer to these questions is somewhat complicated. Common stocks have indeed done better than bonds over a long period of time in the past. The rise of the DJIA from an average of 77 in 1915 to an average of 753 in 1970 works out at an annual compounded rate of just about 4%, to which we may add another 4% for average dividend return. (The corresponding figures for the S & P composite are about the same.) These combined figures of 8%

---

* This is one of Graham's rare misjudgments. In 1973, just two years after President Richard Nixon imposed wage and price controls, inflation hit 8.7%, its highest level since the end of World War II. The decade from 1973 through 1982 was the most inflationary in modern American history, as the cost of living more than doubled.

per year are of course much better than the return enjoyed from bonds over the same 55-year period. But they do not exceed that *now* offered by high-grade bonds. This brings us to the next logical question: Is there a persuasive reason to believe that common stocks are likely to do much better in future years than they have in the last five and one-half decades?

Our answer to this crucial question must be a flat *no.* Common stocks *may* do better in the future than in the past, but they are far from certain to do so. We must deal here with two different time elements in investment results. The first covers what is likely to occur over the long-term future—say, the next 25 years. The second applies to what is likely to happen to the investor—both financially and psychologically—over short or intermediate periods, say five years or less. His frame of mind, his hopes and apprehensions, his satisfaction or discontent with what he has done, above all his decisions what to do next, are all determined not in the retrospect of a lifetime of investment but rather by his experience from year to year.

On this point we can be categorical. There is no close time connection between inflationary (or deflationary) conditions and the movement of common-stock earnings and prices. The obvious example is the recent period, 1966–1970. The rise in the cost of living was 22%, the largest in a five-year period since 1946–1950. But both stock earnings and stock prices as a whole have declined since 1965. There are similar contradictions in both directions in the record of previous five-year periods.

Inflation and Corporate Earnings

Another and highly important approach to the subject is by a study of the earnings rate on capital shown by American business. This has fluctuated, of course, with the general rate of economic activity, but it has shown no general tendency to advance with wholesale prices or the cost of living. Actually this rate has fallen rather markedly in the past twenty years in spite of the inflation of the period. (To some degree the decline was due to the charging of more liberal depreciation rates. See Table 2-2.) Our extended studies have led to the conclusion that the investor cannot count on much above the recent five-year rate earned on the DJIA group—

about 10% on net tangible assets (book value) behind the shares.[2] Since the market value of these issues is well above their book value—say, 900 market vs. 560 book in mid-1971—the earnings on current market price work out only at some 6¼%. (This relationship is generally expressed in the reverse, or "times earnings," manner—e.g., that the DJIA price of 900 equals 18 times the actual earnings for the 12 months ended June 1971.)

Our figures gear in directly with the suggestion in the previous chapter* that the investor may assume an average dividend return of about 3.5% on the market value of his stocks, plus an appreciation of, say, 4% annually resulting from reinvested profits. (Note that each dollar added to book value is here assumed to increase the market price by about $1.60.)

The reader will object that in the end our calculations make no allowance for an increase in common-stock earnings and values to result from our projected 3% annual inflation. Our justification is the absence of any sign that the inflation of a comparable amount in the past has had any *direct* effect on reported per-share earnings. The cold figures demonstrate that *all* the large gain in the earnings of the DJIA unit in the past 20 years was due to a proportionately large growth of invested capital coming from reinvested profits. If inflation had operated as a separate favorable factor, its effect would have been to increase the "value" of previously existing capital; this in turn should increase the rate of earnings on such old capital and therefore on the old and new capital combined. But nothing of the kind actually happened in the past 20 years, during which the wholesale price level has advanced nearly 40%. (Business earnings should be influenced more by wholesale prices than by "consumer prices.") The only way that inflation can add to common stock values is by raising the rate of earnings on capital investment. On the basis of the past record this has not been the case.

In the economic cycles of the past, good business was accompanied by a rising price level and poor business by falling prices. It was generally felt that "a little inflation" was helpful to business profits. This view is not contradicted by the history of 1950–1970,

---

* See p. 25.

which reveals a combination of generally continued prosperity and generally rising prices. But the figures indicate that the effect of all this on the *earning power* of common-stock capital ("equity capital") has been quite limited; in fact it has not even served to maintain the rate of earnings on the investment. Clearly there have been important offsetting influences which have prevented any increase in the real profitability of American corporations as a whole. Perhaps the most important of these have been (1) a rise in wage rates exceeding the gains in productivity, and (2) the need for huge amounts of new capital, thus holding down the ratio of sales to capital employed.

Our figures in Table 2-2 indicate that so far from inflation having benefited our corporations and their shareholders, its effect has been quite the opposite. The most striking figures in our table are those for the growth of corporate debt between 1950 and 1969. It is surprising how little attention has been paid by economists and by Wall Street to this development. The debt of corporations has expanded nearly fivefold while their profits before taxes a little more than doubled. With the great rise in interest rates during this period, it is evident that the aggregate corporate debt is now an

TABLE 2-2 Corporate Debt, Profits, and Earnings on Capital, 1950–1969

		Corporate Profits		*Percent Earned on Capital*	
Year	*Net Corporate Debt (billions)*	Before Income Tax (millions)	After Tax (millions)	S & P Data[a]	Other Data[b]
1950	$140.2	$42.6	$17.8	18.3%	15.0%
1955	212.1	48.6	27.0	18.3	12.9
1960	302.8	49.7	26.7	10.4	9.1
1965	453.3	77.8	46.5	10.8	11.8
1969	692.9	91.2	48.5	11.8	11.3

[a] Earnings of Standard & Poor's industrial index divided by average book value for year.

[b] Figures for 1950 and 1955 from Cottle and Whitman; those for 1960–1969 from *Fortune.*

adverse economic factor of some magnitude and a real problem for many individual enterprises. (Note that in 1950 net earnings after interest but before income tax were about 30% of corporate debt, while in 1969 they were only 13.2% of debt. The 1970 ratio must have been even less satisfactory.) In sum it appears that a significant part of the 11% being earned on corporate equities as a whole is accomplished by the use of a large amount of new debt costing 4% or less after tax credit. If our corporations had maintained the debt ratio of 1950, their earnings rate on stock capital would have fallen still lower, in spite of the inflation.

The stock market has considered that the public-utility enterprises have been a chief victim of inflation, being caught between a great advance in the cost of borrowed money and the difficulty of raising the rates charged under the regulatory process. But this may be the place to remark that the very fact that the unit costs of electricity, gas, and telephone services have advanced so much less than the general price index puts these companies in a strong strategic position for the future.[3] They are entitled by law to charge rates sufficient for an adequate return on their invested capital, and this will probably protect their shareholders in the future as it has in the inflations of the past.

All of the above brings us back to our conclusion that the investor has no sound basis for expecting more than an average overall return of, say, 8% on a portfolio of DJIA-type common stocks purchased at the late 1971 price level. But even if these expectations should prove to be understated by a substantial amount, the case would not be made for an all-stock investment program. If there is one thing guaranteed for the future, it is that the earnings and average annual market value of a stock portfolio will *not* grow at the uniform rate of 4%, or any other figure. In the memorable words of the elder J. P. Morgan, *"They will fluctuate."** This means, first, that the common-stock buyer at today's prices—

* John Pierpont Morgan was the most powerful financier of the late nineteenth and early twentieth centuries. Because of his vast influence, he was constantly asked what the stock market would do next. Morgan developed a mercifully short and unfailingly accurate answer: "It will fluctuate." See Jean Strouse, *Morgan: American Financier* (Random House, 1999), p. 11.

or tomorrow's—will be running a real risk of having unsatisfactory results therefrom over a period of years. It took 25 years for General Electric (and the DJIA itself) to recover the ground lost in the 1929–1932 debacle. Besides that, if the investor concentrates his portfolio on common stocks he is very likely to be led astray either by exhilarating advances or by distressing declines. This is particularly true if his reasoning is geared closely to expectations of further inflation. For then, if another bull market comes along, he will take the big rise not as a danger signal of an inevitable fall, not as a chance to cash in on his handsome profits, but rather as a vindication of the inflation hypothesis and as a reason to keep on buying common stocks no matter how high the market level nor how low the dividend return. That way lies sorrow.

Alternatives to Common Stocks as Inflation Hedges

The standard policy of people all over the world who mistrust their currency has been to buy and hold gold. This has been against the law for American citizens since 1935—luckily for them. In the past 35 years the price of gold in the open market has advanced from $35 per ounce to $48 in early 1972—a rise of only 35%. But during all this time the holder of gold has received no income return on his capital, and instead has incurred some annual expense for storage. Obviously, he would have done much better with his money at interest in a savings bank, in spite of the rise in the general price level.

The near-complete failure of gold to protect against a loss in the purchasing power of the dollar must cast grave doubt on the ability of the ordinary investor to protect himself against inflation by putting his money in "things."* Quite a few categories of valuable

* The investment philosopher Peter L. Bernstein feels that Graham was "dead wrong" about precious metals, particularly gold, which (at least in the years after Graham wrote this chapter) has shown a robust ability to outpace inflation. Financial adviser William Bernstein agrees, pointing out that a tiny allocation to a precious-metals fund (say, 2% of your total assets) is too small to hurt your overall returns when gold does poorly. But, when gold does well, its returns are often so spectacular–sometimes exceeding 100%

objects have had striking advances in market value over the years—such as diamonds, paintings by masters, first editions of books, rare stamps and coins, etc. But in many, perhaps most, of these cases there seems to be an element of the artificial or the precarious or even the unreal about the quoted prices. Somehow it is hard to think of paying $67,500 for a U.S. silver dollar dated 1804 (but not even minted that year) as an "investment operation."[4] We acknowledge we are out of our depth in this area. Very few of our readers will find the swimming safe and easy there.

The outright ownership of real estate has long been considered as a sound long-term investment, carrying with it a goodly amount of protection against inflation. Unfortunately, real-estate values are also subject to wide fluctuations; serious errors can be made in location, price paid, etc.; there are pitfalls in salesmen's wiles. Finally, diversification is not practical for the investor of moderate means, except by various types of participations with others and with the special hazards that attach to new flotations—not too different from common-stock ownership. This too is not our field. All we should say to the investor is, "Be sure it's yours before you go into it."

Conclusion

Naturally, we return to the policy recommended in our previous chapter. Just because of the uncertainties of the future the investor cannot afford to put all his funds into one basket—neither in the bond basket, despite the unprecedentedly high returns that bonds have recently offered; nor in the stock basket, despite the prospect of continuing inflation.

The more the investor depends on his portfolio and the income therefrom, the more necessary it is for him to guard against the

---

in a year—that it can, all by itself, set an otherwise lackluster portfolio glittering. However, the intelligent investor avoids investing in gold directly, with its high storage and insurance costs; instead, seek out a well-diversified mutual fund specializing in the stocks of precious-metal companies and charging below 1% in annual expenses. Limit your stake to 2% of your total financial assets (or perhaps 5% if you are over the age of 65).

unexpected and the disconcerting in this part of his life. It is axiomatic that the conservative investor should seek to minimize his risks. We think strongly that the risks involved in buying, say, a telephone-company bond at yields of nearly 7½% are much less than those involved in buying the DJIA at 900 (or any stock list equivalent thereto). But the possibility of *large-scale* inflation remains, and the investor must carry some insurance against it. There is no certainty that a stock component will insure adequately against such inflation, but it should carry more protection than the bond component.

This is what we said on the subject in our 1965 edition (p. 97), and we would write the same today:

> It must be evident to the reader that we have no enthusiasm for common stocks at these levels (892 for the DJIA). For reasons already given we feel that the defensive investor cannot afford to be without an appreciable proportion of common stocks in his portfolio, even if we regard them as the lesser of two evils—the greater being the risks in an all-bond holding.

COMMENTARY ON CHAPTER 2

Americans are getting stronger. Twenty years ago, it took two people to carry ten dollars' worth of groceries. Today, a five-year-old can do it.

–*Henny Youngman*

Inflation? Who cares about *that*?

After all, the annual rise in the cost of goods and services averaged less than 2.2% between 1997 and 2002–and economists believe that even that rock-bottom rate may be overstated.[1] (Think, for instance, of how the prices of computers and home electronics have plummeted–and how the quality of many goods has risen, meaning that consumers are getting better value for their money.) In recent years, the true rate of inflation in the United States has probably run around 1% annually–an increase so infinitesimal that many pundits have proclaimed that "inflation is dead."[2]

---

[1] The U.S. Bureau of Labor Statistics, which calculates the Consumer Price Index that measures inflation, maintains a comprehensive and helpful website at www.bls.gov/cpi/home.htm.

[2] For a lively discussion of the "inflation is dead" scenario, see www.pbs.org/newshour/bb/economy/july-dec97/inflation_12-16.html. In 1996, the Boskin Commission, a group of economists asked by the government to investigate whether the official rate of inflation is accurate, estimated that it has been overstated, often by nearly two percentage points per year. For the commission's report, see www.ssa.gov/history/reports/boskinrpt.html. Many investment experts now feel that deflation, or falling prices, is an even greater threat than inflation; the best way to hedge against that risk is by including bonds as a permanent component of your portfolio. (See the commentary on Chapter 4.)

THE MONEY ILLUSION

There's another reason investors overlook the importance of inflation: what psychologists call the "money illusion." If you receive a 2% raise in a year when inflation runs at 4%, you will almost certainly feel better than you will if you take a 2% pay cut during a year when inflation is zero. Yet both changes in your salary leave you in a virtually identical position–2% worse off after inflation. So long as the *nominal* (or absolute) change is positive, we view it as a good thing–even if the *real* (or after-inflation) result is negative. And any change in your own salary is more vivid and specific than the generalized change of prices in the economy as a whole.[3] Likewise, investors were delighted to earn 11% on bank certificates of deposit (CDs) in 1980 and are bitterly disappointed to be earning only around 2% in 2003–even though they were losing money after inflation back then but are keeping up with inflation now. The nominal rate we earn is printed in the bank's ads and posted in its window, where a high number makes us feel good. But inflation eats away at that high number in secret. Instead of taking out ads, inflation just takes away our wealth. That's why inflation is so easy to overlook–and why it's so important to measure your investing success not just by what you make, but by how much you keep after inflation.

More basically still, the intelligent investor must always be on guard against whatever is unexpected and underestimated. There are three good reasons to believe that inflation is not dead:

- As recently as 1973–1982, the United States went through one of the most painful bursts of inflation in our history. As measured by the Consumer Price Index, prices more than doubled over that period, rising at an annualized rate of nearly 9%. In 1979 alone, inflation raged at 13.3%, paralyzing the economy in what became known as "stagflation"–and leading many commentators to question whether America could compete in the global market-

---

[3] For more insights into this behavioral pitfall, see Eldar Shafir, Peter Diamond, and Amos Tversky, "Money Illusion," in Daniel Kahneman and Amos Tversky, eds., *Choices, Values, and Frames* (Cambridge University Press, 2000), pp. 335–355.

place.[4] Goods and services priced at $100 in the beginning of 1973 cost $230 by the end of 1982, shriveling the value of a dollar to less than 45 cents. No one who lived through it would scoff at such destruction of wealth; no one who is prudent can fail to protect against the risk that it might recur.

- Since 1960, 69% of the world's market-oriented countries have suffered at least one year in which inflation ran at an annualized rate of 25% or more. On average, those inflationary periods destroyed 53% of an investor's purchasing power.[5] We would be crazy not to hope that America is somehow exempt from such a disaster. But we would be even crazier to conclude that it can never happen here.[6]
- Rising prices allow Uncle Sam to pay off his debts with dollars that have been cheapened by inflation. Completely eradicating inflation runs against the economic self-interest of any government that regularly borrows money.[7]

---

[4] That year, President Jimmy Carter gave his famous "malaise" speech, in which he warned of "a crisis in confidence" that "strikes at the very heart and soul and spirit of our national will" and "threatens to destroy the social and the political fabric of America."

[5] See Stanley Fischer, Ratna Sahay, and Carlos A. Vegh, "Modern Hyper- and High Inflations," National Bureau of Economic Research, Working Paper 8930, at www.nber.org/papers/w8930.

[6] In fact, the United States has had two periods of hyperinflation. During the American Revolution, prices roughly tripled every year from 1777 through 1779, with a pound of butter costing $12 and a barrel of flour fetching nearly $1,600 in Revolutionary Massachusetts. During the Civil War, inflation raged at annual rates of 29% (in the North) and nearly 200% (in the Confederacy). As recently as 1946, inflation hit 18.1% in the United States.

[7] I am indebted to Laurence Siegel of the Ford Foundation for this cynical, but accurate, insight. Conversely, in a time of deflation (or steadily falling prices) it's more advantageous to be a lender than a borrower–which is why most investors should keep at least a small portion of their assets in bonds, as a form of insurance against deflating prices.

HALF A HEDGE

What, then, can the intelligent investor do to guard against inflation? The standard answer is "buy stocks"–but, as common answers so often are, it is not entirely true.

Figure 2-1 shows, for each year from 1926 through 2002, the relationship between inflation and stock prices.

As you can see, in years when the prices of consumer goods and services fell, as on the left side of the graph, stock returns were terrible–with the market losing up to 43% of its value.[8] When inflation shot above 6%, as in the years on the right end of the graph, stocks also stank. The stock market lost money in eight of the 14 years in which inflation exceeded 6%; the average return for those 14 years was a measly 2.6%.

While mild inflation allows companies to pass the increased costs of their own raw materials on to customers, high inflation wreaks havoc–forcing customers to slash their purchases and depressing activity throughout the economy.

The historical evidence is clear: Since the advent of accurate stock-market data in 1926, there have been 64 five-year periods (i.e., 1926–1930, 1927–1931, 1928–1932, and so on through 1998–2002). In 50 of those 64 five-year periods (or 78% of the time), stocks outpaced inflation.[9] That's impressive, but imperfect; it means that stocks failed to keep up with inflation about one-fifth of the time.

---

[8] When inflation is negative, it is technically termed "deflation." Regularly falling prices may at first sound appealing, until you think of the Japanese example. Prices have been deflating in Japan since 1989, with real estate and the stock market dropping in value year after year–a relentless water torture for the world's second-largest economy.

[9] Ibbotson Associates, *Stocks, Bonds, Bills, and Inflation, 2003 Handbook* (Ibbotson Associates, Chicago, 2003), Table 2-8. The same pattern is evident outside the United States: In Belgium, Italy, and Germany, where inflation was especially high in the twentieth century, "inflation appears to have had a negative impact on both stock and bond markets," note Elroy Dimson, Paul Marsh, and Mike Staunton in *Triumph of the Optimists: 101 Years of Global Investment Returns* (Princeton University Press, 2002), p. 53.

FIGURE 2-1

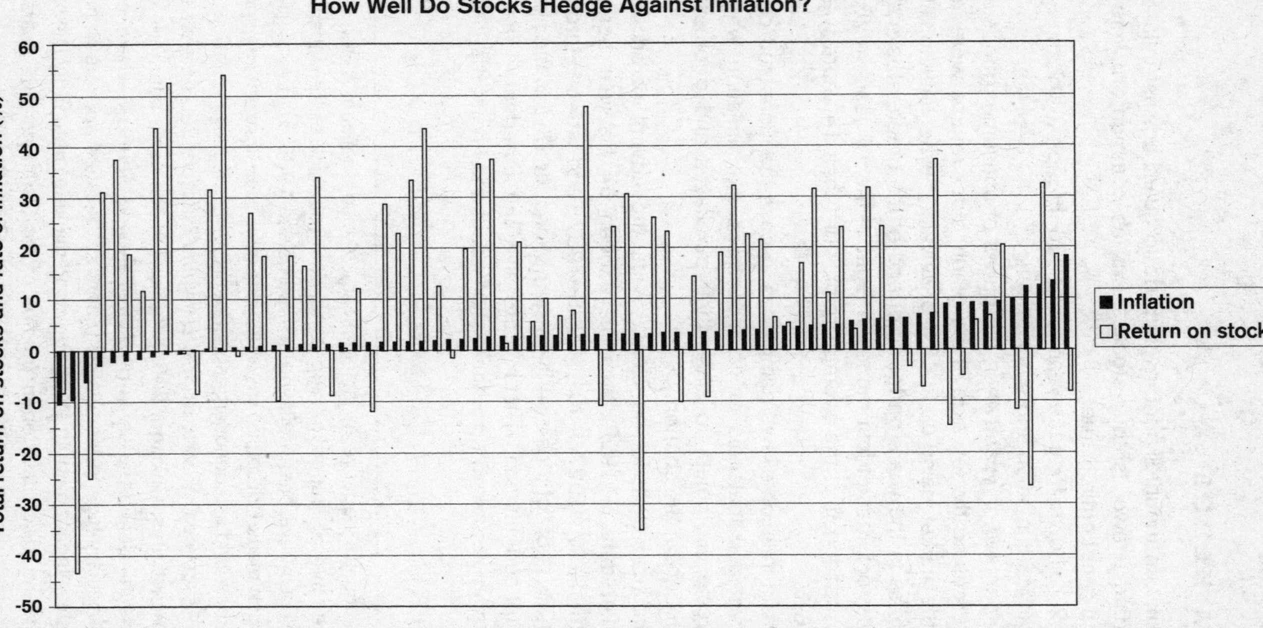

This graph shows inflation and stock returns for each year between 1926 and 2002—arrayed not in chronological order but from the lowest annual inflation rates to the highest. When inflation is highly negative (see far left), stocks do very poorly. When inflation is moderate, as it was in most years during this period, stocks generally do well. But when inflation heats up to very high levels (see far right), stocks perform erratically, often losing at least 10%.

Source: Ibbotson Associates

TWO ACRONYMS TO THE RESCUE

Fortunately, you can bolster your defenses against inflation by branching out beyond stocks. Since Graham last wrote, two inflation-fighters have become widely available to investors:

REITs. Real Estate Investment Trusts, or REITs (pronounced "reets"), are companies that own and collect rent from commercial and residential properties.[10] Bundled into real-estate mutual funds, REITs do a decent job of combating inflation. The best choice is Vanguard REIT Index Fund; other relatively low-cost choices include Cohen & Steers Realty Shares, Columbia Real Estate Equity Fund, and Fidelity Real Estate Investment Fund.[11] While a REIT fund is unlikely to be a foolproof inflation-fighter, in the long run it should give you some defense against the erosion of purchasing power without hampering your overall returns.

TIPS. Treasury Inflation-Protected Securities, or TIPS, are U.S. government bonds, first issued in 1997, that automatically go up in value when inflation rises. Because the full faith and credit of the United States stands behind them, all Treasury bonds are safe from the risk of default (or nonpayment of interest). But TIPS also guarantee that the value of your investment won't be eroded by inflation. In one easy package, you insure yourself against financial loss and the loss of purchasing power.[12]

There is one catch, however. When the value of your TIPS bond rises as inflation heats up, the Internal Revenue Service regards that increase in value as taxable income–even though it is purely a paper

---

[10] Thorough, if sometimes outdated, information on REITs can be found at www.nareit.com.

[11] For further information, see www.vanguard.com, www.cohenandsteers.com, www.columbiafunds.com, and www.fidelity.com. The case for investing in a REIT fund is weaker if you own a home, since that gives you an inherent stake in real-estate ownership.

[12] A good introduction to TIPS can be found at www.publicdebt.treas.gov/of/ofinflin.htm. For more advanced discussions, see www.federalreserve.gov/Pubs/feds/2002/200232/200232pap.pdf, www.tiaa-crefinstitute.org/Publications/resdiags/73_09-2002.htm, and www.bwater.com/research_ibonds.htm.

gain (unless you sold the bond at its newly higher price). Why does this make sense to the IRS? The intelligent investor will remember the wise words of financial analyst Mark Schweber: "The one question never to ask a bureaucrat is 'Why?' " Because of this exasperating tax complication, TIPS are best suited for a tax-deferred retirement account like an IRA, Keogh, or 401(k), where they will not jack up your taxable income.

You can buy TIPS directly from the U.S. government at www.publicdebt.treas.gov/of/ofinflin.htm, or in a low-cost mutual fund like Vanguard Inflation-Protected Securities or Fidelity Inflation-Protected Bond Fund.[13] Either directly or through a fund, TIPS are the ideal substitute for the proportion of your retirement funds you would otherwise keep in cash. Do not trade them: TIPS can be volatile in the short run, so they work best as a permanent, lifelong holding. For most investors, allocating at least 10% of your retirement assets to TIPS is an intelligent way to keep a portion of your money absolutely safe—and entirely beyond the reach of the long, invisible claws of inflation.

---

[13] For details on these funds, see www.vanguard.com or www.fidelity.com.

CHAPTER 3

A Century of Stock-Market History: The Level of Stock Prices in Early 1972

The investor's portfolio of common stocks will represent a small cross-section of that immense and formidable institution known as the stock market. Prudence suggests that he have an adequate idea of stock-market history, in terms particularly of the major fluctuations in its price level and of the varying relationships between stock prices as a whole and their earnings and dividends. With this background he may be in a position to form some worthwhile judgment of the attractiveness or dangers of the level of the market as it presents itself at different times. By a coincidence, useful statistical data on prices, earnings, and dividends go back just 100 years, to 1871. (The material is not nearly as full or dependable in the first half-period as in the second, but it will serve.) In this chapter we shall present the figures, in highly condensed form, with two objects in view. The first is to show the general manner in which stocks have made their underlying advance through the many cycles of the past century. The second is to view the picture in terms of successive ten-year averages, not only of stock prices but of earnings and dividends as well, to bring out the varying relationship between the three important factors. With this wealth of material as a background we shall pass to a consideration of the level of stock prices at the beginning of 1972.

The long-term history of the stock market is summarized in two tables and a chart. Table 3-1 sets forth the low and high points of nineteen bear- and bull-market cycles in the past 100 years. We have used two indexes here. The first represents a combination of an early study by the Cowles Commission going back to 1870, which has been spliced on to and continued to date in the well-

TABLE 3-1 Major Stock-Market Swings Between 1871 and 1971

	Cowles-Standard 500 Composite			*Dow-Jones Industrial Average*		
Year	High	Low	Decline	High	Low	Decline
1871		4.64				
1881	6.58					
1885		4.24	28%			
1887	5.90					
1893		4.08	31			
1897					38.85	
1899				77.6		
1900					53.5	31%
1901	8.50			78.3		
1903		6.26	26		43.2	45
1906	10.03			103		
1907		6.25	38		53	48
1909	10.30			100.5		
1914		7.35	29		53.2	47
1916–18	10.21			110.2		
1917		6.80	33		73.4	33
1919	9.51			119.6		
1921		6.45	32		63.9	47
1929	31.92			381		
1932		4.40	86		41.2	89
1937	18.68			197.4		
1938		8.50	55		99	50
1939	13.23			158		
1942		7.47	44		92.9	41
1946	19.25			212.5		
1949		13.55	30		161.2	24
1952	26.6			292		
1952–53		22.7	15		256	13
1956	49.7			521		
1957		39.0	24		420	20
1961	76.7			735		
1962		54.8	29		536	27
1966–68	108.4			995		
1970		69.3	36		631	37
early 1972	100		—	900		—

known Standard & Poor's composite index of 500 stocks. The second is the even more celebrated Dow Jones Industrial Average (the DJIA, or "the Dow"), which dates back to 1897; it contains 30 companies, of which one is American Telephone & Telegraph and the other 29 are large industrial enterprises.[1]

Chart I, presented by courtesy of Standard & Poor's, depicts the market fluctuations of its 425-industrial-stock index from 1900 through 1970. (A corresponding chart available for the DJIA will look very much the same.) The reader will note three quite distinct patterns, each covering about a third of the 70 years. The first runs from 1900 to 1924, and shows for the most part a series of rather similar market cycles lasting from three to five years. The annual advance in this period averaged just about 3%. We move on to the "New Era" bull market, culminating in 1929, with its terrible aftermath of collapse, followed by quite irregular fluctuations until 1949. Comparing the average level of 1949 with that of 1924, we find the annual rate of advance to be a mere 1½%; hence the close of our second period found the public with no enthusiasm at all for common stocks. By the rule of opposites the time was ripe for the beginning of the greatest bull market in our history, presented in the last third of our chart. This phenomenon may have reached its culmination in December 1968 at 118 for Standard & Poor's 425 industrials (and 108 for its 500-stock composite). As Table 3-1 shows, there were fairly important setbacks between 1949 and 1968 (especially in 1956–57 and 1961–62), but the recoveries therefrom were so rapid that they had to be denominated (in the long-accepted semantics) as recessions in a single bull market, rather than as separate market cycles. Between the low level of 162 for "the Dow" in mid-1949 and the high of 995 in early 1966, the advance had been more than sixfold in 17 years—which is at the average compounded rate of 11% per year, not counting dividends of, say, 3½% per annum. (The advance for the Standard & Poor's composite index was somewhat greater than that of the DJIA—actually from 14 to 96.)

These 14% and better returns were documented in 1963, and later, in a much publicized study.*[2] It created a natural satisfaction

---

* The study, in its final form, was Lawrence Fisher and James H. Lorie, "Rates of Return on Investments in Common Stock: the Year-by-Year

CHART 1

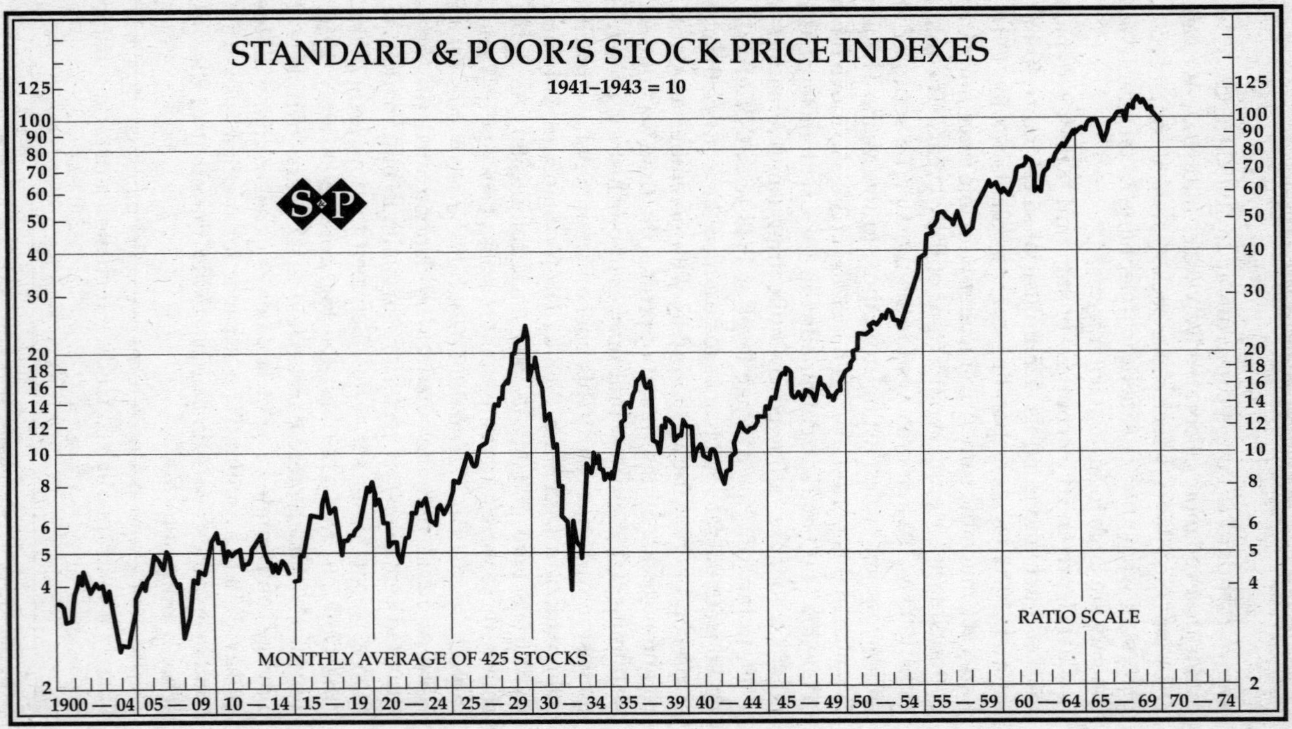

STANDARD & POOR'S STOCK PRICE INDEXES

1941–1943 = 10

S P

MONTHLY AVERAGE OF 425 STOCKS

RATIO SCALE

125 100 90 80 70 60 50 40 30 20 18 16 14 12 10 8 6 5 4 2

1900 — 04 | 05 — 09 | 10 — 14 | 15 — 19 | 20 — 24 | 25 — 29 | 30 — 34 | 35 — 39 | 40 — 44 | 45 — 49 | 50 — 54 | 55 — 59 | 60 — 64 | 65 — 69 | 70 — 74

on Wall Street with such fine achievements, and a quite illogical and dangerous conviction that equally marvelous results could be expected for common stocks in the future. Few people seem to have been bothered by the thought that the very extent of the rise might indicate that it had been overdone. The subsequent decline from the 1968 high to the 1970 low was 36% for the Standard & Poor's composite (and 37% for the DJIA), the largest since the 44% suffered in 1939–1942, which had reflected the perils and uncertainties after Pearl Harbor. In the dramatic manner so characteristic of Wall Street, the low level of May 1970 was followed by a massive and speedy recovery of both averages, and the establishment of a new all-time high for the Standard & Poor's industrials in early 1972. The annual rate of price advance between 1949 and 1970 works out at about 9% for the S & P composite (or the industrial index), using the average figures for both years. That rate of climb was, of course, much greater than for any similar period before 1950. (But in the last decade the rate of advance was much lower—5¼% for the S & P composite index and only the once familiar 3% for the DJIA.)

The record of price movements should be supplemented by corresponding figures for earnings and dividends, in order to provide an overall view of what has happened to our share economy over the ten decades. We present a conspectus of this kind in our Table 3-2 (p. 71). It is a good deal to expect from the reader that he study all these figures with care, but for some we hope they will be interesting and instructive.

Let us comment on them as follows: The full decade figures smooth out the year-to-year fluctuations and leave a general picture of persistent growth. Only two of the nine decades after the first show a decrease in earnings and average prices (in 1891–1900 and 1931–1940), and no decade after 1900 shows a decrease in average dividends. But the rates of growth in all three categories are quite variable. In general the performance since World War II has been superior to that of earlier decades, but the advance in the 1960s was less pronounced than that of the 1950s. Today's investor

---

Record, 1926–65," *The Journal of Business*, vol. XLI, no. 3 (July, 1968), pp. 291–316. For a summary of the study's wide influence, see http://library.dfaus.com/reprints/work_of_art/.

cannot tell from this record what percentage gain in earnings dividends and prices he may expect in the next ten years, but it does supply all the encouragement he needs for a consistent policy of common-stock investment.

However, a point should be made here that is not disclosed in our table. The year 1970 was marked by a definite deterioration in the overall earnings posture of our corporations. The rate of profit on invested capital fell to the lowest percentage since the World War years. Equally striking is the fact that a considerable number of companies reported net losses for the year; many became "financially troubled," and for the first time in three decades there were quite a few important bankruptcy proceedings. These facts as much as any others have prompted the statement made above* that the great boom era may have come to an end in 1969–1970.

A striking feature of Table 3-2 is the change in the price/earnings ratios since World War II.† In June 1949 the S & P composite index sold at only 6.3 times the applicable earnings of the past 12 months; in March 1961 the ratio was 22.9 times. Similarly, the dividend yield on the S & P index had fallen from over 7% in 1949 to only 3.0% in 1961, a contrast heightened by the fact that interest rates on high-grade bonds had meanwhile risen from 2.60% to 4.50%. This is certainly the most remarkable turnabout in the public's attitude in all stock-market history.

To people of long experience and innate caution the passage from one extreme to another carried a strong warning of trouble ahead. They could not help thinking apprehensively of the 1926–1929 bull market and its tragic aftermath. But these fears have not been confirmed by the event. True, the closing price of the DJIA

---

* See pp. 50–52.

† The "price/earnings ratio" of a stock, or of a market average like the S & P 500-stock index, is a simple tool for taking the market's temperature. If, for instance, a company earned $1 per share of net income over the past year, and its stock is selling at $8.93 per share, its price/earnings ratio would be 8.93; if, however, the stock is selling at $69.70, then the price/earnings ratio would be 69.7. In general, a price/earnings ratio (or "P/E" ratio) below 10 is considered low, between 10 and 20 is considered moderate, and greater than 20 is considered expensive. (For more on P/E ratios, see p. 168.)

TABLE 3-2 A Picture of Stock-Market Performance, 1871–1970[a]

Period	*Average Price*	*Average Earnings*	*Average P/E Ratio*	*Dividend Average*	*Average Yield*	*Average Payout*	*Annual Growth Rate*[b]	
							Earnings	Dividends
1871–1880	3.58	0.32	11.3	0.21	6.0%	67%	—	—
1881–1890	5.00	0.32	15.6	0.24	4.7	75	– 0.64%	–0.66%
1891–1900	4.65	0.30	15.5	0.19	4.0	64	– 1.04	–2.23
1901–1910	8.32	0.63	13.1	0.35	4.2	58	+ 6.91	+5.33
1911–1920	8.62	0.86	10.0	0.50	5.8	58	+ 3.85	+3.94
1921–1930	13.89	1.05	13.3	0.71	5.1	68	+ 2.84	+2.29
1931–1940	11.55	0.68	17.0	0.78	5.1	85	– 2.15	–0.23
1941–1950	13.90	1.46	9.5	0.87	6.3	60	+10.60	+3.25
1951–1960	39.20	3.00	13.1	1.63	4.2	54	+ 6.74	+5.90
1961–1970	82.50	4.83	17.1	2.68	3.2	55	+ 5.80[c]	+5.40[c]
1954–1956	38.19	2.56	15.1	1.64	4.3	65	+ 2.40[d]	+7.80[d]
1961–1963	66.10	3.66	18.1	2.14	3.2	58	+ 5.15[d]	+4.42[d]
1968–1970	93.25	5.60	16.7	3.13	3.3	56	+ 6.30[d]	+5.60[d]

[a] The following data based largely on figures appearing in N. Molodovsky's article, "Stock Values and Stock Prices," *Financial Analysts Journal*, May 1960. These, in turn, are taken from the Cowles Commission book *Common Stock Indexes* for years before 1926 and from the spliced-on Standard & Poor's 500-stock composite index for 1926 to date.

[b] The annual growth-rate figures are Molodovsky compilations covering successive 21-year periods ending in 1890, 1900, etc.

[c] Growth rate for 1968–1970 vs. 1958–1960.

[d] These growth-rate figures are for 1954–1956 vs. 1947–1949, 1961–1963 vs. 1954–1956, and for 1968–1970 vs. 1958–1960.

in 1970 was the same as it was 6½ years earlier, and the much heralded "Soaring Sixties" proved to be mainly a march up a series of high hills and then down again. But nothing has happened either to business or to stock prices that can compare with the bear market and depression of 1929–1932.

The Stock-Market Level in Early 1972

With a century-long conspectus of stock, prices, earnings, and dividends before our eyes, let us try to draw some conclusions about the level of 900 for the DJIA and 100 for the S & P composite index in January 1972.

In each of our former editions we have discussed the level of the stock market at the time of writing, and endeavored to answer the question whether it was too high for conservative purchase. The reader may find it informing to review the conclusions we reached on these earlier occasions. This is not entirely an exercise in self-punishment. It will supply a sort of connecting tissue that links the various stages of the stock market in the past twenty years and also a taken-from-life picture of the difficulties facing anyone who tries to reach an informed and critical judgment of current market levels. Let us, first, reproduce the summary of the 1948, 1953, and 1959 analyses that we gave in the 1965 edition:

> In 1948 we applied conservative standards to the Dow Jones level of 180, and found no difficulty in reaching the conclusion that "it was not too high in relation to underlying values." When we approached this problem in 1953 the average market level for that year had reached 275, a gain of over 50% in five years. We asked ourselves the same question—namely, "whether in our opinion the level of 275 for the Dow Jones Industrials was or was not too high for sound investment." In the light of the subsequent spectacular advance, it may seem strange to have to report that it was by no means easy for us to reach a definitive conclusion as to the attractiveness of the 1953 level. We did say, positively enough, that "from the standpoint of value indications—our chief investment guide—the conclusion about 1953 stock prices must be favorable." But we were concerned about the fact that in 1953, the averages had advanced for a longer period than in most bull markets of the

past, and that its absolute level was historically high. Setting these factors against our favorable value judgment, we advised a cautious or compromise policy. As it turned out, this was not a particularly brilliant counsel. A good prophet would have foreseen that the market level was due to advance an additional 100% in the next five years. Perhaps we should add in self-defense that few if any of those whose business was stock-market forecasting—as ours was not—had any better inkling than we did of what lay ahead.

At the beginning of 1959 we found the DJIA at an all-time high of 584. Our lengthy analysis made from all points of view may be summarized in the following (from page 59 of the 1959 edition): "In sum, we feel compelled to express the conclusion that the present level of stock prices is a dangerous one. It may well be perilous because prices are already far too high. But even if this is not the case the market's momentum is such as inevitably to carry it to unjustifiable heights. Frankly, we cannot imagine a market of the future in which there will never be any serious losses, and in which, every tyro will be guaranteed a large profit on his stock purchases."

The caution we expressed in 1959 was somewhat better justified by the sequel than was our corresponding attitude in 1954. Yet it was far from fully vindicated. The DJIA advanced to 685 in 1961; then fell a little below our 584 level (to 566) later in the year; advanced again to 735 in late 1961; and then declined in near panic to 536 in May 1962, showing a loss of 27% within the brief period of six months. At the same time there was a far more serious shrinkage in the most popular "growth stocks"—as evidenced by the striking fall of the indisputable leader, International Business Machines, from a high of 607 in December 1961 to a low of 300 in June 1962.

This period saw a complete debacle in a host of newly launched common stocks of small enterprises—the so-called hot issues—which had been offered to the public at ridiculously high prices and then had been further pushed up by needless speculation to levels little short of insane. Many of these lost 90% and more of the quotations in just a few months.

The collapse in the first half of 1962 was disconcerting, if not disastrous, to many self-acknowledged speculators and perhaps to many more imprudent people who called themselves "investors." But the turnabout that came later that year was equally unsuspected by the financial community. The stock-market averages resumed their upward course, producing the following sequence:

	DJIA	*Standard & Poor's 500-Stock Composite*
December 1961	735	72.64
June 1962	536	52.32
November 1964	892	86.28

The recovery and new ascent of common-stock prices was indeed remarkable and created a corresponding revision of Wall Street sentiment. At the low level of June 1962 predictions had appeared predominantly bearish, and after the partial recovery to the end of that year they were mixed, leaning to the skeptical side. But at the outset of 1964 the natural optimism of brokerage firms was again manifest; nearly all the forecasts were on the bullish side, and they so continued through the 1964 advance.

We then approached the task of appraising the November 1964 levels of the stock market (892 for the DJIA). After discussing it learnedly from numerous angles we reached three main conclusions. The first was that "old standards (of valuation) appear inapplicable; new standards have not yet been tested by time." The second was that the investor "must base his policy on the existence of major uncertainties. The possibilities compass the extremes, on the one hand, of a protracted and further advance in the market's level—say by 50%, or to 1350 for the DJIA; or, on the other hand, of a largely unheralded collapse of the same magnitude, bringing the average in the neighborhood of, say, 450" (p. 63). The third was expressed in much more definite terms. We said: "Speaking bluntly, if the 1964 price level is not too high how could we say that *any* price level is too high?" And the chapter closed as follows:

WHAT COURSE TO FOLLOW

Investors should not conclude that the 1964 market level is dangerous merely because they read it in this book. They must weigh our reasoning against the contrary reasoning they will hear from most competent and experienced people on Wall Street. In the end each one must make his own decision and accept responsibility therefor. We suggest, however, that if the investor is in doubt as to which course to pursue he should choose the path of caution. The principles of investment, as set forth herein, would call for the following policy under 1964 conditions, in order of urgency:

1. No borrowing to buy or hold securities.
2. No increase in the proportion of funds held in common stocks.
3. A reduction in common-stock holdings where needed to bring it down to a maximum of 50 per cent of the total portfolio. The capital-gains tax must be paid with as good grace as possible, and the proceeds invested in first-quality bonds or held as a savings deposit.

Investors who for some time have been following a bona fide dollar-cost averaging plan can in logic elect either to continue their periodic purchases unchanged or to suspend them until they feel the market level is no longer dangerous. We should advise rather strongly against the initiation of a new dollar-averaging plan at the late 1964 levels, since many investors would not have the stamina to pursue such a scheme if the results soon after initiation should appear highly unfavorable.

This time we can say that our caution was vindicated. The DJIA advanced about 11% further, to 995, but then fell irregularly to a low of 632 in 1970, and finished that year at 839. The same kind of debacle took place in the price of "hot issues"—i.e., with declines running as much as 90%—as had happened in the 1961–62 setback. And, as pointed out in the Introduction, the whole financial picture appeared to have changed in the direction of less enthusiasm and greater doubts. A single fact may summarize the story: The DJIA closed 1970 at a level lower than six years before—the first time such a thing had happened since 1944.

Such were our efforts to evaluate former stock-market levels. Is there anything we and our readers can learn from them? We considered the market level favorable for investment in 1948 and 1953 (but too cautiously in the latter year), "dangerous" in 1959 (at 584 for DJIA), and "too high" (at 892) in 1964. All of these judgments could be defended even today by adroit arguments. But it is doubtful if they have been as useful as our more pedestrian counsels—in favor of a consistent and controlled common-stock policy on the one hand, and discouraging endeavors to "beat the market" or to "pick the winners" on the other.

Nonetheless we think our readers may derive some benefit from a renewed consideration of the level of the stock market—this time as of late 1971—even if what we have to say will prove more interesting than practically useful, or more indicative than conclusive. There is a fine passage near the beginning of Aristotle's *Ethics* that goes: "It is the mark of an educated mind to expect that amount of exactness which the nature of the particular subject admits. It is equally unreasonable to accept merely probable conclusions from a mathematician and to demand strict demonstration from an orator." The work of a financial analyst falls somewhere in the middle between that of a mathematician and of an orator.

At various times in 1971 the Dow Jones Industrial Average stood at the 892 level of November 1964 that we considered in our previous edition. But in the present statistical study we have decided to use the price level and the related data for the Standard & Poor's composite index (or S & P 500), because it is more comprehensive and representative of the general market than the 30-stock DJIA. We shall concentrate on a comparison of this material near the four dates of our former editions—namely the year-ends of 1948, 1953, 1958 and 1963—plus 1968; for the current price level we shall take the convenient figure of 100, which was registered at various times in 1971 and in early 1972. The salient data are set forth in Table 3-3. For our earnings figures we present both the last year's showing and the average of three calendar years; for 1971 dividends we use the last twelve months' figures; and for 1971 bond interest and wholesale prices those of August 1971.

The 3-year price/earnings ratio for the market was lower in October 1971 than at year-end 1963 and 1968. It was about the same as in 1958, but much higher than in the early years of the long bull

TABLE 3-3 Data Relating to Standard & Poor's Composite Index in Various Years

Year[a]	*1948*	*1953*	*1958*	*1963*	*1968*	*1971*
Closing price	15.20	24.81	55.21	75.02	103.9	100[d]
Earned in current year	2.24	2.51	2.89	4.02	5.76	5.23
Average earnings of last 3 years	1.65	2.44	2.22	3.63	5.37	5.53
Dividend in current year	.93	1.48	1.75	2.28	2.99	3.10
High-grade bond interest[a]	2.77%	3.08%	4.12%	4.36%	6.51%	7.57%
Wholesale-price index	87.9	92.7	100.4	105.0	108.7	114.3
Ratios:						
Price/last year's earnings	6.3 ×	9.9 ×	18.4 ×	18.6 ×	18.0 ×	19.2 ×
Price/3-years' earnings	9.2 ×	10.2 ×	17.6 ×	20.7 ×	19.5 ×	18.1 ×
3-Years' "earnings yield"[c]	10.9 %	9.8 %	5.8 %	4.8 %	5.15%	5.53%
Dividend yield	5.6 %	5.5 %	3.3 %	3.04%	2.87%	3.11%
Stock-earnings yield/bond yield	3.96×	3.20×	1.41×	1.10×	.80×	.72×
Dividend yield/bond yield	2.1 ×	1.8 ×	.80×	.70×	.44×	.41×
Earnings/book value[e]	11.2 %	11.8 %	12.8 %	10.5 %	11.5 %	11.5 %

[a] Yield on S & P AAA bonds.

[b] Calendar years in 1948–1968, plus year ended June 1971.

[c] "Earnings yield" means the earnings divided by the price, in %.

[d] Price in Oct. 1971, equivalent to 900 for the DJIA.

[e] Three-year average figures.

market. This important indicator, taken by itself, could not be construed to indicate that the market was especially high in January 1972. But when the interest yield on high-grade bonds is brought into the picture, the implications become much less favorable. The reader will note from our table that the ratio of stock returns (earnings/price) to bond returns has grown worse during the entire period, so that the January 1972 figure was less favorable to stocks, by this criterion, than in any of the previous years examined. When dividend yields are compared with bond yields we find that the relationship was completely reversed between 1948 and 1972. In the early year stocks yielded twice as much as bonds; now bonds yield twice as much, and more, than stocks.

Our final judgment is that the adverse change in the bond-yield/stock-yield ratio fully offsets the better price/earnings ratio for late 1971, based on the 3-year earnings figures. Hence our view of the early 1972 market level would tend to be the same as it was some 7 years ago—i.e., that it is an unattractive one from the standpoint of conservative investment. (This would apply to most of the 1971 price range of the DJIA: between, say, 800 and 950.)

In terms of historical market swings the 1971 picture would still appear to be one of irregular recovery from the bad setback suffered in 1969–1970. In the past such recoveries have ushered in a new stage of the recurrent and persistent bull market that began in 1949. (This was the expectation of Wall Street generally during 1971.) After the terrible experience suffered by the public buyers of low-grade common-stock offerings in the 1968–1970 cycle, it is too early (in 1971) for another twirl of the new-issue merry-go-round. Hence that dependable sign of imminent danger in the market is lacking now, as it was at the 892 level of the DJIA in November 1964, considered in our previous edition. Technically, then, the outlook would appear to favor another substantial rise far beyond the 900 DJIA level before the next serious setback or collapse. But we cannot quite leave the matter there, as perhaps we should. To us, the early-1971-market's disregard of the harrowing experiences of less than a year before is a disquieting sign. Can such heedlessness go unpunished? We think the investor must be prepared for difficult times ahead—perhaps in the form of a fairly quick replay of the the 1969–1970 decline, or perhaps in the form of another bull-market fling, to be followed by a more catastrophic collapse.[3]

What Course to Follow

Turn back to what we said in the last edition, reproduced on p. 75. This is our view at the same price level—say 900—for the DJIA in early 1972 as it was in late 1964.

COMMENTARY ON CHAPTER 3

You've got to be careful if you don't know where you're going, 'cause you might not get there.

—Yogi Berra

BULL-MARKET BALONEY

In this chapter, Graham shows how prophetic he can be. He looks two years ahead, foreseeing the "catastrophic" bear market of 1973–1974, in which U.S. stocks lost 37% of their value.[1] He also looks more than two decades into the future, eviscerating the logic of market gurus and best-selling books that were not even on the horizon in his lifetime.

The heart of Graham's argument is that the intelligent investor must never forecast the future exclusively by extrapolating the past. Unfortunately, that's exactly the mistake that one pundit after another made in the 1990s. A stream of bullish books followed Wharton finance professor Jeremy Siegel's *Stocks for the Long Run* (1994)—culminating, in a wild crescendo, with James Glassman and Kevin Hassett's *Dow 36,000,* David Elias' *Dow 40,000,* and Charles Kadlec's *Dow 100,000* (all published in 1999). Forecasters argued that stocks had returned an annual average of 7% after inflation ever since 1802. Therefore, they concluded, that's what investors should expect in the future.

Some bulls went further. Since stocks had "always" beaten bonds over any period of at least 30 years, stocks must be less risky than bonds or even cash in the bank. And if you can eliminate all the risk of owning stocks simply by hanging on to them long enough, then why

---

[1] If dividends are not included, stocks fell 47.8% in those two years.

quibble over how much you pay for them in the first place? (To find out why, see the sidebar on p. 82.)

In 1999 and early 2000, bull-market baloney was everywhere:

- On December 7, 1999, Kevin Landis, portfolio manager of the Firsthand mutual funds, appeared on CNN's *Moneyline* telecast. Asked if wireless telecommunication stocks were overvalued–with many trading at infinite multiples of their earnings–Landis had a ready answer. "It's not a mania," he shot back. "Look at the outright growth, the absolute value of the growth. It's big."
- On January 18, 2000, Robert Froelich, chief investment strategist at the Kemper Funds, declared in the *Wall Street Journal:* "It's a new world order. We see people discard all the right companies with all the right people with the right vision because their stock price is too high–that's the worst mistake an investor can make."
- In the April 10, 2000, issue of *BusinessWeek,* Jeffrey M. Applegate, then the chief investment strategist at Lehman Brothers, asked rhetorically: "Is the stock market riskier today than two years ago simply because prices are higher? The answer is *no.*"

But the answer is *yes.* It always has been. It always will be.

And when Graham asked, "Can such heedlessness go unpunished?" he knew that the eternal answer to that question is *no.* Like an enraged Greek god, the stock market crushed everyone who had come to believe that the high returns of the late 1990s were some kind of divine right. Just look at how those forecasts by Landis, Froelich, and Applegate held up:

- From 2000 through 2002, the most stable of Landis's pet wireless stocks, Nokia, lost "only" 67%–while the worst, Winstar Communications, lost 99.9%.
- Froelich's favorite stocks–Cisco Systems and Motorola–fell more than 70% by late 2002. Investors lost over $400 billion on Cisco alone–more than the annual economic output of Hong Kong, Israel, Kuwait, and Singapore combined.
- In April 2000, when Applegate asked his rhetorical question, the Dow Jones Industrials stood at 11,187; the NASDAQ Composite Index was at 4446. By the end of 2002, the Dow was hobbling around the 8,300 level, while NASDAQ had withered to roughly 1300–eradicating all its gains over the previous six years.

SURVIVAL OF THE FATTEST

There was a fatal flaw in the argument that stocks have "always" beaten bonds in the long run: Reliable figures before 1871 do not exist. The indexes used to represent the U.S. stock market's earliest returns contain as few as seven (yes, 7!) stocks.[1] By 1800, however, there were some 300 companies in America (many in the Jeffersonian equivalents of the Internet: wooden turnpikes and canals). Most went bankrupt, and their investors lost their knickers.

But the stock indexes ignore all the companies that went bust in those early years, a problem technically known as "survivorship bias." Thus these indexes wildly overstate the results earned by real-life investors—who lacked the 20/20 hindsight necessary to know exactly which seven stocks to buy. A lonely handful of companies, including Bank of New York and J. P. Morgan Chase, have prospered continuously since the 1790s. But for every such miraculous survivor, there were thousands of financial disasters like the Dismal Swamp Canal Co., the Pennsylvania Cultivation of Vines Co., and the Snickers's Gap Turnpike Co.—all omitted from the "historical" stock indexes.

Jeremy Siegel's data show that, after inflation, from 1802 through 1870 stocks gained 7.0% per year, bonds 4.8%, and cash 5.1%. But Elroy Dimson and his colleagues at London Business School estimate that the pre-1871 stock returns are overstated by at least two percentage points per year.[2] In the real world, then, stocks did no better than cash and bonds—and perhaps a bit worse. Anyone who claims that the long-term record "proves" that stocks are guaranteed to outperform bonds or cash is an ignoramus.

---

[1] By the 1840s, these indexes had widened to include a maximum of seven financial stocks and 27 railroad stocks—still an absurdly unrepresentative sample of the rambunctious young American stock market.

[2] See Jason Zweig, "New Cause for Caution on Stocks," *Time,* May 6, 2002, p. 71. As Graham hints on p. 65, even the stock indexes between 1871 and the 1920s suffer from survivorship bias, thanks to the hundreds of automobile, aviation, and radio companies that went bust without a trace. These returns, too, are probably overstated by one to two percentage points.

THE HIGHER THEY GO, THE HARDER THEY FALL

As the enduring antidote to this kind of bull-market baloney, Graham urges the intelligent investor to ask some simple, skeptical questions. Why should the future returns of stocks always be the same as their past returns? When every investor comes to believe that stocks are guaranteed to make money in the long run, won't the market end up being wildly overpriced? And once that happens, how can future returns possibly be high?

Graham's answers, as always, are rooted in logic and common sense. The value of any investment is, and always must be, a function of the price you pay for it. By the late 1990s, inflation was withering away, corporate profits appeared to be booming, and most of the world was at peace. But that did not mean–nor could it ever mean–that stocks were worth buying *at any price.* Since the profits that companies can earn are finite, the price that investors should be willing to pay for stocks must also be finite.

Think of it this way: Michael Jordan may well have been the greatest basketball player of all time, and he pulled fans into Chicago Stadium like a giant electromagnet. The Chicago Bulls got a bargain by paying Jordan up to $34 million a year to bounce a big leather ball around a wooden floor. But that does not mean the Bulls would have been justified paying him $340 million, or $3.4 billion, or $34 billion, per season.

THE LIMITS OF OPTIMISM

Focusing on the market's recent returns when they have been rosy, warns Graham, will lead to "a quite illogical and dangerous conclusion that equally marvelous results could be expected for common stocks in the future." From 1995 through 1999, as the market rose by at least 20% each year–a surge unprecedented in American history–stock buyers became ever more optimistic:

- In mid-1998, investors surveyed by the Gallup Organization for the PaineWebber brokerage firm expected their portfolios to earn an average of roughly 13% over the year to come. By early 2000, their average expected return had jumped to more than 18%.

- "Sophisticated professionals" were just as bullish, jacking up their own assumptions of future returns. In 2001, for instance, SBC Communications raised the projected return on its pension plan from 8.5% to 9.5%. By 2002, the average assumed rate of return on the pension plans of companies in the Standard & Poor's 500-stock index had swollen to a record-high 9.2%.

A quick follow-up shows the awful aftermath of excess enthusiasm:

- Gallup found in 2001 and 2002 that the average expectation of one-year returns on stocks had slumped to 7%–even though investors could now buy at prices nearly 50% lower than in 2000.[2]
- Those gung-ho assumptions about the returns on their pension plans will cost the companies in the S & P 500 a bare minimum of $32 billion between 2002 and 2004, according to recent Wall Street estimates.

Even though investors all know they're supposed to buy low and sell high, in practice they often end up getting it backwards. Graham's warning in this chapter is simple: "By the rule of opposites," the more enthusiastic investors become about the stock market in the long run, the more certain they are to be proved wrong in the short run. On March 24, 2000, the total value of the U.S. stock market peaked at $14.75 trillion. By October 9, 2002, just 30 months later, the total U.S. stock market was worth $7.34 trillion, or 50.2% less–a loss of $7.41 trillion. Meanwhile, many market pundits turned sourly bearish, predicting flat or even negative market returns for years–even decades–to come.

At this point, Graham would ask one simple question: Considering how calamitously wrong the "experts" were the last time they agreed on something, why on earth should the intelligent investor believe them now?

---

[2] Those cheaper stock prices do not mean, of course, that investors' expectation of a 7% stock return will be realized.

WHAT'S NEXT?

Instead, let's tune out the noise and think about future returns as Graham might. The stock market's performance depends on three factors:

- real growth (the rise of companies' earnings and dividends)
- inflationary growth (the general rise of prices throughout the economy)
- speculative growth–or decline (any increase or decrease in the investing public's appetite for stocks)

In the long run, the yearly growth in corporate earnings per share has averaged 1.5% to 2% (not counting inflation).[3] As of early 2003, inflation was running around 2.4% annually; the dividend yield on stocks was 1.9%. So,

$$\begin{array}{r} 1.5\% \text{ to } 2\% \\ +\,2.4\% \\ +\,1.9\% \\ \hline =5.8\% \text{ to } 6.3\% \end{array}$$

In the long run, that means you can reasonably expect stocks to average roughly a 6% return (or 4% after inflation). If the investing public gets greedy again and sends stocks back into orbit, then that speculative fever will temporarily drive returns higher. If, instead, investors are full of fear, as they were in the 1930s and 1970s, the returns on stocks will go temporarily lower. (That's where we are in 2003.)

Robert Shiller, a finance professor at Yale University, says Graham inspired his valuation approach: Shiller compares the current price of the Standard & Poor's 500-stock index against average corporate profits over the past 10 years (after inflation). By scanning the historical record, Shiller has shown that when his ratio goes well above 20, the market usually delivers poor returns afterward; when it drops well

[3] See Jeremy Siegel, *Stocks for the Long Run* (McGraw-Hill, 2002), p. 94, and Robert Arnott and William Bernstein, "The Two Percent Dilution," working paper, July, 2002.

below 10, stocks typically produce handsome gains down the road. In early 2003, by Shiller's math, stocks were priced at about 22.8 times the average inflation-adjusted earnings of the past decade–still in the danger zone, but way down from their demented level of 44.2 times earnings in December 1999.

How has the market done in the past when it was priced around today's levels? Figure 3-1 shows the previous periods when stocks were at similar highs, and how they fared over the 10-year stretches that followed:

FIGURE 3-1

Year	Price/earnings ratio	Total return over next 10 years
1898	21.4	9.2
1900	20.7	7.1
1901	21.7	5.9
1905	19.6	5.0
1929	22.0	−0.1
1936	21.1	4.4
1955	18.9	11.1
1959	18.6	7.8
1961	22.0	7.1
1962	18.6	9.9
1963	21.0	6.0
1964	22.8	1.2
1965	23.7	3.3
1966	19.7	6.6
1967	21.8	3.6
1968	22.3	3.2
1972	18.6	6.7
1992	20.4	9.3
Averages	**20.8**	**6.0**

Sources: http://aida.econ.yale.edu/~shiller/data/ie_data.htm; Jack Wilson and Charles Jones, "An Analysis of the S & P 500 Index and Cowles' Extensions: Price Index and Stock Returns, 1870–1999," *The Journal of Business*, vol. 75, no. 3, July, 2002, pp. 527–529; Ibbotson Associates.

Notes: Price/earnings ratio is Shiller calculation (10-year average real earnings of S & P 500-stock index divided by December 31 index value). Total return is nominal annual average.

So, from valuation levels similar to those of early 2003, the stock market has sometimes done very well in the ensuing 10 years, sometimes poorly, and muddled along the rest of the time. I think Graham, ever the conservative, would split the difference between the lowest and highest past returns and project that over the next decade stocks will earn roughly 6% annually, or 4% after inflation. (Interestingly, that projection matches the estimate we got earlier when we added together real growth, inflationary growth, and speculative growth.) Compared to the 1990s, 6% is chicken feed. But it's a whisker better than the gains that bonds are likely to produce–and reason enough for most investors to hang on to stocks as part of a diversified portfolio.

But there is a second lesson in Graham's approach. The only thing you can be confident of while forecasting future stock returns is that you will probably turn out to be wrong. The only indisputable truth that the past teaches us is that the future will always surprise us–always! And the corollary to that law of financial history is that the markets will most brutally surprise the very people who are most certain that their views about the future are right. Staying humble about your forecasting powers, as Graham did, will keep you from risking too much on a view of the future that may well turn out to be wrong.

So, by all means, you should lower your expectations–but take care not to depress your spirit. For the intelligent investor, hope always springs eternal, because *it should.* In the financial markets, the worse the future looks, the better it usually turns out to be. A cynic once told G. K. Chesterton, the British novelist and essayist, "Blessed is he who expecteth nothing, for he shall not be disappointed." Chesterton's rejoinder? "Blessed is he who expecteth nothing, for he shall enjoy everything."

CHAPTER 4

General Portfolio Policy: The Defensive Investor

The basic characteristics of an investment portfolio are usually determined by the position and characteristics of the owner or owners. At one extreme we have had savings banks, life-insurance companies, and so-called legal trust funds. A generation ago their investments were limited by law in many states to high-grade bonds and, in some cases, high-grade preferred stocks. At the other extreme we have the well-to-do and experienced businessman, who will include any kind of bond or stock in his security list provided he considers it an attractive purchase.

It has been an old and sound principle that those who cannot afford to take risks should be content with a relatively low return on their invested funds. From this there has developed the general notion that the rate of return which the investor should aim for is more or less proportionate to the degree of risk he is ready to run. Our view is different. The rate of return sought should be dependent, rather, on the amount of intelligent effort the investor is willing and able to bring to bear on his task. The minimum return goes to our passive investor, who wants both safety and freedom from concern. The maximum return would be realized by the alert and enterprising investor who exercises maximum intelligence and skill. In 1965 we added: "In many cases there may be less real risk associated with buying a 'bargain issue' offering the chance of a large profit than with a conventional bond purchase yielding about 4½%." This statement had more truth in it than we ourselves suspected, since in subsequent years even the best long-term bonds lost a substantial part of their market value because of the rise in interest rates.

The Basic Problem of Bond-Stock Allocation

We have already outlined in briefest form the portfolio policy of the defensive investor.* He should divide his funds between high-grade bonds and high-grade common stocks.

We have suggested as a fundamental guiding rule that the investor should never have less than 25% or more than 75% of his funds in common stocks, with a consequent inverse range of between 75% and 25% in bonds. There is an implication here that the standard division should be an equal one, or 50–50, between the two major investment mediums. According to tradition the sound reason for increasing the percentage in common stocks would be the appearance of the "bargain price" levels created in a protracted bear market. Conversely, sound procedure would call for reducing the common-stock component below 50% when in the judgment of the investor the market level has become dangerously high.

These copybook maxims have always been easy to enunciate and always difficult to follow—because they go against that very human nature which produces that excesses of bull and bear markets. It is almost a contradiction in terms to suggest as a feasible policy for the *average* stockowner that he lighten his holdings when the market advances beyond a certain point and add to them after a corresponding decline. It is because the average man operates, and apparently must operate, in opposite fashion that we have had the great advances and collapses of the past; and—this writer believes—we are likely to have them in the future.

If the division between investment and speculative operations were as clear now as once it was, we might be able to envisage investors as a shrewd, experienced group who sell out to the heedless, hapless speculators at high prices and buy back from them at depressed levels. This picture may have had some verisimilitude in bygone days, but it is hard to identify it with financial developments since 1949. There is no indication that such professional operations as those of the mutual funds have been conducted in this fashion. The percentage of the portfolio held in equities by the

---

* See Graham's "Conclusion" to Chapter 2, p. 56–57.

two major types of funds—"balanced" and "common-stock"—has changed very little from year to year. Their selling activities have been largely related to endeavors to switch from less to more promising holdings.

If, as we have long believed, the stock market has lost contact with its old bounds, and if new ones have not yet been established, then we can give the investor no reliable rules by which to reduce his common-stock holdings toward the 25% minimum and rebuild them later to the 75% maximum. We can urge that in general the investor should not have more than one-half in equities unless he has strong confidence in the soundness of his stock position and is sure that he could view a market decline of the 1969–70 type with equanimity. It is hard for us to see how such strong confidence can be justified at the levels existing in early 1972. Thus we would counsel against a greater than 50% apportionment to common stocks at this time. But, for complementary reasons, it is almost equally difficult to advise a reduction of the figure well below 50%, unless the investor is disquieted *in his own mind* about the current market level, and will be satisfied also to limit his participation in any further rise to, say, 25% of his total funds.

We are thus led to put forward for most of our readers what may appear to be an oversimplified 50–50 formula. Under this plan the guiding rule is to maintain as nearly as practicable an equal division between bond and stock holdings. When changes in the market level have raised the common-stock component to, say, 55%, the balance would be restored by a sale of one-eleventh of the stock portfolio and the transfer of the proceeds to bonds. Conversely, a fall in the common-stock proportion to 45% would call for the use of one-eleventh of the bond fund to buy additional equities.

Yale University followed a somewhat similar plan for a number of years after 1937, but it was geared around a 35% "normal holding" in common stocks. In the early 1950s, however, Yale seems to have given up its once famous formula, and in 1969 held 61% of its portfolio in equities (including some convertibles). (At that time the endowment funds of 71 such institutions, totaling $7.6 billion, held 60.3% in common stocks.) The Yale example illustrates the almost lethal effect of the great market advance upon the once popular *formula approach* to investment. Nonetheless we are convinced that our 50–50 version of this approach makes good sense for the defensive investor. It is extremely simple; it aims unquestionably in the right direction; it gives the follower the feeling that he is at least making some moves in response to market developments; most important of all, it will restrain him from being drawn more and more heavily into common stocks as the market rises to more and more dangerous heights.

Furthermore, a truly conservative investor will be satisfied with the gains shown on half his portfolio in a rising market, while in a severe decline he may derive much solace from reflecting how much better off he is than many of his more venturesome friends.

While our proposed 50–50 division is undoubtedly the simplest "all-purpose program" devisable, it may not turn out to be the best in terms of results achieved. (Of course, no approach, mechanical or otherwise, can be advanced with any assurance that it will work out better than another.) The much larger income return now offered by good bonds than by representative stocks is a potent argument for favoring the bond component. The investor's choice between 50% or a lower figure in stocks may well rest mainly on his own temperament and attitude. If he can act as a cold-blooded weigher of the odds, he would be likely to favor the low 25% stock component at this time, with the idea of waiting until the DJIA dividend yield was, say, two-thirds of the bond yield before he would establish his median 50–50 division between bonds and stocks. Starting from 900 for the DJIA and dividends of $36 on the unit, this would require either a fall in taxable bond yields from 7½% to about 5.5% without any change in the present return on leading stocks, or a fall in the DJIA to as low as 660 if there is no reduction in bond yields and no increase in dividends. A combination of intermediate changes could produce the same "buying point." A program of that kind is not especially complicated; the hard part is to adopt it and to stick to it not to mention the possibility that it may turn out to have been much too conservative.

The Bond Component

The choice of issues in the bond component of the investor's portfolio will turn about two main questions: Should he buy taxable or tax-free bonds, and should he buy shorter- or longer-term maturities? The tax decision should be mainly a matter of arithmetic, turning on the difference in yields as compared with the investor's tax bracket. In January 1972 the choice in 20-year maturities was between obtaining, say, 7½% on "grade Aa" corporate bonds and 5.3% on prime tax-free issues. (The term "municipals" is generally applied to all species of tax-exempt bonds, including state obligations.) There was thus for this maturity a loss in income of some 30% in passing from the corporate to the municipal field. Hence if the investor was in a maximum tax bracket higher than 30% he would have a net saving after taxes by choosing the municipal bonds; the opposite, if his maximum tax was less than 30%. A single person starts paying a 30% rate when his income after deductions passes $10,000; for a married couple the rate applies when combined taxable income passes $20,000. It is evident that a large proportion of individual investors would obtain a higher return after taxes from good municipals than from good corporate bonds.

The choice of longer versus shorter maturities involves quite a different question, viz.: Does the investor want to assure himself against a decline in the price of his bonds, but at the cost of (1) a lower annual yield and (2) loss of the possibility of an appreciable *gain* in principal value? We think it best to discuss this question in Chapter 8, The Investor and Market Fluctuations.

For a period of many years in the past the only sensible bond purchases for individuals were the U.S. savings issues. Their safety was—and is—unquestioned; they gave a higher return than other bond investments of first quality; they had a money-back option and other privileges which added greatly to their attractiveness. In our earlier editions we had an entire chapter entitled "U.S. Savings Bonds: A Boon to Investors."

As we shall point out, U.S. savings bonds still possess certain unique merits that make them a suitable purchase by any individual investor. For the man of modest capital—with, say, not more than $10,000 to put into bonds—we think they are still the easiest and the best choice. But those with larger funds may find other mediums more desirable.

Let us list a few major types of bonds that deserve investor consideration, and discuss them briefly with respect to general description, safety, yield, market price, risk, income-tax status, and other features.

1. U.S. SAVINGS BONDS, SERIES E AND SERIES H. We shall first summarize their important provisions, and then discuss briefly the numerous advantages of these unique, attractive, and exceedingly convenient investments. The Series H bonds pay interest semiannually, as do other bonds. The rate is 4.29% for the first year, and then a flat 5.10% for the next nine years to maturity. Interest on the Series E bonds is not paid out, but accrues to the holder through increase in redemption value. The bonds are sold at 75% of their face value, and mature at 100% in 5 years 10 months after purchase. If held to maturity the yield works out at 5%, compounded semiannually. If redeemed earlier, the yield moves up from a minimum of 4.01% in the first year to an average of 5.20% in the next 4⅚ years.

Interest on the bonds is subject to Federal income tax, but is exempt from state income tax. However, Federal income tax on the Series E bonds may be paid at the holder's option either annually as the interest accrues (through higher redemption value), or not until the bond is actually disposed of.

Owners of Series E bonds may cash them in at any time (shortly after purchase) at their current redemption value. Holders of Series H bonds have similar rights to cash them in at par value (cost). Series E bonds are exchangeable for Series H bonds, with certain tax advantages. Bonds lost, destroyed, or stolen may be replaced without cost. There are limitations on annual purchases, but liberal provisions for co-ownership by family members make it possible for most investors to buy as many as they can afford. *Comment:* There is no other investment that combines (1) absolute assurance of principal and interest payments, (2) the right to demand full "money back" at any time, and (3) guarantee of at least a 5% interest rate for at least ten years. Holders of the earlier issues of Series E bonds have had the right to extend their bonds at maturity, and thus to continue to accumulate annual values at successively higher rates. The deferral of income-tax payments over these long periods has been of great dollar advantage; we calculate it has increased the effective net-after-tax rate received by as much as a third in typical cases. Conversely, the right to cash in the bonds at cost price or better has given the purchasers in former years of low interest rates complete protection against the shrinkage in principal value that befell many bond investors; otherwise stated, it gave them the possibility of *benefiting* from the rise in interest rates by switching their low-interest holdings into very-high-coupon issues on an even-money basis.

In our view the special advantages enjoyed by owners of savings bonds now will more than compensate for their lower current return as compared with other direct government obligations.

2. OTHER UNITED STATES BONDS. A profusion of these issues exists, covering a wide variety of coupon rates and maturity dates. All of them are completely safe with respect to payment of interest and principal. They are subject to Federal income taxes but free from state income tax. In late 1971 the long-term issues—over ten years—showed an average yield of 6.09%, intermediate issues (three to five years) returned 6.35%, and short issues returned 6.03%.

In 1970 it was possible to buy a number of old issues at large discounts. Some of these are accepted at par in settlement of estate taxes. Example: The U.S. Treasury 3½s due 1990 are in this category; they sold at 60 in 1970, but closed 1970 above 77.

It is interesting to note also that in many cases the indirect obligations of the U.S. government yield appreciably more than its direct obligations of the same maturity. As we write, an offering appears of 7.05% of "Certificates Fully Guaranteed by the Secretary of Transportation of the Department of Transportation of the United States." The yield was fully 1% more than that on direct obligations of the U.S., maturing the same year (1986). The certificates were actually issued in the name of the Trustees of the Penn Central Transportation Co., but they were sold on the basis of a statement by the U.S. Attorney General that the guarantee "brings into being a general obligation of the United States, backed by its full faith and credit." Quite a number of indirect obligations of this sort have been assumed by the U.S. government in the past, and all of them have been scrupulously honored.

The reader may wonder why all this hocus-pocus, involving an apparently "personal guarantee" by our Secretary of Transportation, and a higher cost to the taxpayer in the end. The chief reason for the indirection has been the debt limit imposed on government borrowing by the Congress. Apparently guarantees by the government are not regarded as debts—a semantic windfall for shrewder investors. Perhaps the chief impact of this situation has been the creation of tax-free Housing Authority bonds, enjoying the equivalent of a U.S. guarantee, and virtually the only tax-exempt issues that are equivalent to government bonds. Another type of government-backed issues is the recently created New Community Debentures, offered to yield 7.60% in September 1971.

3. STATE AND MUNICIPAL BONDS. These enjoy exemption from Federal income tax. They are also ordinarily free of income tax in the state of issue but not elsewhere. They are either direct obligations of a state or subdivision, or "revenue bonds" dependent for interest payments on receipts from a toll road, bridge, building lease, etc. Not all tax-free bonds are strongly enough protected to justify their purchase by a defensive investor. He may be guided in his selection by the rating given to each issue by Moody's or Standard & Poor's. One of three highest ratings by both services—Aaa (AAA), Aa (AA), or A—should constitute a sufficient indication of adequate safety. The yield on these bonds will vary both with the quality and the maturity, with the shorter maturities giving the lower return. In late 1971 the issues represented in Standard & Poor's municipal bond index averaged AA in quality rating, 20 years in maturity, and 5.78% in yield. A typical offering of Vineland, N.J., bonds, rated AA for A and gave a yield of only 3% on the one-year maturity, rising to 5.8% to the 1995 and 1996 maturities.[1]

4. CORPORATION BONDS. These bonds are subject to both Federal and state tax. In early 1972 those of highest quality yielded 7.19% for a 25-year maturity, as reflected in the published yield of Moody's Aaa corporate bond index. The so-called lower-medium-grade issues—rated Baa—returned 8.23% for long maturities. In each class shorter-term issues would yield somewhat less than longer-term obligations.

Comment. The above summaries indicate that the average investor has several choices among high-grade bonds. Those in high income-tax brackets can undoubtedly obtain a better net yield from good tax-free issues than from taxable ones. For others the early 1972 range of taxable yield would seem to be from 5.00% on U.S. savings bonds, with their special options, to about 7½% on high-grade corporate issues.

Higher-Yielding Bond Investments

By sacrificing quality an investor can obtain a higher income return from his bonds. Long experience has demonstrated that the ordinary investor is wiser to keep away from such high-yield bonds. While, taken as a whole, they may work out somewhat better in terms of overall return than the first-quality issues, they expose the owner to too many individual risks of untoward developments, ranging from disquieting price declines to actual default. (It is true that bargain opportunities occur fairly often in lower-grade bonds, but these require special study and skill to exploit successfully.)*

Perhaps we should add here that the limits imposed by Congress on direct bond issues of the United States have produced at least two sorts of "bargain opportunities" for investors in the purchase of government-backed obligations. One is provided by the tax-exempt "New Housing" issues, and the other by the recently created (taxable) "New Community debentures." An offering of New Housing issues in July 1971 yielded as high as 5.8%, free from both Federal and state taxes, while an issue of (taxable) New Community debentures sold in September 1971 yielded 7.60%. Both obligations have the "full faith and credit" of the United States government behind them and hence are safe without question. And—on a net basis—they yield considerably more than ordinary United States bonds.†

---

* Graham's objection to high-yield bonds is mitigated today by the widespread availability of mutual funds that spread the risk and do the research of owning "junk bonds." See the commentary on Chapter 6 for more detail.

† The "New Housing" bonds and "New Community debentures" are no more. New Housing Authority bonds were backed by the U.S. Department of Housing and Urban Development (HUD) and were exempt from income tax, but they have not been issued since 1974. New Community debentures, also backed by HUD, were authorized by a Federal law passed in 1968. About $350 million of these debentures were issued through 1975, but the program was terminated in 1983.

Savings Deposits in Lieu of Bonds

An investor may now obtain as high an interest rate from a savings deposit in a commercial or savings bank (or from a bank certificate of deposit) as he can from a first-grade bond of short maturity. The interest rate on bank savings accounts may be lowered in the future, but under present conditions they are a suitable substitute for short-term bond investment by the individual.

Convertible Issues

These are discussed in Chapter 16. The price variability of bonds in general is treated in Chapter 8, The Investor and Market Fluctuations.

Call Provisions

In previous editions we had a fairly long discussion of this aspect of bond financing, because it involved a serious but little noticed injustice to the investor. In the typical case bonds were callable fairly soon after issuance, and at modest premiums—say 5%—above the issue price. This meant that during a period of wide fluctuations in the underlying interest rates the investor had to bear the full brunt of unfavorable changes and was deprived of all but a meager participation in favorable ones.

EXAMPLE: Our standard example has been the issue of American Gas & Electric 100-year 5% debentures, sold to the public at 101 in 1928. Four years later, under near-panic conditions, the price of these good bonds fell to 62½, yielding 8%. By 1946, in a great reversal, bonds of this type could be sold to yield only 3%, and the 5% issue *should* have been quoted at close to 160. But at that point the company took advantage of the call provision and redeemed the issue at a mere 106.

The call feature in these bond contracts was a thinly disguised instance of "heads I win, tails you lose." At long last, the bond-buying institutions refused to accept this unfair arrangement; in recent years most long-term high-coupon issues have been protected against redemption for ten years or more after issuance. This still limits their possible price rise, but not inequitably.

In practical terms, we advise the investor in long-term issues to sacrifice a small amount of yield to obtain the assurance of noncallability—say for 20 or 25 years. Similarly, there is an advantage in buying a low-coupon bond* at a discount rather than a high-coupon bond selling at about par and callable in a few years. For the discount—e.g., of a 3½% bond at 63½%, yielding 7.85%—carries full protection against adverse call action.

Straight—i.e., Nonconvertible—Preferred Stocks

Certain general observations should be made here on the subject of preferred stocks. Really good preferred stocks can and do exist, but they are good in spite of their investment form, which is an inherently bad one. The typical preferred shareholder is dependent for his safety on the ability and desire of the company to pay dividends on its *common stock.* Once the common dividends are omitted, or even in danger, his own position becomes precarious, for the directors are under no obligation to continue paying him unless they also pay on the common. On the other hand, the typical preferred stock carries no share in the company's profits beyond the fixed dividend rate. Thus the preferred holder lacks both the legal claim of the bondholder (or creditor) and the profit possibilities of a common shareholder (or partner).

These weaknesses in the legal position of preferred stocks tend to come to the fore recurrently in periods of depression. Only a small percentage of all preferred issues are so strongly entrenched as to maintain an unquestioned investment status through all vicissitudes. Experience teaches that the time to buy preferred stocks is when their price is unduly depressed by temporary adversity. (At such times they may be well suited to the aggressive investor but too unconventional for the defensive investor.)

In other words, they should be bought on a bargain basis or not at all. We shall refer later to convertible and similarly privileged issues, which carry some special possibilities of profits. These are not ordinarily selected for a conservative portfolio.

Another peculiarity in the general position of preferred stocks

---

* A bond's "coupon" is its interest rate; a "low-coupon" bond pays a rate of interest income below the market average.

deserves mention. They have a much better tax status for corporation buyers than for individual investors. Corporations pay income tax on only 15% of the income they receive in dividends, but on the full amount of their ordinary interest income. Since the 1972 corporate rate is 48%, this means that $100 received as preferred-stock dividends is taxed only $7.20, whereas $100 received as bond interest is taxed $48. On the other hand, individual investors pay exactly the same tax on preferred-stock investments as on bond interest, except for a recent minor exemption. Thus, in strict logic, all investment-grade preferred stocks should be bought by corporations, just as all tax-exempt bonds should be bought by investors who pay income tax.*

Security Forms

The bond form and the preferred-stock form, as hitherto discussed, are well-understood and relatively simple matters. A bondholder is entitled to receive fixed interest and payment of principal on a definite date. The owner of a preferred stock is entitled to a fixed dividend, and no more, which must be paid before any common dividend. His principal value does not come due on any specified date. (The dividend may be cumulative or noncumulative. He may or may not have a vote.)

The above describes the standard provisions and, no doubt, the majority of bond and preferred issues, but there are innumerable departures from these forms. The best-known types are convertible and similar issues, and income bonds. In the latter type, interest does not have to be paid unless it is earned by the company. (Unpaid interest may accumulate as a charge against future earnings, but the period is often limited to three years.)

Income bonds should be used by corporations much more

---

* While Graham's logic remains valid, the numbers have changed. Corporations can currently deduct 70% of the income they receive from dividends, and the standard corporate tax rate is 35%. Thus, a corporation would pay roughly $24.50 in tax on $100 in dividends from preferred stock versus $35 in tax on $100 in interest income. Individuals pay the same rate of income tax on dividend income that they do on interest income, so preferred stock offers them no tax advantage.

extensively than they are. Their avoidance apparently arises from a mere accident of economic history—namely, that they were first employed in quantity in connection with railroad reorganizations, and hence they have been associated from the start with financial weakness and poor investment status. But the form itself has several practical advantages, especially in comparison with and in substitution for the numerous (convertible) preferred-stock issues of recent years. Chief of these is the deductibility of the interest paid from the company's taxable income, which in effect cuts the cost of that form of capital in half. From the investor's standpoint it is probably best for him in most cases that he should have (1) an unconditional right to receive interest payments *when they are earned* by the company, and (2) a right to *other* forms of protection than bankruptcy proceedings if interest is not earned and paid. The terms of income bonds can be tailored to the advantage of both the borrower and the lender in the manner best suited to both. (Conversion privileges can, of course, be included.) The acceptance by everybody of the inherently weak preferred-stock form and the rejection of the stronger income-bond form is a fascinating illustration of the way in which traditional institutions and habits often tend to persist on Wall Street despite new conditions calling for a fresh point of view. With every new wave of optimism or pessimism, we are ready to abandon history and time-tested principles, but we cling tenaciously and unquestioningly to our prejudices.

COMMENTARY ON CHAPTER 4

When you leave it to chance, then all of a sudden you don't have any more luck.

–Basketball coach Pat Riley

How aggressive should your portfolio be?

That, says Graham, depends less on what kinds of investments you own than on what kind of investor you are. There are two ways to be an intelligent investor:

- by continually researching, selecting, and monitoring a dynamic mix of stocks, bonds, or mutual funds;
- or by creating a permanent portfolio that runs on autopilot and requires no further effort (but generates very little excitement).

Graham calls the first approach "active" or "enterprising"; it takes lots of time and loads of energy. The "passive" or "defensive" strategy takes little time or effort but requires an almost ascetic detachment from the alluring hullabaloo of the market. As the investment thinker Charles Ellis has explained, the enterprising approach is physically and intellectually taxing, while the defensive approach is emotionally demanding.[1]

If you have time to spare, are highly competitive, think like a sports fan, and relish a complicated intellectual challenge, then the active

---

[1] For more about the distinction between physically and intellectually difficult investing on the one hand, and emotionally difficult investing on the other, see Chapter 8 and also Charles D. Ellis, "Three Ways to Succeed as an Investor," in Charles D. Ellis and James R. Vertin, eds., *The Investor's Anthology* (John Wiley & Sons, 1997), p. 72.

approach is up your alley. If you always feel rushed, crave simplicity, and don't relish thinking about money, then the passive approach is for you. (Some people will feel most comfortable combining both methods—creating a portfolio that is mainly active and partly passive, or vice versa.)

Both approaches are equally intelligent, and you can be successful with either—but only if you know yourself well enough to pick the right one, stick with it over the course of your investing lifetime, and keep your costs and emotions under control. Graham's distinction between active and passive investors is another of his reminders that financial risk lies not only where most of us look for it—in the economy or in our investments—but also within ourselves.

CAN YOU BE BRAVE, OR WILL YOU CAVE?

How, then, should a defensive investor get started? The first and most basic decision is how much to put in stocks and how much to put in bonds and cash. (Note that Graham deliberately places this discussion after his chapter on inflation, forearming you with the knowledge that inflation is one of your worst enemies.)

The most striking thing about Graham's discussion of how to allocate your assets between stocks and bonds is that he never mentions the word "age." That sets his advice firmly against the winds of conventional wisdom—which holds that how much investing risk you ought to take depends mainly on how old you are.[2] A traditional rule of thumb was to subtract your age from 100 and invest that percentage of your assets in stocks, with the rest in bonds or cash. (A 28-year-old would put 72% of her money in stocks; an 81-year-old would put only 19% there.) Like everything else, these assumptions got overheated in the late 1990s. By 1999, a popular book argued that if you were younger than 30 you should put 95% of your money in stocks—even if you had only a "moderate" tolerance for risk![3]

---

[2] A recent Google search for the phrase "age and asset allocation" turned up more than 30,000 online references.

[3] James K. Glassman and Kevin A. Hassett, *Dow 36,000: The New Strategy for Profiting from the Coming Rise in the Stock Market* (Times Business, 1999), p. 250.

Unless you've allowed the proponents of this advice to subtract 100 from your IQ, you should be able to tell that something is wrong here. Why should your age determine how much risk you can take? An 89-year-old with $3 million, an ample pension, and a gaggle of grandchildren would be foolish to move most of her money into bonds. She already has plenty of income, and her grandchildren (who will eventually inherit her stocks) have decades of investing ahead of them. On the other hand, a 25-year-old who is saving for his wedding and a house down payment would be out of his mind to put all his money in stocks. If the stock market takes an Acapulco high dive, he will have no bond income to cover his downside—or his backside.

What's more, no matter how young you are, you might suddenly need to yank your money out of stocks not 40 years from now, but 40 minutes from now. Without a whiff of warning, you could lose your job, get divorced, become disabled, or suffer who knows what other kind of surprise. The unexpected can strike anyone, at any age. Everyone must keep some assets in the riskless haven of cash.

Finally, many people stop investing precisely *because* the stock market goes down. Psychologists have shown that most of us do a very poor job of predicting today how we will feel about an emotionally charged event in the future.[4] When stocks are going up 15% or 20% a year, as they did in the 1980s and 1990s, it's easy to imagine that you and your stocks are married for life. But when you watch every dollar you invested getting bashed down to a dime, it's hard to resist bailing out into the "safety" of bonds and cash. Instead of buying and holding their stocks, many people end up buying high, selling low, and holding nothing but their own head in their hands. Because so few investors have the guts to cling to stocks in a falling market, Graham insists that everyone should keep a minimum of 25% in bonds. That cushion, he argues, will give you the courage to keep the rest of your money in stocks even when stocks stink.

To get a better feel for how much risk you can take, think about the fundamental circumstances of your life, when they will kick in, when they might change, and how they are likely to affect your need for cash:

---

[4] For a fascinating essay on this psychological phenomenon, see Daniel Gilbert and Timothy Wilson's "Miswanting," at www.wjh.harvard.edu/~dtg/Gilbert_&_Wilson(Miswanting).pdf.

- Are you single or married? What does your spouse or partner do for a living?
- Do you or will you have children? When will the tuition bills hit home?
- Will you inherit money, or will you end up financially responsible for aging, ailing parents?
- What factors might hurt your career? (If you work for a bank or a homebuilder, a jump in interest rates could put you out of a job. If you work for a chemical manufacturer, soaring oil prices could be bad news.)
- If you are self-employed, how long do businesses similar to yours tend to survive?
- Do you need your investments to supplement your cash income? (In general, bonds will; stocks won't.)
- Given your salary and your spending needs, how much money can you afford to lose on your investments?

If, after considering these factors, you feel you can take the higher risks inherent in greater ownership of stocks, you belong around Graham's minimum of 25% in bonds or cash. If not, then steer mostly clear of stocks, edging toward Graham's maximum of 75% in bonds or cash. (To find out whether you can go up to 100%, see the sidebar on p. 105.)

Once you set these target percentages, change them only as your life circumstances change. Do not buy more stocks because the stock market has gone up; do not sell them because it has gone down. The very heart of Graham's approach is to replace guesswork with discipline. Fortunately, through your 401(k), it's easy to put your portfolio on permanent autopilot. Let's say you are comfortable with a fairly high level of risk–say, 70% of your assets in stocks and 30% in bonds. If the stock market rises 25% (but bonds stay steady), you will now have just under 75% in stocks and only 25% in bonds.[5] Visit your 401(k)'s website (or call its toll-free number) and sell enough of your stock funds to "rebalance" back to your 70–30 target. The key is to rebalance on a predictable, patient schedule–not so often that you will

---

[5] For the sake of simplicity, this example assumes that stocks rose instantaneously.

WHY *NOT* 100% STOCKS?

Graham advises you never to have more than 75% of your total assets in stocks. But is putting all your money into the stock market inadvisable for *everyone*? For a tiny minority of investors, a 100%-stock portfolio may make sense. You are one of them if you:

- have set aside enough cash to support your family for at least one year
- will be investing steadily for at least 20 years to come
- survived the bear market that began in 2000
- did not sell stocks during the bear market that began in 2000
- bought more stocks during the bear market that began in 2000
- have read Chapter 8 in this book and implemented a formal plan to control your own investing behavior.

Unless you can honestly pass all these tests, you have no business putting all your money in stocks. Anyone who panicked in the last bear market is going to panic in the next one—and will regret having no cushion of cash and bonds.

drive yourself crazy, and not so seldom that your targets will get out of whack. I suggest that you rebalance every six months, no more and no less, on easy-to-remember dates like New Year's and the Fourth of July.

The beauty of this periodic rebalancing is that it forces you to base your investing decisions on a simple, objective standard—Do I now own more of this asset than my plan calls for?—instead of the sheer guesswork of where interest rates are heading or whether you think the Dow is about to drop dead. Some mutual-fund companies, including T. Rowe Price, may soon introduce services that will automatically rebalance your 401(k) portfolio to your preset targets, so you will never need to make an active decision.

THE INS AND OUTS OF INCOME INVESTING

In Graham's day, bond investors faced two basic choices: Taxable or tax-free? Short-term or long-term? Today there is a third: Bonds or bond funds?

Taxable or tax-free? Unless you're in the lowest tax bracket,[6] you should buy only tax-free (municipal) bonds outside your retirement accounts. Otherwise too much of your bond income will end up in the hands of the IRS. The only place to own taxable bonds is inside your 401(k) or another sheltered account, where you will owe no current tax on their income—and where municipal bonds have no place, since their tax advantage goes to waste.[7]

Short-term or long-term? Bonds and interest rates teeter on opposite ends of a seesaw: If interest rates rise, bond prices fall—although a short-term bond falls far less than a long-term bond. On the other hand, if interest rates fall, bond prices rise—and a long-term bond will outperform shorter ones.[8] You can split the difference simply

---

[6] For the 2003 tax year, the bottom Federal tax bracket is for single people earning less than $28,400 or married people (filing jointly) earning less than $47,450.

[7] Two good online calculators that will help you compare the after-tax income of municipal and taxable bonds can be found at www.investinginbonds.com/cgi-bin/calculator.pl and www.lebenthal.com/index_infocenter.html. To decide if a "muni" is right for you, find the "taxable equivalent yield" generated by these calculators, then compare that number to the yield currently available on Treasury bonds (http://money.cnn.com/markets/bondcenter/ or www.bloomberg.com/markets/C13.html). If the yield on Treasury bonds is higher than the taxable equivalent yield, munis are not for you. In any case, be warned that municipal bonds and funds produce lower income, and more price fluctuation, than most taxable bonds. Also, the alternative minimum tax, which now hits many middle-income Americans, can negate the advantages of municipal bonds.

[8] For an excellent introduction to bond investing, see http://flagship.vanguard.com/web/planret/AdvicePTIBInvestmentsInvestingInBonds.html#InterestRates. For an even simpler explanation of bonds, see http://money.cnn.com/pf/101/lessons/7/. A "laddered" portfolio, holding bonds across a range of maturities, is another way of hedging interest-rate risk.

by buying intermediate-term bonds maturing in five to 10 years—which do not soar when their side of the seesaw rises, but do not slam into the ground either. For most investors, intermediate bonds are the simplest choice, since they enable you to get out of the game of guessing what interest rates will do.

Bonds or bond funds? Since bonds are generally sold in $10,000 lots and you need a bare minimum of 10 bonds to diversify away the risk that any one of them might go bust, buying individual bonds makes no sense unless you have at least $100,000 to invest. (The only exception is bonds issued by the U.S. Treasury, since they're protected against default by the full force of the American government.)

Bond funds offer cheap and easy diversification, along with the convenience of monthly income, which you can reinvest right back into the fund at current rates without paying a commission. For most investors, bond funds beat individual bonds hands down (the main exceptions are Treasury securities and some municipal bonds). Major firms like Vanguard, Fidelity, Schwab, and T. Rowe Price offer a broad menu of bond funds at low cost.[9]

The choices for bond investors have proliferated like rabbits, so let's update Graham's list of what's available. As of 2003, interest rates have fallen so low that investors are starved for yield, but there are ways of amplifying your interest income without taking on excessive risk.[10] Figure 4-1 summarizes the pros and cons.

Now let's look at a few types of bond investments that can fill special needs.

CASH IS NOT TRASH

How can you wring more income out of your cash? The intelligent investor should consider moving out of bank certificates of deposit or money-market accounts—which have offered meager returns lately—into some of these cash alternatives:

Treasury securities, as obligations of the U.S. government, carry

---

[9] For more information, see www.vanguard.com, www.fidelity.com, www.schwab.com, and www.troweprice.com.

[10] For an accessible online summary of bond investing, see www.aaii.com/promo/20021118/bonds.shtml.

FIGURE 4-1 The Wide World of Bonds

Type	Maturity	Minimum purchase	Risk of default
Treasury bills	Less than one year	$1,000 (D)	Extremely low
Treasury notes	Between one and 10 years	$1,000 (D)	Extremely low
Treasury bonds	More than 10 yrs	$1,000 (D)	Extremely low
Savings bonds	Up to 30 years	$25 (D)	Extremely low
Certificates of deposit	One month to 5 yrs	Usually $500	Very low; insured up to $100,000
Money-market funds	397 days or less	Usually $2,500	Very low
Mortgage debt	One to 30 yrs	$2,000–3,000 (F)	Generally moderate but can be high
Municipal bonds	One to 30 yrs or more	$5,000 (D); $2,000–$3,000 (F)	Generally moderate but can be high
Preferred stock	Indefinite	None	High
High-yield ("junk") bonds	Seven to 20 yrs	$2,000–$3,000 (F)	High
Emerging-markets debt	Up to 30 yrs	$2,000–$3,000 (F)	High

Sources: Bankrate.com, Bloomberg, Lehman Brothers, Merrill Lynch, Morningstar, www.savingsbonds.gov

Notes: (D): purchased directly. (F): purchased through a mutual fund. "Ease of sale before maturity" indicates how readily you can sell at a fair price before maturity date; mutual funds typically offer better ease of sale than individual bonds. Money-market funds are Federally insured up to $100,000 if purchased at an FDIC-member bank, but otherwise carry only an implicit pledge not to lose value. Federal income tax on savings bonds is deferred until redemption or maturity. Municipal bonds are generally exempt from state income tax only in the state where they were issued.

Risk if interest rates rise	Ease of sale before maturity	Exempt from most state income taxes?	Exempt from Federal income tax?	Benchmark	Yield 12/31/2002
Very low	High	Y	N	90-day	1.2
Moderate	High	Y	N	5-year	2.7
				10 year	3.8
High	High	Y	N	30-year	4.8
Very low	Low	Y	N	EE bond Series bought after May 1995	4.2
Low	Low	N	N	1-year nat'l. avg.	1.5
Low	High	N	N	Taxable money market avg.	0.8
Moderate to high	Moderate to low	N	N	Lehman Bros. MBS Index	4.6
Moderate to high	Moderate to low	N	Y	National Long-Term Mutual Fund avg.	4.3
High	Moderate to low	N	N	None	Highly variable
Moderate	Low	N	N	Merrill Lynch High Yield Index	11.9
Moderate	Low	N	N	Emerg. Mkts Bond fund avg.	8.8

virtually no credit risk–since, instead of defaulting on his debts, Uncle Sam can just jack up taxes or print more money at will. Treasury bills mature in four, 13, or 26 weeks. Because of their very short maturities, T-bills barely get dented when rising interest rates knock down the prices of other income investments; longer-term Treasury debt, however, suffers severely when interest rates rise. The interest income on Treasury securities is generally free from state (but not Federal) income tax. And, with $3.7 trillion in public hands, the market for Treasury debt is immense, so you can readily find a buyer if you need your money back before maturity. You can buy Treasury bills, short-term notes, and long-term bonds directly from the government, with no brokerage fees, at www.publicdebt.treas.gov. (For more on inflation-protected TIPS, see the commentary on Chapter 2.)

Savings bonds, unlike Treasuries, are not marketable; you cannot sell them to another investor, and you'll forfeit three months of interest if you redeem them in less than five years. Thus they are suitable mainly as "set-aside money" to meet a future spending need–a gift for a religious ceremony that's years away, or a jump start on putting your newborn through Harvard. They come in denominations as low as $25, making them ideal as gifts to grandchildren. For investors who can confidently leave some cash untouched for years to come, inflation-protected "I-bonds" recently offered an attractive yield of around 4%. To learn more, see www.savingsbonds.gov.

MOVING BEYOND UNCLE SAM

Mortgage securities. Pooled together from thousands of mortgages around the United States, these bonds are issued by agencies like the Federal National Mortgage Association ("Fannie Mae") or the Government National Mortgage Association ("Ginnie Mae"). However, they are not backed by the U.S. Treasury, so they sell at higher yields to reflect their greater risk. Mortgage bonds generally underperform when interest rates fall and bomb when rates rise. (Over the long run, those swings tend to even out and the higher average yields pay off.) Good mortgage-bond funds are available from Vanguard, Fidelity, and Pimco. But if a broker ever tries to sell you an individual mortgage bond or "CMO," tell him you are late for an appointment with your proctologist.

Annuities. These insurance-like investments enable you to defer current taxes and capture a stream of income after you retire. Fixed annuities offer a set rate of return; variable ones provide a fluctuating return. But what the defensive investor really needs to defend against here are the hard-selling insurance agents, stockbrokers, and financial planners who peddle annuities at rapaciously high costs. In most cases, the high expenses of owning an annuity–including "surrender charges" that gnaw away at your early withdrawals–will overwhelm its advantages. The few good annuities are bought, not sold; if an annuity produces fat commissions for the seller, chances are it will produce meager results for the buyer. Consider only those you can buy directly from providers with rock-bottom costs like Ameritas, TIAA-CREF, and Vanguard.[11]

---

[11] In general, variable annuities are not attractive for investors under the age of 50 who expect to be in a high tax bracket during retirement or who have

Preferred stock. Preferred shares are a worst-of-both-worlds investment. They are less secure than bonds, since they have only a secondary claim on a company's assets if it goes bankrupt. And they offer less profit potential than common stocks do, since companies typically "call" (or forcibly buy back) their preferred shares when interest rates drop or their credit rating improves. Unlike the interest payments on most of its bonds, an issuing company cannot deduct preferred dividend payments from its corporate tax bill. Ask yourself: If this company is healthy enough to deserve my investment, why is it paying a fat dividend on its preferred stock instead of issuing bonds and getting a tax break? The likely answer is that the company is not healthy, the market for its bonds is glutted, and you should approach its preferred shares as you would approach an unrefrigerated dead fish.

Common stock. A visit to the stock screener at http://screen.yahoo.com/stocks.html in early 2003 showed that 115 of the stocks in the Standard & Poor's 500 index had dividend yields of 3.0% or greater. No intelligent investor, no matter how starved for yield, would ever buy a stock for its dividend income alone; the company and its businesses must be solid, and its stock price must be reasonable. But, thanks to the bear market that began in 2000, some leading stocks are now outyielding Treasury bonds. So even the most defensive investor should realize that selectively adding stocks to an all-bond or mostly-bond portfolio can *increase* its income yield–and raise its potential return.[12]

---

not already contributed the maximum to their existing 401(k) or IRA accounts. Fixed annuities (with the notable exception of those from TIAA-CREF) can change their "guaranteed" rates and smack you with nasty surrender fees. For thorough and objective analysis of annuities, see two superb articles by Walter Updegrave: "Income for Life," *Money,* July, 2002, pp. 89–96, and "Annuity Buyer's Guide," *Money,* November, 2002, pp. 104–110.

[12] For more on the role of dividends in a portfolio, see Chapter 19.

CHAPTER 5

The Defensive Investor and Common Stocks

Investment Merits of Common Stocks

In our first edition (1949) we found it necessary at this point to insert a long exposition of the case for including a substantial common-stock component in all investment portfolios.* Common stocks were generally viewed as highly speculative and therefore unsafe; they had declined fairly substantially from the high levels of 1946, but instead of attracting investors to them because of their reasonable prices, this fall had had the opposite effect of undermining confidence in equity securities. We have commented on the converse situation that has developed in the ensuing 20 years, whereby the big advance in stock prices made them appear safe and profitable investments at record high levels which might actually carry with them a considerable degree of risk.†

The argument we made for common stocks in 1949 turned on

---

* At the beginning of 1949, the average annual return produced by stocks over the previous 20 years was 3.1%, versus 3.9% for long-term Treasury bonds—meaning that $10,000 invested in stocks would have grown to $18,415 over that period, while the same amount in bonds would have turned into $21,494. Naturally enough, 1949 turned out to be a fabulous time to buy stocks: Over the next decade, the Standard & Poor's 500-stock index gained an average of 20.1% per year, one of the best long-term returns in the history of the U.S. stock market.

† Graham's earlier comments on this subject appear on pp. 19–20. Just imagine what he would have thought about the stock market of the late 1990s, in which each new record-setting high was considered further "proof" that stocks were the riskless way to wealth!

two main points. The first was that they had offered a considerable degree of protection against the erosion of the investor's dollar caused by inflation, whereas bonds offered no protection at all. The second advantage of common stocks lay in their higher average return to investors over the years. This was produced both by an average dividend income exceeding the yield on good bonds and by an underlying tendency for market value to increase over the years in consequence of the reinvestment of undistributed profits.

While these two advantages have been of major importance—and have given common stocks a far better record than bonds over the long-term past—we have consistently warned that these benefits could be lost by the stock buyer if he pays too high a price for his shares. This was clearly the case in 1929, and it took 25 years for the market level to climb back to the ledge from which it had abysmally fallen in 1929–1932.* Since 1957 common stocks have once again, through their high prices, lost their traditional advantage in dividend yield over bond interest rates.† It remains to

---

* The Dow Jones Industrial Average closed at a then-record high of 381.17 on September 3, 1929. It did not close above that level until November 23, 1954–more than a quarter of a century later–when it hit 382.74. (When you say you intend to own stocks "for the long run," do you realize just how long the long run can be–or that many investors who bought in 1929 were no longer even alive by 1954?) However, for patient investors who reinvested their income, stock returns were positive over this otherwise dismal period, simply because dividend yields averaged more than 5.6% per year. According to professors Elroy Dimson, Paul Marsh, and Mike Staunton of London Business School, if you had invested $1 in U.S. stocks in 1900 and spent all your dividends, your stock portfolio would have grown to $198 by 2000. But if you had reinvested all your dividends, your stock portfolio would have been worth $16,797! Far from being an afterthought, dividends are the greatest force in stock investing.

† Why do the "high prices" of stocks affect their dividend yields? A stock's yield is the ratio of its cash dividend to the price of one share of common stock. If a company pays a $2 annual dividend when its stock price is $100 per share, its yield is 2%. But if the stock price doubles while the dividend stays constant, the dividend yield will drop to 1%. In 1959, when the trend Graham spotted in 1957 became noticeable to everyone, most Wall Street

be seen whether the inflation factor and the economic-growth factor will make up in the future for this significantly adverse development.

It should be evident to the reader that we have no enthusiasm for common stocks in general at the 900 DJIA level of late 1971. For reasons already given* we feel that the defensive investor cannot afford to be without an appreciable proportion of common stocks in his portfolio, even if he must regard them as the lesser of two evils—the greater being the risks attached to an all-bond holding.

Rules for the Common-Stock Component

The selection of common stocks for the portfolio of the defensive investor should be a relatively simple matter. Here we would suggest four rules to be followed:

1. There should be adequate though not excessive diversification. This might mean a minimum of ten different issues and a maximum of about thirty.†

2. Each company selected should be large, prominent, and conservatively financed. Indefinite as these adjectives must be, their general sense is clear. Observations on this point are added at the end of the chapter.

3. Each company should have a long record of continuous dividend payments. (All the issues in the Dow Jones Industrial Aver-

---

pundits declared that it could not possibly last. Never before had stocks yielded less than bonds; after all, since stocks are riskier than bonds, why would anyone buy them at all unless they pay extra dividend income to compensate for their greater risk? The experts argued that bonds would outyield stocks for a few months at most, and then things would revert to "normal." More than four decades later, the relationship has never been normal again; the yield on stocks has (so far) continuously stayed below the yield on bonds.

* See pp. 56–57 and 88–89.

† For another view of diversification, see the sidebar in the commentary on Chapter 14 (p. 368).

age met this dividend requirement in 1971.) To be specific on this point we would suggest the requirement of continuous dividend payments beginning at least in 1950.*

4. The investor should impose some limit on the price he will pay for an issue in relation to its average earnings over, say, the past seven years. We suggest that this limit be set at 25 times such average earnings, and not more than 20 times those of the last twelve-month period. But such a restriction would eliminate nearly all the strongest and most popular companies from the portfolio. In particular, it would ban virtually the entire category of "growth stocks," which have for some years past been the favorites of both speculators and institutional investors. We must give our reasons for proposing so drastic an exclusion.

Growth Stocks and the Defensive Investor

The term "growth stock" is applied to one which has increased its per-share earnings in the past at well above the rate for common stocks generally and is expected to continue to do so in the future. (Some authorities would say that a true growth stock should be expected at least to double its per-share earnings in ten years—i.e., to increase them at a compounded annual rate of over 7.1%.)† Obviously stocks of this kind are attractive to buy and to own, provided the price paid is not excessive. The problem lies there, of

---

* Today's defensive investor should probably insist on at least 10 years of continuous dividend payments (which would eliminate from consideration only one member of the Dow Jones Industrial Average–Microsoft–and would still leave at least 317 stocks to choose from among the S & P 500 index). Even insisting on 20 years of uninterrupted dividend payments would not be overly restrictive; according to Morgan Stanley, 255 companies in the S & P 500 met that standard as of year-end 2002.

† The "Rule of 72" is a handy mental tool. To estimate the length of time an amount of money takes to double, simply divide its assumed growth rate into 72. At 6%, for instance, money will double in 12 years (72 divided by 6 = 12). At the 7.1% rate cited by Graham, a growth stock will double its earnings in just over 10 years (72/7.1 = 10.1 years).

course, since growth stocks have long sold at high prices in relation to current earnings and at much higher multiples of their average profits over a past period. This has introduced a speculative element of considerable weight in the growth-stock picture and has made successful operations in this field a far from simple matter.

The leading growth issue has long been International Business Machines, and it has brought phenomenal rewards to those who bought it years ago and held on to it tenaciously. But we have already pointed out* that this "best of common stocks" actually lost 50% of its market price in a six-months' decline during 1961–62 and nearly the same percentage in 1969–70. Other growth stocks have been even more vulnerable to adverse developments; in some cases not only has the price fallen back but the earnings as well, thus causing a double discomfiture to those who owned them. A good second example for our purpose is Texas Instruments, which in six years rose from 5 to 256, without paying a dividend, while its earnings increased from 40 cents to $3.91 per share. (Note that the price advanced five times as fast as the profits; this is characteristic of popular common stocks.) But two years later the earnings had dropped off by nearly 50% and the price by *four-fifths*, to 49.†

The reader will understand from these instances why we regard growth stocks as a whole as too uncertain and risky a vehicle for the defensive investor. Of course, wonders can be accomplished with the right individual selections, bought at the right levels, and later sold after a huge rise and before the probable decline. But the average investor can no more expect to accomplish this than to find money growing on trees. In contrast we think that the group of

---

* Graham makes this point on p. 73.

† To show that Graham's observations are perennially true, we can substitute Microsoft for IBM and Cisco for Texas Instruments. Thirty years apart, the results are uncannily similar: Microsoft's stock dropped 55.7% from 2000 through 2002, while Cisco's stock–which had risen roughly 50-fold over the previous six years–lost 76% of its value from 2000 through 2002. As with Texas Instruments, the drop in Cisco's stock price was sharper than the fall in its earnings, which dropped just 39.2% (comparing the three-year average for 1997–1999 against 2000–2002). As always, the hotter they are, the harder they fall.

large companies that are relatively unpopular, and therefore obtainable at reasonable earnings multipliers,* offers a sound if unspectacular area of choice by the general public. We shall illustrate this idea in our chapter on portfolio selection.

Portfolio Changes

It is now standard practice to submit all security lists for periodic inspection in order to see whether their quality can be improved. This, of course, is a major part of the service provided for clients by investment counselors. Nearly all brokerage houses are ready to make corresponding suggestions, without special fee, in return for the commission business involved. Some brokerage houses maintain investment services on a fee basis.

Presumably our defensive investor should obtain—at least once a year—the same kind of advice regarding changes in his portfolio as he sought when his funds were first committed. Since he will have little expertness of his own on which to rely, it is essential that he entrust himself only to firms of the highest reputation; otherwise he may easily fall into incompetent or unscrupulous hands. It is important, in any case, that at every such consultation he make clear to his adviser that he wishes to adhere closely to the four rules of common-stock selection given earlier in this chapter. Incidentally, if his list has been competently selected in the first instance, there should be no need for frequent or numerous changes.†

---

* "Earnings multiplier" is a synonym for P/E or price/earnings ratios, which measure how much investors are willing to pay for a stock compared to the profitability of the underlying business. (See footnote † on p. 70 in Chapter 3.)

† Investors can now set up their own automated system to monitor the quality of their holdings by using interactive "portfolio trackers" at such websites as www.quicken.com, moneycentral.msn.com, finance.yahoo.com, and www.morningstar.com. Graham would, however, warn against relying exclusively on such a system; you must use your own judgment to supplement the software.

Dollar-Cost Averaging

The New York Stock Exchange has put considerable effort into popularizing its "monthly purchase plan," under which an investor devotes the same dollar amount each month to buying one or more common stocks. This is an application of a special type of "formula investment" known as dollar-cost averaging. During the predominantly rising-market experience since 1949 the results from such a procedure were certain to be highly satisfactory, especially since they prevented the practitioner from concentrating his buying at the wrong times.

In Lucile Tomlinson's comprehensive study of formula investment plans,[1] the author presented a calculation of the results of dollar-cost averaging in the group of stocks making up the Dow Jones industrial index. Tests were made covering 23 ten-year purchase periods, the first ending in 1929, the last in 1952. Every test showed a profit either at the close of the purchase period or within five years thereafter. The average indicated profit at the end of the 23 buying periods was 21.5%, exclusive of dividends received. Needless to say, in some instances there was a substantial temporary depreciation at market value. Miss Tomlinson ends her discussion of this ultrasimple investment formula with the striking sentence: "No one has yet discovered any other formula for investing which can be used with so much confidence of ultimate success, regardless of what may happen to security prices, as Dollar Cost Averaging."

It may be objected that dollar-cost averaging, while sound in principle, is rather unrealistic in practice, because few people are so situated that they can have available for common-stock investment the same amount of money each year for, say, 20 years. It seems to me that this apparent objection has lost much of its force in recent years. Common stocks are becoming generally accepted as a necessary component of a sound savings-investment program. Thus, systematic and uniform purchases of common stocks may present no more psychological and financial difficulties than similar continuous payments for United States savings bonds and for life insurance—to which they should be complementary. The monthly amount may be small, but the results after 20 or more years can be impressive and important to the saver.

The Investor's Personal Situation

At the beginning of this chapter we referred briefly to the position of the individual portfolio owner. Let us return to this matter, in the light of our subsequent discussion of general policy. To what extent should the type of securities selected by the investor vary with his circumstances? As concrete examples representing widely different conditions, we shall take: (1) a widow left $200,000 with which to support herself and her children; (2) a successful doctor in mid-career, with savings of $100,000 and yearly accretions of $10,000; and (3) a young man earning $200 per week and saving $1,000 a year.*

For the widow, the problem of living on her income is a very difficult one. On the other hand the need for conservatism in her investments is paramount. A division of her fund about equally between United States bonds and first-grade common stocks is a compromise between these objectives and corresponds to our general prescription for the defensive investor. (The stock component may be placed as high as 75% if the investor is psychologically prepared for this decision, and if she can be almost certain she is not buying at too high a level. Assuredly this is *not* the case in early 1972.)

We do not preclude the possibility that the widow may qualify as an enterprising investor, in which case her objectives and methods will be quite different. The one thing the widow must *not* do is to take speculative chances in order to "make some extra income." By this we mean trying for profits or high income without the necessary equipment to warrant full confidence in overall success. It would be far better for her to draw $2,000 per year out of her principal, in order to make both ends meet, than to risk half of it in poorly grounded, and therefore speculative, ventures.

The prosperous doctor has none of the widow's pressures and compulsions, yet we believe that his choices are pretty much the same. Is he willing to take a serious interest in the business of investment? If he lacks the impulse or the flair, he will do best to

---

* To update Graham's figures, take each dollar amount in this section and multiply it by five.

accept the easy role of the defensive investor. The division of his portfolio should then be no different from that of the "typical" widow, and there would be the same area of personal choice in fixing the size of the stock component. The annual savings should be invested in about the same proportions as the total fund.

The average doctor may be more likely than the average widow to elect to become an enterprising investor, and he is perhaps more likely to succeed in the undertaking. He has one important handicap, however—the fact that he has less time available to give to his investment education and to the administration of his funds. In fact, medical men have been notoriously unsuccessful in their security dealings. The reason for this is that they usually have an ample confidence in their own intelligence and a strong desire to make a good return on their money, without the realization that to do so successfully requires both considerable attention to the matter and something of a professional approach to security values.

Finally, the young man who saves $1,000 a year—and expects to do better gradually—finds himself with the same choices, though for still different reasons. Some of his savings should go automatically into Series E bonds. The balance is so modest that it seems hardly worthwhile for him to undergo a tough educational and temperamental discipline in order to qualify as an aggressive investor. Thus a simple resort to our standard program for the defensive investor would be at once the easiest and the most logical policy.

Let us not ignore human nature at this point. Finance has a fascination for many bright young people with limited means. They would like to be both intelligent and enterprising in the placement of their savings, even though investment income is much less important to them than their salaries. This attitude is all to the good. There is a great advantage for the young capitalist to begin his financial education and experience early. If he is going to operate as an aggressive investor he is certain to make some mistakes and to take some losses. Youth can stand these disappointments and profit by them. We urge the beginner in security buying not to waste his efforts and his money in trying to beat the market. Let him study security values and initially test out his judgment on price versus value with the smallest possible sums.

Thus we return to the statement, made at the outset, that the kind of securities to be purchased and the rate of return to be sought depend not on the investor's financial resources but on his financial equipment in terms of knowledge, experience, and temperament.

Note on the Concept of "Risk"

It is conventional to speak of good bonds as less risky than good preferred stocks and of the latter as less risky than good common stocks. From this was derived the popular prejudice against common stocks because they are not "safe," which was demonstrated in the Federal Reserve Board's survey of 1948. We should like to point out that the words "risk" and "safety" are applied to securities in two different senses, with a resultant confusion in thought.

A bond is clearly proved unsafe when it defaults its interest or principal payments. Similarly, if a preferred stock or even a common stock is bought with the expectation that a given rate of dividend will be continued, then a reduction or passing of the dividend means that it has proved unsafe. It is also true that an investment contains a risk if there is a fair possibility that the holder may have to sell at a time when the price is well below cost.

Nevertheless, the idea of risk is often extended to apply to a possible decline in the price of a security, even though the decline may be of a cyclical and temporary nature and even though the holder is unlikely to be forced to sell at such times. These chances are present in all securities, other than United States savings bonds, and to a greater extent in the general run of common stocks than in senior issues as a class. But we believe that what is here involved is not a true risk in the useful sense of the term. The man who holds a mortgage on a building might have to take a substantial loss if he were forced to sell it at an unfavorable time. That element is not taken into account in judging the safety or risk of ordinary real-estate mortgages, the only criterion being the certainty of punctual payments. In the same way the risk attached to an ordinary commercial business is measured by the chance of its losing money, not by what would happen if the owner were forced to sell.

In Chapter 8 we shall set forth our conviction that the bona fide investor does not lose money merely because the market price of his holdings declines; hence the fact that a decline may occur does not mean that he is running a true risk of loss. If a group of well-selected common-stock investments shows a satisfactory overall return, as measured through a fair number of years, then this group investment has proved to be "safe." During that period its market value is bound to fluctuate, and as likely as not it will sell for a while under the buyer's cost. If that fact makes the investment "risky," it would then have to be called both risky and safe at the same time. This confusion may be avoided if we apply the concept of risk solely to a loss of value which either is realized through actual sale, or is caused by a significant deterioration in the company's position—or, more frequently perhaps, is the result of the payment of an excessive price in relation to the intrinsic worth of the security.[2]

Many common stocks do involve risks of such deterioration. But it is our thesis that a properly executed group investment in common stocks does not carry any substantial risk of this sort and that therefore it should not be termed "risky" merely because of the element of price fluctuation. But such risk is present if there is danger that the price may prove to have been clearly too high by intrinsic-value standards—even if any subsequent severe market decline may be recouped many years later.

Note on the Category of "Large, Prominent, and Conservatively Financed Corporations"

The quoted phrase in our caption was used earlier in the chapter to describe the kind of common stocks to which defensive investors should limit their purchases—provided also that they had paid continuous dividends for a considerable number of years. A criterion based on adjectives is always ambiguous. Where is the dividing line for size, for prominence, and for conservatism of financial structure? On the last point we can suggest a specific standard that, though arbitrary, is in line with accepted thinking. An industrial company's finances are not conservative unless the common stock (at book value) represents at least half of the total capitalization, including all bank debt.[3] For a railroad or public utility the figure should be at least 30%.

The words "large" and "prominent" carry the notion of substantial size combined with a leading position in the industry. Such companies are often referred to as "primary"; all other common stocks are then called "secondary," except that growth stocks are ordinarily placed in a separate class by those who buy them as such. To supply an element of concreteness here, let us suggest that to be "large" in present-day terms a company should have $50 million of assets or do $50 million of business.* Again to be "prominent" a company should rank among the first quarter or first third in size within its industry group.

It would be foolish, however, to insist upon such arbitrary criteria. They are offered merely as guides to those who may ask for guidance. But any rule which the investor may set for himself and which does no violence to the common-sense meanings of "large" and "prominent" should be acceptable. By the very nature of the case there must be a large group of companies that some will and others will not include among those suitable for defensive investment. There is no harm in such diversity of opinion and action. In fact, it has a salutary effect upon stock-market conditions, because it permits a gradual differentiation or transition between the categories of primary and secondary stock issues.

---

* In today's markets, to be considered large, a company should have a total stock value (or "market capitalization") of at least $10 billion. According to the online stock screener at http://screen.yahoo.com/stocks.html, that gave you roughly 300 stocks to choose from as of early 2003.

COMMENTARY ON CHAPTER 5

Human felicity is produc'd not so much by great Pieces of good Fortune that seldom happen, as by little Advantages that occur every day.

–Benjamin Franklin

THE BEST DEFENSE IS A GOOD OFFENSE

After the stock-market bloodbath of the past few years, why would any defensive investor put a dime into stocks?

First, remember Graham's insistence that how defensive you should be depends less on your tolerance for risk than on your willingness to put time and energy into your portfolio. And if you go about it the right way, investing in stocks is just as easy as parking your money in bonds and cash. (As we'll see in Chapter 9, you can buy a stock-market index fund with no more effort than it takes to get dressed in the morning.)

Amidst the bear market that began in 2000, it's understandable if you feel burned–and if, in turn, that feeling makes you determined never to buy another stock again. As an old Turkish proverb says, "After you burn your mouth on hot milk, you blow on your yogurt." Because the crash of 2000–2002 was so terrible, many investors now view stocks as scaldingly risky; but, paradoxically, the very act of crashing has taken much of the risk out of the stock market. It was hot milk before, but it is room-temperature yogurt now.

Viewed logically, the decision of whether to own stocks today has nothing to do with how much money you might have lost by owning them a few years ago. When stocks are priced reasonably enough to give you future growth, then you should own them, regardless of the losses they may have cost you in the recent past. That's all the more true when bond yields are low, reducing the future returns on income-producing investments.

As we have seen in Chapter 3, stocks are (as of early 2003) only mildly overpriced by historical standards. Meanwhile, at recent prices, bonds offer such low yields that an investor who buys them for their supposed safety is like a smoker who thinks he can protect himself against lung cancer by smoking low-tar cigarettes. No matter how defensive an investor you are—in Graham's sense of low maintenance, or in the contemporary sense of low risk—today's values mean that you must keep at least some of your money in stocks.

Fortunately, it's never been easier for a defensive investor to buy stocks. And a permanent autopilot portfolio, which effortlessly puts a little bit of your money to work every month in predetermined investments, can defend you against the need to dedicate a large part of your life to stock picking.

SHOULD YOU "BUY WHAT YOU KNOW"?

But first, let's look at something the defensive investor must always defend against: the belief that you can pick stocks without doing any homework. In the 1980s and early 1990s, one of the most popular investing slogans was "buy what you know." Peter Lynch—who from 1977 through 1990 piloted Fidelity Magellan to the best track record ever compiled by a mutual fund—was the most charismatic preacher of this gospel. Lynch argued that amateur investors have an advantage that professional investors have forgotten how to use: "the power of common knowledge." If you discover a great new restaurant, car, toothpaste, or jeans—or if you notice that the parking lot at a nearby business is always full or that people are still working at a company's headquarters long after Jay Leno goes off the air—then you have a personal insight into a stock that a professional analyst or portfolio manager might never pick up on. As Lynch put it, "During a lifetime of buying cars or cameras, you develop a sense of what's good and what's bad, what sells and what doesn't . . . and the most important part is, you know it before Wall Street knows it."[1]

Lynch's rule—"You can outperform the experts if you use your edge by investing in companies or industries you already understand"—isn't

---

[1] Peter Lynch with John Rothchild, *One Up on Wall Street* (Penguin, 1989), p. 23.

totally implausible, and thousands of investors have profited from it over the years. But Lynch's rule can work only if you follow its corollary as well: "Finding the promising company is only the first step. The next step is doing the research." To his credit, Lynch insists that no one should ever invest in a company, no matter how great its products or how crowded its parking lot, without studying its financial statements and estimating its business value.

Unfortunately, most stock buyers have ignored that part.

Barbra Streisand, the day-trading diva, personified the way people abuse Lynch's teachings. In 1999 she burbled, "We go to Starbucks every day, so I buy Starbucks stock." But the Funny Girl forgot that no matter how much you love those tall skinny lattes, you still have to analyze Starbucks's financial statements and make sure the stock isn't even more overpriced than the coffee. Countless stock buyers made the same mistake by loading up on shares of Amazon.com because they loved the website or buying e*Trade stock because it was their own online broker.

"Experts" gave the idea credence too. In an interview televised on CNN in late 1999, portfolio manager Kevin Landis of the Firsthand Funds was asked plaintively, "How do you do it? Why can't I do it, Kevin?" (From 1995 through the end of 1999, the Firsthand Technology Value fund produced an astounding 58.2% average annualized gain.) "Well, you *can* do it," Landis chirped. "All you really need to do is focus on the things that you know, and stay close to an industry, and talk to people who work in it every day."[2]

The most painful perversion of Lynch's rule occurred in corporate retirement plans. If you're supposed to "buy what you know," then what could possibly be a better investment for your 401(k) than your own company's stock? After all, you work there; don't you know more about the company than an outsider ever could? Sadly, the employees

---

[2] Kevin Landis interview on CNN *In the Money,* November 5, 1999, 11 A.M. eastern standard time. If Landis's own record is any indication, focusing on "the things that you know" is not "all you really need to do" to pick stocks successfully. From the end of 1999 through the end of 2002, Landis's fund (full of technology companies that he claimed to know "firsthand" from his base in Silicon Valley) lost 73.2% of its value, an even worse pounding than the average technology fund suffered over that period.

of Enron, Global Crossing, and WorldCom–many of whom put nearly all their retirement assets in their own company's stock, only to be wiped out–learned that insiders often possess only the illusion of knowledge, not the real thing.

Psychologists led by Baruch Fischhoff of Carnegie Mellon University have documented a disturbing fact: becoming more familiar with a subject does not significantly reduce people's tendency to exaggerate how much they actually know about it.[3] That's why "investing in what you know" can be so dangerous; the more you know going in, the less likely you are to probe a stock for weaknesses. This pernicious form of overconfidence is called "home bias," or the habit of sticking to what is already familiar:

- Individual investors own three times more shares in their local phone company than in all other phone companies combined.
- The typical mutual fund owns stocks whose headquarters are 115 miles closer to the fund's main office than the average U.S. company is.
- 401(k) investors keep between 25% and 30% of their retirement assets in the stock of their own company.[4]

In short, familiarity breeds complacency. On the TV news, isn't it always the neighbor or the best friend or the parent of the criminal who says in a shocked voice, "He was such a nice guy"? That's because whenever we are too close to someone or something, we take our beliefs for granted, instead of questioning them as we do when we confront something more remote. The more familiar a stock is, the more likely it is to turn a defensive investor into a lazy one who thinks there's no need to do any homework. Don't let that happen to you.

---

[3] Sarah Lichtenstein and Baruch Fischhoff, "Do Those Who Know More Also Know More about How Much They Know?" *Organizational Behavior and Human Performance,* vol. 20, no. 2, December, 1977, pp. 159–183.

[4] See Gur Huberman, "Familiarity Breeds Investment"; Joshua D. Coval and Tobias J. Moskowitz, "The Geography of Investment"; and Gur Huberman and Paul Sengmuller, "Company Stock in 401(k) Plans," all available at http://papers.ssrn.com.

CAN YOU ROLL YOUR OWN?

Fortunately, for a defensive investor who is willing to do the required homework for assembling a stock portfolio, this is the Golden Age: Never before in financial history has owning stocks been so cheap and convenient.[5]

Do it yourself. Through specialized online brokerages like www.sharebuilder.com, www.foliofn.com, and www.buyandhold.com, you can buy stocks automatically even if you have very little cash to spare. These websites charge as little as $4 for each periodic purchase of any of the thousands of U.S. stocks they make available. You can invest every week or every month, reinvest the dividends, and even trickle your money into stocks through electronic withdrawals from your bank account or direct deposit from your paycheck. Sharebuilder charges more to sell than to buy–reminding you, like a little whack across the nose with a rolled-up newspaper, that rapid selling is an investing no-no–while FolioFN offers an excellent tax-tracking tool.

Unlike traditional brokers or mutual funds that won't let you in the door for less than $2,000 or $3,000, these online firms have no minimum account balances and are tailor-made for beginning investors who want to put fledgling portfolios on autopilot. To be sure, a transaction fee of $4 takes a monstrous 8% bite out of a $50 monthly investment–but if that's all the money you can spare, then these microinvesting sites are the only game in town for building a diversified portfolio.

You can also buy individual stocks straight from the issuing companies. In 1994, the U.S. Securities and Exchange Commission loosened the handcuffs it had long ago clamped onto the direct sale of stocks to the public. Hundreds of companies responded by creating Internet-based programs allowing investors to buy shares without going through a broker. Some helpful online sources of information on buying stocks directly include www.dripcentral.com, www.netstockdirect.com (an affiliate of Sharebuilder), and www.stockpower.com.

---

[5] According to finance professor Charles Jones of Columbia Business School, the cost of a small, one-way trade (either a buy or a sell) in a New York Stock Exchange–listed stock dropped from about 1.25% in Graham's day to about 0.25% in 2000. For institutions like mutual funds, those costs are actually higher. (See Charles M. Jones, "A Century of Stock Market Liquidity and Trading Costs," at http://papers.ssrn.com.)

You may often incur a variety of nuisance fees that can exceed $25 per year. Even so, direct-stock purchase programs are usually cheaper than stockbrokers.

Be warned, however, that buying stocks in tiny increments for years on end can set off big tax headaches. If you are not prepared to keep a permanent and exhaustively detailed record of your purchases, do not buy in the first place. Finally, don't invest in only one stock—or even just a handful of different stocks. Unless you are not willing to spread your bets, you shouldn't bet at all. Graham's guideline of owning between 10 and 30 stocks remains a good starting point for investors who want to pick their own stocks, but you must make sure that you are not overexposed to one industry.[6] (For more on how to pick the individual stocks that will make up your portfolio, see pp. 114–115 and Chapters 11, 14, and 15.)

If, after you set up such an online autopilot portfolio, you find yourself trading more than twice a year—or spending more than an hour or two per month, total, on your investments—then something has gone badly wrong. Do not let the ease and up-to-the-minute feel of the Internet seduce you into becoming a speculator. A defensive investor runs—and wins—the race by sitting still.

Get some help. A defensive investor can also own stocks through a discount broker, a financial planner, or a full-service stockbroker. At a discount brokerage, you'll need to do most of the stock-picking work yourself; Graham's guidelines will help you create a core portfolio requiring minimal maintenance and offering maximal odds of a steady return. On the other hand, if you cannot spare the time or summon the interest to do it yourself, there's no reason to feel any shame in hiring someone to pick stocks or mutual funds for you. But there's one responsibility that you must never delegate. You, and no one but you, must investigate (*before* you hand over your money) whether an adviser is trustworthy and charges reasonable fees. (For more pointers, see Chapter 10.)

Farm it out. Mutual funds are the ultimate way for a defensive investor to capture the upside of stock ownership without the down-

---

[6] To help determine whether the stocks you own are sufficiently diversified across different industrial sectors, you can use the free "Instant X-Ray" function at www.morningstar.com or consult the sector information (Global Industry Classification Standard) at www.standardandpoors.com.

side of having to police your own portfolio. At relatively low cost, you can buy a high degree of diversification and convenience–letting a professional pick and watch the stocks for you. In their finest form–index portfolios–mutual funds can require virtually no monitoring or maintenance whatsoever. Index funds are a kind of Rip Van Winkle investment that is highly unlikely to cause any suffering or surprises even if, like Washington Irving's lazy farmer, you fall asleep for 20 years. They are a defensive investor's dream come true. For more detail, see Chapter 9.

FILLING IN THE POTHOLES

As the financial markets heave and crash their way up and down day after day, the defensive investor can take control of the chaos. Your very refusal to be active, your renunciation of any pretended ability to predict the future, can become your most powerful weapons. By putting every investment decision on autopilot, you drop any self-delusion that you know where stocks are headed, and you take away the market's power to upset you no matter how bizarrely it bounces.

As Graham notes, "dollar-cost averaging" enables you to put a fixed amount of money into an investment at regular intervals. Every week, month, or calendar quarter, you buy more–whether the markets have gone (or are about to go) up, down, or sideways. Any major mutual fund company or brokerage firm can automatically and safely transfer the money electronically for you, so you never have to write a check or feel the conscious pang of payment. It's all out of sight, out of mind.

The ideal way to dollar-cost average is into a portfolio of index funds, which own every stock or bond worth having. That way, you renounce not only the guessing game of where the market is going but which sectors of the market–and which particular stocks or bonds within them–will do the best.

Let's say you can spare $500 a month. By owning and dollar-cost averaging into just three index funds–$300 into one that holds the total U.S. stock market, $100 into one that holds foreign stocks, and $100 into one that holds U.S. bonds–you can ensure that you own almost every investment on the planet that's worth owning.[7] Every

---

[7] For more on the rationale for keeping a portion of your portfolio in foreign stocks, see pp. 186–187.

month, like clockwork, you buy more. If the market has dropped, your preset amount goes further, buying you more shares than the month before. If the market has gone up, then your money buys you fewer shares. By putting your portfolio on permanent autopilot this way, you prevent yourself from either flinging money at the market just when it is seems most alluring (and is actually most dangerous) or refusing to buy more after a market crash has made investments truly cheaper (but seemingly more "risky").

According to Ibbotson Associates, the leading financial research firm, if you had invested $12,000 in the Standard & Poor's 500-stock index at the beginning of September 1929, 10 years later you would have had only $7,223 left. But if you had started with a paltry $100 and simply invested another $100 every single month, then by August 1939, your money would have grown to $15,571! *That's* the power of disciplined buying–even in the face of the Great Depression and the worst bear market of all time.[8]

Figure 5-1 shows the magic of dollar-cost averaging in a more recent bear market.

Best of all, once you build a permanent autopilot portfolio with index funds as its heart and core, you'll be able to answer every market question with the most powerful response a defensive investor could ever have: "I don't know and I don't care." If someone asks whether bonds will outperform stocks, just answer, "I don't know and I don't care"–after all, you're automatically buying both. Will health-care stocks make high-tech stocks look sick? "I don't know and I don't care"–you're a permanent owner of both. What's the next Microsoft? "I don't know and I don't care"–as soon as it's big enough to own, your index fund will have it, and you'll go along for the ride. Will foreign stocks beat U.S. stocks next year? "I don't know and I don't care"–if they do, you'll capture that gain; if they don't, you'll get to buy more at lower prices.

By enabling you to say "I don't know and I don't care," a permanent autopilot portfolio liberates you from the feeling that you need to forecast what the financial markets are about to do–and the illusion that

---

[8] Source: spreadsheet data provided courtesy of Ibbotson Associates. Although it was not possible for retail investors to buy the entire S & P 500 index until 1976, the example nevertheless proves the power of buying more when stock prices go down.

FIGURE 5-1

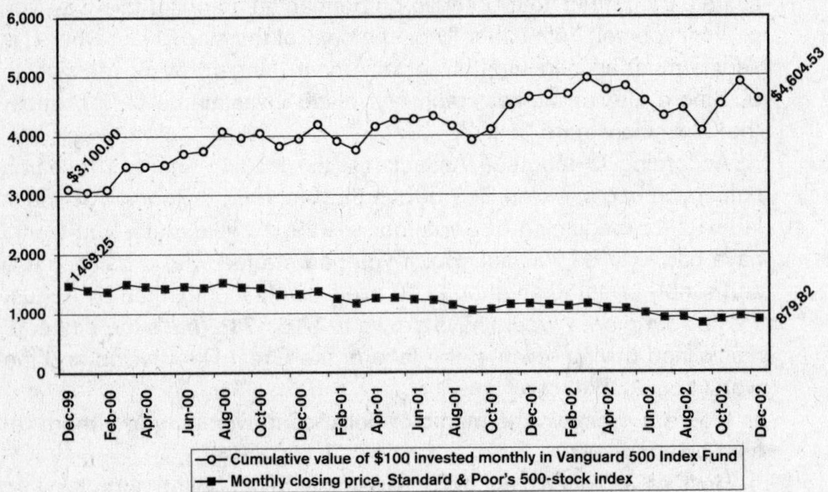

From the end of 1999 through the end of 2002, the S & P 500-stock average fell relentlessly. But if you had opened an index-fund account with a $3,000 minimum investment and added $100 every month, your total outlay of $6,600 would have lost 30.2%–considerably less than the 41.3% plunge in the market. Better yet, your steady buying at lower prices would build the base for an explosive recovery when the market rebounds.

Source: The Vanguard Group

anyone else can. The knowledge of how little you can know about the future, coupled with the acceptance of your ignorance, is a defensive investor's most powerful weapon.

CHAPTER 6

Portfolio Policy for the Enterprising Investor: Negative Approach

The "aggressive" investor should start from the same base as the defensive investor, namely, a division of his funds between high-grade bonds and high-grade common stocks bought at reasonable prices.* He will be prepared to branch out into other kinds of security commitments, but in each case he will want a well-reasoned justification for the departure. There is a difficulty in discussing this topic in orderly fashion, because there is no single or ideal pattern for aggressive operations. The field of choice is wide; the selection should depend not only on the individual's competence and equipment but perhaps equally well upon his interests and preferences.

The most useful generalizations for the enterprising investor are of a negative sort. Let him leave high-grade preferred stocks to corporate buyers. Let him also avoid inferior types of bonds and preferred stocks unless they can be bought at bargain levels—which means ordinarily at prices at least 30% under par for high-coupon

---

* Here Graham has made a slip of the tongue. After insisting in Chapter 1 that the definition of an "enterprising" investor depends not on the amount of risk you seek, but the amount of work you are willing to put in, Graham falls back on the conventional notion that enterprising investors are more "aggressive." The rest of the chapter, however, makes clear that Graham stands by his original definition. (The great British economist John Maynard Keynes appears to have been the first to use the term "enterprise" as a synonym for analytical investment.)

issues, and much less for the lower coupons.* He will let someone else buy foreign-government bond issues, even though the yield may be attractive. He will also be wary of all kinds of new issues, including convertible bonds and preferreds that seem quite tempting and common stocks with excellent earnings confined to the recent past.

For standard bond investments the aggressive investor would do well to follow the pattern suggested to his defensive confrere, and make his choice between high-grade taxable issues, which can now be selected to yield about 7¼%, and good-quality tax-free bonds, which yield up to 5.30% on longer maturities.†

Second-Grade Bonds and Preferred Stocks

Since in late-1971 it is possible to find first-rate corporate bonds to yield 7¼%, and even more, it would not make much sense to buy second-grade issues merely for the higher return they offer. In fact corporations with relatively poor credit standing have found it virtually impossible to sell "straight bonds"—i.e., nonconvertibles—to the public in the past two years. Hence their debt financing has been done by the sale of convertible bonds (or bonds with warrants attached), which place them in a separate category. It follows that virtually all the nonconvertible bonds of inferior rating represent older issues which are selling at a large discount. Thus they offer the possibility of a substantial gain in principal value under favorable future conditions—which would mean here a combination of an improved credit rating for the company and lower general interest rates.

---

* "High-coupon issues" are corporate bonds paying above-average interest rates (in today's markets, at least 8%) or preferred stocks paying large dividend yields (10% or more). If a company must pay high rates of interest in order to borrow money, that is a fundamental signal that it is risky. For more on high-yield or "junk" bonds, see pp. 145–147.

† As of early 2003, the equivalent yields are roughly 5.1% on high-grade corporate bonds and 4.7% on 20-year tax-free municipal bonds. To update these yields, see www.bondsonline.com/asp/news/composites/html or www.bloomberg.com/markets/rates.html and www.bloomberg.com/markets/psamuni.html.

But even in the matter of price discounts and resultant chance of principal gain, the second-grade bonds are in competition with better issues. Some of the well-entrenched obligations with "old-style" coupon rates (2½% to 4%) sold at about 50 cents on the dollar in 1970. Examples: American Telephone & Telegraph 2⅝s, due 1986 sold at 51; Atchison Topeka & Santa Fe RR 4s, due 1995, sold at 51; McGraw-Hill 3⅞s, due 1992, sold at 50½.

Hence under conditions of late-1971 the enterprising investors can probably get from good-grade bonds selling at a large discount all that he should reasonably desire in the form of both income and chance of appreciation.

Throughout this book we refer to the possibility that any well-defined and protracted market situation of the past may return in the future. Hence we should consider what policy the aggressive investor might have to choose in the bond field if prices and yields of high-grade issues should return to former normals. For this reason we shall reprint here our observations on that point made in the 1965 edition, when high-grade bonds yielded only 4½%.

Something should be said now about investing in second-grade issues, which can readily be found to yield any specified return up to 8% or more. The main difference between first- and second-grade bonds is usually found in the number of times the interest charges have been covered by earnings. Example: In early 1964 Chicago, Milwaukee, St. Paul and Pacific 5% income debenture bonds, at 68, yielded 7.35%. But the total interest charges of the road, before income taxes, were earned only 1.5 times in 1963, against our requirement of 5 times for a well-protected railroad issue.[1]

Many investors buy securities of this kind because they "need income" and cannot get along with the meager return offered by top-grade issues. Experience clearly shows that it is unwise to buy a bond or a preferred which lacks adequate safety merely because the yield is attractive.* (Here the word "merely" implies that the issue is not selling at a large discount and thus does not offer an opportunity for a substantial gain in principal value.) Where such securities are bought at full prices—that is, not many points under

---

* For a recent example that painfully reinforces Graham's point, see p. 146 below.

100*—the chances are very great that at some future time the holder will see much lower quotations. For when bad business comes, or just a bad market, issues of this kind prove highly susceptible to severe sinking spells; often interest or dividends are suspended or at least endangered, and frequently there is a pronounced price weakness even though the operating results are not at all bad.

As a specific illustration of this characteristic of second-quality senior issues, let us summarize the price behavior of a group of ten railroad *income bonds* in 1946–47. These comprise all of those which sold at 96 or more in 1946, their high prices averaging 102½. By the following year the group had registered low prices averaging only 68, a loss of one-third of the market value in a very short time. Peculiarly enough, the railroads of the country were showing much better earnings in 1947 than in 1946; hence the drastic price decline ran counter to the business picture and was a reflection of the selloff in the general market. But it should be pointed out that the shrinkage in these income bonds was proportionately larger than that in the *common stocks* in the Dow Jones industrial list (about 23%). Obviously the purchaser of these bonds at a cost above 100 could not have expected to participate to any extent in a further rise in the securities market. The only attractive feature was the income yield, averaging about 4.25% (against 2.50% for first-grade bonds, an advantage of 1.75% in annual income). Yet the sequel showed all too soon and too plainly that for the minor advantage in annual income the buyer of these second-grade bonds was risking the loss of a substantial part of his principal.

The above example permits us to pay our respects to the popular fallacy that goes under the sobriquet of a "businessman's investment." That involves the purchase of a security showing a larger yield than is obtainable on a high-grade issue and carrying a correspondingly greater risk. It is bad business to accept an

* Bond prices are quoted in percentages of "par value," or 100. A bond priced at "85" is selling at 85% of its principal value; a bond originally offered for $10,000, but now selling at 85, will cost $8,500. When bonds sell below 100, they are called "discount" bonds; above 100, they become "premium" bonds.

acknowledged possibility of a loss of principal in exchange for a mere 1 or 2% of additional yearly income. If you are willing to assume some risk you should be certain that you can realize a really substantial gain in principal value if things go well. Hence a second-grade 5.5 or 6% bond *selling at par* is almost always a bad purchase. The same issue at 70 might make more sense—and if you are patient you will probably be able to buy it at that level.

Second-grade bonds and preferred stocks possess two contradictory attributes which the intelligent investor must bear clearly in mind. Nearly all suffer severe sinking spells in bad markets. On the other hand, a large proportion recover their position when favorable conditions return, and these ultimately "work out all right." This is true even of (cumulative) preferred stocks that fail to pay dividends for many years. There were a number of such issues in the early 1940s, as a consequence of the long depression of the 1930s. During the postwar boom period of 1945–1947 many of these large accumulations were paid off either in cash or in new securities, and the principal was often discharged as well. As a result, large profits were made by people who, a few years previously, had bought these issues when they were friendless and sold at low prices.[2]

It may well be true that, in an overall accounting, the higher yields obtainable on second-grade senior issues will prove to have offset those principal losses that were irrecoverable. In other words, an investor who bought all such issues at their offering prices might conceivably fare as well, *in the long run,* as one who limited himself to first-quality securities; or even somewhat better.[3]

But for practical purposes the question is largely irrelevant. Regardless of the outcome, the buyer of second-grade issues at full prices will be worried and discommoded when their price declines precipitately. Furthermore, he cannot buy enough issues to assure an "average" result, nor is he in a position to set aside a portion of his larger income to offset or "amortize" those principal losses which prove to be permanent. Finally, it is mere common sense to abstain from buying securities at around 100 if long experience indicates that they can probably be bought at 70 or less in the next weak market.

Foreign Government Bonds

All investors with even small experience know that foreign bonds, as a whole, have had a bad investment history since 1914. This was inevitable in the light of two world wars and an intervening world depression of unexampled depth. Yet every few years market conditions are sufficiently favorable to permit the sale of some new foreign issues at a price of about par. This phenomenon tells us a good deal about the working of the average investor's mind—and not only in the field of bonds.

We have no *concrete reason* to be concerned about the future history of well-regarded foreign bonds such as those of Australia or Norway. But we do know that, if and when trouble should come, the owner of foreign obligations has no legal or other means of enforcing his claim. Those who bought Republic of Cuba 4½s as high as 117 in 1953 saw them default their interest and then sell as low as 20 cents on the dollar in 1963. The New York Stock Exchange bond list in that year also included Belgian Congo 5¼s at 36, Greek 7s at 30, and various issues of Poland as low as 7. How many readers have any idea of the repeated vicissitudes of the 8% bonds of Czechoslovakia, since they were first offered in this country in 1922 at 96½? They advanced to 112 in 1928, declined to 67¾ in 1932, recovered to 106 in 1936, collapsed to 6 in 1939, recovered (unbelievably) to 117 in 1946, fell promptly to 35 in 1948, and sold as low as 8 in 1970!

Years ago an argument of sorts was made for the purchase of foreign bonds here on the grounds that a rich creditor nation such as ours was under moral obligation to lend abroad. Time, which brings so many revenges, now finds us dealing with an intractable balance-of-payments problem of our own, part of which is ascribable to the large-scale purchase of foreign bonds by American investors seeking a small advantage in yield. For many years past we have questioned the inherent attractiveness of such investments from the standpoint of the buyer; perhaps we should add now that the latter would benefit both his country and himself if he declined these opportunities.

New Issues Generally

It might seem ill-advised to attempt any broad statements about new issues as a class, since they cover the widest possible range of quality and attractiveness. Certainly there will be exceptions to any suggested rule. Our one recommendation is that all investors should be *wary* of new issues—which means, simply, that these should be subjected to careful examination and unusually severe tests before they are purchased.

There are two reasons for this double caveat. The first is that new issues have special salesmanship behind them, which calls therefore for a special degree of sales resistance.* The second is that most new issues are sold under "favorable market conditions"—which means favorable for the seller and consequently less favorable for the buyer.†

The effect of these considerations becomes steadily more important as we go down the scale from the highest-quality bonds through second-grade senior issues to common-stock flotations at the bottom. A tremendous amount of financing, consisting of the repayment of existing bonds at call price and their replacement by new issues with lower coupons, was done in the past. Most of this was in the category of high-grade bonds and preferred stocks. The buyers were largely financial institutions, amply qualified to protect their interests. Hence these offerings were carefully priced to

---

* New issues of common stock–initial public offerings or IPOs–normally are sold with an "underwriting discount" (a built-in commission) of 7%. By contrast, the buyer's commission on older shares of common stock typically ranges below 4%. Whenever Wall Street makes roughly twice as much for selling something new as it does for selling something old, the new will get the harder sell.

† Recently, finance professors Owen Lamont of the University of Chicago and Paul Schultz of the University of Notre Dame have shown that corporations choose to offer new shares to the public when the stock market is near a peak. For technical discussion of these issues, see Lamont's "Evaluating Value Weighting: Corporate Events and Market Timing" and Schultz's "Pseudo Market Timing and the Long-Run Performance of IPOs" at http://papers.ssrn.com.

meet the going rate for comparable issues, and high-powered salesmanship had little effect on the outcome. As interest rates fell lower and lower the buyers finally came to pay too high a price for these issues, and many of them later declined appreciably in the market. This is one aspect of the general tendency to sell new securities of all types when conditions are most favorable to the issuer; but in the case of first-quality issues the ill effects to the purchaser are likely to be unpleasant rather than serious.

The situation proves somewhat different when we study the lower-grade bonds and preferred stocks sold during the 1945–46 and 1960–61 periods. Here the effect of the selling effort is more apparent, because most of these issues were probably placed with individual and inexpert investors. It was characteristic of these offerings that they did not make an adequate showing when judged by the performance of the companies over a sufficient number of years. They did look safe enough, for the most part, if it could be assumed that the recent earnings would continue without a serious setback. The investment bankers who brought out these issues presumably accepted this assumption, and their salesmen had little difficulty in persuading themselves and their customers to a like effect. Nevertheless it was an unsound approach to investment, and one likely to prove costly.

Bull-market periods are usually characterized by the transformation of a large number of privately owned businesses into companies with quoted shares. This was the case in 1945–46 and again beginning in 1960. The process then reached extraordinary proportions until brought to a catastrophic close in May 1962. After the usual "swearing-off" period of several years the whole tragicomedy was repeated, step by step, in 1967–1969.*

---

* In the two years from June 1960, through May 1962, more than 850 companies sold their stock to the public for the first time–an average of more than one per day. In late 1967 the IPO market heated up again; in 1969 an astonishing 781 new stocks were born. That oversupply helped create the bear markets of 1969 and 1973–1974. In 1974 the IPO market was so dead that only nine new stocks were created all year; 1975 saw only 14 stocks born. That undersupply, in turn, helped feed the bull market of the 1980s, when roughly 4,000 new stocks flooded the market–helping to trigger the over-

New Common-Stock Offerings

The following paragraphs are reproduced unchanged from the 1959 edition, with comment added:

> Common-stock financing takes two different forms. In the case of companies already listed, additional shares are offered pro rata to the existing stockholders. The subscription price is set below the current market, and the "rights" to subscribe have an initial money value.* The sale of the new shares is almost always underwritten by one or more investment banking houses, but it is the general hope and expectation that all the new shares will be taken by the exercise of the subscription rights. Thus the sale of additional common stock of listed companies does not ordinarily call for active selling effort on the part of distributing firms.
>
> The second type is the placement with the public of common stock of what were formerly privately owned enterprises. Most of this stock is sold for the account of the controlling interests to enable them to cash in on a favorable market and to diversify their

---

enthusiasm that led to the 1987 crash. Then the cycle swung the other way again as IPOs dried up in 1988–1990. That shortage contributed to the bull market of the 1990s–and, right on cue, Wall Street got back into the business of creating new stocks, cranking out nearly 5,000 IPOs. Then, after the bubble burst in 2000, only 88 IPOs were issued in 2001–the lowest annual total since 1979. In every case, the public has gotten burned on IPOs, has stayed away for at least two years, but has always returned for another scalding. For as long as stock markets have existed, investors have gone through this manic-depressive cycle. In America's first great IPO boom, back in 1825, a man was said to have been squeezed to death in the stampede of speculators trying to buy shares in the new Bank of Southwark; the wealthiest buyers hired thugs to punch their way to the front of the line. Sure enough, by 1829, stocks had lost roughly 25% of their value.

* Here Graham is describing rights offerings, in which investors who already own a stock are asked to pony up even more money to maintain the same proportional interest in the company. This form of financing, still widespread in Europe, has become rare in the United States, except among closed-end funds.

own finances. (When new money is raised for the business it comes often via the sale of preferred stock, as previously noted.) This activity follows a well-defined pattern, which by the nature of the security markets must bring many losses and disappointments to the public. The dangers arise both from the character of the businesses that are thus financed and from the market conditions that make the financing possible.

In the early part of the century a large proportion of our leading companies were introduced to public trading. As time went on, the number of enterprises of first rank that remained closely held steadily diminished; hence original common-stock flotations have tended to be concentrated more and more on relatively small concerns. By an unfortunate correlation, during the same period the stock-buying public has been developing an ingrained preference for the major companies and a similar prejudice against the minor ones. This prejudice, like many others, tends to become weaker as bull markets are built up; the large and quick profits shown by common stocks as a whole are sufficient to dull the public's critical faculty, just as they sharpen its acquisitive instinct. During these periods, also, quite a number of privately owned concerns can be found that are enjoying excellent results—although most of these would not present too impressive a record if the figures were carried back, say, ten years or more.

When these factors are put together the following consequences emerge: Somewhere in the middle of the bull market the first common-stock flotations make their appearance. These are priced not unattractively, and some large profits are made by the buyers of the early issues. As the market rise continues, this brand of financing grows more frequent; the quality of the companies becomes steadily poorer; the prices asked and obtained verge on the exorbitant. One fairly dependable sign of the approaching end of a bull swing is the fact that new common stocks of small and nondescript companies are offered at prices somewhat higher than the current level for many medium-sized companies with a long market history. (It should be added that very little of this common-stock financing is ordinarily done by banking houses of prime size and reputation.)*

* In Graham's day, the most prestigious investment banks generally steered clear of the IPO business, which was regarded as an undignified exploita-

The heedlessness of the public and the willingness of selling organizations to sell whatever may be profitably sold can have only one result—price collapse. In many cases the new issues lose 75% and more of their offering price. The situation is worsened by the aforementioned fact that, at bottom, the public has a real aversion to the very kind of small issue that it bought so readily in its careless moments. Many of these issues fall, proportionately, as much below their true value as they formerly sold above it.

An elementary requirement for the intelligent investor is an ability to resist the blandishments of salesmen offering new common-stock issues during bull markets. Even if one or two can be found that can pass severe tests of quality and value, it is probably bad policy to get mixed up in this sort of business. Of course the salesman will point to many such issues which have had good-sized market advances—including some that go up spectacularly the very day they are sold. But all this is part of the speculative atmosphere. It is easy money. For every dollar you make in this way you will be lucky if you end up by losing only two.

Some of these issues may prove excellent buys—a few years later, when nobody wants them and they can be had at a small fraction of their true worth.

In the 1965 edition we continued our discussion of this subject as follows:

While the broader aspects of the stock market's behavior since 1949 have not lent themselves well to analysis based on long experience, the development of new common-stock flotations proceeded exactly in accordance with ancient prescription. It is doubtful whether we ever before had so many new issues offered, of such low quality, and with such extreme price collapses, as we

---

tion of naïve investors. By the peak of the IPO boom in late 1999 and early 2000, however, Wall Street's biggest investment banks had jumped in with both feet. Venerable firms cast off their traditional prudence and behaved like drunken mud wrestlers, scrambling to foist ludicrously overvalued stocks on a desperately eager public. Graham's description of how the IPO process works is a classic that should be required reading in investment-banking ethics classes, if there are any.

> experienced in 1960–1962.[4] The ability of the stock market as a whole to disengage itself rapidly from that disaster is indeed an extraordinary phenomenon, bringing back long-buried memories of the similar invulnerability it showed to the great Florida real-estate collapse in 1925.
>
> Must there be a return of the new-stock-offering madness before the present bull market can come to its definitive close? Who knows? But we do know that an intelligent investor will not forget what happened in 1962 and will let others make the next batch of quick profits in this area and experience the consequent harrowing losses.

We followed these paragraphs in the 1965 edition by citing "A Horrible Example," namely, the sale of stock of Aetna Maintenance Co. at $9 in November 1961. In typical fashion the shares promptly advanced to $15; the next year they fell to 2⅜, and in 1964 to ⅞. The later history of this company was on the extraordinary side, and illustrates some of the strange metamorphoses that have taken place in American business, great and small, in recent years. The curious reader will find the older and newer history of this enterprise in Appendix 5.

It is by no means difficult to provide even more harrowing examples taken from the more recent version of "the same old story," which covered the years 1967–1970. Nothing could be more pat to our purpose than the case of AAA Enterprises, which happens to be the first company then listed in Standard & Poor's *Stock Guide.* The shares were sold to the public at $14 in 1968, promptly advanced to 28, but in early 1971 were quoted at a dismal 25¢. (Even this price represented a gross overvaluation of the enterprise, since it had just entered the bankruptcy court in a hopeless condition.) There is so much to be learned, and such important warnings to be gleaned, from the story of this flotation that we have reserved it for detailed treatment below, in Chapter 17.

COMMENTARY ON CHAPTER 6

The punches you miss are the ones that wear you out.

—Boxing trainer Angelo Dundee

For the aggressive as well as the defensive investor, what you don't do is as important to your success as what you do. In this chapter, Graham lists his "don'ts" for aggressive investors. Here is a list for today.

JUNKYARD DOGS?

High-yield bonds—which Graham calls "second-grade" or "lower-grade" and today are called "junk bonds"—get a brisk thumbs-down from Graham. In his day, it was too costly and cumbersome for an individual investor to diversify away the risks of default.[1] (To learn how bad a default can be, and how carelessly even "sophisticated" professional bond investors can buy into one, see the sidebar on p. 146.) Today, however, more than 130 mutual funds specialize in junk bonds. These funds buy junk by the cartload; they hold dozens of different bonds. That mitigates Graham's complaints about the difficulty of diversifying. (However, his bias against high-yield preferred stock remains valid, since there remains no cheap and widely available way to spread their risks.)

Since 1978, an annual average of 4.4% of the junk-bond market has gone into default—but, even after those defaults, junk bonds have

---

[1] In the early 1970s, when Graham wrote, there were fewer than a dozen junk-bond funds, nearly all of which charged sales commissions of up to 8.5%; some even made investors pay a fee for the privilege of reinvesting their monthly dividends back into the fund.

A WORLD OF HURT FOR WORLDCOM BONDS

Buying a bond only for its yield is like getting married only for the sex. If the thing that attracted you in the first place dries up, you'll find yourself asking, "What else is there?" When the answer is "Nothing," spouses and bondholders alike end up with broken hearts.

On May 9, 2001, WorldCom, Inc. sold the biggest offering of bonds in U.S. corporate history–$11.9 billion worth. Among the eager beavers attracted by the yields of up to 8.3% were the California Public Employees' Retirement System, one of the world's largest pension funds; Retirement Systems of Alabama, whose managers later explained that "the higher yields" were "very attractive to us at the time they were purchased"; and the Strong Corporate Bond Fund, whose comanager was so fond of WorldCom's fat yield that he boasted, "we're getting paid more than enough extra income for the risk."[1]

But even a 30-second glance at WorldCom's bond prospectus would have shown that these bonds had nothing to offer *but* their yield–and everything to lose. In two of the previous five years WorldCom's pretax income (the company's profits before it paid its dues to the IRS) fell short of covering its fixed charges (the costs of paying interest to its bondholders) by a stupendous $4.1 billion. WorldCom could cover those bond payments only by borrowing more money from banks. And now, with this mountainous new helping of bonds, WorldCom was fattening its interest costs by another $900 million per year![2] Like Mr. Creosote in *Monty Python's The Meaning of Life,* WorldCom was gorging itself to the bursting point.

No yield could ever be high enough to compensate an investor for risking that kind of explosion. The WorldCom bonds did produce fat yields of up to 8% for a few months. Then, as Graham would have predicted, the yield suddenly offered no shelter:

- WorldCom filed bankruptcy in July 2002.
- WorldCom admitted in August 2002 that it had overstated its earnings by more than $7 billion.[3]

- WorldCom's bonds defaulted when the company could no longer cover their interest charges; the bonds lost more than 80% of their original value.

---

[1] See www.calpers.ca.gov/whatshap/hottopic/worldcom_faqs.htm and www.calpers.ca.gov/whatsnew/press/2002/0716a.htm; Retirement Systems of Alabama Quarterly Investment Report for May 31, 2001, at www.rsa.state.al.us/Investments/quarterly_report.htm; and John Bender, Strong Corporate Bond Fund comanager, quoted in www.businessweek.com/magazine/content/01_22/b3734118.htm.

[2] These numbers are all drawn from WorldCom's prospectus, or sales document, for the bond offering. Filed May 11, 2001, it can be viewed at www.sec.gov/edgar/searchedgar/companysearch.html (in "Company name" window, enter "WorldCom"). Even without today's 20/20 hindsight knowledge that WorldCom's earnings were fraudulently overstated, WorldCom's bond offering would have appalled Graham.

[3] For documentation on the collapse of WorldCom, see www.worldcom.com/infodesk.

still produced an annualized return of 10.5%, versus 8.6% for 10-year U.S. Treasury bonds.[2] Unfortunately, most junk-bond *funds* charge high fees and do a poor job of preserving the original principal amount of your investment. A junk fund could be appropriate if you are retired, are looking for extra monthly income to supplement your pension, and can tolerate temporary tumbles in value. If you work at a bank or other financial company, a sharp rise in interest rates could limit your raise or even threaten your job security—so a junk fund, which tends to outperform most other bond funds when interest rates rise, might make sense as a counterweight in your 401(k). A junk-bond fund, though, is only a minor option—not an obligation—for the intelligent investor.

---

[2] Edward I. Altman and Gaurav Bana, "Defaults and Returns on High-Yield Bonds," research paper, Stern School of Business, New York University, 2002.

THE VODKA-AND-BURRITO PORTFOLIO

Graham considered foreign bonds no better a bet than junk bonds.[3] Today, however, one variety of foreign bond may have some appeal for investors who can withstand plenty of risk. Roughly a dozen mutual funds specialize in bonds issued in emerging-market nations (or what used to be called "Third World countries") like Brazil, Mexico, Nigeria, Russia, and Venezuela. No sane investor would put more than 10% of a total bond portfolio in spicy holdings like these. But emerging-markets bond funds seldom move in synch with the U.S. stock market, so they are one of the rare investments that are unlikely to drop merely because the Dow is down. That can give you a small corner of comfort in your portfolio just when you may need it most.[4]

DYING A TRADER'S DEATH

As we've already seen in Chapter 1, day trading–holding stocks for a few hours at a time–is one of the best weapons ever invented for committing financial suicide. Some of your trades might make money, most of your trades will lose money, but your broker will always make money.

And your own eagerness to buy or sell a stock can lower your return. Someone who is desperate to buy a stock can easily end up having to bid 10 cents higher than the most recent share price before any sellers will be willing to part with it. That extra cost, called "market impact," never shows up on your brokerage statement, but it's real. If you're overeager to buy 1,000 shares of a stock and you drive its price

---

[3] Graham did not criticize foreign bonds lightly, since he spent several years early in his career acting as a New York–based bond agent for borrowers in Japan.

[4] Two low-cost, well-run emerging-markets bond funds are Fidelity New Markets Income Fund and T. Rowe Price Emerging Markets Bond Fund; for more information, see www.fidelity.com, www.troweprice.com, and www.morningstar.com. Do not buy any emerging-markets bond fund with annual operating expenses higher than 1.25%, and be forewarned that some of these funds charge short-term redemption fees to discourage investors from holding them for less than three months.

up by just five cents, you've just cost yourself an invisible but very real $50. On the flip side, when panicky investors are frantic to sell a stock and they dump it for less than the most recent price, market impact hits home again.

The costs of trading wear away your returns like so many swipes of sandpaper. Buying or selling a hot little stock can cost 2% to 4% (or 4% to 8% for a "round-trip" buy-and-sell transaction).[5] If you put $1,000 into a stock, your trading costs could eat up roughly $40 before you even get started. Sell the stock, and you could fork over another 4% in trading expenses.

Oh, yes–there's one other thing. When you trade instead of invest, you turn long-term gains (taxed at a maximum capital-gains rate of 20%) into ordinary income (taxed at a maximum rate of 38.6%).

Add it all up, and a stock trader needs to gain at least 10% *just to break even* on buying and selling a stock.[6] Anyone can do that once, by luck alone. To do it often enough to justify the obsessive attention it requires–plus the nightmarish stress it generates–is impossible.

Thousands of people have tried, and the evidence is clear: The more you trade, the less you keep.

Finance professors Brad Barber and Terrance Odean of the University of California examined the trading records of more than 66,000 customers of a major discount brokerage firm. From 1991 through 1996, these clients made more than 1.9 million trades. Before the costs of trading sandpapered away at their returns, the people in the study actually outperformed the market by an average of at least half a percentage point per year. But after trading costs, the most active of these traders–who shifted more than 20% of their stock holdings per

---

[5] The definitive source on brokerage costs is the Plexus Group of Santa Monica, California, and its website, www.plexusgroup.com. Plexus argues persuasively that, just as most of the mass of an iceberg lies below the ocean surface, the bulk of brokerage costs are invisible–misleading investors into believing that their trading costs are insignificant if commission costs are low. The costs of trading NASDAQ stocks are considerably higher for individuals than the costs of trading NYSE-listed stocks (see p. 128, footnote 5).

[6] Real-world conditions are still more harsh, since we are ignoring state income taxes in this example.

month–went from beating the market to underperforming it by an abysmal 6.4 percentage points per year. The most patient investors, however–who traded a minuscule 0.2% of their total holdings in an average month–managed to outperform the market by a whisker, even after their trading costs. Instead of giving a huge hunk of their gains away to their brokers and the IRS, they got to keep almost everything.[7] For a look at these results, see Figure 6-1.

The lesson is clear: Don't just do something, stand there. It's time for everyone to acknowledge that the term "long-term investor" is redundant. A long-term investor is the only kind of investor there is. Someone who can't hold on to stocks for more than a few months at a time is doomed to end up not as a victor but as a victim.

THE EARLY BIRD GETS WORMED

Among the get-rich-quick toxins that poisoned the mind of the investing public in the 1990s, one of the most lethal was the idea that you can build wealth by buying IPOs. An IPO is an "initial public offering," or the first sale of a company's stock to the public. At first blush, investing in IPOs sounds like a great idea–after all, if you'd bought 100 shares of Microsoft when it went public on March 13, 1986, your $2,100 investment would have grown to $720,000 by early 2003.[8] And finance professors Jay Ritter and William Schwert have shown that if you had spread a total of only $1,000 across every IPO in January 1960, at its offering price, sold out at the end of that month, then invested anew in each successive month's crop of IPOs, your portfolio would have been worth more than $533 decillion by year-end 2001.

(On the printed page, that looks like this: $533,000,000,000,000,000,000,000,000,000,000,000.)

---

[7] Barber and Odean's findings are available at http://faculty.haas.berkeley.edu/odean/Current%20Research.htm and http://faculty.gsm.ucdavis.edu/~bmbarber/research/default.html. Numerous studies, incidentally, have found virtually identical results among professional money managers–so this is not a problem limited to "naïve" individuals.

[8] See www.microsoft.com/msft/stock.htm, "IPO investment results."

FIGURE 6-1

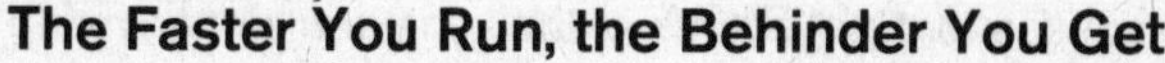

The Faster You Run, the Behinder You Get

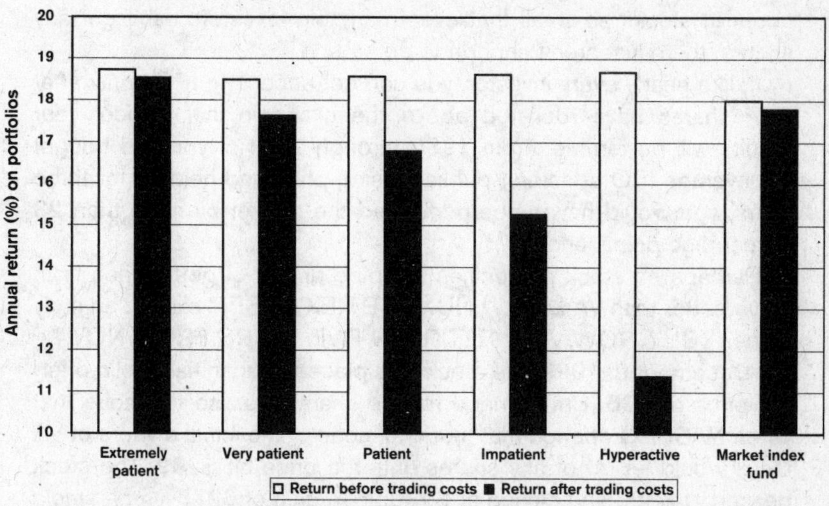

Researchers Brad Barber and Terrance Odean divided thousands of traders into five tiers based on how often they turned over their holdings. Those who traded the least (at the left) kept most of their gains. But the impatient and hyperactive traders made their brokers rich, not themselves. (The bars at the far right show a market index fund for comparison.)

Source: Profs. Brad Barber, University of California at Davis, and Terrance Odean, University of California at Berkeley

Unfortunately, for every IPO like Microsoft that turns out to be a big winner, there are thousands of losers. The psychologists Daniel Kahnerman and Amos Tversky have shown when humans estimate the likelihood or frequency of an event, we make that judgment based not on how often the event has actually occurred, but on how vivid the past examples are. We all want to buy "the next Microsoft"—precisely because we know we missed buying the first Microsoft. But we conveniently overlook the fact that most other IPOs were terrible investments. You could have earned that $533 decillion gain only if you never missed a single one of the IPO market's rare winners—a practical impossibility. Finally, most of the high returns on IPOs are captured by members of an exclusive private club—the big investment banks and fund houses that get shares at the initial (or "underwriting") price, before the stock begins public trading. The biggest "run-ups" often occur in stocks so small that even many big investors can't get any shares; there just aren't enough to go around.

If, like nearly every investor, you can get access to IPOs only *after* their shares have rocketed above the exclusive initial price, your results will be terrible. From 1980 through 2001, if you had bought the average IPO at its first public closing price and held on for three years, you would have underperformed the market by more than 23 percentage points annually.[9]

Perhaps no stock personifies the pipe dream of getting rich from IPOs better than VA Linux. "LNUX THE NEXT MSFT," exulted an early owner; "BUY NOW, AND RETIRE IN FIVE YEARS FROM NOW."[10] On December 9, 1999, the stock was placed at an initial public offering price of $30. But demand for the shares was so ferocious that when NASDAQ opened that morning, none of the initial owners of VA Linux would let go of any shares until the price hit $299. The stock peaked at $320 and closed at $239.25, a gain of 697.5% *in a single day.* But that gain was earned by only a handful of institutional traders; individual investors were almost entirely frozen out.

More important, buying IPOs is a bad idea because it flagrantly violates one of Graham's most fundamental rules: No matter how many other people want to buy a stock, you should buy only if the stock is a cheap way to own a desirable business. At the peak price on day one, investors were valuing VA Linux's shares at a total of $12.7 billion. What was the company's business worth? Less than five years old, VA Linux had sold a cumulative total of $44 million worth of its software and services—but had lost $25 million in the process. In its most recent fiscal quarter, VA Linux had generated $15 million in sales but

---

[9] Jay R. Ritter and Ivo Welch, "A Review of IPO Activity, Pricing, and Allocations," *Journal of Finance,* August, 2002, p. 1797. Ritter's website, at http://bear.cba.ufl.edu/ritter/, and Welch's home page, at http://welch.som.yale.edu/, are gold mines of data for anyone interested in IPOs.

[10] Message no. 9, posted by "GoldFingers69," on the VA Linux (LNUX) message board at messages.yahoo.com, dated December 16, 1999. MSFT is the ticker symbol for Microsoft Corp.

had lost $10 million on them. This business, then, was losing almost 70 cents on every dollar it took in. VA Linux's accumulated deficit (the amount by which its total expenses had exceeded its income) was $30 million.

If VA Linux were a private company owned by the guy who lives next door, and he leaned over the picket fence and asked you how much you would pay to take his struggling little business off his hands, would you answer, "Oh, $12.7 billion sounds about right to me"? Or would you, instead, smile politely, turn back to your barbecue grill, and wonder what on earth your neighbor had been smoking? Relying exclusively on our own judgment, none of us would be caught dead agreeing to pay nearly $13 billion for a money-loser that was already $30 million in the hole.

But when we're in public instead of in private, when valuation suddenly becomes a popularity contest, the price of a stock seems more important than the value of the business it represents. As long as someone else will pay even more than you did for a stock, why does it matter what the business is worth?

This chart shows why it matters.

FIGURE 6-2

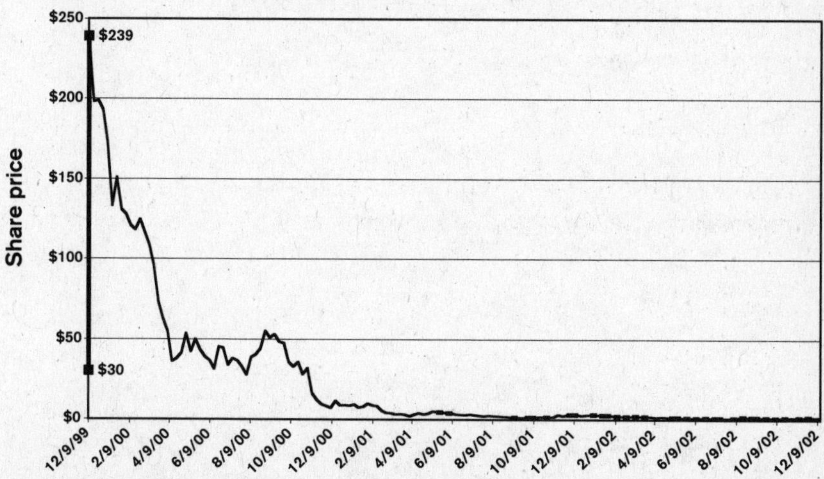

Sources: VA Linux Systems Inc.; www.morningstar.com

After going up like a bottle rocket on that first day of trading, VA Linux came down like a buttered brick. By December 9, 2002, three years to the day after the stock was at $239.50, VA Linux closed at $1.19 per share.

Weighing the evidence objectively, the intelligent investor should conclude that IPO does not stand only for "initial public offering." More accurately, it is also shorthand for:

It's Probably Overpriced,
Imaginary Profits Only,
Insiders' Private Opportunity, or
Idiotic, Preposterous, and Outrageous.

CHAPTER 7

Portfolio Policy for the Enterprising Investor: The Positive Side

The enterprising investor, by definition, will devote a fair amount of his attention and efforts toward obtaining a better than run-of-the-mill investment result. In our discussion of general investment policy we have made some suggestions regarding *bond investments* that are addressed chiefly to the enterprising investor. He might be interested in special opportunities of the following kinds:

(1) Tax-free New Housing Authority bonds effectively guaranteed by the United States government.
(2) Taxable but high-yielding New Community bonds, also guaranteed by the United States government.
(3) Tax-free industrial bonds issued by municipalities, but serviced by lease payments made by strong corporations.

References have been made to these unusual types of bond issues in Chapter 4.*

At the other end of the spectrum there may be lower-quality bonds obtainable at such low prices as to constitute true bargain opportunities. But these would belong in the "special situation" area, where no true distinction exists between bonds and common stocks.†

---

* As already noted (see p. 96, footnote †), the New Housing Authority and New Community bonds are no longer issued.

† Today these "lower-quality bonds" in the "special situation" area are known as distressed or defaulted bonds. When a company is in (or

Operations in Common Stocks

The activities specially characteristic of the enterprising investor in the common-stock field may be classified under four heads:

1. Buying in low markets and selling in high markets
2. Buying carefully chosen "growth stocks"
3. Buying bargain issues of various types
4. Buying into "special situations"

General Market Policy—Formula Timing

We reserve for the next chapter our discussion of the possibilities and limitations of a policy of entering the market when it is depressed and selling out in the advanced stages of a boom. For many years in the past this bright idea appeared both simple and feasible, at least from first inspection of a market chart covering its periodic fluctuations. We have already admitted ruefully that the market's action in the past 20 years has not lent itself to operations of this sort on any mathematical basis. The fluctuations that have taken place, while not inconsiderable in extent, would have required a special talent or "feel" for trading to take advantage of them. This is something quite different from the intelligence which we are assuming in our readers, and we must exclude operations based on such skill from our terms of reference.

The 50–50 plan, which we proposed to the defensive investor and described on p. 90, is about the best specific or automatic formula we can recommend to all investors under the conditions of 1972. But we have retained a broad leeway between the 25% mini-

---

approaching) bankruptcy, its common stock becomes essentially worthless, since U.S. bankruptcy law entitles bondholders to a much stronger legal claim than shareholders. But if the company reorganizes successfully and comes out of bankruptcy, the bondholders often receive stock in the new firm, and the value of the bonds usually recovers once the company is able to pay interest again. Thus the bonds of a troubled company can perform almost as well as the common stock of a healthy company. In these special situations, as Graham puts it, "no true distinction exists between bonds and common stocks."

mum and the 75% maximum in common stocks, which we allow to those investors who have strong convictions about either the danger or the attractiveness of the general market level. Some 20 years ago it was possible to discuss in great detail a number of clear-cut formulas for varying the percentage held in common stocks, with confidence that these plans had practical utility.[1] The times seem to have passed such approaches by, and there would be little point in trying to determine new levels for buying and selling out of the market patterns since 1949. That is too short a period to furnish any reliable guide to the future.*

Growth-Stock Approach

Every investor would like to select the stocks of companies that will do better than the average over a period of years. A growth stock may be defined as one that has done this in the past and is expected to do so in the future.[2] Thus it seems only logical that the intelligent investor should concentrate upon the selection of growth stocks. Actually the matter is more complicated, as we shall try to show.

It is a mere statistical chore to identify companies that have "outperformed the averages" in the past. The investor can obtain a list of 50 or 100 such enterprises from his broker.† Why, then, should he not merely pick out the 15 or 20 most likely looking issues of this group and lo! he has a guaranteed-successful stock portfolio?

---

* Note very carefully what Graham is saying here. Writing in 1972, he contends that the period since 1949—a stretch of more than 22 years—is too short a period from which to draw reliable conclusions! With his mastery of mathematics, Graham never forgets that objective conclusions require very long samples of large amounts of data. The charlatans who peddle "time-tested" stock-picking gimmicks almost always base their findings on smaller samples than Graham would ever accept. (Graham often used 50-year periods to analyze past data.)

† Today, the enterprising investor can assemble such a list over the Internet by visiting such websites as www.morningstar.com (try the Stock Quickrank tool), www.quicken.com/investments/stocks/search/full, and http://yahoo.marketguide.com.

There are two catches to this simple idea. The first is that common stocks with good records and apparently good prospects sell at correspondingly high prices. The investor may be right in his judgment of their prospects and still not fare particularly well, merely because he has paid in full (and perhaps overpaid) for the expected prosperity. The second is that his judgment as to the future may prove wrong. Unusually rapid growth cannot keep up forever; when a company has already registered a brilliant expansion, its very increase in size makes a repetition of its achievement more difficult. At some point the growth curve flattens out, and in many cases it turns downward.

It is obvious that if one confines himself to a few chosen instances, based on hindsight, he could demonstrate that fortunes can readily be either made or lost in the growth-stock field. How can one judge fairly of the overall results obtainable here? We think that reasonably sound conclusions can be drawn from a study of the results achieved by the investment funds specializing in the growth-stock approach. The authoritative manual entitled *Investment Companies,* published annually by Arthur Wiesenberger & Company, members of the New York Stock Exchange, computes the annual performance of some 120 such "growth funds" over a period of years. Of these, 45 have records covering ten years or more. The average overall gain for these companies—unweighted for size of fund—works out at 108% for the decade 1961–1970, compared with 105% for the S & P composite and 83% for the DJIA.[3] In the two years 1969 and 1970 the majority of the 126 "growth funds" did worse than either index. Similar results were found in our earlier studies. The implication here is that no outstanding rewards came from diversified investment in growth companies as compared with that in common stocks generally.*

---

* Over the 10 years ending December 31, 2002, funds investing in large growth companies–today's equivalent of what Graham calls "growth funds"–earned an annual average of 5.6%, underperforming the overall stock market by an average of 3.7 percentage points per year. However, "large value" funds investing in more reasonably priced big companies also underperformed the market over the same period (by a full percentage point per year). Is the problem merely that growth funds cannot reliably select

There is no reason at all for thinking that the average intelligent investor, even with much devoted effort, can derive better results over the years from the purchase of growth stocks than the investment companies specializing in this area. Surely these organizations have more brains and better research facilities at their disposal than you do. Consequently we should advise against the usual type of growth-stock commitment for the enterprising investor.* This is one in which the excellent prospects are fully recognized in the market and already reflected in a current price-earnings ratio of, say, higher than 20. (For the defensive investor we suggested an upper limit of purchase price at 25 times average earnings of the past seven years. The two criteria would be about equivalent in most cases.)†

---

stocks that will outperform the market in the future? Or is it that the high costs of running the average fund (whether it buys growth or "value" companies) exceed any extra return the managers can earn with their stock picks? To update fund performance by type, see www.morningstar.com, "Category Returns." For an enlightening reminder of how perishable the performance of different investment styles can be, see www.callan.com/resource/periodic_table/pertable.pdf.

* Graham makes this point to remind you that an "enterprising" investor is not one who takes more risk than average or who buys "aggressive growth" stocks; an enterprising investor is simply one who is willing to put in extra time and effort in researching his or her portfolio.

† Notice that Graham insists on calculating the price/earnings ratio based on a multiyear average of past earnings. That way, you lower the odds that you will overestimate a company's value based on a temporarily high burst of profitability. Imagine that a company earned $3 per share over the past 12 months, but an average of only 50 cents per share over the previous six years. Which number–the sudden $3 or the steady 50 cents–is more likely to represent a sustainable trend? At 25 times the $3 it earned in the most recent year, the stock would be priced at $75. But at 25 times the average earnings of the past seven years ($6 in total earnings, divided by seven, equals 85.7 cents per share in average annual earnings), the stock would be priced at only $21.43. Which number you pick makes a big difference. Finally, it's worth noting that the prevailing method on Wall Street today–basing price/earnings ratios primarily on "next year's earnings"–would be

The striking thing about growth stocks as a class is their tendency toward wide swings in market price. This is true of the largest and longest-established companies—such as General Electric and International Business Machines—and even more so of newer and smaller successful companies. They illustrate our thesis that the main characteristic of the stock market since 1949 has been the injection of a highly speculative element into the shares of companies which have scored the most brilliant successes, and which themselves would be entitled to a high investment rating. (Their credit standing is of the best, and they pay the lowest interest rates on their borrowings.) The investment caliber of such a *company* may not change over a long span of years, but the risk characteristics of its *stock* will depend on what happens to it in the stock market. The more enthusiastic the public grows about it, and the faster its advance as compared with the actual growth in its earnings, the riskier a proposition it becomes.*

But is it not true, the reader may ask, that the really big fortunes from common stocks have been garnered by those who made a substantial commitment in the early years of a company in whose future they had great confidence, and who held their original shares unwaveringly while they increased 100-fold or more in value? The answer is "Yes." But the big fortunes from single-company investments are almost always realized by persons who

---

anathema to Graham. How can you value a company based on earnings it hasn't even generated yet? That's like setting house prices based on a rumor that Cinderella will be building her new castle right around the corner.

* Recent examples hammer Graham's point home. On September 21, 2000, Intel Corp., the maker of computer chips, announced that it expected its revenues to grow by up to 5% in the next quarter. At first blush, that sounds great; most big companies would be delighted to increase their sales by 5% in just three months. But in response, Intel's stock dropped 22%, a one-day loss of nearly $91 billion in total value. Why? Wall Street's analysts had expected Intel's revenue to rise by up to 10%. Similarly, on February 21, 2001, EMC Corp., a data-storage firm, announced that it expected its revenues to grow by at least 25% in 2001—but that a new caution among customers "may lead to longer selling cycles." On that whiff of hesitation, EMC's shares lost 12.8% of their value in a single day.

TABLE 7-1 Average Results of "Growth Funds," 1961–1970[a]

	1 year 1970	*5 years* 1966–1970	*10 years* 1961–1970	*1970* Dividend Return
17 large growth funds	– 7.5%	+23.2%	+121.1%	2.3%
106 smaller growth funds—group A	–17.7	+20.3	+102.1	1.6
38 smaller growth funds—group B	– 4.7	+23.2	+106.7	1.4
15 funds with "growth" in their name	–14.2	+13.8	+ 97.4	1.7
Standard & Poor's composite	+ 3.5%	+16.1	+104.7	3.4
Dow Jones Industrial Average	+ 8.7	+ 2.9	+ 83.0	3.7

[a] These figures are supplied by Wiesenberger Financial Services.

have a close relationship with the particular company—through employment, family connection, etc.—which justifies them in placing a large part of their resources in one medium and holding on to this commitment through all vicissitudes, despite numerous temptations to sell out at apparently high prices along the way. An investor without such close personal contact will constantly be faced with the question of whether too large a portion of his funds are in this one medium.* Each decline—however temporary it proves in the sequel—will accentuate his problem; and internal and external pressures are likely to force him to take what seems to be a goodly profit, but one far less than the ultimate bonanza.[4]

Three Recommended Fields for "Enterprising Investment"

To obtain better than average investment results over a long pull requires a policy of selection or operation possessing a twofold merit: (1) It must meet objective or rational tests of underlying soundness; and (2) it must be different from the policy followed by most investors or speculators. Our experience and study leads us to recommend three investment approaches that meet these criteria. They differ rather widely from one another, and each may require a different type of knowledge and temperament on the part of those who assay it.

---

* Today's equivalent of investors "who have a close relationship with the particular company" are so-called control persons–senior managers or directors who help run the company and own huge blocks of stock. Executives like Bill Gates of Microsoft or Warren Buffett of Berkshire Hathaway have direct control over a company's destiny–and outside investors want to see these chief executives maintain their large shareholdings as a vote of confidence. But less-senior managers and rank-and-file workers cannot influence the company's share price with their individual decisions; thus they should not put more than a small percentage of their assets in their own employer's stock. As for outside investors, no matter how well they think they know the company, the same objection applies.

The Relatively Unpopular Large Company

If we assume that it is the habit of the market to overvalue common stocks which have been showing excellent growth or are glamorous for some other reason, it is logical to expect that it will undervalue—relatively, at least—companies that are out of favor because of unsatisfactory developments of a temporary nature. This may be set down as a fundamental law of the stock market, and it suggests an investment approach that should prove both conservative and promising.

The key requirement here is that the enterprising investor concentrate on the larger companies that are going through a period of unpopularity. While small companies may also be undervalued for similar reasons, and in many cases may later increase their earnings and share price, they entail the risk of a definitive loss of profitability and also of protracted neglect by the market in spite of better earnings. The large companies thus have a double advantage over the others. First, they have the resources in capital and brain power to carry them through adversity and back to a satisfactory earnings base. Second, the market is likely to respond with reasonable speed to any improvement shown.

A remarkable demonstration of the soundness of this thesis is found in studies of the price behavior of the unpopular issues in the Dow Jones Industrial Average. In these it was assumed that an investment was made each year in either the six or the ten issues in the DJIA which were selling at the lowest multipliers of their current or previous year's earnings. These could be called the "cheapest" stocks in the list, and their cheapness was evidently the reflection of relative unpopularity with investors or traders. It was assumed further that these purchases were sold out at the end of holding periods ranging from one to five years. The results of these investments were then compared with the results shown in either the DJIA as a whole or in the highest multiplier (i.e., the most popular) group.

The detailed material we have available covers the results of annual purchases assumed in each of the past 53 years.[5] In the early period, 1917–1933, this approach proved unprofitable. But since 1933 the method has shown highly successful results. In 34 tests

TABLE 7-2 Average Annual Percentage Gain or Loss on Test Issues, 1937–1969

Period	*10 Low-Multiplier Issues*	*10 High-Multiplier Issues*	*30 DJIA Stocks*
1937–1942	– 2.2	–10.0	– 6.3
1943–1947	17.3	8.3	14.9
1948–1952	16.4	4.6	9.9
1953–1957	20.9	10.0	13.7
1958–1962	10.2	– 3.3	3.6
1963–1969 (8 years)	8.0	4.6	4.0

made by Drexel & Company (now Drexel Firestone)* of one-year holding—from 1937 through 1969—the cheap stocks did definitely worse than the DJIA in only three instances; the results were about the same in six cases; and the cheap stocks clearly outperformed the average in 25 years. The consistently better performance of the low-multiplier stocks is shown (Table 7-2) by the average results for successive five-year periods, when compared with those of the DJIA and of the ten high-multipliers.

The Drexel computation shows further that an original investment of $10,000 made in the low-multiplier issues in 1936, and switched each year in accordance with the principle, would have grown to $66,900 by 1962. The same operations in high-multiplier stocks would have ended with a value of only $25,300; while an operation in all thirty stocks would have increased the original fund to $44,000.†

The concept of buying "unpopular large companies" and its

---

* Drexel Firestone, a Philadelphia investment bank, merged in 1973 with Burnham & Co. and later became Drexel Burnham Lambert, famous for its junk-bond financing of the 1980s takeover boom.

† This strategy of buying the cheapest stocks in the Dow Jones Industrial Average is now nicknamed the "Dogs of the Dow" approach. Information on the "Dow 10" is available at www.djindexes.com/jsp/dow510Faq.jsp.

execution on a group basis, as described above, are both quite simple. But in considering individual companies a special factor of opposite import must sometimes to be taken into account. Companies that are inherently speculative because of widely varying earnings tend to sell both at a relatively high price and at a relatively low multiplier in their good years, and conversely at low prices and high multipliers in their bad years. These relationships are illustrated in Table 7-3, covering fluctuations of Chrysler Corp. common. In these cases the market has sufficient skepticism as to the continuation of the unusually high profits to value them conservatively, and conversely when earnings are low or nonexistent. (Note that, by the arithmetic, if a company earns "next to nothing" its shares must sell at a high multiplier of these minuscule profits.)

As it happens Chrysler has been quite exceptional in the DJIA list of leading companies, and hence it did not greatly affect the the low-multiplier calculations. It would be quite easy to avoid inclusion of such anomalous issues in a low-multiplier list by requiring also that the price be low in relation to past *average* earnings or by some similar test.

While writing this revision we tested the results of the DJIA-low-multiplier method applied to a group assumed to be bought at

TABLE 7-3 Chrysler Common Prices and Earnings, 1952–1970

Year	*Earnings Per Share*	*High or Low Price*	*P/E Ratio*
1952	$ 9.04	H 98	10.8
1954	2.13	L 56	26.2
1955	11.49	H 101½	8.8
1956	2.29	L 52 (in 1957)	22.9
1957	13.75	H 82	6.7
1958	(def.) 3.88	L 44[a]	—
1968	24.92[b]	H 294[b]	11.8
1970	def.	L 65[b]	—

[a] 1962 low was 37½.

[b] Adjusted for stock splits. def.: Net loss.

the end of 1968 and revalued on June 30, 1971. This time the figures proved quite disappointing, showing a sharp loss for the low-multiplier six or ten and a good profit for the high-multiplier selections. This one bad instance should not vitiate conclusions based on 30-odd experiments, but its recent happening gives it a special adverse weight. Perhaps the aggressive investor should start with the "low-multiplier" idea, but add other quantitative and qualitative requirements thereto in making up his portfolio.

Purchase of Bargain Issues

We define a bargain issue as one which, on the basis of facts established by analysis, appears to be worth considerably more than it is selling for. The genus includes bonds and preferred stocks selling well under par, as well as common stocks. To be as concrete as possible, let us suggest that an issue is not a true "bargain" unless the indicated value is at least 50% more than the price. What kind of facts would warrant the conclusion that so great a discrepancy exists? How do bargains come into existence, and how does the investor profit from them?

There are two tests by which a bargain common stock is detected. The first is by the method of appraisal. This relies largely on estimating future earnings and then multiplying these by a factor appropriate to the particular issue. If the resultant value is sufficiently above the market price—and if the investor has confidence in the technique employed—he can tag the stock as a bargain. The second test is the value of the business to a private owner. This value also is often determined chiefly by expected future earnings—in which case the result may be identical with the first. But in the second test more attention is likely to be paid to the realizable value of the *assets,* with particular emphasis on the net current assets or working capital.

At low points in the general market a large proportion of common stocks are bargain issues, as measured by these standards. (A typical example was General Motors when it sold at less than 30 in 1941, equivalent to only 5 for the 1971 shares. It had been earning in excess of $4 and paying $3.50, or more, in dividends.) It is true that current earnings and the immediate prospects may both be poor, but a levelheaded appraisal of average future conditions would indicate values far above ruling prices. Thus the wisdom of having courage in depressed markets is vindicated not only by the voice of experience but also by application of plausible techniques of value analysis.

The same vagaries of the market place that recurrently establish a bargain condition in the general list account for the existence of many individual bargains at almost all market levels. The market is fond of making mountains out of molehills and exaggerating ordinary vicissitudes into major setbacks.* Even a mere lack of interest or enthusiasm may impel a price decline to absurdly low levels. Thus we have what appear to be two major sources of undervaluation: (1) currently disappointing results and (2) protracted neglect or unpopularity.

However, neither of these causes, if considered by itself alone, can be relied on as a guide to successful common-stock investment. How can we be sure that the currently disappointing results are indeed going to be only temporary? True, we can supply excellent examples of that happening. The steel stocks used to be famous for their cyclical quality, and the shrewd buyer could acquire them at low prices when earnings were low and sell them out in boom years at a fine profit. A spectacular example is supplied by Chrysler Corporation, as shown by the data in Table 7-3.

If this were the *standard* behavior of stocks with fluctuating earnings, then making profits in the stock market would be an easy matter. Unfortunately, we could cite many examples of declines in

---

* Among the steepest of the mountains recently made out of molehills: In May 1998, Pfizer Inc. and the U.S. Food and Drug Administration announced that six men taking Pfizer's anti-impotence drug Viagra had died of heart attacks while having sex. Pfizer's stock immediately went flaccid, losing 3.4% in a single day on heavy trading. But Pfizer's shares surged ahead when research later showed that there was no cause for alarm; the stock gained roughly a third over the next two years. In late 1997, shares of Warner-Lambert Co. fell by 19% in a day when sales of its new diabetes drug were temporarily halted in England; within six months, the stock had nearly doubled. In late 2002, Carnival Corp., which operates cruise ships, lost roughly 10% of its value after tourists came down with severe diarrhea and vomiting–on ships run by other companies.

earnings and price which were not followed automatically by a handsome recovery of both. One such was Anaconda Wire and Cable, which had large earnings up to 1956, with a high price of 85 in that year. The earnings then declined irregularly for six years; the price fell to 23½ in 1962, and the following year it was taken over by its parent enterprise (Anaconda Corporation) at the equivalent of only 33.

The many experiences of this type suggest that the investor would need more than a mere falling off in both earnings and price to give him a sound basis for purchase. He should require an indication of at least reasonable stability of earnings over the past decade or more—i.e., no year of earnings deficit—plus sufficient size and financial strength to meet possible setbacks in the future. The ideal combination here is thus that of a large and prominent company selling both well below its past average price and its past average price/earnings multiplier. This would no doubt have ruled out most of the profitable opportunities in companies such as Chrysler, since their low-price years are generally accompanied by high price/earnings ratios. But let us assure the reader now—and no doubt we shall do it again—that there is a world of difference between "hindsight profits" and "real-money profits." We doubt seriously whether the Chrysler type of roller coaster is a suitable medium for operations by our enterprising investor.

We have mentioned protracted neglect or unpopularity as a second cause of price declines to unduly low levels. A current case of this kind would appear to be National Presto Industries. In the bull market of 1968 it sold at a high of 45, which was only 8 times the $5.61 earnings for that year. The per-share profits increased in both 1969 and 1970, but the price declined to only 21 in 1970. This was less than 4 times the (record) earnings in that year and less than its net-current-asset value. In March 1972 it was selling at 34, still only 5½ times the last reported earnings, and at about its enlarged net-current-asset value.

Another example of this type is provided currently by Standard Oil of California, a concern of major importance. In early 1972 it was selling at about the same price as 13 years before, say 56. Its earnings had been remarkably steady, with relatively small growth but with only one small decline over the entire period. Its book value was about equal to the market price. With this conservatively favorable 1958–71 record the company has never shown an average annual price as high as 15 times its current earnings. In early 1972 the price/earnings ratio was only about 10.

A third cause for an unduly low price for a common stock may be the market's failure to recognize its true earnings picture. Our classic example here is Northern Pacific Railway which in 1946–47 declined from 36 to 13½. The true earnings of the road in 1947 were close to $10 per share. The price of the stock was held down in great part by its $1 dividend. It was neglected also because much of its earnings power was concealed by accounting methods peculiar to railroads.

The type of bargain issue that can be most readily identified is a common stock that sells for less than the company's net working capital alone, after deducting all prior obligations.* This would mean that the buyer would pay nothing at all for the fixed assets—buildings, machinery, etc., or any good-will items that might exist. Very few companies turn out to have an ultimate value less than the working capital alone, although scattered instances may be found. The surprising thing, rather, is that there have been so many enterprises obtainable which have been valued in the market on this bargain basis. A compilation made in 1957, when the market's level was by no means low, disclosed about 150 of such common stocks. In Table 7-4 we summarize the result of buying, on December 31, 1957, one share of each of the 85 companies in that list for which data appeared in Standard & Poor's *Monthly Stock Guide,* and holding them for two years.

By something of a coincidence, each of the groups advanced in the two years to somewhere in the neighborhood of the aggregate net-current-asset value. The gain for the entire "portfolio" in that period was 75%, against 50% for Standard & Poor's 425 industrials. What is more remarkable is that none of the issues showed significant losses, seven held about even, and 78 showed appreciable gains.

Our experience with this type of investment selection—on a

* By "net working capital," Graham means a company's current assets (such as cash, marketable securities, and inventories) minus its total liabilities (including preferred stock and long-term debt).

TABLE 7-4 Profit Experience of Undervalued Stocks, 1957–1959

Location of Market	*Number of Companies*	*Aggregate Net Current Assets Per Share*	*Aggregate Price Dec. 1957*	*Aggregate Price Dec. 1959*
New York S.E.	35	$ 748	$ 419	$ 838
American S.E.	25	495	289	492
Midwest S.E.	5	163	87	141
Over the counter	20	425	288	433
Total	85	$1,831	$1,083	$1,904

diversified basis—was uniformly good for many years prior to 1957. It can probably be affirmed without hesitation that it constitutes a safe and profitable method of determining and taking advantage of undervalued situations. However, during the general market advance after 1957 the number of such opportunities became extremely limited, and many of those available were showing small operating profits or even losses. The market decline of 1969–70 produced a new crop of these "sub-working-capital" stocks. We discuss this group in Chapter 15, on stock selection for the enterprising investor.

Bargain-Issue Pattern in Secondary Companies. We have defined a secondary company as one that is not a leader in a fairly important industry. Thus it is usually one of the smaller concerns in its field, but it may equally well be the chief unit in an unimportant line. By way of exception, any company that has established itself as a growth stock is not ordinarily considered "secondary."

In the great bull market of the 1920s relatively little distinction was drawn between industry leaders and other listed issues, provided the latter were of respectable size. The public felt that a middle-sized company was strong enough to weather storms and that it had a better chance for really spectacular expansion than one that was already of major dimensions. The depression years 1931–32, however, had a particularly devastating impact on the companies below the first rank either in size or in inherent stability. As a result of that experience investors have since developed a pronounced preference for industry leaders and a corresponding lack of interest most of the time in the ordinary company of secondary importance. This has meant that the latter group have usually sold at much lower prices in relation to earnings and assets than have the former. It has meant further that in many instances the price has fallen so low as to establish the issue in the bargain class.

When investors rejected the stocks of secondary companies, even though these sold at relatively low prices, they were expressing a belief or fear that such companies faced a dismal future. In fact, at least subconsciously, they calculated that *any* price was too high for them because they were heading for extinction—just as in 1929 the companion theory for the "blue chips" was that no price was too high for them because their future possibilities were limitless. Both of these views were exaggerations and were productive of serious investment errors. Actually, the typical middle-sized listed company is a large one when compared with the average privately owned business. There is no sound reason why such companies should not continue indefinitely in operation, undergoing the vicissitudes characteristic of our economy but earning on the whole a fair return on their invested capital.

This brief review indicates that the stock market's attitude toward secondary companies tends to be unrealistic and consequently to create in normal times innumerable instances of major undervaluation. As it happens, the World War II period and the postwar boom were more beneficial to the smaller concerns than to the larger ones, because then the normal competition for sales was suspended and the former could expand sales and profit margins more spectacularly. Thus by 1946 the market's pattern had completely reversed itself from that before the war. Whereas the leading stocks in the Dow Jones Industrial Average had advanced only 40% from the end of 1938 to the 1946 high, Standard & Poor's index of low-priced stocks had shot up no less than 280% in the same period. Speculators and many self-styled investors—with the proverbial short memories of people in the stock market—were eager to buy both old and new issues of unimportant companies at inflated levels. Thus the pendulum had swung clear to the opposite extreme. The very class of secondary issues that had formerly supplied by far the largest proportion of bargain opportunities was now presenting the greatest number of examples of overenthusiasm and overvaluation. In a different way this phenomenon was repeated in 1961 and 1968—the emphasis now being placed on new offerings of the shares of small companies of less than secondary character, and on nearly all companies in certain favored fields such as "electronics," "computers," "franchise" concerns, and others.*

As was to be expected the ensuing market declines fell most heavily on these overvaluations. In some cases the pendulum swing may have gone as far as definite *under*valuation.

If most secondary issues tend normally to be undervalued, what reason has the investor to believe that he can profit from such a situation? For if it persists indefinitely, will he not always be in the same market position as when he bought the issue? The answer here is somewhat complicated. Substantial profits from the purchase of secondary companies at bargain prices arise in a variety of ways. First, the dividend return is relatively high. Second, the reinvested earnings are substantial in relation to the price paid and will ultimately affect the price. In a five- to seven-year period these advantages can bulk quite large in a well-selected list. Third, a bull market is ordinarily most generous to low-priced issues; thus it tends to raise the typical bargain issue to at least a reasonable level. Fourth, even during relatively featureless market periods a continuous process of price adjustment goes on, under which secondary issues that were undervalued may rise at least to the normal level for their type of security. Fifth, the specific factors that in many

---

* From 1975 through 1983, small ("secondary") stocks outperformed large stocks by an amazing average of 17.6 percentage points per year. The investing public eagerly embraced small stocks, mutual fund companies rolled out hundreds of new funds specializing in them, and small stocks obliged by *underperforming* large stocks by five percentage points per year over the next decade. The cycle recurred in 1999, when small stocks beat big stocks by nearly nine percentage points, inspiring investment bankers to sell hundreds of hot little high-tech stocks to the public for the first time. Instead of "electronics," "computers," or "franchise" in their names, the new buzzwords were ".com," "optical," "wireless," and even prefixes like "e-" and "I-." Investing buzzwords always turn into buzz saws, tearing apart anyone who believes in them.

cases made for a disappointing record of earnings may be corrected by the advent of new conditions, or the adoption of new policies, or by a change in management.

An important new factor in recent years has been the acquisition of smaller companies by larger ones, usually as part of a diversification program. In these cases the consideration paid has almost always been relatively generous, and much in excess of the bargain levels existing not long before.

When interest rates were much lower than in 1970, the field of bargain issues extended to bonds and preferred stocks that sold at large discounts from the amount of their claim. Currently we have a different situation in which even well-secured issues sell at large discounts if carrying coupon rates of, say, 4½% or less. Example: American Telephone & Telegraph 2⅝s, due 1986, sold as low as 51 in 1970; Deere & Co. 4½s, due 1983, sold as low as 62. These may well turn out to have been bargain opportunities before very long—if ruling interest rates should decline substantially. For a bargain bond issue in the more traditional sense perhaps we shall have to turn once more to the first-mortgage bonds of railroads now in financial difficulties, which sell in the 20s or 30s. Such situations are not for the inexpert investor; lacking a real sense of values in this area, he may burn his fingers. But there is an underlying tendency for market decline in this field to be overdone; consequently the group as a whole offers an especially rewarding invitation to careful and courageous analysis. In the decade ending in 1948 the billion-dollar group of defaulted railroad bonds presented numerous and spectacular opportunities in this area. Such opportunities have been quite scarce since then; but they seem likely to return in the 1970s.*

---

* Defaulted railroad bonds do not offer significant opportunities today. However, as already noted, distressed and defaulted junk bonds, as well as convertible bonds issued by high-tech companies, may offer real value in the wake of the 2000–2002 market crash. But diversification in this area is essential–and impractical without at least $100,000 to dedicate to distressed securities alone. Unless you are a millionaire several times over, this kind of diversification is not an option.

Special Situations, or "Workouts"

Not so long ago this was a field which could almost guarantee an attractive rate of return to those who knew their way around in it; and this was true under almost any sort of general market situation. It was not actually forbidden territory to members of the general public. Some who had a flair for this sort of thing could learn the ropes and become pretty capable practitioners without the necessity of long academic study or apprenticeship. Others have been keen enough to recognize the underlying soundness of this approach and to attach themselves to bright young men who handled funds devoted chiefly to these "special situations." But in recent years, for reasons we shall develop later, the field of "arbitrages and workouts" became riskier and less profitable. It may be that in years to come conditions in this field will become more propitious. In any case it is worthwhile outlining the general nature and origin of these operations, with one or two illustrative examples.

The typical "special situation" has grown out of the increasing number of acquisitions of smaller firms by large ones, as the gospel of diversification of products has been adopted by more and more managements. It often appears good business for such an enterprise to acquire an existing company in the field it wishes to enter rather than to start a new venture from scratch. In order to make such acquisition possible, and to obtain acceptance of the deal by the required large majority of shareholders of the smaller company, it is almost always necessary to offer a price considerably above the current level. Such corporate moves have been producing interesting profit-making opportunities for those who have made a study of this field, and have good judgment fortified by ample experience.

A great deal of money was made by shrewd investors not so many years ago through the purchase of bonds of railroads in bankruptcy—bonds which they knew would be worth much more than their cost when the railroads were finally reorganized. After promulgation of the plans of reorganization a "when issued" market for the new securities appeared. These could almost always be sold for considerably more than the cost of the old issues which were to be exchanged therefor. There were risks of nonconsummation of the plans or of unexpected delays, but on the whole such "arbitrage operations" proved highly profitable.

There were similar opportunities growing out of the breakup of public-utility holding companies pursuant to 1935 legislation. Nearly all these enterprises proved to be worth considerably more when changed from holding companies to a group of separate operating companies.

The underlying factor here is the tendency of the security markets to undervalue issues that are involved in any sort of complicated legal proceedings. An old Wall Street motto has been: "Never buy into a lawsuit." This may be sound advice to the speculator seeking quick action on his holdings. But the adoption of this attitude by the general public is bound to create bargain opportunities in the securities affected by it, since the prejudice against them holds their prices down to unduly low levels.*

The exploitation of special situations is a technical branch of investment which requires a somewhat unusual mentality and equipment. Probably only a small percentage of our enterprising investors are likely to engage in it, and this book is not the appropriate medium for expounding its complications.[6]

Broader Implications of Our Rules for Investment

Investment policy, as it has been developed here, depends in the first place on a choice by the investor of either the defensive (passive) or aggressive (enterprising) role. The aggressive investor must have a considerable knowledge of security values—enough, in fact, to warrant viewing his security operations as equivalent to a business enterprise. There is no room in this philosophy for a

---

* A classic recent example is Philip Morris, whose stock lost 23% in two days after a Florida court authorized jurors to consider punitive damages of up to $200 billion against the company–which had finally admitted that cigarettes may cause cancer. Within a year, Philip Morris's stock had doubled–only to fall back after a later multibillion-dollar judgment in Illinois. Several other stocks have been virtually destroyed by liability lawsuits, including Johns Manville, W. R. Grace, and USG Corp. Thus, "never buy into a lawsuit" remains a valid rule for all but the most intrepid investors to live by.

middle ground, or a series of gradations, between the passive and aggressive status. Many, perhaps most, investors seek to place themselves in such an intermediate category; in our opinion that is a compromise that is more likely to produce disappointment than achievement.

As an investor you cannot soundly become "half a businessman," expecting thereby to achieve half the normal rate of business profits on your funds.

It follows from this reasoning that the majority of security owners should elect the defensive classification. They do not have the time, or the determination, or the mental equipment to embark upon investing as a quasi-business. They should therefore be satisfied with the excellent return now obtainable from a defensive portfolio (and with even less), and they should stoutly resist the recurrent temptation to increase this return by deviating into other paths.

The enterprising investor may properly embark upon any security operation for which his training and judgment are adequate and which appears sufficiently promising *when measured by established business standards.*

In our recommendations and caveats for this group of investors we have attempted to apply such business standards. In those for the defensive investor we have been guided largely by the three requirements of underlying safety, simplicity of choice, and promise of satisfactory results, in terms of psychology as well as arithmetic. The use of these criteria has led us to exclude from the field of recommended investment a number of security classes that are normally regarded as suitable for various kinds of investors. These prohibitions were listed in our first chapter on p. 30.

Let us consider a little more fully than before what is implied in these exclusions. We have advised against the purchase at "full prices" of three important categories of securities: (1) foreign bonds, (2) ordinary preferred stocks, and (3) secondary common stocks, including, of course, original offerings of such issues. By "full prices" we mean prices close to par for bonds or preferred stocks, and prices that represent about the fair business value of the enterprise in the case of common stocks. The greater number of defensive investors are to avoid these categories regardless of price; the enterprising investor is to buy them only when obtainable at bargain prices—which we define as prices not more than two-thirds of the appraisal value of the securities.

What would happen if all investors were guided by our advice in these matters? That question was considered in regard to foreign bonds, on p. 138, and we have nothing to add at this point. Investment-grade preferred stocks would be bought solely by corporations, such as insurance companies, which would benefit from the special income-tax status of stock issues owned by them.

The most troublesome consequence of our policy of exclusion is in the field of secondary common stocks. If the majority of investors, being in the defensive class, are not to buy them at all, the field of possible buyers becomes seriously restricted. Furthermore, if aggressive investors are to buy them only at bargain levels, then these issues would be doomed to sell for less than their fair value, except to the extent that they were purchased unintelligently.

This may sound severe and even vaguely unethical. Yet in truth we are merely recognizing what has actually happened in this area for the greater part of the past 40 years. Secondary issues, for the most part, *do* fluctuate about a central level which is well below their fair value. They reach and even surpass that value at times; but this occurs in the upper reaches of bull markets, when the lessons of practical experience would argue against the soundness of paying the prevailing prices for common stocks.

Thus we are suggesting only that the aggressive investor recognize the facts of life as it is lived by secondary issues and that they accept the central market levels that are normal for that class as their guide in fixing their own levels for purchase.

There is a paradox here, nevertheless. The average well-selected secondary company may be fully as promising as the average industrial leader. What the smaller concern lacks in inherent stability it may readily make up in superior possibilities of growth. Consequently it may appear illogical to many readers to term "unintelligent" the purchase of such secondary issues at their full "enterprise value." We think that the strongest logic is that of experience. Financial history says clearly that the investor may expect satisfactory results, on the average, from secondary common stocks only if he buys them for less than their value to a private owner, that is, on a bargain basis.

The last sentence indicates that this principle relates to the ordinary *outside* investor. Anyone who can *control* a secondary company, or who is part of a cohesive group with such control, is fully justified in buying the shares on the same basis as if he were investing in a "close corporation" or other private business. The distinction between the position, and consequent investment policy, of insiders and of outsiders becomes more important as the enterprise itself becomes *less* important. It is a basic characteristic of a primary or leading company that a single detached share is ordinarily worth as much as a share in a controlling block. In secondary companies the *average* market value of a detached share is substantially less than its worth to a controlling owner. Because of this fact, the matter of shareholder-management relations and of those between inside and outside shareholders tends to be much more important and controversial in the case of secondary than in that of primary companies.

At the end of Chapter 5 we commented on the difficulty of making any hard and fast distinction between primary and secondary companies. The many common stocks in the boundary area may properly exhibit an intermediate price behavior. It would not be illogical for an investor to buy such an issue at a *small* discount from its indicated or appraisal value, on the theory that it is only a small distance away from a primary classification and that it may acquire such a rating unqualifiedly in the not too distant future.

Thus the distinction between primary and secondary issues need not be made too precise; for, if it were, then a small difference in quality must produce a large differential in justified purchase price. In saying this we are admitting a middle ground in the classification of common stocks, although we counseled against such a middle ground in the classification of investors. Our reason for this apparent inconsistency is as follows: No great harm comes from some uncertainty of viewpoint regarding a single security, because such cases are exceptional and not a great deal is at stake in the matter. But the investor's choice as between the defensive or the aggressive status is of major consequence to him, and he should not allow himself to be confused or compromised in this basic decision.

COMMENTARY ON CHAPTER 7

> It requires a great deal of boldness and a great deal of caution to make a great fortune; and when you have got it, it requires ten times as much wit to keep it.
>
> —*Nathan Mayer Rothschild*

TIMING IS NOTHING

In an ideal world, the intelligent investor would hold stocks only when they are cheap and sell them when they become overpriced, then duck into the bunker of bonds and cash until stocks again become cheap enough to buy. From 1966 through late 2001, one study claimed, $1 held continuously in stocks would have grown to $11.71. But if you had gotten out of stocks right before the five worst days of each year, your original $1 would have grown to $987.12.[1]

Like most magical market ideas, this one is based on sleight of hand. How, exactly, would you (or anyone) figure out which days will be the worst days—*before* they arrive? On January 7, 1973, the *New York Times* featured an interview with one of the nation's top financial forecasters, who urged investors to buy stocks without hesitation: "It's very rare that you can be as unqualifiedly bullish as you can now." That forecaster was named Alan Greenspan, and it's very rare that anyone

[1] "The Truth About Timing," *Barron's*, November 5, 2001, p. 20. The headline of this article is a useful reminder of an enduring principle for the intelligent investor. Whenever you see the word "truth" in an article about investing, brace yourself; many of the quotes that follow are likely to be lies. (For one thing, an investor who bought stocks in 1966 and held them through late 2001 would have ended up with at least $40, not $11.71; the study cited in *Barron's* appears to have ignored the reinvestment of dividends.)

has ever been so unqualifiedly wrong as the future Federal Reserve chairman was that day: 1973 and 1974 turned out to be the worst years for economic growth and the stock market since the Great Depression.[2]

Can professionals time the market any better than Alan Greenspan? "I see no reason not to think the majority of the decline is behind us," declared Kate Leary Lee, president of the market-timing firm of R. M. Leary & Co., on December 3, 2001. "This is when you want to be in the market," she added, predicting that stocks "look good" for the first quarter of 2002.[3] Over the next three months, stocks earned a measly 0.28% return, underperforming cash by 1.5 percentage points.

Leary is not alone. A study by two finance professors at Duke University found that if you had followed the recommendations of the best 10% of all market-timing newsletters, you would have earned a 12.6% annualized return from 1991 through 1995. But if you had ignored them and kept your money in a stock index fund, you would have earned 16.4%.[4]

As the Danish philosopher Søren Kierkegaard noted, life can only be understood backwards–but it must be lived forwards. Looking back, you can always see exactly when you should have bought and sold your stocks. But don't let that fool you into thinking you can see, in real time, just when to get in and out. In the financial markets, hindsight is forever 20/20, but foresight is legally blind. And thus, for most investors, market timing is a practical and emotional impossibility.[5]

---

[2] The *New York Times*, January 7, 1973, special "Economic Survey" section, pp. 2, 19, 44.

[3] Press release, "It's a good time to be in the market, says R. M. Leary & Company," December 3, 2001.

[4] You would also have saved thousands of dollars in annual subscription fees (which have not been deducted from the calculations of these newsletters' returns). And brokerage costs and short-term capital gains taxes are usually much higher for market timers than for buy-and-hold investors. For the Duke study, see John R. Graham and Campbell R. Harvey, "Grading the Performance of Market-Timing Newsletters," *Financial Analysts Journal*, November/December, 1997, pp. 54–66, also available at www.duke.edu/~charvey/research.htm.

[5] For more on sensible alternatives to market timing–rebalancing and dollar-cost averaging–see Chapters 5 and 8.

WHAT GOES UP . . .

Like spacecraft that pick up speed as they rise into the Earth's stratosphere, growth stocks often seem to defy gravity. Let's look at the trajectories of three of the hottest growth stocks of the 1990s: General Electric, Home Depot, and Sun Microsystems. (See Figure 7-1.)

In every year from 1995 through 1999, each grew bigger and more profitable. Revenues doubled at Sun and more than doubled at Home Depot. According to Value Line, GE's revenues grew 29%; its earnings rose 65%. At Home Depot and Sun, earnings per share roughly tripled.

But something else was happening–and it wouldn't have surprised Graham one bit. The faster these companies grew, the more expensive their stocks became. And when stocks grow faster than companies, investors always end up sorry. As Figure 7-2 shows:

A great company is not a great investment if you pay too much for the stock.

The more a stock has gone up, the more it seems likely to keep going up. But that instinctive belief is flatly contradicted by a fundamental law of financial physics: The bigger they get, the slower they grow. A $1-billion company can double its sales fairly easily; but where can a $50-billion company turn to find another $50 billion in business?

Growth stocks are worth buying when their prices are reasonable, but when their price/earnings ratios go much above 25 or 30 the odds get ugly:

- Journalist Carol Loomis found that, from 1960 through 1999, only eight of the largest 150 companies on the *Fortune* 500 list managed to raise their earnings by an annual average of at least 15% for two decades.[6]
- Looking at five decades of data, the research firm of Sanford C. Bernstein & Co. showed that only 10% of large U.S. companies had increased their earnings by 20% for at least five consecutive years; only 3% had grown by 20% for at least 10 years straight; and not a single one had done it for 15 years in a row.[7]

---

[6] Carol J. Loomis, "The 15% Delusion," *Fortune,* February 5, 2001, pp. 102–108.

[7] See Jason Zweig, "A Matter of Expectations," *Money,* January, 2001, pp. 49–50.

FIGURE 7-1 Up, Up, and Away

		1995	1996	1997	1998	1999
General Electric	Revenues ($ millions)	43,013	46,119	48,952	51,546	55,645
	Earnings per share ($)	0.65	0.73	0.83	0.93	1.07
	Yearly stock return (%)	44.5	40.0	50.6	40.7	53.2
	Year-end price/earnings ratio	18.4	22.8	29.9	36.4	47.9
Home Depot	Revenues ($ millions)	15,470	19,536	24,156	30,219	38,434
	Earnings per share ($)	0.34	0.43	0.52	0.71	1.00
	Yearly stock return (%)	4.2	5.5	76.8	108.3	68.8
	Year-end price/earnings ratio	32.3	27.6	37.5	61.8	73.7
Sun Microsystems	Revenues ($ millions)	5,902	7,095	8,598	9,791	11,726
	Earnings per share ($)	0.11	0.17	0.24	0.29	0.36
	Yearly stock return (%)	157.0	12.6	55.2	114.7	261.7
	Year-end price/earnings ratio	20.3	17.7	17.9	34.5	97.7

Sources: Bloomberg, Value Line

Notes: Revenues and earnings for fiscal years; stock return for calendar years; price/earnings ratio is December 31 price divided by reported earnings for previous four quarters.

FIGURE 7-2 Look Out Below

	Stock price 12/31/99	Stock price 12/31/02	P/E ratio 12/31/99	P/E ratio March 2003
General Electric	$51.58	$24.35	48.1	15.7
Home Depot	$68.75	$23.96	97.4	14.3
Sun Microsystems	$38.72	$3.11	123.3	n/a

n/a: Not applicable; Sun had net loss in 2002.
Sources: www.morningstar.com, yahoo.marketguide.com

- An academic study of thousands of U.S. stocks from 1951 through 1998 found that over all 10-year periods, net earnings grew by an average of 9.7% annually. But for the biggest 20% of companies, earnings grew by an annual average of just 9.3%.[8]

Even many corporate leaders fail to understand these odds (see sidebar on p. 184). The intelligent investor, however, gets interested in big growth stocks not when they are at their most popular–but when something goes wrong. In July 2002, Johnson & Johnson announced that Federal regulators were investigating accusations of false record keeping at one of its drug factories, and the stock lost 16% in a single day. That took J & J's share price down from 24 times the previous 12 months' earnings to just 20 times. At that lower level, Johnson & Johnson might once again have become a growth stock with room to grow–making it an example of what Graham calls "the relatively unpopular large company."[9] This kind of temporary unpopularity can create lasting wealth by enabling you to buy a great company at a good price.

---

[8] Louis K. C. Chan, Jason Karceski, and Josef Lakonishok, "The Level and Persistence of Growth Rates," National Bureau of Economic Research, Working Paper No. 8282, May, 2001, available at www.nber.org/papers/w8282.

[9] Almost exactly 20 years earlier, in October 1982, Johnson & Johnson's stock lost 17.5% of its value in a week when several people died after ingesting Tylenol that had been laced with cyanide by an unknown outsider. Johnson & Johnson responded by pioneering the use of tamper-proof packaging, and the stock went on to be one of the great investments of the 1980s.

HIGH POTENTIAL FOR HYPE POTENTIAL

Investors aren't the only people who fall prey to the delusion that hyper-growth can go on forever. In February 2000, chief executive John Roth of Nortel Networks was asked how much bigger his giant fiber-optics company could get. "The industry is growing 14% to 15% a year," Roth replied, "and we're going to grow six points faster than that. For a company our size, that's pretty heady stuff." Nortel's stock, up nearly 51% annually over the previous six years, was then trading at 87 times what Wall Street was guessing it might earn in 2000. Was the stock overpriced? "It's getting up there," shrugged Roth, "but there's still plenty of room to grow our valuation as we execute on the wireless strategy." (After all, he added, Cisco Systems was trading at 121 times its projected earnings!)[1]

As for Cisco, in November 2000, its chief executive, John Chambers, insisted that his company could keep growing at least 50% annually. "Logic," he declared, "would indicate this is a breakaway." Cisco's stock had come way down–it was then trading at a mere 98 times its earnings over the previous year–and Chambers urged investors to buy. "So who you going to bet on?" he asked. "Now may be the opportunity."[2]

Instead, these growth companies shrank–and their overpriced stocks shriveled. Nortel's revenues fell by 37% in 2001, and the company lost more than $26 billion that year. Cisco's revenues did rise by 18% in 2001, but the company ended up with a net loss of more than $1 billion. Nortel's stock, at $113.50 when Roth spoke, finished 2002 at $1.65. Cisco's shares, at $52 when Chambers called his company a "breakaway," crumbled to $13.

Both companies have since become more circumspect about forecasting the future.

---

[1] Lisa Gibbs, "Optic Uptick," *Money,* April, 2000, pp. 54–55.

[2] Brooke Southall, "Cisco's Endgame Strategy," *InvestmentNews,* November 30, 2000, pp. 1, 23.

SHOULD YOU PUT ALL YOUR EGGS IN ONE BASKET?

"Put all your eggs into one basket and then watch that basket," proclaimed Andrew Carnegie a century ago. "Do not scatter your shot. . . . The great successes of life are made by concentration." As Graham points out, "the really big fortunes from common stocks" have been made by people who packed all their money into one investment they knew supremely well.

Nearly all the richest people in America trace their wealth to a concentrated investment in a single industry or even a single company (think Bill Gates and Microsoft, Sam Walton and Wal-Mart, or the Rockefellers and Standard Oil). The *Forbes* 400 list of the richest Americans, for example, has been dominated by undiversified fortunes ever since it was first compiled in 1982.

However, almost no small fortunes have been made this way–and not many big fortunes have been *kept* this way. What Carnegie neglected to mention is that concentration also makes most of the great *failures* of life. Look again at the *Forbes* "Rich List." Back in 1982, the average net worth of a *Forbes* 400 member was $230 million. To make it onto the 2002 *Forbes* 400, the average 1982 member needed to earn only a 4.5% average annual return on his wealth–during a period when even bank accounts yielded far more than that and the stock market gained an annual average of 13.2%.

So how many of the *Forbes* 400 fortunes from 1982 remained on the list 20 years later? Only 64 of the original members–a measly 16%–were still on the list in 2002. By keeping all their eggs in the one basket that had gotten them onto the list in the first place–once-booming industries like oil and gas, or computer hardware, or basic manufacturing–all the other original members fell away. When hard times hit, none of these people–despite all the huge advantages that great wealth can bring–were properly prepared. They could only stand by and wince at the sickening crunch as the constantly changing economy crushed their only basket and all their eggs.[10]

---

[10] For the observation that it is amazingly difficult to remain on the *Forbes* 400, I am indebted to investment manager Kenneth Fisher (himself a *Forbes* columnist).

THE BARGAIN BIN

You might think that in our endlessly networked world, it would be a cinch to build and buy a list of stocks that meet Graham's criteria for bargains (p. 169). Although the Internet is a help, you'll still have to do much of the work by hand.

Grab a copy of today's *Wall Street Journal,* turn to the "Money & Investing" section, and take a look at the NYSE and NASDAQ Scorecards to find the day's lists of stocks that have hit new lows for the past year–a quick and easy way to search for companies that might pass Graham's net-working-capital tests. (Online, try http://quote.morningstar.com/highlow.html?msection=HighLow.)

To see whether a stock is selling for less than the value of net working capital (what Graham's followers call "net nets"), download or request the most recent quarterly or annual report from the company's website or from the EDGAR database at www.sec.gov. From the company's current assets, subtract its total liabilities, including any preferred stock and long-term debt. (Or consult your local public library's copy of the Value Line Investment Survey, saving yourself a costly annual subscription. Each issue carries a list of "Bargain Basement Stocks" that come close to Graham's definition.) Most of these stocks lately have been in bombed-out areas like high-tech and telecommunications.

As of October 31, 2002, for instance, Comverse Technology had $2.4 billion in current assets and $1.0 billion in total liabilities, giving it $1.4 billion in net working capital. With fewer than 190 million shares of stock, and a stock price under $8 per share, Comverse had a total market capitalization of just under $1.4 billion. With the stock priced at no more than the value of Comverse's cash and inventories, the company's ongoing business was essentially selling for nothing. As Graham knew, you can still lose money on a stock like Comverse–which is why you should buy them only if you can find a couple dozen at a time and hold them patiently. But on the very rare occasions when Mr. Market generates that many true bargains, you're all but certain to make money.

WHAT'S YOUR FOREIGN POLICY?

Investing in foreign stocks may not be mandatory for the intelligent investor, but it is definitely advisable. Why? Let's try a little thought experiment. It's the end of 1989, and you're Japanese. Here are the facts:

- Over the past 10 years, your stock market has gained an annual average of 21.2%, well ahead of the 17.5% annual gains in the United States.
- Japanese companies are buying up everything in the United States from the Pebble Beach golf course to Rockefeller Center; meanwhile, American firms like Drexel Burnham Lambert, Financial Corp. of America, and Texaco are going bankrupt.
- The U.S. high-tech industry is dying. Japan's is booming.

In 1989, in the land of the rising sun, you can only conclude that investing outside of Japan is the dumbest idea since sushi vending machines. Naturally, you put all your money in Japanese stocks.

The result? Over the next decade, you lose roughly two-thirds of your money.

The lesson? It's not that you should never invest in foreign markets like Japan; it's that the Japanese should never have kept all their money at home. And neither should you. If you live in the United States, work in the United States, and get paid in U.S. dollars, you are already making a multilayered bet on the U.S. economy. To be prudent, you should put some of your investment portfolio elsewhere–simply because no one, anywhere, can ever know what the future will bring at home or abroad. Putting up to a third of your stock money in mutual funds that hold foreign stocks (including those in emerging markets) helps insure against the risk that our own backyard may not always be the best place in the world to invest.

CHAPTER 8

The Investor and Market Fluctuations

To the extent that the investor's funds are placed in high-grade bonds of relatively short maturity—say, of seven years or less—he will not be affected significantly by changes in market prices and need not take them into account. (This applies also to his holdings of U.S. savings bonds, which he can always turn in at his cost price or more.) His longer-term bonds may have relatively wide price swings during their lifetimes, and his common-stock portfolio is almost certain to fluctuate in value over any period of several years.

The investor should know about these possibilities and should be prepared for them both financially and psychologically. He will want to benefit from changes in market levels—certainly through an advance in the value of his stock holdings as time goes on, and perhaps also by making purchases and sales at advantageous prices. This interest on his part is inevitable, and legitimate enough. But it involves the very real danger that it will lead him into speculative attitudes and activities. It is easy for us to tell you not to speculate; the hard thing will be for you to follow this advice. Let us repeat what we said at the outset: If you want to speculate do so with your eyes open, knowing that you will probably lose money in the end; be sure to limit the amount at risk and to separate it completely from your investment program.

We shall deal first with the more important subject of price changes in common stocks, and pass later to the area of bonds. In Chapter 3 we supplied a historical survey of the stock market's action over the past hundred years. In this section we shall return to that material from time to time, in order to see what the past record promises the investor—in either the form of long-term appreciation of a portfolio held relatively unchanged through successive rises and declines, or in the possibilities of buying near bear-market lows and selling not too far below bull-market highs.

Market Fluctuations as a Guide to Investment Decisions

Since common stocks, even of investment grade, are subject to recurrent and wide fluctuations in their prices, the intelligent investor should be interested in the possibilities of profiting from these pendulum swings. There are two possible ways by which he may try to do this: the way of *timing* and the way of *pricing.* By timing we mean the endeavor to anticipate the action of the stock market—to buy or hold when the future course is deemed to be upward, to sell or refrain from buying when the course is downward. By pricing we mean the endeavor to buy stocks when they are quoted below their fair value and to sell them when they rise above such value. A less ambitious form of pricing is the simple effort to make sure that when you buy you do not pay too much for your stocks. This may suffice for the defensive investor, whose emphasis is on long-pull holding; but as such it represents an essential minimum of attention to market levels.[1]

We are convinced that the intelligent investor can derive satisfactory results from pricing of either type. We are equally sure that if he places his emphasis on timing, in the sense of forecasting, he will end up as a speculator and with a speculator's financial results. This distinction may seem rather tenuous to the layman, and it is not commonly accepted on Wall Street. As a matter of business practice, or perhaps of thoroughgoing conviction, the stock brokers and the investment services seem wedded to the principle that both investors and speculators in common stocks should devote careful attention to market forecasts.

The farther one gets from Wall Street, the more skepticism one will find, we believe, as to the pretensions of stock-market forecasting or timing. The investor can scarcely take seriously the innumerable predictions which appear almost daily and are his for the asking. Yet in many cases he pays attention to them and even acts upon them. Why? Because he has been persuaded that it is important for him to form *some* opinion of the future course of the stock market, and because he feels that the brokerage or service forecast is at least more dependable than his own.*

We lack space here to discuss in detail the pros and cons of market forecasting. A great deal of brain power goes into this field, and undoubtedly *some people* can make money by being good stock-market analysts. But it is absurd to think that the *general public* can ever make money out of market forecasts. For who will buy when the general public, at a given signal, rushes to sell out at a profit? If you, the reader, expect to get rich over the years by following some system or leadership in market forecasting, you must be expecting to try to do what countless others are aiming at, and to be able to do it better than your numerous competitors in the market. There is no basis either in logic or in experience for assuming that any typical or average investor can anticipate market movements more successfully than the general public, of which he is himself a part.

There is one aspect of the "timing" philosophy which seems to have escaped everyone's notice. Timing is of great psychological importance to the speculator because he wants to make his profit in

---

* In the late 1990s, the forecasts of "market strategists" became more influential than ever before. They did not, unfortunately, become more accurate. On March 10, 2000, the very day that the NASDAQ composite index hit its all-time high of 5048.62, Prudential Securities's chief technical analyst Ralph Acampora said in *USA Today* that he expected NASDAQ to hit 6000 within 12 to 18 months. Five weeks later, NASDAQ had already shriveled to 3321.29–but Thomas Galvin, a market strategist at Donaldson, Lufkin & Jenrette, declared that "there's only 200 or 300 points of downside for the NASDAQ and 2000 on the upside." It turned out that there were no points on the upside and more than 2000 on the downside, as NASDAQ kept crashing until it finally scraped bottom on October 9, 2002, at 1114.11. In March 2001, Abby Joseph Cohen, chief investment strategist at Goldman, Sachs & Co., predicted that the Standard & Poor's 500-stock index would close the year at 1,650 and that the Dow Jones Industrial Average would finish 2001 at 13,000. "We do not expect a recession," said Cohen, "and believe that corporate profits are likely to grow at close to trend growth rates later this year." The U.S. economy was sinking into recession even as she spoke, and the S & P 500 ended 2001 at 1148.08, while the Dow finished at 10,021.50–30% and 23% below her forecasts, respectively.

a hurry. The idea of waiting a year before his stock moves up is repugnant to him. But a waiting period, as such, is of no consequence to the investor. What advantage is there to him in having his money uninvested until he receives some (presumably) trustworthy signal that the time has come to buy? He enjoys an advantage only if by waiting he succeeds in buying later at a sufficiently *lower price* to offset his loss of dividend income. What this means is that timing is of no real value to the investor unless it coincides with pricing—that is, unless it enables him to repurchase his shares at substantially under his previous selling price.

In this respect the famous Dow theory for timing purchases and sales has had an unusual history.* Briefly, this technique takes its signal to buy from a special kind of "breakthrough" of the stock averages on the up side, and its selling signal from a similar breakthrough on the down side. The calculated—not necessarily actual—results of using this method showed an almost unbroken series of profits in operations from 1897 to the early 1960s. On the basis of this presentation the practical value of the Dow theory would have appeared firmly established; the doubt, if any, would apply to the dependability of this published "record" as a picture of what a Dow theorist would actually have done in the market.

A closer study of the figures indicates that the quality of the results shown by the Dow theory changed radically after 1938—a few years after the theory had begun to be taken seriously on Wall Street. Its spectacular achievement had been in giving a sell signal, at 306, about a month before the 1929 crash and in keeping its followers out of the long bear market until things had pretty well righted themselves, at 84, in 1933. But from 1938 on the Dow theory operated mainly by taking its practitioners out at a pretty good price but then putting them back in again at a higher price. For nearly 30 years thereafter, one would have done appreciably better by just buying and holding the DJIA.[2]

In our view, based on much study of this problem, the change in the Dow-theory results is not accidental. It demonstrates an inherent characteristic of forecasting and trading formulas in the fields of business and finance. Those formulas that gain adherents and

---

* See p. 3.

importance do so because they have worked well over a period, or sometimes merely because they have been plausibly adapted to the statistical record of the past. But as their acceptance increases, their reliability tends to diminish. This happens for two reasons: First, the passage of time brings new conditions which the old formula no longer fits. Second, in stock-market affairs the popularity of a trading theory has itself an influence on the market's behavior which detracts in the long run from its profit-making possibilities. (The popularity of something like the Dow theory may seem to create its own vindication, since it would make the market advance or decline by the very action of its followers when a buying or selling signal is given. A "stampede" of this kind is, of course, much more of a danger than an advantage to the public trader.)

Buy-Low–Sell-High Approach

We are convinced that the average investor cannot deal successfully with price movements by endeavoring to forecast them. Can he benefit from them *after* they have taken place—i.e., by buying after each major decline and selling out after each major advance? The fluctuations of the market over a period of many years prior to 1950 lent considerable encouragement to that idea. In fact, a classic definition of a "shrewd investor" was "one who bought in a bear market when everyone else was selling, and sold out in a bull market when everyone else was buying." If we examine our Chart I, covering the fluctuations of the Standard & Poor's composite index between 1900 and 1970, and the supporting figures in Table 3-1 (p. 66), we can readily see why this viewpoint appeared valid until fairly recent years.

Between 1897 and 1949 there were ten complete market cycles, running from bear-market low to bull-market high and back to bear-market low. Six of these took no longer than four years, four ran for six or seven years, and one—the famous "new-era" cycle of 1921–1932—lasted eleven years. The percentage of advance from the lows to highs ranged from 44% to 500%, with most between about 50% and 100%. The percentage of subsequent declines ranged from 24% to 89%, with most found between 40% and 50%. (It should be remembered that a decline of 50% fully offsets a preceding advance of 100%.)

Nearly all the bull markets had a number of well-defined characteristics in common, such as (1) a historically high price level, (2) high price/earnings ratios, (3) low dividend yields as against bond yields, (4) much speculation on margin, and (5) many offerings of new common-stock issues of poor quality. Thus to the student of stock-market history it appeared that the intelligent investor should have been able to identify the recurrent bear and bull markets, to buy in the former and sell in the latter, and to do so for the most part at reasonably short intervals of time. Various methods were developed for determining buying and selling levels of the general market, based on either value factors or percentage movements of prices or both.

But we must point out that even prior to the unprecedented bull market that began in 1949, there were sufficient variations in the successive market cycles to complicate and sometimes frustrate the desirable process of buying low and selling high. The most notable of these departures, of course, was the great bull market of the late 1920s, which threw all calculations badly out of gear.* Even in 1949, therefore, it was by no means a certainty that the investor could base his financial policies and procedures mainly on the endeavor to buy at low levels in bear markets and to sell out at high levels in bull markets.

It turned out, in the sequel, that the opposite was true. The

---

* Without bear markets to take stock prices back down, anyone waiting to "buy low" will feel completely left behind–and, all too often, will end up abandoning any former caution and jumping in with both feet. That's why Graham's message about the importance of *emotional discipline* is so important. From October 1990 through January 2000, the Dow Jones Industrial Average marched relentlessly upward, never losing more than 20% and suffering a loss of 10% or more only three times. The total gain (not counting dividends): 395.7%. According to Crandall, Pierce & Co., this was the second-longest uninterrupted bull market of the past century; only the 1949–1961 boom lasted longer. The longer a bull market lasts, the more severely investors will be afflicted with amnesia; after five years or so, many people no longer believe that bear markets are even possible. All those who forget are doomed to be reminded; and, in the stock market, recovered memories are always unpleasant.

market's behavior in the past 20 years has not followed the former pattern, nor obeyed what once were well-established danger signals, nor permitted its successful exploitation by applying old rules for buying low and selling high. Whether the old, fairly regular bull-and-bear-market pattern will eventually return we do not know. But it seems unrealistic to us for the investor to endeavor to base his present policy on the classic formula—i.e., to wait for demonstrable bear-market levels before buying *any* common stocks. Our recommended policy has, however, made provision for changes in the *proportion* of common stocks to bonds in the portfolio, if the investor chooses to do so, according as the level of stock prices appears less or more attractive by value standards.*

Formula Plans

In the early years of the stock-market rise that began in 1949–50 considerable interest was attracted to various methods of taking advantage of the stock market's cycles. These have been known as "formula investment plans." The essence of all such plans—except the simple case of dollar averaging—is that the investor automatically does *some* selling of common stocks when the market advances substantially. In many of them a very large rise in the market level would result in the sale of all common-stock holdings; others provided for retention of a minor proportion of equities under all circumstances.

This approach had the double appeal of sounding logical (and conservative) and of showing excellent results when applied retrospectively to the stock market over many years in the past. Unfortunately, its vogue grew greatest at the very time when it was destined to work least well. Many of the "formula planners" found themselves entirely or nearly out of the stock market at some level in the middle 1950s. True, they had realized excellent profits, but in a broad sense the market "ran away" from them thereafter, and

---

* Graham discusses this "recommended policy" in Chapter 4 (pp. 89–91). This policy, now called "tactical asset allocation," is widely followed by institutional investors like pension funds and university endowments.

their formulas gave them little opportunity to buy back a common-stock position.*

There is a similarity between the experience of those adopting the formula-investing approach in the early 1950s and those who embraced the purely mechanical version of the Dow theory some 20 years earlier. In both cases the advent of popularity marked almost the exact moment when the system ceased to work well. We have had a like discomfiting experience with our own "central value method" of determining indicated buying and selling levels of the Dow Jones Industrial Average. The moral seems to be that any approach to moneymaking in the stock market which can be easily described and followed by a lot of people is by its terms too simple and too easy to last.† Spinoza's concluding remark applies to Wall Street as well as to philosophy: "All things excellent are as difficult as they are rare."

Market Fluctuations of the Investor's Portfolio

Every investor who owns common stocks must expect to see them fluctuate in value over the years. The behavior of the DJIA since our last edition was written in 1964 probably reflects pretty well what has happened to the stock portfolio of a conservative investor who limited his stock holdings to those of large, prominent, and conservatively financed corporations. The overall value advanced from an average level of about 890 to a high of 995 in

---

* Many of these "formula planners" would have sold all their stocks at the end of 1954, after the U.S. stock market rose 52.6%, the second-highest yearly return then on record. Over the next five years, these market-timers would likely have stood on the sidelines as stocks doubled.

† Easy ways to make money in the stock market fade for two reasons: the natural tendency of trends to reverse over time, or "regress to the mean," and the rapid adoption of the stock-picking scheme by large numbers of people, who pile in and spoil all the fun of those who got there first. (Note that, in referring to his "discomfiting experience," Graham is—as always—honest in admitting his own failures.) See Jason Zweig, "Murphy Was an Investor," *Money*, July, 2002, pp. 61–62, and Jason Zweig, "New Year's Play," *Money*, December, 2000, pp. 89–90.

1966 (and 985 again in 1968), fell to 631 in 1970, and made an almost full recovery to 940 in early 1971. (Since the individual issues set their high and low marks at different times, the fluctuations in the Dow Jones group as a whole are less severe than those in the separate components.) We have traced through the price fluctuations of other types of diversified and conservative common-stock portfolios and we find that the overall results are not likely to be markedly different from the above. In general, the shares of second-line companies* fluctuate more widely than the major ones, but this does not necessarily mean that a group of well-established but smaller companies will make a poorer showing over a fairly long period. In any case the investor may as well resign himself in advance to the probability rather than the mere possibility that most of his holdings will advance, say, 50% or more from their low point and decline the equivalent one-third or more from their high point at various periods in the next five years.†

A serious investor is not likely to believe that the day-to-day or even month-to-month fluctuations of the stock market make him richer or poorer. But what about the longer-term and wider changes? Here practical questions present themselves, and the psychological problems are likely to grow complicated. A substantial rise in the market is at once a legitimate reason for satisfaction and a cause for prudent concern, but it may also bring a strong temptation toward imprudent action. Your shares have advanced, good!

---

* Today's equivalent of what Graham calls "second-line companies" would be any of the thousands of stocks not included in the Standard & Poor's 500-stock index. A regularly revised list of the 500 stocks in the S & P index is available at www.standardandpoors.com.

† Note carefully what Graham is saying here. It is not just possible, but probable, that most of the stocks you own will gain at least 50% from their lowest price and lose at least 33% from their highest price—regardless of which stocks you own or whether the market as a whole goes up or down. If you can't live with that—or you think your portfolio is somehow magically exempt from it—then you are not yet entitled to call yourself an investor. (Graham refers to a 33% decline as the "equivalent one-third" because a 50% gain takes a $10 stock to $15. From $15, a 33% loss [or $5 drop] takes it right back to $10, where it started.)

You are richer than you were, good! But has the price risen *too* high, and should you think of selling? Or should you kick yourself for not having bought more shares when the level was lower? Or—worst thought of all—should you now give way to the bull-market atmosphere, become infected with the enthusiasm, the overconfidence and the greed of the great public (of which, after all, you are a part), and make larger and dangerous commitments? Presented thus in print, the answer to the last question is a self-evident *no,* but even the intelligent investor is likely to need considerable will power to keep from following the crowd.

It is for these reasons of human nature, even more than by calculation of financial gain or loss, that we favor some kind of mechanical method for varying the proportion of bonds to stocks in the investor's portfolio. The chief advantage, perhaps, is that such a formula will give him *something to do.* As the market advances he will from time to time make sales out of his stockholdings, putting the proceeds into bonds; as it declines he will reverse the procedure. These activities will provide some outlet for his otherwise too-pent-up energies. If he is the right kind of investor he will take added satisfaction from the thought that his operations are exactly opposite from those of the crowd.*

Business Valuations versus Stock-Market Valuations

The impact of market fluctuations upon the investor's true situation may be considered also from the standpoint of the shareholder as the part owner of various businesses. The holder of marketable shares actually has a double status, and with it the privilege of taking advantage of either at his choice. On the one hand his position is analogous to that of a minority shareholder or silent partner in a private business. Here his results are entirely dependent on the profits of the enterprise or on a change in the underlying value of its assets. He would usually determine the value of such a private-business interest by calculating his share of the net worth as shown in the most recent balance sheet. On the

---

* For today's investor, the ideal strategy for pursuing this "formula" is rebalancing, which we discuss on pp. 104–105.

other hand, the common-stock investor holds a piece of paper, an engraved stock certificate, which can be sold in a matter of minutes at a price which varies from moment to moment—when the market is open, that is—and often is far removed from the balance-sheet value.*

The development of the stock market in recent decades has made the typical investor more dependent on the course of price quotations and less free than formerly to consider himself merely a business owner. The reason is that the successful enterprises in which he is likely to concentrate his holdings sell almost constantly at prices well above their net asset value (or book value, or "balance-sheet value"). In paying these market premiums the investor gives precious hostages to fortune, for he must depend on the stock market itself to validate his commitments.†

This is a factor of prime importance in present-day investing, and it has received less attention than it deserves. The whole structure of stock-market quotations contains a built-in contradiction. The better a company's record and prospects, the less relationship the price of its shares will have to their book value. But the greater the premium above book value, the less certain the basis of determining its intrinsic value—i.e., the more this "value" will depend on the changing moods and measurements of the stock market. Thus we reach the final paradox, that the more successful the company, the greater are likely to be the fluctuations in the price of its shares. This really means that, in a very real sense, the better the

---

* Most companies today provide "an engraved stock certificate" only upon special request. Stocks exist, for the most part, in purely electronic form (much as your bank account contains computerized credits and debits, not actual currency) and thus have become even easier to trade than they were in Graham's day.

† Net asset value, book value, balance-sheet value, and tangible-asset value are all synonyms for net worth, or the total value of a company's physical and financial assets minus all its liabilities. It can be calculated using the balance sheets in a company's annual and quarterly reports; from total shareholders' equity, subtract all "soft" assets such as goodwill, trademarks, and other intangibles. Divide by the fully diluted number of shares outstanding to arrive at book value per share.

quality of a common stock, the more *speculative* it is likely to be—at least as compared with the unspectacular middle-grade issues.* (What we have said applies to a comparison of the leading growth companies with the bulk of well-established concerns; we exclude from our purview here those issues which are highly speculative because the businesses themselves are speculative.)

The argument made above should explain the often erratic price behavior of our most successful and impressive enterprises. Our favorite example is the monarch of them all—International Business Machines. The price of its shares fell from 607 to 300 in seven months in 1962–63; after two splits its price fell from 387 to 219 in 1970. Similarly, Xerox—an even more impressive earnings gainer in recent decades—fell from 171 to 87 in 1962–63, and from 116 to 65 in 1970. These striking losses did not indicate any doubt about the future long-term growth of IBM or Xerox; they reflected instead a lack of confidence in the premium valuation that the stock market itself had placed on these excellent prospects.

The previous discussion leads us to a conclusion of practical importance to the conservative investor in common stocks. If he is to pay some special attention to the selection of his portfolio, it might be best for him to concentrate on issues selling at a reasonably close approximation to their tangible-asset value—say, at not more than one-third above that figure. Purchases made at such levels, or lower, may with logic be regarded as related to the

---

* Graham's use of the word "paradox" is probably an allusion to a classic article by David Durand, "Growth Stocks and the Petersburg Paradox," *The Journal of Finance,* vol. XII, no. 3, September, 1957, pp. 348–363, which compares investing in high-priced growth stocks to betting on a series of coin flips in which the payoff escalates with each flip of the coin. Durand points out that if a growth stock could continue to grow at a high rate for an indefinite period of time, an investor should (in theory) be willing to pay an infinite price for its shares. Why, then, has no stock ever sold for a price of infinity dollars per share? Because the higher the assumed future growth rate, and the longer the time period over which it is expected, the wider the margin for error grows, and the higher the cost of even a tiny miscalculation becomes. Graham discusses this problem further in Appendix 4 (p. 570).

company's balance sheet, and as having a justification or support independent of the fluctuating market prices. The premium over book value that may be involved can be considered as a kind of extra fee paid for the advantage of stock-exchange listing and the marketability that goes with it.

A caution is needed here. A stock does not become a sound investment merely because it can be bought at close to its asset value. The investor should demand, in addition, a satisfactory ratio of earnings to price, a sufficiently strong financial position, and the prospect that its earnings will at least be maintained over the years. This may appear like demanding a lot from a modestly priced stock, but the prescription is not hard to fill under all but dangerously high market conditions. Once the investor is willing to forgo brilliant prospects—i.e., better than average expected growth—he will have no difficulty in finding a wide selection of issues meeting these criteria.

In our chapters on the selection of common stocks (Chapters 14 and 15) we shall give data showing that more than half of the DJIA issues met our asset-value criterion at the end of 1970. The most widely held investment of all—American Tel. & Tel.—actually sells below its tangible-asset value as we write. Most of the light-and-power shares, in addition to their other advantages, are now (early 1972) available at prices reasonably close to their asset values.

The investor with a stock portfolio having such book values behind it can take a much more independent and detached view of stock-market fluctuations than those who have paid high multipliers of both earnings and tangible assets. As long as the earning power of his holdings remains satisfactory, he can give as little attention as he pleases to the vagaries of the stock market. More than that, at times he can use these vagaries to play the master game of buying low and selling high.

The A. & P. Example

At this point we shall introduce one of our original examples, which dates back many years but which has a certain fascination for us because it combines so many aspects of corporate and investment experience. It involves the Great Atlantic & Pacific Tea Co. Here is the story:

A. & P. shares were introduced to trading on the "Curb" market, now the American Stock Exchange, in 1929 and sold as high as 494. By 1932 they had declined to 104, although the company's earnings were nearly as large in that generally catastrophic year as previously. In 1936 the range was between 111 and 131. Then in the business recession and bear market of 1938 the shares fell to a new low of 36.

That price was extraordinary. It meant that the preferred and common were together selling for $126 million, although the company had just reported that it held $85 million in cash alone and a working capital (or net current assets) of $134 million. A. & P. was the largest retail enterprise in America, if not in the world, with a continuous and impressive record of large earnings for many years. Yet in 1938 this outstanding business was considered on Wall Street to be worth less than its current assets alone—which means less as a going concern than if it were liquidated. Why? First, because there were threats of special taxes on chain stores; second, because net profits had fallen off in the previous year; and, third, because the general market was depressed. The first of these reasons was an exaggerated and eventually groundless fear; the other two were typical of temporary influences.

Let us assume that the investor had bought A. & P. common in 1937 at, say, 12 times its five-year average earnings, or about 80. We are far from asserting that the ensuing decline to 36 was of no importance to him. He would have been well advised to scrutinize the picture with some care, to see whether he had made any miscalculations. But if the results of his study were reassuring—as they should have been—he was entitled then to disregard the market decline as a temporary vagary of finance, unless he had the funds and the courage to take advantage of it by buying more on the bargain basis offered.

Sequel and Reflections

The following year, 1939, A. & P. shares advanced to 117½, or three times the low price of 1938 and well above the average of 1937. Such a turnabout in the behavior of common stocks is by no means uncommon, but in the case of A. & P. it was more striking than most. In the years after 1949 the grocery chain's shares rose with the general market until in 1961 the split-up stock (10 for 1) reached a high of 70½ which was equivalent to 705 for the 1938 shares.

This price of 70½ was remarkable for the fact it was 30 times the earnings of 1961. Such a price/earnings ratio—which compares with 23 times for the DJIA in that year—must have implied expectations of a brilliant growth in earnings. This optimism had no justification in the company's earnings record in the preceding years, and it proved completely wrong. Instead of advancing rapidly, the course of earnings in the ensuing period was generally downward. The year after the 70½ high the price fell by more than half to 34. But this time the shares did not have the bargain quality that they showed at the low quotation in 1938. After varying sorts of fluctuations the price fell to another low of 21½ in 1970 and 18 in 1972—having reported the first quarterly *deficit* in its history.

We see in this history how wide can be the vicissitudes of a major American enterprise in little more than a single generation, and also with what miscalculations and excesses of optimism and pessimism the public has valued its shares. In 1938 the business was really being given away, with no takers; in 1961 the public was clamoring for the shares at a ridiculously high price. After that came a quick loss of half the market value, and some years later a substantial further decline. In the meantime the company was to turn from an outstanding to a mediocre earnings performer; its profit in the boom-year 1968 was to be less than in 1958; it had paid a series of confusing small stock dividends not warranted by the current additions to surplus; and so forth. A. & P. was a larger company in 1961 and 1972 than in 1938, but not as well-run, not as profitable, and not as attractive.*

There are two chief morals to this story. The first is that the stock market often goes far wrong, and sometimes an alert and coura-

* The more recent history of A & P is no different. At year-end 1999, its share price was $27.875; at year-end 2000, $7.00; a year later, $23.78; at year-end 2002, $8.06. Although some accounting irregularities later came to light at A & P, it defies all logic to believe that the value of a relatively stable business like groceries could fall by three-fourths in one year, triple the next year, then drop by two-thirds the year after that.

geous investor can take advantage of its patent errors. The other is that most businesses change in character and quality over the years, sometimes for the better, perhaps more often for the worse. The investor need not watch his companies' performance like a hawk; but he should give it a good, hard look from time to time.

Let us return to our comparison between the holder of marketable shares and the man with an interest in a private business. We have said that the former has the *option* of considering himself merely as the part owner of the various businesses he has invested in, or as the holder of shares which are salable at any time he wishes at their quoted market price.

But note this important fact: The true investor scarcely ever *is forced to sell* his shares, and at all other times he is free to disregard the current price quotation. He need pay attention to it and act upon it only to the extent that it suits his book, and no more.* Thus the investor who permits himself to be stampeded or unduly worried by unjustified market declines in his holdings is perversely transforming his basic advantage into a basic disadvantage. That man would be better off if his stocks had no market quotation at all, for he would then be spared the mental anguish caused him by *other persons'* mistakes of judgment.†

Incidentally, a widespread situation of this kind actually existed during the dark depression days of 1931–1933. There was then a psychological advantage in owning business interests that had no quoted market. For example, people who owned first mortgages on real estate that continued to pay interest were able to tell themselves that their investments had kept their full value, there being no market quotations to indicate otherwise. On the other hand, many listed corporation bonds of even better quality and greater

---

* "Only to the extent that it suits his book" means "only to the extent that the price is favorable enough to justify selling the stock." In traditional brokerage lingo, the "book" is an investor's ledger of holdings and trades.

† This may well be the single most important paragraph in Graham's entire book. In these 113 words Graham sums up his lifetime of experience. You cannot read these words too often; they are like Kryptonite for bear markets. If you keep them close at hand and let them guide you throughout your investing life, you will survive whatever the markets throw at you.

underlying strength suffered severe shrinkages in their market quotations, thus making their owners believe they were growing distinctly poorer. In reality the owners were better off with the listed securities, despite the low prices of these. For if they had wanted to, or were compelled to, they could at least have sold the issues—possibly to exchange them for even better bargains. Or they could just as logically have ignored the market's action as temporary and basically meaningless. But it is self-deception to tell yourself that you have suffered no shrinkage in value *merely because* your securities have no quoted market at all.

Returning to our A. & P. shareholder in 1938, we assert that as long as he held on to his shares he suffered no loss in their price decline, beyond what his own judgment may have told him was occasioned by a shrinkage in their underlying or intrinsic value. If no such shrinkage had occurred, he had a right to expect that in due course the market quotation would return to the 1937 level or better—as in fact it did the following year. In this respect his position was at least as good as if he had owned an interest in a private business with no quoted market for its shares. For in that case, too, he might or might not have been justified in mentally lopping off part of the cost of his holdings because of the impact of the 1938 recession—depending on what had happened to his company.

Critics of the value approach to stock investment argue that listed common stocks cannot properly be regarded or appraised in the same way as an interest in a similar private enterprise, because the presence of an organized security market "injects into equity ownership the new and extremely important attribute of liquidity." But what this liquidity really means is, first, that the investor has the benefit of the stock market's daily and changing appraisal of his holdings, *for whatever that appraisal may be worth*, and, second, that the investor is able to increase or decrease his investment at the market's daily figure—*if he chooses.* Thus the existence of a quoted market gives the investor *certain options* that he does not have if his security is unquoted. But it does not impose the current quotation on an investor who prefers to take his idea of value from some other source.

Let us close this section with something in the nature of a parable. Imagine that in some private business you own a small share that cost you $1,000. One of your partners, named Mr. Market, is very obliging indeed. Every day he tells you what he thinks your interest is worth and furthermore offers either to buy you out or to sell you an additional interest on that basis. Sometimes his idea of value appears plausible and justified by business developments and prospects as you know them. Often, on the other hand, Mr. Market lets his enthusiasm or his fears run away with him, and the value he proposes seems to you a little short of silly.

If you are a prudent investor or a sensible businessman, will you let Mr. Market's daily communication determine your view of the value of a $1,000 interest in the enterprise? Only in case you agree with him, or in case you want to trade with him. You may be happy to sell out to him when he quotes you a ridiculously high price, and equally happy to buy from him when his price is low. But the rest of the time you will be wiser to form your own ideas of the value of your holdings, based on full reports from the company about its operations and financial position.

The true investor is in that very position when he owns a listed common stock. He can take advantage of the daily market price or leave it alone, as dictated by his own judgment and inclination. He must take cognizance of important price movements, for otherwise his judgment will have nothing to work on. Conceivably they may give him a warning signal which he will do well to heed—this in plain English means that he is to sell his shares *because* the price has gone down, foreboding worse things to come. In our view such signals are misleading at least as often as they are helpful. Basically, price fluctuations have only one significant meaning for the true investor. They provide him with an opportunity to buy wisely when prices fall sharply and to sell wisely when they advance a great deal. At other times he will do better if he forgets about the stock market and pays attention to his dividend returns and to the operating results of his companies.

Summary

The most realistic distinction between the investor and the speculator is found in their attitude toward stock-market movements. The speculator's primary interest lies in anticipating and profiting from market fluctuations. The investor's primary interest lies in acquiring and holding suitable securities at suitable prices. Market movements are important to him in a practical sense, because they alternately create low price levels at which he would be wise to buy and high price levels at which he certainly should refrain from buying and probably would be wise to sell.

It is far from certain that the typical investor should regularly hold off buying until low market levels appear, because this may involve a long wait, very likely the loss of income, and the possible missing of investment opportunities. On the whole it may be better for the investor to do his stock buying whenever he has money to put in stocks, *except* when the general market level is much higher than can be justified by well-established standards of value. If he wants to be shrewd he can look for the ever-present bargain opportunities in individual securities.

Aside from forecasting the movements of the general market, much effort and ability are directed on Wall Street toward selecting stocks or industrial groups that in matter of price will "do better" than the rest over a fairly short period in the future. Logical as this endeavor may seem, we do not believe it is suited to the needs or temperament of the true investor—particularly since he would be competing with a large number of stock-market traders and first-class financial analysts who are trying to do the same thing. As in all other activities that emphasize price movements first and underlying values second, the work of many intelligent minds constantly engaged in this field tends to be self-neutralizing and self-defeating over the years.

The investor with a portfolio of sound stocks should expect their prices to fluctuate and should neither be concerned by sizable declines nor become excited by sizable advances. He should always remember that market quotations are there for his convenience, either to be taken advantage of or to be ignored. He should never buy a stock *because* it has gone up or sell one *because* it has gone down. He would not be far wrong if this motto read more simply: "Never buy a stock immediately after a substantial rise or sell one immediately after a substantial drop."

An Added Consideration

Something should be said about the significance of average market prices as a measure of managerial competence. The shareholder judges whether his own investment has been successful in terms both of dividends received and of the long-range trend of the average market value. The same criteria should logically be applied in testing the effectiveness of a company's management and the soundness of its attitude toward the owners of the business.

This statement may sound like a truism, but it needs to be emphasized. For as yet there is no accepted technique or approach by which management is brought to the bar of market opinion. On the contrary, managements have always insisted that they have no responsibility *of any kind* for what happens to the market value of their shares. It is true, of course, that they are not accountable for those *fluctuations* in price which, as we have been insisting, bear no relationship to underlying conditions and values. But it is only the lack of alertness and intelligence among the rank and file of shareholders that permits this immunity to extend to the entire realm of market quotations, including the permanent establishment of a depreciated and unsatisfactory price level. Good managements produce a good average market price, and bad managements produce bad market prices.*

Fluctuations in Bond Prices

The investor should be aware that even though safety of its principal and interest may be unquestioned, a long-term bond could vary widely in market price in response to changes in interest rates. In Table 8-1 we give data for various years back to 1902 covering yields for high-grade corporate and tax-free issues. As individual illustrations we add the price fluctuations of two representative railroad issues for a similar period. (These are the Atchison, Topeka & Santa Fe general mortgage 4s, due 1995, for generations one of our premier noncallable bond issues, and the Northern Pacific Ry. 3s, due 2047—originally a 150-year maturity!—long a typical Baa-rated bond.)

Because of their inverse relationship the low yields correspond to the high prices and vice versa. The decline in the Northern

---

* Graham has much more to say on what is now known as "corporate governance." See the commentary on Chapter 19.

Pacific 3s in 1940 represented mainly doubts as to the safety of the issue. It is extraordinary that the price recovered to an all-time high in the next few years, and then lost two-thirds of its price chiefly because of the rise in general interest rates. There have been startling variations, as well, in the price of even the highest-grade bonds in the past forty years.

Note that bond prices do not fluctuate in the same (inverse) proportion as the calculated yields, because their fixed maturity value of 100% exerts a moderating influence. However, for very long maturities, as in our Northern Pacific example, prices and yields change at close to the same rate.

Since 1964 record movements *in both directions* have taken place in the high-grade bond market. Taking "prime municipals" (tax-free) as an example, their yield more than doubled, from 3.2% in January 1965 to 7% in June 1970. Their price index declined, correspondingly, from 110.8 to 67.5. In mid-1970 the yields on high-grade long-term bonds were higher than *at any time in the nearly 200 years of this country's economic history.** Twenty-five years earlier, just before our protracted bull market began, bond yields were at their *lowest* point in history; long-term municipals returned as little as 1%, and industrials gave 2.40% compared with the 4½ to 5% formerly considered "normal." Those of us with a long experience on Wall Street had seen Newton's law of "action and reaction, equal and opposite" work itself out repeatedly in the stock market—the most noteworthy example being the rise in the DJIA from 64 in 1921 to 381 in 1929, followed by a record collapse to 41 in 1932. But this time the widest pendulum swings took place in the usually staid and slow-moving array of high-grade bond prices and yields. Moral: Nothing important on Wall Street can be counted on to occur exactly in the same way as it happened before. This repre-

---

* By what Graham called "the rule of opposites," in 2002 the yields on long-term U.S. Treasury bonds hit their *lowest* levels since 1963. Since bond yields move inversely to prices, those low yields meant that prices had risen—making investors most eager to buy just as bonds were at their most expensive and as their future returns were almost guaranteed to be low. This provides another proof of Graham's lesson that the intelligent investor must refuse to make decisions based on market fluctuations.

TABLE 8-1 Fluctuations in Bond Yields, and in Prices of Two Representative Bond Issues, 1902–1970

	Bond Yields			*Bond Prices*	
	S & P AAA Composite	S & P Municipals		A. T. & S. F. 4s, 1995	Nor. Pac. 3s, 2047
1902 low	4.31%	3.11%	1905 high	105½	79
1920 high	6.40	5.28	1920 low	69	49½
1928 low	4.53	3.90	1930 high	105	73
1932 high	5.52	5.27	1932 low	75	46¾
1946 low	2.44	1.45	1936 high	117¼	85¼
1970 high	8.44	7.06	1939–40 low	99½	31½
1971 close	7.14	5.35	1946 high	141	94¾
			1970 low	51	32¾
			1971 close	64	37¼

sents the first half of our favorite dictum: "*The more it changes,* the more it's the same thing."

If it is virtually impossible to make worthwhile predictions about the price movements of stocks, it is completely impossible to do so for bonds.* In the old days, at least, one could often find a useful clue to the coming end of a bull or bear market by studying the prior action of bonds, but no similar clues were given to a coming change in interest rates and bond prices. Hence the investor must choose between long-term and short-term bond investments on the basis chiefly of his personal preferences. If he wants to be certain that the market values will not decrease, his best choices are probably U.S. savings bonds, Series E or H, which were described above, p. 93. Either issue will give him a 5% yield (after the first year), the Series E for up to 5⅚ years, the Series H for up to ten years, with a guaranteed resale value of cost or better.

If the investor wants the 7.5% now available on good long-term corporate bonds, or the 5.3% on tax-free municipals, he must be prepared to see them fluctuate in price. Banks and insurance companies have the privilege of valuing high-rated bonds of this type on the mathematical basis of "amortized cost," which disregards market prices; it would not be a bad idea for the individual investor to do something similar.

The price fluctuations of *convertible* bonds and preferred stocks are the resultant of three different factors: (1) variations in the price of the related common stock, (2) variations in the credit standing of the company, and (3) variations in general interest rates. A good many of the convertible issues have been sold by companies that have credit ratings well below the best.[3] Some of these were badly affected by the financial squeeze in 1970. As a result, convertible issues as a whole have been subjected to triply unsettling influences in recent years, and price variations have been unusually wide. In the typical case, therefore, the investor would delude himself if he expected to find in convertible issues that ideal combination of the safety of a high-grade bond and price

---

* An updated analysis for today's readers, explaining recent yields and the wider variety of bonds and bond funds available today, can be found in the commentary on Chapter 4.

protection plus a chance to benefit from an advance in the price of the common.

This may be a good place to make a suggestion about the "long-term bond of the future." Why should not the effects of changing interest rates be divided on some practical and equitable basis between the borrower and the lender? One possibility would be to sell long-term bonds with interest payments that vary with an appropriate index of the going rate. The main results of such an arrangement would be: (1) the investor's bond would always have a principal value of about 100, if the company maintains its credit rating, but the interest received will vary, say, with the rate offered on conventional new issues; (2) the corporation would have the advantages of long-term debt—being spared problems and costs of frequent renewals of refinancing—but its interest costs would change from year to year.[4]

Over the past decade the bond investor has been confronted by an increasingly serious dilemma: Shall he choose complete stability of principal value, but with varying and usually low (short-term) interest rates? Or shall he choose a fixed-interest income, with considerable variations (usually downward, it seems) in his principal value? It would be good for most investors if they could compromise between these extremes, and be assured that neither their interest return nor their principal value will fall below a stated minimum over, say, a 20-year period. This could be arranged, without great difficulty, in an appropriate bond contract of a new form. Important note: In effect the U.S. government has done a similar thing in its combination of the original savings-bonds contracts with their extensions at higher interest rates. The suggestion we make here would cover a longer fixed investment period than the savings bonds, and would introduce more flexibility in the interest-rate provisions.*

It is hardly worthwhile to talk about nonconvertible preferred stocks, since their special tax status makes the safe ones much more desirable holdings by corporations—e.g., insurance companies—

---

* As mentioned in the commentary on Chapters 2 and 4, Treasury Inflation-Protected Securities, or TIPS, are a new and improved version of what Graham is suggesting here.

than by individuals. The poorer-quality ones almost always fluctuate over a wide range, percentagewise, not too differently from common stocks. We can offer no other useful remark about them. Table 16-2 below, p. 406, gives some information on the price changes of lower-grade nonconvertible preferreds between December 1968 and December 1970. The average decline was 17%, against 11.3% for the S & P composite index of common stocks.

COMMENTARY ON CHAPTER 8

> The happiness of those who want to be popular depends on others; the happiness of those who seek pleasure fluctuates with moods outside their control; but the happiness of the wise grows out of their own free acts.
>
> *—Marcus Aurelius*

DR. JEKYLL AND MR. MARKET

Most of the time, the market is mostly accurate in pricing most stocks. Millions of buyers and sellers haggling over price do a remarkably good job of valuing companies—on average. But sometimes, the price is not right; occasionally, it is very wrong indeed. And at such times, you need to understand Graham's image of Mr. Market, probably the most brilliant metaphor ever created for explaining how stocks can become mispriced.[1] The manic-depressive Mr. Market does not always price stocks the way an appraiser or a private buyer would value a business. Instead, when stocks are going up, he happily pays more than their objective value; and, when they are going down, he is desperate to dump them for less than their true worth.

Is Mr. Market still around? Is he still bipolar? You bet he is.

On March 17, 2000, the stock of Inktomi Corp. hit a new high of $231.625. Since they first came on the market in June 1998, shares in the Internet-searching software company had gained roughly 1,900%. Just in the few weeks since December 1999, the stock had nearly tripled.

What was going on at Inktomi the business that could make Inktomi the stock so valuable? The answer seems obvious: phenomenally fast

---

[1] See Graham's text, pp. 204–205.

growth. In the three months ending in December 1999, Inktomi sold $36 million in products and services, more than it had in the entire year ending in December 1998. If Inktomi could sustain its growth rate of the previous 12 months for just five more years, its revenues would explode from $36 million a quarter to $5 billion a month. With such growth in sight, the faster the stock went up, the farther up it seemed certain to go.

But in his wild love affair with Inktomi's stock, Mr. Market was overlooking something about its business. The company was losing money–lots of it. It had lost $6 million in the most recent quarter, $24 million in the 12 months before that, and $24 million in the year before that. In its entire corporate lifetime, Inktomi had never made a dime in profits. Yet, on March 17, 2000, Mr. Market valued this tiny business at a total of $25 billion. (Yes, that's *billion,* with a *B.*)

And then Mr. Market went into a sudden, nightmarish depression. On September 30, 2002, just two and a half years after hitting $231.625 per share, Inktomi's stock closed at 25 cents–collapsing from a total market value of $25 billion to less than $40 million. Had Inktomi's business dried up? Not at all; over the previous 12 months, the company had generated $113 million in revenues. So what had changed? Only Mr. Market's mood: In early 2000, investors were so wild about the Internet that they priced Inktomi's shares at 250 times the company's revenues. Now, however, they would pay only 0.35 times its revenues. Mr. Market had morphed from Dr. Jekyll to Mr. Hyde and was ferociously trashing every stock that had made a fool out of him.

But Mr. Market was no more justified in his midnight rage than he had been in his manic euphoria. On December 23, 2002, Yahoo! Inc. announced that it would buy Inktomi for $1.65 per share. That was nearly seven times Inktomi's stock price on September 30. History will probably show that Yahoo! got a bargain. When Mr. Market makes stocks so cheap, it's no wonder that entire companies get bought right out from under him.[2]

---

[2] As Graham noted in a classic series of articles in 1932, the Great Depression caused the shares of dozens of companies to drop below the value of their cash and other liquid assets, making them "worth more dead than alive."

THINK FOR YOURSELF

Would you willingly allow a certifiable lunatic to come by at least five times a week to tell you that you should feel exactly the way he feels? Would you ever agree to be euphoric just because he is—or miserable just because he thinks you should be? Of course not. You'd insist on your right to take control of your own emotional life, based on your experiences and your beliefs. But, when it comes to their financial lives, millions of people let Mr. Market tell them how to feel and what to do—despite the obvious fact that, from time to time, he can get nuttier than a fruitcake.

In 1999, when Mr. Market was squealing with delight, American employees directed an average of 8.6% of their paychecks into their 401(k) retirement plans. By 2002, after Mr. Market had spent three years stuffing stocks into black garbage bags, the average contribution rate had dropped by nearly one-quarter, to just 7%.[3] The cheaper stocks got, the less eager people became to buy them—because they were imitating Mr. Market, instead of thinking for themselves.

The intelligent investor shouldn't ignore Mr. Market entirely. Instead, you should do business with him—but only to the extent that it serves your interests. Mr. Market's job is to provide you with prices; your job is to decide whether it is to your advantage to act on them. *You do not have to trade with him just because he constantly begs you to.*

By refusing to let Mr. Market be your master, you transform him into your servant. After all, even when he seems to be destroying values, he is creating them elsewhere. In 1999, the Wilshire 5000 index—the broadest measure of U.S. stock performance—gained 23.8%, powered by technology and telecommunications stocks. But 3,743 of the 7,234 stocks in the Wilshire index went down in value even as the average was rising. While those high-tech and telecom stocks were hotter than the hood of a race car on an August afternoon, thousands of "Old Economy" shares were frozen in the mud—getting cheaper and cheaper.

The stock of CMGI, an "incubator" or holding company for Internet

---

[3] News release, The Spectrem Group, "Plan Sponsors Are Losing the Battle to Prevent Declining Participation and Deferrals into Defined Contribution Plans," October 25, 2002.

FIGURE 8-1 From Stinkers to Stars

Company	Business	Total Return				Final value of $1,000 invested
		1999	2000	2001	2002	1/1/1999
Angelica	industrial uniforms	–43.7	1.8	19.3	94.1	1,328
Ball Corp.	metal & plastic packaging	–12.7	19.2	55.3	46.0	2,359
Checkers Drive-In Restaurants	fast food	–45.5	63.9	66.2	2.1	1,517
Family Dollar Stores	discount retailer	–25.1	33.0	41.1	5.0	1,476
International Game Technology	gambling equipment	–16.3	136.1	42.3	11.2	3,127
J B Hunt Transportation	trucking	–39.1	21.9	38.0	26.3	1,294
Jos. A. Bank Clothiers	apparel	–62.5	50.0	57.1	201.6	2,665
Lockheed Martin	defense & aerospace	–46.9	58.0	39.0	24.7	1,453
Pier 1 Imports	home furnishings	–33.2	63.9	70.5	10.3	2,059
UST Inc.	snuff tobacco	–23.5	21.6	32.2	1.0	1,241
Wilshire Internet Index		139.1	–55.5	–46.2	–45.0	315
Wilshire 5000 index (total stock market)		23.8	–10.9	–11.0	–20.8	778

Sources: Aronson + Johnson + Ortiz, L.P.; www.wilshire.com

start-up firms, went up an astonishing 939.9% in 1999. Meanwhile, Berkshire Hathaway–the holding company through which Graham's greatest disciple, Warren Buffett, owns such Old Economy stalwarts as Coca-Cola, Gillette, and the Washington Post Co.–dropped by 24.9%.[4]

But then, as it so often does, the market had a sudden mood swing. Figure 8-1 offers a sampling of how the stinkers of 1999 became the stars of 2000 through 2002.

As for those two holding companies, CMGI went on to lose 96% in 2000, another 70.9% in 2001, and still 39.8% more in 2002–a cumulative loss of 99.3%. Berkshire Hathaway went up 26.6% in 2000 and 6.5% in 2001, then had a slight 3.8% loss in 2002–a cumulative gain of 30%.

CAN YOU BEAT THE PROS AT THEIR OWN GAME?

One of Graham's most powerful insights is this: "The investor who permits himself to be stampeded or unduly worried by unjustified market declines in his holdings is perversely transforming his basic advantage into a basic disadvantage."

What does Graham mean by those words "basic advantage"? He means that the intelligent individual investor has the full freedom to choose whether or not to follow Mr. Market. You have the luxury of being able to think for yourself.[5]

---

[4] A few months later, on March 10, 2000–the very day that NASDAQ hit its all-time high–online trading pundit James J. Cramer wrote that he had "repeatedly" been tempted in recent days to sell Berkshire Hathaway short, a bet that Buffett's stock had farther to fall. With a vulgar thrust of his rhetorical pelvis, Cramer even declared that Berkshire's shares were "ripe for the banging." That same day, market strategist Ralph Acampora of Prudential Securities asked, "Norfolk Southern or Cisco Systems: Where do you want to be in the future?" Cisco, a key to tomorrow's Internet superhighway, seemed to have it all over Norfolk Southern, part of yesterday's railroad system. (Over the next year, Norfolk Southern gained 35%, while Cisco lost 70%.)

[5] When asked what keeps most individual investors from succeeding, Graham had a concise answer: "The primary cause of failure is that they pay too much attention to what the stock market is doing currently." See "Benjamin Graham: Thoughts on Security Analysis" [transcript of lecture at Northeast Missouri State University Business School, March, 1972], *Financial History* magazine, no. 42, March, 1991, p. 8.

The typical money manager, however, has no choice but to mimic Mr. Market's every move—buying high, selling low, marching almost mindlessly in his erratic footsteps. Here are some of the handicaps mutual-fund managers and other professional investors are saddled with:

- With billions of dollars under management, they must gravitate toward the biggest stocks—the only ones they can buy in the multimillion-dollar quantities they need to fill their portfolios. Thus many funds end up owning the same few overpriced giants.
- Investors tend to pour more money into funds as the market rises. The managers use that new cash to buy more of the stocks they already own, driving prices to even more dangerous heights.
- If fund investors ask for their money back when the market drops, the managers may need to sell stocks to cash them out. Just as the funds are forced to buy stocks at inflated prices in a rising market, they become forced sellers as stocks get cheap again.
- Many portfolio managers get bonuses for beating the market, so they obsessively measure their returns against benchmarks like the S & P 500 index. If a company gets added to an index, hundreds of funds compulsively buy it. (If they don't, and that stock then does well, the managers look foolish; on the other hand, if they buy it and it does poorly, no one will blame them.)
- Increasingly, fund managers are expected to specialize. Just as in medicine the general practitioner has given way to the pediatric allergist and the geriatric otolaryngologist, fund managers must buy only "small growth" stocks, or only "mid-sized value" stocks, or nothing but "large blend" stocks.[6] If a company gets too big, or too small, or too cheap, or an itty bit too expensive, the fund has to sell it—even if the manager loves the stock.

So there's no reason you can't do as well as the pros. What you cannot do (despite all the pundits who say you can) is to "beat the pros at their own game." *The pros can't even win their own game!* Why should you want to play it at all? If you follow their rules, you will lose—since you will end up as much a slave to Mr. Market as the professionals are.

---

[6] Never mind what these terms mean, or are supposed to mean. While in public these classifications are treated with the utmost respect, in private most people in the investment business regard them with the contempt normally reserved for jokes that aren't funny.

Instead, recognize that investing intelligently is about controlling the controllable. You can't control whether the stocks or funds you buy will outperform the market today, next week, this month, or this year; in the short run, your returns will always be hostage to Mr. Market and his whims. But you *can* control:

- **your brokerage costs,** by trading rarely, patiently, and cheaply
- **your ownership costs,** by refusing to buy mutual funds with excessive annual expenses
- **your expectations,** by using realism, not fantasy, to forecast your returns[7]
- **your risk,** by deciding how much of your total assets to put at hazard in the stock market, by diversifying, and by rebalancing
- **your tax bills,** by holding stocks for at least one year and, whenever possible, for at least five years, to lower your capital-gains liability
- and, most of all, **your own behavior.**

If you listen to financial TV, or read most market columnists, you'd think that investing is some kind of sport, or a war, or a struggle for survival in a hostile wilderness. *But investing isn't about beating others at their game. It's about controlling yourself at your own game.* The challenge for the intelligent investor is not to find the stocks that will go up the most and down the least, but rather to prevent yourself from being your own worst enemy–from buying high just because Mr. Market says "Buy!" and from selling low just because Mr. Market says "Sell!"

If you investment horizon is long–at least 25 or 30 years–there is only one sensible approach: Buy every month, automatically, and whenever else you can spare some money. The single best choice for this lifelong holding is a total stock-market index fund. Sell only when you need the cash (for a psychological boost, clip out and sign your "Investment Owner's Contract"–which you can find on p. 225).

To be an intelligent investor, you must also refuse to judge your financial success by how a bunch of total strangers are doing. You're not one penny poorer if someone in Dubuque or Dallas or Denver

---

[7] See the brilliant column by Walter Updegrave, "Keep It Real," *Money,* February, 2002, pp. 53–56.

beats the S & P 500 and you don't. No one's gravestone reads "HE BEAT THE MARKET."

I once interviewed a group of retirees in Boca Raton, one of Florida's wealthiest retirement communities. I asked these people–mostly in their seventies–if they had beaten the market over their investing lifetimes. Some said yes, some said no; most weren't sure. Then one man said, "Who cares? All I know is, my investments earned enough for me to end up in Boca."

Could there be a more perfect answer? After all, the whole point of investing is not to earn more money than average, but to earn enough money to meet your own needs. The best way to measure your investing success is not by whether you're beating the market but by whether you've put in place a financial plan and a behavioral discipline that are likely to get you where you want to go. In the end, what matters isn't crossing the finish line before anybody else but just making sure that you do cross it.[8]

YOUR MONEY AND YOUR BRAIN

Why, then, do investors find Mr. Market so seductive? It turns out that our brains are hardwired to get us into investing trouble; humans are pattern-seeking animals. Psychologists have shown that if you present people with a random sequence–and tell them that it's unpredictable–they will nevertheless insist on trying to guess what's coming next. Likewise, we "know" that the next roll of the dice will be a seven, that a baseball player is due for a base hit, that the next winning number in the Powerball lottery will definitely be 4-27-9-16-42-10–and that this hot little stock is the next Microsoft.

Groundbreaking new research in neuroscience shows that our brains are designed to perceive trends even where they might not exist. After an event occurs just two or three times in a row, regions of the human brain called the anterior cingulate and nucleus accumbens automatically anticipate that it will happen again. If it does repeat, a natural chemical called dopamine is released, flooding your brain with a soft euphoria. Thus, if a stock goes up a few times in a row, you reflexively expect it to keep going–and your brain chemistry changes

---

[8] See Jason Zweig, "Did You Beat the Market?" *Money,* January, 2000, pp. 55–58.

as the stock rises, giving you a "natural high." You effectively become addicted to your own predictions.

But when stocks drop, that financial loss fires up your amygdala–the part of the brain that processes fear and anxiety and generates the famous "fight or flight" response that is common to all cornered animals. Just as you can't keep your heart rate from rising if a fire alarm goes off, just as you can't avoid flinching if a rattlesnake slithers onto your hiking path, you can't help feeling fearful when stock prices are plunging.[9]

In fact, the brilliant psychologists Daniel Kahneman and Amos Tversky have shown that the pain of financial loss is more than twice as intense as the pleasure of an equivalent gain. Making $1,000 on a stock feels great–but a $1,000 loss wields an emotional wallop more than twice as powerful. Losing money is so painful that many people, terrified at the prospect of any further loss, sell out near the bottom or refuse to buy more.

That helps explain why we fixate on the raw magnitude of a market decline and forget to put the loss in proportion. So, if a TV reporter hollers, "The market is *plunging*–the Dow is down *100 points!*" most people instinctively shudder. But, at the Dow's recent level of 8,000, that's a drop of just 1.2%. Now think how ridiculous it would sound if, on a day when it's 81 degrees outside, the TV weatherman shrieked, "The temperature is *plunging*–it's dropped from *81 degrees* to *80 degrees!*" That, too, is a 1.2% drop. When you forget to view changing market prices in percentage terms, it's all too easy to panic over minor vibrations. (If you have decades of investing ahead of you, there's a better way to visualize the financial news broadcasts; see the sidebar on p. 222.)

In the late 1990s, many people came to feel that they were in the dark unless they checked the prices of their stocks several times a day. But, as Graham puts it, the typical investor "would be better off if his stocks had no market quotation at all, for he would then be spared the mental anguish caused him by *other persons'* mistakes of judg-

---

[9] The neuroscience of investing is explored in Jason Zweig, "Are You Wired for Wealth?" *Money,* October, 2002, pp. 74–83, also available at http://money.cnn.com/2002/09/25/pf/investing/agenda_brain _short/index.htm. See also Jason Zweig, "The Trouble with Humans," *Money,* November, 2000, pp. 67–70.

NEWS YOU COULD USE

Stocks are crashing, so you turn on the television to catch the latest market news. But instead of CNBC or CNN, imagine that you can tune in to the Benjamin Graham Financial Network. On BGFN, the audio doesn't capture that famous sour clang of the market's closing bell; the video doesn't home in on brokers scurrying across the floor of the stock exchange like angry rodents. Nor does BGFN run any footage of investors gasping on frozen sidewalks as red arrows whiz overhead on electronic stock tickers.

Instead, the image that fills your TV screen is the facade of the New York Stock Exchange, festooned with a huge banner reading: "SALE! 50% OFF!" As intro music, Bachman-Turner Overdrive can be heard blaring a few bars of their old barnburner, "You Ain't Seen Nothin' Yet." Then the anchorman announces brightly, "Stocks became more attractive *yet again* today, as the Dow dropped *another* 2.5% on heavy volume—the *fourth day in a row* that stocks have gotten *cheaper.* Tech investors fared *even better,* as leading companies like Microsoft *lost nearly 5% on the day,* making them *even more affordable.* That comes on *top* of the *good* news of the past year, in which stocks have *already* lost *50%,* putting them at *bargain* levels not seen in *years.* And *some* prominent analysts are *optimistic* that prices may drop *still further* in the weeks and months to come."

The newscast cuts over to market strategist Ignatz Anderson of the Wall Street firm of Ketchum & Skinner, who says, "My forecast is for stocks to lose *another 15%* by June. I'm cautiously *optimistic* that if *everything goes well,* stocks could lose *25%,* maybe *more.*"

"Let's hope Ignatz Anderson is *right,*" the anchor says cheerily. "*Falling* stock prices would be *fabulous* news for *any* investor with a very long *horizon.* And now over to *Wally Wood* for our *exclusive* AccuWeather forecast."

ment." If, after checking the value of your stock portfolio at 1:24 P.M., you feel compelled to check it all over again at 1:37 P.M., ask yourself these questions:

- Did I call a real-estate agent to check the market price of my house at 1:24 P.M.? Did I call back at 1:37 P.M.?
- If I had, would the price have changed? If it did, would I have rushed to sell my house?
- By not checking, or even knowing, the market price of my house from minute to minute, do I prevent its value from rising over time?[10]

The only possible answer to these questions is *of course not!* And you should view your portfolio the same way. Over a 10- or 20- or 30-year investment horizon, Mr. Market's daily dipsy-doodles simply do not matter. In any case, for anyone who will be investing for years to come, falling stock prices are good news, not bad, since they enable you to buy more for less money. The longer and further stocks fall, and the more steadily you keep buying as they drop, the more money you will make in the end–*if* you remain steadfast until the end. Instead of fearing a bear market, you should embrace it. The intelligent investor should be perfectly comfortable owning a stock or mutual fund even if the stock market stopped supplying daily prices for the next 10 years.[11]

Paradoxically, "you will be much more in control," explains neuroscientist Antonio Damasio, "if you realize how much you are not in control." By acknowledging your biological tendency to buy high and sell low, you can admit the need to dollar-cost average, rebalance, and sign an investment contract. By putting much of your portfolio on permanent autopilot, you can fight the prediction addiction, focus on your long-term financial goals, and tune out Mr. Market's mood swings.

---

[10] It's also worth asking whether you could enjoy living in your house if its market price was reported to the last penny every day in the newspapers and on TV.

[11] In a series of remarkable experiments in the late 1980s, a psychologist at Columbia and Harvard, Paul Andreassen, showed that investors who received frequent news updates on their stocks earned half the returns of investors who got no news at all. See Jason Zweig, "Here's How to Use the News and Tune Out the Noise," *Money*, July, 1998, pp. 63–64.

WHEN MR. MARKET GIVES YOU LEMONS, MAKE LEMONADE

Although Graham teaches that you should buy when Mr. Market is yelling "sell," there's one exception the intelligent investor needs to understand. Selling into a bear market can make sense if it creates a tax windfall. The U.S. Internal Revenue Code allows you to use your realized losses (any declines in value that you lock in by selling your shares) to offset up to $3,000 in ordinary income.[12] Let's say you bought 200 shares of Coca-Cola stock in January 2000 for $60 a share–a total investment of $12,000. By year-end 2002, the stock was down to $44 a share, or $8,800 for your lot–a loss of $3,200.

You could have done what most people do–either whine about your loss, or sweep it under the rug and pretend it never happened. Or you could have taken control. Before 2002 ended, you could have sold all your Coke shares, locking in the $3,200 loss. Then, after waiting 31 days to comply with IRS rules, you would buy 200 shares of Coke all over again. The result: You would be able to reduce your taxable income by $3,000 in 2002, and you could use the remaining $200 loss to offset your income in 2003. And better yet, you would still own a company whose future you believe in–but now you would own it for almost one-third less than you paid the first time.[13]

With Uncle Sam subsidizing your losses, it can make sense to sell and lock in a loss. If Uncle Sam wants to make Mr. Market look logical by comparison, who are we to complain?

---

[12] Federal tax law is subject to constant change. The example of Coca-Cola stock given here is valid under the provisions of the U.S. tax code as it stood in early 2003.

[13] This example assumes that the investor had no realized capital gains in 2002 and did not reinvest any Coke dividends. Tax swaps are not to be undertaken lightly, since they can be mishandled easily. Before doing a tax swap, read IRS Publication 550 (www.irs.gov/pub/irspdf/p550.pdf). A good guide to managing your investment taxes is Robert N. Gordon with Jan M. Rosen, *Wall Street Secrets for Tax-Efficient Investing* (Bloomberg Press, Princeton, New Jersey, 2001). Finally, before you pull the trigger, consult a professional tax adviser.

INVESTMENT OWNER'S CONTRACT

I, ___________ ________________, hereby state that I am an investor who is seeking to accumulate wealth for many years into the future.

I know that there will be many times when I will be tempted to invest in stocks or bonds because they have gone (or "are going") up in price, and other times when I will be tempted to sell my investments because they have gone (or "are going") down.

I hereby declare my refusal to let a herd of strangers make my financial decisions for me. I further make a solemn commitment never to invest because the stock market has gone up, and never to sell because it has gone down. Instead, I will invest $_____.00 per month, every month, through an automatic investment plan or "dollar-cost averaging program," into the following mutual fund(s) or diversified portfolio(s):

____________________________,

____________________________,

____________________________.

I will also invest additional amounts whenever I can afford to spare the cash (and can afford to lose it in the short run).

I hereby declare that I will hold each of these investments continually through at least the following date (which must be a minimum of 10 years after the date of this contact): ______________ _____, 20__. The only exceptions allowed under the terms of this contract are a sudden, pressing need for cash, like a health-care emergency or the loss of my job, or a planned expenditure like a housing down payment or a tuition bill.

I am, by signing below, stating my intention not only to abide by the terms of this contract, but to re-read this document whenever I am tempted to sell any of my investments.

This contract is valid only when signed by at least one witness, and must be kept in a safe place that is easily accessible for future reference.

Signed: Date:

___________ ________________ _____________ ____, 20__

Witnesses:

___________ ________________

___________ ________________

CHAPTER 9

Investing in Investment Funds

One course open to the defensive investor is to put his money into investment-company shares. Those that are redeemable on demand by the holder, at net asset value, are commonly known as "mutual funds" (or "open-end funds"). Most of these are actively selling additional shares through a corps of salesmen. Those with nonredeemable shares are called "closed-end" companies or funds; the number of their shares remains relatively constant. All of the funds of any importance are registered with the Securities & Exchange Commission (SEC), and are subject to its regulations and controls.*

The industry is a very large one. At the end of 1970 there were 383 funds registered with the SEC, having assets totaling $54.6 billions. Of these 356 companies, with $50.6 billions, were mutual funds, and 27 companies with $4.0 billions, were closed-end.†

There are different ways of classifying the funds. One is by the broad division of their portfolio; they are "balanced funds" if they have a significant (generally about one-third) component of bonds, or "stock-funds" if their holdings are nearly all common stocks. (There are some other varieties here, such as "bond funds," "hedge

---

* It is a violation of Federal law for an open-end mutual fund, a closed-end fund, or an exchange-traded fund to sell shares to the public unless it has "registered" (or made mandatory financial filings) with the SEC.

† The fund industry has gone from "very large" to immense. At year-end 2002, there were 8,279 mutual funds holding $6.56 trillion; 514 closed-end funds with $149.6 billion in assets; and 116 exchange-trade funds or ETFs with $109.7 billion. These figures exclude such fund-like investments as variable annuities and unit investment trusts.

funds," "letter-stock funds," etc.)* Another is by their objectives, as their primary aim is for income, price stability, or capital appreciation ("growth"). Another distinction is by their method of sale. "Load funds" add a selling charge (generally about 9% of asset value on minimum purchases) to the value before charge.[1] Others, known as "no-load" funds, make no such charge; the managements are content with the usual investment-counsel fees for handling the capital. Since they cannot pay salesmen's commissions, the size of the no-load funds tends to be on the low side.† The buying and selling prices of the *closed-end* funds are not fixed by the companies, but fluctuate in the open market as does the ordinary corporate stock.

Most of the companies operate under special provisions of the income-tax law, designed to relieve the shareholders from double taxation on their earnings. In effect, the funds must pay out virtually all their ordinary income—i.e., dividends and interest received, less expenses. In addition they can pay out their realized long-term profits on sales of investments—in the form of "capital-gains dividends"—which are treated by the shareholder as if they were his own security profits. (There is another option here, which we omit to avoid clutter.)‡ Nearly all the funds have but one class

---

* Lists of the major types of mutual funds can be found at www.ici.org/pdf/g2understanding.pdf and http://news.morningstar.com/fundReturns/CategoryReturns.html. Letter-stock funds no longer exist, while hedge funds are generally banned by SEC rules from selling shares to any investor whose annual income is below $200,000 or whose net worth is below $1 million.

† Today, the maximum sales load on a stock fund tends to be around 5.75%. If you invest $10,000 in a fund with a flat 5.75% sales load, $575 will go to the person (and brokerage firm) that sold it to you, leaving you with an initial net investment of $9,425. The $575 sales charge is actually 6.1% of that amount, which is why Graham calls the standard way of calculating the charge a "sales gimmick." Since the 1980s, no-load funds have become popular, and they no longer tend to be smaller than load funds.

‡ Nearly every mutual fund today is taxed as a "regulated investment company," or RIC, which is exempt from corporate income tax so long as it pays out essentially all of its income to its shareholders. In the "option" that

of security outstanding. A new wrinkle, introduced in 1967, divides the capitalization into a preferred issue, which will receive all the ordinary income, and a capital issue, or common stock, which will receive all the profits on security sales. (These are called "dual-purpose funds.")*

Many of the companies that state their primary aim is for capital gains concentrate on the purchase of the so-called "growth stocks," and they often have the word "growth" in their name. Some specialize in a designated area such as chemicals, aviation, overseas investments; this is usually indicated in their titles.

The investor who wants to make an intelligent commitment in fund shares has thus a large and somewhat bewildering variety of choices before him—not too different from those offered in direct investment. In this chapter we shall deal with some major questions, viz:

1. Is there any way by which the investor can assure himself of better than average results by choosing the right funds? (Subquestion: What about the "performance funds"?)†

2. If not, how can he avoid choosing funds that will give him worse than average results?

3. Can he make intelligent choices between different types of funds—e.g., balanced versus all-stock, open-end versus closed-end, load versus no-load?

Graham omits "to avoid clutter," a fund can ask the SEC for special permission to distribute one of its holdings directly to the fund's shareholders–as his Graham-Newman Corp. did in 1948, parceling out shares in GEICO to Graham-Newman's own investors. This sort of distribution is extraordinarily rare.

* Dual-purpose funds, popular in the late 1980s, have essentially disappeared from the marketplace–a shame, since they offered investors a more flexible way to take advantage of the skills of great stock pickers like John Neff. Perhaps the recent bear market will lead to a renaissance of this attractive investment vehicle.

† "Performance funds" were all the rage in the late 1960s. They were equivalent to the aggressive growth funds of the late 1990s, and served their investors no better.

Investment-Fund Performance as a Whole

Before trying to answer these questions we should say something about the performance of the fund industry as a whole. Has it done a good job for its shareholders? In the most general way, how have fund investors fared as against those who made their investments directly? We are quite certain that the funds in the aggregate have served a useful purpose. They have promoted good habits of savings and investment; they have protected countless individuals against costly mistakes in the stock market; they have brought their participants income and profits commensurate with the overall returns from common stocks. On a comparative basis we would hazard the guess that the average individual who put his money exclusively in investment-fund shares in the past ten years has fared better than the average person who made his common-stock purchases directly.

The last point is probably true even though the actual performance of the funds seems to have been no better than that of common stocks as a whole, and even though the cost of investing in mutual funds may have been greater than that of direct purchases. The real choice of the average individual has not been between constructing and acquiring a well-balanced common-stock portfolio or doing the same thing, a bit more expensively, by buying into the funds. More likely his choice has been between succumbing to the wiles of the doorbell-ringing mutual-fund salesman on the one hand, as against succumbing to the even wilier and much more dangerous peddlers of second- and third-rate new offerings. We cannot help thinking, too, that the average individual who opens a brokerage account with the idea of making conservative common-stock investments is likely to find himself beset by untoward influences in the direction of speculation and speculative losses; these temptations should be much less for the mutual-fund buyer.

But how have the investment funds performed as against the general market? This is a somewhat controversial subject, but we shall try to deal with it in simple but adequate fashion. Table 9-1 gives some calculated results for 1961–1970 of our ten largest stock funds at the end of 1970, but choosing only the largest one from each management group. It summarizes the overall return of each of these funds for 1961–1965, 1966–1970, and for the single years

TABLE 9-1 Management Results of Ten Large Mutual Funds[a]

	(Indicated) 5 years, 1961–1965 (all +)	*5 years, 1966–1970*	*10 years, 1961–1970 (all +)*	*1969*	*1970*	*Net Assets, December 1970 (millions)*
Affiliated Fund	71%	+19.7%	105.3%	–14.3%	+2.2%	$1,600
Dreyfus	97	+18.7	135.4	–11.9	–6.4	2,232
Fidelity Fund	79	+31.8	137.1	–7.4	+2.2	819
Fundamental Inv.	79	+ 1.0	81.3	–12.7	–5.8	1,054
Invest. Co. of Am.	82	+37.9	152.2	–10.6	+2.3	1,168
Investors Stock Fund	54	+ 5.6	63.5	–80.0	–7.2	2,227
Mass. Inv. Trust	18	+16.2	44.2	– 4.0	+0.6	1,956
National Investors	61	+31.7	112.2	+ 4.0	–9.1	747
Putnam Growth	62	+22.3	104.0	–13.3	–3.8	684
United Accum.	74	– 2.0	72.7	–10.3	–2.9	1,141
Average	72	18.3	105.8	– 8.9	–2.2	$13,628 (total)
Standard & Poor's composite index	77	+16.1	104.7	– 8.3	+3.5	
DJIA	78	+ 2.9	83.0	–11.6	+8.7	

[a] These are the stock funds with the largest net assets at the end of 1970, but using only one fund from each management group. Data supplied by Wiesenberger Financial Services.

1969 and 1970. We also give average results based on the sum of one share of each of the ten funds. These companies had combined assets of over $15 billion at the end of 1969, or about one-third of all the common-stock funds. Thus they should be fairly representative of the industry as a whole. (In theory, there should be a bias in this list on the side of better than industry performance, since these better companies should have been entitled to more rapid expansion than the others; but this may not be the case in practice.)

Some interesting facts can be gathered from this table. First, we find that the overall results of these ten funds for 1961–1970 were not appreciably different from those of the Standard & Poor's 500-stock composite average (or the S & P 425-industrial stock average). But they were definitely better than those of the DJIA. (This raises the intriguing question as to why the 30 giants in the DJIA did worse than the much more numerous and apparently rather miscellaneous list used by Standard & Poor's.)* A second point is that the funds' aggregate performance as against the S & P index has improved somewhat in the last five years, compared with the preceding five. The funds' gain ran a little lower than S & P's in 1961–1965 and a little higher than S & P's in 1966–1970. The third point is that a wide difference exists between the results of the individual funds.

We do not think the mutual-fund industry can be criticized for doing no better than the market as a whole. Their managers and their professional competitors administer so large a portion of all marketable common stocks that what happens to the market as a whole must necessarily happen (approximately) to the sum of their funds. (Note that the trust assets of insured commercial banks included $181 billion of common stocks at the end of 1969; if we add to this the common stocks in accounts handled by investment advisers, plus the $56 billion of mutual and similar funds, we must conclude that the combined decisions of these professionals pretty well determine the movements of the stock averages, and that the

---

* For periods as long as 10 years, the returns of the Dow and the S & P 500 can diverge by fairly wide margins. Over the course of the typical investing lifetime, however—say 25 to 50 years—their returns have tended to converge quite closely.

movement of the stock averages pretty well determines the funds' aggregate results.)

Are there better than average funds and can the investor select these so as to obtain superior results for himself? Obviously all investors could not do this, since in that case we would soon be back where we started, with no one doing better than anyone else. Let us consider the question first in a simplified fashion. Why shouldn't the investor find out what fund has made the best showing of the lot over a period of sufficient years in the past, assume from this that its management is the most capable and will therefore do better than average in the future, and put his money in that fund? This idea appears the more practicable because, in the case of the mutual funds, he could obtain this "most capable management" without paying any special premium for it as against the other funds. (By contrast, among noninvestment corporations the best-managed companies sell at correspondingly high prices in relation to their current earnings and assets.)

The evidence on this point has been conflicting over the years. But our Table 9-1 covering the ten largest funds indicates that the results shown by the top five performers of 1961–1965 carried over *on the whole* through 1966–1970, even though two of this set did not do as well as two of the other five. Our studies indicate that the investor in mutual-fund shares may properly consider comparative performance over a period of years in the past, say at least five, *provided* the data do not represent a large net upward movement of the market as a whole. In the latter case spectacularly favorable results may be achieved in unorthodox ways—as will be demonstrated in our following section on "performance" funds. Such results in themselves may indicate only that the fund managers are taking undue speculative risks, and getting away with same *for the time being*.

"Performance" Funds

One of the new phenomena of recent years was the appearance of the cult of "performance" in the management of investment funds (and even of many trust funds). We must start this section with the important disclaimer that it does not apply to the large majority of well-established funds, but only to a relatively small section of the industry which has attracted a disproportionate amount of attention. The story is simple enough. Some of those in charge set out to get much better than average (or DJIA) results. They succeeded in doing this for a while, garnering considerable publicity and additional funds to manage. The aim was legitimate enough; unfortunately, it appears that, in the context of investing really sizable funds, the aim cannot be accomplished without incurring sizable risks. And in a comparatively short time the risks came home to roost.

Several of the circumstances surrounding the "performance" phenomenon caused ominous headshaking by those of us whose experience went far back—even to the 1920s—and whose views, for that very reason, were considered old-fashioned and irrelevant to this (second) "New Era." In the first place, and on this very point, nearly all these brilliant performers were young men—in their thirties and forties—whose direct financial experience was limited to the all but continuous bull market of 1948–1968. Secondly, they often acted as if the definition of a "sound investment" was a stock that was likely to have a good rise in the market in the next few months. This led to large commitments in newer ventures at prices completely disproportionate to their assets or recorded earnings. They could be "justified" only by a combination of naïve hope in the future accomplishments of these enterprises with an apparent shrewdness in exploiting the speculative enthusiasms of the uninformed and greedy public.

This section will not mention people's names. But we have every reason to give concrete examples of companies. The "performance fund" most in the public's eye was undoubtedly Manhattan Fund, Inc., organized at the end of 1965. Its first offering was of 27 million shares at $9.25 to $10 per share. The company started out with $247 million of capital. Its emphasis was, of course, on capital gains. Most of its funds were invested in issues selling at high multipliers of current earnings, paying no dividends (or very small ones), with a large speculative following and spectacular price movements. The fund showed an overall gain of 38.6% in 1967, against 11% for the S & P composite index. But thereafter its performance left much to be desired, as is shown in Table 9-2.

TABLE 9-2 A Performance-Fund Portfolio and Performance
(Larger Holdings of Manhattan Fund, December 31, 1969)

Shares Held (thousands)	*Issue*	*Price*	*Earned 1969*	*Dividend 1969*	*Market Value (millions)*
60	Teleprompter	99	$ .99	none	$ 6.0
190	Deltona	60½	2.32	none	11.5
280	Fedders	34	1.28	$ .35	9.5
105	Horizon Corp.	53½	2.68	none	5.6
150	Rouse Co.	34	.07	none	5.1
130	Mattel Inc.	64¼	1.11	.20	8.4
120	Polaroid	125	1.90	.32	15.0
244[a]	Nat'l Student Mkt'g	28½	.32	none	6.1
56	Telex Corp.	90½	.68	none	5.0
100	Bausch & Lomb	77¾	1.92	.80	7.8
190	Four Seasons Nursing	66	.80	none	12.3[b]
20	Int. Bus. Machines	365	8.21	3.60	7.3
41.5	Nat'l Cash Register	160	1.95	1.20	6.7
100	Saxon Ind.	109	3.81	none	10.9
105	Career Academy	50	.43	none	5.3
285	King Resources	28	.69	none	8.1
					$130.6
			Other common stocks		93.8
			Other holdings		19.6
			Total investments[c]		$244.0

[a] After 2-for-1 split.
[b] Also $1.1 million of affiliated stocks.
[c] Excluding cash equivalents.

Annual Performance Compared with S & P Composite Index

	1966	*1967*	*1968*	*1969*	*1970*	*1971*
Manhattan Fund	– 6 %	+38.6%	– 7.3%	–13.3%	–36.9%	+ 9.6%
S & P Composite	–10.1%	+23.0%	+10.4%	– 8.3%	+ 3.5%	+13.5%

The portfolio of Manhattan Fund at the end of 1969 was unorthodox to say the least. It is an extraordinary fact that two of its largest investments were in companies that filed for bankruptcy within six months thereafter, and a third faced creditors' actions in 1971. It is another extraordinary fact that shares of at least one of these doomed companies were bought not only by investment funds but by university endowment funds, the trust departments of large banking institutions, and the like.* A third extraordinary fact was that the founder-manager of Manhattan Fund sold his stock in a separately organized management company to another large concern for over $20 million in its stock; at that time the management company sold had less than $1 million in assets. This is undoubtedly one of the greatest disparities of all times between the results for the "manager" and the "managees."

A book published at the end of 1969[2] provided profiles of nineteen men "who are tops at the demanding game of managing billions of dollars of other people's money." The summary told us further that "they are young . . . some earn more than a million dollars a year . . . they are a new financial breed . . . they all have a total fascination with the market . . . and a spectacular knack for coming up with winners." A fairly good idea of the accomplishments of this top group can be obtained by examining the published results of the funds they manage. Such results are available for funds directed by twelve of the nineteen persons described in *The Money Managers.* Typically enough, they showed up well in 1966, and brilliantly in 1967. In 1968 their performance was still good in the aggregate, but mixed as to individual funds. In 1969 they all showed losses, with only one managing to do a bit better than the S & P composite index. In 1970 their comparative performance was even worse than in 1969.

---

* One of the "doomed companies" Graham refers to was National Student Marketing Corp., a con game masquerading as a stock, whose saga was told brilliantly in Andrew Tobias's *The Funny Money Game* (Playboy Press, New York, 1971). Among the supposedly sophisticated investors who were snookered by NSM's charismatic founder, Cort Randell, were the endowment funds of Cornell and Harvard and the trust departments at such prestigious banks as Morgan Guaranty and Bankers Trust.

We have presented this picture in order to point a moral, which perhaps can best be expressed by the old French proverb: *Plus ça change, plus c'est la même chose.* Bright, energetic people—usually quite young—have promised to perform miracles with "other people's money" since time immemorial. They have usually been able to do it for a while—or at least to appear to have done it—and they have inevitably brought losses to their public in the end.* About a half century ago the "miracles" were often accompanied by flagrant manipulation, misleading corporate reporting, outrageous capitalization structures, and other semifraudulent financial practices. All this brought on an elaborate system of financial controls by the SEC, as well as a cautious attitude toward common stocks on the part of the general public. The operations of the new "money managers" in 1965–1969 came a little more than one full generation after the shenanigans of 1926–1929.† The specific malpractices banned after the 1929 crash were no longer resorted to—they involved the risk of jail sentences. But in many corners of Wall Street they were replaced by newer gadgets and gimmicks that produced very similar results in the end. Outright manipulation of prices disappeared, but there were many other methods of drawing the gullible public's attention to the profit possibilities in "hot" issues. Blocks of "letter stock"[3] could be bought well below the quoted market price, subject to undisclosed restrictions on their sale; they could immediately be carried in the reports at their full market value, showing a lovely and illusory profit. And so on. It is

---

* As only the latest proof that "the more things change, the more they stay the same," consider that Ryan Jacob, a 29-year-old boy wonder, launched the Jacob Internet Fund at year-end 1999, after producing a 216% return at his previous dot-com fund. Investors poured nearly $300 million into Jacob's fund in the first few weeks of 2000. It then proceeded to lose 79.1% in 2000, 56.4% in 2001, and 13% in 2002–a cumulative collapse of 92%. That loss may have made Mr. Jacob's investors even older and wiser than it made him.

† Intriguingly, the disastrous boom and bust of 1999–2002 also came roughly 35 years after the previous cycle of insanity. Perhaps it takes about 35 years for the investors who remember the last "New Economy" craze to become less influential than those who do not. If this intuition is correct, the intelligent investor should be particularly vigilant around the year 2030.

amazing how, in a completely different atmosphere of regulation and prohibitions, Wall Street was able to duplicate so much of the excesses and errors of the 1920s.

No doubt there will be new regulations and new prohibitions. The specific abuses of the late 1960s will be fairly adequately banned from Wall Street. But it is probably too much to expect that the urge to speculate will ever disappear, or that the exploitation of that urge can ever be abolished. It is part of the armament of the intelligent investor to know about these "Extraordinary Popular Delusions,"[4] and to keep as far away from them as possible.

The picture of most of the performance funds is a poor one if we start *after* their spectacular record in 1967. With the 1967 figures included, their overall showing is not at all disastrous. On that basis one of "The Money Managers" operators did quite a bit better than the S & P composite index, three did distinctly worse, and six did about the same. Let us take as a check another group of performance funds—the ten that made the best showing in 1967, with gains ranging from 84% up to 301% in that single year. Of these, four gave a better overall four-year performance than the S & P index, if the 1967 gains are included; and two excelled the index in 1968–1970. None of these funds was large, and the average size was about $60 million. Thus, there is a strong indication that smaller size is a necessary factor for obtaining continued outstanding results.

The foregoing account contains the implicit conclusion that there may be special risks involved in looking for superior performance by investment-fund managers. All financial experience up to now indicates that large funds, soundly managed, can produce at best only slightly better than average results over the years. If they are unsoundly managed they can produce spectacular, but largely illusory, profits for a while, followed inevitably by calamitous losses. There have been instances of funds that have consistently outperformed the market averages for, say, ten years or more. But these have been scarce exceptions, having most of their operations in specialized fields, with self-imposed limits on the capital employed—and not actively sold to the public.*

---

* Today's equivalent of Graham's "scarce exceptions" tend to be open-end funds that are closed to new investors–meaning that the managers have

Closed-End versus Open-End Funds

Almost all the mutual funds or open-end funds, which offer their holders the right to cash in their shares at each day's valuation of the portfolio, have a corresponding machinery for selling new shares. By this means most of them have grown in size over the years. The closed-end companies, nearly all of which were organized a long time ago, have a fixed capital structure, and thus have diminished in relative dollar importance. Open-end companies are being sold by many thousands of energetic and persuasive salesmen, the closed-end shares have no one especially interested in distributing them. Consequently it has been possible to sell most "mutual funds" to the public at a fixed premium of about 9% above net asset value (to cover salesmen's commissions, etc.), while the majority of close-end shares have been consistently obtainable at *less* than their asset value. This price discount has varied among individual companies, and the average discount for the group as a whole has also varied from one date to another. Figures on this point for 1961–1970 are given in Table 9-3.

It does not take much shrewdness to suspect that the lower relative price for closed-end as against open-end shares has very little to do with the difference in the overall investment results between the two groups. That this is true is indicated by the comparison of the annual results for 1961–1970 of the two groups included in Table 9-3.

Thus we arrive at one of the few clearly evident rules for investors' choices. If you want to put money in investment funds, buy a group of closed-end shares at a discount of, say, 10% to 15% from asset value, instead of paying a premium of about 9% above asset value for shares of an open-end company. Assuming that the future dividends and changes in asset values continue to be about the same for the two groups, you will thus obtain about one-fifth more for your money from the closed-end shares.

The mutual-fund salesman will be quick to counter with the

---

stopped taking in any more cash. While that reduces the management fees they can earn, it maximizes the returns their existing shareholders can earn. Because most fund managers would rather look out for No. 1 than be No. 1, closing a fund to new investors is a rare and courageous step.

TABLE 9-3 Certain Data on Closed-End Funds, Mutual Funds, and S & P Composite Index

Year	*Average Discount of Closed-End Funds*	*Average Results of Closed-End Funds*[a]	*Average Results of Mutual Stock Funds*[b]	*Results of S & P Index*[c]
1970	– 6%	even	– 5.3%	+ 3.5%
1969		– 7.9%	–12.5	– 8.3
1968	(+ 7)[d]	+13.3	+15.4	+10.4
1967	– 5	+28.2	+37.2	+23.0
1966	–12	– 5.9	– 4.1	–10.1
1965	–14	+14.0	+24.8	+12.2
1964	–10	+16.9	+13.6	+14.8
1963	– 8	+20.8	+19.3	+24.0
1962	– 4	–11.6	–14.6	– 8.7
1961	– 3	+23.6	+25.7	+27.0
Average of 10 yearly figures:		+ 9.14%	+ 9.95%	+ 9.79%

[a] Wiesenberger average of ten diversified companies.

[b] Average of five Wiesenberger averages of common-stock funds each year.

[c] In all cases distributions are added back.

[d] Premium.

argument: "Ah, but if you own closed-end shares you can never be sure what price you can sell them for. The discount can be greater than it is today, and you will suffer from the wider spread. With our shares you are guaranteed the right to turn in your shares at 100% of asset value, never less." Let us examine this argument a bit; it will be a good exercise in logic and plain common sense. Question: Assuming that the discount on closed-end shares does widen, how likely is it that you will be worse off with those shares than with an otherwise equivalent purchase of open-end shares?

This calls for a little arithmetic. Assume that Investor A buys some open-end shares at 109% of asset value, and Investor B buys closed-end shares at 85% thereof, plus 1½% commission. Both sets of shares earn and pay 30% of this asset value in, say, four years,

TABLE 9-4 Average Results of Diversified Closed-End Funds, 1961–1970[a]

	1970	5 years, 1966–1970	1961–1970	Premium or Discount, December 1970
Three funds selling at premiums	–5.2%	+25.4%	+115.0%	11.4% premium
Ten funds selling at discounts	+1.3	+22.6	+102.9	9.2% discount

[a] Data from Wiesenberger Financial Services.

and end up with the same value as at the beginning. Investor A redeems his shares at 100% of value, losing the 9% premium he paid. His overall return for the period is 30% less 9%, or 21% on asset value. This, in turn, is 19% on his investment. How much must Investor B realize on his closed-end shares to obtain the same return on his investment as Investor A? The answer is 73%, or a discount of 27% from asset value. In other words, the closed-end man could suffer a widening of 12 points in the market discount (about double) before his return would get down to that of the open-end investor. An adverse change of this magnitude has happened rarely, if ever, in the history of closed-end shares. Hence it is very unlikely that you will obtain a lower overall return from a (representative) closed-end company, bought at a discount, if its investment performance is about equal to that of a representative mutual fund. If a small-load (or no-load) fund is substituted for one with the usual "8½%" load, the advantage of the closed-end investment is of course reduced, but it remains an advantage.

The fact that a few closed-end funds are selling at *premiums* greater than the true 9% charge on most mutual funds introduces a separate question for the investor. Do these premium companies enjoy superior management of sufficient proven worth to warrant their elevated prices? If the answer is sought in the comparative results for the past five or ten years, the answer would appear to be no. Three of the six premium companies have mainly foreign investments. A striking feature of these is the large variation in

TABLE 9-5 Comparison of Two Leading Closed-End Companies[a]

	1970	*5 years, 1966–1970*	*10 years, 1961–1970*	*Premium or Discount, December 1970*
General Am. Investors Co.	–0.3%	+34.0%	+165.6%	7.6% discount
Lehman Corp.	–7.2	+20.6	+108.0	13.9% premium

[a] Data from Wiesenberger Financial Services.

prices in a few years' time; at the end of 1970 one sold at only one-quarter of its high, another at a third, another at less than half. If we consider the three domestic companies selling above asset value, we find that the average of their ten-year overall returns was somewhat better than that of ten discount funds, but the opposite was true in the last five years. A comparison of the 1961–1970 record of Lehman Corp. and of General American Investors, two of our oldest and largest closed-end companies, is given in Table 9-5. One of these sold 14% above and the other 7.6% below its net-asset value at the end of 1970. The difference in price to net-asset relationships did not appear warranted by these figures.

Investment in Balanced Funds

The 23 balanced funds covered in the Wiesenberger Report had between 25% and 59% of their assets in preferred stocks and bonds, the average being just 40%. The balance was held in common stocks. It would appear more logical for the typical investor to make his bond-type investments directly, rather than to have them form part of a mutual-fund commitment. The average income return shown by these balanced funds in 1970 was only 3.9% per annum on asset value, or say 3.6% on the offering price. The better choice for the bond component would be the purchase of United States savings bonds, or corporate bonds rated A or better, or tax-free bonds, for the investor's bond portfolio.

COMMENTARY ON CHAPTER 9

> The schoolteacher asks Billy Bob: "If you have twelve sheep and one jumps over the fence, how many sheep do you have left?"
>
> Billy Bob answers, "None."
>
> "Well," says the teacher, "you sure don't know your subtraction."
>
> "Maybe not," Billy Bob replies, "but I darn sure know my sheep."
>
> *–As told by Prof. Henry T. C. Hu of the University of Texas School of Law*

ALMOST PERFECT

A purely American creation, the mutual fund was introduced in 1924 by a former salesman of aluminum pots and pans named Edward G. Leffler. Mutual funds are quite cheap, very convenient, generally diversified, professionally managed, and tightly regulated under some of the toughest provisions of Federal securities law. By making investing easy and affordable for almost anyone, the funds have brought some 54 million American families (and millions more around the world) into the investing mainstream–probably the greatest advance in financial democracy ever achieved.

But mutual funds aren't perfect; they are *almost* perfect, and that word makes all the difference. Because of their imperfections, most funds underperform the market, overcharge their investors, create tax headaches, and suffer erratic swings in performance. The intelligent investor must choose funds with great care in order to avoid ending up owning a big fat mess.

TOP OF THE CHARTS

Most investors simply buy a fund that has been going up fast, on the assumption that it will keep on going. And why not? Psychologists have shown that humans have an inborn tendency to believe that the long run can be predicted from even a short series of outcomes. What's more, we know from our own experience that some plumbers are far better than others, that some baseball players are much more likely to hit home runs, that our favorite restaurant serves consistently superior food, and that smart kids get consistently good grades. Skill and brains and hard work are recognized, rewarded–and consistently repeated–all around us. So, if a fund beats the market, our intuition tells us to expect it to keep right on outperforming.

Unfortunately, in the financial markets, luck is more important than skill. If a manager happens to be in the right corner of the market at just the right time, he will look brilliant–but all too often, what was hot suddenly goes cold and the manager's IQ seems to shrivel by 50 points. Figure 9-1 shows what happened to the hottest funds of 1999.

This is yet another reminder that the market's hottest market sector–in 1999, that was technology–often turns as cold as liquid nitrogen, with blinding speed and utterly no warning.[1] And it's a reminder that buying funds based purely on their past performance is one of the stupidest things an investor can do. Financial scholars have been studying mutual-fund performance for at least a half century, and they are virtually unanimous on several points:

- the average fund does not pick stocks well enough to overcome its costs of researching and trading them;
- the higher a fund's expenses, the lower its returns;
- the more frequently a fund trades its stocks, the less it tends to earn;

---

[1] Sector funds specializing in almost every imaginable industry are available–and date back to the 1920s. After nearly 80 years of history, the evidence is overwhelming: The most lucrative, and thus most popular, sector of any given year often turns out to be among the worst performers of the following year. Just as idle hands are the devil's workshop, sector funds are the investor's nemesis.

FIGURE 9-1 The Crash-and-Burn Club

Fund	Total Return				Value on 12/31/02 of $10,000 invested on 1/1/1999
	1999	2000	2001	2002	
Van Wagoner Emerging Growth	291.2	–20.9	–59.7	–64.6	4,419
Monument Internet	273.1	–56.9	–52.2	–51.2	3,756
Amerindo Technology	248.9	–64.8	–50.8	–31.0	4,175
PBHG Technology & Communications	243.9	–43.7	–52.4	–54.5	4,198
Van Wagoner Post-Venture	237.2	–30.3	–62.1	–67.3	2,907
ProFunds Ultra OTC	233.2	–73.7	–69.1	–69.4	829
Van Wagoner Technology	223.8	–28.1	–61.9	–65.8	3,029
Thurlow Growth	213.2	–56.0	–26.1	–31.0	7,015
Firsthand Technology Innovators	212.3	–37.9	–29.1	–54.8	6,217
Janus Global Technology	211.6	–33.7	–40.0	–40.9	7,327
Wilshire 5000 index (total stock market)	23.8	–10.9	–11.0	–20.8	7,780

Source: Lipper

Note: Monument Internet was later renamed Orbitex Emerging Technology.

These 10 funds were among the hottest performers of 1999—and, in fact, among the highest annual performers of all time. But the next three years erased all the giant gains of 1999, and then some.

- highly volatile funds, which bounce up and down more than average, are likely to stay volatile;
- funds with high past returns are unlikely to remain winners for long.[2]

Your chances of selecting the top-performing funds of the future on the basis of their returns in the past are about as high as the odds that Bigfoot and the Abominable Snowman will both show up in pink ballet slippers at your next cocktail party. In other words, your chances are not zero—but they're pretty close. (See sidebar, p. 255.)

But there's good news, too. First of all, understanding why it's so hard to find a good fund will help you become a more intelligent investor. Second, while past performance is a poor predictor of future returns, there are other factors that you can use to increase your odds of finding a good fund. Finally, a fund can offer excellent value even if it doesn't beat the market—by providing an economical way to diversify your holdings and by freeing up your time for all the other things you would rather be doing than picking your own stocks.

THE FIRST SHALL BE LAST

Why don't more winning funds stay winners?

The better a fund performs, the more obstacles its investors face:

Migrating managers. When a stock picker seems to have the Midas touch, everyone wants him—including rival fund companies. If you bought Transamerica Premier Equity Fund to cash in on the skills of Glen Bickerstaff, who gained 47.5% in 1997, you were quickly out of luck; TCW snatched him away in mid-1998 to run its TCW Galileo Select Equities Fund, and the Transamerica fund lagged the market in three of the next four years. If you bought Fidelity Aggressive Growth Fund in early 2000 to capitalize on the high returns of Erin Sullivan, who had nearly tripled her shareholders' money since 1997, oh well: She quit to start her own hedge fund in

---

[2] The research on mutual fund performance is too voluminous to cite. Useful summaries and links can be found at: www.investorhome.com/mutual.htm#do, www.ssrn.com (enter "mutual fund" in the search window), and www.stanford.edu/~wfsharpe/art/art.htm.

2000, and her former fund lost more than three-quarters of its value over the next three years.[3]

Asset elephantiasis. When a fund earns high returns, investors notice—often pouring in hundreds of millions of dollars in a matter of weeks. That leaves the fund manager with few choices—all of them bad. He can keep that money safe for a rainy day, but then the low returns on cash will crimp the fund's results if stocks keep going up. He can put the new money into the stocks he already owns—which have probably gone up since he first bought them and will become dangerously overvalued if he pumps in millions of dollars more. Or he can buy new stocks he didn't like well enough to own already—but he will have to research them from scratch and keep an eye on far more companies than he is used to following.

Finally, when the $100-million Nimble Fund puts 2% of its assets (or $2 million) in Minnow Corp., a stock with a total market value of $500 million, it's buying up less than one-half of 1% of Minnow. But if hot performance swells the Nimble Fund to $10 billion, then an investment of 2% of its assets would total $200 million—nearly half the entire value of Minnow, a level of ownership that isn't even permissible under Federal law. If Nimble's portfolio manager still wants to own small stocks, he will have to spread his money over vastly more companies—and probably end up spreading his attention too thin.

No more fancy footwork. Some companies specialize in "incubating" their funds—test-driving them privately before selling them publicly. (Typically, the only shareholders are employees and affiliates of the fund company itself.) By keeping them tiny, the sponsor can use these incubated funds as guinea pigs for risky strategies that work best with small sums of money, like buying truly tiny stocks or rapid-fire trading of initial public offerings. If its strategy succeeds, the fund can lure public investors en masse by publicizing its private returns. In other cases, the fund manager "waives" (or skips charging) management fees, raising the net return—then slaps the fees on later after the high returns attract plenty of customers. Almost without exception, the returns of incubated and fee-waived funds have faded into mediocrity after outside investors poured millions of dollars into them.

---

[3] That's not to say that these funds would have done better if their "superstar" managers had stayed in place; all we can be sure of is that the two funds did poorly without them.

Rising expenses. It often costs more to trade stocks in very large blocks than in small ones; with fewer buyers and sellers, it's harder to make a match. A fund with $100 million in assets might pay 1% a year in trading costs. But, if high returns send the fund mushrooming up to $10 billion, its trades could easily eat up at least 2% of those assets. The typical fund holds on to its stocks for only 11 months at a time, so trading costs eat away at returns like a corrosive acid. Meanwhile, the other costs of running a fund rarely fall–and sometimes even rise–as assets grow. With operating expenses averaging 1.5%, and trading costs at around 2%, the typical fund has to beat the market by 3.5 percentage points per year before costs just to match it after costs!

Sheepish behavior. Finally, once a fund becomes successful, its managers tend to become timid and imitative. As a fund grows, its fees become more lucrative–making its managers reluctant to rock the boat. The very risks that the managers took to generate their initial high returns could now drive investors away–and jeopardize all that fat fee income. So the biggest funds resemble a herd of identical and overfed sheep, all moving in sluggish lockstep, all saying "baaaa" at the same time. Nearly every growth fund owns Cisco and GE and Microsoft and Pfizer and Wal-Mart–and in almost identical proportions. This behavior is so prevalent that finance scholars simply call it herding.[4] But by protecting their own fee income, fund managers compromise their ability to produce superior returns for their outside investors.

---

[4] There's a second lesson here: To succeed, the individual investor must either avoid shopping from the same list of favorite stocks that have already been picked over by the giant institutions, or own them far more patiently. See Erik R. Sirri and Peter Tufano, "Costly Search and Mutual Fund Flows," *The Journal of Finance,* vol. 53, no. 8, October, 1998, pp. 1589–1622; Keith C. Brown, W. V. Harlow, and Laura Starks, "Of Tournaments and Temptations," *The Journal of Finance,* vol. 51, no. 1, March, 1996, pp. 85–110; Josef Lakonishok, Andrei Shleifer, and Robert Vishny, "What Do Money Managers Do?" working paper, University of Illinois, February, 1997; Stanley Eakins, Stanley Stansell, and Paul Wertheim, "Institutional Portfolio Composition," *Quarterly Review of Economics and Finance,* vol. 38, no. 1, Spring, 1998, pp. 93–110; Paul Gompers and Andrew Metrick, "Institutional Investors and Equity Prices," *The Quarterly Journal of Economics,* vol. 116, no. 1, February, 2001, pp. 229–260.

FIGURE 9-2 The Funnel of Fund Performance

Looking back from December 31, 2002, how many U.S. stock funds outperformed Vanguard 500 Index Fund?

One year:
1,186 of 2,423 funds (or 48.9%)

Three years:
1,157 of 1,944 funds (or 59.5%)

Five years:
768 of 1,494 funds (or 51.4%)

Ten years:
227 of 728 funds (or 31.2%)

Fifteen years:
125 of 445 funds (or 28.1%)

Twenty years:
37 of 248 funds (or 14.9%)

Source: Lipper Inc.

Because of their fat costs and bad behavior, most funds fail to earn their keep. No wonder high returns are nearly as perishable as unrefrigerated fish. What's more, as time passes, the drag of their excessive expenses leaves most funds farther and farther behind, as Figure 9.2 shows.[5]

What, then, should the intelligent investor do?

First of all, recognize that an index fund–which owns all the stocks

[5] Amazingly, this illustration *understates* the advantage of index funds, since the database from which it is taken does not include the track records of hundreds of funds that disappeared over these periods. Measured more accurately, the advantage of indexing would be overpowering.

in the market, all the time, without any pretense of being able to select the "best" and avoid the "worst"—will beat most funds over the long run. (If your company doesn't offer a low-cost index fund in your 401(k), organize your coworkers and petition to have one added.) Its rock-bottom overhead—operating expenses of 0.2% annually, and yearly trading costs of just 0.1%—give the index fund an insurmountable advantage. If stocks generate, say, a 7% annualized return over the next 20 years, a low-cost index fund like Vanguard Total Stock Market will return just under 6.7%. (That would turn a $10,000 investment into more than $36,000.) But the average stock fund, with its 1.5% in operating expenses and roughly 2% in trading costs, will be lucky to gain 3.5% annually. (That would turn $10,000 into just under $20,000—or *nearly 50% less* than the result from the index fund.)

Index funds have only one significant flaw: They are boring. You'll never be able to go to a barbecue and brag about how you own the top-performing fund in the country. You'll never be able to boast that you beat the market, because the job of an index fund is to match the market's return, not to exceed it. Your index-fund manager is not likely to "roll the dice" and gamble that the next great industry will be teleportation, or scratch-'n'-sniff websites, or telepathic weight-loss clinics; the fund will always own every stock, not just one manager's best guess at the next new thing. But, as the years pass, the cost advantage of indexing will keep accruing relentlessly. Hold an index fund for 20 years or more, adding new money every month, and you are all but certain to outperform the vast majority of professional and individual investors alike. Late in his life, Graham praised index funds as the best choice for individual investors, as does Warren Buffett.[6]

---

[6] See Benjamin Graham, *Benjamin Graham: Memoirs of the Dean of Wall Street,* Seymour Chatman, ed. (McGraw-Hill, New York, 1996), p. 273, and Janet Lowe, *The Rediscovered Benjamin Graham: Selected Writings of the Wall Street Legend* (John Wiley & Sons, New York, 1999), p. 273. As Warren Buffett wrote in his 1996 annual report: "Most investors, both institutional and individual, will find that the best way to own common stocks is through an index fund that charges minimal fees. Those following this path are sure to beat the net results (after fees and expenses) delivered by the great majority of investment professionals." (See www.berkshirehathaway.com/1996ar/1996.html.)

TILTING THE TABLES

When you add up all their handicaps, the wonder is not that so few funds beat the index, but that any do. And yet, some do. What qualities do they have in common?

Their managers are the biggest shareholders. The conflict of interest between what's best for the fund's managers and what's best for its investors is mitigated when the managers are among the biggest owners of the fund's shares. Some firms, like Longleaf Partners, even forbid their employees from owning anything but their own funds. At Longleaf and other firms like Davis and FPA, the managers own so much of the funds that they are likely to manage your money as if it were their own–lowering the odds that they will jack up fees, let the funds swell to gargantuan size, or whack you with a nasty tax bill. A fund's proxy statement and Statement of Additional Information, both available from the Securities and Exchange Commission through the EDGAR database at www.sec.gov, disclose whether the managers own at least 1% of the fund's shares.

They are cheap. One of the most common myths in the fund business is that "you get what you pay for"–that high returns are the best justification for higher fees. There are two problems with this argument. First, it isn't true; decades of research have proven that funds with higher fees earn *lower* returns over time. Secondly, high returns are temporary, while high fees are nearly as permanent as granite. If you buy a fund for its hot returns, you may well end up with a handful of cold ashes–but your costs of owning the fund are almost certain *not* to decline when its returns do.

They dare to be different. When Peter Lynch ran Fidelity Magellan, he bought whatever seemed cheap to him–regardless of what other fund managers owned. In 1982, his biggest investment was Treasury bonds; right after that, he made Chrysler his top holding, even though most experts expected the automaker to go bankrupt; then, in 1986, Lynch put almost 20% of Fidelity Magellan in foreign stocks like Honda, Norsk Hydro, and Volvo. So, before you buy a U.S. stock fund, compare the holdings listed in its latest report against the roster of the S & P 500 index; if they look like Tweedledee and Tweedledum, shop for another fund.[7]

---

[7] A complete listing of the S & P 500's constituent companies is available at www.standardandpoors.com.

They shut the door. The best funds often close to new investors–permitting only their existing shareholders to buy more. That stops the feeding frenzy of new buyers who want to pile in at the top and protects the fund from the pains of asset elephantiasis. It's also a signal that the fund managers are not putting their own wallets ahead of yours. But the closing should occur before–not after–the fund explodes in size. Some companies with an exemplary record of shutting their own gates are Longleaf, Numeric, Oakmark, T. Rowe Price, Vanguard, and Wasatch.

They don't advertise. Just as Plato says in *The Republic* that the ideal rulers are those who do not want to govern, the best fund managers often behave as if they don't want your money. They don't appear constantly on financial television or run ads boasting of their No. 1 returns. The steady little Mairs & Power Growth Fund didn't even have a website until 2001 and still sells its shares in only 24 states. The Torray Fund has never run a retail advertisement since its launch in 1990.

What else should you watch for? Most fund buyers look at past performance first, then at the manager's reputation, then at the riskiness of the fund, and finally (if ever) at the fund's expenses.[8]

The intelligent investor looks at those same things–but in the opposite order.

Since a fund's expenses are far more predictable than its future risk or return, you should make them your first filter. There's no good reason ever to pay more than these levels of annual operating expenses, by fund category:

- Taxable and municipal bonds: 0.75%
- U.S. equities (large and mid-sized stocks): 1.0%
- High-yield (junk) bonds: 1.0%

---

[8] See Noel Capon, Gavan Fitzsimons, and Russ Alan Prince, "An Individual Level Analysis of the Mutual Fund Investment Decision," *Journal of Financial Services Research,* vol. 10, 1996, pp. 59–82; Investment Company Institute, "Understanding Shareholders' Use of Information and Advisers," Spring, 1997, at www.ici.org/pdf/rpt_undstnd_share.pdf, p. 21; Gordon Alexander, Jonathan Jones, and Peter Nigro, "Mutual Fund Shareholders: Characteristics, Investor Knowledge, and Sources of Information," OCC working paper, December, 1997, at www.occ.treas.gov/ftp/workpaper/wp97-13.pdf.

- U.S. equities (small stocks): 1.25%
- Foreign stocks: 1.50%[9]

Next, evaluate risk. In its prospectus (or buyer's guide), every fund must show a bar graph displaying its worst loss over a calendar quarter. If you can't stand losing at least that much money in three months, go elsewhere. It's also worth checking a fund's Morningstar rating. A leading investment research firm, Morningstar awards "star ratings" to funds, based on how much risk they took to earn their returns (one star is the worst, five is the best). But, just like past performance itself, these ratings look back in time; they tell you which funds were the best, not which are going to be. Five-star funds, in fact, have a disconcerting habit of going on to underperform one-star funds. So first find a low-cost fund whose managers are major shareholders, dare to be different, don't hype their returns, and have shown a willingness to shut down before they get too big for their britches. Then, and only then, consult their Morningstar rating.[10]

Finally, look at past performance, remembering that it is only a pale predictor of future returns. As we've already seen, yesterday's winners often become tomorrow's losers. But researchers have shown that one thing is almost certain: Yesterday's losers almost never become tomorrow's winners. So avoid funds with consistently poor past returns—especially if they have above-average annual expenses.

THE CLOSED WORLD OF CLOSED-END FUNDS

Closed-end stock funds, although popular during the 1980s, have slowly atrophied. Today, there are only 30 diversified domestic

---

[9] Investors can search easily for funds that meet these expense hurdles by using the fund-screening tools at www.morningstar.com and http://money.cnn.com.

[10] See Matthew Morey, "Rating the Raters: An Investigation of Mutual Fund Rating Services," *Journal of Investment Consulting,* vol. 5, no. 2, November/December, 2002. While its star ratings are a weak predictor of future results, Morningstar is the single best source of information on funds for individual investors.

equity funds, many of them tiny, trading only a few hundred shares a day, with high expenses and weird strategies (like Morgan Fun-Shares, which specializes in the stocks of "habit-forming" industries like booze, casinos, and cigarettes). Research by closed-end fund expert Donald Cassidy of Lipper Inc. reinforces Graham's earlier observations: Diversified closed-end stock funds trading at a discount not only tend to outperform those trading at a premium but are likely to have a better return than the average open-end mutual fund. Sadly, however, diversified closed-end stock funds are not always available at a discount in what has become a dusty, dwindling market.[11]

But there are hundreds of closed-end bond funds, with especially strong choices available in the municipal-bond area. When these funds trade at a discount, their yield is amplified and they can be attractive, so long as their annual expenses are below the thresholds listed above.[12]

The new breed of exchange-traded index funds can be worth exploring as well. These low-cost "ETFs" sometimes offer the only means by which an investor can gain entrée to a narrow market like, say, companies based in Belgium or stocks in the semiconductor industry. Other index ETFs offer much broader market exposure. However, they are generally not suitable for investors who wish to add money regularly, since most brokers will charge a separate commission on every new investment you make.[13]

---

[11] Unlike a mutual fund, a closed-end fund does not issue new shares directly to anyone who wants to buy them. Instead, an investor must buy shares not from the fund itself, but from another shareholder who is willing to part with them. Thus, the price of the shares fluctuates above and below their net asset value, depending on supply and demand.

[12] For more information, see www.morningstar.com and www.etfconnect.com.

[13] Unlike index mutual funds, index ETFs are subject to standard stock commissions when you buy and sell them—and these commissions are often assessed on any additional purchases or reinvested dividends. Details are available at www.ishares.com, www.streettracks.com, www.amex.com, and www.indexfunds.com.

KNOW WHEN TO FOLD 'EM

Once you own a fund, how can you tell when it's time to sell? The standard advice is to ditch a fund if it underperforms the market (or similar portfolios) for one–or is it two?–or is it three?–years in a row. But this advice makes no sense. From its birth in 1970 through 1999, the Sequoia Fund underperformed the S & P 500 index in 12 out of its 29 years–or more than 41% of the time. Yet Sequoia gained more than 12,500% over that period, versus 4,900% for the index.[14]

The performance of most funds falters simply because the type of stocks they prefer temporarily goes out of favor. If you hired a manager to invest in a particular way, why fire him for doing what he promised? By selling when a style of investing is out of fashion, you not only lock in a loss but lock yourself out of the all-but-inevitable recovery. One study showed that mutual-fund investors underperformed their own funds by 4.7 percentage points annually from 1998 through 2001–simply by buying high and selling low.[15]

So when should you sell? Here a few definite red flags:

- **a sharp and unexpected change in strategy,** such as a "value" fund loading up on technology stocks in 1999 or a "growth" fund buying tons of insurance stocks in 2002;
- **an increase in expenses,** suggesting that the managers are lining their own pockets;
- **large and frequent tax bills** generated by excessive trading;
- **suddenly erratic returns,** as when a formerly conservative fund generates a big loss (or even produces a giant gain).

---

[14] See Sequoia's June 30, 1999, report to shareholders at www.sequoiafund.com/Reports/Quarterly/SemiAnn99.htm. Sequoia has been closed to new investors since 1982, which has reinforced its superb performance.

[15] Jason Zweig, "What Fund Investors Really Need to Know," *Money,* June, 2002, pp. 110–115.

WHY WE LOVE OUR OUIJA BOARDS

Believing—or even just hoping—that we can pick the best funds of the future makes us feel better. It gives us the pleasing sensation that we are in charge of our own investment destiny. This "I'm-in-control-here" feeling is part of the human condition; it's what psychologists call overconfidence. Here are just a few examples of how it works:

- In 1999, *Money* Magazine asked more than 500 people whether their portfolios had beaten the market. One in four said yes. When asked to specify their returns, however, 80% of those investors reported gains *lower* than the market's. (Four percent had no idea how much their portfolios rose—but were sure they had beaten the market anyway!)
- A Swedish study asked drivers who had been in severe car crashes to rate their own skills behind the wheel. These people—including some the police had found responsible for the accidents and others who had been so badly injured that they answered the survey from their hospital beds—insisted they were better-than-average drivers.
- In a poll taken in late 2000, *Time* and CNN asked more than 1,000 likely voters whether they thought they were in the top 1% of the population by income. Nineteen percent placed themselves among the richest 1% of Americans.
- In late 1997, a survey of 750 investors found that 74% believed their mutual-fund holdings would "consistently beat the Standard & Poor's 500 each year"—even though most funds fail to beat the S & P 500 in the long run and many fail to beat it in *any* year.[1]

While this kind of optimism is a normal sign of a healthy psyche, that doesn't make it good investment policy. It makes sense to believe you can predict something only if it actually *is* predictable. Unless you are realistic, your quest for self-esteem will end up in self-defeat.

---

[1] See Jason Zweig, "Did You Beat the Market?" *Money*, January, 2000, pp. 55–58; *Time*/CNN poll #15, October 25–26, 2000, question 29.

As the investment consultant Charles Ellis puts it, "If you're not prepared to stay married, you shouldn't *get* married."[16] Fund investing is no different. If you're not prepared to stick with a fund through at least three lean years, you shouldn't buy it in the first place. Patience is the fund investor's single most powerful ally.

[16] See interview with Ellis in Jason Zweig, "Wall Street's Wisest Man," *Money,* June, 2001, pp. 49–52.

CHAPTER 10

The Investor and His Advisers

The investment of money in securities is unique among business operations in that it is almost always based in some degree on advice received from others. The great bulk of investors are amateurs. Naturally they feel that in choosing their securities they can profit by professional guidance. Yet there are peculiarities inherent in the very concept of investment advice.

If the reason people invest is to make money, then in seeking advice they are asking others to tell them how to make money. That idea has some element of naïveté. Businessmen seek professional advice on various elements of their business, but they do not expect to be told how to make a profit. That is their own bailiwick. When they, or nonbusiness people, rely on others to make *investment profits* for them, they are expecting a kind of result for which there is no true counterpart in ordinary business affairs.

If we assume that there are normal or standard *income* results to be obtained from investing money in securities, then the role of the adviser can be more readily established. He will use his superior training and experience to protect his clients against mistakes and to make sure that they obtain the results to which their money is entitled. It is when the investor demands more than an average return on his money, or when his adviser undertakes to do better for him, that the question arises whether more is being asked or promised than is likely to be delivered.

Advice on investments may be obtained from a variety of sources. These include: (1) a relative or friend, presumably knowledgeable in securities; (2) a local (commercial) banker; (3) a brokerage firm or investment banking house; (4) a financial service or periodical; and (5) an investment counselor.* The miscellaneous character of this list suggests that no logical or systematic approach in this matter has crystallized, as yet, in the minds of investors.

Certain common-sense considerations relate to the criterion of normal or standard results mentioned above. Our basic thesis is this: If the investor is to rely chiefly on the advice of others in handling his funds, then either he must limit himself and his advisers strictly to standard, conservative, and even unimaginative forms of investment, or he must have an unusually intimate and favorable knowledge of the person who is going to direct his funds into other channels. But if the ordinary business or professional relationship exists between the investor and his advisers, he can be receptive to *less conventional* suggestions only to the extent that he himself has grown in knowledge and experience and has therefore become competent to pass independent judgment on the recommendations of others. He has then passed from the category of defensive or unenterprising investor into that of aggressive or enterprising investor.

Investment Counsel and Trust Services of Banks

The truly professional investment advisers—that is, the well-established investment counsel firms, who charge substantial annual fees—are quite modest in their promises and pretentions. For the most part they place their clients' funds in standard interest- and dividend-paying securities, and they rely mainly on normal investment experience for their overall results. In the typical case it is doubtful whether more than 10% of the total fund is ever invested in securities other than those of leading companies, plus

---

* The list of sources for investment advice remains as "miscellaneous" as it was when Graham wrote. A survey of investors conducted in late 2002 for the Securities Industry Association, a Wall Street trade group, found that 17% of investors depended most heavily for investment advice on a spouse or friend; 2% on a banker; 16% on a broker; 10% on financial periodicals; and 24% on a financial planner. The only difference from Graham's day is that 8% of investors now rely heavily on the Internet and 3% on financial television. (See www.sia.com.)

government bonds (including state and municipal issues); nor do they make a serious effort to take advantage of swings in the general market.

The leading investment-counsel firms make no claim to being brilliant; they do pride themselves on being careful, conservative, and competent. Their primary aim is to conserve the principal value over the years and produce a conservatively acceptable rate of income. Any accomplishment beyond that—and they do strive to better the goal—they regard in the nature of extra service rendered. Perhaps their chief value to their clients lies in shielding them from costly mistakes. They offer as much as the defensive investor has the right to expect from any counselor serving the general public.

What we have said about the well-established investment-counsel firms applies generally to the trust and advisory services of the larger banks.*

Financial Services

The so-called financial services are organizations that send out uniform bulletins (sometimes in the form of telegrams) to their subscribers. The subjects covered may include the state and prospects of business, the behavior and prospect of the securities markets, and information and advice regarding individual issues. There is often an "inquiry department" which will answer questons affecting an individual subscriber. The cost of the service averages much less than the fee that investment counselors charge their individual clients. Some organizations—notably Babson's and Standard & Poor's—operate on separate levels as a financial service and as investment counsel. (Incidentally, other organiza-

* The character of investment counseling firms and trust banks has not changed, but today they generally do not offer their services to investors with less than $1 million in financial assets; in some cases, $5 million or more is required. Today thousands of independent financial-planning firms perform very similar functions, although (as analyst Robert Veres puts it) the mutual fund has replaced blue-chip stocks as the investment of choice and diversification has replaced "quality" as the standard of safety.

tions—such as Scudder, Stevens & Clark—operate separately as investment counsel and as one or more investment funds.)

The financial services direct themselves, on the whole, to a quite different segment of the public than do the investment-counsel firms. The latters' clients generally wish to be relieved of bother and the need for making decisions. The financial services offer information and guidance to those who are directing their own financial affairs or are themselves advising others. Many of these services confine themselves exclusively, or nearly so, to forecasting market movements by various "technical" methods. We shall dismiss these with the observation that their work does not concern "investors" as the term is used in this book.

On the other hand, some of the best known—such as Moody's Investment Service and Standard & Poor's—are identified with statistical organizations that compile the voluminous statistical data that form the basis for all serious security analysis. These services have a varied clientele, ranging from the most conservative-minded investor to the rankest speculator. As a result they must find it difficult to adhere to any clear-cut or fundamental philosophy in arriving at their opinions and recommendations.

An old-established service of the type of Moody's and the others must obviously provide something worthwhile to a broad class of investors. What is it? Basically they address themselves to the matters in which the average active investor-speculator is interested, and their views on these either command some measure of authority or at least appear more reliable than those of the unaided client.

For years the financial services have been making stock-market forecasts without anyone taking this activity very seriously. Like everyone else in the field they are sometimes right and sometimes wrong. Wherever possible they hedge their opinions so as to avoid the risk of being proved completely wrong. (There is a well-developed art of Delphic phrasing that adjusts itself successfully to whatever the future brings.) In our view—perhaps a prejudiced one—this segment of their work has no real significance except for the light it throws on human nature in the securities markets. Nearly everyone interested in common stocks wants to be told by someone else what he thinks the market is going to do. The demand being there, it must be supplied.

Their interpretations and forecasts of business conditions, of course, are much more authoritative and informing. These are an important part of the great body of economic intelligence which is spread continuously among buyers and sellers of securities and tends to create fairly rational prices for stocks and bonds under most circumstances. Undoubtedly the material published by the financial services adds to the store of information available and fortifies the investment judgment of their clients.

It is difficult to evaluate their recommendations of individual securities. Each service is entitled to be judged separately, and the verdict could properly be based only on an elaborate and inclusive study covering many years. In our own experience we have noted among them a pervasive attitude which we think tends to impair what could otherwise be more useful advisory work. This is their general view that a stock should be bought if the near-term prospects of the business are favorable and should be sold if these are unfavorable—*regardless of the current price.* Such a superficial principle often prevents the services from doing the sound analytical job of which their staffs are capable—namely, to ascertain whether a given stock appears over- or undervalued at the current price in the light of its indicated long-term future earning power.

The intelligent investor will not do his buying and selling solely on the basis of recommendations received from a financial service. Once this point is established, the role of the financial service then becomes the useful one of supplying information and offering suggestions.

Advice from Brokerage Houses

Probably the largest volume of information and advice to the security-owning public comes from stockbrokers. These are members of the New York Stock Exchange, and of other exchanges, who execute buying and selling orders for a standard commission. Practically all the houses that deal with the public maintain a "statistical" or analytical department, which answers inquiries and makes recommendations. A great deal of analytical literature, some of it elaborate and expensive, is distributed gratis to the firms' customers—more impressively referred to as clients.

A great deal is at stake in the innocent-appearing question whether "customers" or "clients" is the more appropriate name. A business has customers; a professional person or organization has clients. The Wall Street brokerage fraternity has probably the highest ethical standards of any *business,* but it is still feeling its way toward the standards and standing of a true profession.*

In the past Wall Street has thrived mainly on speculation, and stock-market speculators as a class were almost certain to lose money. Hence it has been logically impossible for brokerage houses to operate on a thoroughly professional basis. To do that would have required them to direct their efforts toward reducing rather than increasing their business.

The farthest that certain brokerage houses have gone in that direction—and could have been expected to go—is to refrain from inducing or encouraging anyone to speculate. Such houses have confined themselves to executing orders given them, to supplying financial information and analyses, and to rendering opinions on the investment merits of securities. Thus, in theory at least, they are devoid of all responsibility for either the profits or the losses of their speculative customers.†

Most stock-exchange houses, however, still adhere to the old-time slogans that they are in business to make commissions and that the way to succeed in business is to give the customers what they want. Since the most profitable customers want speculative advice and suggestions, the thinking and activities of the typical firm are pretty closely geared to day-to-day trading in the market. Thus it tries hard to help its customers make money in a field where they are condemned almost by mathematical law to lose in the end.‡ By this we mean that the speculative part of their operations cannot be profitable over the long run for most brokerage-

---

* Overall, Graham was as tough and cynical an observer as Wall Street has ever seen. In this rare case, however, he was not nearly cynical enough. Wall Street may have higher ethical standards than *some* businesses (smuggling, prostitution, Congressional lobbying, and journalism come to mind) but the investment world nevertheless has enough liars, cheaters, and thieves to keep Satan's check-in clerks frantically busy for decades to come.

† The thousands of people who bought stocks in the late 1990s in the belief that Wall Street analysts were providing unbiased and valuable advice have learned, in a painful way, how right Graham is on this point.

‡ Interestingly, this stinging criticism, which in his day Graham was directing at full-service brokers, ended up applying to discount Internet brokers in the

house customers. But to the extent that their operations resemble true investing they may produce investment gains that more than offset the speculative losses.

The investor obtains advice and information from stock-exchange houses through two types of employees, now known officially as "customers' brokers" (or "account executives") and financial analysts.

The customer's broker, also called a "registered representative," formerly bore the less dignified title of "customer's man." Today he is for the most part an individual of good character and considerable knowledge of securities, who operates under a rigid code of right conduct. Nevertheless, since his business is to earn commissions, he can hardly avoid being speculation-minded. Thus the security buyer who wants to avoid being influenced by speculative considerations will ordinarily have to be careful and explicit in his dealing with his customer's broker; he will have to show clearly, by word and deed, that he is not interested in anything faintly resembling a stock-market "tip." Once the customer's broker understands clearly that he has a real investor on his hands, he will respect this point of view and cooperate with it.

The financial analyst, formerly known chiefly as security analyst, is a person of particular concern to the author, who has been one himself for more than five decades and has helped educate countless others. At this stage we refer only to the financial analysts employed by brokerage houses. The function of the security analyst is clear enough from his title. It is he who works up the detailed studies of individual securities, develops careful comparisons of various issues in the same field, and forms an expert opinion of the safety or attractiveness or intrinsic value of all the different kinds of stocks and bonds.

---

late 1990s. These firms spent millions of dollars on flashy advertising that goaded their customers into trading more and trading faster. Most of those customers ended up picking their own pockets, instead of paying someone else to do it for them—and the cheap commissions on that kind of transaction are a poor consolation for the result. More traditional brokerage firms, meanwhile, began emphasizing financial planning and "integrated asset management," instead of compensating their brokers only on the basis of how many commissions they could generate.

By what must seem a quirk to the outsider there are no formal requirements for being a security analyst. Contrast with this the facts that a customer's broker must pass an examination, meet the required character tests, and be duly accepted and registered by the New York Stock Exchange. As a practical matter, nearly all the younger analysts have had extensive business-school training, and the oldsters have acquired at least the equivalent in the school of long experience. In the great majority of cases, the employing brokerage house can be counted on to assure itself of the qualifications and competence of its analysts.*

The customer of the brokerage firm may deal with the security analysts directly, or his contact may be an indirect one via the customer's broker. In either case the analyst is available to the client for a considerable amount of information and advice. Let us make an emphatic statement here. The value of the security analyst to the investor depends largely on the investor's own attitude. If the investor asks the analyst the right questions, he is likely to get the right—or at least valuable—answers. The analysts hired by brokerage houses, we are convinced, are greatly handicapped by the general feeling that they are supposed to be market analysts as well. When they are asked whether a given common stock is "sound," the question often means, "Is this stock likely to advance during the next few months?" As a result many of them are com-

---

* This remains true, although many of Wall Street's best analysts hold the title of chartered financial analyst. The CFA certification is awarded by the Association of Investment Management & Research (formerly the Financial Analysts Federation) only after the candidate has completed years of rigorous study and passed a series of difficult exams. More than 50,000 analysts worldwide have been certified as CFAs. Sadly, a recent survey by Professor Stanley Block found that most CFAs ignore Graham's teachings: Growth potential ranks higher than quality of earnings, risks, and dividend policy in determining P/E ratios, while far more analysts base their buy ratings on recent price than on the long-term outlook for the company. See Stanley Block, "A Study of Financial Analysts: Practice and Theory," *Financial Analysts Journal*, July/August, 1999, at www.aimrpubs.org. As Graham was fond of saying, his own books have been read by–and ignored by–more people than any other books in finance.

pelled to analyze with one eye on the stock ticker—a pose not conducive to sound thinking or worthwhile conclusions.*

In the next section of this book we shall deal with some of the concepts and possible achievements of security analysis. A great many analysts working for stock exchange firms could be of prime assistance to the bona fide investor who wants to be sure that he gets full value for his money, and possibly a little more. As in the case of the customers' brokers, what is needed at the beginning is a clear understanding by the analyst of the investor's attitude and objectives. Once the analyst is convinced that he is dealing with a man who is value-minded rather than quotation-minded, there is an excellent chance that his recommendations will prove of real overall benefit.

The CFA Certificate for Financial Analysts

An important step was taken in 1963 toward giving professional standing and responsibility to financial analysts. The official title of chartered financial analyst (CFA) is now awarded to those senior practitioners who pass required examinations and meet other tests of fitness.[1] The subjects covered include security analysis and portfolio management. The analogy with the long-established professional title of certified public accountant (CPA) is evident and intentional. This relatively new apparatus of recognition and control should serve to elevate the standards of financial analysts and eventually to place their work on a truly professional basis.†

---

* It is highly unusual today for a security analyst to allow mere commoners to contact him directly. For the most part, only the nobility of institutional investors are permitted to approach the throne of the almighty Wall Street analyst. An individual investor might, perhaps, have some luck calling analysts who work at "regional" brokerage firms headquartered outside of New York City. The investor relations area at the websites of most publicly traded companies will provide a list of analysts who follow the stock. Websites like www.zacks.com and www.multex.com offer access to analysts' research reports–but the intelligent investor should remember that most analysts do not analyze businesses. Instead, they engage in guesswork about future stock prices.

† Benjamin Graham was the prime force behind the establishment of the CFA program, which he advocated for nearly two decades before it became a reality.

Dealings with Brokerage Houses

One of the most disquieting developments of the period in which we write this revision has been the financial embarrassment—in plain words, bankruptcy or near-bankruptcy—of quite a few New York Stock Exchange firms, including at least two of considerable size.* This is the first time in half a century or more that such a thing has happened, and it is startling for more than one reason. For many decades the New York Stock Exchange has been moving in the direction of closer and stricter controls over the operations and financial condition of its members—including minimum capital requirements, surprise audits, and the like. Besides this, we have had 37 years of control over the exchanges and their members by the Securities and Exchange Commission. Finally, the stock-brokerage industry itself has operated under favorable conditions—namely, a huge increase in volume, fixed minimum commission rates (largely eliminating competitive fees), and a limited number of member firms.

The first financial troubles of the brokerage houses (in 1969) were attributed to the increase in volume itself. This, it was claimed, overtaxed their facilities, increased their overhead, and produced many troubles in making financial settlements. It should be pointed out this was probably the first time in history that important enterprises have gone broke because they had more business than they could handle. In 1970, as brokerage failures increased, they were blamed chiefly on "the falling off in volume." A strange complaint when one reflects that the turnover of the

---

* The two firms Graham had in mind were probably Du Pont, Glore, Forgan & Co. and Goodbody & Co. Du Pont (founded by the heirs to the chemical fortune) was saved from insolvency in 1970 only after Texas entrepreneur H. Ross Perot lent more than $50 million to the firm; Goodbody, the fifth-largest brokerage firm in the United States, would have failed in late 1970 had Merrill Lynch not acquired it. Hayden, Stone & Co. would also have gone under if it had not been acquired. In 1970, no fewer than seven brokerage firms went bust. The farcical story of Wall Street's frenzied overexpansion in the late 1960s is beautifully told in John Brooks's *The Go-Go Years* (John Wiley & Sons, New York, 1999).

NYSE in 1970 totaled 2,937 million shares, the *largest* volume in its history and well over twice as large as in any year before 1965. During the 15 years of the bull market ending in 1964 the annual volume had averaged "only" 712 million shares—one quarter of the 1970 figure—but the brokerage business had enjoyed the greatest prosperity in its history. If, as it appears, the member firms as a whole had allowed their overhead and other expenses to increase at a rate that could not sustain even a mild reduction in volume during part of a year, this does not speak well for either their business acumen or their financial conservatism.

A third explanation of the financial trouble finally emerged out of a mist of concealment, and we suspect that it is the most plausible and significant of the three. It seems that a good part of the capital of certain brokerage houses was held in the form of common stocks owned by the individual partners. Some of these seem to have been highly speculative and carried at inflated values. When the market declined in 1969 the quotations of such securities fell drastically and a substantial part of the capital of the firms vanished with them.[2] In effect the partners were speculating with the capital that was supposed to protect the customers against the ordinary financial hazards of the brokerage business, in order to make a double profit thereon. This was inexcusable; we refrain from saying more.

The investor should use his intelligence not only in formulating his financial policies but also in the associated details. These include the choice of a reputable broker to execute his orders. Up to now it was sufficient to counsel our readers to deal only with a member of the New York Stock Exchange, unless he had compelling reasons to use a nonmember firm. Reluctantly, we must add some further advice in this area. We think that people who do not carry margin accounts—and in our vocabulary this means *all* nonprofessional *investors*—should have the delivery and receipt of their securities handled by their bank. When giving a buying order to your brokers you can instruct them to deliver the securities bought to your bank against payment therefor by the bank; conversely, when selling you can instruct your bank to deliver the securities to the broker against payment of the proceeds. These services will cost a little extra but they should be well worth the expense in terms of safety and peace of mind. This advice may be disregarded, as no longer called for, after the investor is sure that all the problems of stock-exchange firms have been disposed of, but not before.*

Investment Bankers

The term "investment banker" is applied to a firm that engages to an important extent in originating, underwriting, and selling new issues of stocks and bonds. (To underwrite means to guarantee to the issuing corporation, or other issuer, that the security will be fully sold.) A number of the brokerage houses carry on a certain amount of underwriting activity. Generally this is confined to participating in underwriting groups formed by leading investment bankers. There is an additional tendency for brokerage firms to originate and sponsor a minor amount of new-issue financing, particularly in the form of smaller issues of common stocks when a bull market is in full swing.

Investment banking is perhaps the most respectable department of the Wall Street community, because it is here that finance plays its constructive role of supplying new capital for the expansion of industry. In fact, much of the theoretical justification for maintaining active stock markets, notwithstanding their frequent speculative excesses, lies in the fact that organized security exchanges facilitate the sale of new issues of bonds and stocks. If investors or speculators could not expect to see a ready market for a new security offered them, they might well refuse to buy it.

The relationship between the investment banker and the

* Nearly all brokerage transactions are now conducted electronically, and securities are no longer physically "delivered." Thanks to the establishment of the Securities Investor Protection Corporation, or SIPC, in 1970, investors are generally assured of recovering their full account values if their brokerage firm becomes insolvent. SIPC is a government-mandated consortium of brokers; all the members agree to pool their assets to cover losses incurred by the customers of any firm that becomes insolvent. SIPC's protection eliminates the need for investors to make payment and take delivery through a bank intermediary, as Graham urges.

investor is basically that of the salesman to the prospective buyer. For many years past the great bulk of the new offerings in dollar value has consisted of bond issues that were purchased in the main by financial institutions such as banks and insurance companies. In this business the security salesmen have been dealing with shrewd and experienced buyers. Hence any recommendations made by the investment bankers to these customers have had to pass careful and skeptical scrutiny. Thus these transactions are almost always effected on a businesslike footing.

But a different situation obtains in a relationship between the *individual* security buyer and the investment banking firms, including the stockbrokers acting as underwriters. Here the purchaser is frequently inexperienced and seldom shrewd. He is easily influenced by what the salesman tells him, especially in the case of common-stock issues, since often his unconfessed desire in buying is chiefly to make a quick profit. The effect of all this is that the public investor's protection lies less in his own critical faculty than in the scruples and ethics of the offering houses.[3]

It is a tribute to the honesty and competence of the underwriting firms that they are able to combine fairly well the discordant roles of adviser and salesman. But it is imprudent for the buyer to trust himself to the judgment of the seller. In 1959 we stated at this point: "The bad results of this unsound attitude show themselves recurrently in the underwriting field and with notable effects in the sale of new common stock issues during periods of active speculation." Shortly thereafter this warning proved urgently needed. As already pointed out, the years 1960–61 and, again, 1968–69 were marked by an unprecedented outpouring of issues of lowest quality, sold to the public at absurdly high offering prices and in many cases pushed much higher by heedless speculation and some semi-manipulation. A number of the more important Wall Street houses have participated to some degree in these less than creditable activities, which demonstrates that the familiar combination of greed, folly, and irresponsibility has not been exorcized from the financial scene.

The intelligent investor will pay attention to the advice and recommendations received from investment banking houses, especially those known by him to have an excellent reputation; but he will be sure to bring sound and independent judgment to bear upon these suggestions—either his own, if he is competent, or that of some other type of adviser.*

Other Advisers

It is a good old custom, especially in the smaller towns, to consult one's local banker about investments. A commercial banker may not be a thoroughgoing expert on security values, but he is experienced and conservative. He is especially useful to the unskilled investor, who is often tempted to stray from the straight and unexciting path of a defensive policy and needs the steadying influence of a prudent mind. The more alert and aggressive investor, seeking counsel in the selection of security bargains, will not ordinarily find the commercial banker's viewpoint to be especially suited to his own objectives.†

We take a more critical attitude toward the widespread custom of asking investment advice from relatives or friends. The inquirer always thinks he has good reason for assuming that the person consulted has superior knowledge or experience. Our own observation indicates that it is almost as difficult to select satisfactory lay advisers as it is to select the proper securities unaided. Much bad advice is given free.

Summary

Investors who are prepared to pay a fee for the management of their funds may wisely select some well-established and well-recommended investment-counsel firm. Alternatively, they may use the investment department of a large trust company or the supervisory service supplied on a fee basis by a few of the leading New York Stock Exchange houses. The results to be expected are in no wise exceptional, but they are commensurate with those of the average well-informed and cautious investor.

---

* Those who heeded Graham's advice would not have been suckered into buying Internet IPOs in 1999 and 2000.

† This traditional role of bankers has for the most part been supplanted by accountants, lawyers, or financial planners.

Most security buyers obtain advice without paying for it specifically. It stands to reason, therefore, that in the majority of cases they are not entitled to and should not expect better than average results. They should be wary of all persons, whether customers' brokers or security salesmen, who promise spectacular income or profits. This applies both to the selection of securities and to guidance in the elusive (and perhaps illusive) art of trading in the market.

Defensive investors, as we have defined them, will not ordinarily be equipped to pass independent judgment on the security recommendations made by their advisers. But they can be explicit—and even repetitiously so—in stating the kind of securities they want to buy. If they follow our prescription they will confine themselves to high-grade bonds and the common stocks of leading corporations, preferably those that can be purchased at individual price levels that are not high in the light of experience and analysis. The security analyst of any reputable stock-exchange house can make up a suitable list of such common stocks and can certify to the investor whether or not the existing price level therefor is a reasonably conservative one as judged by past experience.

The aggressive investor will ordinarily work in active cooperation with his advisers. He will want their recommendations explained in detail, and he will insist on passing his own judgment upon them. This means that the investor will gear his expectations and the character of his security operations to the development of his own knowledge and experience in the field. Only in the exceptional case, where the integrity and competence of the advisers have been thoroughly demonstrated, should the investor act upon the advice of others without understanding and approving the decision made.

There have always been unprincipled stock salesmen and fly-by-night stock brokers, and—as a matter of course—we have advised our readers to confine their dealings, if possible, to members of the New York Stock Exchange. But we are reluctantly compelled to add the extra-cautious counsel that security deliveries and payments be made through the intermediary of the investor's bank. The distressing Wall Street brokerage-house picture may have cleared up completely in a few years, but in late 1971 we still suggest, "Better safe than sorry."

COMMENTARY ON CHAPTER 10

> I feel grateful to the Milesian wench who, seeing the philosopher Thales continually spending his time in contemplation of the heavenly vault and always keeping his eyes raised upward, put something in his way to make him stumble, to warn him that it would be time to amuse his thoughts with things in the clouds when he had seen to those at his feet. Indeed she gave him or her good counsel, to look rather to himself than to the sky.
>
> *–Michel de Montaigne*

DO YOU NEED HELP?

In the glory days of the late 1990s, many investors chose to go it alone. By doing their own research, picking stocks themselves, and placing their trades through an online broker, these investors bypassed Wall Street's costly infrastructure of research, advice, and trading. Unfortunately, many do-it-yourselfers asserted their independence right before the worst bear market since the Great Depression–making them feel, in the end, that they were fools for going it alone. That's not necessarily true, of course; people who delegated every decision to a traditional stockbroker lost money, too.

But many investors do take comfort from the experience, judgment, and second opinion that a good financial adviser can provide. Some investors may need an outsider to show them what rate of return they need to earn on their investments, or how much extra money they need to save, in order to meet their financial goals. Others may simply benefit from having someone else to blame when their investments go down; that way, instead of beating yourself up in an agony of self-doubt, you get to criticize someone who typically can defend him or herself and encourage you at the same time. That may provide just the psychological boost you need to keep investing steadily at a time

…t as there's no
…'s no shame in

…e signals:
…of its value from
…n you did even
…t itself. It hardly
…or just unlucky;
…help.
…ake ends meet,
…ble to save on a
…lls on time, then
…you get a grip on
…plan that will out-
save, and invest.
…t they were diver-
…different" Internet
…ds. But that's like
…inging "Old Man
how many sopra-
…ll those low notes
…our holdings go up
…that true diversifi-
can help.
…ed and need to set
…ve their finances in
…an adviser can not
…uine improvements
…ed professional can
…staggering complex-

…ing you into trusting
…m. Before you place

…ues, see Walter Upde-
…53–55.

your financial future in the
find someone who not only
is beyond reproach. As R
ify." Start off by thinking of
trust the most. Then ask if
trust and who, they feel,
confidence from someone y

Once you have the nam
specialty—is he a stockbrok
ance agent?—you can begin
adviser and his or her firm i
to see if anything comes up
"lawsuit," "disciplinary actio
stockbroker or insurance a
securities commissioner (a
www.nasaa.org) to ask whe
complaints have been filed a
an accountant who also fun
accounting regulators (whom
ciation of State Boards of A
you whether his or her record

Financial planners (or their
Securities and Exchange Cor
state where their practice is
adviser must file a two-part do
able to view and download it
com, or the website of your
attention to the Disclosure Re
disclose any disciplinary actio

---

[2] If you're unable to get a referral
to find a fee-only financial planner
org), whose members are genera
integrity.

[3] By itself, a customer complaint is
your consideration; but a persisten
nary action by state or Federal re
adviser. Another source for checkir
com/PDPI.

when other investors' hearts may fail them. All in all, just as there's no reason you can't manage your own portfolio, so there's no shame in seeking professional help in managing it.[1]

How can you tell if you need a hand? Here are some signals:

Big losses. If your portfolio lost more than 40% of its value from the beginning of 2000 through the end of 2002, then you did even worse than the dismal performance of the stock market itself. It hardly matters whether you blew it by being lazy, reckless, or just unlucky; after such a giant loss, your portfolio is crying out for help.

Busted budgets. If you perennially struggle to make ends meet, have no idea where your money goes, find it impossible to save on a regular schedule, and chronically fail to pay your bills on time, then your finances are out of control. An adviser can help you get a grip on your money by designing a comprehensive financial plan that will outline how—and how much—you should spend, borrow, save, and invest.

Chaotic portfolios. All too many investors thought they were diversified in the late 1990s because they owned 39 "different" Internet stocks, or seven "different" U.S. growth-stock funds. But that's like thinking that an all-soprano chorus can handle singing "Old Man River" better than a soprano soloist can. No matter how many sopranos you add, that chorus will never be able to nail all those low notes until some baritones join the group. Likewise, if all your holdings go up and down together, you lack the investing harmony that true diversification brings. A professional "asset-allocation" plan can help.

Major changes. If you've become self-employed and need to set up a retirement plan, your aging parents don't have their finances in order, or college for your kids looks unaffordable, an adviser can not only provide peace of mind but help you make genuine improvements in the quality of your life. What's more, a qualified professional can ensure that you benefit from and comply with the staggering complexity of the tax laws and retirement rules.

TRUST, THEN VERIFY

Remember that financial con artists thrive by talking you into trusting them and by talking you out of investigating them. Before you place

---

[1] For a particularly thoughtful discussion of these issues, see Walter Updegrave, "Advice on Advice," *Money,* January, 2003, pp. 53–55.

your financial future in the hands of an adviser, it's imperative that you find someone who not only makes you comfortable but whose honesty is beyond reproach. As Ronald Reagan used to say, "Trust, then verify." Start off by thinking of the handful of people you know best and trust the most. Then ask if they can refer you to an adviser whom *they* trust and who, they feel, delivers good value for his fees. A vote of confidence from someone you admire is a good start.[2]

Once you have the name of the adviser and his firm, as well as his specialty–is he a stockbroker? financial planner? accountant? insurance agent?–you can begin your due diligence. Enter the name of the adviser and his or her firm into an Internet search engine like Google to see if anything comes up (watch for terms like "fine," "complaint," "lawsuit," "disciplinary action," or "suspension"). If the adviser is a stockbroker or insurance agent, contact the office of your state's securities commissioner (a convenient directory of online links is at www.nasaa.org) to ask whether any disciplinary actions or customer complaints have been filed against the adviser.[3] If you're considering an accountant who also functions as a financial adviser, your state's accounting regulators (whom you can find through the National Association of State Boards of Accountancy at www.nasba.org) will tell you whether his or her record is clean.

Financial planners (or their firms) must register with either the U.S. Securities and Exchange Commission or securities regulators in the state where their practice is based. As part of that registration, the adviser must file a two-part document called Form ADV. You should be able to view and download it at www.advisorinfo.sec.gov, www.iard.com, or the website of your state securities regulator. Pay special attention to the Disclosure Reporting Pages, where the adviser must disclose any disciplinary actions by regulators. (Because unscrupu-

---

[2] If you're unable to get a referral from someone you trust, you may be able to find a fee-only financial planner through www.napfa.org (or www.feeonly.org), whose members are generally held to high standards of service and integrity.

[3] By itself, a customer complaint is not enough to disqualify an adviser from your consideration; but a persistent pattern of complaints is. And a disciplinary action by state or Federal regulators usually tells you to find another adviser. Another source for checking a broker's record is http://pdpi.nasdr.com/PDPI.

lous advisers have been known to remove those pages before handing an ADV to a prospective client, you should independently obtain your own complete copy.) It's a good idea to cross-check a financial planner's record at www.cfp-board.org, since some planners who have been disciplined outside their home state can fall through the regulatory cracks. For more tips on due diligence, see the sidebar below.

WORDS OF WARNING

The need for due diligence doesn't stop once you hire an adviser. Melanie Senter Lubin, securities commissioner for the State of Maryland, suggests being on guard for words and phrases that can spell trouble. If your adviser keeps saying them—or twisting your arm to do anything that makes you uncomfortable—"then get in touch with the authorities very quickly," warns Lubin. Here's the kind of lingo that should set off warning bells:

- "offshore"
- "the opportunity of a lifetime"
- "prime bank"
- "This baby's gonna move."
- "guaranteed"
- "You need to hurry."
- "It's a sure thing."
- "our proprietary computer model"
- "The smart money is buying it."
- "options strategy"
- "It's a no-brainer."
- "You can't afford not to own it."
- "We can beat the market."
- "You'll be sorry if you don't . . ."
- "exclusive"
- "You should focus on performance, not fees."
- "Don't you want to be rich?"
- "can't lose"
- "The upside is huge."
- "There's no downside."
- "I'm putting my mother in it."
- "Trust me."
- "commodities trading"
- "monthly returns"
- "active asset-allocation strategy"
- "We can cap your downside."
- "No one else knows how to do this."

GETTING TO KNOW YOU

A leading financial-planning newsletter recently canvassed dozens of advisers to get their thoughts on how you should go about interviewing them.[4] In screening an adviser, your goals should be to:

- determine whether he or she cares about helping clients, or just goes through the motions
- establish whether he or she understands the fundamental principles of investing as they are outlined in this book
- assess whether he or she is sufficiently educated, trained, and experienced to help you.

Here are some of the questions that prominent financial planners recommended any prospective client should ask:

Why are you in this business? What is the mission statement of your firm? Besides your alarm clock, what makes you get up in the morning?

What is your investing philosophy? Do you use stocks or mutual funds? Do you use technical analysis? Do you use market timing? (A "yes" to either of the last two questions is a "no" signal to you.)

Do you focus solely on asset management, or do you also advise on taxes, estate and retirement planning, budgeting and debt management, and insurance? How do your education, experience, and credentials qualify you to give those kinds of financial advice?[5]

What needs do your clients typically have in common? How can you help me achieve my goals? How will you track and report my progress? Do you provide a checklist that I can use to monitor the implementation of any financial plan we develop?

---

[4] Robert Veres, editor and publisher of the *Inside Information* newsletter, generously shared these responses for this book. Other checklists of questions can be found at www.cfp-board.org and www.napfa.org.

[5] Credentials like the CFA, CFP, or CPA tell you that the adviser has taken and passed a rigorous course of study. (Most of the other "alphabet soup" of credentials brandished by financial planners, including the "CFM" or the "CMFC," signify very little.) More important, by contacting the organization that awards the credential, you can verify his record and check that he has not been disciplined for violations of rules or ethics.

How do you choose investments? What investing approach do you believe is most successful, and what evidence can you show me that you have achieved that kind of success for your clients? What do you do when an investment performs poorly for an entire year? (Any adviser who answers "sell" is not worth hiring.)

Do you, when recommending investments, accept any form of compensation from any third party? Why or why not? Under which circumstances? How much, in actual dollars, do you estimate I would pay for your services the first year? What would make that number go up or down over time? (If fees will consume more than 1% of your assets annually, you should probably shop for another adviser.[6])

How many clients do you have, and how often do you communicate with them? What has been your proudest achievement for a client? What characteristics do your favorite clients share? What's the worst experience you've had with a client, and how did you resolve it? What determines whether a client speaks to you or to your support staff? How long do clients typically stay with you?

Can I see a sample account statement? (If you can't understand it, ask the adviser to explain it. If you can't understand his explanation, he's not right for you.)

Do you consider yourself financially successful? Why? How do you define financial success?

How high an average annual return do you think is feasible on my investments? (Anything over 8% to10% is unrealistic.)

Will you provide me with your résumé, your Form ADV, and at least three references? (If the adviser or his firm is required to file an ADV, and he will not provide you a copy, get up and leave–and keep one hand on your wallet as you go.)

Have you ever had a formal complaint filed against you? Why did the last client who fired you do so?

---

[6] If you have less than $100,000 to invest, you may not be able to find a financial adviser who will take your account. In that case, buy a diversified basket of low-cost index funds, follow the behavioral advice throughout this book, and your portfolio should eventually grow to the level at which you can afford an adviser.

DEFEATING YOUR OWN WORST ENEMY

Finally, bear in mind that great financial advisers do not grow on trees. Often, the best already have as many clients as they can handle—and may be willing to take you on only if you seem like a good match. So they will ask you some tough questions as well, which might include:

Why do you feel you need a financial adviser?

What are your long-term goals?

What has been your greatest frustration in dealing with other advisers (including yourself)?

Do you have a budget? Do you live within your means? What percentage of your assets do you spend each year?

When we look back a year from now, what will I need to have accomplished in order for you to be happy with your progress?

How do you handle conflicts or disagreements?

How did you respond emotionally to the bear market that began in 2000?

What are your worst financial fears? Your greatest financial hopes?

What rate of return on your investments do you consider reasonable? (Base your answer on Chapter 3.)

An adviser who doesn't ask questions like these—and who does not show enough interest in you to sense intuitively what other questions you consider to be the right ones—is not a good fit.

Above all else, you should trust your adviser enough to permit him or her to protect you from your worst enemy—yourself. "You hire an adviser," explains commentator Nick Murray, "not to manage money but to manage you."

"If the adviser is a line of defense between you and your worst impulsive tendencies," says financial-planning analyst Robert Veres, "then he or she should have systems in place that will help the two of you control them." Among those systems:

- a **comprehensive financial plan** that outlines how you will earn, save, spend, borrow, and invest your money;
- an **investment policy statement** that spells out your fundamental approach to investing;
- an **asset-allocation plan** that details how much money you will keep in different investment categories.

These are the building blocks on which good financial decisions must be founded, and they should be created mutually–by you and the adviser–rather than imposed unilaterally. You should not invest a dollar or make a decision until you are satisfied that these foundations are in place and in accordance with your wishes.

CHAPTER 11

Security Analysis for the Lay Investor: General Approach

Financial analysis is now a well-established and flourishing profession, or semiprofession. The various societies of analysts that make up the National Federation of Financial Analysts have over 13,000 members, most of whom make their living out of this branch of mental activity. Financial analysts have textbooks, a code of ethics, and a quarterly journal.* They also have their share of unresolved problems. In recent years there has been a tendency to replace the general concept of "security analysis" by that of "financial analysis." The latter phrase has a broader implication and is better suited to describe the work of most senior analysts on Wall Street. It would be useful to think of security analysis as limiting itself pretty much to the examination and evaluation of stocks and bonds, whereas financial analysis would comprise that work, plus the determination of investment policy (portfolio selection), plus a substantial amount of general economic analysis.[1] In this chapter we shall use whatever designation is most applicable, with chief emphasis on the work of the security analyst proper.

The security analyst deals with the past, the present, and the future of any given security issue. He describes the business; he summarizes its operating results and financial position; he sets forth its strong and weak points, its possibilities and risks; he estimates its future earning power under various assumptions, or as a

* The National Federation of Financial Analysts is now the Association for Investment Management and Research; its "quarterly" research publication, the *Financial Analysts Journal*, now appears every other month.

"best guess." He makes elaborate comparisons of various companies, or of the same company at various times. Finally, he expresses an opinion as to the safety of the issue, if it is a bond or investment-grade preferred stock, or as to its attractiveness as a purchase, if it is a common stock.

In doing all these things the security analyst avails himself of a number of techniques, ranging from the elementary to the most abstruse. He may modify substantially the figures in the company's annual statements, even though they bear the sacred *imprimatur* of the certified public accountant. He is on the lookout particularly for items in these reports that may mean a good deal more or less than they say.

The security analyst develops and applies standards of safety by which we can conclude whether a given bond or preferred stock may be termed sound enough to justify purchase for investment. These standards relate primarily to past average earnings, but they are concerned also with capital structure, working capital, asset values, and other matters.

In dealing with common stocks the security analyst until recently has only rarely applied standards of value as well defined as were his standards of safety for bonds and preferred stocks. Most of the time he contended himself with a summary of past performances, a more or less general forecast of the future—with particular emphasis on the next 12 months—and a rather arbitrary conclusion. The latter was, and still is, often drawn with one eye on the stock ticker or the market charts. In the past few years, however, much attention has been given by practicing analysts to the problem of valuing growth stocks. Many of these have sold at such high prices in relation to past and current earnings that those recommending them have felt a special obligation to justify their purchase by fairly definite projections of expected earnings running fairly far into the future. Certain mathematical techniques of a rather sophisticated sort have perforce been invoked to support the valuations arrived at.

We shall deal with these techniques, in foreshortened form, a little later. However, we must point out a troublesome paradox here, which is that the mathematical valuations have become most prevalent precisely in those areas where one might consider them least reliable. For the more dependent the valuation becomes on

anticipations of the future—and the less it is tied to a figure demonstrated by past performance—the more vulnerable it becomes to possible miscalculation and serious error. A large part of the value found for a high-multiplier growth stock is derived from future projections which differ markedly from past performance—except perhaps in the growth rate itself. Thus it may be said that security analysts today find themselves compelled to become most mathematical and "scientific" in the very situations which lend themselves least auspiciously to exact treatment.*

Let us proceed, nonetheless, with our discussion of the more important elements and techniques of security analysis. The present highly condensed treatment is directed to the needs of the nonprofessional investor. At the minimum he should understand what the security analyst is talking about and driving at; beyond that, he should be equipped, if possible, to distinguish between superficial and sound analysis.

Security analysis for the lay investor is thought of as beginning

---

* The higher the growth rate you project, and the longer the future period over which you project it, the more sensitive your forecast becomes to the slightest error. If, for instance, you estimate that a company earning $1 per share can raise that profit by 15% a year for the next 15 years, its earnings would end up at $8.14. If the market values the company at 35 times earnings, the stock would finish the period at roughly $285. But if earnings grow at 14% instead of 15%, the company would earn $7.14 at the end of the period–and, in the shock of that shortfall, investors would no longer be willing to pay 35 times earnings. At, say, 20 times earnings, the stock would end up around $140 per share, or more than 50% less. Because advanced mathematics gives the appearance of precision to the inherently iffy process of foreseeing the future, investors must be highly skeptical of anyone who claims to hold any complex computational key to basic financial problems. As Graham put it: "In 44 years of Wall Street experience and study, I have never seen dependable calculations made about common-stock values, or related investment policies, that went beyond simple arithmetic or the most elementary algebra. Whenever calculus is brought in, or higher algebra, you could take it as a warning signal that the operator was trying to substitute theory for experience, and usually also to give to speculation the deceptive guise of investment." (See p. 570.)

with the interpretation of a company's annual financial report. This is a subject which we have covered for laymen in a separate book, entitled *The Interpretation of Financial Statements.*[2] We do not consider it necessary or appropriate to traverse the same ground in this chapter, especially since the emphasis in the present book is on principles and attitudes rather than on information and description. Let us pass on to two basic questions underlying the selection of investments. What are the primary tests of safety of a corporate bond or preferred stock? What are the chief factors entering into the valuation of a common stock?

Bond Analysis

The most dependable and hence the most respectable branch of security analysis concerns itself with the safety, or quality, of bond issues and investment-grade preferred stocks. The chief criterion used for corporate bonds is the number of times that total interest charges have been covered by available earnings for some years in the past. In the case of preferred stocks, it is the number of times that bond interest and preferred dividends combined have been covered.

The exact standards applied will vary with different authorities. Since the tests are at bottom arbitrary, there is no way to determine precisely the most suitable criteria. In the 1961 revision of our textbook, *Security Analysis,* we recommend certain "coverage" standards, which appear in Table 11-1.*

Our basic test is applied only to the *average* results for a period of years. Other authorities require also that a *minimum* coverage be shown for every year considered. We approve a "poorest-year" test

---

* In 1972, an investor in corporate bonds had little choice but to assemble his or her own portfolio. Today, roughly 500 mutual funds invest in corporate bonds, creating a convenient, well-diversified bundle of securities. Since it is not feasible to build a diversified bond portfolio on your own unless you have at least $100,000, the typical intelligent investor will be best off simply buying a low-cost bond fund and leaving the painstaking labor of credit research to its managers. For more on bond funds, see the commentary on Chapter 4.

TABLE 11-1 Recommended Minimum "Coverage" for Bonds and Preferred Stocks

A. For Investment-grade Bonds

Minimum Ratio of Earnings to Total Fixed Charges:

	Before Income Taxes		*After Income Taxes*	
Type of enterprise	Average of Past 7 Years	Alternative: Measured by "Poorest Year"	Average of Past 7 Years	Alternative: Measured by "Poorest Year"
Public-utility operating company	4 times	3 times	2.65 times	2.10 times
Railroad	5	4	3.20	2.65
Industrial	7	5	4.30	3.20
Retail concern	5	4	3.20	2.65

B. *For Investment-grade Preferred Stocks*

The same minimum figures as above are required to be shown by the ratio of earnings *before* income taxes to the sum of fixed charges plus twice preferred dividends.

NOTE: The inclusion of twice the preferred dividends allows for the fact that preferred dividends are not income-tax deductible, whereas interest charges are so deductible.

C. *Other Categories of Bonds and Preferreds*

The standards given above are not applicable to (1) public-utility holding companies, (2) financial companies, (3) real-estate companies. Requirements for these special groups are omitted here.

as an *alternative* to the seven-year-average test; it would be sufficient if the bond or preferred stock met either of these criteria.

It may be objected that the large increase in bond interest rates since 1961 would justify some offsetting reduction in the coverage of charges required. Obviously it would be much harder for an industrial company to show a seven-times coverage of interest charges at 8% than at 4½%. To meet this changed situation we now suggest an alternative requirement related to the percent earned on the *principal* amount of the debt. These figures might be 33% before taxes for an industrial company, 20% for a public utility, and 25% for a railroad. It should be borne in mind here that the rate actually paid by most companies on their total debt is considerably less than the current 8% figures, since they have the benefit of older issues bearing lower coupons. The "poorest year" requirement could be set at about two-thirds of the seven-year requirement.

In addition to the earnings-coverage test, a number of others are generally applied. These include the following:

1. *Size of Enterprise.* There is a minimum standard in terms of volume of business for a corporation—varying as between industrials, utilities, and railroads—and of population for a municipality.

2. *Stock/Equity Ratio.* This is the ratio of the market price of the junior stock issues* to the total face amount of the debt, or the debt plus preferred stock. It is a rough measure of the protection, or "cushion," afforded by the presence of a junior investment that must first bear the brunt of unfavorable developments. This factor includes the market's appraisal of the future prospects of the enterprise.

3. *Property Value.* The asset values, as shown on the balance sheet or as appraised, were formerly considered the chief security and protection for a bond issue. Experience has shown that in most cases safety resides in the earning power, and if this is deficient the assets lose most of their reputed value. Asset values, however, retain importance as a separate test of ample security for bonds and preferred stocks in three enterprise groups: public utilities (because rates may depend largely on the property investment), real-estate concerns, and investment companies.

At this point the alert investor should ask, "How dependable are tests of safety that are measured by past and present performance, in view of the fact that payment of interest and principal depends upon what the future will bring forth?" The answer can be founded

* By "junior stock issues" Graham means shares of common stock. Preferred stock is considered "senior" to common stock because the company must pay all dividends on the preferred before paying any dividends on the common.

only on experience. Investment history shows that bonds and preferred stocks that have met stringent tests of safety, based on the past, have in the great majority of cases been able to face the vicissitudes of the future successfully. This has been strikingly demonstrated in the major field of railroad bonds—a field that has been marked by a calamitous frequency of bankruptcies and serious losses. In nearly every case the roads that got into trouble had long been overbonded, had shown an inadequate coverage of fixed charges in periods of average prosperity, and would thus have been ruled out by investors who applied strict tests of safety. Conversely, practically every road that has met such tests has escaped financial embarrassment. Our premise was strikingly vindicated by the financial history of the numerous railroads reorganized in the 1940s and in 1950. All of these, with one exception, started their careers with fixed charges reduced to a point where the current coverage of fixed-interest requirements was ample, or at least respectable. The exception was the New Haven Railroad, which in its reorganization year, 1947, earned its new charges only about 1.1 times. In consequence, while all the other roads were able to come through rather difficult times with solvency unimpaired, the New Haven relapsed into trusteeship (for the third time) in 1961.

In Chapter 17 below we shall consider some aspects of the bankruptcy of the Penn Central Railroad, which shook the financial community in 1970. An elementary fact in this case was that the coverage of fixed charges did not meet conservative standards as early as 1965; hence a prudent bond investor would have avoided or disposed of the bond issues of the system long before its financial collapse.

Our observations on the adequacy of the past record to judge future safety apply, and to an even greater degree, to the public utilities, which constitute a major area for bond investment. Receivership of a soundly capitalized (electric) utility company or system is almost impossible. Since Securities and Exchange Commission control was instituted,* along with the breakup of most of

* After investors lost billions of dollars on the shares of recklessly assembled utility companies in 1929–1932, Congress authorized the SEC to regulate the issuance of utility stocks under the Public Utility Holding Company Act of 1935.

the holding-company systems, public-utility financing has been sound and bankruptcies unknown. The financial troubles of electric and gas utilities in the 1930s were traceable almost 100% to financial excesses and mismanagement, which left their imprint clearly on the companies' capitalization structures. Simple but stringent tests of safety, therefore, would have warned the investor away from the issues that were later to default.

Among industrial bond issues the long-term record has been different. Although the industrial group as a whole has shown a better growth of earning power than either the railroads or the utilities, it has revealed a lesser degree of inherent stability for individual companies and lines of business. Thus in the past, at least, there have been persuasive reasons for confining the purchase of industrial bonds and preferred stocks to companies that not only are of major size but also have shown an ability in the past to withstand a serious depression.

Few defaults of industrial bonds have occurred since 1950, but this fact is attributable in part to the absence of a major depression during this long period. Since 1966 there have been adverse developments in the financial position of many industrial companies. Considerable difficulties have developed as the result of unwise expansion. On the one hand this has involved large additions to both bank loans and long-term debt; on the other it has frequently produced operating losses instead of the expected profits. At the beginning of 1971 it was calculated that in the past seven years the interest payments of all nonfinancial firms had grown from $9.8 billion in 1963 to $26.1 billion in 1970, and that interest payments had taken 29% of the aggregate profits before interest and taxes in 1971, against only 16% in 1963.[3] Obviously, the burden on many individual firms had increased much more than this. Overbonded companies have become all too familiar. There is every reason to repeat the caution expressed in our 1965 edition:

> We are not quite ready to suggest that the investor may count on an indefinite continuance of this favorable situation, and hence relax his standards of bond selection in the industrial or any other group.

Common-Stock Analysis

The ideal form of common-stock analysis leads to a valuation of the issue which can be compared with the current price to determine whether or not the security is an attractive purchase. This valuation, in turn, would ordinarily be found by estimating the average earnings over a period of years in the *future* and then multiplying that estimate by an appropriate "capitalization factor."

The now-standard procedure for estimating future earning power starts with average *past* data for physical volume, prices received, and operating margin. Future sales in dollars are then projected on the basis of assumptions as to the amount of change in volume and price level over the previous base. These estimates, in turn, are grounded first on general economic forecasts of gross national product, and then on special calculations applicable to the industry and company in question.

An illustration of this method of valuation may be taken from our 1965 edition and brought up to date by adding the sequel. The Value Line, a leading investment service, makes forecasts of future earnings and dividends by the procedure outlined above, and then derives a figure of "price potentiality" (or projected market value) by applying a valuation formula to each issue based largely on certain past relationships. In Table 11-2 we reproduce the projections for 1967–1969 made in June 1964, and compare them with the earnings, and average market price actually realized in 1968 (which approximates the 1967–1969 period).

The combined forecasts proved to be somewhat on the low side, but not seriously so. The corresponding predictions made six years before had turned out to be overoptimistic on earnings and dividends; but this had been offset by use of a low multiplier, with the result that the "price potentiality" figure proved to be about the same as the actual average price for 1963.

The reader will note that quite a number of the individual forecasts were wide of the mark. This is an instance in support of our general view that composite or group estimates are likely to be a good deal more dependable than those for individual companies. Ideally, perhaps, the security analyst should pick out the three or four companies whose future he thinks he knows the best, and concentrate his own and his clients' interest on what he forecasts for

TABLE 11-2 The Dow Jones Industrial Average

(The Value Line's Forecast for 1967–1969 (Made in Mid-1964) Compared With Actual Results in 1968)

	Earnings Forecast 1967–1969	Actual 1968[a]	Price June 30 1964	Price Forecast 1967–1969	Average Price 1968[a]
Allied Chemical	$3.70	$1.46	54½	67	36½
Aluminum Corp. of Am.	3.85	4.75	71½	85	79
American Can	3.50	4.25	47	57	48
American Tel. & Tel.	4.00	3.75	73½	68	53
American Tobacco	3.00	4.38	51½	33	37
Anaconda	6.00	8.12	44½	70	106
Bethlehem Steel	3.25	3.55	36½	45	31
Chrysler	4.75	6.23	48½	45	60
Du Pont	8.50	7.82	253	240	163
Eastman Kodak	5.00	9.32	133	100	320
General Electric	4.50	3.95	80	90	90½
General Foods	4.70	4.16	88	71	84½
General Motors	6.25	6.02	88	78	81½
Goodyear Tire	3.25	4.12	43	43	54
Internat. Harvester	5.75	5.38	82	63	69
Internat. Nickel	5.20	3.86	79	83	76
Internat. Paper	2.25	2.04	32	36	33
Johns Manville	4.00	4.78	57½	54	71½
Owens-Ill. Glass	5.25	6.20	99	100	125½
Procter & Gamble	4.20	4.30	83	70	91
Sears Roebuck	4.70	5.46	118	78	122½
Standard Oil of Cal.	5.25	5.59	64½	60	67
Standard Oil of N.J.	6.00	5.94	87	73	76
Swift & Co.	3.85	3.41[b]	54	50	57
Texaco	5.50	6.04	79½	70	81
Union Carbide	7.35	5.20	126½	165	90
United Aircraft	4.00	7.65	49½	50	106
U.S. Steel	4.50	4.69	57½	60	42
Westinghouse Elec.	3.25	3.49	30½	50	69
Woolworth	2.25	2.29	29½	32	29½
Total	138.25	149.20	2222	2186	2450
DJIA (Total % 2.67)	52.00	56.00	832	820	918[c]
DJIA Actual 1968	57.89				906[c]
DJIA Actual 1967–1969	56.26				

[a] Adjusted for stock-splits since 1964.
[b] Average 1967–1969.
[c] Difference due to changed divisor.

them. Unfortunately, it appears to be almost impossible to distinguish in advance between those individual forecasts which can be relied upon and those which are subject to a large chance of error. At bottom, this is the reason for the wide diversification practiced by the investment funds. For it is undoubtedly better to concentrate on one stock that you *know* is going to prove highly profitable, rather than dilute your results to a mediocre figure, merely for diversification's sake. But this is not done, because it cannot be done *dependably*.[4] The prevalence of wide diversification is in itself a pragmatic repudiation of the fetish of "selectivity," to which Wall Street constantly pays lip service.*

Factors Affecting the Capitalization Rate

Though average future earnings are supposed to be the chief determinant of value, the security analyst takes into account a number of other factors of a more or less definite nature. Most of these will enter into his capitalization rate, which can vary over a wide range, depending upon the "quality" of the stock issue. Thus, although two companies may have the same figure of expected

---

* In more recent years, most mutual funds have almost robotically mimicked the Standard & Poor's 500-stock index, lest any different holdings cause their returns to deviate from that of the index. In a countertrend, some fund companies have launched what they call "focused" portfolios, which own 25 to 50 stocks that the managers declare to be their "best ideas." That leaves investors wondering whether the other funds run by the same managers contain their worst ideas. Considering that most of the "best idea" funds do not markedly outperform the averages, investors are also entitled to wonder whether the managers' ideas are even worth having in the first place. For indisputably skilled investors like Warren Buffett, wide diversification would be foolish, since it would water down the concentrated force of a few great ideas. But for the typical fund manager or individual investor, *not* diversifying is foolish, since it is so difficult to select a limited number of stocks that will include most winners and exclude most losers. As you own more stocks, the damage any single loser can cause will decline, and the odds of owning all the big winners will rise. The ideal choice for most investors is a total stock market index fund, a low-cost way to hold every stock worth owning.

earnings per share in 1973–1975—say $4—the analyst may value one as low as 40 and the other as high as 100. Let us deal briefly with some of the considerations that enter into these divergent multipliers.

1. *General Long-Term Prospects.* No one really knows anything about what will happen in the distant future, but analysts and investors have strong views on the subject just the same. These views are reflected in the substantial differentials between the price/earnings ratios of individual companies and of industry groups. At this point we added in our 1965 edition:

> For example, at the end of 1963 the chemical companies in the DJIA were selling at considerably higher multipliers than the oil companies, indicating stronger confidence in the prospects of the former than of the latter. Such distinctions made by the market are often soundly based, but when dictated mainly by past performance they are as likely to be wrong as right.

We shall supply here, in Table 11-3, the 1963 year-end material on the chemical and oil company issues in the DJIA, and carry their earnings to the end of 1970. It will be seen that the chemical companies, despite their high multipliers, made practically no gain in earnings in the period after 1963. The oil companies did much better than the chemicals and about in line with the growth implied in their 1963 multipliers.[5] Thus our chemical-stock example proved to be one of the cases in which the market multipliers were proven wrong.*

---

* Graham's point about chemical and oil companies in the 1960s applies to nearly every industry in nearly every time period. Wall Street's consensus view of the future for any given sector is usually either too optimistic or too pessimistic. Worse, the consensus is at its most cheery just when the stocks are most overpriced–and gloomiest just when they are cheapest. The most recent example, of course, is technology and telecommunications stocks, which hit record highs when their future seemed brightest in 1999 and early 2000, and then crashed all the way through 2002. History proves that Wall Street's "expert" forecasters are equally inept at predicting the

TABLE 11-3 Performance of Chemical and Oil Stocks in the DJIA, 1970 versus 1964

	1963			*1970*		
	Closing Price	Earned Per Share	P/E Ratio	Closing Price	Earned Per Share	P/E Ratio
Chemical companies:						
Allied Chemical	55	2.77	19.8 ×	24⅛	1.56	15.5 ×
Du Pont[a]	77	6.55	23.5	133½	6.76	19.8
Union Carbide[b]	60¼	2.66	22.7	40	2.60	15.4
			25.3 ave.			
Oil companies:						
Standard Oil of Cal.	59½	4.50	13.2 ×	54½	5.36	10.2 ×
Standard Oil of N.J.	76	4.74	16.0	73½	5.90	12.4
Texaco[b]	35	2.15	16.3	35	3.02	11.6
			15.3 ave.			

[a] 1963 figures adjusted for distribution of General Motors shares.

[b] 1963 figures adjusted for subsequent stock splits.

2. *Management.* On Wall Street a great deal is constantly said on this subject, but little that is really helpful. Until objective, quantitative, and reasonably reliable tests of managerial competence are devised and applied, this factor will continue to be looked at through a fog. It is fair to assume that an outstandingly successful company has unusually good management. This will have shown itself already in the past record; it will show up again in the estimates for the next five years, and once more in the previously discussed factor of long-term prospects. The tendency to count it still another time as a separate bullish consideration can easily lead to expensive overvaluations. The management factor is most useful, we think, in those cases in which a recent change has taken place that has not yet had the time to show its significance in the actual figures.

Two spectacular occurrences of this kind were associated with the Chrysler Motor Corporation. The first took place as far back as 1921, when Walter Chrysler took command of the almost moribund Maxwell Motors, and in a few years made it a large and highly profitable enterprise, while numerous other automobile companies were forced out of business. The second happened as recently as 1962, when Chrysler had fallen far from its once high estate and the stock was selling at its lowest price in many years. Then new interests, associated with Consolidation Coal, took over the reins. The earnings advanced from the 1961 figure of $1.24 per share to the equivalent of $17 in 1963, and the price rose from a low of 38½ in 1962 to the equivalent of nearly 200 the very next year.[6]

3. *Financial Strength and Capital Structure.* Stock of a company with a lot of surplus cash and nothing ahead of the common is clearly a better purchase (at the same price) than another one with the same per share earnings but large bank loans and senior securities. Such factors are properly and carefully taken into account by security analysts. A modest amount of bonds or preferred stock,

---

performance of 1) the market as a whole, 2) industry sectors, and 3) specific stocks. As Graham points out, the odds that individual investors can do any better are not good. The intelligent investor excels by making decisions that are not dependent on the accuracy of anybody's forecasts, including his or her own. (See Chapter 8.)

however, is not necessarily a disadvantage to the common, nor is the moderate use of seasonal bank credit. (Incidentally, a top-heavy structure—too little common stock in relation to bonds and preferred—may under favorable conditions make for a huge *speculative* profit in the common. This is the factor known as "leverage.")

4. *Dividend Record.* One of the most persuasive tests of high quality is an uninterrupted record of dividend payments going back over many years. We think that a record of continuous dividend payments for the last 20 years or more is an important plus factor in the company's quality rating. Indeed the defensive investor might be justified in limiting his purchases to those meeting this test.

5. *Current Dividend Rate.* This, our last additional factor, is the most difficult one to deal with in satisfactory fashion. Fortunately, the majority of companies have come to follow what may be called a standard dividend policy. This has meant the distribution of about two-thirds of their average earnings, except that in the recent period of high profits and inflationary demands for more capital the figure has tended to be lower. (In 1969 it was 59.5% for the stocks in the Dow Jones average, and 55% for all American corporations.)* Where the dividend bears a normal relationship to the earnings, the valuation may be made on either basis without substantially affecting the result. For example, a typical secondary company with expected average earnings of $3 and an expected dividend of $2 may be valued at either 12 times its earnings or 18 times its dividend, to yield a value of 36 in both cases.

However, an increasing number of growth companies are departing from the once standard policy of paying out 60% or more of earnings in dividends, on the grounds that the sharehold-

---

* This figure, now known as the "dividend payout ratio," has dropped considerably since Graham's day as American tax law discouraged investors from seeking, and corporations from paying, dividends. As of year-end 2002, the payout ratio stood at 34.1% for the S & P 500-stock index and, as recently as April 2000, it hit an all-time low of just 25.3%. (See www.barra.com/research/fundamentals.asp.) We discuss dividend policy more thoroughly in the commentary on Chapter 19.

ers' interests will be better served by retaining nearly all the profits to finance expansion. The issue presents problems and requires careful distinctions. We have decided to defer our discussion of the vital question of proper dividend policy to a later section—Chapter 19—where we shall deal with it as a part of the general problem of management-shareholder relations.

Capitalization Rates for Growth Stocks

Most of the writing of security analysts on formal appraisals relates to the valuation of growth stocks. Our study of the various methods has led us to suggest a foreshortened and quite simple formula for the valuation of growth stocks, which is intended to produce figures fairly close to those resulting from the more refined mathematical calculations. Our formula is:

Value = Current (Normal) Earnings × (8.5 plus twice the expected annual growth rate)

The growth figure should be that expected over the next seven to ten years.[7]

In Table 11-4 we show how our formula works out for various rates of assumed growth. It is easy to make the converse calculation and to determine what rate of growth is anticipated by the current market price, assuming our formula is valid. In our last edition we made that calculation for the DJIA and for six important stock issues. These figures are reproduced in Table 11-5. We commented at the time:

> The difference between the implicit 32.4% annual growth rate for Xerox and the extremely modest 2.8% for General Motors is indeed striking. It is explainable in part by the stock market's feeling that General Motors' 1963 earnings—the largest for any corporation in history—can be maintained with difficulty and exceeded only modestly at best. The price earnings ratio of Xerox, on the other hand, is quite representative of speculative enthusiasm fastened upon a company of great achievement and perhaps still greater promise.
>
> The implicit or expected growth rate of 5.1% for the DJIA com-

TABLE 11-4 Annual Earnings Multipliers Based on Expected Growth Rates, Based on a Simplified Formula

Expected growth rate	0.0%	2.5%	5.0%	7.2%	10.0%	14.3%	20.0%
Growth in 10 years	0.0	28.0%	63.0%	100.0%	159.0%	280.0%	319.0%
Multiplier of current earnings	8.5	13.5	18.5	22.9	28.5	37.1	48.5

TABLE 11-5 Implicit or Expected Growth Rates, December 1963 and December 1969

Issue	*P/E Ratio, 1963*	*Projected[a] Growth Rate, 1963*	*Earned Per Share 1963*	*Earned Per Share 1969*	*Actual Annual Growth, 1963–1969*	*P/E Ratio, 1969*	*Projected[a] Growth Rate, 1969*
American Tel. & Tel.	23.0 ×	7.3%	3.03	4.00	4.75%	12.2 ×	1.8%
General Electric	29.0	10.3	3.00	3.79[b]	4.0	20.4	6.0
General Motors	14.1	2.8	5.55	5.95	1.17	11.6	1.6
IBM	38.5	15.0	3.48[c]	8.21	16.0	44.4	17.9
International Harvester	13.2	2.4	2.29[c]	2.30	0.1	10.8	1.1
Xerox	25.0	32.4	.38[c]	2.08	29.2	50.8	21.2
DJIA	18.6	5.1	41.11	57.02	5.5	14.0	2.8

[a] Based on formula on p. 295.

[b] Average of 1968 and 1970, since 1969 earnings were reduced by strike.

[c] Adjusted for stock splits.

pares with an actual annual increase of 3.4% (compounded) between 1951–1953 and 1961–1963.

We should have added a caution somewhat as follows: The valuations of expected high-growth stocks are necessarily on the low side, if we were to assume these growth rates will actually be realized. In fact, according to the arithmetic, if a company could be assumed to grow at a rate of 8% or more *indefinitely* in the future its value would be infinite, and no price would be too high to pay for the shares. What the valuer actually does in these cases is to introduce a *margin of safety* into his calculations—somewhat as an engineer does in his specifications for a structure. On this basis the purchases would realize his assigned objective (in 1963, a future overall return of 7½% per annum) even if the growth rate actually realized proved substantially less than that projected in the formula. Of course, then, if that rate were actually realized the investor would be sure to enjoy a handsome additional return. There is really no way of valuing a high-growth company (with an expected rate above, say, 8% annually), in which the analyst can make realistic assumptions of *both* the proper multiplier for the current earnings and the expectable multiplier for the future earnings.

As it happened the actual growth for Xerox and IBM proved very close to the high rates implied from our formula. As just explained, this fine showing inevitably produced a large advance in the price of both issues. The growth of the DJIA itself was also about as projected by the 1963 closing market price. But the moderate rate of 5% did not involve the mathematical dilemma of Xerox and IBM. It turned out that the 23% price rise to the end of 1970, plus the 28% in aggregate dividend return received, gave not far from the 7½% annual overall gain posited in our formula. In the case of the other four companies it may suffice to say that their growth did not equal the expectations implied in the 1963 price and that their quotations failed to rise as much as the DJIA. *Warning:* This material is supplied for illustrative purposes only, and because of the inescapable necessity in security analysis to project the future growth rate for most companies studied. Let the reader not be misled into thinking that such projections have any high degree of reliability or, conversely, that future prices can be counted on to behave accordingly as the prophecies are realized, surpassed, or disappointed.

We should point out that any "scientific," or at least reasonably dependable, stock evaluation based on anticipated future results must take future interest rates into account. A given schedule of expected earnings, or dividends, would have a smaller present value if we assume a higher than if we assume a lower interest structure.* Such assumptions have always been difficult to make with any degree of confidence, and the recent violent swings in long-term interest rates render forecasts of this sort almost presumptuous. Hence we have retained our old formula above, simply because no new one would appear more plausible.

Industry Analysis

Because the general prospects of the enterprise carry major weight in the establishment of market prices, it is natural for the security analyst to devote a great deal of attention to the economic position of the industry and of the individual company in its industry. Studies of this kind can go into unlimited detail. They are sometimes productive of valuable insights into important factors that will be operative in the future and are insufficiently appreciated by the current market. Where a conclusion of that kind can be drawn with a fair degree of confidence, it affords a sound basis for investment decisions.

Our own observation, however, leads us to minimize somewhat the practical value of most of the industry studies that are made available to investors. The material developed is ordinarily of a kind with which the public is already fairly familiar and that has already exerted considerable influence on market quotations.

---

* Why is this? By "the rule of 72," at 10% interest a given amount of money doubles in just over seven years, while at 7% it doubles in just over 10 years. When interest rates are high, the amount of money you need to set aside today to reach a given value in the future is *lower*–since those high interest rates will enable it to grow at a more rapid rate. Thus a rise in interest rates today makes a future stream of earnings or dividends less valuable–since the alternative of investing in bonds has become relatively more attractive.

Rarely does one find a brokerage-house study that points out, with a convincing array of facts, that a popular industry is heading for a fall or that an unpopular one is due to prosper. Wall Street's view of the longer future is notoriously fallible, and this necessarily applies to that important part of its investigations which is directed toward the forecasting of the course of profits in various industries.

We must recognize, however, that the rapid and pervasive growth of technology in recent years is not without major effect on the attitude and the labors of the security analyst. More so than in the past, the progress or retrogression of the typical company in the coming decade may depend on its relation to new products and new processes, which the analyst may have a chance to study and evaluate *in advance.* Thus there is doubtless a promising area for effective work by the analyst, based on field trips, interviews with research men, and on intensive technological investigation on his own. There are hazards connected with investment conclusions derived chiefly from such glimpses into the future, and not supported by presently demonstrable value. Yet there are perhaps equal hazards in sticking closely to the limits of value set by sober calculations resting on actual results. The investor cannot have it both ways. He can be imaginative and play for the big profits that are the reward for vision proved sound by the event; but then he must run a substantial risk of major or minor miscalculation. Or he can be conservative, and refuse to pay more than a minor premium for possibilities as yet unproved; but in that case he must be prepared for the later contemplation of golden opportunities foregone.

A Two-Part Appraisal Process

Let us return for a moment to the idea of valuation or appraisal of a common stock, which we began to discuss above on p. 288. A great deal of reflection on the subject has led us to conclude that this better be done quite differently than is now the established practice. We suggest that analysts work out first what we call the "past-performance value," which is based solely on the past record. This would indicate what the stock would be worth—absolutely, or as a percentage of the DJIA or of the S & P composite—if it is assumed that its relative past performance will continue unchanged in the future. (This includes the assumption that its relative growth rate, as shown in the last seven years, will also continue unchanged over the next seven years.) This process could be carried out mechanically by applying a formula that gives individual weights to past figures for profitability, stability, and growth, and also for current financial condition. The second part of the analysis should consider to what extent the value based solely on past performance should be modified because of new conditions expected in the future.

Such a procedure would divide the work between senior and junior analysts as follows: (1) The senior analyst would set up the formula to apply to all companies generally for determining past-performance value. (2) The junior analysts would work up such factors for the designated companies—pretty much in mechanical fashion. (3) The senior analyst would then determine to what extent a company's performance—absolute or relative—is likely to differ from its past record, and what change should be made in the value to reflect such anticipated changes. It would be best if the senior analyst's report showed both the original valuation and the modified one, with his reasons for the change.

Is a job of this kind worth doing? Our answer is in the affirmative, but our reasons may appear somewhat cynical to the reader. We doubt whether the valuations so reached will prove sufficiently dependable in the case of the typical industrial company, great or small. We shall illustrate the difficulties of this job in our discussion of Aluminum Company of America (ALCOA) in the next chapter. Nonetheless it should be done for such common stocks. Why? First, many security analysts are bound to make current or projected valuations, as part of their daily work. The method we propose should be an improvement on those generally followed today. Secondly, because it should give useful experience and insight to the analysts who practice this method. Thirdly, because work of this kind could produce an invaluable body of recorded experience—as has long been the case in medicine—that may lead to better methods of procedure and a useful knowledge of its possibilities and limitations. The public-utility stocks might well prove an important area in which this approach will show real pragmatic value. Eventually the intelligent analyst will confine himself to those groups in which the future appears reasonably predictable,* or where the margin of safety of past-performance value over current price is so large that he can take his chances on future variations—as he does in selecting well-secured senior securities.

In subsequent chapters we shall supply concrete examples of the application of analytical techniques. But they will only be illustrations. If the reader finds the subject interesting he should pursue it systematically and thoroughly before he considers himself qualified to pass a final buy-or-sell judgment of his own on a security issue.

---

* These industry groups, ideally, would not be overly dependent on such unforeseeable factors as fluctuating interest rates or the future direction of prices for raw materials like oil or metals. Possibilities might be industries like gaming, cosmetics, alcoholic beverages, nursing homes, or waste management.

COMMENTARY ON CHAPTER 11

"Would you tell me, please, which way I ought to go from here?"
"That depends a good deal on where you want to get to," said the Cat.

—*Lewis Carroll,* Alice's Adventures in Wonderland

Putting a Price on the Future

Which factors determine how much you should be willing to pay for a stock? What makes one company worth 10 times earnings and another worth 20 times? How can you be reasonably sure that you are not overpaying for an apparently rosy future that turns out to be a murky nightmare?

Graham feels that five elements are decisive.[1] He summarizes them as:

- the company's "general long-term prospects"
- the quality of its management
- its financial strength and capital structure
- its dividend record
- and its current dividend rate.

Let's look at these factors in the light of today's market.

The long-term prospects. Nowadays, the intelligent investor should begin by downloading at least five years' worth of annual reports (Form 10-K) from the company's website or from the EDGAR

---

[1] Because so few of today's individual investors buy—or should buy—individual bonds, we will limit this discussion to stock analysis. For more on bond funds, see the commentary on Chapter 4.

database at www.sec.gov.[2] Then comb through the financial statements, gathering evidence to help you answer two overriding questions. What makes this company grow? Where do (and where will) its profits come from? Among the problems to watch for:

- The company is a "serial acquirer." An average of more than two or three acquisitions a year is a sign of potential trouble. After all, if the company itself would rather buy the stock of other businesses than invest in its own, shouldn't you take the hint and look elsewhere too? And check the company's track record as an acquirer. Watch out for corporate bulimics–firms that wolf down big acquisitions, only to end up vomiting them back out. Lucent, Mattel, Quaker Oats, and Tyco International are among the companies that have had to disgorge acquisitions at sickening losses. Other firms take chronic write-offs, or accounting charges proving that they overpaid for their past acquisitions. That's a bad omen for future deal making.[3]
- The company is an OPM addict, borrowing debt or selling stock to raise boatloads of Other People's Money. These fat infusions of OPM are labeled "cash from financing activities" on the statement of cash flows in the annual report. They can make a sick company appear to be growing even if its underlying businesses are not generating enough cash–as Global Crossing and WorldCom showed not long ago.[4]

---

[2] You should also get at least one year's worth of quarterly reports (on Form 10-Q). By definition, we are assuming that you are an "enterprising" investor willing to devote a considerable amount of effort to your portfolio. If the steps in this chapter sound like too much work to you, then you are not temperamentally well suited to picking your own stocks. You cannot reliably obtain the results you imagine unless you put in the kind of effort we describe.

[3] You can usually find details on acquisitions in the "Management's Discussion and Analysis" section of Form 10-K; cross-check it against the footnotes to the financial statements. For more on "serial acquirers," see the commentary on Chapter 12.

[4] To determine whether a company is an OPM addict, read the "Statement of Cash Flows" in the financial statements. This page breaks down the

- The company is a Johnny-One-Note, relying on one customer (or a handful) for most of its revenues. In October 1999, fiber-optics maker Sycamore Networks, Inc. sold stock to the public for the first time. The prospectus revealed that one customer, Williams Communications, accounted for 100% of Sycamore's $11 million in total revenues. Traders blithely valued Sycamore's shares at $15 billion. Unfortunately, Williams went bankrupt just over two years later. Although Sycamore picked up other customers, its stock lost 97% between 2000 and 2002.

As you study the sources of growth and profit, stay on the lookout for positives as well as negatives. Among the good signs:

- The company has a wide "moat," or competitive advantage. Like castles, some companies can easily be stormed by marauding competitors, while others are almost impregnable. Several forces can widen a company's moat: a strong *brand identity* (think of Harley Davidson, whose buyers tattoo the company's logo onto their bodies); a *monopoly* or near-monopoly on the market; *economies of scale,* or the ability to supply huge amounts of goods or services cheaply (consider Gillette, which churns out razor blades by the billion); a unique *intangible asset* (think of Coca-Cola, whose secret formula for flavored syrup has no real physical value but maintains a priceless hold on consumers); a *resistance to substitution* (most businesses have no alternative to electricity, so utility companies are unlikely to be supplanted any time soon).[5]

---

company's cash inflows and outflows into "operating activities," "investing activities," and "financing activities." If cash from operating activities is consistently negative, while cash from financing activities is consistently positive, the company has a habit of craving more cash than its own businesses can produce–and you should not join the "enablers" of that habitual abuse. For more on Global Crossing, see the commentary on Chapter 12. For more on WorldCom, see the sidebar in the commentary on Chapter 6.

[5] For more insight into "moats," see the classic book *Competitive Strategy* by Harvard Business School professor Michael E. Porter (Free Press, New York, 1998).

- The company is a marathoner, not a sprinter. By looking back at the income statements, you can see whether revenues and net earnings have grown smoothly and steadily over the previous 10 years. A recent article in the *Financial Analysts Journal* confirmed what other studies (and the sad experience of many investors) have shown: that the fastest-growing companies tend to overheat and flame out.[6] If earnings are growing at a long-term rate of 10% pretax (or 6% to 7% after-tax), that may be sustainable. But the 15% growth hurdle that many companies set for themselves is delusional. And an even higher rate—or a sudden burst of growth in one or two years—is all but certain to fade, just like an inexperienced marathoner who tries to run the whole race as if it were a 100-meter dash.
- The company sows *and* reaps. No matter how good its products or how powerful its brands, a company must spend some money to develop new business. While research and development spending is not a source of growth today, it may well be tomorrow—particularly if a firm has a proven record of rejuvenating its businesses with new ideas and equipment. The average budget for research and development varies across industries and companies. In 2002, Procter & Gamble spent about 4% of its net sales on R & D, while 3M spent 6.5% and Johnson & Johnson 10.9%. In the long run, a company that spends nothing on R & D is at least as vulnerable as one that spends too much.

The quality and conduct of management. A company's executives should say what they will do, then do what they said. Read the past annual reports to see what forecasts the managers made and if they fulfilled them or fell short. Managers should forthrightly admit their failures and take responsibility for them, rather than blaming all-purpose scapegoats like "the economy," "uncertainty," or "weak demand." Check whether the tone and substance of the chairman's letter stay constant, or fluctuate with the latest fads on Wall Street. (Pay special attention to boom years like 1999: Did the executives of

---

[6] See Cyrus A. Ramezani, Luc Soenen, and Alan Jung, "Growth, Corporate Profitability, and Value Creation," *Financial Analysts Journal*, November/December, 2002, pp. 56–67; also available at http://cyrus.cob.calpoly.edu/.

a cement or underwear company suddenly declare that they were "on the leading edge of the transformative software revolution"?)

These questions can also help you determine whether the people who run the company will act in the interests of the people who *own* the company:

- Are they looking out for No. 1?

  A firm that pays its CEO $100 million in a year had better have a very good reason. (Perhaps he discovered–and patented–the Fountain of Youth? Or found El Dorado and bought it for $1 an acre? Or contacted life on another planet and negotiated a contract obligating the aliens to buy all their supplies from only one company on Earth?) Otherwise, this kind of obscenely obese payday suggests that the firm is run by the managers, *for* the managers.

  If a company reprices (or "reissues" or "exchanges") its stock options for insiders, stay away. In this switcheroo, a company cancels existing (and typically worthless) stock options for employees and executives, then replaces them with new ones at advantageous prices. If their value is never allowed to go to zero, while their potential profit is always infinite, how can options encourage good stewardship of corporate assets? Any established company that reprices options–as dozens of high-tech firms have–is a disgrace. And any investor who buys stock in such a company is a sheep begging to be sheared.

  By looking in the annual report for the mandatory footnote about stock options, you can see how large the "option overhang" is. AOL Time Warner, for example, reported in the front of its annual report that it had 4.5 billion shares of common stock outstanding as of December 31, 2002–but a footnote in the bowels of the report reveals that the company had issued options on 657 million more shares. So AOL's future earnings will have to be divided among 15% more shares. You should factor in the potential flood of new shares from stock options whenever you estimate a company's future value.[7]

  "Form 4," available through the EDGAR database at www.sec.

---

[7] Jason Zweig is an employee of AOL Time Warner and holds options in the company. For more about how stock options work, see the commentary on Chapter 19, p. 507.

gov, shows whether a firm's senior executives and directors have been buying or selling shares. There can be legitimate reasons for an insider to sell–diversification, a bigger house, a divorce settlement–but repeated big sales are a bright red flag. A manager can't legitimately be your partner if he keeps selling while you're buying.

- Are they managers or promoters?

  Executives should spend most of their time managing their company in private, not promoting it to the investing public. All too often, CEOs complain that their stock is undervalued no matter how high it goes–forgetting Graham's insistence that managers should try to keep the stock price from going either too low *or* too high.[8] Meanwhile, all too many chief financial officers give "earnings guidance," or guesstimates of the company's quarterly profits. And some firms are hype-o-chondriacs, constantly spewing forth press releases boasting of temporary, trivial, or hypothetical "opportunities."

  A handful of companies–including Coca-Cola, Gillette, and USA Interactive–have begun to "just say no" to Wall Street's short-term thinking. These few brave outfits are providing more detail about their current budgets and long-term plans, while refusing to speculate about what the next 90 days might hold. (For a model of how a company can communicate candidly and fairly with its shareholders, go to the EDGAR database at www.sec.gov and view the 8-K filings made by Expeditors International of Washington, which periodically posts its superb question-and-answer dialogues with shareholders there.)

  Finally, ask whether the company's accounting practices are designed to make its financial results transparent–or opaque. If "nonrecurring" charges keep recurring, "extraordinary" items crop up so often that they seem ordinary, acronyms like EBITDA take priority over net income, or "pro forma" earnings are used to cloak actual losses, you may be looking at a firm that has not yet learned how to put its shareholders' long-term interests first.[9]

---

[8] See note 19 in the commentary on Chapter 19, p. 508.

[9] For more on these issues, see the commentary on Chapter 12 and the superb essay by Joseph Fuller and Michael C. Jensen, "Just Say No to Wall Street," at http://papers.ssrn.com.

Financial strength and capital structure. The most basic possible definition of a good business is this: It generates more cash than it consumes. Good managers keep finding ways of putting that cash to productive use. In the long run, companies that meet this definition are virtually certain to grow in value, no matter what the stock market does.

Start by reading the statement of cash flows in the company's annual report. See whether cash from operations has grown steadily throughout the past 10 years. Then you can go further. Warren Buffett has popularized the concept of *owner earnings,* or net income plus amortization and depreciation, minus normal capital expenditures. As portfolio manager Christopher Davis of Davis Selected Advisors puts it, "If you owned 100% of this business, how much cash would you have in your pocket at the end of the year?" Because it adjusts for accounting entries like amortization and depreciation that do not affect the company's cash balances, owner earnings can be a better measure than reported net income. To fine-tune the definition of owner earnings, you should also subtract from reported net income:

- any costs of granting stock options, which divert earnings away from existing shareholders into the hands of new inside owners
- any "unusual," "nonrecurring," or "extraordinary" charges
- any "income" from the company's pension fund.

If owner earnings per share have grown at a steady average of at least 6% or 7% over the past 10 years, the company is a stable generator of cash, and its prospects for growth are good.

Next, look at the company's capital structure. Turn to the balance sheet to see how much debt (including preferred stock) the company has; in general, long-term debt should be under 50% of total capital. In the footnotes to the financial statements, determine whether the long-term debt is fixed-rate (with constant interest payments) or variable (with payments that fluctuate, which could become costly if interest rates rise).

Look in the annual report for the exhibit or statement showing the "ratio of earnings to fixed charges." That exhibit to Amazon.com's 2002 annual report shows that Amazon's earnings fell $145 million short of covering its interest costs. In the future, Amazon will either have to earn much more from its operations or find a way to borrow money at lower rates. Otherwise, the company could end up being owned not by its shareholders but by its bondholders, who can lay claim to Amazon's assets if they have no other way of securing the interest payments they are owed. (To be fair, Amazon's ratio of earnings to fixed charges was far healthier in 2002 than two years earlier, when earnings fell $1.1 billion short of covering debt payments.)

A few words on dividends and stock policy (for more, please see Chapter 19):

- The burden of proof is on the company to show that you are better off if it does not pay a dividend. If the firm has consistently outperformed the competition in good markets and bad, the managers are clearly putting the cash to optimal use. If, however, business is faltering or the stock is underperforming its rivals, then the managers and directors are misusing the cash by refusing to pay a dividend.
- Companies that repeatedly split their shares–and hype those splits in breathless press releases–treat their investors like dolts. Like Yogi Berra, who wanted his pizza cut into four slices because "I don't think I can eat eight," the shareholders who love stock splits miss the point. Two shares of a stock at $50 are not worth more than one share at $100. Managers who use splits to promote their stock are aiding and abetting the worst instincts of the investing public, and the intelligent investor will think twice before turning any money over to such condescending manipulators.[10]
- Companies should buy back their shares when they are cheap–not when they are at or near record highs. Unfortunately, it recently has become all too common for companies to repurchase their stock *when it is overpriced.* There is no more cynical waste of a company's cash–since the real purpose of that maneuver is to enable top executives to reap multimillion-dollar paydays by selling their own stock options in the name of "enhancing shareholder value."

A substantial amount of anecdotal evidence, in fact, suggests that managers who talk about "enhancing shareholder value" seldom do. In investing, as with life in general, ultimate victory usually goes to the doers, not to the talkers.

---

[10] Stock splits are discussed further in the commentary on Chapter 13.

CHAPTER 12

Things to Consider About Per-Share Earnings

This chapter will begin with two pieces of advice to the investor that cannot avoid being contradictory in their implications. The first is: Don't take a single year's earnings seriously. The second is: If you do pay attention to short-term earnings, look out for booby traps in the per-share figures. If our first warning were followed strictly the second would be unnecessary. But it is too much to expect that most shareholders can relate all their common-stock decisions to the long-term record and the long-term prospects. The quarterly figures, and especially the annual figures, receive major attention in financial circles, and this emphasis can hardly fail to have its impact on the investor's thinking. He may well need some education in this area, for it abounds in misleading possibilities.

As this chapter is being written the earnings report of Aluminum Company of America (ALCOA) for 1970 appears in the *Wall Street Journal*. The first figures shown are

	1970	1969
Share earnings[a]	$5.20	$5.58

The little [a] at the outset is explained in a footnote to refer to "primary earnings," before special charges. There is much more footnote material; in fact it occupies twice as much space as do the basic figures themselves.

For the December quarter alone, the "earnings per share" are given as $1.58 in 1970 against $1.56 in 1969.

The investor or speculator interested in ALCOA shares, reading those figures, might say to himself: "Not so bad. I knew that 1970 was a recession year in aluminum. But the fourth quarter shows a gain over 1969, with earnings at the rate of $6.32 per year. Let me see. The stock is selling at 62. Why, that's less than ten times earnings. That makes it look pretty cheap, compared with 16 times for International Nickel, etc., etc."

But if our investor-speculator friend had bothered to read all the material in the footnote, he would have found that instead of one figure of earnings per share for the year 1970 there were actually *four,* viz.:

	1970	*1969*
Primary earnings	$5.20	$5.58
Net income (after special charges)	4.32	5.58
Fully diluted, before special charges	5.01	5.35
Fully diluted, after special charges	4.19	5.35

For the fourth quarter alone only two figures are given:

Primary earnings	$1.58	$1.56
Net income (after special charges)	.70	1.56

What do all these additional earnings mean? Which earnings are true earnings for the year and the December quarter? If the latter should be taken at 70 cents—the net income after special charges—the annual rate would be $2.80 instead of $6.32, and the price 62 would be "22 times earnings," instead of the 10 times we started with.

Part of the question as to the "true earnings" of ALCOA can be answered quite easily. The reduction from $5.20 to $5.01, to allow for the effects of "dilution," is clearly called for. ALCOA has a large bond issue convertible into common stock; to calculate the "earning power" of the common, based on the 1970 results, it must be assumed that the conversion privilege will be exercised if it should prove profitable to the bondholders to do so. The amount involved in the ALCOA picture is relatively small, and hardly deserves detailed comment. But in other cases, making allowance for conversion rights—and the existence of stock-purchase warrants—can reduce the apparent earnings by half, or more. We shall present examples of a really significant dilution factor below (page 411). (The financial services are not always consistent in their allowance for the dilution factor in their reporting and analyses.)*

Let us turn now to the matter of "special charges." This figure of $18,800,000, or 88 cents per share, deducted in the fourth quarter, is not unimportant. Is it to be ignored entirely, or fully recognized as an earnings reduction, or partly recognized and partly ignored? The alert investor might ask himself also how does it happen that there was a virtual epidemic of such special charge-offs appearing after the close of 1970, but not in previous years? Could there possibly have been some fine Italian hands† at work with the accounting—but always, of course, within the limits of the permissible? When we look closely we may find that such losses, charged off before they actually occur, can be charmed away, as it were, with no unhappy effect on either past or future "primary earnings." In some extreme cases they might be availed of to make subsequent earnings appear nearly twice as large as in reality—by a more or less prestidigitous treatment of the tax credit involved.

---

* "Dilution" is one of many words that describe stocks in the language of fluid dynamics. A stock with high trading volume is said to be "liquid." When a company goes public in an IPO, it "floats" its shares. And, in earlier days, a company that drastically diluted its shares (with large amounts of convertible debt or multiple offerings of common stock) was said to have "watered" its stock. This term is believed to have originated with the legendary market manipulator Daniel Drew (1797–1879), who began as a livestock trader. He would drive his cattle south toward Manhattan, force-feeding them salt along the way. When they got to the Harlem River, they would guzzle huge volumes of water to slake their thirst. Drew would then bring them to market, where the water they had just drunk would increase their weight. That enabled him to get a much higher price, since cattle on the hoof is sold by the pound. Drew later watered the stock of the Erie Railroad by massively issuing new shares without warning.

† Graham is referring to the precise craftsmanship of the immigrant Italian stone carvers who ornamented the otherwise plain facades of buildings throughout New York in the early 1900s. Accountants, likewise, can transform simple financial facts into intricate and even incomprehensible patterns.

In dealing with ALCOA's special charges, the first thing to establish is how they arose. The footnotes are specific enough. The deductions came from four sources, viz.:

1. Management's estimate of the anticipated costs of closing down the manufactured products division.
2. Ditto for closing down ALCOA Castings Co.'s plants.
3. Ditto for losses in phasing out ALCOA Credit Co.
4. Also, estimated costs of $5.3 million associated with completion of the contract for a "curtain wall."

All of these items are related to future costs and losses. It is easy to say that they are not part of the "regular operating results" of 1970—but if so, where do they belong? Are they so "extraordinary and nonrecurring" as to belong nowhere? A widespread enterprise such as ALCOA, doing a $1.5 billion business annually, must have a lot of divisions, departments, affiliates, and the like. Would it not be normal rather than extraordinary for one or more to prove unprofitable, and to require closing down? Similarly for such things as a contract to build a wall. Suppose that any time a company had a loss on any part of its business it had the bright idea of charging it off as a "special item," and thus reporting its "primary earnings" per share so as to include only its profitable contracts and operations? Like King Edward VII's sundial, that marked only the "sunny hours."*

---

* The king probably took his inspiration from a once-famous essay by the English writer William Hazlitt, who mused about a sundial near Venice that bore the words *Horas non numero nisi serenas*, or "I count only the hours that are serene." Companies that chronically exclude bad news from their financial results on the pretext that negative events are "extraordinary" or "nonrecurring" are taking a page from Hazlitt, who urged his readers "to take no note of time but by its benefits, to watch only for the smiles and neglect the frowns of fate, to compose our lives of bright and gentle moments, turning away to the sunny side of things, and letting the rest slip from our imaginations, unheeded or forgotten!" (William Hazlitt, "On a Sun-Dial," ca. 1827.) Unfortunately, investors must always count the sunny and dark hours alike.

The reader should note two ingenious aspects of the ALCOA procedure we have been discussing. The first is that by *anticipating future losses* the company escapes the necessity of allocating the losses themselves to an identifiable year. They don't belong in 1970, because they were not actually taken in that year. And they won't be *shown* in the year when they are actually taken, because they have already been provided for. Neat work, but might it not be just a little misleading?

The ALCOA footnote says nothing about the future tax saving from these losses. (Most other statements of this sort state specifically that only the "after-tax effect" has been charged off.) If the ALCOA figure represents future losses before the related tax credit, then not only will future earnings be freed from the weight of these charges (as they are actually incurred), but they will be *increased* by a tax credit of some 50% thereof. It is difficult to believe that the accounts will be handled that way. But it is a fact that certain companies which have had large losses in the past have been able to report future earnings without charging the normal taxes against them, in that way making a very fine profits appearance indeed—based paradoxically enough on their past disgraces. (Tax credits resulting from *past years'* losses are now being shown separately as "special items," but they will enter into future statistics as part of the final "net-income" figure. However, a reserve now set up for *future* losses, if *net* of expected tax credit, should not create an addition of this sort to the net income of later years.)

The other ingenious feature is the use by ALCOA and many other companies of the 1970 year-end for making these special charge-offs. The stock market took what appeared to be a blood bath in the first half of 1970. Everyone expected relatively poor results for the year for most companies. Wall Street was now anticipating better results in 1971, 1972, etc. What a nice arrangement, then, to charge as much as possible to the bad year, which had already been written off mentally and had virtually receded into the past, leaving the way clear for nicely fattened figures in the next few years! Perhaps this is good accounting, good business policy, and good for management-shareholder relationships. But we have lingering doubts.

The combination of widely (or should it be wildly?) diversified operations with the impulse to clean house at the end of 1970 has produced some strange-looking footnotes to the annual reports. The reader may be amused by the following explanation given by a New York Stock Exchange company (which shall remain unnamed) of its "special items" aggregating $2,357,000, or about a third of the income before charge-offs: "Consists of provision for closing Spalding United Kingdom operations; provision for reorganizational expenses of a division; costs of selling a small baby-pants and bib manufacturing company, disposing of part interest in a Spanish car-leasing facility, and liquidation of a ski-boot operation."*

Years ago the strong companies used to set up "contingency reserves" out of the profits of *good years* to absorb some of the bad effects of depression years to come. The underlying idea was to equalize the reported earnings, more or less, and to improve the stability factor in the company's record. A worthy motive, it would seem; but the accountants quite rightly objected to the practice as misstating the true earnings. They insisted that each year's results be presented as they were, good or bad, and the shareholders and analysts be allowed to do the averaging or equalizing for themselves. We seem now to be witnessing the opposite phenomenon, with everyone charging off as much as possible against forgotten 1970, so as to start 1971 with a slate not only clean but specially prepared to show pleasing per-share figures in the coming years.

It is time to return to our first question. What then were the true earnings of ALCOA in 1970? The accurate answer would be: The $5.01 per share, after "dilution," *less* that part of the 82 cents of "special charges" that may properly be attributed to occurrences in 1970. But we do not know what that portion is, and *hence we cannot properly state the true earnings for the year.* The management and the auditors should have given us their best judgment on this point, but they did not do so. And furthermore, the management and the auditors should have provided for deduction of the balance of these charges from the *ordinary earnings* of a suitable number of

---

* The company to which Graham refers so coyly appears to be American Machine & Foundry (or AMF Corp.), one of the most jumbled conglomerates of the late 1960s. It was a predecessor of today's AMF Bowling Worldwide, which operates bowling alleys and manufactures bowling equipment.

future years—say, not more than five. This evidently they will not do either, since they have already conveniently disposed of the entire sum as a 1970 special charge.

The more seriously investors take the per-share earnings figures as published, the more necessary it is for them to be on their guard against accounting factors of one kind and another that may impair the true comparability of the numbers. We have mentioned three sorts of these factors: the use of *special charges,* which may never be reflected in the per-share earnings, the reduction in the normal *income-tax* deduction by reason of past losses, and the *dilution* factor implicit in the existence of substantial amounts of convertible securities or warrants.[1] A fourth item that has had a significant effect on reported earnings in the past is the method of treating depreciation—chiefly as between the "straight-line" and the "accelerated" schedules. We refrain from details here. But as an example current as we write, let us mention the 1970 report of Trane Co. This firm showed an increase of nearly 20% in per-share earnings over 1969—$3.29 versus $2.76—but half of this came from returning to the older straight-line depreciation rates, less burdensome on earnings than the accelerated method used the year before. (The company will continue to use the accelerated rate on its income-tax return, thus deferring income-tax payments on the difference.) Still another factor, important at times, is the choice between charging off research and development costs in the year they are incurred or amortizing them over a period of years. Finally, let us mention the choice between the FIFO (first-in-first-out) and LIFO (last-in-first-out) methods of valuing inventories.*

---

* Nowadays, investors need to be aware of several other "accounting factors" that can distort reported earnings. One is "pro forma" or "as if" financial statements, which report a company's earnings as if Generally Accepted Accounting Principles (GAAP) did not apply. Another is the dilutive effect of issuing millions of stock options for executive compensation, then buying back millions of shares to keep those options from reducing the value of the common stock. A third is unrealistic assumptions of return on the company's pension funds, which can artificially inflate earnings in good years and depress them in bad. Another is "Special Purpose Entities," or affiliated firms or partnerships that buy risky assets or liabilities of the com-

An obvious remark here would be that investors should not pay any attention to these accounting variables if the amounts involved are relatively small. But Wall Street being as it is, even items quite minor in themselves can be taken seriously. Two days before the ALCOA report appeared in the *Wall Street Journal,* the paper had quite a discussion of the corresponding statement of Dow Chemical. It closed with the observation that "many analysts" had been troubled by the fact that Dow had included a 21-cent item in regular profits for 1969, instead of treating it as an item of "extraordinary income." Why the fuss? Because, evidently, evaluations of Dow Chemical involving many millions of dollars in the aggregate seemed to depend on exactly what was the percentage gain for 1969 over 1968—in this case either 9% or 4½%. This strikes us as rather absurd; it is very unlikely that small differences involved in one year's results could have any bearing on future average profits or growth, and on a conservative, realistic valuation of the enterprise.

By contrast, consider another statement also appearing in January 1971. This concerned Northwest Industries Inc.'s report for 1970.* The company was planning to write off, as a special charge, not less than $264 million in one fell swoop. Of this, $200 million represents the loss to be taken on the proposed sale of the railroad subsidiary to its employees and the balance a write-down of a recent stock purchase. These sums would work out to a loss of about $35 per share of common before dilution offsets, or twice its then current market price. Here we have something really signifi-

---

pany and thus "remove" those financial risks from the company's balance sheet. Another element of distortion is the treatment of marketing or other "soft" costs as assets of the company, rather than as normal expenses of doing business. We will briefly examine such practices in the commentary that accompanies this chapter.

* Northwest Industries was the holding company for, among other businesses, the Chicago and Northwestern Railway Co. and Union Underwear (the maker of both BVD and Fruit of the Loom briefs). It was taken over in 1985 by overindebted financier William Farley, who ran the company into the ground. Fruit of the Loom was bought in a bankruptcy proceeding by Warren Buffett's Berkshire Hathaway Inc. in early 2002.

cant. If the transaction goes through, and if the tax laws are not changed, this loss provided for in 1970 will permit Northwest Industries to realize about $400 million of future profits (within five years) from its other diversified interests without paying income tax thereon.* What will then be the real earnings of that enterprise; should they be calculated with or without provision for the nearly 50% in income taxes which it will not actually have to pay? In our opinion, the proper mode of calculation would be first to consider the indicated earning power on the basis of full income-tax liability, and to derive some broad idea of the stock's value based on that estimate. To this should be added some bonus figure, representing the value per share of the important but temporary tax exemption the company will enjoy. (Allowance must be made, also, for a possible large-scale dilution in this case. Actually, the convertible preferred issues and warrants would more than double the outstanding common shares if the privileges are exercised.)

All this may be confusing and wearisome to our readers, but it belongs in our story. Corporate accounting is often tricky; security analysis can be complicated; stock valuations are really dependable only in exceptional cases.† For most investors it would be probably best to assure themselves that they are getting good value for the prices they pay, and let it go at that.

---

* Graham is referring to the provision of Federal tax law that allows corporations to "carry forward" their net operating losses. As the tax code now stands, these losses can be carried forward for up to 20 years, reducing the company's tax liability for the entire period (and thus raising its earnings after tax). Therefore, investors should consider whether recent severe losses could actually *improve* the company's net earnings in the future.

† Investors should keep these words at hand and remind themselves of them frequently: "Stock valuations are really dependable only in exceptional cases." While the prices of most stocks are approximately right most of the time, the price of a stock and the value of its business are almost never identical. The market's judgment on price is often unreliable. Unfortunately, the margin of the market's pricing errors is often not wide enough to justify the expense of trading on them. The intelligent investor must carefully evaluate the costs of trading and taxes before attempting to take advantage of any price discrepancy–and should never count on being able to sell for the exact price currently quoted in the market.

Use of Average Earnings

In former times analysts and investors paid considerable attention to the average earnings over a fairly long period in the past—usually from seven to ten years. This "mean figure"* was useful for ironing out the frequent ups and downs of the business cycle, and it was thought to give a better idea of the company's earning power than the results of the latest year alone. One important advantage of such an averaging process is that it will solve the problem of what to do about nearly all the special charges and credits. They should be *included* in the average earnings. For certainly most of these losses and gains represent a part of the company's operating history. If we do this for ALCOA, the average earnings for 1961–1970 (ten years) would appear as $3.62 and for the seven years 1964–1970 as $4.62 per share. If such figures are used in conjunction with ratings for growth and stability of earnings during the same period, they could give a really informing picture of the company's past performance.

Calculation of the Past Growth Rate

It is of prime importance that the growth factor in a company's record be taken adequately into account. Where the growth has been large the recent earnings will be well above the seven- or ten-year average, and analysts may deem these long-term figures irrelevant. This need not be the case. The earnings can be given in terms *both* of the average and the latest figure. We suggest that the growth rate itself be calculated by comparing the *average* of the last three years with corresponding figures ten years earlier. (Where there is a problem of "special charges or credits" it may be dealt with on some compromise basis.) Note the following calculation for the growth of ALCOA as against that of Sears Roebuck and the DJIA group as a whole.

Comment: These few figures could be made the subject of a long discussion. They probably show as well as any others, derived by elaborate mathematical treatment, the actual growth of earnings

* "Mean figure" refers to the simple, or arithmetic, average that Graham describes in the preceding sentence.

TABLE 12-1

	ALCOA	Sears Roebuck	DJIA
Average earnings 1968–1970	$4.95[a]	$2.87	$55.40
Average earnings 1958–1960	2.08	1.23	31.49
Growth	141.0%	134.0%	75.0%
Annual rate (compounded)	9.0%	8.7%	5.7%

[a] Three-fifths of special charges of 82 cents in 1970 deducted here.

for the long period 1958–1970. But how relevant is this figure, generally considered central in common-stock valuations, to the case of ALCOA? Its past growth rate was excellent, actually a bit better than that of acclaimed Sears Roebuck and much higher than that of the DJIA composite. But the market price at the beginning of 1971 seemed to pay no attention to this fine performance. ALCOA sold at only 11½ times the recent three-year average, while Sears sold at 27 times and the DJIA itself at 15+ times. How did this come about? Evidently Wall Street has fairly pessimistic views about the future course of ALCOA's earnings, in contrast with its past record. Surprisingly enough, the high price for ALCOA was made as far back as 1959. In that year it sold at 116, or 45 times its earnings. (This compares with a 1959 adjusted high price of 25½ for Sears Roebuck, or 20 times its then earnings.) Even though ALCOA's profits did show excellent growth thereafter, it is evident that in this case the future possibilities were greatly overestimated in the market price. It closed 1970 at exactly half of the 1959 high, while Sears tripled in price and the DJIA moved up nearly 30%.

It should be pointed out that ALCOA's earnings on capital funds* had been only average or less, and this may be the decisive factor here. High multipliers have been *maintained* in the stock market only if the company has maintained better than average profitability.

---

* Graham appears to be using "earnings on capital funds" in the traditional sense of return on book value—essentially, net income divided by the company's tangible net assets.

Let us apply at this point to ALCOA the suggestion we made in the previous chapter for a "two-part appraisal process."* Such an approach might have produced a "past-performance value" for ALCOA of 10% of the DJIA, or $84 per share relative to the closing price of 840 for the DJIA in 1970. On this basis the shares would have appeared quite attractive at their price of 57¼.

To what extent should the senior analyst have marked down the "past-performance value" to allow for adverse developments that he saw in the future? Frankly, we have no idea. Assume he had reason to believe that the 1971 earnings would be as low as $2.50 per share—a large drop from the 1970 figure, as against an advance expected for the DJIA. Very likely the stock market would take this poor performance quite seriously, but would it really establish the once mighty Aluminum Company of America as a relatively *unprofitable* enterprise, to be valued at less than its tangible assets behind the shares?† (In 1971 the price declined from a high of 70 in May to a low of 36 in December, against a book value of 55.)

ALCOA is surely a representative industrial company of huge size, but we think that its price-and-earnings history is more unusual, even contradictory, than that of most other large enterprises. Yet this instance supports to some degree, the doubts we expressed in the last chapter as to the dependability of the appraisal procedure when applied to the typical industrial company.

---

* See pp. 299–301.

† Recent history–and a mountain of financial research–have shown that the market is unkindest to rapidly growing companies that suddenly report a fall in earnings. More moderate and stable growers, as ALCOA was in Graham's day or Anheuser-Busch and Colgate-Palmolive are in our time, tend to suffer somewhat milder stock declines if they report disappointing earnings. Great expectations lead to great disappointment if they are not met; a failure to meet moderate expectations leads to a much milder reaction. Thus, one of the biggest risks in owning growth stocks is not that their growth will stop, but merely that it will slow down. And in the long run, that is not merely a risk, but a virtual certainty.

COMMENTARY ON CHAPTER 12

You can get ripped off easier by a dude with a pen than you can by a dude with a gun.

—Bo Diddley

THE NUMBERS GAME

Even Graham would have been startled by the extent to which companies and their accountants pushed the limits of propriety in the past few years. Compensated heavily through stock options, top executives realized that they could become fabulously rich merely by increasing their company's earnings for just a few years running.[1] Hundreds of companies violated the spirit, if not the letter, of accounting principles—turning their financial reports into gibberish, tarting up ugly results with cosmetic fixes, cloaking expenses, or manufacturing earnings out of thin air. Let's look at some of these unsavory practices.

AS IF!

Perhaps the most widespread bit of accounting hocus-pocus was the "pro forma" earnings fad. There's an old saying on Wall Street that every bad idea starts out as a good idea, and pro forma earnings presentation is no different. The original point was to provide a truer picture of the long-term growth of earnings by adjusting for short-term deviations from the trend or for supposedly "nonrecurring" events. A pro forma press release might, for instance, show what a company would have earned over the past year if another firm it just acquired had been part of the family for the entire 12 months.

---

[1] For more on how stock options can enrich corporate managers—but not necessarily outside shareholders—see the commentary on Chapter 19.

But, as the Naughty 1990s advanced, companies just couldn't leave well enough alone. Just look at these examples of pro forma flim-flam:

- For the quarter ended September 30, 1999, InfoSpace, Inc. presented its pro forma earnings as if it had not paid $159.9 million in preferred-stock dividends.
- For the quarter ended October 31, 2001, BEA Systems, Inc. presented its pro forma earnings as if it had not paid $193 million in payroll taxes on stock options exercised by its employees.
- For the quarter ended March 31, 2001, JDS Uniphase Corp. presented its pro forma earnings as if it had not paid $4 million in payroll taxes, had not lost $7 million investing in lousy stocks, and had not incurred *$2.5 billion* in charges related to mergers and goodwill.

In short, pro forma earnings enable companies to show how well they might have done if they hadn't done as badly as they did.[2] As an intelligent investor, the only thing you should do with pro forma earnings is ignore them.

HUNGRY FOR RECOGNITION

In 2000, Qwest Communications International Inc., the telecommunications giant, looked strong. Its shares dropped less than 5% even as the stock market lost more than 9% that year.

But Qwest's financial reports held an odd little revelation. In late 1999, Qwest decided to recognize the revenues from its telephone directories as soon as the phone books were published–even though, as anyone who has ever taken out a Yellow Pages advertisement knows, many businesses pay for those ads in monthly installments.

---

[2] All the above examples are taken directly from press releases issued by the companies themselves. For a brilliant satire on what daily life would be like if we all got to justify our behavior the same way companies adjust their reported earnings, see "My Pro Forma Life," by Rob Walker, at http://slate.msn.com/?id=2063953. (". . . a recent post-workout lunch of a 22-ounce, bone-in rib steak at Smith & Wollensky and three shots of bourbon is treated here as a nonrecurring expense. I'll never do that again!")

Abracadabra! That piddly-sounding "change in accounting principle" pumped up 1999 net income by $240 million after taxes–a fifth of all the money Qwest earned that year.

Like a little chunk of ice crowning a submerged iceberg, aggressive revenue recognition is often a sign of dangers that run deep and loom large–and so it was at Qwest. By early 2003, after reviewing its previous financial statements, the company announced that it had prematurely recognized profits on equipment sales, improperly recorded the costs of services provided by outsiders, inappropriately booked costs as if they were capital assets rather than expenses, and unjustifiably treated the exchange of assets as if they were outright sales. All told, Qwest's revenues for 2000 and 2001 had been overstated by $2.2 billion–including $80 million from the earlier "change in accounting principle," which was now reversed.[3]

CAPITAL OFFENSES

In the late 1990s, Global Crossing Ltd. had unlimited ambitions. The Bermuda-based company was building what it called the "first integrated global fiber optic network" over more than 100,000 miles of

---

[3] In 2002, Qwest was one of 330 publicly-traded companies to restate past financial statements, an all-time record, according to Huron Consulting Group. All information on Qwest is taken from its financial filings with the U.S. Securities and Exchange Commission (annual report, Form 8K, and Form 10-K) found in the EDGAR database at www.sec.gov. No hindsight was required to detect the "change in accounting principle," which Qwest fully disclosed at the time. How did Qwest's shares do over this period? At year-end 2000, the stock had been at $41 per share, a total market value of $67.9 billion. By early 2003, Qwest was around $4, valuing the entire company at less than $7 billion–a 90% loss. The drop in share price is not the only cost associated with bogus earnings; a recent study found that a sample of 27 firms accused of accounting fraud by the SEC had overpaid $320 million in Federal income tax. Although much of that money will eventually be refunded by the IRS, most shareholders are unlikely to stick around to benefit from the refunds. (See Merle Erickson, Michelle Hanlon, and Edward Maydew, "How Much Will Firms Pay for Earnings that Do Not Exist?" at http://papers.ssrn.com.)

cables, largely laid across the floor of the world's oceans. After wiring the world, Global Crossing would sell other communications companies the right to carry their traffic over its network of cables. In 1998 alone, Global Crossing spent more than $600 million to construct its optical web. That year, nearly a third of the construction budget was charged against revenues as an expense called "cost of capacity sold." If not for that $178 million expense, Global Crossing–which reported a net loss of $96 million–could have reported a net profit of roughly $82 million.

The next year, says a bland footnote in the 1999 annual report, Global Crossing "initiated service contract accounting." The company would no longer charge most construction costs as expenses against the immediate revenues it received from selling capacity on its network. Instead, a major chunk of those construction costs would now be treated not as an operating expense but as a capital expenditure–thereby increasing the company's total assets, instead of decreasing its net income.[4]

Poof! In one wave of the wand, Global Crossing's "property and equipment" assets rose by $575 million, while its cost of sales increased by a mere $350 million–even though the company was spending money like a drunken sailor.

Capital expenditures are an essential tool for managers to make a good business grow bigger and better. But malleable accounting rules permit managers to inflate reported profits by transforming nor-

---

[4] Global Crossing formerly treated much of its construction costs as an expense to be charged against the revenue generated from the sale or lease of usage rights on its network. Customers generally paid for their rights up front, although some could pay in installments over periods of up to four years. But Global Crossing did not book most of the revenues up front, instead deferring them over the lifetime of the lease. Now, however, because the networks had an estimated usable life of up to 25 years, Global Crossing began treating them as depreciable, long-lived capital assets. While this treatment conforms with Generally Accepted Accounting Principles, it is unclear why Global Crossing did not use it before October 1, 1999, or what exactly prompted the change. As of March 2001, Global Crossing had a total stock valuation of $12.6 billion; the company filed for bankruptcy on January 28, 2002, rendering its common stock essentially worthless.

mal operating expenses into capital assets. As the Global Crossing case shows, the intelligent investor should be sure to understand what, and why, a company capitalizes.

AN INVENTORY STORY

Like many makers of semiconductor chips, Micron Technology, Inc. suffered a drop in sales after 2000. In fact, Micron was hit so hard by the plunge in demand that it had to start writing down the value of its inventories–since customers clearly did not want them at the prices Micron had been asking. In the quarter ended May 2001, Micron slashed the recorded value of its inventories by $261 million. Most investors interpreted the write-down not as a normal or recurring cost of operations, but as an unusual event.

But look what happened after that:

FIGURE 12-1

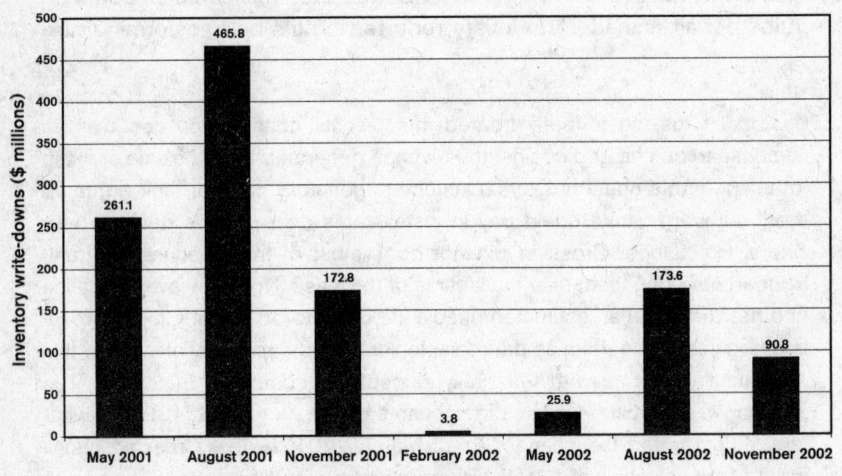

Source: Micron Technology's financial reports.

Micron booked further inventory write-downs in every one of the next six fiscal quarters. Was the devaluation of Micron's inventory a nonrecurring event, or had it become a chronic condition? Reasonable minds can differ on this particular case, but one thing is clear: The intelligent investor must always be on guard for "nonrecurring" costs that, like the Energizer bunny, just keep on going.[5]

THE PENSION DIMENSION

In 2001, SBC Communications, Inc., which owns interests in Cingular Wireless, PacTel, and Southern New England Telephone, earned $7.2 billion in net income–a stellar performance in a bad year for the overextended telecom industry. But that gain didn't come only from SBC's business. Fully $1.4 billion of it–13% of the company's net income–came from SBC's pension plan.

Because SBC had more money in the pension plan than it estimated was necessary to pay its employees' future benefits, the company got to treat the difference as current income. One simple reason for that surplus: In 2001, SBC raised the rate of return it expected to earn on the pension plan's investments from 8.5% to 9.5%–lowering the amount of money it needed to set aside today.

SBC explained its rosy new expectations by noting that "for each of the three years ended 2001, our actual 10-year return on investments exceeded 10%." In other words, our past returns have been high, so let's assume that our future returns will be too. But that not only flunked the most rudimentary tests of logic, it flew in the face of the fact that interest rates were falling to near-record lows, depressing the future returns on the bond portion of a pension portfolio.

The same year, in fact, Warren Buffett's Berkshire Hathaway *lowered* the expected rate of return on its pension assets from 8.3% to 6.5%. Was SBC being realistic in assuming that its pension-fund managers could significantly outperform the world's greatest investor? Probably not: In 2001, Berkshire Hathaway's pension fund gained 9.8%, but SBC's pension fund lost 6.9%.[6]

---

[5] I am grateful to Howard Schilit and Mark Hamel of the Center for Financial Research and Analysis for providing this example.

[6] Returns are approximated by dividing the total net value of plan assets at the beginning of the year by "actual return on plan assets."

Here are some quick considerations for the intelligent investor: Is the "net pension benefit" more than 5% of the company's net income? *(If so, would you still be comfortable with the company's other earnings if those pension gains went away in future years?)* Is the assumed "long-term rate of return on plan assets" reasonable? *(As of 2003, anything above 6.5% is implausible, while a rising rate is downright delusional.)*

CAVEAT INVESTOR

A few pointers will help you avoid buying a stock that turns out to be an accounting time bomb:

Read backwards. When you research a company's financial reports, start reading on the last page and slowly work your way toward the front. Anything that the company doesn't want you to find is buried in the back–which is precisely why you should look there first.

Read the notes. *Never* buy a stock without reading the footnotes to the financial statements in the annual report. Usually labeled "summary of significant accounting policies," one key note describes how the company recognizes revenue, records inventories, treats installment or contract sales, expenses its marketing costs, and accounts for the other major aspects of its business.[7] In the other footnotes,

[7] Do not be put off by the stupefyingly boring verbiage of accounting footnotes. They are designed expressly to deter normal people from actually reading them–which is why you must persevere. A footnote to the 1996 annual report of Informix Corp., for instance, disclosed that "The Company generally recognizes license revenue from sales of software licenses upon delivery of the software product to a customer. However, for certain computer hardware manufacturers and end-user licensees with amounts payable within twelve months, the Company will recognize revenue at the time the customer makes a contractual commitment for a minimum nonrefundable license fee, if such computer hardware manufacturers and end-user licensees meet certain criteria established by the Company." In plain English, Informix was saying that it would credit itself for revenues on products even if they had not yet been resold to "end-users" (the actual customers for Informix's software). Amid allegations by the U.S. Securities and

watch for disclosures about debt, stock options, loans to customers, reserves against losses, and other "risk factors" that can take a big chomp out of earnings. Among the things that should make your antennae twitch are technical terms like "capitalized," "deferred," and "restructuring"–and plain-English words signaling that the company has altered its accounting practices, like "began," "change," and "however." None of those words mean you should not buy the stock, but all mean that you need to investigate further. Be sure to compare the footnotes with those in the financial statements of at least one firm that's a close competitor, to see how aggressive your company's accountants are.

Read more. If you are an enterprising investor willing to put plenty of time and energy into your portfolio, then you owe it to yourself to learn more about financial reporting. That's the only way to minimize your odds of being misled by a shifty earnings statement. Three solid books full of timely and specific examples are Martin Fridson and Fernando Alvarez's *Financial Statement Analysis,* Charles Mulford and Eugene Comiskey's *The Financial Numbers Game,* and Howard Schilit's *Financial Shenanigans.*[8]

Exchange Commission that Informix had committed accounting fraud, the company later restated its revenues, wiping away $244 million in such "sales." This case is a keen reminder of the importance of reading the fine print with a skeptical eye. I am indebted to Martin Fridson for suggesting this example.

[8] Martin Fridson and Fernando Alvarez, *Financial Statement Analysis: A Practitioner's Guide* (John Wiley & Sons, New York, 2002); Charles W. Mulford and Eugene E. Comiskey, *The Financial Numbers Game: Detecting Creative Accounting Practices* (John Wiley & Sons, New York, 2002); Howard Schilit, *Financial Shenanigans* (McGraw-Hill, New York, 2002). Benjamin Graham's own book, *The Interpretation of Financial Statements* (HarperBusiness, New York, 1998 reprint of 1937 edition), remains an excellent brief introduction to the basic principles of earnings and expenses, assets and liabilities.

CHAPTER 13

A Comparison of Four Listed Companies

In this chapter we should like to present a sample of security analysis in operation. We have selected, more or less at random, four companies which are found successively on the New York Stock Exchange list. These are ELTRA Corp. (a merger of Electric Autolite and Mergenthaler Linotype enterprises), Emerson Electric Co. (a manufacturer of electric and electronic products), Emery Air Freight (a domestic forwarder of air freight), and Emhart Corp. (originally a maker of bottling machinery only, but now also in builders' hardware).* There are some broad resemblances between the three manufacturing firms, but the differences will seem more significant. There should be sufficient variety in the financial and operating data to make the examination of interest.

In Table 13-1 we present a summary of what the four companies were selling for in the market at the end of 1970, and a few figures on their 1970 operations. We then detail certain key ratios, which relate on the one hand to *performance* and on the other to *price.* Comment is called for on how various aspects of the performance pattern agree with the relative price pattern. Finally, we shall pass the four companies in review, suggesting some comparisons and relationships and evaluating each in terms of the requirements of a conservative common-stock investor.

---

* Of Graham's four examples, only Emerson Electric still exists in the same form. ELTRA Corp. is no longer an independent company; it merged with Bunker Ramo Corp. in the 1970s, putting it in the business of supplying stock quotes to brokerage firms across an early network of computers. What remains of ELTRA's operations is now part of Honeywell Corp. The firm formerly known as Emery Air Freight is now a division of CNF Inc. Emhart Corp. was acquired by Black & Decker Corp. in 1989.

TABLE 13-1 A Comparison of Four Listed Companies

	ELTRA	*Emerson Electric*	*Emery Air Freight*	*Emhart Corp.*
A. Capitalization				
Price of common, Dec. 31, 1970	27	66	57¾	32¾
Number of shares of common	7,714,000	24,884,000[a]	3,807,000	4,932,000
Market value of common	$208,300,000	$1,640,000,000	$220,000,000	$160,000,000
Bonds and preferred stock	8,000,000	42,000,000		9,200,000
Total capitalization	216,300,000	1,682,000,000	220,000,000	169,200,000
B. Income Items				
Sales, 1970	$454,000,000	$657,000,000	$108,000,000	$227,000,000
Net income, 1970	20,773,000	54,600,000	5,679,000	13,551,000
Earned per share, 1970	$2.70	$2.30	$1.49	$2.75[b]
Earned per share, ave., 1968–1970	2.78	2.10	1.28	2.81
Earned per share, ave., 1963–1965	1.54	1.06	.54	2.46
Earned per share, ave., 1958–1960	.54	.57	.17	1.21
Current dividend	1.20	1.16	1.00	1.20
C. Balance-sheet Items, 1970				
Current assets	$205,000,000	$307,000,000	$20,400,000	$121,000,000
Current liabilities	71,000,000	72,000,000	11,800,000	34,800,000
Net assets for common stock	207,000,000	257,000,000	15,200,000	133,000,000
Book value per share	$27.05	$10.34	$3.96	$27.02

[a] Assuming conversion of preferred stock.

[b] After special charge of 13 cents per share.

[c] Year ended Sept. 1970.

TABLE 13-2 A Comparison of Four Listed Companies (*continued*)

	ELTRA	*Emerson Electric*	*Emery Air Freight*	*Emhart Corp.*
B. Ratios				
Price/earnings, 1970	10.0 ×	30.0 ×	38.5 ×	11.9 ×
Price/earnings, 1968–1970	9.7 ×	33.0 ×	45.0 ×	11.7 ×
Price/book value	1.00 ×	6.37 ×	14.3 ×	1.22 ×
Net/sales, 1970	4.6 %	8.5 %	5.4 %	5.7 %
Net per share/book value	10.0 %	22.2 %	34.5 %	10.2 %
Dividend yield	4.45 %	1.78 %	1.76 %	3.65 %
Current assets to current liabilities	2.9 ×	4.3 ×	1.7 ×	3.4 ×
Working capital/debt	Very large	5.6 ×	no debt	3.4 ×
Earnings growth per share:				
1968–1970 vs. 1963–1965	+ 81%	+ 87%	+ 135%	+14 %
1968–1970 vs. 1958–1970	+400%	+250%	Very large	+132%
C. Price Record				
1936–1968 Low	¾	1	⅛	3⅝
High	50¾	61½	66	58¼
1970 Low	18⅝	42⅛	41	23½
1971 High	29⅜	78¾	72	44⅜

The most striking fact about the four companies is that the current price/earnings ratios vary much more widely than their operating performance or financial condition. Two of the enterprises—ELTRA and Emhart—were modestly priced at only 9.7 times and 12 times the average earnings for 1968–1970, as against a similar figure of 15.5 times for the DJIA. The other two—Emerson and Emery—showed very high multiples of 33 and 45 times such earnings. There is bound to be some explanation of a difference such as this, and it is found in the superior growth of the favored companies' profits in recent years, especially by the freight forwarder. (But the growth figures of the other two firms were not unsatisfactory.)

For more comprehensive treatment let us review briefly the chief elements of performance as they appear from our figures.

1. *Profitability.* (*a*) All the companies show satisfactory earnings on their book value, but the figures for Emerson and Emery are much higher than for the other two. A high rate of return on invested capital often goes along with a high annual growth rate in earnings per share.* All the companies except Emery showed better earnings on book value in 1969 than in 1961; but the Emery figure was exceptionally large in both years. (*b*) For manufacturing companies, the profit figure per dollar of sales is usually an indication of comparative strength or weakness. We use here the "ratio of operating income to sales," as given in Standard & Poor's *Listed Stock Reports.* Here again the results are satisfactory for all four companies, with an especially impressive showing by Emerson. The changes between 1961 and 1969 vary considerably among the companies.

2. *Stability.* This we measure by the maximum decline in per-share earnings in any one of the past ten years, as against the average of the three preceding years. No decline translates into 100% stability, and this was registered by the two popular concerns. But the shrinkages of ELTRA and Emhart were quite moderate in the "poor year" 1970, amounting to only 8% each by our measurement, against 7% for the DJIA.

3. *Growth.* The two low-multiplier companies show quite satisfactory growth rates, in both cases doing better than the Dow Jones group. The ELTRA figures are especially impressive when set against its low price/earnings ratio. The growth is of course more impressive for the high-multiplier pair.

4. *Financial Position.* The three manufacturing companies are in sound financial condition, having better than the standard ratio of $2 of current assets for $1 of current liabilities. Emery Air Freight has a lower ratio; but it falls in a different category, and with its fine record it would have no problem raising needed cash. All the companies have relatively low long-term debt. "Dilution" note: Emerson Electric had $163 million of market value of low-dividend

---

* This measure is captured in the line "Net per share/book value" in Table 13-2, which measures the companies' net income as a percentage of their tangible book value.

convertible preferred shares outstanding at the end of 1970. In our analysis we have made allowance for the dilution factor in the usual way by treating the preferred as if converted into common. This decreased recent earnings by about 10 cents per share, or some 4%.

5. *Dividends.* What really counts is the history of continuance without interruption. The best record here is Emhart's, which has not suspended a payment since 1902. ELTRA's record is very good, Emerson's quite satisfactory, Emery Freight is a newcomer. The variations in payout percentage do not seem especially significant. The current dividend yield is twice as high on the "cheap pair" as on the "dear pair," corresponding to the price/earnings ratios.

6. *Price History.* The reader should be impressed by the percentage advance shown in the price of all four of these issues, as measured from the lowest to the highest points during the past 34 years. (In all cases the low price has been adjusted for subsequent stock splits.) Note that for the DJIA the range from low to high was on the order of 11 to 1; for our companies the spread has varied from "only" 17 to 1 for Emhart to no less than 528 to 1 for Emery Air Freight.* These manifold price advances are characteristic of most of our older common-stock issues, and they proclaim the great opportunities of profit that have existed in the stock markets of the past. (But they may indicate also how overdone were the declines in the bear markets before 1950 when the low prices were registered.) Both ELTRA and Emhart sustained price shrinkages of more than 50% in the 1969–70 price break. Emerson and Emery had serious, but less distressing, declines; the former rebounded to a new all-time high before the end of 1970, the latter in early 1971.

---

* In each case, Graham is referring to Section C of Table 13-2 and dividing the high price during the 1936–1968 period by the low price. For example, Emery's high price of 66 divided by its low price of 1/8 equals 528, or a ratio of 528 to 1 between the high and low.

General Observations on the Four Companies

Emerson Electric has an enormous total market value, dwarfing the other three companies combined.* It is one of our "good-will giants," to be commented on later. A financial analyst blessed (or handicapped) with a good memory will think of an analogy between Emerson Electric and Zenith Radio, and that would not be reassuring. For Zenith had a brilliant growth record for many years; it too sold in the market for $1.7 billion (in 1966); but its profits fell from $43 million in 1968 to only half as much in 1970, and in that year's big selloff its price declined to 22½ against the previous top of 89. High valuations entail high risks.

Emery Air Freight must be the most promising of the four companies in terms of future growth, if the price/earnings ratio of nearly 40 times its highest reported earnings is to be even partially justified. The past growth, of course, has been most impressive. But these figures may not be so significant for the future if we consider that they started quite small, at only $570,000 of net earnings in 1958. It often proves much more difficult to continue to grow at a high rate after volume and profits have already expanded to big totals. The most surprising aspect of Emery's story is that its earnings and market price continued to grow apace in 1970, which was the worst year in the domestic air-passenger industry. This is a remarkable achievement indeed, but it raises the question whether future profits may not be vulnerable to adverse developments, through increased competition, pressure for new arrangements between forwarders and airlines, etc. An elaborate study might be needed before a sound judgment could be passed on these points, but the conservative investor cannot leave them out of his general reckoning.

Emhart and ELTRA. Emhart has done better in its business than in the stock market over the past 14 years. In 1958 it sold as high as 22 times the current earnings—about the same ratio as for the DJIA. Since then its profits tripled, as against a rise of less than 100% for the Dow, but its closing price in 1970 was only a third above the

* At the end of 1970, Emerson's $1.6 billion in market value truly was "enormous," given average stock sizes at the time. At year-end 2002, Emerson's common stock had a total market value of approximately $21 billion.

1958 high, versus 43% for the Dow. The record of ELTRA is somewhat similar. It appears that neither of these companies possesses glamour, or "sex appeal," in the present market; but in all the statistical data they show up surprisingly well. Their future prospects? We have no sage remarks to make here, but this is what Standard & Poor's had to say about the four companies in 1971:

ELTRA—"Long-term Prospects: Certain operations are cyclical, but an established competitive position and diversification are offsetting factors."

Emerson Electric—"While adequately priced (at 71) on the current outlook, the shares have appeal for the long term. . . . A continued acquisition policy together with a strong position in industrial fields and an accelerated international program suggests further sales and earnings progress."

Emery Air Freight—"The shares appear amply priced (at 57) on current prospects, but are well worth holding for the long pull."

Emhart—"Although restricted this year by lower capital spending in the glass-container industry, earnings should be aided by an improved business environment in 1972. The shares are worth holding (at 34)."

Conclusions: Many financial analysts will find Emerson and Emery more interesting and appealing stocks than the other two—primarily, perhaps, because of their better "market action," and secondarily because of their faster recent growth in earnings. Under our principles of conservative investment the first is not a valid reason for selection—that is something for the speculators to play around with. The second has validity, but within limits. Can the past growth and the presumably good prospects of Emery Air Freight justify a price more than 60 times its recent earnings?[1] Our answer would be: Maybe for someone who has made an in-depth study of the possibilities of this company and come up with exceptionally firm and optimistic conclusions. But *not* for the careful investor who wants to be reasonably sure in advance that he is not committing the typical Wall Street error of overenthusiasm for good performance in earnings and in the stock market.* The same

---

* Graham was right. Of the "Nifty Fifty" stocks that were most fashionable and highly valued in 1972, Emery fared among the worst. The March 1,

cautionary statements seem called for in the case of Emerson Electric, with a special reference to the market's current valuation of over a billion dollars for the intangible, or earning-power, factor here. We should add that the "electronics industry," once a fair-haired child of the stock market, has in general fallen on disastrous days. Emerson is an outstanding exception, but it will have to continue to be such an exception for a great many years in the future before the 1970 closing price will have been fully justified by its subsequent performance.

By contrast, both ELTRA at 27 and Emhart at 33 have the earmarks of companies with sufficient value behind their price to constitute reasonably protected investments. Here the investor can, if he wishes, consider himself basically a part owner of these businesses, at a cost corresponding to what the balance sheet shows to be the money invested therein.* The rate of earnings on invested capital has long been satisfactory; the stability of profits also; the past growth rate surprisingly so. The two companies will meet our seven *statistical* requirements for inclusion in a defensive investor's portfolio. These will be developed in the next chapter, but we summarize them as follows:

1. Adequate size.
2. A sufficiently strong financial condition.
3. Continued dividends for at least the past 20 years.
4. No earnings deficit in the past ten years.

1982, issue of *Forbes* reported that since 1972 Emery had lost 72.8% of its value after inflation. By late 1974, according to the investment researchers at the Leuthold Group in Minneapolis, Emery's stock had already fallen 58% and its price/earnings ratio had plummeted from 64 times to just 15. The "overenthusiasm" Graham had warned against was eviscerated in short order. Can the passage of time make up for this kind of excess? Not always: Leuthold calculated that $1000 invested in Emery in 1972 would be worth only $839 as of 1999. It's likely that the people who overpaid for Internet stocks in the late 1990s will not break even for decades–if ever (see the commentary on Chapter 20).

* Graham's point is that, based on their prices at the time, an investor could buy shares in these two companies for little more than their book value, as shown in the third line of Section B in Table 13-2.

5. Ten-year growth of at least one-third in per-share earnings.
6. Price of stock no more than 1½ times net asset value.
7. Price no more than 15 times average earnings of the past three years.

We make no predictions about the future earnings performance of ELTRA or Emhart. In the investor's diversified list of common stocks there are bound to be some that prove disappointing, and this may be the case for one or both of this pair. But the diversified list itself, based on the above principles of selection, plus whatever other sensible criteria the investor may wish to apply, should perform well enough across the years. At least, long experience tells us so.

A final observation: An experienced security analyst, even if he accepted our general reasoning on these four companies, would have hesitated to recommend that a holder of Emerson or Emery *exchange* his shares for ELTRA or Emhart at the end of 1970—unless the holder understood clearly the philosophy behind the recommendation. There was no reason to expect that in any short period of time the low-multiplier duo would outperform the high-multipliers. The latter were well thought of in the market and thus had a considerable degree of momentum behind them, which might continue for an indefinite period. The sound basis for preferring ELTRA and Emhart to Emerson and Emery would be the client's considered conclusion that he preferred value-type investments to glamour-type investments. Thus, to a substantial extent, common-stock investment policy must depend on the attitude of the individual investor. This approach is treated at greater length in our next chapter.

COMMENTARY ON CHAPTER 13

> In the Air Force we have a rule: check six. A guy is flying along, looking in all directions, and feeling very safe. Another guy flies up behind him (at "6 o'clock"–"12 o'clock" is directly in front) and shoots. Most airplanes are shot down that way. Thinking that you're safe is very dangerous! Somewhere, there's a weakness you've got to find. You must always check six o'clock.
>
> *–U.S. Air Force Gen. Donald Kutyna*

E-BUSINESS

As Graham did, let's compare and contrast four stocks, using their reported numbers as of December 31, 1999–a time that will enable us to view some of the most drastic extremes of valuation ever recorded in the stock market.

Emerson Electric Co. (ticker symbol: EMR) was founded in 1890 and is the only surviving member of Graham's original quartet; it makes a wide array of products, including power tools, air-conditioning equipment, and electrical motors.

EMC Corp. (ticker symbol: EMC) dates back to 1979 and enables companies to automate the storage of electronic information over computer networks.

Expeditors International of Washington, Inc. (ticker symbol: EXPD), founded in Seattle in 1979, helps shippers organize and track the movement of goods around the world.

Exodus Communications, Inc. (ticker symbol: EXDS) hosts and manages websites for corporate customers, along with other Internet services; it first sold shares to the public in March 1998.

This table summarizes the price, performance, and valuation of these companies as of year-end 1999:

FIGURE 13-1 E-valuations

	Emerson Electric	EMC Corp.	Exodus Communications, Inc.	Expeditors International of Washington
Capitalization				
Closing price, 12/31/99, $ per share	57.37	54.62	44.41	21.68
Total return, 1999 (%)	–3.1	157.1	1005.8	109.1
Total market cap, 12/31/99, $ millions	24845.9	111054.3	14358.4	2218.8
Total debt (including preferred stock), $ millions	4600.1	27.1	2555.7	0
Earnings				
Total revenues, 1999, $ millions	14385.8	6715.6	242.1	1444.6
Net income, 1999, $ millions	1313.6	1010.6	–130.3	59.2
Earnings growth, 1995 through 1999 (average annual %)	7.7	28.8	NM	19.8
Earnings per share (EPS), 1999 ($ fully diluted)	3.00	0.53	–0.38	0.55
EPS growth rate, 1995–1999 (average annual %)	8.3	28.8	NM	25.8
Annual dividend ($ per share), 1999	1.30	0	0	0.08
Balance sheet				
Current assets, $ millions	5124.4	4320.4	1093.2	402.7
Current liabilities, $ millions	4590.4	1397.9	150.6	253.1
Book value per share ($ 12/31/99)	14.27	2.38	0.05	2.79
Valuation				
Price/earnings ratio (×)	17.7	103.1	NM	39.4
Price/book value (×)	3.7	22.9	888.1	7.8
Net income/revenues (% net profit margin)	9.2	17.4	NM	4.1
Net income/book value (%)	21.0	22.2	NM	19.7
Working capital/debt (×)	0.1	107.8	0.4	no debt
Market cap/revenues (×)	1.7	16.5	59.3	1.5

Sources: Value Line, Thomson/Baseline, Bloomberg, finance.yahoo.com, the companies' SEC filings

Notes: All figures adjusted for later stock splits. Debt, revenue, and earnings are for fiscal years. Market cap: total value of common stock. NM: not meaningful.

ELECTRIC, NOT ELECTRIFYING

The most expensive of Graham's four stocks, Emerson Electric, ended up as the cheapest in our updated group. With its base in Old Economy industries, Emerson looked boring in the late 1990s. (In the Internet Age, who cared about Emerson's heavy-duty wet-dry vacuums?) The company's shares went into suspended animation. In 1998 and 1999, Emerson's stock lagged the S & P 500 index by a cumulative 49.7 percentage points, a miserable underperformance.

But that was Emerson the stock. What about Emerson the company? In 1999, Emerson sold $14.4 billion worth of goods and services, up nearly $1 billion from the year before. On those revenues Emerson earned $1.3 billion in net income, or 6.9% more than in 1998. Over the previous five years, earnings per share had risen at a robust average rate of 8.3%. Emerson's dividend had more than doubled to $1.30 per share; book value had gone from $6.69 to $14.27 per share. According to Value Line, throughout the 1990s, Emerson's net profit margin and return on capital–key measures of its efficiency as a business–had stayed robustly high, around 9% and 18% respectively. What's more, Emerson had increased its earnings for 42 years in a row and had raised its dividend for 43 straight years–one of the longest runs of steady growth in American business. At year-end, Emerson's stock was priced at 17.7 times the company's net income per share. Like its power tools, Emerson was never flashy, but it was reliable–and showed no sign of overheating.

COULD EMC GROW PDQ?

EMC Corp. was one of the best-performing stocks of the 1990s, rising–or should we say levitating?–more than 81,000%. If you had invested $10,000 in EMC's stock at the beginning of 1990, you would have ended 1999 with just over $8.1 million. EMC's shares returned 157.1% in 1999 alone–more than Emerson's stock had gained in the eight years from 1992 through 1999 combined. EMC had never paid a dividend, instead retaining all its earnings "to provide funds for the continued growth of the company."[1] At their December

---

[1] As we will see in Chapter 19, this rationale often means, in practice, "to provide funds for the continued growth of the company's top managers' wealth."

31 price of $54.625, EMC's shares were trading at 103 times the earnings the company would report for the full year–nearly six times the valuation level of Emerson's stock.

What about EMC the business? Revenues grew 24% in 1999, rising to $6.7 billion. Its earnings per share soared to 92 cents from 61 cents the year before, a 51% increase. Over the five years ending in 1999, EMC's earnings had risen at a sizzling annual rate of 28.8%. And, with everyone expecting the tidal wave of Internet commerce to keep rolling, the future looked even brighter. Throughout 1999, EMC's chief executive repeatedly predicted that revenues would hit $10 billion by 2001–up from $5.4 billion in 1998.[2] That would require average annual growth of 23%, a monstrous rate of expansion for so big a company. But Wall Street's analysts, and most investors, were sure EMC could do it. After all, over the previous five years, EMC had more than doubled its revenues and better than tripled its net income.

But from 1995 through 1999, according to Value Line, EMC's net profit margin slid from 19.0% to 17.4%, while its return on capital dropped from 26.8% to 21%. Although still highly profitable, EMC was already slipping. And in October 1999, EMC acquired Data General Corp., which added roughly $1.1 billion to EMC's revenues that year. Simply by subtracting the extra revenues brought in from Data General, we can see that the volume of EMC's existing businesses grew from $5.4 billion in 1998 to just $5.6 billion in 1999, a rise of only 3.6%. In other words, EMC's true growth rate was almost nil–even in a year when the scare over the "Y2K" computer bug had led many companies to spend record amounts on new technology.[3]

---

[2] Appearing on CNBC on December 30, 1999, EMC's chief executive, Michael Ruettgers, was asked by host Ron Insana whether "2000 and beyond" would be as good as the 1990s had been. "It actually looks like it's accelerating," boasted Ruettgers. When Insana asked if EMC's stock was overvalued, Ruettgers answered: "I think when you look at the opportunity we have in front of us, it's almost unlimited. . . . So while it's hard to predict whether these things are overpriced, there's such a major change taking place that if you could find the winners today–and I certainly think EMC is one of those people–you'll be well rewarded in the future."

[3] The "Y2K bug" or the "Year 2000 Problem" was the belief that millions of computers worldwide would stop functioning at one second past midnight

A SIMPLE TWIST OF FREIGHT

Unlike EMC, Expeditors International hadn't yet learned to levitate. Although the firm's shares had risen 30% annually in the 1990s, much of that big gain had come at the very end, as the stock raced to a 109.1% return in 1999. The year before, Expeditors' shares had gone up just 9.5%, trailing the S & P 500 index by more than 19 percentage points.

What about the business? Expeditors was growing expeditiously indeed: Since 1995, its revenues had risen at an average annual rate of 19.8%, nearly tripling over the period to finish 1999 at $1.4 billion. And earnings per share had grown by 25.8% annually, while dividends had risen at a 27% annual clip. Expeditors had no long-term debt, and its working capital had nearly doubled since 1995. According to Value Line, Expeditors' book value per share had increased 129% and its return on capital had risen by more than one-third to 21%.

By any standard, Expeditors was a superb business. But the little freight-forwarding company, with its base in Seattle and much of its operations in Asia, was all-but-unknown on Wall Street. Only 32% of the shares were owned by institutional investors; in fact, Expeditors had only 8,500 shareholders. After doubling in 1999, the stock was priced at 39 times the net income Expeditors would earn for the year—no longer anywhere near cheap, but well below the vertiginous valuation of EMC.

THE PROMISED LAND?

By the end of 1999, Exodus Communications seemed to have taken its shareholders straight to the land of milk and honey. The stock soared 1,005.8% in 1999—enough to turn a $10,000 investment on January 1 into more than $110,000 by December 31. Wall Street's leading Internet-stock analysts, including the hugely influential Henry

---

on the morning of January 1, 2000, because programmers in the 1960s and 1970s had not thought to allow for the possibility of any date past 12/31/1999 in their operating code. U.S. companies spent billions of dollars in 1999 to ensure that their computers would be "Y2K-compliant." In the end, at 12:00:01 A.M. on January 1, 2000, everything worked just fine.

Blodget of Merrill Lynch, were predicting that the stock would rise another 25% to 125% over the coming year.

And best of all, in the eyes of the online traders who gorged on Exodus's gains, was the fact that the stock had split 2-for-1 three times during 1999. In a 2-for-1 stock split, a company doubles the number of its shares and halves their price—so a shareholder ends up owning twice as many shares, each priced at half the former level. What's so great about that? Imagine that you handed me a dime, and I then gave you back two nickels and asked, "Don't you feel richer now?" You would probably conclude either that I was an idiot, or that I had mistaken you for one. And yet, in 1999's frenzy over dot-com stocks, online traders acted exactly as if two nickels were more valuable than one dime. In fact, just the news that a stock would be splitting 2-for-1 could instantly drive its shares up 20% or more.

Why? Because getting more shares makes people *feel* richer. Someone who bought 100 shares of Exodus in January watched them turn into 200 when the stock split in April; then those 200 turned into 400 in August; then the 400 became 800 in December. It was thrilling for these people to realize that they had gotten 700 more shares just for owning 100 in the first place. To them, that felt like "found money"—never mind that the price per share had been cut in half with each split.[4] In December, 1999, one elated Exodus shareholder, who went by the handle "givemeadollar," exulted on an online message board: "I'm going to hold these shares until I'm 80, [because] after it splits hundreds of times over the next years, I'll be close to becoming CEO."[5]

What about Exodus the business? Graham wouldn't have touched it with a 10-foot pole and a haz-mat suit. Exodus's revenues were exploding—growing from $52.7 million in 1998 to $242.1 million in 1999—but it lost $130.3 million on those revenues in 1999, nearly double its loss the year before. Exodus had $2.6 billion in total debt—and was so starved for cash that it borrowed $971 million in the

---

[4] For more on the folly of stock splits, see Jason Zweig, "Splitsville," *Money*, March, 2001, pp. 55–56.

[5] Posting no. 3622, December 7, 1999, at the Exodus Communications message board on the Raging Bull website (http://ragingbull.lycos.com/mboard/boards.cgi?board=EXDS&read=3622).

month of December alone. According to Exodus's annual report, that new borrowing would add more than $50 million to its interest payments in the coming year. The company started 1999 with $156 million in cash and, even after raising $1.3 billion in new financing, finished the year with a cash balance of $1 billion—meaning that its businesses had devoured more than $400 million in cash during 1999. How could such a company ever pay its debts?

But, of course, online traders were fixated on how far and fast the *stock* had risen, not on whether the *company* was healthy. "This stock," bragged a trader using the screen name of "Launch_Pad1999," "will just continue climbing to infinity and beyond."[6]

The absurdity of Launch_Pad's prediction—what is "beyond" infinity?—is the perfect reminder of one of Graham's classic warnings. "Today's investor," Graham tells us,

> is so concerned with anticipating the future that he is already paying handsomely for it in advance. Thus what he has projected with so much study and care may actually happen and still not bring him any profit. If it should fail to materialize to the degree expected he may in fact be faced with a serious temporary and perhaps even permanent loss."[7]

WHERE THE Es ENDED UP

How did these four stocks perform after 1999?

Emerson Electric went on to gain 40.7% in 2000. Although the shares lost money in both 2001 and 2002, they nevertheless ended 2002 less than 4% below their final price of 1999.

EMC also rose in 2000, gaining 21.7%. But then the shares lost 79.4% in 2001 and another 54.3% in 2002. That left them 88% below their level at year-end 1999. What about the forecast of $10 billion in revenues by 2001? EMC finished that year with revenues of just $7.1 billion (and a net loss of $508 million).

---

[6] Posting no. 3910, December 15, 1999, at the Exodus Communications message board on the Raging Bull website (http://ragingbull.lycos.com/mboard/boards.cgi?board=EXDS&read=3910).

[7] See Graham's speech, "The New Speculation in Common Stocks," in the Appendix, p. 563.

Meanwhile, as if the bear market did not even exist, Expeditors International's shares went on to gain 22.9% in 2000, 6.5% in 2001, and another 15.1% in 2002–finishing that year nearly 51% higher than their price at the end of 1999.

Exodus's stock lost 55% in 2000 and 99.8% in 2001. On September 26, 2001, Exodus filed for Chapter 11 bankruptcy protection. Most of the company's assets were bought by Cable & Wireless, the British telecommunications giant. Instead of delivering its shareholders to the promised land, Exodus left them exiled in the wilderness. As of early 2003, the last trade in Exodus's stock was at one penny a share.

CHAPTER 14

Stock Selection for the Defensive Investor

It is time to turn to some broader applications of the techniques of security analysis. Since we have already described in general terms the investment policies recommended for our two categories of investors,* it would be logical for us now to indicate how security analysis comes into play in order to implement these policies. The defensive investor who follows our suggestions will purchase only high-grade bonds plus a diversified list of leading common stocks. He is to make sure that the price at which he bought the latter is not unduly high as judged by applicable standards.

In setting up this diversified list he has a choice of two approaches, the DJIA-type of portfolio and the quantitatively-tested portfolio. In the first he acquires a true cross-section sample of the leading issues, which will include both some favored growth companies, whose shares sell at especially high multipliers, and also less popular and less expensive enterprises. This could be done, most simply perhaps, by buying the same amounts of all thirty of the issues in the Dow-Jones Industrial Average (DJIA). Ten shares of each, at the 900 level for the average, would cost an aggregate of about $16,000.[1] On the basis of the past record he might expect approximately the same future results by buying shares of several representative investment funds.†

His second choice would be to apply a set of standards to each

---

* Graham describes his recommended investment policies in Chapters 4 through 7.

† As we have discussed in the commentaries on Chapters 5 and 9, today's defensive investor can achieve this goal simply by buying a low-cost index fund, ideally one that tracks the return of the total U.S. stock market.

purchase, to make sure that he obtains (1) a minimum of *quality* in the past performance and current financial position of the company, and also (2) a minimum of *quantity* in terms of earnings and assets per dollar of price. At the close of the previous chapter we listed seven such quality and quantity criteria suggested for the selection of specific common stocks. Let us describe them in order.

1. *Adequate Size of the Enterprise*

All our minimum figures must be arbitrary and especially in the matter of size required. Our idea is to exclude small companies which may be subject to more than average vicissitudes especially in the industrial field. (There are often good possibilities in such enterprises but we do not consider them suited to the needs of the defensive investor.) Let us use round amounts: not less than $100 million of annual sales for an industrial company and, not less than $50 million of total assets for a public utility.

2. *A Sufficiently Strong Financial Condition*

For industrial companies current assets should be at least twice current liabilities—a so-called two-to-one current ratio. Also, long-term debt should not exceed the net current assets (or "working capital"). For public utilities the debt should not exceed twice the stock equity (at book value).

3. *Earnings Stability*

Some earnings for the common stock in each of the past ten years.

4. *Dividend Record*

Uninterrupted payments for at least the past 20 years.

5. *Earnings Growth*

A minimum increase of at least one-third in per-share earnings in the past ten years using three-year averages at the beginning and end.

6. Moderate Price/Earnings Ratio

Current price should not be more than 15 times average earnings of the past three years.

7. Moderate Ratio of Price to Assets

Current price should not be more than 1½ times the book value last reported. However, a multiplier of earnings below 15 could justify a correspondingly higher multiplier of assets. As a rule of thumb we suggest that the *product* of the multiplier times the ratio of price to book value should not exceed 22.5. (This figure corresponds to 15 times earnings and 1½ times book value. It would admit an issue selling at only 9 times earnings and 2.5 times asset value, etc.)

General Comments: These requirements are set up especially for the needs and the temperament of defensive investors. They will eliminate the great majority of common stocks as candidates for the portfolio, and in two opposite ways. On the one hand they will exclude companies that are (1) too small, (2) in relatively weak financial condition, (3) with a deficit stigma in their ten-year record, and (4) not having a long history of continuous dividends. Of these tests the most severe under recent financial conditions are those of financial strength. A considerable number of our large and formerly strongly entrenched enterprises have weakened their current ratio or overexpanded their debt, or both, in recent years.

Our last two criteria are exclusive in the opposite direction, by demanding more earnings and more assets per dollar of price than the popular issues will supply. This is by no means the standard viewpoint of financial analysts; in fact most will insist that even conservative investors should be prepared to pay generous prices for stocks of the choice companies. We have expounded our contrary view above; it rests largely on the absence of an adequate *factor of safety* when too large a portion of the price must depend on ever-increasing earnings in the future. The reader will have to decide this important question for himself—after weighing the arguments on both sides.

We have nonetheless opted for the inclusion of a modest requirement of growth over the past decade. Without it the typical company would show retrogression, at least in terms of profit per dollar of invested capital. There is no reason for the defensive investor to include such companies—though if the price is low enough they could qualify as bargain opportunities.

The suggested *maximum* figure of 15 times earnings might well result in a typical portfolio with an *average* multiplier of, say, 12 to 13 times. Note that in February 1972 American Tel. & Tel. sold at 11 times its three-year (and current) earnings, and Standard Oil of California at less than 10 times latest earnings. Our basic recommendation is that the stock portfolio, when acquired, should have an overall earnings/price ratio—the reverse of the P/E ratio—at least as high as the current high-grade bond rate. This would mean a P/E ratio no higher than 13.3 against an AA bond yield of 7.5%.*

Application of Our Criteria to the DJIA at the End of 1970

All of our suggested criteria were satisfied by the DJIA issues at the end of 1970, but two of them just barely. Here is a survey based on the closing price of 1970 and the relevant figures. (The basic data for each company are shown in Tables 14-1 and 14-2.)

1. Size is more than ample for each company.
2. Financial condition is adequate in the *aggregate,* but not for every company.[2]
3. Some dividend has been paid by every company since at least 1940. Five of the dividend records go back to the last century.

---

* In early 2003, the yield on 10-year, AA-rated corporate bonds was around 4.6%, suggesting–by Graham's formula–that a stock portfolio should have an earnings-to-price ratio at least that high. Taking the inverse of that number (by dividing 4.6 into 100), we can derive a "suggested maximum" P/E ratio of 21.7. At the beginning of this paragraph Graham recommends that the "average" stock be priced about 20% below the "maximum" ratio. That suggests that–in general–Graham would consider stocks selling at no more than 17 times their three-year average earnings to be potentially attractive given today's interest rates and market conditions. As of December 31, 2002, more than 200–or better than 40%–of the stocks in the S & P 500-stock index had three-year average P/E ratios of 17.0 or lower. Updated AA bond yields can be found at www.bondtalk.com.

TABLE 14-1 Basic Data on 30 Stocks in the Dow Jones Industrial Average at September 30, 1971

		"Earnings Per Share"[a]					
	Price Sept. 30, 1971	Sept. 30, 1971	Ave. 1968–1970	Ave. 1958–1960	Div. Since	Net Asset Value	Current Div.
Allied Chemical	32½	1.40	1.82	2.14	1887	26.02	1.20
Aluminum Co. of Am.	45½	4.25	5.18	2.08	1939	55.01	1.80
Amer. Brands	43½	4.32	3.69	2.24	1905	13.46	2.10
Amer. Can	33¼	2.68	3.76	2.42	1923	40.01	2.20
Amer. Tel. & Tel.	43	4.03	3.91	2.52	1881	45.47	2.60
Anaconda	15	2.06	3.90	2.17	1936	54.28	none
Bethlehem Steel	25½	2.64	3.05	2.62	1939	44.62	1.20
Chrysler	28½	1.05	2.72	(0.13)	1926	42.40	0.60
DuPont	154	6.31	7.32	8.09	1904	55.22	5.00
Eastman Kodak	87	2.45	2.44	0.72	1902	13.70	1.32
General Electric	61¼	2.63	1.78	1.37	1899	14.92	1.40
General Foods	34	2.34	2.23	1.13	1922	14.13	1.40
General Motors	83	3.33	4.69	2.94	1915	33.39	3.40
Goodyear	33½	2.11	2.01	1.04	1937	18.49	0.85
Inter. Harvester	28½	1.16	2.30	1.87	1910	42.06	1.40
Inter. Nickel	31	2.27	2.10	0.94	1934	14.53	1.00
Inter. Paper	33	1.46	2.22	1.76	1946	23.68	1.50
Johns-Manville	39	2.02	2.33	1.62	1935	24.51	1.20
Owens-Illinois	52	3.89	3.69	2.24	1907	43.75	1.35
Procter & Gamble	71	2.91	2.33	1.02	1891	15.41	1.50
Sears Roebuck	68½	3.19	2.87	1.17	1935	23.97	1.55
Std. Oil of Calif.	56	5.78	5.35	3.17	1912	54.79	2.80
Std. Oil of N.J.	72	6.51	5.88	2.90	1882	48.95	3.90
Swift & Co.	42	2.56	1.66	1.33	1934	26.74	0.70
Texaco	32	3.24	2.96	1.34	1903	23.06	1.60
Union Carbide	43½	2.59	2.76	2.52	1918	29.64	2.00
United Aircraft	30½	3.13	4.35	2.79	1936	47.00	1.80
U. S. Steel	29½	3.53	3.81	4.85	1940	65.54	1.60
Westinghouse	96½	3.26	3.44	2.26	1935	33.67	1.80
Woolworth	49	2.47	2.38	1.35	1912	25.47	1.20

[a] Adjusted for stock dividends and stock splits.
[b] Typically for the 12 months ended June 30, 1971.

TABLE 14-2 Significant Ratios of DJIA Stocks at September 30, 1971

	Price to Earnings		Current	Earnings Growth			Price/
	Sept. 1971	1968–1970	Div. Yield	1968–1970 vs. 1958–1960	CA/CL[a]	NCA/ Debt[b]	Net Asset Value
Allied Chemical	18.3 ×	18.0 ×	3.7%	(–15.0%)	2.1 ×	74%	125%
Aluminum Co. of Am.	10.7	8.8	4.0	149.0%	2.7	51	84
Amer. Brands	10.1	11.8	5.1	64.7	2.1	138	282
Amer. Can	12.4	8.9	6.6	52.5	2.1	91	83
Amer. Tel. & Tel.	10.8	11.0	6.0	55.2	1.1	—[c]	94
Anaconda	5.7	3.9	—	80.0	2.9	80	28
Bethlehem Steel	12.4	8.1	4.7	16.4	1.7	68	58
Chrysler	27.0	10.5	2.1	—[d]	1.4	78	67
DuPont	24.5	21.0	3.2	(–9.0)	3.6	609	280
Eastman Kodak	35.5	35.6	1.5	238.9	2.4	1764	635
General Electric	23.4	34.4	2.3	29.9	1.3	89	410
General Foods	14.5	15.2	4.1	97.3	1.6	254	240
General Motors	24.4	17.6	4.1	59.5	1.9	1071	247
Goodyear	15.8	16.7	2.5	93.3	2.1	129	80
Inter. Harvester	24.5	12.4	4.9	23.0	2.2	191	66
Inter. Nickel	13.6	16.2	3.2	123.4	2.5	131	213

Inter. Paper	22.5	14.0	4.6	26.1	2.2	62	139
Johns-Manville	19.3	16.8	3.0	43.8	2.6	—	158
Owens-Illinois	13.2	14.0	2.6	64.7	1.6	51	118
Procter & Gamble	24.2	31.6	2.1	128.4	2.4	400	460
Sears Roebuck	21.4	23.8	1.7	145.3	1.6	322	285
Std. Oil of Calif.	9.7	10.5	5.0	68.8	1.5	79	102
Std. Oil of N.J.	11.0	12.2	5.4	102.8	1.5	94	115
Swift & Co.	16.4	25.5	1.7	24.8	2.4	138	158
Texaco	9.9	10.8	5.0	120.9	1.7	128	138
Union Carbide	16.6	15.8	4.6	9.5	2.2	86	146
United Aircraft	9.7	7.0	5.9	55.9	1.5	155	65
U. S. Steel	8.3	6.7	5.4	(–21.5)	1.7	51	63
Westinghouse El.	29.5	28.0	1.9	52.2	1.8	145	2.86
Woolworth	19.7	20.5	2.4	76.3	1.8	185	1.90

[a] Figures taken for fiscal 1970 year-end co. results.
[b] Figures taken from *Moody's Industrial Manual* (1971).
[c] Debit balance for NCA. (NCA = net current assets.)
[d] Reported deficit for 1958–1960.

4. The aggregate earnings have been quite stable in the past decade. None of the companies reported a deficit during the prosperous period 1961–69, but Chrysler showed a small deficit in 1970.
5. The total growth—comparing three-year averages a decade apart—was 77%, or about 6% per year. But five of the firms did not grow by one-third.
6. The ratio of year-end price to three-year average earnings was 839 to $55.5 or 15 to 1—right at our suggested upper limit.
7. The ratio of price to net asset value was 839 to 562—also just within our suggested limit of 1½ to 1.

If, however, we wish to apply the same seven criteria to each individual company, we would find that only five of them would meet *all* our requirements. These would be: American Can, American Tel. & Tel., Anaconda, Swift, and Woolworth. The totals for these five appear in Table 14-3. Naturally they make a much better statistical showing than the DJIA as a whole, except in the past growth rate.[3]

Our application of specific criteria to this select group of industrial stocks indicates that the number meeting every one of our tests will be a relatively small percentage of *all* listed industrial issues. We hazard the guess that about 100 issues of this sort could have been found in the Standard & Poor's *Stock Guide* at the end of 1970, just about enough to provide the investor with a satisfactory range of personal choice.*

The Public-Utility "Solution"

If we turn now to the field of public-utility stocks we find a much more comfortable and inviting situation for the investor.†

---

* An easy-to-use online stock screener that can sort the stocks in the S & P 500 by most of Graham's criteria is available at: www.quicken.com/investments/stocks/search/full.

† When Graham wrote, only one major mutual fund specializing in utility stocks–Franklin Utilities–was widely available. Today there are more than 30. Graham could not have anticipated the financial havoc wrought by can-

TABLE 14-3 DJIA Issues Meeting Certain Investment Criteria at the End of 1970

	American Can	American Tel. & Tel.	Anaconda	Swift	Woolworth	Average, 5 Companies
Price Dec. 31, 1970	39¾	48⅞	21	30⅛	36½	
Price/earnings, 1970	11.0 ×	12.3 ×	6.7 ×	13.5 ×	14.4 ×	11.6 ×
Price/earnings, 3 years	10.5 ×	12.5 ×	5.4 ×	18.1 ×[b]	15.1 ×	12.3 ×
Price/book value	99%	108%	38%	113%	148%	112%
Current assets/current liabilities	2.2 ×	n.a.	2.9 ×	2.3 ×	1.8 ×[c]	2.3 ×
Net current assets/debt	110%	n.a.	120%	141%	190%	140%
Stability index[a]	85	100	72	77	99	86
Growth[a]	55%	53%	78%	25%	73%	57%

[a] See definition on p. 338.

[b] In view of Swift's good showing in the poor year 1970, we waive the 1968–1970 deficiency here.

[c] The small deficiency here below 2 to 1 was offset by margin for additional debt financing.

n.a. = not applicable. American Tel. & Tel.'s debt was less than its stock equity.

Here the vast majority of issues appear to be cut out, by their performance record and their price ratios, in accordance with the defensive investor's needs as we judge them. We exclude one criterion from our tests of public-utility stocks—namely, the ratio of current assets to current liabilities. The working-capital factor takes care of itself in this industry as part of the continuous financing of its growth by sales of bonds and shares. We do require an adequate proportion of stock capital to debt.[4]

In Table 14-4 we present a résumé of the 15 issues in the Dow Jones public-utility average. For comparison, Table 14-5 gives a similar picture of a random selection of fifteen other utilities taken from the New York Stock Exchange list.

As 1972 began the defensive investor could have had quite a wide choice of utility common stocks, each of which would have met our requirements for both performance and price. These companies offered him everything he had a right to demand from simply chosen common-stock investments. In comparison with prominent industrial companies as represented by the DJIA, they offered almost as good a record of past growth, plus smaller fluctuations in the annual figures—both at a lower price in relation to earnings and assets. The dividend return was significantly higher. The position of the utilities as regulated monopolies is assuredly more of an advantage than a disadvantage for the conservative investor. Under law they are entitled to charge rates sufficiently remunerative to attract the capital they need for their continuous expansion, and this implies adequate offsets to inflated costs. While the process of regulation has often been cumbersome and perhaps dilatory, it has not prevented the utilities from earning a fair return on their rising invested capital over many decades.

---

celed and decommissioned nuclear energy plants; nor did he foresee the consequences of bungled regulation in California. Utility stocks are vastly more volatile than they were in Graham's day, and most investors should own them only through a well-diversified, low-cost fund like the Dow Jones U.S. Utilities Sector Index Fund (ticker symbol: IDU) or Utilities Select Sector SPDR (XLU). For more information, see: www.ishares.com and www.spdrindex.com/spdr/. (Be sure your broker will not charge commissions to reinvest your dividends.)

TABLE 14-4 Data on the Fifteen Stocks in the Dow Jones Utility Average at September 30, 1971

	Price Sept. 30, 1971	*Earned*[a]	*Dividend*	*Book Value*	*Price/ Earnings*	*Price/ Book Value*	*Div. Yield*	*Earns. Per Share 1970 vs. 1960*
Am. Elec. Power	26	2.40	1.70	18.86	11×	138%	6.5%	+87%
Cleveland El. Ill.	34¾	3.10	2.24	22.94	11	150	6.4	86
Columbia Gas System	33	2.95	1.76	25.58	11	129	5.3	85
Commonwealth Edison	35½	3.05	2.20	27.28	12	130	6.2	56
Consolidated Edison	24½	2.40	1.80	30.63	10	80	7.4	19
Consd. Nat. Gas	27¾	3.00	1.88	32.11	9	86	6.8	53
Detroit Edison	19¼	1.80	1.40	22.66	11	84	7.3	40
Houston Ltg. & Power	42¾	2.88	1.32	19.02	15	222	3.1	135
Niagara-Mohawk Pwr.	15½	1.45	1.10	16.46	11	93	7.2	32
Pacific Gas & Electric	29	2.65	1.64	25.45	11	114	5.6	79
Panhandle E. Pipe L.	32½	2.90	1.80	19.95	11	166	5.5	79
Peoples Gas Co.	31½	2.70	2.08	30.28	8	104	6.6	23
Philadelphia El.	20½	2.00	1.64	19.74	10	103	8.0	29
Public Svs. El. & Gas	25½	2.80	1.64	21.81	9	116	6.4	80
Sou. Calif. Edison	29¼	2.80	1.50	27.28	10	107	5.1	85
Average	28½	2.66	1.71	23.83	10.7×	121%	6.2%	+65%

[a] Estimated for year 1971.

TABLE 14-5 Data on a Second List of Public-Utility Stocks at September 30, 1971

	Price Sept. 30, 1971	*Earned*	*Dividend*	*Book Value*	*Price/ Earnings*	*Price/ Book Value*	*Div. Yield*	*Earns. Per Share 1970 vs. 1960*
Alabama Gas	15½	1.50	1.10	17.80	10 ×	87%	7.1%	+34%
Allegheny Power	22½	2.15	1.32	16.88	10	134	6.0	71
Am. Tel. & Tel.	43	4.05	2.60	45.47	11	95	6.0	47
Am. Water Works	14	1.46	.60	16.80	10	84	4.3	187
Atlantic City Elec.	20½	1.85	1.36	14.81	11	138	6.6	74
Baltimore Gas & Elec.	30¼	2.85	1.82	23.03	11	132	6.0	86
Brooklyn Union Gas	23½	2.00	1.12	20.91	12	112	7.3	29
Carolina Pwr. & Lt.	22½	1.65	1.46	20.49	14	110	6.5	39
Cen. Hudson G. & E.	22¼	2.00	1.48	20.29	11	110	6.5	13
Cen. Ill. Lt.	25¼	2.50	1.56	22.16	10	114	6.5	55
Cen. Maine Pwr.	17¾	1.48	1.20	16.35	12	113	6.8	62
Cincinnati Gas & Elec.	23¼	2.20	1.56	16.13	11	145	6.7	102
Consumers Power	29½	2.80	2.00	32.59	11	90	6.8	89
Dayton Pwr. & Lt.	23	2.25	1.66	16.79	10	137	7.2	94
Delmarva Pwr. & Lt.	16½	1.55	1.12	14.04	11	117	6.7	78
Average	23½	2.15	1.50	21.00	11 ×	112%	6.5%	+71%

For the defensive investor the central appeal of the public-utility stocks at this time should be their availability at a moderate price in relation to book value. This means that he can ignore stockmarket considerations, if he wishes, and consider himself primarily as a part owner of well-established and well-earning businesses. The market quotations are always there for him to take advantage of when times are propitious—either for purchases at unusually attractive low levels, or for sales when their prices seem definitely too high.

The market record of the public-utility indexes—condensed in Table 14-6, along with those of other groups—indicates that there have been ample possibilities of profit in these investments in the past. While the rise has not been as great as in the industrial index, the individual utilities have shown more price stability in most periods than have other groups.* It is striking to observe in this table that the relative price/earnings ratios of the industrials and the utilities have changed places during the past two decades.

TABLE 14-6 Development of Prices and Price/Earnings Ratios for Various Standard & Poor's Averages, 1948–1970.

	Industrials		*Railroads*		*Utilities*	
Year	Price[a]	P/E Ratio	Price[a]	P/E Ratio	Price[a]	P/E Ratio
1948	15.34	6.56	15.27	4.55	16.77	10.03
1953	24.84	9.56	22.60	5.42	24.03	14.00
1958	58.65	19.88	34.23	12.45	43.13	18.59
1963	79.25	18.18	40.65	12.78	66.42	20.44
1968	113.02	17.80	54.15	14.21	69.69	15.87
1970	100.00	17.84	34.40	12.83	61.75	13.16

[a] Prices are at the close of the year.

* In a remarkable confirmation of Graham's point, the dull-sounding Standard & Poor's Utility Index outperformed the vaunted NASDAQ Composite Index for the 30 years ending December 31, 2002.

These reversals will have more meaning for the active than for the passive investor. But they suggest that even defensive portfolios should be changed from time to time, especially if the securities purchased have an apparently excessive advance and can be replaced by issues much more reasonably priced. Alas! there will be capital-gains taxes to pay—which for the typical investor seems to be about the same as the Devil to pay. Our old ally, experience, tells us here that it is better to sell and pay the tax than not sell and repent.

Investing in Stocks of Financial Enterprises

A considerable variety of concerns may be ranged under the rubric of "financial companies." These would include banks, insurance companies, savings and loan associations, credit and small-loan companies, mortgage companies, and "investment companies" (e.g., mutual funds).* It is characteristic of all these enterprises that they have a relatively small part of their assets in the form of material things—such as fixed assets and merchandise inventories—but on the other hand most categories have short-term obligations well in excess of their stock capital. The question of financial soundness is, therefore, more relevant here than in the case of the typical manufacturing or commercial enterprise. This, in turn, has given rise to various forms of regulation and supervision, with the design and general result of assuring against unsound financial practices.

Broadly speaking, the shares of financial concerns have produced investment results similar to those of other types of common shares. Table 14-7 shows price changes between 1948 and 1970 in six groups represented in the Standard & Poor's stock-price indexes. The average for 1941–1943 is taken as 10, the base level.

---

* Today the financial-services industry is made up of even more components, including commercial banks; savings & loan and mortgage-financing companies; consumer-finance firms like credit-card issuers; money managers and trust companies; investment banks and brokerages; insurance companies; and firms engaged in developing or owning real estate, including real-estate investment trusts. Although the sector is much more diversified today, Graham's caveats about financial soundness apply more than ever.

TABLE 14-7 Relative Price Movements of Stocks of Various Types of Financial Companies Between 1948 and 1970

	1948	1953	1958	1963	1968	1970
Life insurance	17.1	59.5	156.6	318.1	282.2	218.0
Property and liability insurance	13.7	23.9	41.0	64.7	99.2	84.3
New York City banks	11.2	15.0	24.3	36.8	49.6	44.3
Banks outside New York City	16.9	33.3	48.7	75.9	96.9	83.3
Finance companies	15.6	27.1	55.4	64.3	92.8	78.3
Small-loan companies	18.4	36.4	68.5	118.2	142.8	126.8
Standard & Poor's composite	13.2	24.8	55.2	75.0	103.9	92.2

[a] Year-end figures from Standard & Poor's stock-price indexes. Average of 1941–1943 = 10.

The year-end 1970 figures ranged between 44.3 for the 9 New York banks and 218 for the 11 life-insurance stocks. During the subintervals there was considerable variation in the respective price movements. For example, the New York City bank stocks did quite well between 1958 and 1968; conversely the spectacular life-insurance group actually lost ground between 1963 and 1968. These cross-movements are found in many, perhaps most, of the numerous industry groups in the Standard & Poor's indexes.

We have no very helpful remarks to offer in this broad area of investment—other than to counsel that the same arithmetical standards for price in relation to earnings and book value be applied to the choice of companies in these groups as we have suggested for industrial and public-utility investments.

Railroad Issues

The railroad story is a far different one from that of the utilities. The carriers have suffered severely from a combination of severe competition and strict regulation. (Their labor-cost problem has of course been difficult as well, but that has not been confined to railroads.) Automobiles, buses, and airlines have drawn off most of their passenger business and left the rest highly unprofitable; the trucks have taken a good deal of their freight traffic. More than half of the railroad mileage of the country has been in bankruptcy (or "trusteeship") at various times during the past 50 years.

But this half-century has not been all downhill for the carriers. There have been prosperous periods for the industry, especially the war years. Some of the lines have managed to maintain their earning power and their dividends despite the general difficulties.

The Standard & Poor's index advanced sevenfold from the low of 1942 to the high of 1968, not much below the percentage gain in the public-utility index. The bankruptcy of the Penn Central Transportation Co., our most important railroad, in 1970 shocked the financial world. Only a year and two years previously the stock sold at close to the highest price level in its long history, and it had paid continuous dividends for more than 120 years! (On p. 423 below we present a brief analysis of this railroad to illustrate how a competent student could have detected the developing weaknesses in the company's picture and counseled against ownership of its securities.) The market level of railroad shares as a whole was seriously affected by this financial disaster.

It is usually unsound to make blanket recommendations of whole classes of securities, and there are equal objections to broad condemnations. The record of railroad share prices in Table 14-6 shows that the group as a whole has often offered chances for a large profit. (But in our view the great advances were in themselves largely unwarranted.) Let us confine our suggestion to this: There is no compelling reason for the investor to own railroad shares; before he buys any he should make sure that he is getting so much value for his money that it would be unreasonable to look for something else instead.*

---

* Only a few major rail stocks now remain, including Burlington Northern, CSX, Norfolk Southern, and Union Pacific. The advice in this section is at least as relevant to airline stocks today–with their massive current losses and a half-century of almost incessantly poor results–as it was to railroads in Graham's day.

Selectivity for the Defensive Investor

Every investor would like his list to be better or more promising than the average. Hence the reader will ask whether, if he gets himself a competent adviser or security analyst, he should not be able to count on being supplied with an investment package of really superior merits. "After all," he may say, "the rules you have outlined are pretty simple and easygoing. A highly trained analyst ought to be able to use all his skill and techniques to improve substantially on something as obvious as the Dow Jones list. If not, what good are all his statistics, calculations, and pontifical judgments?"

Suppose, as a practical test, we had asked a hundred security analysts to choose the "best" five stocks in the Dow Jones Average, to be bought at the end of 1970. Few would have come up with identical choices and many of the lists would have differed completely from each other.

This is not so surprising as it may at first appear. The underlying reason is that the current price of each prominent stock pretty well reflects the salient factors in its financial record plus the general opinion as to its future prospects. Hence the view of any analyst that one stock is a better buy than the rest must arise to a great extent from his personal partialities and expectations, or from the placing of his emphasis on one set of factors rather than on another in his work of evaluation. If all analysts were agreed that one particular stock was better than all the rest, that issue would quickly advance to a price which would offset all of its previous advantages.*

---

* Graham is summarizing the "efficient markets hypothesis," or EMH, an academic theory claiming that the price of each stock incorporates all publicly available information about the company. With millions of investors scouring the market every day, it is unlikely that severe mispricings can persist for long. An old joke has two finance professors walking along the sidewalk; when one spots a $20 bill and bends over to pick it up, the other grabs his arm and says, "Don't bother. If it was really a $20 bill, someone would have taken it already." While the market is not perfectly efficient, it is pretty close most of the time–so the intelligent investor will stoop to pick up the stock market's $20 bills only after researching them thoroughly and minimizing the costs of trading and taxes.

Our statement that the current price reflects both known facts and future expectations was intended to emphasize the double basis for market valuations. Corresponding with these two kinds of value elements are two basically different approaches to security analysis. To be sure, every competent analyst looks forward to the future rather than backward to the past, and he realizes that his work will prove good or bad depending on what *will* happen and not on what *has* happened. Nevertheless, the future itself can be approached in two different ways, which may be called the way of *prediction* (or projection) and the way of *protection*.*

Those who emphasize prediction will endeavor to anticipate fairly accurately just what the company will accomplish in future years—in particular whether earnings will show pronounced and persistent growth. These conclusions may be based on a very careful study of such factors as supply and demand in the industry—or volume, price, and costs—or else they may be derived from a rather naïve projection of the line of past growth into the future. If these authorities are convinced that the fairly long-term prospects are unusually favorable, they will almost always recommend the stock for purchase without paying too much regard to the level at which it is selling. Such, for example, was the general attitude with respect to the air-transport stocks—an attitude that persisted for many years despite the distressingly bad results often shown after 1946. In the Introduction we have commented on the disparity between the strong price action and the relatively disappointing earnings record of this industry.

---

* This is one of the central points of Graham's book. All investors labor under a cruel irony: We invest *in* the present, but we invest *for* the future. And, unfortunately, the future is almost entirely uncertain. Inflation and interest rates are undependable; economic recessions come and go at random; geopolitical upheavals like war, commodity shortages, and terrorism arrive without warning; and the fate of individual companies and their industries often turns out to be the opposite of what most investors expect. Therefore, investing on the basis of *projection* is a fool's errand; even the forecasts of the so-called experts are less reliable than the flip of a coin. For most people, investing on the basis of *protection*–from overpaying for a stock and from overconfidence in the quality of their own judgment–is the best solution. Graham expands on this concept in Chapter 20.

By contrast, those who emphasize protection are always especially concerned with the price of the issue at the time of study. Their main effort is to assure themselves of a substantial margin of indicated present value above the market price—which margin could absorb unfavorable developments in the future. Generally speaking, therefore, it is not so necessary for them to be enthusiastic over the company's long-run prospects as it is to be reasonably confident that the enterprise will get along.

The first, or predictive, approach could also be called the qualitative approach, since it emphasizes prospects, management, and other nonmeasurable, albeit highly important, factors that go under the heading of quality. The second, or protective, approach may be called the quantitative or statistical approach, since it emphasizes the measurable relationships between selling price and earnings, assets, dividends, and so forth. Incidentally, the quantitative method is really an extension—into the field of common stocks—of the viewpoint that security analysis has found to be sound in the selection of bonds and preferred stocks for investment.

In our own attitude and professional work we were always committed to the quantitative approach. From the first we wanted to make sure that we were getting ample value for our money in concrete, demonstrable terms. We were not willing to accept the prospects and promises of the future as compensation for a lack of sufficient value in hand. This has by no means been the standard viewpoint among investment authorities; in fact, the majority would probably subscribe to the view that prospects, quality of management, other intangibles, and "the human factor" far outweigh the indications supplied by any study of the past record, the balance sheet, and all the other cold figures.

Thus this matter of choosing the "best" stocks is at bottom a highly controversial one. Our advice to the defensive investor is that he let it alone. Let him emphasize diversification more than individual selection. Incidentally, the universally accepted idea of diversification is, in part at least, the negation of the ambitious pretensions of selectivity. If one *could* select the best stocks unerringly, one would only lose by diversifying. Yet within the limits of the four most general rules of common-stock selection suggested for the defensive investor (on pp. 114–115) there is room for a rather considerable freedom of preference. At the worst the indulgence of such preferences should do no harm; beyond that, it may add something worthwhile to the results. With the increasing impact of technological developments on long-term corporate results, the investor cannot leave them out of his calculations. Here, as elsewhere, he must seek a mean between neglect and overemphasis.

COMMENTARY ON CHAPTER 14

He that resteth upon gains certain, shall hardly grow to great riches; and he that puts all upon adventures, doth oftentimes break and come to poverty: it is good therefore to guard adventures with certainties that may uphold losses.

—*Sir Francis Bacon*

GETTING STARTED

How should you tackle the nitty-gritty work of stock selection? Graham suggests that the defensive investor can, "most simply," buy every stock in the DowJones Industrial Average. Today's defensive investor can do even better—by buying a total stock-market index fund that holds essentially every stock worth having. A low-cost index fund is the best tool ever created for low-maintenance stock investing—and any effort to improve on it takes more work (and incurs more risk and higher costs) than a truly defensive investor can justify.

Researching and selecting your own stocks is not necessary; for most people, it is not even advisable. However, some defensive investors do enjoy the diversion and intellectual challenge of picking individual stocks—and, if you have survived a bear market and *still* enjoy stock picking, then nothing that Graham or I could say will dissuade you. In that case, instead of making a total stock market index fund your complete portfolio, make it the foundation of your portfolio. Once you have that foundation in place, you can experiment around the edges with your own stock choices. Keep 90% of your stock money in an index fund, leaving 10% with which to try picking your own stocks. Only after you build that solid core should you explore. (To learn why such broad diversification is so important, please see the sidebar on the following page.)

WHY DIVERSIFY?

During the bull market of the 1990s, one of the most common criticisms of diversification was that it lowers your potential for high returns. After all, if you could identify the next Microsoft, wouldn't it make sense for you to put all your eggs into that one basket?

Well, sure. As the humorist Will Rogers once said, "Don't gamble. Take all your savings and buy some good stock and hold it till it goes up, then sell it. If it don't go up, don't buy it."

However, as Rogers knew, 20/20 foresight is not a gift granted to most investors. No matter how confident we feel, there's no way to find out whether a stock will go up until *after* we buy it. Therefore, the stock you think is "the next Microsoft" may well turn out to be the next MicroStrategy instead. (That former market star went from $3,130 per share in March 2000 to $15.10 at year-end 2002, an apocalyptic loss of 99.5%).[1] Keeping your money spread across many stocks and industries is the only reliable insurance against the risk of being wrong.

But diversification doesn't just minimize your odds of being wrong. It also maximizes your chances of being right. Over long periods of time, a handful of stocks turn into "superstocks" that go up 10,000% or more. *Money* Magazine identified the 30 best-performing stocks over the 30 years ending in 2002–and, even with 20/20 hindsight, the list is startlingly unpredictable. Rather than lots of technology or health-care stocks, it includes Southwest Airlines, Worthington Steel, Dollar General discount stores, and snuff-tobacco maker UST Inc.[2] If you think you would have been willing to bet big on any of those stocks back in 1972, you are kidding yourself.

Think of it this way: In the huge market haystack, only a few needles ever go on to generate truly gigantic gains. The more of the haystack you own, the higher the odds go that you will end up finding at least one of those needles. By owning the entire haystack (ideally through an index fund that tracks the total U.S. stock market) you can be sure to find every needle, thus capturing the returns of all the superstocks. Especially if you are a defensive investor, why look for the needles when you can own the whole haystack?

---

[1] Adjusted for stock splits. To many people, MicroStrategy really did look like the next Microsoft in early 2000; its stock had gained 566.7% in 1999, and its chairman, Michael Saylor, declared that "our future today is better than it was 18 months ago." The U.S. Securities and Exchange Commission later accused MicroStrategy of accounting fraud, and Saylor paid an $8.3 million fine to settle the charges.

[2] Jon Birger, "The 30 Best Stocks," *Money,* Fall 2002, pp. 88–95.

TESTING, TESTING

Let's briefly update Graham's criteria for stock selection.

Adequate size. Nowadays, "to exclude small companies," most defensive investors should steer clear of stocks with a total market value of less than $2 billion. In early 2003, that still left you with 437 of the companies in the Standard & Poor's 500-stock index to choose from.

However, today's defensive investors–unlike those in Graham's day–can conveniently own small companies by buying a mutual fund specializing in small stocks. Again, an index fund like Vanguard Small-Cap Index is the first choice, although active funds are available at reasonable cost from such firms as Ariel, T. Rowe Price, Royce, and Third Avenue.

Strong financial condition. According to market strategists Steve Galbraith and Jay Lasus of Morgan Stanley, at the beginning of 2003 about 120 of the companies in the S & P 500 index met Graham's test of a 2-to-1 current ratio. With current assets at least twice their current liabilities, these firms had a sizeable cushion of working capital that–on average–should sustain them through hard times.

Wall Street has always abounded in bitter ironies, and the bursting of the growth-stock bubble has created a doozy: In 1999 and 2000, high-tech, bio-tech, and telecommunications stocks were supposed to provide "aggressive growth" and ended up giving most of their investors aggressive shrinkage instead. But, by early 2003, the wheel had come full circle, and many of those aggressive growth stocks had become financially conservative–loaded with working capital, rich in cash, and often debt-free. This table provides a sampler:

FIGURE 14-1 Everything New Is Old Again

Company	Current Assets	Current Liabilities	Ratio of Current Assets to Current Liabilities	Long-Term Debt	Ratio of Long-Term Debt to Working Capital
Applied Micro Circuits	1091.2	61.9	17.6	0	none
Linear Technology	1736.4	148.1	11.7	0	none
QLogic Corp.	713.1	69.6	10.2	0	none
Analog Devices	3711.1	467.3	7.9	1274.5	0.39
Qualcomm Inc.	4368.5	654.9	6.7	156.9	0.04
Maxim Integrated Products	1390.5	212.3	6.5	0	none
Applied Materials	7878.7	1298.4	6.1	573.9	0.09
Tellabs Inc.	1533.6	257.3	6.0	0.5	0.0004
Scientific-Atlanta	1259.8	252.4	5.0	8.8	0.01
Altera Corp.	1176.2	240.5	4.9	0	none
Xilinx Inc.	1108.8	228.1	4.9	0	none
American Power Conversion	1276.3	277.4	4.6	0	none
Chiron Corp.	1393.8	306.7	4.5	414.9	0.38
Biogen Inc.	1194.7	265.4	4.5	39	0.04
Novellus Systems	1633.9	381.6	4.3	0	none
Amgen Inc.	6403.5	1529.2	4.2	3039.7	0.62
LSI Logic Corp.	1626.1	397.8	4.1	1287.1	1.05
Rowan Cos.	469.9	116.0	4.1	494.8	1.40
Biomet Inc.	1000.0	248.6	4.0	0	none
Siebel Systems	2588.4	646.5	4.0	315.6	0.16

All figures in millions of dollars from latest available financial statements as of 12/31/02. Working capital is current assets minus current liabilities.
Long-term debt includes preferred stock, excludes deferred tax liabilities.
Sources: Morgan Stanley; Baseline; EDGAR database at www.sec.gov.

In 1999, most of these companies were among the hottest of the market's darlings, offering the promise of high potential growth. By early 2003, they offered hard evidence of true value.

The lesson here is not that these stocks were "a sure thing," or that you should rush out and buy everything (or anything) in this table.[1] Instead, you should realize that a defensive investor can always prosper by looking patiently and calmly through the wreckage of a bear market. Graham's criterion of financial strength still works: If you build a diversified basket of stocks whose current assets are at least double their current liabilities, and whose long-term debt does not exceed working capital, you should end up with a group of conservatively financed companies with plenty of staying power. The best values today are often found in the stocks that were once hot and have since gone cold. Throughout history, such stocks have often provided the margin of safety that a defensive investor demands.

Earnings stability. According to Morgan Stanley, 86% of all the companies in the S & P 500 index have had positive earnings in every year from 1993 through 2002. So Graham's insistence on "some earnings for the common stock in each of the past ten years" remains a valid test–tough enough to eliminate chronic losers, but not so restrictive as to limit your choices to an unrealistically small sample.

Dividend record. As of early 2003, according to Standard & Poor's, 354 companies in the S & P 500 (or 71% of the total) paid a dividend. No fewer than 255 companies have paid a dividend for at least 20 years in a row. And, according to S & P, 57 companies in the index have *raised* their dividends for at least 25 consecutive years. That's no guarantee that they will do so forever, but it's a comforting sign.

Earnings growth. How many companies in the S & P 500 increased their earnings per share by "at least one third," as Graham requires, over the 10 years ending in 2002? (We'll average each company's earnings from 1991 through 1993, and then determine whether the average earnings from 2000 through 2002 were at least 33% higher.) According to Morgan Stanley, 264 companies in the S & P 500 met that test. But here, it seems, Graham set a very low hurdle; 33% cumulative growth over a decade is less than a 3% average annual increase. Cumulative growth in earnings per share of at least 50%–or a 4% average annual rise–is a bit less conservative. No

---

[1] By the time you read this, much will already have changed since year-end 2002.

FIGURE 14-2 Steady Eddies

These companies have paid higher dividends with each passing year with no exception.

Company	Sector	Cash dividends paid each year since . . .	Number of annual dividend increases in the past 40 years
3M Co	Industrials	1916	40
Abbott Laboratories	Health Care	1926	35
ALLTEL Corp	Telecomm. Services	1961	37
Altria Group (formerly Philip Morris)	Consumer Staples	1928	36
AmSouth Bancorp	Financials	1943	34
Anheuser-Busch Cos	Consumer Staples	1932	39
Archer-Daniels-Midland	Consumer Staples	1927	32
Automatic Data Proc	Industrials	1974	29
Avery Dennison Corp	Industrials	1964	36
Bank of America	Financials	1903	36
Bard (C. R.)	Health Care	1960	36
Becton, Dickinson	Health Care	1926	38
CenturyTel Inc	Telecomm. Services	1974	29
Chubb Corp	Financials	1902	28
Clorox Co	Consumer Staples	1968	30
Coca-Cola Co	Consumer Staples	1893	40
Comerica Inc	Financials	1936	39
ConAgra Foods	Consumer Staples	1976	32
Consolidated Edison	Utilities	1885	31
Donnelley(R. R.) & Sons	Industrials	1911	36
Dover Corp	Industrials	1947	37
Emerson Electric	Industrials	1947	40
Family Dollar Stores	Consumer Discretionary	1976	27
First Tenn Natl	Financials	1895	31
Gannett Co	Consumer Discretionary	1929	35
General Electric	Industrials	1899	35
Grainger (W. W.)	Industrials	1965	33
Heinz (H. J.)	Consumer Staples	1911	38

CHAPTER 15

Stock Selection for the Enterprising Investor

In the previous chapter we have dealt with common-stock selection in terms of broad groups of eligible securities, from which the defensive investor is free to make up any list that he or his adviser prefers, provided adequate diversification is achieved. Our emphasis in selection has been chiefly on exclusions—advising on the one hand against all issues of recognizably poor quality, and on the other against the highest-quality issues if their price is so high as to involve a considerable speculative risk. In this chapter, addressed to the enterprising investor, we must consider the possibilities and the means of making *individual* selections which are likely to prove more profitable than an across-the-board average.

What are the prospects of doing this successfully? We would be less than frank, as the euphemism goes, if we did not at the outset express some grave reservations on this score. At first blush the case for successful selection appears self-evident. To get average results—e.g., equivalent to the performance of the DJIA—should require no special ability of any kind. All that is needed is a portfolio identical with, or similar to, those thirty prominent issues. Surely, then, by the exercise of even a moderate degree of skill—derived from study, experience, and native ability—it should be possible to obtain substantially better results than the DJIA.

Yet there is considerable and impressive evidence to the effect that this is very hard to do, even though the qualifications of those trying it are of the highest. The evidence lies in the record of the numerous investment companies, or "funds," which have been in operation for many years. Most of these funds are large enough to command the services of the best financial or security analysts in the field, together with all the other constituents of an adequate research department. Their expenses of operation, when spread

Household Intl.	Financials	1926	40
Jefferson-Pilot	Financials	1913	36
Johnson & Johnson	Health Care	1944	40
Johnson Controls	Consumer Discretionary	1887	29
KeyCorp	Financials	1963	36
Kimberly-Clark	Consumer Staples	1935	34
Leggett & Platt	Consumer Discretionary	1939	33
Lilly (Eli)	Health Care	1885	38
Lowe's Cos.	Consumer Discretionary	1961	40
May Dept Stores	Consumer Discretionary	1911	31
McDonald's Corp.	Consumer Discretionary	1976	27
McGraw-Hill Cos.	Consumer Discretionary	1937	35
Merck & Co	Health Care	1935	38
Nucor Corp.	Materials	1973	30
PepsiCo Inc.	Consumer Staples	1952	35
Pfizer, Inc.	Health Care	1901	39
PPG Indus.	Materials	1899	37
Procter & Gamble	Consumer Staples	1891	40
Regions Financial	Financials	1968	32
Rohm & Haas	Materials	1927	38
Sigma-Aldrich	Materials	1970	28
Stanley Works	Consumer Discretionary	1877	37
Supervalu Inc.	Consumer Staples	1936	36
Target Corp.	Consumer Discretionary	1965	34
TECO Energy	Utilities	1900	40
U.S. Bancorp	Financials	1999	35
VF Corp.	Consumer Discretionary	1941	35
Wal-Mart Stores	Consumer Discretionary	1973	29
Walgreen Co.	Consumer Staples	1933	31

Source: Standard & Poor's Corp.
Data as of 12/31/2002.

fewer than 245 companies in the S & P 500 index met that criterion as of early 2003, leaving the defensive investor an ample list to choose from. (If you double the cumulative growth hurdle to 100%, or 7% average annual growth, then 198 companies make the cutoff.)

Moderate P/E ratio. Graham recommends limiting yourself to stocks whose current price is no more than 15 times average earnings over the past three years. Incredibly, the prevailing practice on Wall Street today is to value stocks by dividing their current price by something called "next year's earnings." That gives what is sometimes called "the forward P/E ratio." But it's nonsensical to derive a price/earnings ratio by dividing the known current price by unknown future earnings. Over the long run, money manager David Dreman has shown, 59% of Wall Street's "consensus" earnings forecasts miss the mark by a mortifyingly wide margin—either underestimating or overestimating the actual reported earnings by at least 15%.[2] Investing your money on the basis of what these myopic soothsayers predict for the coming year is as risky as volunteering to hold up the bulls-eye at an archery tournament for the legally blind. Instead, calculate a stock's price/earnings ratio yourself, using Graham's formula of current price divided by average earnings over the past three years.[3]

As of early 2003, how many stocks in the Standard & Poor's 500 index were valued at no more than 15 times their average earnings of 2000 through 2002? According to Morgan Stanley, a generous total of 185 companies passed Graham's test.

Moderate price-to-book ratio. Graham recommends a "ratio of price to assets" (or price-to-book-value ratio) of no more than 1.5. In recent years, an increasing proportion of the value of companies has come from intangible assets like franchises, brand names, and patents and trademarks. Since these factors (along with goodwill from acquisitions) are excluded from the standard definition of book value, most companies today are priced at higher price-to-book multiples than in Graham's day. According to Morgan Stanley, 123 of the companies in the S & P 500 (or one in four) are priced below 1.5 times book value.

[2] David Dreman, "Bubbles and the Role of Analysts' Forecasts," *The Journal of Psychology and Financial Markets,* vol. 3, no. 1 (2002), pp. 4–14.

[3] You can calculate this ratio by hand from a company's annual reports or obtain the data at websites like www.morningstar.com or http://finance.yahoo.com.

All told, 273 companies (or 55% of the index) have p
ratios of less than 2.5.

What about Graham's suggestion that you multiply the
the price-to-book ratio and see whether the resulting numb
22.5? Based on data from Morgan Stanley, at least 142 st
S & P 500 could pass that test as of early 2003, inclu
Corp., Electronic Data Systems, Sun Microsystems, and W
Mutual. So Graham's "blended multiplier" still works as
screen to identify reasonably-priced stocks.

DUE DILIGENCE

No matter how defensive an investor you are—in Graham's
wishing to minimize the work you put into picking stocks—th
couple of steps you cannot afford to skip:

Do your homework. Through the EDGAR database at w
gov, you get instant access to a company's annual and
reports, along with the proxy statement that discloses the m
compensation, ownership, and potential conflicts of interest.
least five years' worth.[4]

Check out the neighborhood. Websites like http://qu
morningstar.com, http://finance.yahoo.com and www.quicken.c
readily tell you what percentage of a company's shares are ow
institutions. Anything over 60% suggests that a stock is s
undiscovered and probably "overowned." (When big institutio
they tend to move in lockstep, with disastrous results for the
Imagine all the Radio City Rockettes toppling off the front edge
stage at once and you get the idea.) Those websites will also t
who the largest owners of the stock are. If they are m
management firms that invest in a style similar to your own, th
good sign.

[4] For more on what to look for, see the commentary on Chapters 11, 12
19. If you are not willing to go to the minimal effort of reading the proxy
making basic comparisons of financial health across five years' wor
annual reports, then you are too defensive to be buying individual stoc
all. Get yourself out of the stock-picking business and into an index f
where you belong.

over their ample capital, average about one-half of 1% a year thereon, or less. These costs are not negligible in themselves; but when they are compared with the approximately 15% annual overall return on common stocks generally in the decade 1951–1960, and even the 6% return in 1961–1970, they do not bulk large. A small amount of superior selective ability should easily have overcome that expense handicap and brought in a superior net result for the fund shareholders.

Taken as a whole, however, the all-common-stock funds failed over a long span of years to earn quite as good a return as was shown on Standard & Poor's 500-stock averages or the market as a whole. This conclusion has been substantiated by several comprehensive studies. To quote the latest one before us, covering the period 1960–1968:*

> It appears from these results that random portfolios of New York Stock Exchange stocks with equal investment in each stock performed on the average better over the period than did mutual funds in the same risk class. The differences were fairly substantial for the low- and medium-risk portfolios (3.7% and 2.5% respectively per annum), but quite small for the high-risk portfolios (0.2% per annum).[1]

As we pointed out in Chapter 9, these comparative figures in no way invalidate the usefulness of the investment funds as a financial institution. For they do make available to all members of the

---

* The Friend-Blume-Crockett research covered January 1960, through June 1968, and compared the performance of more than 100 major mutual funds against the returns on portfolios constructed randomly from more than 500 of the largest stocks listed on the NYSE. The funds in the Friend-Blume-Crockett study did better from 1965 to 1968 than they had in the first half of the measurement period, much as Graham found in his own research (see above, pp. 158 and 229–232). But that improvement did not last. And the thrust of these studies—that mutual funds, on average, underperform the market by a margin roughly equal to their operating expenses and trading costs—has been reconfirmed so many times that anyone who doubts them should found a financial chapter of The Flat Earth Society.

investing public the possibility of obtaining approximately average results on their common-stock commitments. For a variety of reasons, most members of the public who put their money in common stocks of their own choice fail to do nearly as well. But to the objective observer the failure of the funds to better the performance of a broad average is a pretty conclusive indication that such an achievement, instead of being easy, is in fact extremely difficult.

Why should this be so? We can think of two different explanations, each of which may be partially applicable. The first is the possibility that the stock market does in fact reflect in the current prices not only all the important facts about the companies' past and current performance, but also whatever expectations can be reasonably formed as to their future. If this is so, then the diverse market movements which subsequently take place—and these are often extreme—must be the result of new developments and probabilities that could not be reliably foreseen. This would make the price movements essentially fortuitous and random. To the extent that the foregoing is true, the work of the security analyst—however intelligent and thorough—must be largely ineffective, because in essence he is trying to predict the unpredictable.

The very multiplication of the number of security analysts may have played an important part in bringing about this result. With hundreds, even thousands, of experts studying the value factors behind an important common stock, it would be natural to expect that its current price would reflect pretty well the consensus of informed opinion on its value. Those who would prefer it to other issues would do so for reasons of personal partiality or optimism that could just as well be wrong as right.

We have often thought of the analogy between the work of the host of security analysts on Wall Street and the performance of master bridge players at a duplicate-bridge tournament. The former try to pick the stocks "most likely to succeed"; the latter to get top score for each hand played. Only a limited few can accomplish either aim. To the extent that all the bridge players have about the same level of expertness, the winners are likely to be determined by "breaks" of various sorts rather than superior skill. On Wall Street the leveling process is helped along by the freemasonry that exists in the profession, under which ideas and discoveries are quite freely shared at the numerous get-togethers of various sorts.

It is almost as if, at the analogous bridge tournament, the various experts were looking over each other's shoulders and arguing out each hand as it was played.

The second possibility is of a quite different sort. Perhaps many of the security analysts are handicapped by a flaw in their basic approach to the problem of stock selection. They seek the industries with the best prospects of growth, and the companies in these industries with the best management and other advantages. The implication is that they will buy into such industries and such companies at any price, however high, and they will avoid less promising industries and companies no matter how low the price of their shares. This would be the only correct procedure if the earnings of the good companies were sure to grow at a rapid rate indefinitely in the future, for then in theory their value would be infinite. And if the less promising companies were headed for extinction, with no salvage, the analysts would be right to consider them unattractive at any price.

The truth about our corporate ventures is quite otherwise. Extremely few companies have been able to show a high rate of uninterrupted growth for long periods of time. Remarkably few, also, of the larger companies suffer ultimate extinction. For most, their history is one of vicissitudes, of ups and downs, of change in their relative standing. In some the variations "from rags to riches and back" have been repeated on almost a cyclical basis—the phrase used to be a standard one applied to the steel industry—for others spectacular changes have been identified with deterioration or improvement of management.*

How does the foregoing inquiry apply to the enterprising investor who would like to make individual selections that will yield superior results? It suggests first of all that he is taking on a

---

* As we discuss in the commentary on Chapter 9, there are several other reasons mutual funds have not been able to outperform the market averages, including the low returns on the funds' cash balances and the high costs of researching and trading stocks. Also, a fund holding 120 companies (a typical number) can trail the S & P 500-stock index if *any* of the other 380 companies in that benchmark turns out to be a great performer. The fewer stocks a fund owns, the more likely it is to miss "the next Microsoft."

difficult and perhaps impracticable assignment. Readers of this book, however intelligent and knowing, could scarcely expect to do a better job of portfolio selection than the top analysts of the country. But if it is true that a fairly large segment of the stock market is often discriminated against or entirely neglected in the standard analytical selections, then the intelligent investor may be in a position to profit from the resultant undervaluations.

But to do so he must follow specific methods that are not generally accepted on Wall Street, since those that are so accepted do not seem to produce the results everyone would like to achieve. It would be rather strange if—with all the brains at work professionally in the stock market—there could be approaches which are both sound and relatively unpopular. Yet our own career and reputation have been based on this unlikely fact.*

A Summary of the Graham-Newman Methods

To give concreteness to the last statement, it should be worthwhile to give a brief account of the types of operations we engaged in during the thirty-year life of Graham-Newman Corporation, between 1926 and 1956.† These were classified in our records as follows:

Arbitrages: The purchase of a security and the simultaneous sale

---

* In this section, as he did also on pp. 363–364, Graham is summarizing the Efficient Market Hypothesis. Recent appearances to the contrary, the problem with the stock market today is not that so many financial analysts are idiots, but rather that so many of them are so smart. As more and more smart people search the market for bargains, that very act of searching makes those bargains rarer–and, in a cruel paradox, makes the analysts look as if they lack the intelligence to justify the search. The market's valuation of a given stock is the result of a vast, continuous, real-time operation of collective intelligence. Most of the time, for most stocks, that collective intelligence gets the valuation approximately right. Only rarely does Graham's "Mr. Market" (see Chapter 8) send prices wildly out of whack.

† Graham launched Graham-Newman Corp. in January 1936, and dissolved it when he retired from active money management in 1956; it was the successor to a partnership called the Benjamin Graham Joint Account, which he ran from January 1926, through December 1935.

of one or more other securities into which it was to be exchanged under a plan of reorganization, merger, or the like.

Liquidations: Purchase of shares which were to receive one or more cash payments in liquidation of the company's assets.

Operations of these two classes were selected on the twin basis of (a) a calculated annual return of 20% or more, and (b) our judgment that the chance of a successful outcome was at least four out of five.

Related Hedges: The purchase of convertible bonds or convertible preferred shares, and the simultaneous sale of the common stock into which they were exchangeable. The position was established at close to a parity basis—i.e., at a small maximum loss if the senior issue had actually to be converted and the operation closed out in that way. But a profit would be made if the common stock fell considerably more than the senior issue, and the position closed out in the market.

Net-Current-Asset (or "Bargain") Issues: The idea here was to acquire as many issues as possible at a cost for each of less than their book value in terms of net-current-assets alone—i.e., giving no value to the plant account and other assets. Our purchases were made typically at two-thirds or less of such stripped-down asset value. In most years we carried a wide diversification here—at least 100 different issues.

We should add that from time to time we had some large-scale acquisitions of the control type, but these are not relevant to the present discussion.

We kept close track of the results shown by each class of operation. In consequence of these follow-ups we discontinued two broader fields, which were found not to have shown satisfactory overall results. The first was the purchase of apparently attractive issues—based on our general analysis—which were not obtainable at less than their working-capital value alone. The second were "unrelated" hedging operations, in which the purchased security was not exchangeable for the common shares sold. (Such operations correspond roughly to those recently embarked on by the new group of "hedge funds" in the investment-company field.* In

---

* An "unrelated" hedge involves buying a stock or bond issued by one company and short-selling (or betting on a decline in) a security issued by a dif-

both cases a study of the results realized by us over a period of ten years or more led us to conclude that the profits were not sufficiently dependable—and the operations not sufficiently "headache proof"—to justify our continuing them.

Hence from 1939 on our operations were limited to "self-liquidating" situations, related hedges, working-capital bargains, and a few control operations. Each of these classes gave us quite consistently satisfactory results from then on, with the special feature that the related hedges turned in good profits in the bear markets when our "undervalued issues" were not doing so well.

We hesitate to prescribe our own diet for any large number of intelligent investors. Obviously, the professional techniques we have followed are not suitable for the defensive investor, who by definition is an amateur. As for the aggressive investor, perhaps only a small minority of them would have the type of temperament needed to limit themselves so severely to only a relatively small part of the world of securities. Most active-minded practitioners would prefer to venture into wider channels. Their natural hunting grounds would be the entire field of securities that they felt (a) were certainly not overvalued by conservative measures, and (b) appeared decidedly more attractive—because of their prospects or past record, or both—than the average common stock. In such choices they would do well to apply various tests of quality and price-reasonableness along the lines we have proposed for the defensive investor. But they should be less inflexible, permitting a considerable plus in one factor to offset a small black mark in another. For example, he might not rule out a company which had shown a deficit in a year such as 1970, if large average earnings and other important attributes made the stock look cheap. The enterprising investor may confine his choice to industries and companies about which he holds an optimistic view, but we counsel strongly against paying a high price for a stock (in relation to earn-

ferent company. A "related" hedge involves buying and selling different stocks or bonds issued by the same company. The "new group" of hedge funds described by Graham were widely available around 1968, but later regulation by the U.S. Securities and Exchange Commission restricted access to hedge funds for the general public.

ings and assets) because of such enthusiasm. If he followed our philosophy in this field he would more likely be the buyer of important cyclical enterprises—such as steel shares perhaps—when the current situation is unfavorable, the near-term prospects are poor, and the low price fully reflects the current pessimism.*

Secondary Companies

Next in order for examination and possible selection would come secondary companies that are making a good showing, have a satisfactory past record, but appear to hold no charm for the public. These would be enterprises on the order of ELTRA and Emhart at their 1970 closing prices. (See Chapter 13 above.) There are various ways of going about locating such companies. We should like to try a novel approach here and give a reasonably detailed exposition of one such exercise in stock selection. Ours is a double purpose. Many of our readers may find a substantial practical value in the method we shall follow, or it may suggest comparable methods to try out. Beyond that what we shall do may help them to come to grips with the real world of common stocks, and introduce them to one of the most fascinating and valuable little volumes in existence. It is Standard & Poor's *Stock Guide,* published monthly, and made available to the general public under annual subscription. In addition many brokerage firms distribute the *Guide* to their clients (on request.)

The great bulk of the *Guide* is given over to about 230 pages of condensed statistical information on the stocks of more than 4,500 companies. These include all the issues listed on the various exchanges, say 3,000, plus some 1,500 unlisted issues. Most of the items needed for a first and even a second look at a given company appear in this compendium. (From our viewpoint the important missing datum is the net-asset-value, or book value, per share, which can be found in the larger Standard & Poor's volumes and elsewhere.)

---

* In 2003, an intelligent investor following Graham's train of thought would be searching for opportunities in the technology, telecommunications, and electric-utility industries. History has shown that yesterday's losers are often tomorrow's winners.

The investor who likes to play around with corporate figures will find himself in clover with the *Stock Guide.* He can open to any page and see before his eyes a condensed panorama of the splendors and miseries of the stock market, with all-time high and low prices going as far back as 1936, when available. He will find companies that have multiplied their price 2,000 times from the minuscule low to the majestic high. (For prestigious IBM the growth was "only" 333 times in that period.) He will find (not so exceptionally) a company whose shares advanced from ⅜ to 68, and then fell back to 3.[2] In the dividend record column he will find one that goes back to 1791—paid by Industrial National Bank of Rhode Island (which recently saw fit to change its ancient corporate name).* If he looks at the *Guide* for the year-end 1969 he will read that Penn Central Co. (as successor to Pennsylvania Railroad) has been paying dividends steadily since 1848; alas!, it was doomed to bankruptcy a few months later. He will find a company selling at only 2 times its last reported earnings, and another selling at 99 times such earnings.[3] In most cases he will find it difficult to tell the line of business from the corporate name; for one U.S. Steel there will be three called such things as ITI Corp. (bakery stuff) or Santa Fe Industries (mainly the large railroad). He can feast on an extraordinary variety of price histories, dividend and earnings histories, financial positions, capitalization setups, and what not. Backward-leaning conservatism, run-of-the-mine featureless companies, the most peculiar combinations of "principal business," all kinds of Wall Street gadgets and widgets—they are all there, waiting to be browsed over, or studied with a serious objective.

The *Guides* give in separate columns the current dividend yields and price/earnings ratios, based on latest 12-month figures, wherever applicable. It is this last item that puts us on the track of our exercise in common-stock selection.

---

* The successor corporation to Industrial National Bank of Rhode Island is FleetBoston Financial Corp. One of its corporate ancestors, the Providence Bank, was founded in 1791.

TABLE 15-1 A Sample Portfolio of Low-Multiplier Industrial Stocks

(The First Fifteen Issues in the *Stock Guide* at December 31, 1971, Meeting Six Requirements)

	Price Dec. 1970	Earned Per Share Last 12 Months	Book Value	S & P Ranking	Price Feb. 1972
Aberdeen Mfg.	10¼	$1.25	$9.33	B	13¾
Alba-Waldensian	6⅜	.68	9.06	B+	6⅜
Albert's Inc.	8½	1.00	8.48	n.r.[a]	14
Allied Mills	24½	2.68	24.38	B+	18¼
Am. Maize Prod.	9¼	1.03	10.68	A	16½
Am. Rubber & Plastics	13¾	1.58	15.06	B	15
Am. Smelt. & Ref.	27½	3.69	25.30	B+	23¼
Anaconda	21	4.19	54.28	B+	19
Anderson Clayton	37¾	4.52	65.74	B+	52½
Archer-Daniels-Mid.	32½	3.51	31.35	B+	32½
Bagdad Copper	22	2.69	18.54	n.r.[a]	32
D. H. Baldwin	28	3.21	28.60	B+	50
Big Bear Stores	18½	2.71	20.57	B+	39½
Binks Mfg.	15¼	1.83	14.41	B+	21½
Bluefield Supply	22¼	2.59	28.66	n.r.[a]	39½[b]

[a] n.r. = not ranked.

[b] Adjusted for stock split.

Single Criteria for Choosing Common Stocks

An inquiring reader might well ask whether the choice of a better than average portfolio could be made a simpler affair than we have just outlined. Could a single plausible criterion be used to good advantage—such as a low price/earnings ratio, or a high dividend return, or a large asset value? The two methods of this sort that we have found to give quite consistently good results in the longer past have been (a) the purchase of low-multiplier stocks of important companies (such as the DJIA list), and (b) the choice of a diversified group of stocks selling under their net-current-asset value (or working-capital value). We have already pointed out that the low-multiplier criterion applied to the DJIA at the end of 1968 worked out badly when the results are measured to mid-1971. The record of common-stock purchases made at a price below their working-capital value has no such bad mark against it; the drawback here has been the drying up of such opportunities during most of the past decade.

What about other bases of choice? In writing this book we have made a series of "experiments," each based on a single, fairly obvious criterion. The data used would be readily found in the Standard & Poor's *Stock Guide.* In all cases a 30-stock portfolio was assumed to have been acquired at the 1968 closing prices and then revalued at June 30, 1971. The separate criteria applied were the following, as applied to otherwise random choices: (1) A low multiplier of recent earnings (not confined to DJIA issues). (2) A high dividend return. (3) A very long dividend record. (4) A very large enterprise, as measured by number of outstanding shares. (5) A strong financial position. (6) A low price in dollars per share. (7) A low price in relation to the previous high price. (8) A high quality-ranking by Standard & Poor's.

It will be noted that the *Stock Guide* has at least one column relating to each of the above criteria. This indicates the publisher's belief that each is of importance in analyzing and choosing common stocks. (As we pointed out above, we should like to see another figure added: the net-asset-value per share.)

The most important fact that emerges from our various tests relates to the performance of stocks bought at random. We have tested this performance for three 30-stock portfolios, each made up of issues found on the first line of the December 31, 1968, *Stock Guide* and also found in the issue for August 31, 1971. Between these two dates the S & P composite was practically unchanged, and the DJIA lost about 5%. But our 90 randomly chosen issues declined an average of 22%, not counting 19 issues that were dropped from the *Guide* and probably showed larger losses. These comparative results undoubtedly reflect the tendency of smaller issues of inferior quality to be relatively overvalued in bull markets, and not only to suffer more serious declines than the stronger issues in the ensuing price collapse, but also to delay their full recovery—in many cases indefinitely. The moral for the intelligent investor is, of course, to avoid second-quality issues in making up a portfolio, unless—for the enterprising investor—they are demonstrable bargains.

Other results gleaned from our portfolio studies may be summarized as follows:

Only three of the groups studied showed up better than the S & P composite (and hence better than the DJIA), viz: (1) Industrials with the highest quality ranking (A+). These advanced 9½% in the period against a decline of 2.4% for the S & P industrials, and 5.6% for the DJIA. (However, the ten public-utility issues rated A+ declined 18% against a decline of 14% for the 55-stock S & P public-utility index.) It is worth remarking that the S & P rankings showed up very well in this single test. In every case a portfolio based on a higher ranking did better than a lower-ranking portfolio. (2) Companies with more than 50 million shares outstanding showed no change on the whole, as against a small decline for the indexes. (3) Strangely enough, stocks selling at a high price per share (over 100) showed a slight (1%) composite advance.

Among our various tests we made one based on book value, a figure not given in the *Stock Guide*. Here we found—contrary to our investment philosophy—that companies that combined major size with a large good-will component in their market price did very well as a whole in the 2½-year holding period. (By "good-will component" we mean the part of the price that exceeds the book value.)* Our list of "good-will giants" was made up of 30 issues, each of which had a good-will component of over a billion dollars, representing more than half of its market price. The total market value of these good-will items at the end of 1968 was more than $120 billions! Despite these optimistic market valuations the group as a whole showed a price advance per share of 15% between December 1968 and August 1971, and acquitted itself best among the 20-odd lists studied.

A fact like this must not be ignored in a work on investment

---

* In Graham's terms, a large amount of goodwill can result from two causes: a corporation can acquire other companies for substantially more than the value of their assets, or its own stock can trade for substantially more than its book value.

policies. It is clear that, at the least, a considerable *momentum* is attached to those companies that combine the virtues of great size, an excellent past record of earnings, the public's expectation of continued earnings growth in the future, and strong market action over many past years. Even if the price may appear excessive by our quantitative standards the underlying market momentum may well carry such issues along more or less indefinitely. (Naturally this assumption does not apply to every individual issue in the category. For example, the indisputable good-will leader, IBM, moved down from 315 to 304 in the 30-month period.) It is difficult to judge to what extent the superior market action shown is due to "true" or objective investment merits and to what extent to long-established popularity. No doubt both factors are important here. Clearly, both the long-term and the recent market action of the good-will giants would recommend them for a diversified portfolio of common stocks. Our own preference, however, remains for other types that show a combination of favorable investment factors, including asset values of at least two-thirds the market price.

The tests using other criteria indicate in general that random lists based on a single favorable factor did better than random lists chosen for the opposite factor—e.g., low-multiplier issues had a smaller decline in this period than high-multiplier issues, and long-term dividend payers lost less than those that were not paying dividends at the end of 1968. To that extent the results support our recommendation that the issues selected meet a combination of quantitative or tangible criteria.

Finally we should comment on the much poorer showing made by our lists as a whole as compared with the price record of the S & P composite. The latter is weighted by the size of each enterprise, whereas our tests are based on taking one share of each company. Evidently the larger emphasis given to giant enterprises by the S & P method made a significant difference in the results, and points up once again their greater price stability as compared with "run-of-the-mine" companies.

Bargain Issues, or Net-Current-Asset Stocks

In the tests discussed above we did not include the results of buying 30 issues at a price less than their net-current-asset value. The reason was that only a handful, at most, of such issues would have been found in the *Stock Guide* at the end of 1968. But the picture changed in the 1970 decline, and at the low prices of that year a goodly number of common stocks could have been bought at below their working-capital value. It always seemed, and still seems, ridiculously simple to say that if one can acquire a diversified group of common stocks at a price less than the applicable net current assets alone—after deducting all prior claims, and counting as *zero* the fixed and other assets—the results should be quite satisfactory. They were so, in our experience, for more than 30 years—say, between 1923 and 1957—excluding a time of real trial in 1930–1932.

Has this approach any relevance at the beginning of 1971? Our answer would be a qualified "yes." A quick runover of the *Stock Guide* would have uncovered some 50 or more issues that appeared to be obtainable at or below net-current-asset value. As might be expected a good many of these had been doing badly in the difficult year 1970. If we eliminated those which had reported net losses in the last 12-month period we would be still left with enough issues to make up a diversified list.

We have included in Table 15-2 some data on five issues that sold at less than their working-capital value* at their *low* prices of

TABLE 15-2 Stocks of Prominent Companies Selling at or Below Net-Current-Asset Value in 1970

Company	*1970 Price*	*Net-Current-Asset Value Per Share*	*Book Value Per Share*	*Earned Per Share, 1970*	*Current Dividend*	*High Price Before 1970*
Cone Mills	13	$18	$39.3	$1.51	$1.00	41½
Jantzen Inc.	11⅛	12	16.3	1.27	.60	37
National Presto	21½	27	31.7	6.15	1.00	45
Parker Pen	9¼	9½	16.6	1.62	.60	31¼
West Point Pepperell	16¼	20½	39.4	1.82	1.50	64

* Technically, the working-capital value of a stock is the current assets per share, minus the current liabilities per share, divided by the number of shares outstanding. Here, however, Graham means "*net* working-capital value," or the per-share value of current assets minus *total* liabilities.

1970. These give some food for reflection on the nature of stock-price fluctuations. How does it come about that well-established companies, whose brands are household names all over the country, could be valued at such low figures—at the same time when other concerns (with better earnings growth of course) were selling for billions of dollars in excess of what their balance sheets showed? To quote the "old days" once more, the idea of good will as an element of intangible value was usually associated with a "trade name." Names such as Lady Pepperell in sheets, Jantzen in swim suits, and Parker in pens would be considered assets of great value indeed. But now, if the "market doesn't like a company," not only renowned trade names but land, buildings, machinery, and what you will, can all count for nothing in its scales. Pascal said that "the heart has its reasons that the reason doesn't understand."* For "heart" read "Wall Street."

There is another contrast that comes to mind. When the going is good and new issues are readily salable, stock offerings of no quality at all make their appearance. They quickly find buyers; their prices are often bid up enthusiastically right after issuance to levels in relation to assets and earnings that would put IBM, Xerox, and Polaroid to shame. Wall Street takes this madness in its stride, with no overt efforts by anyone to call a halt before the inevitable collapse in prices. (The SEC can't do much more than insist on disclosure of information, about which the speculative public couldn't care less, or announce investigations and usually mild punitive actions of various sorts after the letter of the law has been clearly broken.) When many of these minuscule but grossly inflated enterprises disappear from view, or nearly so, it is all taken philosophically enough as "part of the game." Everybody swears off such inexcusable extravagances—until next time.

Thanks for the lecture, says the gentle reader. But what about your "bargain issues"? Can one really make money in them without taking a serious risk? Yes indeed, *if* you can find enough of them to make a diversified group, and *if* you don't lose patience if

---

* *Le coeur a ses raisons que la raison ne connaît point.* This poetic passage is one of the concluding arguments in the great French theologian's discussion of what has come to be known as "Pascal's wager" (see commentary on Chapter 20).

they fail to advance soon after you buy them. Sometimes the patience needed may appear quite considerable. In our previous edition we hazarded a single example (p. 188) which was current as we wrote. It was Burton-Dixie Corp., with stock selling at 20, against net-current-asset value of 30, and book value of about 50. A profit on that purchase would not have been immediate. But in August 1967 all the shareholders were offered 53¾ for their shares, probably at just about book value. A patient holder, who had bought the shares in March 1964 at 20 would have had a profit of 165% in 3½ years—a noncompounded annual return of 47%. Most of the bargain issues in our experience have not taken that long to show good profits–nor have they shown so high a rate. For a somewhat similar situation, current as we write, see our discussion of National Presto Industries above, p. 168.

Special Situations or "Workouts"

Let us touch briefly on this area, since it is theoretically includable in the program of operations of an enterprising investor. It was commented upon above. Here we shall supply some examples of the genre, and some further remarks on what it appears to offer an open-minded and alert investor.

Three such situations, among others, were current early in 1971, and they may be summarized as follows:

Situation 1. Acquisition of Kayser-Roth by Borden's. In January 1971 Borden Inc. announced a plan to acquire control of Kayser-Roth ("diversified apparel") by giving 1⅓ shares of its own stock in exchange for one share of Kayser-Roth. On the following day, in active trading. Borden closed at 26 and Kayser-Roth at 28. If an "operator" had bought 300 shares of Kayser-Roth and sold 400 Borden at these prices and if the deal were later consummated on the announced terms, he would have had a profit of some 24% on the cost of his shares, less commissions and some other items. Assuming the deal had gone through in six months, his final profit might have been at about a 40% per annum rate.

Situation 2. In November 1970 National Biscuit Co. offered to buy control of Aurora Plastics Co. at $11 in cash. The stock was selling at about 8½; it closed the month at 9 and continued to sell there at year-end. Here the gross profit indicated was originally about 25%, subject to the risks of nonconsummation and to the time element.

Situation 3. Universal-Marion Co., which had ceased its business operations, asked its shareholders to ratify dissolution of the concern. The treasurer indicated that the common stock had a book value of about $28½ per share, a substantial part of which was in liquid form. The stock closed 1970 at 21½, indicating a possible gross profit here, if book value was realized in liquidation, of more than 30%.

If operations of this kind, conducted on a diversified basis for spreading the risk, could be counted to yield annual profits of, say, 20% or better, they would undoubtedly be more than merely worthwhile. Since this is not a book on "special situations," we are not going into the details of the business—for it really is a business. Let us point out two contradictory developments there in recent years. On the one hand the number of deals to choose from has increased enormously, as compared with, say, ten years ago. This is a consequence of what might be called a mania of corporations to diversify their activities through various types of acquisitions, etc. In 1970 the number of "merger announcements" aggregated some 5,000, down from over 6,000 in 1969. The total money values involved in these deals amounted to many, many billions. Perhaps only a small fraction of the 5,000 announcements could have presented a clear-cut opportunity for purchase of shares by a special-situations man, but this fraction was still large enough to keep him busy studying, picking, and choosing.

The other side of the picture is that an increasing proportion of the mergers announced failed to be consummated. In such cases, of course, the aimed-for profit is not realized, and is likely to be replaced by a more or less serious loss. Reasons for nonsuccess are numerous, including antitrust intervention, shareholder opposition, change in "market conditions," unfavorable indications from further study, inability to agree on details, and others. The trick here, of course, is to have the judgment, buttressed by experience, to pick the deals most likely to succeed and also those which are likely to occasion the smallest loss if they fail.*

* As discussed in the commentary on Chapter 7, merger arbitrage is wholly inappropriate for most individual investors.

Further Comment on the Examples Above

KAYSER-ROTH. The directors of this company had already rejected (in January 1971) the Borden proposal when this chapter was written. If the operation had been "undone" immediately the overall loss, including commissions, would have been about 12% of the cost of the Kayser-Roth shares.

AURORA PLASTICS. Because of the bad showing of this company in 1970 the takeover terms were renegotiated and the price reduced to 10½. The shares were paid for at the end of May. The annual rate of return realized here was about 25%.

UNIVERSAL-MARION. This company promptly made an initial distribution in cash and stock worth about $7 per share, reducing the investment to say 14½. However the market price fell as low as 13 subsequently, casting doubt on the ultimate outcome of the liquidation.

Assuming that the three examples given are fairly representative of "workout or arbitrage" opportunities as a whole in 1971, it is clear that they are not attractive if entered into upon a random basis. This has become more than ever a field for professionals, with the requisite experience and judgment.

There is an interesting sidelight on our Kayser-Roth example. Late in 1971 the price fell below 20 while Borden was selling at 25, equivalent to 33 for Kayser-Roth under the terms of the exchange offer. It would appear that either the directors had made a great mistake in turning down that opportunity or the shares of Kayser-Roth were now badly undervalued in the market. Something for a security analyst to look into.

COMMENTARY ON CHAPTER 15

> It is easy in the world to live after the world's opinion; it is easy in solitude to live after our own; but the great man is he who in the midst of the crowd keeps with perfect sweetness the independence of solitude.
>
> *–Ralph Waldo Emerson*

PRACTICE, PRACTICE, PRACTICE

Max Heine, founder of the Mutual Series Funds, liked to say that "there are many roads to Jerusalem." What this masterly stock picker meant was that his own value-centered method of selecting stocks was not the only way to be a successful investor. In this chapter we'll look at several techniques that some of today's leading money managers use for picking stocks.

First, though, it's worth repeating that for most investors, selecting individual stocks is unnecessary–if not inadvisable. The fact that most professionals do a poor job of stock picking does not mean that most amateurs can do better. The vast majority of people who try to pick stocks learn that they are not as good at it as they thought; the luckiest ones discover this early on, while the less fortunate take years to learn it. A small percentage of investors can excel at picking their own stocks. Everyone else would be better off getting help, ideally through an index fund.

Graham advised investors to practice first, just as even the greatest athletes and musicians practice and rehearse before every actual performance. He suggested starting off by spending a year tracking and picking stocks (but *not* with real money).[1] In Graham's day, you would

---

[1] Patricia Dreyfus, "Investment Analysis in Two Easy Lessons" (interview with Graham), *Money*, July, 1976, p. 36.

have practiced using a ledger of hypothetical buys and sells on a legal pad; nowadays, you can use "portfolio trackers" at websites like www.morningstar.com, http://finance.yahoo.com, http://money.cnn.com/services/portfolio/ or www.marketocracy.com (at the last site, ignore the "market-beating" hype on its funds and other services).

By test-driving your techniques before trying them with real money, you can make mistakes without incurring any actual losses, develop the discipline to avoid frequent trading, compare your approach against those of leading money managers, and learn what works for you. Best of all, tracking the outcome of all your stock picks will prevent you from forgetting that some of your hunches turn out to be stinkers. That will force you to learn from your winners *and* your losers. After a year, measure your results against how you would have done if you had put all your money in an S & P 500 index fund. If you didn't enjoy the experiment or your picks were poor, no harm done—selecting individual stocks is not for you. Get yourself an index fund and stop wasting your time on stock picking.

If you enjoyed the experiment and earned sufficiently good returns, gradually assemble a basket of stocks—but limit it to a maximum of 10% of your overall portfolio (keep the rest in an index fund). And remember, you can always stop if it no longer interests you or your returns turn bad.

LOOKING UNDER THE RIGHT ROCKS

So how should you go about looking for a potentially rewarding stock? You can use websites like http://finance.yahoo.com and www.morningstar.com to screen stocks with the statistical filters suggested in Chapter 14. Or you can take a more patient, craftsmanlike approach. Unlike most people, many of the best professional investors first get interested in a company when its share price goes down, not up. Christopher Browne of Tweedy Browne Global Value Fund, William Nygren of the Oakmark Fund, Robert Rodriguez of FPA Capital Fund, and Robert Torray of the Torray Fund all suggest looking at the daily list of new 52-week lows in the *Wall Street Journal* or the similar table in the "Market Week" section of *Barron's.* That will point you toward stocks and industries that are unfashionable or unloved and that thus offer the potential for high returns once perceptions change.

Christopher Davis of the Davis Funds and William Miller of Legg

FROM EPS TO ROIC

Net income or earnings per share (EPS) has been distorted in recent years by factors like stock-option grants and accounting gains and charges. To see how much a company is truly earning on the capital it deploys in its businesses, look beyond EPS to ROIC, or return on invested capital. Christopher Davis of the Davis Funds defines it with this formula:

ROIC = Owner Earnings ÷ Invested Capital,

where Owner Earnings is equal to:

Operating profit

plus depreciation

plus amortization of goodwill

minus Federal income tax (paid at the company's average rate)

minus cost of stock options

minus "maintenance" (or essential) capital expenditures

minus any income generated by unsustainable rates of return on pension funds (as of 2003, anything greater than 6.5%)

and where Invested Capital is equal to:

Total assets

minus cash (as well as short-term investments and non-interest-bearing current liabilities)

plus past accounting charges that reduced invested capital.

ROIC has the virtue of showing, after all legitimate expenses, what the company earns from its operating businesses–and how efficiently it has used the shareholders' money to generate that return. An ROIC of at least 10% is attractive; even 6% or 7% can be tempting if the company has good brand names, focused management, or is under a temporary cloud.

Mason Value Trust like to see rising returns on invested capital, or ROIC–a way of measuring how efficiently a company generates what Warren Buffett has called "owner earnings."[2] (See the sidebar on p. 398 for more detail.)

By checking "comparables," or the prices at which similar businesses have been acquired over the years, managers like Oakmark's Nygren and Longleaf Partners' O. Mason Hawkins get a better handle on what a company's parts are worth. For an individual investor, it's painstaking and difficult work: Start by looking at the "Business Segments" footnote in the company's annual report, which typically lists the industrial sector, revenues, and earnings of each subsidiary. (The "Management Discussion and Analysis" may also be helpful.) Then search a news database like Factiva, ProQuest, or LexisNexis for examples of other firms in the same industries that have recently been acquired. Using the EDGAR database at www.sec.gov to locate their past annual reports, you may be able to determine the ratio of purchase price to the earnings of those acquired companies. You can then apply that ratio to estimate how much a corporate acquirer might pay for a similar division of the company you are investigating.

By separately analyzing each of the company's divisions this way, you may be able to see whether they are worth more than the current stock price. Longleaf's Hawkins likes to find what he calls "60-cent dollars," or companies whose stock is trading at 60% or less of the value at which he appraises the businesses. That helps provide the margin of safety that Graham insists on.

WHO'S THE BOSS?

Finally, most leading professional investors want to see that a company is run by people who, in the words of Oakmark's William Nygren, "think like owners, not just managers." Two simple tests: Are the company's financial statements easily understandable, or are they full of obfuscation? Are "nonrecurring" or "extraordinary" or "unusual" charges just that, or do they have a nasty habit of recurring?

Longleaf's Mason Hawkins looks for corporate managers who are

---

[2] See the commentary on Chapter 11.

"good partners"—meaning that they communicate candidly about problems, have clear plans for allocating current and future cash flow, and own sizable stakes in the company's stock (preferably through cash purchases rather than through grants of options). But "if managements talk more about the stock price than about the business," warns Robert Torray of the Torray Fund, "we're not interested." Christopher Davis of the Davis Funds favors firms that limit issuance of stock options to roughly 3% of shares outstanding.

At Vanguard Primecap Fund, Howard Schow tracks "what the company said one year and what happened the next. We want to see not only whether managements are honest with shareholders but also whether they're honest with themselves." (If a company boss insists that all is hunky-dory when business is sputtering, watch out!) Nowadays, you can listen in on a company's regularly scheduled conference calls even if you own only a few shares; to find out the schedule, call the investor relations department at corporate headquarters or visit the company's website.

Robert Rodriguez of FPA Capital Fund turns to the back page of the company's annual report, where the heads of its operating divisions are listed. If there's a lot of turnover in those names in the first one or two years of a new CEO's regime, that's probably a good sign; he's cleaning out the dead wood. But if high turnover continues, the turnaround has probably devolved into turmoil.

KEEPING YOUR EYES ON THE ROAD

There are even more roads to Jerusalem than these. Some leading portfolio managers, like David Dreman of Dreman Value Management and Martin Whitman of the Third Avenue Funds, focus on companies selling at very low multiples of assets, earnings, or cash flow. Others, like Charles Royce of the Royce Funds and Joel Tillinghast of Fidelity Low-Priced Stock Fund, hunt for undervalued small companies. And, for an all-too-brief look at how today's most revered investor, Warren Buffett, selects companies, see the sidebar on p. 401.

One technique that can be helpful: See which leading professional money managers own the same stocks you do. If one or two names keep turning up, go to the websites of those fund companies and download their most recent reports. By seeing which other stocks these investors own, you can learn more about what qualities they

WARREN'S WAY

Graham's greatest student, Warren Buffett, has become the world's most successful investor by putting new twists on Graham's ideas. Buffett and his partner, Charles Munger, have combined Graham's "margin of safety" and detachment from the market with their own innovative emphasis on future growth. Here is an all-too-brief summary of Buffett's approach:

He looks for what he calls "franchise" companies with strong consumer brands, easily understandable businesses, robust financial health, and near-monopolies in their markets, like H & R Block, Gillette, and the Washington Post Co. Buffett likes to snap up a stock when a scandal, big loss, or other bad news passes over it like a storm cloud–as when he bought Coca-Cola soon after its disastrous rollout of "New Coke" and the market crash of 1987. He also wants to see managers who set and meet realistic goals; build their businesses from within rather than through acquisition; allocate capital wisely; and do not pay themselves hundred-million-dollar jackpots of stock options. Buffett insists on steady and sustainable growth in earnings, so the company will be worth more in the future than it is today.

In his annual reports, archived at www.berkshirehathaway.com, Buffett has set out his thinking like an open book. Probably no other investor, Graham included, has publicly revealed more about his approach or written such compellingly readable essays. (One classic Buffett proverb: "When a management with a reputation for brilliance tackles a business with a reputation for bad economics, it is the reputation of the business that remains intact.") Every intelligent investor can–and should–learn by reading this master's own words.

have in common; by reading the managers' commentary, you may get ideas on how to improve your own approach.[3]

No matter which techniques they use in picking stocks, successful investing professionals have two things in common: First, they are disciplined and consistent, refusing to change their approach even when it is unfashionable. Second, they think a great deal about what they do and how to do it, but they pay very little attention to what the market is doing.

[3] There are also many newsletters dedicated to analyzing professional portfolios, but most of them are a waste of time and money for even the most enterprising investor. A shining exception for people who can spare the cash is *Outstanding Investor Digest* (www.oid.com).

CHAPTER 16

Convertible Issues and Warrants

Convertible bonds and preferred stocks have been taking on a predominant importance in recent years in the field of senior financing. As a parallel development, stock-option warrants—which are long-term rights to buy common shares at stipulated prices—have become more and more numerous. More than half the preferred issues now quoted in the Standard & Poor's *Stock Guide* have conversion privileges, and this has been true also of a major part of the corporate *bond* financing in 1968–1970. There are at least 60 different series of stock-option warrants dealt in on the American Stock Exchange. In 1970, for the first time in its history, the New York Stock Exchange listed an issue of long-term warrants, giving rights to buy 31,400,000 American Tel. & Tel. shares at $52 each. With "Mother Bell" now leading that procession, it is bound to be augmented by many new fabricators of warrants. (As we shall point out later, they are a fabrication in more than one sense.)*

In the overall picture the convertible issues rank as much more important than the warrants, and we shall discuss them first. There are two main aspects to be considered from the standpoint of the investor. First, how do they rank as investment opportunities and risks? Second, how does their existence affect the value of the related common-stock issues?

Convertible issues are claimed to be especially advantageous to both the investor and the issuing corporation. The investor receives the superior protection of a bond or preferred stock, plus the opportunity to participate in any substantial rise in the value of the

---

* Graham detested warrants, as he makes clear on pp. 413–416.

common stock. The issuer is able to raise capital at a moderate interest or preferred dividend cost, and if the expected prosperity materializes the issuer will get rid of the senior obligation by having it exchanged into common stock. Thus both sides to the bargain will fare unusually well.

Obviously the foregoing paragraph must overstate the case somewhere, for you cannot by a mere ingenious device make a bargain much better for both sides. In exchange for the conversion privilege the investor usually gives up something important in quality or yield, or both.[1] Conversely, if the company gets its money at lower cost because of the conversion feature, it is surrendering in return part of the common shareholders' claim to future enhancement. On this subject there are a number of tricky arguments to be advanced both pro and con. The safest conclusion that can be reached is that convertible issues are like any other *form* of security, in that their form itself guarantees neither attractiveness nor unattractiveness. That question will depend on all the facts surrounding the individual issue.*

We do know, however, that the group of convertible issues floated during the latter part of a bull market are bound to yield unsatisfactory results as a whole. (It is at such optimistic periods, unfortunately, that most of the convertible financing has been done in the past.) The poor consequences must be inevitable, from the timing itself, since a wide decline in the stock market must invariably make the conversion privilege much less attractive—and often, also, call into question the underlying safety of the issue itself.† As a group illustration we shall retain the example used in

---

* Graham is pointing out that, despite the promotional rhetoric that investors usually hear, convertible bonds do not automatically offer "the best of both worlds." Higher yield and lower risk do *not* always go hand in hand. What Wall Street gives with one hand, it usually takes away with the other. An investment may offer the best of one world, or the worst of another; but the best of both worlds seldom becomes available in a single package.

† According to Goldman Sachs and Ibbotson Associates, from 1998 through 2002, convertibles generated an average annual return of 4.8%. That was considerably better than the 0.6% annual loss on U.S. stocks, but substantially worse than the returns of medium-term corporate bonds (a

TABLE 16-1 Price Record of New Preferred-Stock Issues Offered in 1946

Price Change from Issue Price to Low up to July 1947	"Straight" Issues	Convertible and Participating Issues
	(number of issues)	
No decline	7	0
Declined 0–10%	16	2
10–20%	11	6
20–40%	3	22
40% or more	0	12
	37	42
Average decline	About 9%	About 30%

our first edition of the relative price behavior of convertible and straight (nonconvertible) preferreds offered in 1946, the closing year of the bull market preceding the extraordinary one that began in 1949.

A comparable presentation is difficult to make for the years 1967–1970, because there were virtually no new offerings of nonconvertibles in those years. But it is easy to demonstrate that the average price decline of convertible preferred stocks from December 1967 to December 1970 was greater than that for common stocks as a whole (which lost only 5%). Also the convertibles seem to have done quite a bit worse than the older straight preferred shares during the period December 1968 to December 1970, as is shown by the sample of 20 issues of each kind in Table 16-2. These

---

7.5% annual gain) and long-term corporate bonds (an 8.3% annual gain). In the mid-1990s, according to Merrill Lynch, roughly $15 billion in convertibles were issued annually; by 1999, issuance had more than doubled to $39 billion. In 2000, $58 billion in convertibles were issued, and in 2001, another $105 billion emerged. As Graham warns, convertible securities always come out of the woodwork near the end of a bull market—largely because even poor-quality companies then have stock returns high enough to make the conversion feature seem attractive.

TABLE 16-2 Price Record of Preferred Stocks, Common Stocks, and Warrants, December 1970 versus December 1968

(Based on Random Samples of 20 Issues Each)

	Straight Preferred Stocks Rated A or Better	Rated Below A	Convertible Preferred Stocks	Listed Common Stocks	Listed Warrants
Advances	2	0	1	2	1
Declines:					
0–10%	3	3	3	4	0
10–20%	14	10	2	1	0
20–40%	1	5	5	6	1
40% or more	0	0	9	7	18
Average declines	10%	17%	29%	33%	65%

(Standard & Poor's composite index of 500 common stocks declined 11.3%.)

comparisons would demonstrate that convertible securities as a whole have relatively poor quality as senior issues and also are tied to common stocks that do worse than the general market except during a speculative upsurge. These observations do not apply to all convertible issues, of course. In the 1968 and 1969 particularly, a fair number of strong companies used convertible issues to combat the inordinately high interest rates for even first-quality bonds. But it is noteworthy that in our 20-stock sample of convertible preferreds only one showed an advance and 14 suffered bad declines.*

* Recent structural changes in the convertible market have negated some of these criticisms. Convertible preferred stock, which made up roughly half the total convertible market in Graham's day, now accounts for only an eighth of the market. Maturities are shorter, making convertible bonds less volatile, and many now carry "call protection," or assurances against early redemption. And more than half of all convertibles are now investment grade, a significant improvement in credit quality from Graham's time. Thus, in 2002, the Merrill Lynch All U.S. Convertible Index lost 8.6%—versus the 22.1% loss of the S & P 500-stock index and the 31.3% decline in the NASDAQ Composite stock index.

The conclusion to be drawn from these figures is not that convertible issues are in themselves less desirable than nonconvertible or "straight" securities. Other things being equal, the opposite is true. But we clearly see that other things are *not* equal in practice and that the addition of the conversion privilege often—perhaps generally—betrays an absence of genuine investment quality for the issue.

It is true, of course, that a convertible preferred is safer than the common stock of the same company—that is to say, it carries smaller risk of eventual loss of principal. Consequently those who buy new convertibles instead of the corresponding common stock are logical to that extent. But in most cases the common would not have been an intelligent purchase to begin with, at the ruling price, and the substitution of the convertible preferred did not improve the picture sufficiently. Furthermore, a good deal of the buying of convertibles was done by investors who had no special interest or confidence in the common stock—that is, they would never have thought of buying the common at the time—but who were tempted by what seemed an ideal combination of a prior claim plus a conversion privilege close to the current market. In a number of instances this combination has worked out well, but the statistics seem to show that it is more likely to prove a pitfall.

In connection with the ownership of convertibles there is a special problem which most investors fail to realize. Even when a profit appears it brings a dilemma with it. Should the holder sell on a small rise; should he hold for a much bigger advance; if the issue is called—as often happens when the common has gone up considerably—should he sell out then or convert into and retain the common stock?*

Let us talk in concrete terms. You buy a 6% bond at 100, convertible into stock at 25—that is, at the rate of 40 shares for each $1,000 bond. The stock goes to 30, which makes the bond worth at least 120, and so it sells at 125. You either sell or hold. If you hold, hoping for a higher price, you are pretty much in the position of a com-

---

* A bond is "called" when the issuing corporation forcibly pays it off ahead of the stated maturity date, or final due date for interest payments. For a brief summary of how convertible bonds work, see Note 1 in the commentary on this chapter (p. 418).

mon shareholder, since if the stock goes down your bond will go down too. A conservative person is likely to say that beyond 125 his position has become too speculative, and therefore he sells and makes a gratifying 25% profit.

So far, so good. But pursue the matter a bit. In many cases where the holder sells at 125 the common stock continues to advance, carrying the convertible with it, and the investor experiences that peculiar pain that comes to the man who has sold out much too soon. The next time, he decides to hold for 150 or 200. The issue goes up to 140 and he does not sell. Then the market breaks and his bond slides down to 80. Again he has done the wrong thing.

Aside from the mental anguish involved in making these bad guesses—and they seem to be almost inevitable—there is a real arithmetical drawback to operations in convertible issues. It may be assumed that a stern and uniform policy of selling at 25% or 30% profit will work out best as applied to many holdings. This would then mark the upper limit of profit and would be realized only on the issues that worked out well. But, if—as appears to be true—these issues often lack adequate underlying security and tend to be floated and purchased in the latter stages of a bull market, then a goodly proportion of them will fail to rise to 125 but will not fail to collapse when the market turns downward. Thus the spectacular opportunities in convertibles prove to be illusory in practice, and the overall experience is marked by fully as many substantial losses—at least of a temporary kind—as there are gains of similar magnitude.

Because of the extraordinary length of the 1950–1968 bull market, convertible issues as a whole gave a good account of themselves for some 18 years. But this meant only that the great majority of common stocks enjoyed large advances, in which most convertible issues were able to share. The soundness of investment in convertible issues can only be tested by their performance in a declining stock market—and this has always proved disappointing as a whole.*

In our first edition (1949) we gave an illustration of this special

---

* In recent years, convertibles have tended to outperform the Standard & Poor's 500-stock index during declining stock markets, but they have typically underperformed other bonds–which weakens, but does not fully negate, the criticism Graham makes here.

problem of "what to do" with a convertible when it goes up. We believe it still merits inclusion here. Like several of our references it is based on our own investment operations. We were members of a "select group," mainly of investment funds, who participated in a private offering of convertible 4½% debentures of Eversharp Co. at par, convertible into common stock at $40 per share. The stock advanced rapidly to 65½, and then (after a three-for-two split) to the equivalent of 88. The latter price made the convertible debentures worth no less than 220. During this period the two issues were called at a small premium; hence they were practically all converted into common stock, which was retained by a number of the original investment-fund buyers of the debentures. The price promptly began a severe decline, and in March 1948 the stock sold as low as 7⅜. This represented a value of only 27 for the debenture issues, or a loss of 75% of the original price instead of a profit of over 100%.

The real point of this story is that some of the original purchasers converted their bonds into the stock and held the stock through its great decline. In so doing they ran counter to an old maxim of Wall Street, which runs: "Never convert a convertible bond." Why this advice? Because once you convert you have lost your strategic combination of prior claimant to interest plus a chance for an attractive profit. You have probably turned from investor into speculator, and quite often at an unpropitious time (because the stock has already had a large advance). If "Never convert a convertible" is a good rule, how came it that these experienced fund managers exchanged their Eversharp bonds for stock, to their subsequent embarrassing loss? The answer, no doubt, is that they let themselves be carried away by enthusiasm for the company's prospects as well as by the "favorable market action" of the shares. Wall Street has a few prudent principles; the trouble is that they are always forgotten when they are most needed.* Hence that other famous dictum of the old-timers: "Do as I say, not as I do."

Our general attitude toward new convertible issues is thus a mistrustful one. We mean here, as in other similar observations,

---

* This sentence could serve as the epitaph for the bull market of the 1990s. Among the "few prudent principles" that investors forgot were such market clichés as "Trees don't grow to the sky" and "Bulls make money, bears make money, but pigs get slaughtered."

that the investor should look more than twice before he buys them. After such hostile scrutiny he may find some exceptional offerings that are too good to refuse. The ideal combination, of course, is a strongly secured convertible, exchangeable for a common stock which itself is attractive, and at a price only slightly higher than the current market. Every now and then a new offering appears that meets these requirements. By the nature of the securities markets, however, you are more likely to find such an opportunity in some older issue which has developed into a favorable position rather than in a new flotation. (If a new issue is a really strong one, it is not likely to have a good conversion privilege.)

The fine balance between what is given and what is withheld in a standard-type convertible issue is well illustrated by the extensive use of this type of security in the financing of American Telephone & Telegraph Company. Between 1913 and 1957 the company sold at least nine separate issues of convertible bonds, most of them through subscription rights to shareholders. The convertible bonds had the important advantage to the company of bringing in a much wider class of buyers than would have been available for a stock offering, since the bonds were popular with many financial institutions which possess huge resources but some of which were not permitted to buy stocks. The interest return on the bonds has generally been less than half the corresponding dividend yield on the stock—a factor that was calculated to offset the prior claim of the bondholders. Since the company maintained its $9 dividend rate for 40 years (from 1919 to the stock split in 1959) the result was the eventual conversion of virtually all the convertible issues into common stock. Thus the buyers of these convertibles have fared well through the years—but not quite so well as if they had bought the capital stock in the first place. This example establishes the soundness of American Telephone & Telegraph, but not the intrinsic attractiveness of convertible bonds. To prove them sound in practice we should need to have a number of instances in which the convertible worked out well even though the common stock proved disappointing. Such instances are not easy to find.*

---

* AT&T Corp. no longer is a significant issuer of convertible bonds. Among the largest issuers of convertibles today are General Motors, Merrill Lynch, Tyco International, and Roche.

Effect of Convertible Issues on the Status of the Common Stock

In a large number of cases convertibles have been issued in connection with mergers or new acquisitions. Perhaps the most striking example of this financial operation was the issuance by the NVF Corp. of nearly $100,000,000 of its 5% convertible bonds (plus warrants) in exchange for most of the common stock of Sharon Steel Co. This extraordinary deal is discussed below pp. 429–433. Typically the transaction results in a pro forma increase in the reported earnings per share of common stock; the shares advance in response to their larger earnings, so-called, but also because the management has given evidence of its energy, enterprise, and ability to make more money for the shareholders.* But there are two offsetting factors, one of which is practically ignored and the other entirely so in optimistic markets. The first is the actual dilution of the current and future earnings on the common stock that flows arithmetically from the new conversion rights. This dilution can be quantified by taking the recent earnings, or assuming some other figures, and calculating the adjusted earnings per share if all the convertible shares or bonds were actually converted. In the majority of companies the resulting reduction in per-share figures is not significant. But there are numerous exceptions to this statement, and there is danger that they will grow at an uncomfortable rate. The fast-expanding "conglomerates" have been the chief practitioners of convertible legerdemain. In Table 16-3 we list seven companies with large amounts of stock issuable on conversions or against warrants.†

Indicated Switches from Common into Preferred Stocks

For decades before, say, 1956, common stocks yielded more than the preferred stocks of the same companies; this was particularly

---

* For a further discussion of "pro forma" financial results, see the commentary on Chapter 12.

† In recent years, convertible bonds have been heavily issued by companies in the financial, health-care, and technology industries.

TABLE 16-3 Companies with Large Amounts of Convertible Issues and Warrants at the End of 1969 (Shares in Thousands)

		Additional Common Stock Issuable			
		On Conversion of			Total
	Common Stock Outstanding	Bonds	Preferred Stock	Against Warrants	Additional Common Stock
Avco Corp.	11,470	1,750	10.436	3,085	15,271
Gulf & Western Inc.	14,964	9,671	5,632	6,951	22,260
International Tel. & Tel.	67,393	190	48,115		48,305
Ling-Temco-Vought	4,410[a]	1,180	685	7,564	9,429
National General	4,910	4,530		12,170	16,700
Northwest Industries[b]	7,433		11,467	1,513	12,980
Rapid American	3,591	426	1,503	8,000	9,929

[a] Includes "special stock."
[b] At end of 1970.

true if the preferred stock had a conversion privilege close to the market. The reverse is generally true at present. As a result there are a considerable number of convertible preferred stocks which are clearly more attractive than the related common shares. Owners of the common have nothing to lose and important advantages to gain by switching from their junior shares into the senior issue.

EXAMPLE: A typical example was presented by Studebaker-Worthington Corp. at the close of 1970. The common sold at 57, while the $5 convertible preferred finished at 87½. Each preferred share is exchangeable for 1½ shares of common, then worth 85½. This would indicate a small money difference against the buyer of the preferred. But dividends are being paid on the common at the annual rate of $1.20 (or $1.80 for the 1½ shares), against the $5 obtainable on one share of preferred. Thus the original adverse difference in price would probably be made up in less than a year, after which the preferred would probably return an appreciably higher dividend yield than the common for some time to come. But most important, of course, would be the senior position that the common shareholder would gain from the switch. At the *low* prices of 1968 and again in 1970 the preferred sold 15 points higher than 1½ shares of common. Its conversion privilege guarantees that it could never sell lower than the common package.[2]

Stock-Option Warrants

Let us mince no words at the outset. We consider the recent development of stock-option warrants as a near fraud, an existing menace, and a potential disaster. They have created huge aggregate dollar "values" out of thin air. They have no excuse for existence except to the extent that they mislead speculators and investors. They should be prohibited by law, or at least strictly limited to a minor part of the total capitalization of a company.*

For an analogy in general history and in literature we refer the reader to the section of *Faust* (part 2), in which Goethe describes the invention of paper money. As an ominous precedent on Wall Street history, we may mention the warrants of American & Foreign Power Co., which in 1929 had a quoted market value of over a billion dollars, although they appeared only in a footnote to the company's balance sheet. By 1932 this billion dollars had shrunk to $8 million, and in 1952 the warrants were wiped out in the company's recapitalization—even though it had remained solvent.

Originally, stock-option warrants were attached now and then to bond issues, and were usually equivalent to a partial conversion privilege. They were unimportant in amount, and hence did no harm. Their use expanded in the late 1920s, along with many other financial abuses, but they dropped from sight for long years thereafter. They were bound to turn up again, like the bad pennies they are, and since 1967 they have become familiar "instruments of

---

* Warrants were an extremely widespread technique of corporate finance in the nineteenth century and were fairly common even in Graham's day. They have since diminished in importance and popularity–one of the few recent developments that would give Graham unreserved pleasure. As of year-end 2002, there were only seven remaining warrant issues on the New York Stock Exchange–only the ghostly vestige of a market. Because warrants are no longer commonly used by major companies, today's investors should read the rest of Graham's chapter only to see how his logic works.

finance." In fact a standard procedure has developed for raising the capital for new real-estate ventures, affiliates of large banks, by selling units of an equal number of common shares and warrants to buy additional common shares at the same price. *Example:* In 1971 CleveTrust Realty Investors sold 2,500,000 of these combinations of common stock (or "shares of beneficial interest") and warrants, for $20 per unit.

Let us consider for a moment what is really involved in this financial setup. Ordinarily, a common-stock issue has the first right to buy additional common shares when the company's directors find it desirable to raise capital in this manner. This so-called "preemptive right" is one of the elements of value entering into the ownership of common stock—along with the right to receive dividends, to participate in the company's growth, and to vote for directors. When separate warrants are issued for the right to subscribe additional capital, that action takes away part of the value inherent in an ordinary common share and transfers it to a separate certificate. An analogous thing could be done by issuing separate certificates for the right to receive dividends (for a limited or unlimited period), or the right to share in the proceeds of sale or liquidation of the enterprise, or the right to vote the shares. Why then are these subscription warrants created as part of the original capital structure? Simply because people are inexpert in financial matters. They don't realize that the common stock is worth less with warrants outstanding than otherwise. Hence the package of stock and warrants usually commands a better price in the market than would the stock alone. Note that in the usual company reports the per-share earnings are (or have been) computed without proper allowance for the effect of outstanding warrants. The result is, of course, to overstate the true relationship between the earnings and the market value of the company's capitalization.*

---

* Today, the last remnant of activity in warrants is in the cesspool of the NASDAQ "bulletin board," or over-the-counter market for tiny companies, where common stock is often bundled with warrants into a "unit" (the contemporary equivalent of what Graham calls a "package"). If a stockbroker ever offers to sell you "units" in any company, you can be 95% certain that warrants are involved, and at least 90% certain that the broker is either a thief or an idiot. Legitimate brokers and firms have no business in this area.

The simplest and probably the best method of allowing for the existence of warrants is to add the equivalent of their market value to the common-share capitalization, thus increasing the "true" market price per share. Where large amounts of warrants have been issued in connection with the sale of senior securities, it is customary to make the adjustment by assuming that the proceeds of the stock payment are used to retire the related bonds or preferred shares. This method does not allow adequately for the usual "premium value" of a warrant above exercisable value. In Table 16-4 we compare the effect of the two methods of calculation in the case of National General Corp. for the year 1970.

Does the company itself derive an advantage from the creation of these warrants, in the sense that they assure it in some way of receiving additional capital when it needs some? Not at all. Ordinarily there is no way in which the company can require the warrant-holders to exercise their rights, and thus provide new capital to the company, prior to the expiration date of the warrants. In the meantime, if the company wants to raise additional common-stock funds it must offer the shares to its shareholders in the usual way—which means somewhat under the ruling market price. The warrants are no help in such an operation; they merely complicate the situation by frequently requiring a downward revision in their own subscription price. Once more we assert that large issues of stock-option warrants serve no purpose, except to fabricate imaginary market values.

The paper money that Goethe was familiar with, when he wrote his *Faust,* were the notorious French assignats that had been greeted as a marvelous invention, and were destined ultimately to lose all of their value—as did the billion dollars worth of American & Foreign Power warrants.* Some of the poet's remarks apply

---

* The "notorious French assignats" were issued during the Revolution of 1789. They were originally debts of the Revolutionary government, purportedly secured by the value of the real estate that the radicals had seized from the Catholic church and the nobility. But the Revolutionaries were bad financial managers. In 1790, the interest rate on assignats was cut; soon they stopped paying interest entirely and were reclassified as paper money. But the government refused to redeem them for gold or silver and issued massive amounts of new assignats. They were officially declared worthless in 1797.

TABLE 16-4 Calculation of "True Market Price" and Adjusted Price/Earnings Ratio of a Common Stock with Large Amounts of Warrants Outstanding

(Example: National General Corp. in June 1971)

1. Calculation of "True Market Price."

Market value of 3 issues of warrants, June 30, 1971	$94,000,000
Value of warrants per share of common stock	$18.80
Price of common stock alone	24.50
Corrected price of common, adjusted for warrants	43.30

2. Calculation of P/E Ratio to Allow for Warrant Dilution

	Before	*After Warrant Dilution*	
(1970 earnings)	*Warrant*	Company's	Our
A. Before Special Items.	*Dilution*	Calculation	Calculation
Earned per share	$ 2.33	$ 1.60	$ 2.33
Price of common	24.50	24.50	43.30 (adj.)
P/E ratio	10.5×	15.3×	18.5×
B. After Special Items.			
Earned per share	$ .90	$ 1.33	$ .90
Price of common	24.50	24.50	43.30 (adj.)
P/E ratio	27.2×	18.4×	48.1×

Note that, after special charges, the effect of the company's calculation is to increase the earnings per share and reduce the P/E ratio. This is manifestly absurd. By our suggested method the effect of the dilution is to increase the P/E ratio substantially, as it should be.

equally well to one invention or another—such as the following (in Bayard Taylor's translation):

> FAUST: Imagination in its highest flight
> Exerts itself but cannot grasp it quite.
>
> MEPHISTOPHELES (the inventor): If one needs coin the brokers ready stand.
>
> THE FOOL (finally): The magic paper . . . !

Practical Postscript

The crime of the warrants is in "having been born."* Once born they function as other security forms, and offer chances of profit as well as of loss. Nearly all the newer warrants run for a limited time—generally between five and ten years. The older warrants were often perpetual, and they were likely to have fascinating price histories over the years.

EXAMPLE: The record books will show that Tri-Continental Corp. warrants, which date from 1929, sold at a negligible 1/32 of a dollar each in the depth of the depression. From that lowly estate their price rose to a magnificent 75¾ in 1969, an astronomical advance of some 242,000%. (The warrants then sold considerably higher than the shares themselves; this is the kind of thing that occurs on Wall Street through technical developments, such as stock splits.) A recent example is supplied by Ling-Temco-Vought warrants, which in the first half of 1971 advanced from 2½ to 12½—and then fell back to 4.

No doubt shrewd operations can be carried on in warrants from time to time, but this is too technical a matter for discussion here. We might say that warrants tend to sell relatively higher than the corresponding market components related to the conversion privilege of bonds or preferred stocks. To that extent there is a valid argument for selling bonds with warrants attached rather than creating an equivalent dilution factor by a convertible issue. If the warrant total is relatively small there is no point in taking its theoretical aspect too seriously; if the warrant issue is large relative to the outstanding stock, that would probably indicate that the company has a top-heavy senior capitalization. It should be selling additional common stock instead. Thus the main objective of our attack on warrants as a financial mechanism is not to condemn their use in connection with moderate-size bond issues, but to argue against the wanton creation of huge "paper-money" monstrosities of this genre.

---

* Graham, an enthusiastic reader of Spanish literature, is paraphrasing a line from the play *Life Is a Dream* by Pedro Calderon de la Barca (1600–1681): "The greatest crime of man is having been born."

COMMENTARY ON CHAPTER 16

That which thou sowest is not quickened, except it die.

—*I. Corinthians,* XV:36.

THE ZEAL OF THE CONVERT

Although convertible bonds are called "bonds," they behave like stocks, work like options, and are cloaked in obscurity.

If you own a convertible, you also hold an option: You can either keep the bond and continue to earn interest on it, or you can exchange it for common stock of the issuing company at a predetermined ratio. (An option gives its owner the right to buy or sell another security at a given price within a specific period of time.) Because they are exchangeable into stock, convertibles pay lower rates of interest than most comparable bonds. On the other hand, if a company's stock price soars, a convertible bond exchangeable into that stock will perform much better than a conventional bond. (Conversely, the typical convertible—with its lower interest rate—will fare worse in a falling bond market.)[1]

---

[1] As a brief example of how convertible bonds work in practice, consider the 4.75% convertible subordinated notes issued by DoubleClick Inc. in 1999. They pay $47.50 in interest per year and are each convertible into 24.24 shares of the company's common stock, a "conversion ratio" of 24.24. As of year-end 2002, DoubleClick's stock was priced at $5.66 a share, giving each bond a "conversion value" of $137.20 ($5.66 × 24.24). Yet the bonds traded roughly six times higher, at $881.30—creating a "conversion premium," or excess over their conversion value, of 542%. If you bought at that price, your "break-even time," or "payback period," was very long. (You paid roughly $750 more than the conversion value of the bond, so it will take nearly 16 years of $47.50 interest payments for you to "earn back" that con-

From 1957 through 2002, according to Ibbotson Associates, convertible bonds earned an annual average return of 8.3%–only two percentage points below the total return on stocks, but with steadier prices and shallower losses.[2] More income, less risk than stocks: No wonder Wall Street's salespeople often describe convertibles as a "best of both worlds" investment. But the intelligent investor will quickly realize that convertibles offer less income and more risk than most other *bonds.* So they could, by the same logic and with equal justice, be called a "worst of both worlds" investment. Which side you come down on depends on how you use them.

In truth, convertibles act more like stocks than bonds. The return on convertibles is about 83% correlated to the Standard & Poor's 500-stock index–but only about 30% correlated to the performance of Treasury bonds. Thus, "converts" zig when most bonds zag. For conservative investors with most or all of their assets in bonds, adding a diversified bundle of converts is a sensible way to seek stock-like returns without having to take the scary step of investing in stocks directly. You could call convertible bonds "stocks for chickens."

As convertibles expert F. Barry Nelson of Advent Capital Management points out, this roughly $200 billion market has blossomed since Graham's day. Most converts are now medium-term, in the seven-to-10-year range; roughly half are investment-grade; and many issues now carry some call protection (an assurance against early redemption). All these factors make them less risky than they used to be.[3]

---

version premium.) Since each DoubleClick bond is convertible to just over 24 common shares, the stock will have to rise from $5.66 to more than $36 if conversion is to become a practical option before the bonds mature in 2006. Such a stock return is not impossible, but it borders on the miraculous. The cash yield on this particular bond scarcely seems adequate, given the low probability of conversion.

[2] Like many of the track records commonly cited on Wall Street, this one is hypothetical. It indicates the return you would have earned in an imaginary index fund that owned all major convertibles. It does not include any management fees or trading costs (which are substantial for convertible securities). In the real world, your returns would have been roughly two percentage points lower.

[3] However, most convertible bonds remain junior to other long-term debt and bank loans–so, in a bankruptcy, convertible holders do not have prior

It's expensive to trade small lots of convertible bonds, and diversification is impractical unless you have well over $100,000 to invest in this sector alone. Fortunately, today's intelligent investor has the convenient recourse of buying a low-cost convertible bond fund. Fidelity and Vanguard offer mutual funds with annual expenses comfortably under 1%, while several closed-end funds are also available at a reasonable cost (and, occasionally, at discounts to net asset value).[4]

On Wall Street, cuteness and complexity go hand-in-hand—and convertibles are no exception. Among the newer varieties are a jumble of securities with acronymic nicknames like LYONS, ELKS, EYES, PERCS, MIPS, CHIPS, and YEELDS. These intricate securities put a "floor" under your potential losses, but also cap your potential profits and often compel you to convert into common stock on a fixed date. Like most investments that purport to ensure against loss (see sidebar on p. 421), these things are generally more trouble than they are worth. You can best shield yourself against loss not by buying one of these quirky contraptions, but by intelligently diversifying your entire portfolio across cash, bonds, and U.S. and foreign stocks.

---

claim to the company's assets. And, while they are not nearly as dicey as high-yield "junk" bonds, many converts are still issued by companies with less than sterling credit ratings. Finally, a large portion of the convertible market is held by hedge funds, whose rapid-fire trading can increase the volatility of prices.

[4] For more detail, see www.fidelity.com, www.vanguard.com, and www.morningstar.com. The intelligent investor will *never* buy a convertible bond fund with annual operating expenses exceeding 1.0%.

UNCOVERING COVERED CALLS

As the bear market clawed its way through 2003, it dug up an old fad: writing covered call options. (A recent Google search on "covered call writing" turned up more than 2,600 hits.) What are covered calls, and how do they work? Imagine that you buy 100 shares of Ixnay Corp. at $95 apiece. You then sell (or "write") a call option on your shares. In exchange, you get a cash payment known as a "call premium." (Let's say it's $10 per share.) The buyer of the option, meanwhile, has the contractual right to buy your Ixnay shares at a mutually agreed-upon price–say, $100. You get to keep the stock so long as it stays below $100, and you earn a fat $1,000 in premium income, which will cushion the fall if Ixnay's stock crashes.

Less risk, more income. What's not to like?

Well, now imagine that Ixnay's stock price jumps overnight to $110. Then your option buyer will exercise his rights, yanking your shares away for $100 apiece. You've still got your $1,000 in income, but he's got your Ixnay–and the more it goes up, the harder you will kick yourself.[1]

Since the potential gain on a stock is unlimited, while no loss can exceed 100%, the only person you will enrich with this strategy is your broker. You've put a floor under your losses, but you've also slapped a ceiling over your gains. For individual investors, covering your downside is never worth surrendering most of your upside.

---

[1] Alternatively, you could buy back the call option, but you would have to take a loss on it–and options can have even higher trading costs than stocks.

CHAPTER 17

Four Extremely Instructive Case Histories

The word "extremely" in the title is a kind of pun, because the histories represent extremes of various sorts that were manifest on Wall Street in recent years. They hold instruction, and grave warnings, for everyone who has a serious connection with the world of stocks and bonds—not only for ordinary investors and speculators but for professionals, security analysts, fund managers, trust-account administrators, and even for bankers who lend money to corporations. The four companies to be reviewed, and the different extremes that they illustrate are:

Penn Central (Railroad) Co. An extreme example of the neglect of the most elementary warning signals of financial weakness, by all those who had bonds or shares of this system under their supervision. A crazily high market price for the stock of a tottering giant.

Ling-Temco-Vought Inc. An extreme example of quick and unsound "empire building," with ultimate collapse practically guaranteed; but helped by indiscriminate bank lending.

NVF Corp. An extreme example of one corporate acquisition, in which a small company absorbed another seven times its size, incurring a huge debt and employing some startling accounting devices.

AAA Enterprises. An extreme example of public stock-financing of a small company; its value based on the magic word "franchising," and little else, sponsored by important stock-exchange houses. Bankruptcy followed within two years of the stock sale and the doubling of the initial inflated price in the heedless stock market.

The Penn Central Case

This is the country's largest railroad in assets and gross revenues. Its bankruptcy in 1970 shocked the financial world. It has defaulted on most of its bond issues, and has been in danger of abandoning its operations entirely. Its security issues fell drastically in price, the common stock collapsing from a high level of 86½ as recently as 1968 to a low of 5½ in 1970. (There seems little doubt that these shares will be wiped out in reorganization.)*

Our basic point is that the application of the simplest rules of security analysis and the simplest standards of sound investment would have revealed the fundamental weakness of the Penn Central system long before its bankruptcy—certainly in 1968, when the shares were selling at their post-1929 record, and when most of its bond issues could have been exchanged at even prices for well-secured public-utility obligations with the same coupon rates. The following comments are in order:

1. In the S & P *Bond Guide* the interest charges of the system are shown to have been earned 1.91 times in 1967 and 1.98 times in 1968. The minimum coverage prescribed for railroad bonds in our textbook *Security Analysis* is 5 times before income taxes and 2.9 times after income taxes at regular rates. As far as we know the validity of these standards has never been questioned by any investment authority. On the basis of our requirements for earnings *after taxes,* the Penn Central fell short of the requirements for safety. But our after-tax requirement is based on a before-tax ratio of *five* times, with regular income tax deducted after the bond interest. In the case of Penn Central, it had been paying *no income taxes to speak of* for the past 11 years! Hence the coverage of its interest charges before taxes was less than two times—a totally inadequate figure against our conservative requirement of 5 times.

---

* How "shocked" was the financial world by the Penn Central's bankruptcy, which was filed over the weekend of June 20–21, 1970? The closing trade in Penn Central's stock on Friday, June 19, was $11.25 per share–hardly a going-out-of-business price. In more recent times, stocks like Enron and WorldCom have also sold at relatively high prices shortly before filing for bankruptcy protection.

2. The fact that the company paid no income taxes over so long a period should have raised serious questions about the *validity* of its reported earnings.

3. The bonds of the Penn Central system could have been exchanged in 1968 and 1969, at no sacrifice of price or income, for far better secured issues. For example, in 1969, Pennsylvania RR 4½s, due 1994 (part of Penn Central) had a range of 61 to 74½, while Pennsylvania Electric Co. 4⅜s, due 1994, had a range of 64¼ to 72¼. The public utility had earned its interest 4.20 times before taxes in 1968 against only 1.98 times for the Penn Central system; during 1969 the latter's comparative showing grew steadily worse. An exchange of this sort was clearly called for, and it would have been a lifesaver for a Penn Central bondholder. (At the end of 1970 the railroad 4¼s were in default, and selling at only 18½, while the utility's 4⅜s closed at 66½.)

4. Penn Central reported earnings of $3.80 per share in 1968; its high price of 86½ in that year was 24 times such earnings. But any analyst worth his salt would have wondered how "real" were earnings of this sort reported without the necessity of paying any income taxes thereon.

5. For 1966 the newly merged company* had reported "earnings" of $6.80 a share—in reflection of which the common stock later rose to its peak of 86½. This was a valuation of over $2 billion for the equity. How many of these buyers knew at the time that the so lovely earnings were *before* a special charge of $275 million or $12 per share to be taken in 1971 for "costs and losses" incurred on the merger. O wondrous fairyland of Wall Street where a company can announce "profits" of $6.80 per share in one place and special "costs and losses" of $12 in another, and shareholders and speculators rub their hands with glee!†

---

* Penn Central was the product of the merger, announced in 1966, of the Pennsylvania Railroad and the New York Central Railroad.

† This kind of accounting legerdemain, in which profits are reported as if "unusual" or "extraordinary" or "nonrecurring" charges do not matter, anticipates the reliance on "pro forma" financial statements that became popular in the late 1990s (see the commentary on Chapter 12).

6. A railroad analyst would have long since known that the operating picture of the Penn Central was very bad in comparison with the more profitable roads. For example, its transportation ratio was 47.5% in 1968 against 35.2% for its neighbor, Norfolk & Western.*

7. Along the way there were some strange transactions with peculiar accounting results.[1] Details are too complicated to go into here.

CONCLUSION: Whether better management could have saved the Penn Central bankruptcy may be arguable. But there is no doubt whatever that no bonds and no shares of the Penn Central system should have remained after 1968 at the latest in any securities account watched over by competent security analysts, fund managers, trust officers, or investment counsel. *Moral:* Security analysts should do their elementary jobs before they study stock-market movements, gaze into crystal balls, make elaborate mathematical calculations, or go on all-expense-paid field trips.†

Ling-Temco-Vought Inc.

This is a story of head-over-heels expansion and head-over-heels debt, ending up in terrific losses and a host of financial problems. As usually happens in such cases, a fair-haired boy, or "young genius," was chiefly responsible for both the creation of the great empire and its ignominious downfall; but there is plenty of blame to be accorded others as well.‡

---

* A railroad's "transportation ratio" (now more commonly called its operating ratio) measures the expenses of running its trains divided by the railroad's total revenues. The higher the ratio, the less efficient the railroad. Today even a ratio of 70% would be considered excellent.

† Today, Penn Central is a faded memory. In 1976, it was absorbed into Consolidated Rail Corp. (Conrail), a federally-funded holding company that bailed out several failed railroads. Conrail sold shares to the public in 1987 and, in 1997, was taken over jointly by CSX Corp. and Norfolk Southern Corp.

‡ Ling-Temco-Vought Inc. was founded in 1955 by James Joseph Ling, an electrical contractor who sold his first $1 million worth of shares to the pub-

The rise and fall of Ling-Temco-Vought can be summarized by setting forth condensed income accounts and balance-sheet items for five years between 1958 and 1970. This is done in Table 17-1. The first column shows the company's modest beginnings in 1958, when its sales were only $7 million. The next gives figures for 1960; the enterprise had grown twentyfold in only two years, but it was still comparatively small. Then came the heyday years to 1967 and 1968, in which sales again grew twentyfold to $2.8 billion with the debt figure expanding from $44 million to an awesome $1,653 million. In 1969 came new acquisitions, a further huge increase in debt (to a total of $1,865 million!), and the beginning of serious trouble. A large loss, after extraordinary items, was reported for the year; the stock price declined from its 1967 high of 169½ to a low of 24; the young genius was superseded as the head of the company. The 1970 results were even more dreadful. The enterprise reported a final net loss of close to $70 million; the stock fell away to a low price of 7⅛, and its largest bond issue was quoted at one time at a pitiable 15 cents on the dollar. The company's expansion policy was sharply reversed, various of its important interests were placed on the market, and some headway was made in reducing its mountainous obligations.

The figures in our table speak so eloquently that few comments are called for. But here are some:

---

lic by becoming his own investment banker, hawking prospectuses from a booth set up at the Texas State Fair. His success at that led him to acquire dozens of different companies, almost always using LTV's stock to pay for them. The more companies LTV acquired, the higher its stock went; the higher its stock went, the more companies it could afford to acquire. By 1969, LTV was the 14th biggest firm on the *Fortune* 500 list of major U.S. corporations. And then, as Graham shows, the whole house of cards came crashing down. (LTV Corp., now exclusively a steelmaker, ended up seeking bankruptcy protection in late 2000.) Companies that grow primarily through acquisitions are called "serial acquirers"—and the similarity to the term "serial killers" is no accident. As the case of LTV demonstrates, serial acquirers nearly always leave financial death and destruction in their wake. Investors who understood this lesson of Graham's would have avoided such darlings of the 1990s as Conseco, Tyco, and WorldCom.

TABLE 17-1 Ling-Temco-Vought Inc., 1958–1970 (In Millions of Dollars Except Earned Per Share)

A. Operating Results	1958	1960	1967	1969	1970
Sales	$ 6.9	$143.0	$1,833.0	$3,750.0	$374.0
Net before taxes and interest	0.552	7.287	95.6	124.4	88.0
Interest charges	.1 (est.)	1.5 (est.)	17.7	122.6	128.3
(Times earned)	(5.5 ×)	(4.8 ×)	(54 ×)	(1.02 ×)	(0.68 ×)
Income taxes	0.225	2.686	35.6	*cr.* 15.2	4.9
Special items				*dr.* 40.6	*dr.* 18.8
Net after special items	0.227	3.051	34.0	*dr.* 38.3	*dr.* 69.6
Balance for common stock	0.202	3.051	30.7	*dr.* 40.8	*dr.* 71.3
Earned per share of common	0.17	0.83	5.56	*def.* 10.59	*def.* 17.18
B. Financial Position					
Total assets	6.4	94.5	845.0	2,944.0	2,582.0
Debt payable within 1 year	1.5	29.3	165.0	389.3	301.3
Long-term debt	.5	14.6	202.6	1,500.8	1,394.6
Shareholders' equity	2.7	28.5	245.0†	*def.* 12.0*	*def.* 69.0*
Ratios					
Current assets/current liabilities	1.27 ×	1.45 ×	1.80 ×	1.52 ×	1.45 ×
Equity/long-term debt	5.4 ×	2.0 ×	1.2 ×	0.17 ×	0.13 ×
Market-price range		28–20	169½–109	97¾–24⅛	29½–7⅛

* Excluding debt-discount as an asset and deducting preferred stock at redemption value.

† As published. *cr.:* credit. *dr.:* debit. *def.:* deficit.

1. The company's expansion period was not without an interruption. In 1961 it showed a small operating deficit, but—adopting a practice that was to be seen later in so many reports for 1970—evidently decided to throw all possible charges and reserves into the one bad year.* These amounted to a round $13 million, which was more than the combined net profits of the preceding three years. It was now ready to show "record earnings" in 1962, etc.

2. At the end of 1966 the net tangible assets are given as $7.66 per share of common (adjusted for a 3-for-2 split). Thus the market price in 1967 reached 22 times (!) its reported asset value at the time. At the end of 1968 the balance sheet showed $286 million available for 3,800,000 shares of common and Class AA stock, or about $77 per share. But if we deduct the preferred stock at full value and exclude the good-will items and the huge bond-discount "asset,"† there would remain $13 million for the common—a mere $3 per share. This tangible equity was wiped out by the losses of the following years.

3. Toward the end of 1967 two of our best-regarded banking firms offered 600,000 shares of Ling-Temco-Vought stock at $111 per share. It had been as high as 169½. In less than three years the price fell to 7⅛.‡

---

* The sordid tradition of hiding a company's true earnings picture under the cloak of restructuring charges is still with us. Piling up every possible charge in one year is sometimes called "big bath" or "kitchen sink" accounting. This bookkeeping gimmick enables companies to make an easy show of apparent growth in the following year–but investors should not mistake that for real business health.

† The "bond-discount asset" appears to mean that LTV had purchased some bonds below their par value and was treating that discount as an asset, on the grounds that the bonds could eventually be sold at par. Graham scoffs at this, since there is rarely any way to know what a bond's market price will be on a given date in the future. If the bonds could be sold only at values *below* par, this "asset" would in fact be a liability.

‡ We can only imagine what Graham would have thought of the investment banking firms that brought InfoSpace, Inc. public in December 1998. The stock (adjusted for later splits) opened for trading at $31.25, peaked at

4. At the end of 1967 the bank loans had reached $161 million, and a year later they stood at $414 million—which should have been a frightening figure. In addition, the long-term debt amounted to $1,237 million. By 1969 combined debt reached a total of $1,869 million. This may have been the largest combined debt figure of any industrial company anywhere and at any time, with the single exception of the impregnable Standard Oil of N.J.

5. The losses in 1969 and 1970 far exceeded the total profits since the formation of the company.

MORAL: The primary question raised in our mind by the Ling-Temco-Vought story is how the commercial bankers could have been persuaded to lend the company such huge amounts of money during its expansion period. In 1966 and earlier the company's coverage of interest charges did not meet conservative standards, and the same was true of the ratio of current assets to current liabilities and of stock equity to total debt. But in the next two years the banks advanced the enterprise nearly $400 million additional for further "diversification." This was not good business for them, and it was worse in its implications for the company's shareholders. If the Ling-Temco-Vought case will serve to keep commercial banks from aiding and abetting unsound expansions of this type in the future, some good may come of it at last.*

The NVF Takeover of Sharon Steel (A Collector's Item)

At the end of 1968 NVF Company was a company with $4.6 million of long-term debt, $17.4 million of stock capital, $31 million of sales, and $502,000 of net income (before a special credit of $374,000). Its business was described as "vulcanized fiber and plastics." The management decided to take over the Sharon Steel Corp.,

---

$1305.32 per share in March 2000, and finished 2002 at a princely $8.45 per share.

* Graham would have been disappointed, though surely not surprised, to see that commercial banks have chronically kept supporting "unsound expansions." Enron and WorldCom, two of the biggest collapses in corporate history, were aided and abetted by billions of dollars in bank loans.

which had $43 million of long-term debt, $101 million of stock capital, $219 million of sales, and $2,929,000 of net earnings. The company it wished to acquire was thus seven times the size of NVF. In early 1969 it made an offer for all the shares of Sharon. The terms per share were $70 face amount of NVF junior 5% bonds, due 1994, plus warrants to buy 1½ shares of NVF stock at $22 per share of NVF. The management of Sharon strenuously resisted this takeover attempt, but in vain. NVF acquired 88% of the Sharon stock under the offer, issuing therefore $102 million of its 5% bonds and warrants for 2,197,000 of its shares. Had the offer been 100% operative the consolidated enterprise would, for the year 1968, have had $163 million in debt, only $2.2 million in tangible stock capital, $250 million of sales. The net-earnings question would have been a bit complicated, but the company subsequently stated them as a net loss of 50 cents per share of NVF stocks, before an extraordinary credit, and net earnings of 3 cents per share after such credit.*

First Comment: Among all the takeovers effected in the year 1969 this was no doubt the most extreme in its financial disproportions. The acquiring company had assumed responsibility for a new and top-heavy debt obligation, and it had changed its calculated 1968 earnings from a profit to a loss into the bargain. A measure of the impairment of the company's financial position by this

* In June 1972 (just after Graham finished this chapter), a Federal judge found that NVF's chairman, Victor Posner, had improperly diverted the pension assets of Sharon Steel "to assist affiliated companies in their takeovers of other corporations." In 1977, the U.S. Securities and Exchange Commission secured a permanent injunction against Posner, NVF, and Sharon Steel to prevent them from future violations of Federal laws against securities fraud. The Commission alleged that Posner and his family had improperly obtained $1.7 million in personal perks from NVF and Sharon, overstated Sharon's pretax earnings by $13.9 million, misrecorded inventory, and "shifted income and expenses from one year to another." Sharon Steel, which Graham had singled out with his cold and skeptical eye, became known among Wall Street wags as "Share and Steal." Posner was later a central force in the wave of leveraged buyouts and hostile takeovers that swept the United States in the 1980s, as he became a major customer for the junk bonds underwritten by Drexel Burnham Lambert.

step is found in the fact that the new 5% bonds did not sell higher than 42 cents on the dollar during the year of issuance. This would have indicated grave doubt of the safety of the bonds and of the company's future; however, the management actually exploited the bond price in a way to save the company annual income taxes of about $1,000,000 as will be shown.

The 1968 report, published after the Sharon takeover, contained a condensed picture of its results, carried back to the year-end. This contained two most unusual items:

1. There is listed as an asset $58,600,000 of "deferred debt expense." This sum is greater than the entire "stockholders' equity," placed at $40,200,000.

2. However, not included in the shareholders' equity is an item of $20,700,000 designated as "excess of equity over cost of investment in Sharon."

Second Comment: If we eliminate the debt expense as an asset, which it hardly seems to be, and include the other item in the shareholders' equity (where it would normally belong), then we have a more realistic statement of tangible equity for NVF stock, viz., $2,200,000. Thus the first effect of the deal was to reduce NVF's "real equity" from $17,400,000 to $2,200,000 or from $23.71 per share to about $3 per share, on 731,000 shares. In addition the NVF shareholders had given to others the right to buy 3½ times as many additional shares at six points below the market price at the close of 1968. The initial market value of the warrants was then about $12 each, or a total of some $30 million for those involved in the purchase offer. Actually, the market value of the warrants well exceeded the total market value of the outstanding NVF stock—another evidence of the tail-wagging-dog nature of the transaction.

The Accounting Gimmicks

When we pass from this pro forma balance sheet to the next year's report we find several strange-appearing entries. In addition to the basic interest expense (a hefty $7,500,000), there is deducted $1,795,000 for "amortization of deferred debt expense." But this last is nearly offset on the next line by a very unusual income item indeed: "amortization of equity over cost of investment in subsidiary: Cr. $1,650,000." In one of the footnotes we find an entry, not appearing in any other report that we know of: Part of the stock capital is there designated as "fair market value of warrants issued in connection with acquisition, etc., $22,129,000."

What on earth do all these entries mean? None of them is even referred to in the descriptive text of the 1969 report. The trained security analyst has to figure out these mysteries by himself, almost in detective fashion. He finds that the underlying idea is to derive a tax advantage from the low initial price of the 5% debentures. For readers who may be interested in this ingenious arrangement we set forth our solution in Appendix 6.

Other Unusual Items

1. Right after the close of 1969 the company bought in no less than 650,000 warrants at a price of $9.38 each. This was extraordinary when we consider that (*a*) NVF itself had only $700,000 in cash at the year-end, and had $4,400,000 of debt due in 1970 (evidently the $6 million paid for the warrants had to be borrowed); (*b*) it was buying in this warrant "paper money" at a time when its 5% bonds were selling at less than 40 cents on the dollar—ordinarily a warning that financial difficulties lay ahead.

2. As a partial offset to this, the company had retired $5,100,000 of its bonds along with 253,000 warrants in exchange for a like amount of common stock. This was possible because, by the vagaries of the securities markets, people were selling the 5% bonds at less than 40 while the common sold at an average price of 13½, paying no dividend.

3. The company had plans in operation not only for selling stock to its employees, but also for selling them a larger number of *warrants* to buy the stock. Like the stock purchases the warrants were to be paid for 5% down and the rest over many years in the future. This is the only such employee-purchase plan for *warrants* that we know of. Will someone soon invent and sell on installments a right to buy a right to buy a share, and so on?

4. In the year 1969 the newly controlled Sharon Steel Co. changed its method of arriving at its pension costs, and also

adopted lower depreciation rates. These accounting changes added about $1 per share to the reported earnings of NVF before dilution.

5. At the end of 1970 Standard & Poor's *Stock Guide* reported that NVF shares were selling at a price/earning ratio of only 2, the lowest figure for all the 4,500-odd issues in the booklet. As the old Wall Street saying went, this was "important if true." The ratio was based on the year's closing price of 8¾ and the computed "earnings" of $5.38 per share for the 12 months ended September 1970. (Using these figures the shares were selling at only 1.6 times earnings.) But this ratio did not allow for the large dilution factor,* nor for the adverse results actually realized in the last quarter of 1970. When the full year's figures finally appeared, they showed only $2.03 per share earned for the stock, before allowing for dilution, and $1.80 per share on a diluted basis. Note also that the aggregate market price of the stock and warrants on that date was about $14 million against a bonded debt of $135 million—a skimpy equity position indeed.

AAA Enterprises

History

About 15 years ago a college student named Williams began selling mobile homes (then called "trailers").† In 1965 he incorpo-

---

* The "large dilution factor" would be triggered when NVF employees exercised their warrants to buy common stock. The company would then have to issue more shares, and its net earnings would be divided across a much greater number of shares outstanding.

† Jackie G. Williams founded AAA Enterprises in 1958. On its first day of trading, the stock soared 56% to close at $20.25. Williams later announced that AAA would come up with a new franchising concept every month (if people would step into a mobile home to get their income taxes done by "Mr. Tax of America," just imagine what else they might do inside a trailer!). But AAA ran out of time and money before Williams ran out of ideas. The history of AAA Enterprises is reminiscent of the saga of a later company with charismatic management and scanty assets: ZZZZ Best achieved a stock-market value of roughly $200 million in the late 1980s, even though its purported industrial vacuum-cleaning business was little more than a telephone and a rented office run by a teenager named Barry Minkow. ZZZZ Best went bust and Minkow

rated his business. In that year he sold $5,800,000 of mobile homes and earned $61,000 before corporate tax. By 1968 he had joined the "franchising" movement and was selling others the right to sell mobile homes under his business name. He also conceived the bright idea of going into the business of preparing income-tax returns, using his mobile homes as offices. He formed a subsidiary company called Mr. Tax of America, and of course started to sell franchises to others to use the idea and the name. He multiplied the number of corporate shares to 2,710,000 and was ready for a stock offering. He found that one of our largest stock-exchange houses, along with others, was willing to handle the deal. In March 1969 they offered the public 500,000 shares of AAA Enterprises at $13 per share. Of these, 300,000 were sold for Mr. Williams's personal account and 200,000 were sold for the company account, adding $2,400,000 to its resources. The price of the stock promptly doubled to 28, or a value of $84 million for the equity, against a book value of, say, $4,200,000 and maximum reported earnings of $690,000. The stock was thus selling at a tidy 115 times its current (and largest) earnings per share. No doubt Mr. Williams had selected the name AAA Enterprise so that it might be among the first in the phone books and the yellow pages. A collateral result was that his company was destined to appear as the first name in Standard & Poor's *Stock Guide.* Like Abu-Ben-Adhem's, it led all the rest.* This gives a special reason to select it as a harrowing example of 1969 new financing and "hot issues."

COMMENT: This was not a bad deal for Mr. Williams. The 300,000 shares he sold had a book value in December of 1968 of $180,000 and he netted therefor 20 times as much, or a cool $3,600,000. The underwriters and distributors split $500,000 between them, less expenses.

---

went to jail. Even as you read this, another similar company is being formed, and a new generation of "investors" will be taken for a ride. No one who has read Graham, however, should climb on board.

* In "Abou Ben Adhem," by the British Romantic poet Leigh Hunt (1784–1859), a righteous Muslim sees an angel writing in a golden book "the names of those who love the Lord." When the angel tells Abou that his name is not among them, Abou says, "I pray thee, then, write me as one that loves his fellow men." The angel returns the next night to show Abou the book, in which now "Ben Adhem's name led all the rest."

1. This did not seem so brilliant a deal for the clients of the selling houses. They were asked to pay about ten times the book value of the stock, after the bootstrap operation of increasing their equity per share from 59 cents to $1.35 with their own money.* Before the best year 1968, the company's maximum earnings had been a ridiculous 7 cents per share. There were ambitious plans for the future, of course—but the public was being asked to pay heavily in advance for the hoped-for realization of these plans.

2. Nonetheless, the price of the stock doubled soon after original issuance, and any one of the brokerage-house clients could have gotten out at a handsome profit. Did this fact alter the flotation, or did the advance possibility that it might happen exonerate the original distributors of the issue from responsibility for this public offering and its later sequel? Not an easy question to answer, but it deserves careful consideration by Wall Street and the government regulatory agencies.†

Subsequent History

With its enlarged capital AAA Enterprises went into two additional businesses. In 1969 it opened a chain of retail carpet stores, and it acquired a plant that manufactured mobile homes. The results reported for the first nine months were not exactly brilliant, but they were a little better than the year before—22 cents a share against 14

---

* By purchasing more common stock at a premium to its book value, the investing public increased the value of AAA's equity per share. But investors were only pulling themselves up by their own bootstraps, since most of the rise in shareholders' equity came from the public's own willingness to overpay for the stock.

† Graham's point is that investment banks are not entitled to take credit for the gains a hot stock may produce right after its initial public offering unless they are also willing to take the blame for the stock's performance in the longer term. Many Internet IPOs rose 1,000% or more in 1999 and early 2000; most of them lost more than 95% in the subsequent three years. How could these early gains earned by a few investors justify the massive destruction of wealth suffered by the millions who came later? Many IPOs were, in fact, deliberately underpriced to "manufacture" immediate gains that would attract more attention for the next offering.

cents. What happened in the next months was literally incredible. The company lost $4,365,000, or $1.49 per share. This consumed all its capital before the financing, plus the entire $2,400,000 received on the sale of stock plus two-thirds of the amount reported as earned in the first nine months of 1969. There was left a pathetic $242,000, or 8 cents per share, of capital for the public shareholders who had paid $13 for the new offering only seven months before. Nonetheless the shares closed the year 1969 at 8⅛ bid, or a "valuation" of more than $25 million for the company.

FURTHER COMMENT: 1. It is too much to believe that the company had actually earned $686,000 from January to September 1969 and then lost $4,365,000 in the next three months. There was something sadly, badly, and accusingly wrong about the September 30 report.

2. The year's closing price of 8⅛ bid was even more of a demonstration of the complete heedlessness of stock-market prices than were the original offering price of 13 or the subsequent "hot-issue" advance to a high bid of 28. These latter quotations at least were based on enthusiasm and hope—out of all proportion to reality and common sense, but at least comprehensible. The year-end valuation of $25 million was given to a company that had lost all but a minuscule remnant of its capital, for which a completely insolvent condition was imminent, and for which the words "enthusiasm" or "hope" would be only bitter sarcasms. (It is true the year-end figures had not been published by December 31, but it is the business of Wall Street houses associated with a company to have monthly operating statements and a fairly exact idea of how things are going.)

Final Chapter

For the first half of 1970 the company reported a further loss of $1 million. It now had a good-sized capital deficit. It was kept out of bankruptcy by loans made by Mr. Williams, up to a total of $2,500,000. No further statements seem to have been issued, until in January 1971 AAA Enterprises finally filed a petition in bankruptcy. The quotation for the stock at month-end was still 50 cents a share bid, or $1,500,000 for the entire issue, which evidently had no more than wallpaper value. End of our story.

MORAL AND QUESTIONS: The speculative public is incorrigible. In financial terms it cannot count beyond 3. It will buy anything, at any price, if there seems to be some "action" in progress. It will fall for any company identified with "franchising," computers, electronics, science, technology, or what have you, when the particular fashion is raging. Our readers, sensible investors all, are of course above such foolishness. But questions remain: Should not responsible investment houses be honor-bound to refrain from identifying themselves with such enterprises, nine out of ten of which may be foredoomed to ultimate failure? (This was actually the situation when the author entered Wall Street in 1914. By comparison it would seem that the ethical standards of the "Street" have fallen rather than advanced in the ensuing 57 years, despite all the reforms and all the controls.) Could and should the SEC be given other powers to protect the public, beyond the present ones which are limited to requiring the printing of all important relevant facts in the offering prospectus? Should some kind of box score for public offerings of various types be compiled and published in conspicuous fashion? Should every prospectus, and perhaps every confirmation of sale under an original offering, carry some kind of formal warranty that the offering price for the issue is not substantially out of line with the ruling prices for issues of the same general type already established in the market? As we write this edition a movement toward reform of Wall Street abuses is under way. It will be difficult to impose worthwhile changes in the field of new offerings, because the abuses are so largely the result of the public's own heedlessness and greed. But the matter deserves long and careful consideration.*

---

* The first four sentences of Graham's paragraph could read as the official epitaph of the Internet and telecommunications bubble that burst in early 2000. Just as the Surgeon General's warning on the side of a cigarette pack does not stop everyone from lighting up, no regulatory reform will ever prevent investors from overdosing on their own greed. (Not even Communism can outlaw market bubbles; the Chinese stock market shot up 101.7% in the first half of 1999, then crashed.) Nor can investment banks ever be entirely cleansed of their own compulsion to sell any stock at any price the market will bear. The circle can only be broken one investor, and one financial adviser, at a time. Mastering Graham's principles (see especially Chapters 1, 8, and 20) is the best way to start.

COMMENTARY ON CHAPTER 17

> The wisdom god, Woden, went out to the king of the trolls, got him in an armlock, and demanded to know of him how order might triumph over chaos. "Give me your left eye," said the troll, "and I'll tell you." Without hesitation, Woden gave up his left eye. "Now tell me." The troll said, "The secret is, 'Watch with both eyes!' "
>
> *—John Gardner*

THE MORE THINGS CHANGE . . .

Graham highlights four extremes:

- an overpriced "tottering giant"
- an empire-building conglomerate
- a merger in which a tiny firm took over a big one
- an initial public offering of shares in a basically worthless company

The past few years have provided enough new cases of Graham's extremes to fill an encyclopedia. Here is a sampler:

LUCENT, NOT TRANSPARENT

In mid-2000, Lucent Technologies Inc. was owned by more investors than any other U.S. stock. With a market capitalization of $192.9 billion, it was the 12th-most-valuable company in America.

Was that giant valuation justified? Let's look at some basics from Lucent's financial report for the fiscal quarter ended June 30, 2000:[1]

---

[1] This document, like all the financial reports cited in this chapter, is readily available to the public through the EDGAR Database at www.sec.gov.

FIGURE 17-1 Lucent Technologies Inc.

	For the quarter ended . . .	
	June 30, 2000	June 30, 1999
Income		
Revenues	8,713	7,403
Income (loss) from continuing operations	(14)	622
Income (loss) from discontinued operations	(287)	141
Net income	(301)	763
Assets		
Cash	710	1,495
Receivables	10,101	9,486
Goodwill	8,736	3,340*
Capitalized software development costs	576	412
Total assets	46,340	37,156

All numbers in millions of dollars. * Other assets, which includes goodwill.
Source: Lucent quarterly financial reports (Form 10-Q).

A closer reading of Lucent's report sets alarm bells jangling like an unanswered telephone switchboard:

- Lucent had just bought an optical equipment supplier, Chromatis Networks, for $4.8 billion–of which $4.2 billion was "goodwill" (or cost above book value). Chromatis had 150 employees, no customers, and zero revenues, so the term "goodwill" seems inadequate; perhaps "hope chest" is more accurate. If Chromatis's embryonic products did not work out, Lucent would have to reverse the goodwill and charge it off against future earnings.
- A footnote discloses that Lucent had lent $1.5 billion to purchasers of its products. Lucent was also on the hook for $350 million in guarantees for money its customers had borrowed elsewhere. The total of these "customer financings" had doubled in a year–suggesting that purchasers were running out of cash to buy Lucent's products. What if they ran out of cash to pay their debts?
- Finally, Lucent treated the cost of developing new software as a "capital asset." Rather than an asset, wasn't that a routine business expense that should come out of earnings?

CONCLUSION: In August 2001, Lucent shut down the Chromatis division after its products reportedly attracted only two customers.[2] In fiscal year 2001, Lucent lost $16.2 billion; in fiscal year 2002, it lost another $11.9 billion. Included in those losses were $3.5 billion in "provisions for bad debts and customer financings," $4.1 billion in "impairment charges related to goodwill," and $362 million in charges "related to capitalized software."

Lucent's stock, at $51.062 on June 30, 2000, finished 2002 at $1.26–a loss of nearly $190 billion in market value in two-and-a-half years.

THE ACQUISITION MAGICIAN

To describe Tyco International Ltd., we can only paraphrase Winston Churchill and say that never has so much been sold by so many to so few. From 1997 through 2001, this Bermuda-based conglomerate spent a total of more than $37 billion–most of it in shares of Tyco stock–buying companies the way Imelda Marcos bought shoes. In fiscal year 2000 alone, according to its annual report, Tyco acquired "approximately 200 companies"–an average of more than one every other day.

The result? Tyco grew phenomenally fast; in five years, revenues went from $7.6 billion to $34 billion, and operating income shot from a $476 million loss to a $6.2 billion gain. No wonder the company had a total stock-market value of $114 billion at the end of 2001.

But Tyco's financial statements were at least as mind-boggling as its growth. Nearly every year, they featured hundreds of millions of dollars in acquisition-related charges. These expenses fell into three main categories:

1) "merger" or "restructuring" or "other nonrecurring" costs,
2) "charges for the impairment of long-lived assets," and
3) "write-offs of purchased in-process research and development."

For the sake of brevity, let's refer to the first kind of charge as MORON, the second as CHILLA, and the third as WOOPIPRAD. How did they show up over time?

---

[2] The demise of the Chromatis acquisition is discussed in *The Financial Times*, August 29, 2001, p. 1, and September 1/September 2, 2001, p. XXIII.

FIGURE 17-2 Tyco International Ltd.

	Fiscal year	MORON	CHILLA	WOOPIPRAD
	1997	918	148	361
	1998	0	0	0
	1999	1,183	335	0
	2000	4175	99	0
	2001	234	120	184
Totals		2,510	702	545

All figures are as originally reported, stated in hundreds of millions of dollars.
"Mergers & acquisitions" totals do not include pooling-of-interests deals.
Source: Tyco International annual reports (Form 10-K).

As you can see, the MORON charges—*which are supposed to be nonrecurring*—showed up in four out of five years and totaled a whopping $2.5 billion. CHILLA cropped up just as chronically and amounted to more than $700 million. WOOPIPRAD came to another half-billion dollars.[3]

The intelligent investor would ask:

- If Tyco's strategy of growth-through-acquisition was such a neat idea, how come it had to spend an average of $750 million a year cleaning up after itself?
- If, as seems clear, Tyco was not in the business of making things—but rather in the business of buying other companies that make things—then why were its MORON charges "nonrecurring"? Weren't they just part of Tyco's normal costs of doing business?
- And with accounting charges for past acquisitions junking up every year's earnings, who could tell what next year's would be?

[3] When accounting for acquisitions, loading up on WOOPIPRAD enabled Tyco to reduce the portion of the purchase price that it allocated to goodwill. Since WOOPIPRAD can be expensed up front, while goodwill (under the accounting rules then in force) had to be written off over multi-year periods, this maneuver enabled Tyco to minimize the impact of goodwill charges on its future earnings.

In fact, an investor couldn't even tell what Tyco's *past* earnings were. In 1999, after an accounting review by the U.S. Securities and Exchange Commission, Tyco retroactively added $257 million in MORON charges to its 1998 expenses—meaning that those "nonrecurring" costs had actually recurred in that year, too. At the same time, the company rejiggered its originally reported 1999 charges: MORON dropped to $929 million while CHILLA rose to $507 million.

Tyco was clearly growing in size, but was it growing more profitable? No outsider could safely tell.

CONCLUSION: In fiscal year 2002, Tyco lost $9.4 billion. The stock, which had closed at $58.90 at year-end 2001, finished 2002 at $17.08—a loss of 71% in twelve months.[4]

A MINNOW SWALLOWS A WHALE

On January 10, 2000, America Online, Inc. and Time Warner Inc. announced that they would merge in a deal initially valued at $156 billion.

As of December 31, 1999, AOL had $10.3 billion in assets, and its revenues over the previous 12 months had amounted to $5.7 billion. Time Warner, on the other hand, had $51.2 billion in assets and revenues of $27.3 billion. Time Warner was a vastly bigger company by any measure except one: the valuation of its stock. Because America Online bedazzled investors simply by being in the Internet industry, its stock sold for a stupendous 164 times its earnings. Stock in Time Warner, a grab bag of cable television, movies, music, and magazines, sold for around 50 times earnings.

In announcing the deal, the two companies called it a "strategic merger of equals." Time Warner's chairman, Gerald M. Levin, declared that "the opportunities are limitless for everyone connected to AOL Time Warner"—above all, he added, for its shareholders.

Ecstatic that their stock might finally get the cachet of an Internet

---

[4] In 2002, Tyco's former chief executive, L. Dennis Kozlowski, was charged by state and Federal legal authorities with income tax fraud and improperly diverting Tyco's corporate assets for his own use, including the appropriation of $15,000 for an umbrella stand and $6,000 for a shower curtain. Kozlowski denied all charges.

darling, Time Warner shareholders overwhelmingly approved the deal. But they overlooked a few things:

- This "merger of equals" was designed to give America Online's shareholders 55% of the combined company–even though Time Warner was five times bigger.
- For the second time in three years, the U.S. Securities and Exchange Commission was investigating whether America Online had improperly accounted for marketing costs.
- Nearly half of America Online's total assets–$4.9 billion worth–was made up of "available-for-sale equity securities." If the prices of publicly-traded technology stocks fell, that could wipe out much of the company's asset base.

CONCLUSION: On January 11, 2001, the two firms finalized their merger. AOL Time Warner Inc. lost $4.9 billion in 2001 and–in the most gargantuan loss ever recorded by a corporation–another $98.7 billion in 2002. Most of the losses came from writing down the value of America Online. By year-end 2002, the shareholders for whom Levin predicted "unlimited" opportunities had nothing to show but a roughly 80% loss in the value of their shares since the deal was first announced.[5]

CAN YOU FLUNK INVESTING KINDERGARTEN?

On May 20, 1999, eToys Inc. sold 8% of its stock to the public. Four of Wall Street's most prestigious investment banks–Goldman, Sachs & Co.; BancBoston Robertson Stephens; Donaldson, Lufkin & Jenrette; and Merrill Lynch & Co.–underwrote 8,320,000 shares at $20 apiece, raising $166.4 million. The stock roared up, closing at $76.5625, a 282.8% gain in its first day of trading. At that price, eToys (with its 102 million shares) had a market value of $7.8 billion.[6]

---

[5] Disclosure: Jason Zweig is an employee of Time Inc., formerly a division of Time Warner and now a unit of AOL Time Warner Inc.

[6] eToys' prospectus had a gatefold cover featuring an original cartoon of Arthur the aardvark, showing in comic style how much easier it would be to

What kind of business did buyers get for that price? eToys' sales had risen 4,261% in the previous year, and it had added 75,000 customers in the last quarter alone. But, in its 20 months in business, eToys had produced total sales of $30.6 million, on which it had run a net loss of $30.8 million–meaning that eToys was spending $2 to sell every dollar's worth of toys.

The IPO prospectus also disclosed that eToys would use some proceeds of the offering to acquire another online operation, BabyCenter, Inc., which had lost $4.5 million on $4.8 million in sales over the previous year. (To land this prize, eToys would pay a mere $205 million.) And eToys would "reserve" 40.6 million shares of common stock for future issuance to its management. So, if eToys ever made money, its net income would have to be divided not among 102 million shares, but among 143 million–diluting any future earnings per share by nearly one-third.

A comparison of eToys with Toys "R" Us, Inc.–its biggest rival–is shocking. In the preceding three months, Toys "R" Us had earned $27 million in net income and had sold over 70 times more goods than eToys had sold in an entire year. And yet as Figure 17-3 shows, the stock market valued eToys at nearly $2 billion *more* than Toys "R" Us.

CONCLUSION: On March 7, 2001, eToys filed for bankruptcy protection after racking up net losses of more than $398 million in its brief life as a public company. The stock, which peaked at $86 per share in October 1999, last traded for a penny.

---

buy tchotchkes for children at eToys than at a traditional toy store. As analyst Gail Bronson of IPO Monitor told the Associated Press on the day of eToys' stock offering, "eToys has very, very smartly managed the development of the company last year and positioned themselves to be the children's center of the Internet." Added Bronson: "The key to a successful IPO, especially a dot-com IPO, is good marketing and branding." Bronson was partly right: That's the key to a successful IPO for the issuing company and its bankers. Unfortunately, for *investors* the key to a successful IPO is earnings, which eToys didn't have.

FIGURE 17-3 A Toy Story

	eToys Inc. Fiscal year ended 3/31/1999	Toys "R" Us, Inc. Fiscal quarter ended 5/1/1999
Net sales	30	2,166
Net income	(29)	27
Cash	20	289
Total assets	31	8,067
Market value of common stock (5/20/1999)	7,780	5,650

All amounts in millions of dollars.

Sources: The companies' SEC filings.

CHAPTER 18

A Comparison of Eight Pairs of Companies

In this chapter we shall attempt a novel form of exposition. By selecting eight pairs of companies which appear next to each other, or nearly so, on the stock-exchange list we hope to bring home in a concrete and vivid manner some of the many varieties of character, financial structure, policies, performance, and vicissitudes of corporate enterprises, and of the investment and speculative attitudes found on the financial scene in recent years. In each comparison we shall comment only on those aspects that have a special meaning and import.

Pair I: Real Estate Investment Trust (stores, offices, factories, etc.) and Realty Equities Corp. of New York (real estate investment; general construction)

In this first comparison we depart from the alphabetical order used for the other pairs. It has a special significance for us, since it seems to encapsulate, on the one hand, all that has been reasonable, stable, and generally good in the traditional methods of handling other people's money, in contrast—in the other company—with the reckless expansion, the financial legerdemain, and the roller-coaster changes so often found in present-day corporate operations. The two enterprises have similar names, and for many years they appeared side by side on the American Stock Exchange list. Their stock-ticker symbóls—REI and REC—could easily have been confused. But one of them is a staid New England trust, administered by three trustees, with operations dating back nearly a century, and with dividends paid continuously since 1889. It has kept throughout to the same type of prudent investments, limiting its expansion to a moderate rate and its debt to an easily manageable figure.*

The other is a typical New York-based sudden-growth venture, which in eight years blew up its assets from $6.2 million to $154 million, and its debts in the same proportion; which moved out from ordinary real-estate operations to a miscellany of ventures, including two racetracks, 74 movie theaters, three literary agencies, a public-relations firm, hotels, supermarkets, and a 26% interest in a large cosmetics firm (which went bankrupt in 1970).† This conglomeration of business ventures was matched by a corresponding variety of corporate devices, including the following:

1. A preferred stock entitled to $7 annual dividends, but with a par value of only $1, and carried as a liability at $1 per share.
2. A stated common-stock value of $2,500,000 ($1 per share), more than offset by a deduction of $5,500,000 as the cost of 209,000 shares of reacquired stock.
3. Three series of stock-option warrants, giving rights to buy a total of 1,578,000 shares.
4. At least six different kinds of debt obligations, in the form of mortgages, debentures, publicly held notes, notes payable to banks, "notes, loans, and contracts payable," and loans payable to the Small Business Administration, adding up to over $100 million in March 1969. In addition it had the usual taxes and accounts payable.

Let us present first a few figures of the two enterprises as they appeared in 1960 (Table 18-1A). Here we find the Trust shares selling in the market for nine times the aggregate value of Equities stock. The Trust enterprise had a smaller relative debt and a better

---

* Here Graham is describing Real Estate Investment Trust, which was acquired by San Francisco Real Estate Investors in 1983 for $50 a share. The next paragraph describes Realty Equities Corp. of New York.

† The actor Paul Newman was briefly a major shareholder in Realty Equities Corp. of New York after it bought his movie-production company, Kayos, Inc., in 1969.

TABLE 18-1A. Pair 1. Real Estate Investment Trust vs. Realty Equities Corp. in 1960

	Real Estate Investment Trust	*Realty Equities Corp. of New York*
Gross revenues	$ 3,585,000	$1,484,000
Net income	485,000	150,000
Earned per share	.66	.47
Dividend per share	none	.10
Book value per share	$20.	$4.
Price range	20–12	5⅜–4¾
Total assets	$22,700,000	$6,200,000
Total liabilities	7,400,000	5,000,000
Book value of common	15,300,000	1,200,000
Average market value of common	12,200,000	1,360,000

ratio of net to gross, but the price of the common was higher in relation to per-share earnings.

In Table 18-1B we present the situation about eight years later. The Trust had "kept the noiseless tenor of its way," increasing both its revenues and its per-share earnings by about three-quarters.* But Realty Equities had been metamorphosed into something monstrous and vulnerable.

How did Wall Street react to these diverse developments? By paying as little attention as possible to the Trust and a lot to Realty Equities. In 1968 the latter shot up from 10 to 37¾ and the listed warrants from 6 to 36½, on combined sales of 2,420,000 shares. While this was happening the Trust shares advanced sedately from 20 to 30¼ on modest volume. The March 1969 balance sheet of Equities was to show an asset value of only $3.41 per share, less than a tenth of its high price that year. The book value of the Trust shares was $20.85.

---

* Graham, an avid reader of poetry, is quoting Thomas Gray's "Elegy Written in a Country Churchyard."

TABLE 18-1B. Pair 1.

	Real Estate Investment Trust	*Realty Equities Corp. of New York*
Price, December 31, 1968	26½	32½
Number of shares of common	1,423,000	2,311,000 (March '69)
Market value of common	$37,800,000	$75,000,000
Estimated market value of warrants	—	30,000,000[a]
Estimated market value of common and warrants	—	105,000,000
Debt	9,600,000	100,800,000
Preferred stock	—	2,900,000
Total capitalization	$47,400,000	$208,700,000
Market value per share of common, adjusted for warrants	—	45 (est.)
Book value per share	$20.85 (Nov.)	$3.41
	November 1968	March 1969
Revenues	$6,281,000	$39,706,000
Net for interest	2,696,000	11,182,000
Interest charges	590,000	6,684,000
Income tax	58,000[b]	2,401,000
Preferred dividend		174,000
Net for common	2,048,000	1,943,000
Special items	245,000 cr.	1,896,000 dr.
Final net for common	2,293,000	47,000
Earned per share before special items	$1.28	$1.00
Earned per share after special items	1.45	.20
Dividend on common	1.20	.30
Interest charges earned	4.6 ×	1.8 ×

[a] There were warrants to buy 1,600,000 or more shares at various prices. A listed issue sold at 30½ per warrant.

[b] As a realty trust, this enterprise was not subjected to Federal income tax in 1968.

The next year it became clear that all was not well in the Equities picture, and the price fell to 9½. When the report for March 1970 appeared the shareholders must have felt shell-shocked as they read that the enterprise had sustained a net loss of $13,200,000, or $5.17 per share—virtually wiping out their former slim equity. (This disastrous figure included a reserve of $8,800,000 for future losses on investments.) Nonetheless the directors had bravely (?) declared an extra dividend of 5 cents right after the close of the fiscal year. But more trouble was in sight. The company's auditors refused to certify the financial statements for 1969–70, and the shares were suspended from trading on the American Stock Exchange. In the over-the-counter market the bid price dropped below $2 per share.*

Real Estate Investment Trust shares had typical price fluctuations after 1969. The low in 1970 was 16½, with a recovery to 26⅝ in early 1971. The latest reported earnings were $1.50 per share, and the stock was selling moderately above its 1970 book value of $21.60. The issue may have been somewhat overpriced at its record high in 1968, but the shareholders have been honestly and well served by their trustees. The Real Estate Equities story is a different and a sorry one.

Pair 2: Air Products and Chemicals (industrial and medical gases, etc.) and Air Reduction Co. (industrial gases and equipment; chemicals)

Even more than our first pair, these two resemble each other in both name and line of business. The comparison they invite is thus of the conventional type in security analysis, while most of our other pairs are more heteroclite in nature.† "Products" is a newer

* Realty Equities was delisted from the American Stock Exchange in September 1973. In 1974, the U.S. Securities and Exchange Commission sued Realty Equities' accountants for fraud. Realty Equities' founder, Morris Karp, later pleaded guilty to one count of grand larceny. In 1974–1975, the overindebtedness that Graham criticizes led to a financial crisis among large banks, including Chase Manhattan, that had lent heavily to the most aggressive realty trusts.

† "Heteroclite" is a technical term from classical Greek that Graham uses to mean abnormal or unusual.

company than "Reduction," and in 1969 had less than half the other's volume.* Nonetheless its equity issues sold for 25% more in the aggregate than Air Reduction's stock. As Table 18-2 shows, the reason can be found both in Air Reduction's greater profitability and in its stronger growth record. We find here the typical consequences of a better showing of "quality." Air Products sold at 16½ times its latest earnings against only 9.1 times for Air Reduction. Also Air Products sold well above its asset backing, while Air Reduction could be bought at only 75% of its book value.† Air Reduction paid a more liberal dividend; but this may be deemed to reflect the greater desirability for Air Products to retain its earnings. Also, Air Reduction had a more comfortable working-capital position. (On this point we may remark that a profitable company can always put its current position in shape by some form of permanent financing. But by our standards Air Products was somewhat overbonded.)

If the analyst were called on to choose between the two companies he would have no difficulty in concluding that the prospects of Air Products looked more promising than those of Air Reduction. But did this make Air Products more attractive at its considerably higher relative price? We doubt whether this question can be answered in a definitive fashion. In general Wall Street sets "quality" above "quantity" in its thinking, and probably the majority of security analysts would opt for the "better" but dearer Air Products as against the "poorer" but cheaper Air Reduction. Whether this preference is to prove right or wrong is more likely to depend on the unpredictable future than on any demonstrable investment principle. In this instance, Air Reduction appears to belong to the group of important companies in the low-multiplier class. If, as the studies referred to above†† would seem to indicate, that group *as a*

---

* By "volume," Graham is referring to sales or revenues–the total dollar amount of each company's business.

† "Asset backing" and book value are synonyms. In Table 18-2, the relationship of price to asset or book value can be seen by dividing the first line ("Price, December 31, 1969") by "Book value per share."

†† Graham is citing his research on value stocks, which he discusses in Chapter 15 (see p. 389). Since Graham completed his studies, a vast body of scholarly work has confirmed that value stocks outperform *(cont'd on p. 453)*

whole is likely to give a better account of itself than the high-multiplier stocks, then Air Reduction should logically be given the preference—but only as part of a diversified operation. (Also, a thorough-going study of the individual companies could lead the analyst to the opposite conclusion; but that would have to be for reasons beyond those already reflected in the past showing.)

SEQUEL: Air Products stood up better than Air Reduction in the

TABLE 18-2. Pair 2.

	Air Products & Chemicals 1969	*Air Reduction 1969*
Price, December 31, 1969	39½	16⅜
Number of shares of common	5,832,000[a]	11,279,000
Market value of common	$231,000,000	$185,000,000
Debt	113,000,000	179,000,000
Total capitalization at market	344,000,000	364,000,000
Book value per share	$22.89	$21.91
Sales	$221,500,000	$487,600,000
Net income	13,639,000	20,326,000
Earned per share, 1969	$2.40	$1.80
Earned per share, 1964	1.51	1.51
Earned per share, 1959	.52	1.95
Current dividend rate	.20	.80
Dividend since	1954	1917
Ratios:		
Price/earnings	16.5 ×	9.1 ×
Price/book value	165.0%	75.0%
Dividend yield	0.5%	4.9%
Net/sales	6.2%	4.25%
Earnings/book value	11.0%	8.2%
Current assets/liabilities	1.53 ×	3.77 ×
Working capital/debt	.32 ×	.85 ×
Growth in per-share earnings		
1969 versus 1964	+59%	+19%
1969 versus 1959	+362%	decrease

[a] Assuming conversion of preferred stock.

1970 break, with a decline of 16% against 24%. However, Reduction made a better comeback in early 1971, rising to 50% above its 1969 close, against 30% for Products. In this case the low-multiplier issue scored the advantage—for the time being, at least.*

Pair 3: American Home Products Co. (drugs, cosmetics, household products, candy) and American Hospital Supply Co. (distributor and manufacturer of hospital supplies and equipment)

These were two "billion-dollar good-will" companies at the end of 1969, representing different segments of the rapidly growing and immensely profitable "health industry." We shall refer to them as Home and Hospital, respectively. Selected data on both are presented in Table 18-3. They had the following favorable points in common: excellent growth, with no setbacks since 1958 (i.e., 100% earnings stability); and strong financial condition. The growth rate of Hospital up to the end of 1969 was considerably higher than Home's. On the other hand, Home enjoyed substantially better profitability on both sales and capital.† (In fact, the relatively low rate of Hospital's earnings on its capital in 1969—only 9.7%—raises the intriguing question whether the business then was in fact a highly profitable one, despite its remarkable past growth rate in sales and earnings.)

When comparative price is taken into account, Home offered

(cont'd from p. 451) growth stocks over long periods. (Much of the best research in modern finance simply provides independent confirmation of what Graham demonstrated decades ago.) See, for instance, James L. Davis, Eugene F. Fama, and Kenneth R. French, "Characteristics, Covariances, and Average Returns: 1929–1997," at http://papers.ssrn.com.

* Air Products and Chemicals, Inc., still exists as a publicly-traded stock and is included in the Standard & Poor's 500-stock index. Air Reduction Co. became a wholly-owned subsidiary of The BOC Group (then known as British Oxygen) in 1978.

† You can determine profitability, as measured by return on sales and return on capital, by referring to the "Ratios" section of Table 18-3. "Net/sales" measures return on sales; "Earnings/book value" measures return on capital.

TABLE 18-3. Pair 3.

	American Home Products 1969	*American Hospital Supply 1969*
Price, December 31, 1969	72	45⅛
Number of shares of common	52,300,000	33,600,000
Market value of common	$3,800,000,000	$1,516,000,000
Debt	11,000,000	18,000,000
Total capitalization at market	3,811,000,000	1,534,000,000
Book value per share	$5.73	$7.84
Sales	$1,193,000,000	$446,000,000
Net income	123,300,000	25,000,000
Earned per share, 1969	$2.32	$.77
Earned per share, 1964	1.37	.31
Earned per share, 1959	.92	.15
Current dividend rate	1.40	.24
Dividends since	1919	1947
Ratios:		
Price/earnings	31.0 ×	58.5 ×
Price/book value	1250.0%	575.0%
Dividend yield	1.9%	0.55%
Net/sales	10.7%	5.6%
Earnings/book value	41.0%	9.5%
Current assets/liabilities	2.6 ×	4.5 ×
Growth in per-share earnings		
1969 versus 1964	+75%	+142%
1969 versus 1959	+161%	+405%

much more for the money in terms of current (or past) earnings and dividends. The very low book value of Home illustrates a basic ambiguity or contradiction in common-stock analysis. On the one hand, it means that the company is earning a high return on its capital—which in general is a sign of strength and prosperity. On the other, it means that the investor at the current price would be especially vulnerable to any important adverse change in the company's earnings situation. Since Hospital was selling at over four times its book value in 1969, this cautionary remark must be applied to both companies.

CONCLUSIONS: Our clear-cut view would be that both companies were too "rich" at their current prices to be considered by the investor who decides to follow our ideas of conservative selection. This does not mean that the companies were lacking in promise. The trouble is, rather, that their price contained too much "promise" and not enough actual performance. For the two enterprises combined, the 1969 price reflected almost $5 billion of good-will valuation. How many years of excellent future earnings would it take to "realize" that good-will factor in the form of dividends or tangible assets?

SHORT-TERM SEQUEL: At the end of 1969 the market evidently thought more highly of the earnings prospects of Hospital than of Home, since it gave the former almost twice the multiplier of the latter. As it happened the favored issue showed a microscopic *decline* in earnings in 1970, while Home turned in a respectable 8% gain. The market price of Hospital reacted significantly to this one-year disappointment. It sold at 32 in February 1971—a loss of about 30% from its 1969 close—while Home was quoted slightly above its corresponding level.*

Pair 4: H & R Block, Inc. (income-tax service) and Blue Bell, Inc., (manufacturers of work clothes, uniforms, etc.)

These companies rub shoulders as relative newcomers to the New York Stock Exchange, where they represent two very different genres of success stories. Blue Bell came up the hard way in a highly competitive industry, in which eventually it became the largest factor. Its earnings have fluctuated somewhat with industry conditions, but their growth since 1965 has been impressive. The company's operations go back to 1916 and its continuous dividend record to 1923. At the end of 1969 the stock market showed no enthusiasm for the issue, giving it a price/earnings ratio of only 11, against about 17 for the S & P composite index.

By contrast, the rise of H & R Block has been meteoric. Its first

---

* American Home Products Co. is now known as Wyeth; the stock is included in the Standard & Poor's 500-stock index. American Hospital Supply Co. was acquired by Baxter Healthcare Corp. in 1985.

published figures date only to 1961, in which year it earned $83,000 on revenues of $610,000. But eight years later, on our comparison date, its revenues had soared to $53.6 million and its net to $6.3 million. At that time the stock market's attitude toward this fine performer appeared nothing less than ecstatic. The price of 55 at the close of 1969 was more than 100 times the last reported 12-months' earnings—which of course were the largest to date. The aggregate market value of $300 million for the stock issue was nearly 30 times the tangible assets behind the shares.* This was almost unheard of in the annals of serious stock-market valuations. (At that time IBM was selling at about 9 times and Xerox at 11 times book value.)

Our Table 18-4 sets forth in dollar figures and in ratios the extraordinary discrepancy in the comparative valuations of Block and Blue Bell. True, Block showed twice the profitability of Blue Bell per dollar of capital, and its percentage growth in earnings over the past five years (from practically nothing) was much higher. But as a stock enterprise Blue Bell was selling for less than one-third the total value of Block, although Blue Bell was doing four times as much business, earning 2½ times as much for its stock, had 5½ times as much in tangible investment, and gave nine times the dividend yield on the price.

Indicated Conclusions: An experienced analyst would have conceded great momentum to Block, implying excellent prospects for future growth. He might have had some qualms about the dangers of serious competition in the income-tax-service field, lured by the handsome return on capital realized by Block.[1] But mindful of the continued success of such outstanding companies as Avon Products in highly competitive areas, he would have hesitated to predict a speedy flattening out of the Block growth curve. His chief

---

* "Nearly 30 times" is reflected in the entry of 2920% under "Price/book value" in the Ratios section of Table 18-4. Graham would have shaken his head in astonishment during late 1999 and early 2000, when many high-tech companies sold for hundreds of times their asset value (see the commentary on this chapter). Talk about "almost unheard of in the annals of serious stock-market valuations"! H & R Block remains a publicly-traded company, while Blue Bell was taken private in 1984 at $47.50 per share.

TABLE 18-4. Pair 4.

	H & R Block 1969	*Blue Bell 1969*
Price, December 31, 1969	55	49¾
Number of shares of common	5,426,000	1,802,000[a]
Market value of common	$298,000,000	$89,500,000
Debt	—	17,500,000
Total capitalization at market	298,000,000	107,000,000
Book value per share	$1.89	$34.54
Sales	$53,600,000	$202,700,000
Net income	6,380,000	7,920,000
Earned per share, 1969	$.51 (October)	$4.47
Earned per share, 1964	.07	2.64
Earned per share, 1959	—	1.80
Current dividend rate	.24	1.80
Dividends since	1962	1923
Ratios:		
Price/earnings	108.0 ×	11.2 ×
Price/book value	2920 %	142 %
Dividend yield	0.4 %	3.6 %
Net/sales	11.9 %	3.9 %
Earnings/book value	27 %	12.8 %
Current assets/liabilities	3.2 ×	2.4 ×
Working capital/debt	no debt	3.75 ×
Growth in per-share earnings		
1969 versus 1964	+630%	+68%
1969 versus 1959	—	+148%

[a] Assuming conversion of preferred stock.

concern would be simply whether the $300 million valuation for the company had not already fully valued and perhaps overvalued all that one could reasonably expect from this excellent business. By contrast the analyst should have had little difficulty in recommending Blue Bell as a fine company, quite conservatively priced.

SEQUEL TO MARCH 1971. The 1970 near-panic lopped one-quarter off the price of Blue Bell and about one-third from that of Block. Both then joined in the extraordinary recovery of the general market. The price of Block rose to 75 in February 1971, but Blue Bell advanced considerably more—to the equivalent of 109 (after a three-for-two split). Clearly Blue Bell proved a better buy than Block as of the end of 1969. But the fact that Block was able to advance some 35% from that apparently inflated value indicates how wary analysts and investors must be to sell good companies short—either by word or deed—no matter how high the quotation may seem.*

Pair 5: International Flavors & Fragrances (flavors, etc., for other businesses) and International Harvester Co. (truck manufacturer, farm machinery, construction machinery)

This comparison should carry more than one surprise. Everyone knows of International Harvester, one of the 30 giants in the Dow Jones Industrial Average.† How many of our readers have even heard of International Flavors & Fragrances, next-door neighbor to Harvester on the New York Stock Exchange list? Yet, *mirabile dictu*, IFF was actually selling at the end of 1969 for a higher aggregate market value than Harvester—$747 million versus $710 million. This is the more amazing when one reflects that Harvester had 17 times the stock capital of Flavors and 27 times the annual sales. In

---

* Graham is alerting readers to a form of the "gambler's fallacy," in which investors believe that an overvalued stock must drop in price purely because it is overvalued. Just as a coin does not become more likely to turn up heads after landing on tails for nine times in a row, so an overvalued stock (or stock market!) can stay overvalued for a surprisingly long time. That makes short-selling, or betting that stocks will drop, too risky for mere mortals.

† International Harvester was the heir to McCormick Harvesting Machine Co., the manufacturer of the McCormick reaper that helped make the midwestern states the "breadbasket of the world." But International Harvester fell on hard times in the 1970s and, in 1985, sold its farm-equipment business to Tenneco. After changing its name to Navistar, the remaining company was booted from the Dow in 1991 (although it remains a member of the S & P 500 index). International Flavors & Fragrances, also a constituent of the S & P 500, had a total stock-market value of $3 billion in early 2003, versus $1.6 billion for Navistar.

TABLE 18-5. Pair 5.

	International Flavors & Fragrances 1969	*International Harvester 1969*
Price, December 31, 1969	65½	24¾
Number of shares of common	11,400,000	27,329,000
Market value of common	$747,000,000	$710,000,000
Debt	4,000,000	313,000,000
Total capitalization at market	751,000,000	1,023,000,000
Book value per share	$6.29	$41.70
Sales	$94,200,000	$2,652,000,000
Net income	13,540,000	63,800,000
Earned per share, 1969	$1.19	$2.30
Earned per share, 1964	.62	3.39
Earned per share, 1959	.28	2.83
Current dividend rate	.50	1.80
Dividends since	1956	1910
Ratios:		
Price/earnings	55.0 ×	10.7 ×
Price/book value	1050.0%	59.0%
Dividend yield	0.9%	7.3%
Net/sales	14.3%	2.6%
Earnings/book value	19.7%	5.5%
Current assets/liabilities	3.7 ×	2.0 ×
Working capital/debt	large	1.7 ×
Interest earned	—	(before tax) 3.9 ×
Growth in per-share earnings		
1969 versus 1964	+93%	+9%
1969 versus 1959	+326%	+39%

fact, only three years before, the *net earnings* of Harvester had been larger than the 1969 *sales* of Flavors! How did these extraordinary disparities develop? The answer lies in the two magic words: profitability and growth. Flavors made a remarkable showing in both categories, while Harvester left everything to be desired.

The story is told in Table 18-5. Here we find Flavors with a sensational profit of 14.3% of sales (before income tax the figure was 23%), compared with a mere 2.6% for Harvester. Similarly, Flavors had earned 19.7% on its stock capital against an inadequate 5.5% earned by Harvester. In five years the net earnings of Flavors had nearly doubled, while those of Harvester practically stood still. Between 1969 and 1959 the comparison makes similar reading. These differences in performance produced a typical stock-market divergence in valuation. Flavors sold in 1969 at 55 times its last reported earnings, and Harvester at only 10.7 times. Correspondingly, Flavors was valued at 10.4 times its book value, while Harvester was selling at a 41% *discount* from its net worth.

COMMENT AND CONCLUSIONS: The first thing to remark is that the market success of Flavors was based entirely on the development of its central business, and involved none of the corporate wheeling and dealing, acquisition programs, top-heavy capitalization structures, and other familiar Wall Street practices of recent years. The company has stuck to its extremely profitable knitting, and that is virtually its whole story. The record of Harvester raises an entirely different set of questions, but these too have nothing to do with "high finance." Why have so many great companies become relatively unprofitable even during many years of general prosperity? What is the advantage of doing more than $2½ billion of business if the enterprise cannot earn enough to justify the shareholders' investment? It is not for us to prescribe the solution of this problem. But we insist that not only management but the rank and file of shareholders should be conscious that the problem exists and that it calls for the best brains and the best efforts possible to deal with it.* From the standpoint of common-stock selection, neither issue would have met our standards of sound, reasonably attractive, and moderately priced investment. Flavors was a typical brilliantly successful but lavishly valued company;

* For more of Graham's thoughts on shareholder activism, see the commentary on Chapter 19. In criticizing Harvester for its refusal to maximize shareholder value, Graham uncannily anticipated the behavior of the company's future management. In 2001, a majority of shareholders voted to remove Navistar's restrictions against outside takeover bids—but the board of directors simply refused to implement the shareholders' wishes. It's remarkable that an antidemocratic tendency in the culture of some companies can endure for decades.

Harvester's showing was too mediocre to make it really attractive even at its discount price. (Undoubtedly there were better values available in the reasonably priced class.)

SEQUEL TO 1971: The low price of Harvester at the end of 1969 protected it from a large further decline in the bad break of 1970. It lost only 10% more. Flavors proved more vulnerable and declined to 45, a loss of 30%. In the subsequent recovery both advanced, well above their 1969 close, but Harvester soon fell back to the 25 level.

Pair 6: McGraw Edison (public utility and equipment; housewares) McGraw-Hill, Inc. (books, films, instruction systems; magazine and newspaper publishers; information services)

This pair with so similar names—which at times we shall call Edison and Hill—are two large and successful enterprises in vastly different fields. We have chosen December 31, 1968, as the date of our comparison, developed in Table 18-6. The issues were selling at about the same price, but because of Hill's larger capitalization it was valued at about twice the total figure of the other. This difference should appear somewhat surprising, since Edison had about 50% higher sales and one-quarter larger net earnings. As a result, we find that the key ratio—the multiplier of earnings—was more than twice as great for Hill as for Edison. This phenomenon seems explicable chiefly by the persistence of a strong enthusiasm and partiality exhibited by the market toward shares of book-publishing companies, several of which had been introduced to public trading in the later 1960s.*

Actually, by the end of 1968 it was evident that this enthusiasm had been overdone. The Hill shares had sold at 56 in 1967, more than 40 times the just-reported record earnings for 1966. But a small decline had appeared in 1967 and a further decline in 1968. Thus the current high multiplier of 35 was being applied to a company that

---

* McGraw-Hill remains a publicly-traded company that owns, among other operations, *BusinessWeek* magazine and Standard & Poor's Corp. McGraw–Edison is now a division of Cooper Industries.

TABLE 18-6. Pair 6.

	McGraw Edison 1968	*McGraw-Hill 1968*
Price, December 31, 1968	37⅝	39¾
Number of shares of common	13,717,000	24,200,000[a]
Market value of common	$527,000,000	$962,000,000
Debt	6,000,000	53,000,000
Total capitalization at market	533,000,000	1,015,000,000
Book value per share	$20.53	$5.00
Sales	$568,600,000	$398,300,000
Net income	33,400,000	26,200,000
Earned per share, 1968	$2.44	$1.13
Earned per share, 1963	1.20	.66
Earned per share, 1958	1.02	.46
Current dividend rate	1.40	.70
Dividends since	1934	1937
Ratios:		
Price/earnings	15.5 ×	35.0 ×
Price/book value	183.0%	795.0%
Dividend yield	3.7%	1.8%
Net/sales	5.8%	6.6%
Earnings/book value	11.8%	22.6%
Current assets/liabilities	3.95 ×	1.75 ×
Working capital/debt	large	1.75 ×
Growth in per-share earnings		
1968 versus 1963	+104%	+71%
1968 versus 1958	+139%	+146%

[a] Assuming conversion of preferred stock.

had already shown two years of receding profits. Nonetheless the stock was still valued at more than eight times its tangible asset backing, indicating a good-will component of not far from a billion dollars! Thus the price seemed to illustrate—in Dr. Johnson's famous phrase—"The triumph of hope over experience."

By contrast, McGraw Edison seemed quoted at a reasonable price in relation to the (high) general market level and to the company's overall performance and financial position.

SEQUEL TO EARLY 1971: The decline of McGraw-Hill's earnings continued through 1969 and 1970, dropping to $1.02 and then to $.82 per share. In the May 1970 debacle its price suffered a devastating break to 10—less than a fifth of the figure two years before. It had a good recovery thereafter, but the high of 24 in May 1971 was still only 60% of the 1968 closing price. McGraw Edison gave a better account of itself—declining to 22 in 1970 and recovering fully to 41½ in May 1971.*

McGraw-Hill continues to be a strong and prosperous company. But its price history exemplifies—as do so many other cases—the speculative hazards in such stocks created by Wall Street through its undisciplined waves of optimism and pessimism.

Pair 7: National General Corp. (a large conglomerate) and National Presto Industries (diverse electric appliances, ordnance)

These two companies invite comparison chiefly because they are so different. Let us call them "General" and "Presto." We have selected the end of 1968 for our study, because the write-offs taken by General in 1969 made the figures for that year too ambiguous. The full flavor of General's far-flung activities could not be savored the year before, but it was already conglomerate enough for anyone's taste. The condensed description in the *Stock Guide* read "Nation-wide theatre chain; motion picture and TV production, savings and loan assn., book publishing." To which could be added, then or later, "insurance, investment banking, records, music publishing, computerized services, real estate—and 35% of Performance Systems Inc. (name recently changed from Minnie Pearl's Chicken System Inc.)." Presto had also followed a diversification program, but in comparison with General it was modest indeed. Starting as the leading maker of pressure cookers, it had branched out into various other household and electric appliances. Quite differently, also, it took on a number of ordnance contracts for the U.S. government.

* In "the May 1970 debacle" that Graham refers to, the U.S. stock market lost 5.5%. From the end of March to the end of June 1970, the S & P 500 index lost 19% of its value, one of the worst three-month returns on record.

Our Table 18-7 summarizes the showing of the companies at the end of 1968. The capital structure of Presto was as simple as it could be—nothing but 1,478,000 shares of common stock, selling in the market for $58 million. Contrastingly, General had more than twice as many shares of common, plus an issue of convertible preferred, plus three issues of stock warrants calling for a huge amount of common, plus a towering convertible bond issue (just given in exchange for stock of an insurance company), plus a goodly sum of nonconvertible bonds. All this added up to a market capitalization of $534 million, not counting an impending issue of convertible bonds, and $750 million, including such issue. Despite National General's enormously greater capitalization, it had actually done considerably less gross business than Presto in their fiscal years, and it had shown only 75% of Presto's net income.

The determination of the *true market value* of General's common-stock capitalization presents an interesting problem for security analysts and has important implications for anyone interested in the stock on any basis more serious than outright gambling. The relatively small $4½ convertible preferred can be readily taken care of by assuming its conversion into common, when the latter sells at a suitable market level. This we have done in Table 18-7. But the warrants require different treatment. In calculating the "full dilution" basis the company assumes exercise of all the warrants, and the application of the proceeds to the retirement of debt, plus use of the balance to buy in common at the market. These assumptions actually produced virtually no effect on the earnings per share in calendar 1968—which were reported as $1.51 both before and after allowance for dilution. We consider this treatment illogical and unrealistic. As we see it, the warrants represent a part of the "common-stock package" and their market value is part of the "effective market value" of the common-stock part of the capital. (See our discussion of this point on p. 415 above.) This simple technique of adding the market price of the warrants to that of the common has a radical effect on the showing of National General at the end of 1968, as appears from the calculation in Table 18-7. In fact the "true market price" of the common stock turns out to be more than twice the quoted figure. Hence the true multiplier of the 1968 earnings is more than doubled—to the inherently absurd figure of 69 times. The total market value of the "common-stock equivalents" then

TABLE 18-7. Pair 7.

	National General 1968	*National Presto Industries 1968*
Price, December 31, 1968	44¼	38⅝
Number of shares of common	4,330,000[a]	1,478,000
Market value of common	$192,000,000	$58,000,000
Add market value of 3 issues of warrants	221,000,000	—
Total value of common and warrants	413,000,000	—
Senior issues	121,000,000	—
Total capitalization at market	534,000,000	58,000,000
Market price of common stock adjusted for warrants	98	—
Book value of common	$31.50	$26.30
Sales and revenues	$117,600,000	$152,200,000
Net income	6,121,000	8,206,000
Earned per share, 1968	$1.42 (December)	$5.61
Earned per share, 1963	.96 (September)	1.03
Earned per share, 1958	.48 (September)	.77
Current dividend rate	.20	.80
Dividends since	1964	1945
Ratios:		
Price/earnings	69.0 ×[b]	6.9 ×
Price/book value	310.0%	142.0%
Dividend yield	.5%	2.4%
Net/sales	5.5%	5.4%
Earnings/book value	4.5%	21.4%
Current assets/liabilities	1.63 ×	3.40 ×
Working capital/debt	.21 ×	no debt
Growth in per-share earnings		
1968 versus 1963	+48%	+450%
1968 versus 1960	+195%	+630%

[a] Assuming conversion of preferred stock.

[b] Adjusted for market price of warrants.

becomes $413 million, which is over three times the tangible assets shown therefor.

These figures appear the more anomalous when comparison is made with those of Presto. One is moved to ask how could Presto possibly be valued at only 6.9 times its current earnings when the multiplier for General was nearly 10 times as great. All the ratios of Presto are quite satisfactory—the growth figure suspiciously so, in fact. By that we mean that the company was undoubtedly benefiting considerably from its war work, and the shareholders should be prepared for some falling off in profits under peacetime conditions. But, on balance, Presto met all the requirements of a sound and reasonably priced investment, while General had all the earmarks of a typical "conglomerate" of the late 1960s vintage, full of corporate gadgets and grandiose gestures, but lacking in substantial values behind the market quotations.

SEQUEL: General continued its diversification policy in 1969, with some increase in its debt. But it took a whopping write-off of millions, chiefly in the value of its investment in the Minnie Pearl Chicken deal. The final figures showed a loss of $72 million before tax credit and $46.4 million after tax credit. The price of the shares fell to 16½ in 1969 and as low as 9 in 1970 (only 15% of its 1968 high of 60). Earnings for 1970 were reported as $2.33 per share diluted, and the price recovered to 28½ in 1971. National Presto increased its per-share earnings somewhat in both 1969 and 1970, marking 10 years of uninterrupted growth of profits. Nonetheless its price declined to 21½ in the 1970 debacle. This was an interesting figure, since it was less than four times the last reported earnings, and less than the net current assets available for the stock at the time. Late in 1971 we find the price of National Presto 60% higher, at 34, but the ratios are still startling. The enlarged working capital is still about equal to the current price, which in turn is only 5½ times the last reported earnings. If the investor could now find ten such issues, for diversification, he could be confident of satisfactory results.*

---

* National Presto remains a publicly-traded company. National General was acquired in 1974 by another controversial conglomerate, American Financial Group, which at various times has had interests in cable television, banking, real estate, mutual funds, insurance, and bananas. AFG is also the final resting place of some of the assets of Penn Central Corp. (see Chapter 17).

Pair 8: Whiting Corp. (materials-handling equipment) and Willcox & Gibbs (small conglomerate)

This pair are close but not touching neighbors on the American Stock Exchange list. The comparison—set forth in Table 18-8A—makes one wonder if Wall Street is a rational institution. The company with smaller sales and earnings, and with half the tangible

Table 18-8A. Pair 8.

	Whiting *1969*	*Willcox & Gibbs* *1969*
Price, December 31, 1969	17¾	15½
Number of shares of common	570,000	2,381,000
Market value of common	$10,200,000	$36,900,000
Debt	1,000,000	5,900,000
Preferred stock	—	1,800,000
Total capitalization at market	$11,200,000	$44,600,000
Book value per share	$25.39	$3.29
Sales	$42,200,000	$29,000,000
	(October)	(December)
Net income before special item	1,091,000	347,000
Net income after special item	1,091,000	*def.* 1,639,000
Earned per share, 1969	$1.91 (October)	$.08[a]
Earned per share, 1964	1.90 (April)	.13
Earned per share, 1959	.42 (April)	.13
Current dividend rate	1.50	—
Dividends since	1954	(none since 1957)
Ratios:		
Price/earnings	9.3 ×	very large
Price/book value	70.0%	470.0%
Dividend yield	8.4%	—
Net/sales	3.2%	0.1%[a]
Earnings/book value	7.5%	2.4%[a]
Current assets/liabilities	3.0 ×	1.55 ×
Working capital/debt	9.0 ×	3.6 ×
Growth in per-share earnings		
1969 versus 1964	even	decrease
1969 versus 1959	+354%	decrease

[a] Before special charge. *def.*: deficit.

TABLE 18-8B. Ten-Year Price and Earnings Record of Whiting and Willcox & Gibbs

	Whiting Corp.		*Willcox & Gibbs*	
Year	Earned Per Share[a]	Price Range	Earned Per Share	Price Range
1970	$1.81	22½–16¼	$.34	18½–4½
1969	2.63	37–17¾	.05	20⅝–8¾
1968	3.63	43⅛–28¼	.35	20⅛–8⅓
1967	3.01	36½–25	.47	11–4¾
1966	2.49	30¼–19¼	.41	8–3¾
1965	1.90	20–18	.32	10⅜–6⅛
1964	1.53	14–8	.20	9½–4½
1963	.88	15–9	.13	14–4¾
1962	.46	10–6½	.04	19¾–8¼
1961	.42	12½–7¾	.03	19½–10½

[a] Year ended following April 30.

assets for the common, sold at about four times the aggregate value of the other. The higher-valued company was about to report a large loss after special charges; it had not paid a dividend in thirteen years. The other had a long record of satisfactory earnings, had paid continuous dividends since 1936, and was currently returning one of the highest dividend yields in the entire common-stock list. To indicate more vividly the disparity in the performance of the two companies we append, in Table 18-8B, the earnings and price record for 1961–1970.

The history of the two companies throws an interesting light on the development of medium-sized businesses in this country, in contrast with much larger-sized companies that have mainly appeared in these pages. Whiting was incorporated in 1896, and thus goes back at least 75 years. It seems to have kept pretty faithfully to its materials-handling business and has done quite well with it over the decades. Willcox & Gibbs goes back even farther—to 1866—and was long known in its industry as a prominent maker of industrial sewing machines. During the past decade it adopted a policy of diversification in what seems a rather outlandish form. For on the one hand it has an extraordinarily large number of subsidiary companies (at least 24), making an astonishing variety of products, but on the other hand the entire conglomeration adds up to mighty small potatoes by usual Wall Street standards.

The earnings developments in Whiting are rather characteristic of our business concerns. The figures show steady and rather spectacular growth from 41 cents a share in 1960 to $3.63 in 1968. But they carried no assurance that such growth must continue indefinitely. The subsequent decline to only $1.77 for the 12 months ended January 1971 may have reflected nothing more than the slowing down of the general economy. But the stock price reacted in severe fashion, falling about 60% from its 1968 high (43½) to the close of 1969. Our analysis would indicate that the shares represented a sound and attractive secondary-issue investment—suitable for the enterprising investor as part of a group of such commitments.

SEQUEL: Willcox & Gibbs showed a small operating loss for 1970. Its price declined drastically to a low of 4½, recovering in typical fashion to 9½ in February 1971. It would be hard to justify that price statistically. Whiting had a relatively small decline, to 16¾ in 1970. (At that price it was selling at just about the current assets alone available for the shares). Its earnings held at $1.85 per share to July 1971. In early 1971 the price advanced to 24½, which seemed reasonable enough but no longer a "bargain" by our standards.*

General Observations

The issues used in these comparisons were selected with some malice aforethought, and thus they cannot be said to present a random cross-section of the common-stock list. Also they are limited to the industrial section, and the important areas of public utilities,

* Whiting Corp. ended up a subsidiary of Wheelabrator-Frye, but was taken private in 1983. Willcox & Gibbs is now owned by Group Rexel, an electrical-equipment manufacturer that is a division of Pinault-Printemps-Redoute Group of France. Rexel's shares trade on the Paris Stock Exchange.

transportation companies, and financial enterprises do not appear. But they vary sufficiently in size, lines of business, and qualitative and quantitative aspects to convey a fair idea of the choices confronting an investor in common stocks.

The relationship between price and indicated value has also differed greatly from one case to another. For the most part the companies with better growth records and higher profitability have sold at higher multipliers of current earnings—which is logical enough in

TABLE 18-9. Some Price Fluctuations of Sixteen Common Stocks (Adjusted for Stock Splits Through 1970)

	Price Range 1936–1970	*Decline 1961 to 1962*	*Decline 1968–69 to 1970*
Air Products & Chemicals	1⅜–49	43¼–21⅝	49–31⅜
Air Reduction	9⅜–45¾	22½–12	37–16
American Home Products	⅞–72	44¾–22	72–51⅛
American Hospital Supply	¾–47½	11⅝–5¾	47½–26¾[a]
H & R Block	¼–68½	–	68½–37⅛[a]
Blue Bell	8¾–55	25–16	44¾–26½
International Flavors & Fragrances	4¾–67½	8–4½	66⅜–44⅞
International Harvester	6¼–53	28¾–19¼	38¾–22
McGraw Edison	1¼–46¼	24⅜–14[b]	44¾–21⅝
McGraw-Hill	⅛–56½	21½–9⅛	54⅝–10¼
National General	3⅝–60½	14⅞–4¾[b]	60½–9
National Presto Industries	½–45	20⅝–8¼	45–21½
Real Estate Investment Trust	10½–30¼	25⅛–15¼	30¼–16⅜
Realty Equities of N.Y.	3¾–47¾	6⅞–4½	37¾–2
Whiting	2⅞–43⅜	12½–6½	43⅜–16¾
Willcox & Gibbs	4–20⅝	19½–8¼	20⅜–4½

[a] High and low both in 1970.

[b] 1959 to 1960.

general. Whether the specific differentials in price/earnings ratios are "justified" by the facts—or will be vindicated by future developments—cannot be answered with confidence. On the other hand we do have quite a few instances here in which a worthwhile judgment can be reached. These include virtually all the cases where there has been great market activity in companies of questionable underlying soundness. Such stocks not only were speculative—which means inherently risky—but a good deal of the time they were and are obviously overvalued. Other issues appeared to be worth more than their price, being affected by the opposite sort of market attitude—which we might call "underspeculation"—or by undue pessimism because of a shrinkage in earnings.

In Table 18-9 we provide some data on the price fluctuations of the issues covered in this chapter. Most of them had large declines between 1961 and 1962, as well as from 1969 to 1970. Clearly the investor must be prepared for this type of adverse market movement in future stock markets. In Table 18-10 we show year-to-year

TABLE 18-10. Large Year-to-Year Fluctuations of McGraw-Hill, 1958–1971[a]

From	*To*	*Advances*	*Declines*
1958	1959	39–72	
1959	1960	54–109¾	
1960	1961	21¾–43⅛	
1961	1962	18¼–32¼	43⅛–18¼
1963	1964	23⅜–38⅞	
1964	1965	28⅜–61	
1965	1966	37½–79½	
1966	1967	54½–112	
1967	1968		56¼–37½
1968	1969		54⅝–24
1969	1970		39½–10
1970	1971	10–24⅛	

[a] Prices not adjusted for stock-splits.

fluctuations of McGraw-Hill common stock for the period 1958–1970. It will be noted that in each of the last 13 years the price either advanced or declined over a range of at least three to two from one year to the next. (In the case of National General fluctuations of at least this amplitude both upward and downward were shown in each two-year period.)

In studying the stock list for the material in this chapter, we were impressed once again by the wide difference between the usual objectives of security analysis and those we deem dependable and rewarding. Most security analysts try to select the issues that will give the best account of themselves in the future, in terms chiefly of market action but considering also the development of earnings. We are frankly skeptical as to whether this can be done with satisfactory results. Our preference for the analyst's work would be rather that he should seek the exceptional or minority cases in which he can form a reasonably confident judgment that the price is well below value. He should be able to do this work with sufficient expertness to produce satisfactory average results over the years.

COMMENTARY ON CHAPTER 18

> The thing that hath been, it is that which shall be; and that which is done is that which shall be done: and there is no new thing under the sun. Is there any thing whereof it may be said, See, this is new? it hath been already of old time, which was before us.
>
> —*Ecclesiastes,* I: 9–10.

Let's update Graham's classic write-up of eight pairs of companies, using the same compare-and-contrast technique that he pioneered in his lectures at Columbia Business School and the New York Institute of Finance. Bear in mind that these summaries describe these stocks only at the times specified. The cheap stocks may later become overpriced; the expensive stocks may turn cheap. At some point in its life, almost every stock is a bargain; at another time, it will be expensive. Although there are good and bad companies, there is no such thing as a good stock; there are only good stock prices, which come and go.

PAIR 1: CISCO AND SYSCO

On March 27, 2000, Cisco Systems, Inc., became the world's most valuable corporation as its stock hit $548 billion in total value. Cisco, which makes equipment that directs data over the Internet, first sold its shares to the public only 10 years earlier. Had you bought Cisco's stock in the initial offering and kept it, you would have earned a gain resembling a typographical error made by a madman: 103,697%, or a 217% average annual return. Over its previous four fiscal quarters, Cisco had generated $14.9 billion in revenues and $2.5 billion in earnings. The stock was trading at 219 times Cisco's net income, one of the highest price/earnings ratios ever accorded to a large company.

Then there was Sysco Corp., which supplies food to institutional kitchens and had been publicly traded for 30 years. Over its last four quarters, Sysco served up $17.7 billion in revenues–almost 20% more than Cisco–but "only" $457 million in net income. With a market value of $11.7 billion, Sysco's shares traded at 26 times earnings, well below the market's average P/E ratio of 31.

A word-association game with a typical investor might have gone like this.

Q: What are the first things that pop into your head when I say Cisco Systems?

A: The Internet . . . the industry of the future . . . great stock . . . hot stock . . . Can I please buy some before it goes up even more?

Q: And what about Sysco Corp.?

A: Delivery trucks . . . succotash . . . Sloppy Joes . . . shepherd's pie . . . school lunches . . . *hospital food* . . . no thanks, I'm not hungry anymore.

It's well established that people often assign a mental value to stocks based largely on the emotional imagery that companies evoke.[1] But the intelligent investor always digs deeper. Here's what a skeptical look at Cisco and Sysco's financial statements would have turned up:

- Much of Cisco's growth in revenues and earnings came from acquisitions. Since September alone, Cisco had ponied up $10.2 billion to buy 11 other firms. How could so many companies be mashed together so quickly?[2] Also, tax breaks on stock options

---

[1] Ask yourself which company's stock would be likely to rise more: one that discovered a cure for a rare cancer, or one that discovered a new way to dispose of a common kind of garbage. The cancer cure sounds more exciting to most investors, but a new way to get rid of trash would probably make more money. See Paul Slovic, Melissa Finucane, Ellen Peters, and Donald G. MacGregor, "The Affect Heuristic," in Thomas Gilovich, Dale Griffin, and Daniel Kahneman, eds., *Heuristics and Biases: The Psychology of Intuitive Judgment* (Cambridge University Press, New York, 2002), pp. 397–420, and Donald G. MacGregor, "Imagery and Financial Judgment," *The Journal of Psychology and Financial Markets,* vol. 3, no. 1, 2002, pp. 15–22.

[2] "Serial acquirers," which grow largely by buying other companies, nearly always meet a bad end on Wall Street. See the commentary on Chapter 17 for a longer discussion.

exercised by Cisco's executives and employees amounted to the equivalent of roughly one-third of the company's total earnings over the previous six months. And Cisco had gained $5.8 billion selling "investments," then bought $6 billion more. Was it an Internet company or a mutual fund? What if those "investments" stopped going up?

- Sysco had also acquired several companies over the same period–but paid only about $130 million. Stock options for Sysco's insiders totaled only 1.5% of shares outstanding, versus 6.9% at Cisco. If insiders cashed their options, Sysco's earnings per share would be diluted much less than Cisco's. And Sysco had raised its quarterly dividend from nine cents a share to 10; Cisco paid no dividend.

Finally, as Wharton finance professor Jeremy Siegel pointed out, no company as big as Cisco had ever been able to grow fast enough to justify a price/earnings ratio above 60–let alone a P/E ratio over 200.[3] Once a company becomes a giant, its growth must slow down–or it will end up eating the entire world. The great American satirist Ambrose Bierce coined the word "incompossible" to describe two things that are conceivable separately but cannot exist together. A company can be a giant, or it can deserve a giant P/E ratio, but both together are incompossible.

The wheels soon came off the Cisco juggernaut. First, in 2001, came a $1.2 billion charge to "restructure" some of those acquisitions. Over the next two years, $1.3 billion in losses on those "investments" leaked out. From 2000 through 2002, Cisco's stock lost three-quarters of its value. Sysco, meanwhile, kept dishing out profits, and the stock gained 56% over the same period (see Figure 18-1).

PAIR 2: YAHOO! AND YUM!

On November 30, 1999, Yahoo! Inc.'s stock closed at $212.75, up 79.6% since the year began. By December 7, the stock was at $348–

---

[3] Jeremy Siegel, "Big-Cap Tech Stocks are a Sucker's Bet," *Wall Street Journal,* March 14, 2000 (available at www.jeremysiegel.com).

FIGURE 18-1 Cisco vs. Sysco

	2000	2001	2002
Cisco			
Total return (%)	–28.6	–52.7	–27.7
Net earnings ($ millions)	2,668	–1,014	1,893
Sysco			
Total return (%)	53.5	–11.7	15.5
Net earnings ($ millions)	446	597	680

Note: Total returns for calendar year; net earnings for fiscal year.
Source: www.morningstar.com

a 63.6% gain in five trading days. Yahoo! kept whooping along through year-end, closing at $432.687 on December 31. In a single month, the stock had more than doubled, gaining roughly $58 billion to reach a total market value of $114 billion.[4]

In the previous four quarters, Yahoo! had racked up $433 million in revenues and $34.9 million in net income. So Yahoo!'s stock was now priced at 263 times revenues and 3,264 times earnings. (Remember that a P/E ratio much above 25 made Graham grimace!)[5]

Why was Yahoo! screaming upward? After the market closed on November 30, Standard & Poor's announced that it would add Yahoo! to its S & P 500 index as of December 7. That would make Yahoo! a compulsory holding for index funds and other big investors–and that sudden rise in demand was sure to drive the stock even higher, at least temporarily. With some 90% of Yahoo!'s stock locked up in the hands of employees, venture-capital firms, and other restricted holders, just a fraction of its shares could trade. So thousands of people bought the stock only because they knew other people would have to buy it–and price was no object.

[4] Yahoo!'s stock split two-for-one in February 2000; the share prices given here are not adjusted for that split in order to show the levels the stock actually traded at. But Yahoo!'s percentage return and market value, as cited here, do reflect the split.

[5] Counting the effect of acquisitions, Yahoo!'s revenues were $464 million. Graham criticizes high P/E ratios in (among other places) Chapters 7 and 11.

Meanwhile, Yum! went begging. A former division of PepsiCo that runs thousands of Kentucky Fried Chicken, Pizza Hut, and Taco Bell eateries, Yum! had produced $8 billion in revenues over the previous four quarters, on which it earned $633 million–making it more than 17 times Yahoo!'s size. Yet Yum!'s stock-market value at year-end 1999 was only $5.9 billion, or 1/19 of Yahoo!'s capitalization. At that price, Yum!'s stock was selling at just over nine times its earnings and only 73% of its revenues.[6]

As Graham liked to say, in the short run the market is a voting machine, but in the long run it is a weighing machine. Yahoo! won the short-term popularity contest. But in the end, it's earnings that matter–and Yahoo! barely had any. Once the market stopped voting and started weighing, the scales tipped toward Yum! Its stock rose 25.4% from 2000 through 2002, while Yahoo!'s lost 92.4% cumulatively:

FIGURE 18-2 Yahoo! vs. Yum!

	2000	2001	2002
Yahoo!			
Total return (%)	–86.1	–41.0	–7.8
Net earnings ($ millions)	71	–93	43
Yum!			
Total return (%)	–14.6	49.1	–1.5
Net earnings ($ millions)	413	492	583

Notes: Total returns for calendar year; net earnings for fiscal year. Yahoo!'s net earnings for 2002 include effect of change in accounting principle.

Sources: www.morningstar.com

PAIR 3: COMMERCE ONE AND CAPITAL ONE

In May 2000, Commerce One, Inc., had been publicly traded only since the previous July. In its first annual report, the company (which

[6] Yum! was then known as Tricon Global Restaurants, Inc., although its ticker symbol was YUM. The company changed its name officially to Yum! Brands, Inc. in May 2002.

designs Internet "exchanges" for corporate purchasing departments) showed assets of just $385 million and reported a net loss of $63 million on only $34 million in total revenues. The stock of this minuscule company had risen nearly 900% since its IPO, hitting a total market capitalization of $15 billion. Was it overpriced? "Yes, we have a big market cap," Commerce One's chief executive, Mark Hoffman, shrugged in an interview. "But we have a big market to play in. We're seeing incredible demand. . . . Analysts expect us to make $140 million in revenue this year. And in the past we have exceeded expectations."

Two things jump out from Hoffman's answer:

- Since Commerce One was already losing $2 on every dollar in sales, if it quadrupled its revenues (as "analysts expect"), wouldn't it lose money even more massively?
- How could Commerce One have exceeded expectations "in the past"? *What* past?

Asked whether his company would ever turn a profit, Hoffman was ready: "There is no question we can turn this into a profitable business. We plan on becoming profitable in the fourth quarter of 2001, a year analysts see us making over $250 million in revenues."

There come those analysts again! "I like Commerce One at these levels because it's growing faster than Ariba [a close competitor whose stock was also trading at around 400 times revenues]," said Jeanette Sing, an analyst at the Wasserstein Perella investment bank. "If these growth rates continue, Commerce One will be trading at 60 to 70 times sales in 2001." (In other words, I can name a stock that's more overpriced than Commerce One, so Commerce One is cheap.)[7]

At the other extreme was Capital One Financial Corp., an issuer of MasterCard and Visa credit cards. From July 1999, to May 2000, its stock lost 21.5%. Yet Capital One had $12 billion in total assets and earned $363 million in 1999, up 32% from the year before. With a market value of about $7.3 billion, the stock sold at 20 times Capital One's net earnings. All might not be well at Capital One–the company had barely raised its reserves for loans that might go bad, even though

[7] See "CEO Speaks" and "The Bottom Line," *Money*, May 2000, pp. 42–44.

default rates tend to jump in a recession—but its stock price reflected at least some risk of potential trouble.

What happened next? In 2001, Commerce One generated $409 million in revenues. Unfortunately, it ran a net loss of $2.6 billion—or $10.30 of red ink per share—on those revenues. Capital One, on the other hand, earned nearly $2 billion in net income in 2000 through 2002. Its stock lost 38% in those three years—no worse than the stock market as a whole. Commerce One, however, lost 99.7% of its value.[8]

Instead of listening to Hoffman and his lapdog analysts, traders should have heeded the honest warning in Commerce One's annual report for 1999: "We have never been profitable. We expect to incur net losses for the foreseeable future and we may never be profitable."

PAIR 4: PALM AND 3COM

On March 2, 2000, the data-networking company 3Com Corp. sold 5% of its Palm, Inc. subsidiary to the public. The remaining 95% of Palm's stock would be spun off to 3Com's shareholders in the next few months; for each share of 3Com they held, investors would receive 1.525 shares of Palm.

So there were two ways you could get 100 shares of Palm: By trying to elbow your way into the IPO, or by buying 66 shares of 3Com and waiting until the parent company distributed the rest of the Palm stock. Getting one-and-a-half shares of Palm for each 3Com share, you'd end up with 100 shares of the new company—and you'd still have 66 shares of 3Com.

But who wanted to wait a few months? While 3Com was struggling against giant rivals like Cisco, Palm was a leader in the hot "space" of handheld digital organizers. So Palm's stock shot up from its offering price of $38 to close at $95.06, a 150% first-day return. That valued Palm at more than 1,350 times its earnings over the previous 12 months.

That same day, 3Com's share price *dropped* from $104.13 to $81.81. Where should 3Com have closed that day, given the price of Palm? The arithmetic is easy:

---

[8] In early 2003, Capital One's chief financial officer resigned after securities regulators revealed that they might charge him with violations of laws against insider trading.

- each 3Com share was entitled to receive 1.525 shares of Palm
- each share of Palm closed at $95.06
- 1.525 × $95.06 = $144.97

That's what each 3Com share was worth based on its stake in Palm alone. Thus, at $81.81, traders were saying that all of 3Com's other businesses combined were worth a negative $63.16 per share, *or a total of minus $22 billion!* Rarely in history has any stock been priced more stupidly.[9]

But there was a catch: Just as 3Com wasn't really worth minus $22 billion, Palm wasn't really worth over 1,350 times earnings. By the end of 2002, both stocks were hurting in the high-tech recession, but it was Palm's shareholders who really got smacked—because they abandoned all common sense when they bought in the first place:

FIGURE 18-3

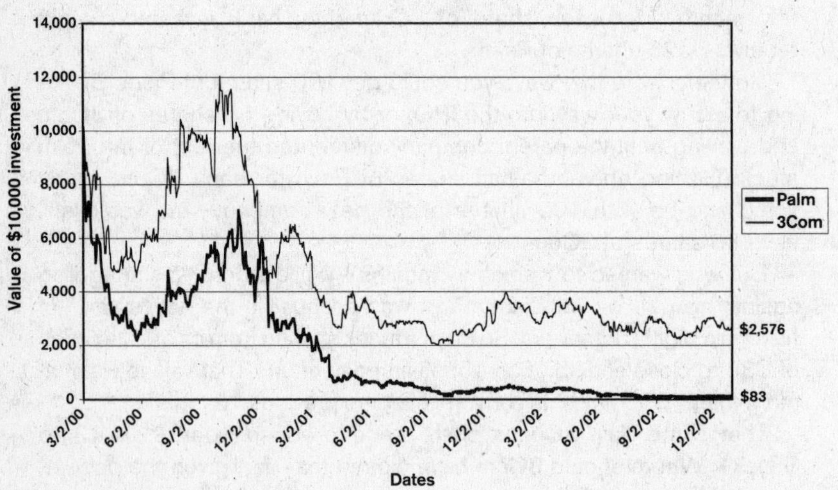

Source: www.morningstar.com

[9] For a more advanced look at this bizarre event, see Owen A. Lamont and Richard H. Thaler, "Can the Market Add and Subtract?" National Bureau of Economic Research working paper no. 8302, at www.nber.org/papers/w8302.

PAIR 5: CMGI AND CGI

The year 2000 started off with a bang for CMGI, Inc., as the stock hit $163.22 on January 3–a gain of 1,126% over its price just one year before. The company, an "Internet incubator," financed and acquired start-up firms in a variety of online businesses–among them such early stars as theglobe.com and Lycos.[10]

In fiscal year 1998, as its stock rose from 98 cents to $8.52, CMGI spent $53.8 million acquiring whole or partial stakes in Internet companies. In fiscal year 1999, as its stock shot from $8.52 to $46.09, CMGI shelled out $104.7 million. And in the last five months of 1999, as its shares zoomed up to $138.44, CMGI spent $4.1 billion on acquisitions. Virtually all the "money" was CMGI's own privately-minted currency: its common stock, now valued at a total of more than $40 billion.

It was a kind of magical money merry-go-round. The higher CMGI's own stock went, the more it could afford to buy. The more CMGI could afford to buy, the higher its stock went. First stocks would go up on the rumor that CMGI might buy them; then, once CMGI acquired them, its own stock would go up because it owned them. No one cared that CMGI had lost $127 million on its operations in the latest fiscal year.

Down in Webster, Massachusetts, less than 70 miles southwest of CMGI's headquarters in Andover, sits the main office of Commerce Group, Inc. CGI was everything CMGI was not: Offering automobile insurance, mainly to drivers in Massachusetts, it was a cold stock in an old industry. Its shares lost 23% in 1999–although its net income, at $89 million, ended up falling only 7% below 1998's level. CGI even paid a dividend of more than 4% (CMGI paid none). With a total market value of $870 million, CGI stock was trading at less than 10 times what the company would earn for 1999.

And then, quite suddenly, everything went into reverse. CMGI's magical money merry-go-round screeched to a halt: Its dot-com

---

[10] CMGI began corporate life as College Marketing Group, which sold information about college professors and courses to academic publishers–a business that bore a faint but disturbing similarity to National Student Marketing, discussed by Graham on p. 235.

stocks stopped rising in price, then went straight down. No longer able to sell them for a profit, CMGI had to take their loss in value as a hit to its earnings. The company lost $1.4 billion in 2000, $5.5 billion in 2001, and nearly $500 million more in 2002. Its stock went from $163.22 at the beginning of 2000 to 98 cents by year-end 2002–a loss of 99.4%. Boring old CGI, however, kept cranking out steady earnings, and its stock rose 8.5% in 2000, 43.6% in 2001, and 2.7% in 2002–a 60% cumulative gain.

PAIR 6: BALL AND STRYKER

Between July 9 and July 23, 2002, Ball Corp.'s stock dropped from $43.69 to $33.48–a loss of 24% that left the company with a stock-market value of $1.9 billion. Over the same two weeks, Stryker Corp.'s shares fell from $49.55 to $45.60, an 8% drop that left Strkyer valued at a total of $9 billion.

What had made these two companies worth so much less in so short a time? Stryker, which manufactures orthopedic implants and surgical equipment, issued only one press release during those two weeks. On July 16, Stryker announced that its sales grew 15% to $734 million in the second quarter, while earnings jumped 31% to $86 million. The stock rose 7% the next day, then rolled right back downhill.

Ball, the original maker of the famous "Ball Jars" used for canning fruits and vegetables, now makes metal and plastic packaging for industrial customers. Ball issued no press releases at all during those two weeks. On July 25, however, Ball reported that it had earned $50 million on sales of $1 billion in the second quarter–a 61% rise in net income over the same period one year earlier. That brought its earnings over the trailing four quarters to $152 million, so the stock was trading at just 12.5 times Ball's earnings. And, with a book value of $1.1 billion, you could buy the stock for 1.7 times what the company's tangible assets were worth. (Ball did, however, have just over $900 million in debt.)

Stryker was in a different league. Over the last four quarters, the company had generated $301 million in net income. Stryker's book value was $570 million. So the company was trading at fat multiples of 30 times its earnings over the past 12 months and nearly 16 times its book value. On the other hand, from 1992 through the end of 2001, Stryker's earnings had risen 18.6% annually; its dividend had grown by nearly 21% per year. And in 2001, Stryker had spent $142 million on research and development to lay the groundwork for future growth.

What, then, had pounded these two stocks down? Between July 9 and July 23, 2002, as WorldCom keeled over into bankruptcy, the Dow Jones Industrial Average fell from 9096.09 to 7702.34, a 15.3% plunge. The good news at Ball and Stryker got lost in the bad headlines and falling markets, which took these two stocks down with them.

Although Ball ended up priced far more cheaply than Stryker, the lesson here is not that Ball was a steal and Stryker was a wild pitch. Instead, the intelligent investor should recognize that market panics can create great prices for good companies (like Ball) and good prices for great companies (like Stryker). Ball finished 2002 at $51.19 a share, up 53% from its July low; Stryker ended the year at $67.12, up 47%. Every once in a while, value and growth stocks alike go on sale. Which choice you prefer depends largely on your own personality, but bargains can be had on either side of the plate.

PAIR 7: NORTEL AND NORTEK

The 1999 annual report for Nortel Networks, the fiber-optic equipment company, boasted that it was "a golden year financially." As of February 2000, at a market value of more than $150 billion, Nortel's stock traded at 87 times the earnings that Wall Street's analysts estimated the company would produce in 2000.

How credible was that estimate? Nortel's accounts receivable—sales to customers that had not yet paid the bill—had shot up by $1 billion in a year. The company said the rise "was driven by increased sales in the fourth quarter of 1999." However, inventories had also ballooned by $1.2 billion—meaning that Nortel was producing equipment even faster than those "increased sales" could unload it.

Meanwhile, Nortel's "long-term receivables"—bills not yet paid for multi-year contracts—jumped from $519 million to $1.4 billion. And Nortel was having a hard time controlling costs; its selling, general, and administrative expense (or overhead) had risen from 17.6% of revenues in 1997 to 18.7% in 1999. All told, Nortel had lost $351 million in 1999.

Then there was Nortek, Inc., which produces stuff at the dim end of the glamour spectrum: vinyl siding, door chimes, exhaust fans, range hoods, trash compactors. In 1999, Nortek earned $49 million on $2 billion in net sales, up from $21 million in net income on $1.1 billion in sales in 1997. Nortek's profit margin (net earnings as a percentage of net sales) had risen by almost a third from 1.9% to 2.5%. And Nortek had cut overhead from 19.3% of revenues to 18.1%.

To be fair, much of Nortek's expansion came from buying other companies, not from internal growth. What's more, Nortek had $1 billion in debt, a big load for a small firm. But, in February 2000, Nortek's stock price–roughly five times its earnings in 1999–included a healthy dose of pessimism.

On the other hand, Nortel's price–87 times the guesstimate of what it might earn in the year to come–was a massive overdose of optimism. When all was said and done, instead of earning the $1.30 per share that analysts had predicted, Nortel lost $1.17 per share in 2000. By the end of 2002, Nortel had bled more than $36 billion in red ink.

Nortek, on the other hand, earned $41.6 million in 2000, $8 million in 2001, and $55 million in the first nine months of 2002. Its stock went from $28 a share to $45.75 by year-end 2002–a 63% gain. In January 2003, Nortek's managers took the company private, buying all the stock from public investors at $46 per share. Nortel's stock, meanwhile, sank from $56.81 in February 2000, to $1.61 at year-end 2002–a 97% loss.

PAIR 8: RED HAT AND BROWN SHOE

On August 11, 1999, Red Hat, Inc., a developer of Linux software, sold stock to the public for the first time. Red Hat was red-hot; initially offered at $7, the shares opened for trading at $23 and closed at $26.031–a 272% gain.[11] In a single day, Red Hat's stock had gone up more than Brown Shoe's had in the previous 18 years. By December 9, Red Hat's shares hit $143.13–up 1,944% in four months.

Brown Shoe, meanwhile, had its laces tied together. Founded in 1878, the company wholesales Buster Brown shoes and runs nearly 1,300 footwear stores in the United States and Canada. Brown Shoe's stock, at $17.50 a share on August 11, stumbled down to $14.31 by December 9. For all of 1999, Brown Shoe's shares lost 17.6%.[12]

---

[11] All stock prices for Red Hat are adjusted for its two-for-one stock split in January 2000.

[12] Ironically, 65 years earlier Graham had singled out Brown Shoe as one of the most stable companies on the New York Stock Exchange. See the 1934 edition of *Security Analysis*, p. 159.

Besides a cool name and a hot stock, what did Red Hat's investors get? Over the nine months ending November 30, the company produced $13 million in revenues, on which it ran a net loss of $9 million.[13] Red Hat's business was barely bigger than a street-corner delicatessen–and a lot less lucrative. But traders, inflamed by the words "software" and "Internet," drove the total value of Red Hat's shares to $21.3 billion by December 9.

And Brown Shoe? Over the previous three quarters, the company had produced $1.2 billion in net sales and $32 million in earnings. Brown Shoe had nearly $5 a share in cash and real estate; kids were still buying Buster Brown shoes. Yet, that December 9, Brown Shoe's stock had a total value of $261 million–barely 1/80 the size of Red Hat even though Brown Shoe had 100 times Red Hat's revenues. At that price, Brown Shoe was valued at 7.6 times its annual earnings and less than one-quarter of its annual sales. Red Hat, on the other hand, had no profits at all, while its stock was selling at more than 1,000 times its annual sales.

Red Hat the company kept right on gushing red ink. Soon enough, the stock did too. Brown Shoe, however, trudged out more profits–and so did its shareholders:

FIGURE 18-4 Red Hat vs. Brown Shoe

	2000	2001	2002
Red Hat			
Total return (%)	–94.1	13.6	–16.8
Net earnings ($ millions)	–43	-87	–140
Brown Shoe			
Total return (%)	–4.6	28.2	49.5
Net earnings ($ millions)	36	36	–4

Note: Total returns for calendar year; net earnings for fiscal year.
Source: www.morningstar.com

[13] We use a nine-month period only because Red Hat's 12-month results could not be determined from its financial statements without including the results of acquisitions.

What have we learned? The market scoffs at Graham's principles in the short run, but they are always revalidated in the end. If you buy a stock purely because its *price* has been going up–instead of asking whether the underlying company's *value* is increasing–then sooner or later you will be extremely sorry. That's not a likelihood. It is a certainty.

CHAPTER 19

Shareholders and Managements: Dividend Policy

Ever since 1934 we have argued in our writings for a more intelligent and energetic attitude by shareholders toward their managements. We have asked them to take a generous attitude toward those who are demonstrably doing a good job. We have asked them also to demand clear and satisfying explanations when the results appear to be worse than they should be, and to support movements to improve or remove clearly unproductive managements. Shareholders are justified in raising questions as to the competence of the management when the results (1) are unsatisfactory in themselves, (2) are poorer than those obtained by other companies that appear similarly situated, and (3) have resulted in an unsatisfactory market price of long duration.

In the last 36 years practically nothing has actually been accomplished through intelligent action by the great body of shareholders. A sensible crusader—if there are any such—would take this as a sign that he has been wasting his time, and that he had better give up the fight. As it happens our cause has not been lost; it has been rescued by an extraneous development—known as take-overs, or take-over bids.* We said in Chapter 8 that poor manage-

* Ironically, takeovers began drying up shortly after Graham's last revised edition appeared, and the 1970s and early 1980s marked the absolute low point of modern American industrial efficiency. Cars were "lemons," televisions and radios were constantly "on the fritz," and the managers of many publicly-traded companies ignored both the present interests of their outside shareholders and the future prospects of their own businesses. All of

ments produce poor market prices. The low market prices, in turn, attract the attention of companies interested in diversifying their operations—and these are now legion. Innumerable such acquisitions have been accomplished by agreement with the existing managements, or else by accumulation of shares in the market and by offers made over the head of those in control. The price bid has usually been within the range of the value of the enterprise under reasonably competent management. Hence, in many cases, the inert public shareholder has been bailed out by the actions of "outsiders"—who at times may be enterprising individuals or groups acting on their own.

It can be stated as a rule with very few exceptions that poor managements are not changed by action of the "public stockholders," but only by the assertion of control by an individual or compact group. This is happening often enough these days to put the management, including the board of directors, of a typical publicly controlled company on notice that if its operating results and the resulting market price are highly unsatisfactory, it may become the target of a successful take-over move. As a consequence, boards of directors have probably become more alive than previously to their fundamental duty to see that their company has a satisfactory top management. Many more changes of presidents have been seen in recent years than formerly.

Not all companies in the unsatisfactory class have benefited from such developments. Also, the change has often occurred after a long period of bad results without remedial action, and has depended on enough disappointed shareholders selling out at low prices to permit the energetic outsiders to acquire a controlling position in the shares. But the idea that public shareholders could really help themselves by supporting moves for improving management and management policies has proved too quixotic to war-

---

this began to change in 1984, when independent oilman T. Boone Pickens launched a hostile takeover bid for Gulf Oil. Soon, fueled by junk-bond financing provided by Drexel Burnham Lambert, "corporate raiders" stalked the landscape of corporate America, scaring long-sclerotic companies into a new regimen of efficiency. While many of the companies involved in buyouts and takeovers were ravaged, the rest of American business emerged both leaner (which was good) and meaner (which sometimes was not).

rant further space in this book. Those individual shareholders who have enough gumption to make their presence felt at annual meetings—generally a completely futile performance—will not need our counsel on what points to raise with the managements. For others the advice would probably be wasted. Nevertheless, let us close this section with the plea that shareholders consider with an open mind and with careful attention any proxy material sent them by fellow-shareholders who want to remedy an obviously unsatisfactory management situation in the company.

Shareholders and Dividend Policy

In the past the dividend policy was a fairly frequent subject of argument between public, or "minority," shareholders and managements. In general these shareholders wanted more liberal dividends, while the managements preferred to keep the earnings in the business "to strengthen the company." They asked the shareholders to sacrifice their present interests for the good of the enterprise and for their own future long-term benefit. But in recent years the attitude of investors toward dividends has been undergoing a gradual but significant change. The basic argument now for paying small rather than liberal dividends is not that the company "needs" the money, but rather that it can use it to the shareholders' direct and immediate advantage by retaining the funds for profitable expansion. Years ago it was typically the weak company that was more or less forced to hold on to its profits, instead of paying out the usual 60% to 75% of them in dividends. The effect was almost always adverse to the market price of the shares. Nowadays it is quite likely to be a strong and growing enterprise that deliberately keeps down its dividend payments, with the approval of investors and speculators alike.*

There was always a strong theoretical case for reinvesting prof-

---

* The irony that Graham describes here grew even stronger in the 1990s, when it almost seemed that the stronger the company was, the less likely it was to pay a dividend–or for its shareholders to want one. The "payout ratio" (or the percentage of their net income that companies paid out as dividends) dropped from "60% to 75%" in Graham's day to 35% to 40% by the end of the 1990s.

its in the business where such retention could be counted on to produce a goodly increase in earnings. But there were several strong counter-arguments, such as: The profits "belong" to the shareholders, and they are entitled to have them paid out within the limits of prudent management; many of the shareholders need their dividend income to live on; the earnings they receive in dividends are "real money," while those retained in the company may or may not show up later as tangible values for the shareholders. These counter-arguments were so compelling, in fact, that the stock market showed a persistent bias in favor of the liberal dividend payers as against the companies that paid no dividends or relatively small ones.[1]

In the last 20 years the "profitable reinvestment" theory has been gaining ground. The better the past record of growth, the readier investors and speculators have become to accept a low-pay-out policy. So much is this true that in many cases of growth favorites the dividend rate—or even the absence of any dividend—has seemed to have virtually no effect on the market price.*

A striking example of this development is found in the history of Texas Instruments, Incorporated. The price of its common stock rose from 5 in 1953 to 256 in 1960, while earnings were advancing from 43 cents to $3.91 per share and while no dividend of any kind was paid. (In 1962 cash dividends were initiated, but by that year the earnings had fallen to $2.14 and the price had shown a spectacular drop to a low of 49.)

Another extreme illustration is provided by Superior Oil. In 1948 the company reported earnings of $35.26 per share, paid $3 in dividends, and sold as high as 235. In 1953 the dividend was reduced to $1, but the high price was 660. In 1957 it *paid no dividend*

---

* In the late 1990s, technology companies were particularly strong advocates of the view that all of their earnings should be "plowed back into the business," where they could earn higher returns than any outside shareholder possibly could by reinvesting the same cash if it were paid out to him or her in dividends. Incredibly, investors never questioned the truth of this patronizing Daddy-Knows-Best principle–or even realized that a company's cash belongs to the shareholders, not its managers. See the commentary on this chapter.

at all, and sold at 2,000! This unusual issue later declined to 795 in 1962, when it earned $49.50 and paid $7.50.*

Investment sentiment is far from crystallized in this matter of dividend policy of growth companies. The conflicting views are well illustrated by the cases of two of our very largest corporations—American Telephone & Telegraph and International Business Machines. American Tel. & Tel. came to be regarded as an issue with good growth possibilities, as shown by the fact that in 1961 it sold at 25 times that year's earnings. Nevertheless, the company's cash dividend policy has remained an investment and speculative consideration of first importance, its quotation making an active response to even *rumors* of an impending increase in the dividend rate. On the other hand, comparatively little attention appears to have been paid to the *cash* dividend on IBM, which in 1960 yielded only 0.5% at the high price of the year and 1.5% at the close of 1970. (But in both cases stock splits have operated as a potent stock-market influence.)

The market's appraisal of cash-dividend policy appears to be developing in the following direction: Where prime emphasis is not placed on growth the stock is rated as an "income issue," and the dividend rate retains its long-held importance as the prime determinant of market price. At the other extreme, stocks clearly recognized to be in the rapid-growth category are valued primarily in terms of the expected growth rate over, say, the next decade, and the cash-dividend rate is more or less left out of the reckoning.

While the above statement may properly describe present tendencies, it is by no means a clear-cut guide to the situation in all common stocks, and perhaps not in the majority of them. For one thing, many companies occupy an intermediate position between growth and nongrowth enterprises. It is hard to say how much importance should be ascribed to the growth factor in such cases, and the market's view thereof may change radically from year to year. Secondly, there seems to be something paradoxical about

* Superior Oil's stock price peaked at $2165 per share in 1959, when it paid a $4 dividend. For many years, Superior was the highest-priced stock listed on the New York Stock Exchange. Superior, controlled by the Keck family of Houston, was acquired by Mobil Corp. in 1984.

requiring the companies showing slower growth to be more liberal with their cash dividends. For these are generally the less prosperous concerns, and in the past the more prosperous the company the greater was the expectation of both liberal and increasing payments.

It is our belief that shareholders should demand of their managements either a normal payout of earnings—on the order, say, of two-thirds—or else a clear-cut demonstration that the reinvested profits have produced a satisfactory increase in per-share earnings. Such a demonstration could ordinarily be made in the case of a recognized growth company. But in many other cases a low payout is clearly the cause of an average market price that is below fair value, and here the shareholders have every right to inquire and probably to complain.

A niggardly policy has often been imposed on a company because its financial position is relatively weak, and it has needed all or most of its earnings (plus depreciation charges) to pay debts and bolster its working-capital position. When this is so there is not much the shareholders can say about it—except perhaps to criticize the management for permitting the company to fall into such an unsatisfactory financial position. However, dividends are sometimes held down by relatively unprosperous companies for the declared purpose of expanding the business. We feel that such a policy is illogical on its face, and should require both a complete explanation and a convincing defense before the shareholders should accept it. In terms of the past record there is no reason a priori to believe that the owners will benefit from expansion moves undertaken with their money by a business showing mediocre results and continuing its old management.

Stock Dividends and Stock Splits

It is important that investors understand the essential difference between a stock dividend (properly so-called) and a stock split. The latter represents a restatement of the common-stock structure—in a typical case by issuing two or three shares for one. The new shares are not related to specific earnings reinvested in a specific past period. Its purpose is to establish a lower market price for the single shares, presumably because such lower price range would be more acceptable to old and new shareholders. A stock split may be carried out by what technically may be called a stock dividend, which involves a transfer of sums from earned surplus to capital account; or else by a change in par value, which does not affect the surplus account.*

What we should call a *proper stock dividend* is one that is paid to shareholders to give them a tangible evidence or representation of *specific* earnings which have been reinvested in the business for their account over some relatively short period in the recent past—say, not more than the two preceding years. It is now approved practice to value such a stock dividend at the approximate value at the time of declaration, and to transfer an amount equal to such value from earned surplus to capital accounts. Thus the amount of a typical stock dividend is relatively small—in most cases not more than 5%. In essence a stock dividend of this sort has the same overall effect as the payment of an equivalent amount of cash out of earnings when accompanied by the sale of additional shares of like total value to the shareholders. However, a straight stock dividend has an important tax advantage over the otherwise equivalent combination of cash dividends with stock subscription rights, which is the almost standard practice for public-utility companies.

The New York Stock Exchange has set the figure of 25% as a practical dividing line between stock splits and stock dividends. Those of 25% or more need not be accompanied by the transfer of their market value from earned surplus to capital, and so forth.† Some companies, especially banks, still follow the old practice of

---

* Today, virtually all stock splits are carried out by a change in value. In a two-for-one split, one share becomes two, each trading at half the former price of the original single share; in a three-for-one split, one share becomes three, each trading at a third of the former price; and so on. Only in very rare cases is a sum transferred "from earned surplus to capital account," as in Graham's day.

† Rule 703 of the New York Stock Exchange governs stock splits and stock dividends. The NYSE now designates stock dividends of greater than 25% and less than 100% as "partial stock splits." Unlike in Graham's day, these stock dividends may now trigger the NYSE's accounting requirement that the amount of the dividend be capitalized from retained earnings.

declaring any kind of stock dividend they please—e.g., one of 10%, not related to recent earnings—and these instances maintain an undesirable confusion in the financial world.

We have long been a strong advocate of a systematic and clearly enunciated policy with respect to the payment of cash and stock dividends. Under such a policy, stock dividends are paid periodically to capitalize all or a stated portion of the earnings reinvested in the business. Such a policy—covering 100% of the reinvested earnings—has been followed by Purex, Government Employees Insurance, and perhaps a few others.*

Stock dividends of all types seem to be disapproved of by most academic writers on the subject. They insist that they are nothing but pieces of paper, that they give the shareholders nothing they did not have before, and that they entail needless expense and inconvenience.† On our side we consider this a completely doctrinaire view, which fails to take into account the practical and psychological realities of investment. True, a periodic stock dividend—say of 5%—changes only the "form" of the owners' investment. He has 105 shares in place of 100; but without the stock dividend the original 100 shares would have represented the same

---

* This policy, already unusual in Graham's day, is extremely rare today. In 1936 and again in 1950, roughly half of all stocks on the NYSE paid a so-called special dividend. By 1970, however, that percentage had declined to less than 10% and, by the 1990s, was well under 5%. See Harry DeAngelo, Linda DeAngelo, and Douglas J. Skinner, "Special Dividends and the Evolution of Dividend Signaling," *Journal of Financial Economics,* vol. 57, no. 3, September, 2000, pp. 309–354. The most plausible explanation for this decline is that corporate managers became uncomfortable with the idea that shareholders might interpret special dividends as a signal that future profits might be low.

† The academic criticism of dividends was led by Merton Miller and Franco Modigliani, whose influential article "Dividend Policy, Growth, and the Valuation of Shares" (1961) helped win them Nobel Prizes in Economics. Miller and Modigliani argued, in essence, that dividends were irrelevant, since an investor should not care whether his return comes through dividends and a rising stock price, or through a rising stock price alone, so long as the total return is the same in either case.

ownership interest now embodied in his 105 shares. Nonetheless, the change of form is actually one of real importance and value to him. If he wishes to cash in his share of the reinvested profits he can do so by selling the new certificate sent him, instead of having to break up his original certificate. He can count on receiving the same cash-dividend rate on 105 shares as formerly on his 100 shares; a 5% rise in the cash-dividend rate without the stock dividend would not be nearly as probable.*

The advantages of a periodic stock-dividend policy are most evident when it is compared with the usual practice of the public-utility companies of paying liberal cash dividends and then taking back a good part of this money from the shareholders by selling them additional stock (through subscription rights).† As we mentioned above, the shareholders would find themselves in exactly the same position if they received stock dividends in lieu of the popular combination of cash dividends followed by stock subscriptions—except that they would save the income tax otherwise paid on the cash dividends. Those who need or wish the maximum annual cash income, with no additional stock, can get this result by selling their stock dividends, in the same way as they sell their subscription rights under present practice.

The aggregate amount of income tax that could be saved by substituting stock dividends for the present stock-dividends-plus-subscription-rights combination is enormous. We urge that this

---

* Graham's argument is no longer valid, and today's investors can safely skip over this passage. Shareholders no longer need to worry about "having to break up" a stock certificate, since virtually all shares now exist in electronic rather than paper form. And when Graham says that a 5% increase in a cash dividend on 100 shares is less "probable" than a constant dividend on 105 shares, it's unclear how he could even calculate that probability.

† Subscription rights, often simply known as "rights," are used less frequently than in Graham's day. They confer upon an existing shareholder the right to buy new shares, sometimes at a discount to market price. A shareholder who does not participate will end up owning proportionately less of the company. Thus, as is the case with so many other things that go by the name of "rights," some coercion is often involved. Rights are most common today among closed-end funds and insurance or other holding companies.

change be made by the public utilities, despite its adverse effect on the U.S. Treasury, because we are convinced that it is completely inequitable to impose a second (personal) income tax on earnings which are not really received by the shareholders, since the companies take the same money back through sales of stock.*

Efficient corporations continuously modernize their facilities, their products, their bookkeeping, their management-training programs, their employee relations. It is high time they thought about modernizing their major financial practices, not the least important of which is their dividend policy.

* The administration of President George W. Bush made progress in early 2003 toward reducing the problem of double-taxation of corporate dividends, although it is too soon to know how helpful any final laws in this area will turn out to be. A cleaner approach would be to make dividend payments tax-deductible to the corporation, but that is not part of the proposed legislation.

COMMENTARY ON CHAPTER 19

The most dangerous untruths are truths slightly distorted.

–G. C. Lichtenberg

WHY DID GRAHAM THROW IN THE TOWEL?

Perhaps no other part of *The Intelligent Investor* was more drastically changed by Graham than this. In the first edition, this chapter was one of a pair that together ran nearly 34 pages. That original section ("The Investor as Business Owner") dealt with shareholders' voting rights, ways of judging the quality of corporate management, and techniques for detecting conflicts of interest between insiders and outside investors. By his last revised edition, however, Graham had pared the whole discussion back to less than eight terse pages about dividends.

Why did Graham cut away more than three-quarters of his original argument? After decades of exhortation, he evidently had given up hope that investors would ever take any interest in monitoring the behavior of corporate managers.

But the latest epidemic of scandal–allegations of managerial misbehavior, shady accounting, or tax maneuvers at major firms like AOL, Enron, Global Crossing, Sprint, Tyco, and WorldCom–is a stark reminder that Graham's earlier warnings about the need for eternal vigilance are more vital than ever. Let's bring them back and discuss them in light of today's events.

THEORY VERSUS PRACTICE

Graham begins his original (1949) discussion of "The Investor as Business Owner" by pointing out that, *in theory,* "the stockholders as a class are king. Acting as a majority they can hire and fire managements and bend them completely to their will." But, *in practice,* says Graham,

> the shareholders are a complete washout. As a class they show neither intelligence nor alertness. They vote in sheeplike fashion for whatever the management recommends and no matter how poor the management's record of accomplishment may be. . . . The only way to inspire the average American shareholder to take any *independently* intelligent action would be by exploding a firecracker under him. . . . We cannot resist pointing out the paradoxical fact that Jesus seems to have been a more practical businessman than are American shareholders.[1]

Graham wants you to realize something basic but incredibly profound: When you buy a stock, you become an owner of the company. Its managers, all the way up to the CEO, work for you. Its board of directors must answer to you. Its cash belongs to you. Its businesses are your property. If you don't like how your company is being managed, you have the right to demand that the managers be fired, the directors be changed, or the property be sold. "Stockholders," declares Graham, "should wake up."[2]

---

[1] Benjamin Graham, *The Intelligent Investor* (Harper & Row, New York, 1949), pp. 217, 219, 240. Graham explains his reference to Jesus this way: "In at least four parables in the Gospels there is reference to a highly critical relationship between a man of wealth and those he puts in charge of his property. Most to the point are the words that "a certain rich man" speaks to his steward or manager, who is accused of wasting his goods: 'Give an account of thy stewardship, for thou mayest be no longer steward.' (*Luke,* 16:2)." Among the other parables Graham seems to have in mind is *Matt.,* 25:15–28.

[2] Benjamin Graham, "A Questionnaire on Stockholder-Management Relationship," *The Analysts Journal,* Fourth Quarter, 1947, p. 62. Graham points out that he had conducted a survey of nearly 600 professional security analysts and found that more than 95% of them believed that shareholders have the right to call for a formal investigation of managers whose leadership does not enhance the value of the stock. Graham adds dryly that "such action is almost unheard of in practice." This, he says, "highlights the wide gulf between what should happen and what does happen in shareholder-management relationships."

THE INTELLIGENT OWNER

Today's investors have forgotten Graham's message. They put most of their effort into buying a stock, a little into selling it–but none into owning it. "Certainly," Graham reminds us, "there is just as much reason to exercise care and judgment in *being* as in *becoming* a stockholder."[3]

So how should you, as an intelligent investor, go about being an intelligent owner? Graham starts by telling us that "there are just two basic questions to which stockholders should turn their attention:

1. Is the management reasonably efficient?
2. Are the interests of the average *outside* shareholder receiving proper recognition?"[4]

You should judge the efficiency of management by comparing each company's profitability, size, and competitiveness against similar firms in its industry. What if you conclude that the managers are no good? Then, urges Graham,

> A few of the more substantial stockholders should become convinced that a change is needed and should be willing to work toward that end. Second, the rank and file of the stockholders should be open-minded enough to read the proxy material and to weigh the arguments on both sides. They must at least be able to know when their company has been unsuccessful and be ready to demand more than artful platitudes as a vindication of the incumbent management. Third, it would be most helpful, when the figures clearly show that the results are well below average, if it became the custom to call in outside business engineers to pass upon the policies and competence of the management.[5]

---

[3] Graham and Dodd, *Security Analysis* (1934 ed.), p. 508.

[4] *The Intelligent Investor,* 1949 edition, p. 218.

[5] 1949 edition, p. 223. Graham adds that a proxy vote would be necessary to authorize an independent committee of outside shareholders to select "the engineering firm" that would submit its report to the shareholders, not to the board of directors. However, the company would bear the costs of this project. Among the kinds of "engineering firms" *(cont'd on p. 501)*

THE ENRON END-RUN

Back in 1999, Enron Corp. ranked seventh on the *Fortune* 500 list of America's top companies. The energy giant's revenues, assets, and earnings were all rising like rockets.

But what if an investor had ignored the glamour and glittering numbers–and had simply put Enron's 1999 proxy statement under the microscope of common sense? Under the heading "Certain Transactions," the proxy disclosed that Enron's chief financial officer, Andrew Fastow, was the "managing member" of two partnerships, LJM1 and LJM2, that bought "energy and communications related investments." And where was LJM1 and LJM2 buying from? Why, where else but from Enron! The proxy reported that the partnerships had already bought $170 million of assets from Enron–sometimes using money borrowed from Enron.

The intelligent investor would immediately have asked:

- Did Enron's directors approve this arrangement? (Yes, said the proxy.)
- Would Fastow get a piece of LJM's profits? (Yes, said the proxy.)
- As Enron's chief financial officer, was Fastow obligated to act exclusively in the interests of Enron's shareholders? (Of course.)
- Was Fastow therefore duty-bound to maximize the price Enron obtained for any assets it sold? (Absolutely.)
- But if LJM paid a high price for Enron's assets, would that lower LJM's potential profits–and Fastow's personal income? (Clearly.)
- On the other hand, if LJM paid a low price, would that raise profits for Fastow and his partnerships, but hurt Enron's income? (Clearly.)
- Should Enron lend Fastow's partnerships any money to buy assets from Enron that might generate a personal profit for Fastow? (Say what?!)
- Doesn't all this constitute profoundly disturbing conflicts of interest? (No other answer is even possible.)

- What does this arrangement say about the judgment of the directors who approved it? (It says you should take your investment dollars elsewhere.)

Two clear lessons emerge from this disaster: Never dig so deep into the numbers that you check your common sense at the door, and always read the proxy statement before (and after) you buy a stock.

What is "proxy material" and why does Graham insist that you read it? In its proxy statement, which it sends to every shareholder, a company announces the agenda for its annual meeting and discloses details about the compensation and stock ownership of managers and directors, along with transactions between insiders and the company. Shareholders are asked to vote on which accounting firm should audit the books and who should serve on the board of directors. If you use your common sense while reading the proxy, this document can be like a canary in a coal mine—an early warning system signaling that something is wrong. (See the Enron sidebar above.)

Yet, on average, between a third and a half of all individual investors cannot be bothered to vote their proxies.[6] Do they even read them?

Understanding and voting your proxy is as every bit as fundamental

---

(cont'd from p. 499) Graham had in mind were money managers, rating agencies and organizations of security analysts. Today, investors could choose from among hundreds of consulting firms, restructuring advisers, and members of entities like the Risk Management Association.

[6] Tabulations of voting results for 2002 by Georgeson Shareholder and ADP's Investor Communication Services, two leading firms that mail proxy solicitations to investors, suggest response rates that average around 80% to 88% (including proxies sent in by stockbrokers on behalf of their clients, which are automatically voted in favor of management unless the clients specify otherwise). Thus the owners of between 12% and 20% of all shares are not voting their proxies. Since individuals own only 40% of U.S. shares by market value, and most institutional investors like pension funds and insurance companies are legally bound to vote on proxy issues, that means that roughly a third of all individual investors are neglecting to vote.

to being an intelligent investor as following the news and voting your conscience is to being a good citizen. It doesn't matter whether you own 10% of a company or, with your piddling 100 shares, just 1/10.000 of 1%. If you've never read the proxy of a stock you own, and the company goes bust, the only person you should blame is yourself. If you do read the proxy and see things that disturb you, then:

- vote against every director to let them know you disapprove
- attend the annual meeting and speak up for your rights
- find an online message board devoted to the stock (like those at http://finance.yahoo.com) and rally other investors to join your cause.

Graham had another idea that could benefit today's investors:

> . . . there are advantages to be gained through the selection of one or more professional and independent directors. These should be men of wide business experience who can turn a fresh and expert eye on the problems of the enterprise. . . . They should submit a separate annual report, addressed directly to the stockholders and containing their views on the major question which concerns the owners of the enterprise: "Is the business showing the results for the outside stockholder which could be expected of it under proper management? If not, why–and what should be done about it?[7]

One can only imagine the consternation that Graham's proposal would cause among the corporate cronies and golfing buddies who constitute so many of today's "independent" directors. (Let's not suggest that it might send a shudder of fear down their spines, since most independent directors do not appear to have a backbone.)

WHOSE MONEY IS IT, ANYWAY?

Now let's look at Graham's second criterion–whether management acts in the best interests of outside investors. Managers have always told shareholders that they–the managers–know best what to do with

---

[7] 1949 edition, p. 224.

the company's cash. Graham saw right through this managerial malarkey:

> A company's management may run the business well and yet not give the outside stockholders the right results for them, because its efficiency is confined to operations and does not extend to the best use of the capital. The objective of efficient *operation* is to produce at low cost and to find the most profitable articles to sell. Efficient *finance* requires that the stockholders' money be working in forms most suitable to their interest. This is a question in which management, as such, has little interest. Actually, it almost always wants as much capital from the owners as it can possibly get, in order to minimize its own financial problems. Thus the typical management will operate with more capital than necessary, if the stockholders permit it—which they often do.[8]

In the late 1990s and into the early 2000s, the managements of leading technology companies took this "Daddy-Knows-Best" attitude to new extremes. The argument went like this: Why should you demand a dividend when we can invest that cash for you and turn it into a rising share price? Just look at the way our stock has been going up—doesn't that prove that we can turn your pennies into dollars better than you can?

Incredibly, investors fell for it hook, line, and sinker. Daddy Knows Best became such gospel that, by 1999, only 3.7% of the companies that first sold their stock to the public that year paid a dividend—down from an average of 72.1% of all IPOs in the 1960s.[9] Just look at how

---

[8] 1949 edition, p. 233.

[9] Eugene F. Fama and Kenneth R. French, "Disappearing Dividends: Changing Firm Characteristics or Lower Propensity to Pay?" *Journal of Financial Economics,* vol. 60, no. 1, April, 2001, pp. 3–43, especially Table 1; see also Elroy Dimson, Paul Marsh, and Mike Staunton, *Triumph of the Optimists* (Princeton Univ. Press, Princeton, 2002), pp. 158–161. Interestingly, the total dollar amount of dividends paid by U.S. stocks has risen since the late 1970s, even after inflation—but the number of stocks that pay a dividend has shrunk by nearly two-thirds. See Harry DeAngelo, Linda DeAngelo, and Douglas J. Skinner, "Are Dividends Disappearing? Dividend Concentration and the Consolidation of Earnings," available at: http://papers.ssrn.com.

the percentage of companies paying dividends (shown in the dark area) has withered away:

FIGURE 19-1

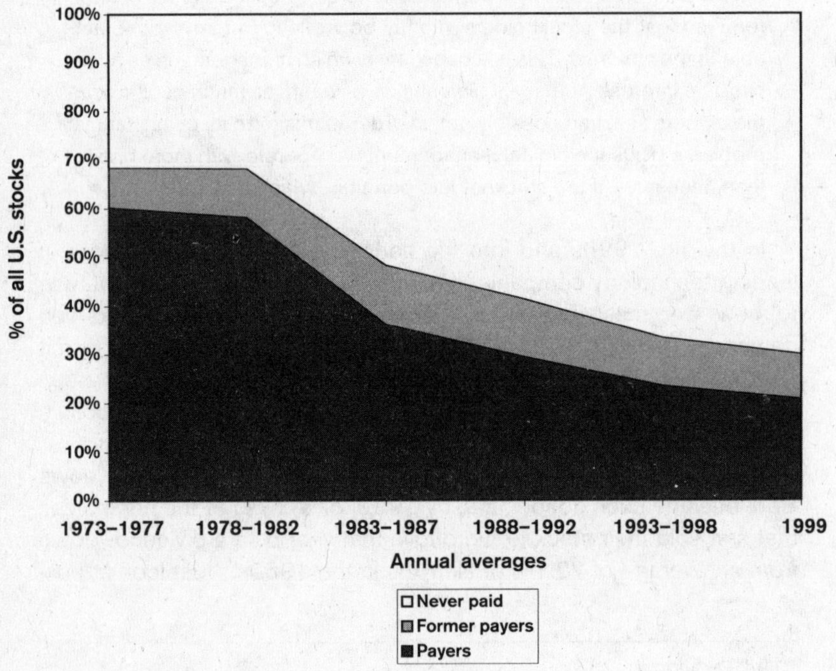

Source: Eugene Fama and Kenneth French, "Disappearing Dividends," Journal of Financial Economics, *April 2001.*

But Daddy Knows Best was nothing but bunk. While some companies put their cash to good use, many more fell into two other categories: those that simply wasted it, and those that piled it up far faster than they could possibly spend it.

In the first group, Priceline.com wrote off $67 million in losses in

2000 after launching goofy ventures into groceries and gasoline, while Amazon.com destroyed at least $233 million of its shareholders' wealth by "investing" in dot-bombs like Webvan and Ashford.com.[10] And the two biggest losses so far on record–JDS Uniphase's $56 billion in 2001 and AOL Time Warner's $99 billion in 2002–occurred after companies chose not to pay dividends but to merge with other firms at a time when their shares were obscenely overvalued.[11]

In the second group, consider that by late 2001, Oracle Corp. had piled up $5 billion in cash. Cisco Systems had hoarded at least $7.5 billion. Microsoft had amassed a mountain of cash $38.2 billion high–and rising by an average of more than $2 million *per hour.*[12] Just how rainy a day was Bill Gates expecting, anyway?

So the anecdotal evidence clearly shows that many companies

---

[10] Perhaps Benjamin Franklin, who is said to have carried his coins around in an asbestos purse so that money wouldn't burn a hole in his pocket, could have avoided this problem if he had been a CEO.

[11] A study by *BusinessWeek* found that from 1995 through 2001, 61% out of more than 300 large mergers ended up destroying wealth for the shareholders of the acquiring company–a condition known as "the winner's curse" or "buyer's remorse." And acquirers using stock rather than cash to pay for the deal underperformed rival companies by 8%. (David Henry, "Mergers: Why Most Big Deals Don't Pay Off," *BusinessWeek,* October 14, 2002, pp. 60–70.) A similar academic study found that acquisitions of private companies and subsidiaries of public companies lead to positive stock returns, but that acquisitions of entire public companies generate losses for the winning bidder's shareholders. (Kathleen Fuller, Jeffry Netter, and Mike Stegemoller, "What Do Returns to Acquiring Firms Tell Us?" *The Journal of Finance,* vol. 57, no. 4, August, 2002, pp. 1763–1793.)

[12] With interest rates near record lows, such a mountain of cash produces lousy returns if it just sits around. As Graham asserts, "So long as this surplus cash remains with the company, the outside stockholder gets little benefit from it" (1949 edition, p. 232). Indeed, by year-end 2002, Microsoft's cash balance had swollen to $43.4 billion–clear proof that the company could find no good use for the cash its businesses were generating. As Graham would say, Microsoft's *operations* were efficient, but its *finance* no longer was. In a step toward redressing this problem, Microsoft declared in early 2003 that it would begin paying a regular quarterly dividend.

don't know how to turn excess cash into extra returns. What does the statistical evidence tell us?

- Research by money managers Robert Arnott and Clifford Asness found that when current dividends are low, future corporate earnings also turn out to be low. And when current dividends are high, so are future earnings. Over 10-year periods, the average rate of earnings growth was 3.9 points greater when dividends were high than when they were low.[13]
- Columbia accounting professors Doron Nissim and Amir Ziv found that companies that raise their dividend not only have better stock returns but that "dividend increases are associated with [higher] future profitability for at least four years after the dividend change."[14]

In short, most managers are wrong when they say that they can put your cash to better use than you can. Paying out a dividend does not guarantee great results, but it does *improve* the return of the typical stock by yanking at least some cash out of the managers' hands before they can either squander it or squirrel it away.

SELLING LOW, BUYING HIGH

What about the argument that companies can put spare cash to better use by buying back their own shares? When a company repurchases some of its stock, that reduces the number of its shares outstanding. Even if its net income stays flat, the company's earnings

---

[13] Robert D. Arnott and Clifford S. Asness, "Surprise! Higher Dividends = Higher Earnings Growth," *Financial Analysts Journal,* January/February, 2003, pp. 70–87.

[14] Doron Nissim and Amir Ziv, "Dividend Changes and Future Profitability," *The Journal of Finance,* vol. 56, no. 6, December, 2001, pp. 2111–2133. Even researchers who disagree with the Arnott-Asness and Nissim-Ziv findings on future earnings agree that dividend increases lead to higher future stock returns; see Shlomo Benartzi, Roni Michaely, and Richard Thaler, "Do Changes in Dividends Signal the Future or the Past?" *The Journal of Finance,* vol. 52, no. 3, July, 1997, pp. 1007–1034.

per share will rise, since its total earnings will be spread across fewer shares. That, in turn, should lift the stock price. Better yet, unlike a dividend, a buyback is tax-free to investors who don't sell their shares.[15] Thus it increases the value of their stock without raising their tax bill. And if the shares are cheap, then spending spare cash to repurchase them is an excellent use of the company's capital.[16]

All this is true in theory. Unfortunately, in the real world, stock buybacks have come to serve a purpose that can only be described as sinister. Now that grants of stock options have become such a large part of executive compensation, many companies—especially in high-tech industries—must issue hundreds of millions of shares to give to the managers who exercise those stock options.[17] But that would jack

---

[15] The tax reforms proposed by President George W. Bush in early 2003 would change the taxability of dividends, but the fate of this legislation was not yet clear by press time.

[16] Historically, companies took a common-sense approach toward share repurchases, reducing them when stock prices were high and stepping them up when prices were low. After the stock market crash of October 19, 1987, for example, 400 companies announced new buybacks over the next 12 days alone—while only 107 firms had announced buyback programs in the earlier part of the year, when stock prices had been much higher. See Murali Jagannathan, Clifford P. Stephens, and Michael S. Weisbach, "Financial Flexibility and the Choice Between Dividends and Stock Repurchases," *Journal of Financial Economics,* vol. 57, no. 3, September, 2000, p. 362.

[17] The stock options granted by a company to its executives and employees give them the right (but not the obligation) to buy shares in the future at a discounted price. That conversion of options to shares is called "exercising" the options. The employees can then sell the shares at the current market price and pocket the difference as profit. Because hundreds of millions of options may be exercised in a given year, the company must increase its supply of shares outstanding. Then, however, the company's total net income would be spread across a much greater number of shares, reducing its earnings per share. Therefore, the company typically feels compelled to buy back other shares to cancel out the stock issued to the option holders. In 1998, 63.5% of chief financial officers admitted that counteracting the dilution from options was a major reason for repurchasing shares (see CFO Forum, "The Buyback Track," *Institutional Investor,* July, 1998).

up the number of shares outstanding and shrink earnings per share. To counteract that dilution, the companies must turn right back around and repurchase millions of shares in the open market. By 2000, companies were spending an astounding 41.8% of their total net income to repurchase their own shares–up from 4.8% in 1980.[18]

Let's look at Oracle Corp., the software giant. Between June 1, 1999, and May 31, 2000, Oracle issued 101 million shares of common stock to its senior executives and another 26 million to employees at a cost of $484 million. Meanwhile, to keep the exercise of earlier stock options from diluting its earnings per share, Oracle spent $5.3 billion–*or 52% of its total revenues that year*–to buy back 290.7 million shares of stock. Oracle issued the stock to insiders at an average price of $3.53 per share and repurchased it at an average price of $18.26. Sell low, buy high: Is this any way to "enhance" shareholder value?[19]

By 2002, Oracle's stock had fallen to less than half its peak in 2000. Now that its shares were cheaper, did Oracle hasten to buy back more stock? Between June 1, 2001, and May 31, 2002, Oracle *cut* its repurchases to $2.8 billion, apparently because its executives and employees exercised fewer options that year. The same sell-low, buy-high pattern is evident at dozens of other technology companies.

What's going on here? Two surprising factors are at work:

---

[18] One of the main factors driving this change was the U.S. Securities and Exchange Commission's decision, in 1982, to relax its previous restrictions on share repurchases. See Gustavo Grullon and Roni Michaely, "Dividends, Share Repurchases, and the Substitution Hypothesis," *The Journal of Finance,* vol. 57, no. 4, August, 2002, pp. 1649–1684.

[19] Throughout his writings, Graham insists that corporate managements have a duty not just to make sure their stock is not undervalued, but also to make sure it never gets overvalued. As he put it in *Security Analysis* (1934 ed., p. 515), "the responsibility of managements to act in the interest of their shareholders includes the obligation to prevent–in so far as they are able–the establishment of either absurdly high or unduly low prices for their securities." Thus, enhancing shareholder value doesn't just mean making sure that the stock price does not go too low; it also means ensuring that the stock price does not go *up* to unjustifiable levels. If only the executives of Internet companies had heeded Graham's wisdom back in 1999!

- Companies get a tax break when executives and employees exercise stock options (which the IRS considers a "compensation expense" to the company).[20] In its fiscal years from 2000 through 2002, for example, Oracle reaped $1.69 billion in tax benefits as insiders cashed in on options. Sprint Corp. pocketed $678 million in tax benefits as its executives and employees locked in $1.9 billion in options profits in 1999 and 2000.
- A senior executive heavily compensated with stock options has a vested interest in favoring stock buybacks over dividends. Why? For technical reasons, options increase in value as the price fluctuations of a stock grow more extreme. But dividends dampen the volatility of a stock's price. So, if the managers increased the dividend, they would lower the value of their own stock options.[21]

No wonder CEOs would much rather buy back stock than pay dividends–regardless of how overvalued the shares may be or how drastically that may waste the resources of the outside shareholders.

---

[20] Incredibly, although options are considered a compensation expense on a company's tax returns, they are not counted as an expense on the income statement in financial reports to shareholders. Investors can only hope that accounting reforms will change this ludicrous practice.

[21] See George W. Fenn and Nellie Liang, "Corporate Payout Policy and Managerial Stock Incentives," *Journal of Financial Economics*, vol. 60, no. 1, April, 2001, pp. 45–72. Dividends make stocks less volatile by providing a stream of current income that cushions shareholders against fluctuations in market value. Several researchers have found that the average profitability of companies with stock-buyback programs (but no cash dividends) is at least twice as volatile as that of companies that pay dividends. Those more variable earnings will, in general, lead to bouncier share prices, making the managers' stock options more valuable–by creating more opportunities when share prices will be temporarily high. Today, about two-thirds of executive compensation comes in the form of options and other noncash awards; thirty years ago, at least two-thirds of compensation came as cash.

KEEPING THEIR OPTIONS OPEN

Finally, drowsy investors have given their companies free rein to overpay executives in ways that are simply unconscionable. In 1997, Steve Jobs, the cofounder of Apple Computer Inc., returned to the company as its "interim" chief executive officer. Already a wealthy man, Jobs insisted on taking a cash salary of $1 per year. At year-end 1999, to thank Jobs for serving as CEO "for the previous 2 1/2 years without compensation," the board presented him with his very own Gulfstream jet, at a cost to the company of a mere $90 million. The next month Jobs agreed to drop "interim" from his job title, and the board rewarded him with options on 20 million shares. (Until then, Jobs had held a grand total of two shares of Apple stock.)

The principle behind such option grants is to align the interests of managers with outside investors. If you are an outside Apple shareholder, you want its managers to be rewarded only if Apple's stock earns superior returns. Nothing else could possibly be fair to you and the other owners of the company. But, as John Bogle, former chairman of the Vanguard funds, points out, nearly all managers *sell* the stock they receive immediately after exercising their options. How could dumping millions of shares for an instant profit possibly align their interests with those of the company's loyal long-term shareholders?

In Jobs' case, if Apple stock rises by just 5% annually through the beginning of 2010, he will be able to cash in his options for $548.3 million. In other words, even if Apple's stock earns no better than half the long-term average return of the overall stock market, Jobs will land a half-a-billion dollar windfall.[22] Does that align his interests with those of Apple's shareholders—or malign the trust that Apple's shareholders have placed in the board of directors?

Reading proxy statements vigilantly, the intelligent owner will vote against any executive compensation plan that uses option grants to turn more than 3% of the company's shares outstanding over to the managers. And you should veto any plan that does not make option grants contingent on a fair and enduring measure of superior results—

---

[22] Apple Computer Inc. proxy statement for April 2001 annual meeting, p. 8 (available at www.sec.gov). Jobs' option grant and share ownership are adjusted for a two-for-one share split.

say, outperforming the average stock in the same industry for a period of at least five years. No CEO ever deserves to make himself rich if he has produced poor results for you.

A FINAL THOUGHT

Let's go back to Graham's suggestion that every company's independent board members should have to report to the shareholders in writing on whether the business is properly managed on behalf of its true owners. What if the independent directors also had to justify the company's policies on dividends and share repurchases? What if they had to describe exactly how they determined that the company's senior management was not overpaid? And what if every investor became an intelligent owner and actually read that report?

CHAPTER 20

"Margin of Safety" as the Central Concept of Investment

In the old legend the wise men finally boiled down the history of mortal affairs into the single phrase, "This too will pass."* Confronted with a like challenge to distill the secret of sound investment into three words, we venture the motto, MARGIN OF SAFETY. This is the thread that runs through all the preceding discussion of investment policy—often explicitly, sometimes in a less direct fashion. Let us try now, briefly, to trace that idea in a connected argument.

All experienced investors recognize that the margin-of-safety concept is essential to the choice of sound bonds and preferred stocks. For example, a railroad should have earned its total fixed charges better than five times (before income tax), taking a period of years, for its bonds to qualify as investment-grade issues. This *past* ability to earn in excess of interest requirements constitutes the margin of safety that is counted on to protect the investor against loss or discomfiture in the event of some *future* decline in net income. (The margin above charges may be stated in other ways—

* "It is said an Eastern monarch once charged his wise men to invent him a sentence, to be ever in view, and which should be true and appropriate in all times and situations. They presented him the words: '*And this, too, shall pass away.*' How much it expresses! How chastening in the hour of pride!–how consoling in the depths of affliction! 'And this, too, shall pass away.' And yet let us hope it is not *quite* true."–Abraham Lincoln, Address to the Wisconsin State Agricultural Society, Milwaukee, September 30, 1859, in *Abraham Lincoln: Speeches and Writings, 1859–1865* (Library of America, 1985), vol. II, p. 101.

for example, in the percentage by which revenues or profits may decline before the balance after interest disappears—but the underlying idea remains the same.)

The bond investor does not expect future average earnings to work out the same as in the past; if he were sure of that, the margin demanded might be small. Nor does he rely to any controlling extent on his judgment as to whether future earnings will be materially better or poorer than in the past, if he did that, he would have to measure his margin in terms of a carefully *projected* income account, instead of emphasizing the margin shown in the past record. Here the function of the margin of safety is, in essence, that of rendering unnecessary an accurate estimate of the future. If the margin is a large one, then it is enough to assume that future earnings will not fall far below those of the past in order for an investor to feel sufficiently protected against the vicissitudes of time.

The margin of safety for bonds may be calculated, alternatively, by comparing the total value of the enterprise with the amount of debt. (A similar calculation may be made for a preferred-stock issue.) If the business owes $10 million and is fairly worth $30 million, there is room for a shrinkage of two-thirds in value—at least theoretically—before the bondholders will suffer loss. The amount of this extra value, or "cushion," above the debt may be approximated by using the average market price of the junior stock issues over a period of years. Since average stock prices are generally related to average earning power, the margin of "enterprise value" over debt and the margin of earnings over charges will in most cases yield similar results.

So much for the margin-of-safety concept as applied to "fixed-value investments." Can it be carried over into the field of common stocks? Yes, but with some necessary modifications.

There are instances where a common stock may be considered sound because it enjoys a margin of safety as large as that of a good bond. This will occur, for example, when a company has outstanding only common stock that under depression conditions is selling for less than the amount of bonds that could safely be issued against its property and earning power.* That was the position of a

---

* "Earning power" is Graham's term for a company's potential profits or, as he puts it, the amount that a firm "might be expected to earn year after year

host of strongly financed industrial companies at the low price levels of 1932–33. In such instances the investor can obtain the margin of safety associated with a bond, *plus* all the chances of larger income and principal appreciation inherent in a common stock. (The only thing he lacks is the legal power to insist on dividend payments "or else"—but this is a small drawback as compared with his advantages.) Common stocks bought under such circumstances will supply an ideal, though infrequent, combination of safety and profit opportunity. As a quite recent example of this condition, let us mention once more National Presto Industries stock, which sold for a total enterprise value of $43 million in 1972. With its $16 millions of recent earnings before taxes the company could easily have supported this amount of bonds.

In the ordinary common stock, bought for investment under normal conditions, the margin of safety lies in an expected earning power considerably above the going rate for bonds. In former editions we elucidated this point with the following figures:

> Assume in a typical case that the earning power is 9% on the price and that the bond rate is 4%; then the stockbuyer will have an average annual margin of 5% accruing in his favor. Some of the excess is paid to him in the dividend rate; even though spent by him, it enters into his overall investment result. The undistributed balance is reinvested in the business for his account. In many cases such reinvested earnings fail to add commensurately to the earning power and value of his stock. (That is why the market has a stubborn habit of valuing earnings disbursed in dividends more generously than the portion retained in the business.)* But, if the picture is viewed as a whole, there is a reasonably close connection

---

if the business conditions prevailing during the period were to continue unchanged" (*Security Analysis*, 1934 ed., p. 354). Some of his lectures make it clear that Graham intended the term to cover periods of five years or more. You can crudely but conveniently approximate a company's earning power per share by taking the inverse of its price/earnings ratio; a stock with a P/E ratio of 11 can be said to have earning power of 9% (or 1 divided by 11). Today "earning power" is often called "earnings yield."

* This problem is discussed extensively in the commentary on Chapter 19.

between the growth of corporate surpluses through reinvested earnings and the growth of corporate values.

Over a ten-year period the typical excess of stock earning power over bond interest may aggregate 50% of the price paid. This figure is sufficient to provide a very real margin of safety—which, under favorable conditions, will prevent or minimize a loss. If such a margin is present in each of a diversified list of twenty or more stocks, the probability of a favorable result under "fairly normal conditions" becomes very large. That is why the policy of investing in representative common stocks does not require high qualities of insight and foresight to work out successfully. If the purchases are made at the average level of the market over a span of years, the prices paid should carry with them assurance of an adequate margin of safety. The danger to investors lies in concentrating their purchases in the upper levels of the market, or in buying nonrepresentative common stocks that carry more than average risk of diminished earning power.

As we see it, the whole problem of common-stock investment under 1972 conditions lies in the fact that "in a typical case" the earning power is now much less than 9% on the price paid.* Let us assume that by concentrating somewhat on the low-multiplier issues among the large companies a defensive investor may now

---

* Graham elegantly summarized the discussion that follows in a lecture he gave in 1972: "The margin of safety is the difference between the percentage rate of the earnings on the stock at the price you pay for it and the rate of interest on bonds, and that margin of safety is the difference which would absorb unsatisfactory developments. At the time the 1965 edition of *The Intelligent Investor* was written the typical stock was selling at 11 times earnings, giving about 9% return as against 4% on bonds. In that case you had a margin of safety of over 100 per cent. Now [in 1972] there is no difference between the earnings rate on stocks and the interest rate on stocks, and I say there is no margin of safety . . . you have a negative margin of safety on stocks . . ." See "Benjamin Graham: Thoughts on Security Analysis" [transcript of lecture at the Northeast Missouri State University business school, March, 1972], *Financial History,* no. 42, March, 1991, p. 9.

acquire equities at 12 times recent earnings—i.e., with an earnings return of 8.33% on cost. He may obtain a dividend yield of about 4%, and he will have 4.33% of his cost reinvested in the business for his account. On this basis, the excess of stock earning power over bond interest over a ten-year basis would still be too small to constitute an adequate margin of safety. For that reason we feel that there are real risks now even in a diversified list of sound common stocks. The risks may be fully offset by the profit possibilities of the list; and indeed the investor may have no choice but to incur them—for otherwise he may run an even greater risk of holding only fixed claims payable in steadily depreciating dollars. Nonetheless the investor would do well to recognize, and to accept as philosophically as he can, that the old package of *good profit possibilities combined with small ultimate risk* is no longer available to him.*

However, the risk of paying too high a price for good-quality stocks—while a real one—is not the chief hazard confronting the average buyer of securities. Observation over many years has taught us that the chief losses to investors come from the purchase of *low-quality* securities at times of favorable business conditions. The purchasers view the current good earnings as equivalent to "earning power" and assume that prosperity is synonymous with safety. It is in those years that bonds and preferred stocks of inferior grade can be sold to the public at a price around par, because they carry a little higher income return or a deceptively attractive conversion privilege. It is then, also, that common stocks of obscure companies can be floated at prices far above the tangible investment, on the strength of two or three years of excellent growth.

These securities do not offer an adequate margin of safety in any admissible sense of the term. Coverage of interest charges and preferred dividends must be tested over a number of years, including preferably a period of subnormal business such as in 1970–71. The same is ordinarily true of common-stock earnings if they are to

---

* This paragraph–which Graham wrote in early 1972–is an uncannily precise description of market conditions in early 2003. (For more detail, see the commentary on Chapter 3.)

qualify as indicators of earning power. Thus it follows that most of the fair-weather investments, acquired at fair-weather prices, are destined to suffer disturbing price declines when the horizon clouds over—and often sooner than that. Nor can the investor count with confidence on an eventual recovery—although this does come about in some proportion of the cases—for he has never had a real safety margin to tide him through adversity.

The philosophy of investment in growth stocks parallels in part and in part contravenes the margin-of-safety principle. The growth-stock buyer relies on an expected earning power that is greater than the average shown in the past. Thus he may be said to substitute these expected earnings for the past record in calculating his margin of safety. In investment theory there is no reason why carefully estimated future earnings should be a less reliable guide than the bare record of the past; in fact, security analysis is coming more and more to prefer a competently executed evaluation of the future. Thus the growth-stock approach may supply as dependable a margin of safety as is found in the ordinary investment—provided the calculation of the future is conservatively made, and provided it shows a satisfactory margin in relation to the price paid.

The danger in a growth-stock program lies precisely here. For such favored issues the market has a tendency to set prices that will not be adequately protected by a *conservative* projection of future earnings. (It is a basic rule of prudent investment that all estimates, when they differ from past performance, must err at least slightly on the side of understatement.) The margin of safety is always dependent on the price paid. It will be large at one price, small at some higher price, nonexistent at some still higher price. If, as we suggest, the average market level of most growth stocks is too high to provide an adequate margin of safety for the buyer, then a simple technique of diversified buying in this field may not work out satisfactorily. A special degree of foresight and judgment will be needed, in order that wise individual selections may overcome the hazards inherent in the customary market level of such issues as a whole.

The margin-of-safety idea becomes much more evident when we apply it to the field of undervalued or bargain securities. We have here, by definition, a favorable difference between price on the one hand and indicated or appraised value on the other. That difference is the safety margin. It is available for absorbing the effect of miscalculations or worse than average luck. The buyer of bargain issues places particular emphasis on the ability of the investment to withstand adverse developments. For in most such cases he has no real enthusiasm about the company's prospects. True, if the prospects are definitely bad the investor will prefer to avoid the security no matter how low the price. But the field of undervalued issues is drawn from the many concerns—perhaps a majority of the total—for which the future appears neither distinctly promising nor distinctly unpromising. If these are bought on a bargain basis, even a moderate decline in the earning power need not prevent the investment from showing satisfactory results. The margin of safety will then have served its proper purpose.

Theory of Diversification

There is a close logical connection between the concept of a safety margin and the principle of diversification. One is correlative with the other. Even with a margin in the investor's favor, an individual security may work out badly. For the margin guarantees only that he has a better chance for profit than for loss—not that loss is impossible. But as the number of such commitments is increased the more certain does it become that the aggregate of the profits will exceed the aggregate of the losses. That is the simple basis of the insurance-underwriting business.

Diversification is an established tenet of conservative investment. By accepting it so universally, investors are really demonstrating their acceptance of the margin-of-safety principle, to which diversification is the companion. This point may be made more colorful by a reference to the arithmetic of roulette. If a man bets $1 on a single number, he is paid $35 profit when he wins—but the chances are 37 to 1 that he will lose. He has a "negative margin of safety." In his case diversification is foolish. The more numbers he bets on, the smaller his chance of ending with a profit. If he regularly bets $1 on every number (including 0 and 00), he is certain to lose $2 on each turn of the wheel. But suppose the winner received $39 profit instead of $35. Then he would have a small but important margin of safety. Therefore, the more numbers he wagers on, the better his chance of gain. And he could be certain of winning $2 on every spin by simply betting $1 each on all the numbers. (Incidentally, the two examples given actually describe the respective positions of the player and proprietor of a wheel with 0 and 00.)*

A Criterion of Investment versus Speculation

Since there is no single definition of investment in general acceptance, authorities have the right to define it pretty much as they please. Many of them deny that there is any useful or dependable difference between the concepts of investment and of speculation. We think this skepticism is unnecessary and harmful. It is injurious because it lends encouragement to the innate leaning of many people toward the excitement and hazards of stock-market speculation. We suggest that the margin-of-safety concept may be used to advantage as the touchstone to distinguish an investment operation from a speculative one.

Probably most speculators believe they have the odds in their favor when they take their chances, and therefore they may lay claim to a safety margin in their proceedings. Each one has the feeling that the time is propitious for his purchase, or that his skill is superior to the crowd's, or that his adviser or system is trustworthy. But such claims are unconvincing. They rest on subjective judgment, unsupported by any body of favorable evidence or any

---

* In "American" roulette, most wheels include 0 and 00 along with numbers 1 through 36, for a total of 38 slots. The casino offers a maximum payout of 35 to 1. What if you bet $1 on every number? Since only one slot can be the one into which the ball drops, you would win $35 on that slot, but lose $1 on each of your other 37 slots, for a net loss of $2. That $2 difference (or a 5.26% spread on your total $38 bet) is the casino's "house advantage," ensuring that, *on average*, roulette players will always lose more than they win. Just as it is in the roulette player's interest to bet as seldom as possible, it is in the casino's interest to keep the roulette wheel spinning. Likewise, the intelligent investor should seek to maximize the number of holdings that offer "a better chance for profit than for loss." For most investors, diversification is the simplest and cheapest way to widen your margin of safety.

conclusive line of reasoning. We greatly doubt whether the man who stakes money on his view that the market is heading up or down can ever be said to be protected by a margin of safety in any useful sense of the phrase.

By contrast, the investor's concept of the margin of safety—as developed earlier in this chapter—rests upon simple and definite arithmetical reasoning from statistical data. We believe, also, that it is well supported by practical investment experience. There is no guarantee that this fundamental quantitative approach will continue to show favorable results under the unknown conditions of the future. But, equally, there is no valid reason for pessimism on this score.

Thus, in sum, we say that to have a true investment there must be present a true margin of safety. And a true margin of safety is one that can be demonstrated by figures, by persuasive reasoning, and by reference to a body of actual experience.

Extension of the Concept of Investment

To complete our discussion of the margin-of-safety principle we must now make a further distinction between conventional and unconventional investments. Conventional investments are appropriate for the typical portfolio. Under this heading have always come United States government issues and high-grade, dividend-paying common stocks. We have added state and municipal bonds for those who will benefit sufficiently by their tax-exempt features. Also included are first-quality corporate bonds when, as now, they can be bought to yield sufficiently more than United States savings bonds.

Unconventional investments are those that are suitable only for the enterprising investor. They cover a wide range. The broadest category is that of undervalued common stocks of secondary companies, which we recommend for purchase when they can be bought at two-thirds or less of their indicated value. Besides these, there is often a wide choice of medium-grade corporate bonds and preferred stocks when they are selling at such depressed prices as to be obtainable also at a considerable discount from their apparent value. In these cases the average investor would be inclined to call the securities speculative, because in his mind their lack of a first-quality rating is synonymous with a lack of investment merit.

It is our argument that a sufficiently low price can turn a security of mediocre quality into a sound investment opportunity—provided that the buyer is informed and experienced and that he practices adequate diversification. For, if the price is low enough to create a substantial margin of safety, the security thereby meets our criterion of investment. Our favorite supporting illustration is taken from the field of real-estate bonds. In the 1920s, billions of dollars' worth of these issues were sold at par and widely recommended as sound investments. A large proportion had so little margin of value over debt as to be in fact highly speculative in character. In the depression of the 1930s an enormous quantity of these bonds defaulted their interest, and their price collapsed—in some cases below 10 cents on the dollar. At that stage the same advisers who had recommended them at par as safe investments were rejecting them as paper of the most speculative and unattractive type. But as a matter of fact the price depreciation of about 90% made many of these securities exceedingly attractive and reasonably safe—for the true values behind them were four or five times the market quotation.*

The fact that the purchase of these bonds actually resulted in what is generally called "a large speculative profit" did not prevent them from having true investment qualities at their low prices. The "speculative" profit was the purchaser's reward for having made an unusually shrewd investment. They could properly be called *investment* opportunities, since a careful analysis would have shown that the excess of value over price provided a large margin of safety. Thus the very class of "fair-weather investments" which we stated above is a chief source of serious loss to naïve security buyers is likely to afford many sound profit opportunities to the sophisticated operator who may buy them later at pretty much his own price.†

---

* Graham is saying that there is no such thing as a good or bad stock; there are only cheap stocks and expensive stocks. Even the best company becomes a "sell" when its stock price goes too high, while the worst company is worth buying if its stock goes low enough.

† The very people who considered technology and telecommunications stocks a "sure thing" in late 1999 and early 2000, when they were hellishly overpriced, shunned them as "too risky" in 2002–even *(cont'd on p. 522)*

The whole field of "special situations" would come under our definition of investment operations, because the purchase is always predicated on a thoroughgoing analysis that promises a larger realization than the price paid. Again there are risk factors in each individual case, but these are allowed for in the calculations and absorbed in the overall results of a diversified operation.

To carry this discussion to a logical extreme, we might suggest that a defensible investment operation could be set up by buying such intangible values as are represented by a group of "common-stock option warrants" selling at historically low prices. (This example is intended as somewhat of a shocker.)* The entire value of these warrants rests on the possibility that the related stocks may some day advance above the option price. At the moment they have no exercisable value. Yet, since all investment rests on reasonable future expectations, it is proper to view these warrants in terms of the mathematical chances that some future bull market will create a large increase in their indicated value and in their price. Such a study might well yield the conclusion that there is much more to be gained in such an operation than to be lost and that the chances of an ultimate profit are much better than those of an ultimate loss. If that is so, there is a safety margin present even

---

(cont'd from p. 521) though, in Graham's exact words from an earlier period, "the price depreciation of about 90% made many of these securities exceedingly attractive and reasonably safe." Similarly, Wall Street's analysts have always tended to call a stock a "strong buy" when its price is high, and to label it a "sell" after its price has fallen–the exact opposite of what Graham (and simple common sense) would dictate. As he does throughout the book, Graham is distinguishing speculation–or buying on the hope that a stock's price will keep going up–from investing, or buying on the basis of what the underlying business is worth.

* Graham uses "common-stock option warrant" as a synonym for "warrant," a security issued directly by a corporation giving the holder a right to purchase the company's stock at a predetermined price. Warrants have been almost entirely superseded by stock options. Graham quips that he intends the example as a "shocker" because, even in his day, warrants were regarded as one of the market's seediest backwaters. (See the commentary on Chapter 16.)

in this unprepossessing security form. A sufficiently enterprising investor could then include an option-warrant operation in his miscellany of unconventional investments.[1]

To Sum Up

Investment is most intelligent when it is most *businesslike*. It is amazing to see how many capable businessmen try to operate in Wall Street with complete disregard of all the sound principles through which they have gained success in their own undertakings. Yet every corporate security may best be viewed, in the first instance, as an ownership interest in, or a claim against, a specific business enterprise. And if a person sets out to make profits from security purchases and sales, he is embarking on a business venture of his own, which must be run in accordance with accepted business principles if it is to have a chance of success.

The first and most obvious of these principles is, "Know what you are doing—know your business." For the investor this means: Do not try to make "business profits" out of securities—that is, returns in excess of normal interest and dividend income—unless you know as much about security values as you would need to know about the value of merchandise that you proposed to manufacture or deal in.

A second business principle: "Do not let anyone else run your business, unless (1) you can supervise his performance with adequate care and comprehension or (2) you have unusually strong reasons for placing implicit confidence in his integrity and ability." For the investor this rule should determine the conditions under which he will permit someone else to decide what is done with his money.

A third business principle: "Do not enter upon an operation—that is, manufacturing or trading in an item—unless a reliable calculation shows that it has a fair chance to yield a reasonable profit. In particular, keep away from ventures in which you have little to gain and much to lose." For the enterprising investor this means that his operations for profit should be based not on optimism but on arithmetic. For every investor it means that when he limits his return to a small figure—as formerly, at least, in a conventional bond or preferred stock—he must demand convincing evidence that he is not risking a substantial part of his principal.

A fourth business rule is more positive: "Have the courage of your knowledge and experience. If you have formed a conclusion from the facts and if you know your judgment is sound, act on it—even though others may hesitate or differ." (You are neither right nor wrong because the crowd disagrees with you. You are right because your data and reasoning are right.) Similarly, in the world of securities, courage becomes the supreme virtue *after* adequate knowledge and a tested judgment are at hand.

Fortunately for the typical investor, it is by no means necessary for his success that he bring these qualities to bear upon his program—*provided* he limits his ambition to his capacity and confines his activities within the safe and narrow path of standard, defensive investment. To achieve *satisfactory* investment results is easier than most people realize; to achieve *superior* results is harder than it looks.

COMMENTARY ON CHAPTER 20

> If we fail to anticipate the unforeseen or expect the unexpected in a universe of infinite possibilities, we may find ourselves at the mercy of anyone or anything that cannot be programmed, categorized, or easily referenced.
>
> –*Agent Fox Mulder,* The X-Files

FIRST, DON'T LOSE

What is risk?

You'll get different answers depending on whom, and when, you ask. In 1999, risk didn't mean losing money; it meant making less money than someone else. What many people feared was bumping into somebody at a barbecue who was getting even richer even quicker by day trading dot-com stocks than they were. Then, quite suddenly, by 2003 risk had come to mean that the stock market might keep dropping until it wiped out whatever traces of wealth you still had left.

While its meaning may seem nearly as fickle and fluctuating as the financial markets themselves, risk has some profound and permanent attributes. The people who take the biggest gambles and make the biggest gains in a bull market are almost always the ones who get hurt the worst in the bear market that inevitably follows. (Being "right" makes speculators even more eager to take extra risk, as their confidence catches fire.) And once you lose big money, you then have to gamble even harder just to get back to where you were, like a racetrack or casino gambler who desperately doubles up after every bad bet. Unless you are phenomenally lucky, that's a recipe for disaster. No wonder, when he was asked to sum up everything he had learned in his long career about how to get rich, the legendary financier J. K.

Klingenstein of Wertheim & Co. answered simply: "Don't lose."[1] This graph shows what he meant:

FIGURE 20-1

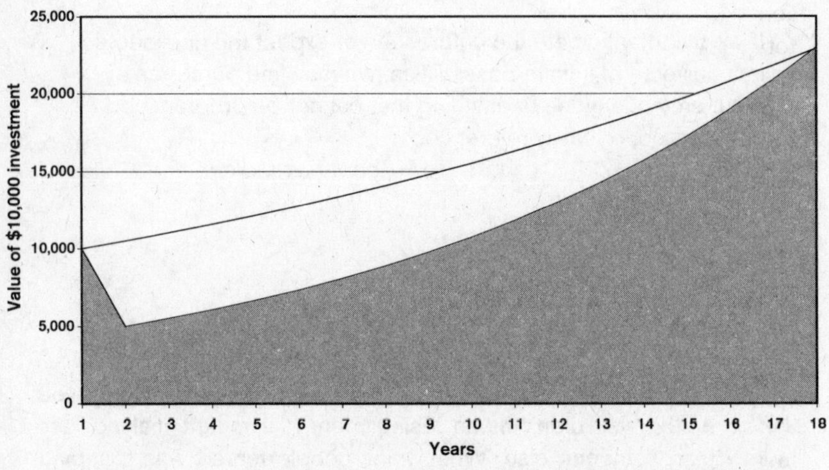

Imagine that you find a stock that you think can grow at 10% a year even if the market only grows 5% annually. Unfortunately, you are so enthusiastic that you pay too high a price, and the stock loses 50% of its value the first year. Even if the stock then generates double the market's return, it will take you more than 16 years *to overtake the market—simply because you paid too much, and lost too much, at the outset.*

Losing *some* money is an inevitable part of investing, and there's nothing you can do to prevent it. But, to be an intelligent investor, you must take responsibility for ensuring that you never lose *most or all* of your money. The Hindu goddess of wealth, Lakshmi, is often portrayed standing on tiptoe, ready to dart away in the blink of an eye. To keep her sym-

[1] As recounted by investment consultant Charles Ellis in Jason Zweig, "Wall Street's Wisest Man," *Money,* June, 2001, pp. 49–52.

bolically in place, some of Lakshmi's devotees will lash her statue down with strips of fabric or nail its feet to the floor. For the intelligent investor, Graham's "margin of safety" performs the same function: By refusing to pay too much for an investment, you minimize the chances that your wealth will ever disappear or suddenly be destroyed.

Consider this: Over the four quarters ending in December 1999, JDS Uniphase Corp., the fiber-optics company, generated $673 million in net sales, on which it lost $313 million. Its tangible assets totaled $1.5 billion. Yet, on March 7, 2000, JDS Uniphase's stock hit $153 a share, giving the company a total market value of roughly $143 billion.[2] And then, like most "New Era" stocks, it crashed. Anyone who bought it that day and still clung to it at the end of 2002 faced these prospects:

FIGURE 20-2

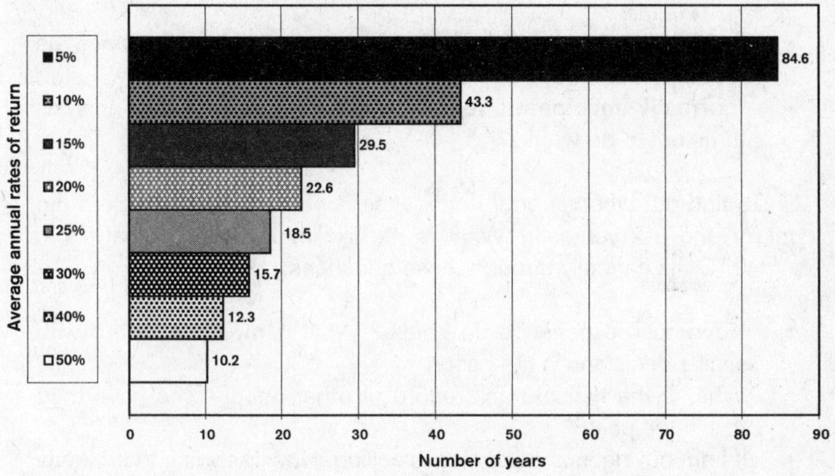

If you had bought JDS Uniphase at its peak price of $153.421 on March 7, 2000, and still held it at year-end 2002 (when it closed at $2.47), how long would it take you to get back to your purchase price at various annual average rates of return?

[2] JDS Uniphase's share price has been adjusted for later splits.

Even at a robust 10% annual rate of return, it will take more than *43 years* to break even on this overpriced purchase!

THE RISK IS NOT IN OUR STOCKS, BUT IN OURSELVES

Risk exists in another dimension: inside you. If you overestimate how well you really understand an investment, or overstate your ability to ride out a temporary plunge in prices, it doesn't matter what you own or how the market does. Ultimately, financial risk resides not in what kinds of investments you have, but in what kind of investor you are. If you want to know what risk really is, go to the nearest bathroom and step up to the mirror. *That's* risk, gazing back at you from the glass.

As you look at yourself in the mirror, what should you watch for? The Nobel-prize–winning psychologist Daniel Kahneman explains two factors that characterize good decisions:

- **"well-calibrated confidence"** (do I understand this investment as well as I think I do?)
- **"correctly-anticipated regret"** (how will I react if my analysis turns out to be wrong?).

To find out whether your confidence is well-calibrated, look in the mirror and ask yourself: "What is the likelihood that my analysis is right?" Think carefully through these questions:

- How much experience do I have? What is my track record with similar decisions in the past?
- What is the typical track record of other people who have tried this in the past?[3]
- If I am buying, someone else is selling. How likely is it that I know something that this other person (or company) does not know?
- If I am selling, someone else is buying. How likely is it that I know something that this other person (or company) does not know?

---

[3] No one who diligently researched the answer to this question, and honestly accepted the results, would ever have day traded or bought IPOs.

- Have I calculated how much this investment needs to go up for me to break even after my taxes and costs of trading?

Next, look in the mirror to find out whether you are the kind of person who correctly anticipates your regret. Start by asking: "Do I fully understand the consequences if my analysis turns out to be wrong?" Answer that question by considering these points:

- If I'm right, I could make a lot of money. But what if I'm wrong? Based on the historical performance of similar investments, how much could I *lose*?
- Do I have other investments that will tide me over if this decision turns out to be wrong? Do I already hold stocks, bonds, or funds with a proven record of going up when the kind of investment I'm considering goes down? Am I putting too much of my capital at risk with this new investment?
- When I tell myself, "You have a high tolerance for risk," how do I know? Have I ever lost a lot of money on an investment? How did it feel? Did I buy more, or did I bail out?
- Am I relying on my willpower alone to prevent me from panicking at the wrong time? Or have I controlled my own behavior in advance by diversifying, signing an investment contract, and dollar-cost averaging?

You should always remember, in the words of the psychologist Paul Slovic, that "risk is brewed from an equal dose of two ingredients–probabilities and consequences."[4] Before you invest, you must ensure that you have realistically assessed your probability of being right *and* how you will react to the consequences of being wrong.

PASCAL'S WAGER

The investment philosopher Peter Bernstein has another way of summing this up. He reaches back to Blaise Pascal, the great French mathematician and theologian (1623–1662), who created a thought

[4] Paul Slovic, "Informing and Educating the Public about Risk," *Risk Analysis,* vol. 6, no. 4 (1986), p. 412.

experiment in which an agnostic must gamble on whether or not God exists. The ante this person must put up for the wager is his conduct in this life; the ultimate payoff in the gamble is the fate of his soul in the afterlife. In this wager, Pascal asserts, "reason cannot decide" the probability of God's existence. Either God exists or He does not–and only faith, not reason, can answer that question. But while the probabilities in Pascal's wager are a toss-up, the consequences are perfectly clear and utterly certain. As Bernstein explains:

> Suppose you act as though God is and [you] lead a life of virtue and abstinence, when in fact there is no god. You will have passed up some goodies in life, but there will be rewards as well. Now suppose you act as though God is not and spend a life of sin, selfishness, and lust when in fact God is. You may have had fun and thrills during the relatively brief duration of your lifetime, but when the day of judgment rolls around you are in big trouble.[5]

Concludes Bernstein: "In making decisions under conditions of uncertainty, the consequences must dominate the probabilities. We never know the future." Thus, as Graham has reminded you in every chapter of this book, the intelligent investor must focus not just on getting the analysis right. You must also ensure against loss if your analysis turns out to be wrong–as even the best analyses will be at least some of the time. The probability of making at least one mistake at some point in your investing lifetime is virtually 100%, and those odds are entirely out of your control. However, you *do* have control over the consequences of being wrong. Many "investors" put essentially all of their money into dot-com stocks in 1999; an online survey of 1,338 Americans by *Money* Magazine in 1999 found that nearly one-tenth of them had at least 85% of their money in Internet stocks. By ignoring Graham's call for a margin of safety, these people took the wrong side of Pascal's wager. Certain that they knew the probabilities of being

---

[5] "The Wager," in Blaise Pascal, *Pensées* (Penguin Books, London and New York, 1995), pp. 122–125; Peter L. Bernstein, *Against the Gods* (John Wiley & Sons, New York, 1996), pp. 68–70; Peter L. Bernstein, "Decision Theory in Iambic Pentameter," *Economics & Portfolio Strategy,* January 1, 2003, p. 2.

right, they did nothing to protect themselves against the consequences of being wrong.

Simply by keeping your holdings permanently diversified, and refusing to fling money at Mr. Market's latest, craziest fashions, you can ensure that the consequences of your mistakes will never be catastrophic. No matter what Mr. Market throws at you, you will always be able to say, with a quiet confidence, "This, too, shall pass away."

Postscript

We know very well two partners who spent a good part of their lives handling their own and other people's funds on Wall Street. Some hard experience taught them it was better to be safe and careful rather than to try to make all the money in the world. They established a rather unique approach to security operations, which combined good profit possibilities with sound values. They avoided anything that appeared overpriced and were rather too quick to dispose of issues that had advanced to levels they deemed no longer attractive. Their portfolio was always well diversified, with more than a hundred different issues represented. In this way they did quite well through many years of ups and downs in the general market; they averaged about 20% per annum on the several millions of capital they had accepted for management, and their clients were well pleased with the results.*

In the year in which the first edition of this book appeared an opportunity was offered to the partners' fund to purchase a half-interest in a growing enterprise. For some reason the industry did not have Wall Street appeal at the time and the deal had been turned down by quite a few important houses. But the pair was impressed by the company's possibilities; what was decisive for them was that the price was moderate in relation to current earnings and asset value. The partners went ahead with the acquisition, amounting in dollars to about one-fifth of their fund. They became closely identified with the new business interest, which prospered.†

---

* The two partners Graham coyly refers to are Jerome Newman and Benjamin Graham himself.

† Graham is describing the Government Employees Insurance Co., or GEICO, in which he and Newman purchased a 50% interest in 1948, right

In fact it did so well that the price of its shares advanced to two hundred times or more the price paid for the half-interest. The advance far outstripped the actual growth in profits, and almost from the start the quotation appeared much too high in terms of the partners' own investment standards. But since they regarded the company as a sort of "family business," they continued to maintain a substantial ownership of the shares despite the spectacular price rise. A large number of participants in their funds did the same, and they became millionaires through their holding in this one enterprise, plus later-organized affiliates.*

Ironically enough, the aggregate of profits accruing from this single investment decision far exceeded the sum of all the others realized through 20 years of wide-ranging operations in the partners' specialized fields, involving much investigation, endless pondering, and countless individual decisions.

Are there morals to this story of value to the intelligent investor? An obvious one is that there are several different ways to make and keep money in Wall Street. Another, not so obvious, is that one lucky break, or one supremely shrewd decision—can we tell them apart?—may count for more than a lifetime of journeyman efforts.[1] But behind the luck, or the crucial decision, there must usually exist a background of preparation and disciplined capacity. One needs to be sufficiently established and recognized so that these opportunities will knock at his particular door. One must

---

around the time he finished writing *The Intelligent Investor.* The $712,500 that Graham and Newman put into GEICO was roughly 25% of their fund's assets at the time. Graham was a member of GEICO's board of directors for many years. In a nice twist of fate, Graham's greatest student, Warren Buffett, made an immense bet of his own on GEICO in 1976, by which time the big insurer had slid to the brink of bankruptcy. It turned out to be one of Buffett's best investments as well.

* Because of a legal technicality, Graham and Newman were directed by the U.S. Securities & Exchange Commission to "spin off," or distribute, Graham-Newman Corp.'s GEICO stake to the fund's shareholders. An investor who owned 100 shares of Graham-Newman at the beginning of 1948 (worth $11,413) and who then held on to the GEICO distribution would have had $1.66 million by 1972. GEICO's "later-organized affiliates" included Government Employees Financial Corp. and Criterion Insurance Co.

have the means, the judgment, and the courage to take advantage of them.

Of course, we cannot promise a like spectacular experience to all intelligent investors who remain both prudent and alert through the years. We are not going to end with J. J. Raskob's slogan that we made fun of at the beginning: "Everybody can be rich." But interesting possibilities abound on the financial scene, and the intelligent and enterprising investor should be able to find both enjoyment and profit in this three-ring circus. Excitement is guaranteed.

COMMENTARY ON POSTSCRIPT

Successful investing is about managing risk, not avoiding it. At first glance, when you realize that Graham put 25% of his fund into a single stock, you might think he was gambling rashly with his investors' money. But then, when you discover that Graham had painstakingly established that he could liquidate GEICO for at least what he paid for it, it becomes clear that Graham was taking very little financial risk. But he needed enormous courage to take the psychological risk of such a big bet on so unknown a stock.[1]

And today's headlines are full of fearful facts and unresolved risks: the death of the 1990s bull market, sluggish economic growth, corporate fraud, the specters of terrorism and war. "Investors don't like uncertainty," a market strategist is intoning right now on financial TV or in today's newspaper. But investors have never liked uncertainty–and yet it is the most fundamental and enduring condition of the investing world. It always has been, and it always will be. At heart, "uncertainty" and "investing" are synonyms. In the real world, no one has ever been given the ability to see that any particular time is the best time to buy stocks. Without a saving faith in the future, no one would ever invest at all. To be an investor, you must be a believer in a better tomorrow.

The most literate of investors, Graham loved the story of Ulysses, told through the poetry of Homer, Alfred Tennyson, and Dante. Late in his life, Graham relished the scene in Dante's *Inferno* when Ulysses describes inspiring his crew to sail westward into the unknown waters beyond the gates of Hercules:

---

[1] Graham's anecdote is also a powerful reminder that those of us who are not as brilliant as he was must always diversify to protect against the risk of putting too much money into a single investment. When Graham himself admits that GEICO was a "lucky break," that's a signal that most of us cannot count on being able to find such a great opportunity. To keep investing from decaying into gambling, you must diversify.

"O brothers," I said, "who after a hundred thousand
perils have reached the west,
in this little waking vigil
that still remains to our senses,
let us not choose to avoid the experience
of the unpeopled world that lies behind the sun.
Consider the seeds from which you sprang:
You were made not to live like beasts,
but to seek virtue and understanding."
With this little oration I made my shipmates
so eager for the voyage
that it would have hurt to hold them back.
And we swung our stern toward the morning
and turned our oars into wings for the wild flight.[2]

Investing, too, is an adventure; the financial future is always an uncharted world. With Graham as your guide, your lifelong investing voyage should be as safe and confident as it is adventurous.

---

[2] Dante Alighieri, *The Inferno,* Canto XXVI, lines 112–125, translated by Jason Zweig.

Appendixes

1. The Superinvestors of Graham-and-Doddsville

by Warren E. Buffett

EDITOR'S NOTE: *This article is an edited transcript of a talk given at Columbia University in 1984 commemorating the fiftieth anniversary of* Security Analysis, *written by Benjamin Graham and David L. Dodd. This specialized volume first introduced the ideas later popularized in* The Intelligent Investor. *Buffett's essay offers a fascinating study of how Graham's disciples have used Graham's value investing approach to realize phenomenal success in the stock market.*

Is the Graham and Dodd "look for values with a significant margin of safety relative to prices" approach to security analysis out of date? Many of the professors who write textbooks today say yes. They argue that the stock market is efficient; that is, that stock prices reflect everything that is known about a company's prospects and about the state of the economy. There are no undervalued stocks, these theorists argue, because there are smart security analysts who utilize all available information to ensure unfailingly appropriate prices. Investors who seem to beat the market year after year are just lucky. "If prices fully reflect available information, this sort of investment adeptness is ruled out," writes one of today's textbook authors.

Well, maybe. But I want to present to you a group of investors who have, year in and year out, beaten the Standard & Poor's 500 stock index. The hypothesis that they do this by pure chance is at least worth examining. Crucial to this examination is the fact that these winners were all well known to me and pre-identified as superior investors, the most recent identification occurring over fifteen years ago. Absent this condition—that is, if I had just recently searched among thousands of records to select a few names for you this morning—I would advise you to stop reading right here. I should add that all these records have been audited. And I should further add that I have known many of those who have invested with these managers, and the checks received by those participants over the years have matched the stated records.

Before we begin this examination, I would like you to imagine a national coin-flipping contest. Let's assume we get 225 million Americans up tomorrow morning and we ask them all to wager a dollar. They go out in the morning at sunrise, and they all call the flip of a coin. If they call correctly, they win a dollar from those who called wrong. Each day the losers drop out, and on the subsequent day the stakes build as all previous winnings are put on the line. After ten flips on ten mornings, there will be approximately 220,000 people in the United States who have correctly called ten flips in a row. They each will have won a little over $1,000.

Now this group will probably start getting a little puffed up about this, human nature being what it is. They may try to be modest, but at cocktail parties they will occasionally admit to attractive members of the opposite sex what their technique is, and what marvelous insights they bring to the field of flipping.

Assuming that the winners are getting the appropriate rewards from the losers, in another ten days we will have 215 people who have successfully called their coin flips 20 times in a row and who, by this exercise, each have turned one dollar into a little over $1 million. $225 million would have been lost, $225 million would have been won.

By then, this group will really lose their heads. They will probably write books on "How I Turned a Dollar into a Million in Twenty Days Working Thirty Seconds a Morning." Worse yet, they'll probably start jetting around the country attending seminars on efficient coin-flipping and tackling skeptical professors with, "If it can't be done, why are there 215 of us?"

But then some business school professor will probably be rude enough to bring up the fact that if 225 million orangutans had engaged in a similar exercise, the results would be much the same—215 egotistical orangutans with 20 straight winning flips.

I would argue, however, that there *are* some important differences in the examples I am going to present. For one thing, if (a) you had taken 225 million orangutans distributed roughly as the U.S. population is; if (b) 215 winners were left after 20 days; and if (c) you found that 40 came from a particular zoo in Omaha, you would be pretty sure you were on to something. So you would probably go out and ask the zookeeper about what he's feeding them, whether they had special exercises, what books they read, and who knows what else. That is, if you found any really extraordinary concentrations of success, you might want to see if you could identify concentrations of unusual characteristics that might be causal factors.

Scientific inquiry naturally follows such a pattern. If you were trying to analyze possible causes of a rare type of cancer—with, say, 1,500 cases a year in the United States—and you found that 400 of them occurred in some little mining town in Montana, you would get very interested in the water there, or the occupation of those afflicted, or other variables. You know that it's not random chance that 400 come from a small area. You would not necessarily know the causal factors, but you would know where to search.

I submit to you that there are ways of defining an origin other than geography. In addition to geographical origins, there can be what I call an *intellectual* origin. I think you will find that a disproportionate number of successful coin-flippers in the investment world came from a very small intellectual village that could be called Graham-and-Doddsville. A concentration of winners that simply cannot be explained by chance can be traced to this particular intellectual village.

Conditions could exist that would make even that concentration unimportant. Perhaps 100 people were simply imitating the coin-flipping call of some terribly persuasive personality. When he called heads, 100 followers automatically called that coin the same way. If the leader was part of the 215 left at the end, the fact that 100 came from the same intellectual origin would mean nothing. You would simply be identifying one case as a hundred cases. Similarly, let's assume that you lived in a strongly patriarchal society and every family in the United States conveniently consisted of ten members. Further assume that the patriarchal culture was so strong that, when the 225 million people went out the first day, every member of the family identified with the father's call. Now, at the end of the 20-day period, you would have 215 winners, and you would find that they came from only 21.5 families. Some naive types might say that this indicates an enormous hereditary factor as an explanation of successful coin-flipping. But, of course, it would have no significance at all because it would simply mean that you didn't have 215 individual winners, but rather 21.5 randomly distributed families who were winners.

In this group of successful investors that I want to consider, there has been a common intellectual patriarch, Ben Graham. But the children who left the house of this intellectual patriarch have called their "flips" in very different ways. They have gone to different places and bought and sold different stocks and companies, yet they have had a combined record that simply can't be explained by random chance. It certainly cannot be explained by the fact that they are all calling flips identically because a leader is signaling the calls to make. The patriarch has merely set forth the intellectual theory for making coin-calling decisions, but each student has decided on his own manner of applying the theory.

The common intellectual theme of the investors from Graham-and-Doddsville is this: they search for discrepancies between the *value* of a business and the *price* of small pieces of that business in the market. Essentially, they exploit those discrepancies without the efficient market theorist's concern as to whether the stocks are bought on Monday or Thursday, or whether it is January or July, etc. Incidentally, when businessmen buy businesses—which is just what our Graham & Dodd investors are doing through the medium of marketable stocks—I doubt that many are cranking into their purchase decision the day of the week or the month in which the transaction is going to occur. If it doesn't make any difference whether all of a business is being bought on a Monday or a Friday, I am baffled why academicians invest extensive time and effort to see whether it makes a difference when buying small pieces of those same businesses. Our Graham & Dodd investors, needless to say, do not discuss beta, the capital asset pricing model, or covariance in returns among securities. These are not subjects of any interest to them. In fact, most of them would have difficulty defining those terms. The investors simply focus on two variables: price and value.

I always find it extraordinary that so many studies are made of price and volume behavior, the stuff of chartists. Can you imagine buying an entire business simply because the price of the business had been marked *up* substantially last week and the week before? Of course, the reason a lot of studies are made of these price and volume variables is that now, in the age of computers, there are almost endless data available about them. It isn't necessarily because such studies have any utility; it's simply that the data are there and academicians have worked hard to learn the mathematical skills needed to manipulate them. Once these skills are acquired, it seems sinful not to use them, even if the usage has no utility or negative utility. As a friend said, to a man with a hammer, everything looks like a nail.

I think the group that we have identified by a common intellectual home is worthy of study. Incidentally, despite all the academic studies of the influence of such variables as price, volume, seasonality, capitalization size, etc., upon stock performance, no interest has been evidenced in studying the methods of this unusual concentration of value-oriented winners.

I begin this study of results by going back to a group of four of us who worked at Graham-Newman Corporation from 1954 through 1956. There were only four—I have not selected these names from among thousands. I offered to go to work at Graham-Newman for nothing after I took Ben Graham's class, but he turned me down as overvalued. He took this value stuff very seriously! After much pestering he finally hired me. There were three partners and four of us at the "peasant" level. All four left between 1955 and 1957 when the firm was wound up, and it's possible to trace the record of three.

The first example (see Table 1, pages 549–550) is that of Walter Schloss. Walter never went to college, but took a course from Ben Graham at night at the New York Institute of Finance. Walter left Graham-Newman in 1955 and achieved the record shown here over 28 years.

Here is what "Adam Smith"—after I told him about Walter—wrote about him in *Supermoney* (1972):

> He has no connections or access to useful information. Practically no one in Wall Street knows him and he is not fed any ideas. He looks up the numbers in the manuals and sends for the annual reports, and that's about it.
>
> In introducing me to [Schloss] Warren had also, to my mind, described himself. "He never forgets that he is handling other people's money and this reinforces his normal strong aversion to loss." He has total integrity and a realistic picture of himself. Money is real to him and stocks are real—and from this flows an attraction to the "margin of safety" principle.

Walter has diversified enormously, owning well over 100 stocks currently. He knows how to identify securities that sell at considerably less than their value to a private owner. *And that's all he does.* He doesn't worry about whether it's January, he doesn't worry about whether it's Monday, he doesn't worry about whether it's an election year. He simply says, if a business is worth a dollar and I can buy it for 40 cents, something good may happen to me. And he does it over and over and over again. He owns many more stocks than I do—and is far less interested in the underlying nature of the business: I don't seem to have very much influence on Walter. That's one of his strengths; no one has much influence on him.

The second case is Tom Knapp, who also worked at Graham-Newman with me. Tom was a chemistry major at Princeton before the war; when he came back from the war, he was a beach bum. And then one day he read that Dave Dodd was giving a night course in investments at Columbia. Tom took it on a noncredit basis, and he got so interested in the subject from taking that course that he came up and enrolled at Columbia Business School, where he got the MBA degree. He took Dodd's course again, and took Ben Graham's course. Incidentally, 35 years later I called Tom to ascertain some of the facts involved here and I found him on the beach again. The only difference is that now he owns the beach!

In 1968 Tom Knapp and Ed Anderson, also a Graham disciple, along with one or two other fellows of similar persuasion, formed Tweedy, Browne Partners, and their investment results appear in Table 2. Tweedy, Browne built that record with very wide diversification. They occasionally bought control of businesses, but the record of the passive investments is equal to the record of the control investments.

Table 3 describes the third member of the group who formed Buffett Partnership in 1957. The best thing he did was to quit in 1969. Since then, in a sense, Berkshire Hathaway has been a continuation of the partnership in some respects. There is no single index I can give you that I would feel would be a fair test of investment management at Berkshire. But I think that any way you figure it, it has been satisfactory.

Table 4 shows the record of the Sequoia Fund, which is managed by a man whom I met in 1951 in Ben Graham's class, Bill Ruane. After getting out of Harvard Business School, he went to Wall Street. Then he realized that he needed to get a real business education so he came up to take Ben's course at Columbia, where we met in early 1951. Bill's record from 1951 to 1970, working with relatively small sums, was far better than average. When I wound up Buffett Partnership I asked Bill if he would set up a fund to handle all our partners, so he set up the Sequoia Fund. He set it up at a terrible time, just when I was quitting. He went right into the two-tier market and all the difficulties that made for comparative performance for value-oriented investors. I am happy to say that my partners, to an amazing degree, not only stayed with him but added money, with the happy result shown.

There's no hindsight involved here. Bill was the only person I recommended to my partners, and I said at the time that if he achieved a four-point-per-annum advantage over the Standard & Poor's, that would be solid performance. Bill has achieved well over that, working with progressively larger sums of money. That makes things much more difficult. Size is the anchor of performance. There is no question about it. It doesn't mean you can't do better than average when you get larger, but the margin shrinks. And if you ever get so you're managing two trillion dollars, and that happens to be the amount of the total equity evaluation in the economy, don't think that you'll do better than average!

I should add that in the records we've looked at so far, throughout this whole period there was practically no duplication in these portfolios. These are men who select securities based on discrepancies between price and value, but they make their selections very differently. Walter's largest holdings have been such stalwarts as Hudson Pulp & Paper and Jeddo Highland Coal and New York Trap Rock Company and all those other names that come instantly to mind to even a casual reader of the business pages. Tweedy

Browne's selections have sunk even well below that level in terms of name recognition. On the other hand, Bill has worked with big companies. The overlap among these portfolios has been very, very low. These records do not reflect one guy calling the flip and fifty people yelling out the same thing after him.

Table 5 is the record of a friend of mine who is a Harvard Law graduate, who set up a major law firm. I ran into him in about 1960 and told him that law was fine as a hobby but he could do better. He set up a partnership quite the opposite of Walter's. His portfolio was concentrated in very few securities and therefore his record was much more volatile but it was based on the same discount-from-value approach. He was willing to accept greater peaks and valleys of performance, and he happens to be a fellow whose whole psyche goes toward concentration, with the results shown. Incidentally, this record belongs to Charlie Munger, my partner for a long time in the operation of Berkshire Hathaway. When he ran his partnership, however, his portfolio holdings were almost completely different from mine and the other fellows mentioned earlier.

Table 6 is the record of a fellow who was a pal of Charlie Munger's—another non–business school type—who was a math major at USC. He went to work for IBM after graduation and was an IBM salesman for a while. After I got to Charlie, Charlie got to him. This happens to be the record of Rick Guerin. Rick, from 1965 to 1983, against a compounded gain of 316 percent for the S&P, came off with 22,200 percent, which, probably because he lacks a business school education, he regards as statistically significant.

One sidelight here: it is extraordinary to me that the idea of buying dollar bills for 40 cents takes immediately with people or it doesn't take at all. It's like an inoculation. If it doesn't grab a person right away, I find that you can talk to him for years and show him records, and it doesn't make any difference. They just don't seem able to grasp the concept, simple as it is. A fellow like Rick Guerin, who had no formal education in business, understands immediately the value approach to investing and he's applying it five minutes later. I've never seen anyone who became a gradual convert over a ten-year period to this approach. It doesn't seem to be a matter of IQ or academic training. It's instant recognition, or it is nothing.

Table 7 is the record of Stan Perlmeter. Stan was a liberal arts major at the University of Michigan who was a partner in the advertising agency of Bozell & Jacobs. We happened to be in the same building in Omaha. In 1965 he figured out I had a better business than he did, so he left advertising. Again, it took five minutes for Stan to embrace the value approach.

Perlmeter does not own what Walter Schloss owns. He does not own what Bill Ruane owns. These are records made *independently.* But every time Perlmeter buys a stock it's because he's getting more for his money than he's paying. That's the only thing he's thinking about. He's not looking at quarterly earnings projections, he's not looking at next year's earnings, he's not thinking about what day of the week it is, he doesn't care what investment research from any place says, he's not interested in price momentum, volume, or anything. He's simply asking: What is the business worth?

Table 8 and Table 9 are the records of two pension funds I've been involved in. They are not selected from dozens of pension funds with which I have had involvement; they are the only two I have influenced. In both cases I have steered them toward value-oriented managers. Very, very few pension funds are managed from a value standpoint. Table 8 is the Washington Post Company's Pension Fund. It was with a large bank some years ago, and I suggested that they would do well to select managers who had a value orientation.

As you can see, overall they have been in the top percentile ever since they made the change. The Post told the managers to keep at least 25 percent of these funds in bonds, which would not have been necessarily the choice of these managers. So I've included the bond performance simply to illustrate that this group has no particular expertise about bonds. They wouldn't have said they did. Even with this drag of 25 percent of their fund in an area that was not their game, they were in the top percentile of fund management. The Washington Post experience does not cover a terribly long period but it does represent many investment decisions by three managers who were not identified retroactively.

Table 9 is the record of the FMC Corporation fund. I don't manage a dime of it myself but I did, in 1974, influence their decision to select value-oriented managers. Prior to that time they had selected managers much the same way as most larger companies. They now rank number one in the Becker survey of pension funds for their size over the period of time subsequent to this "conversion" to the value approach. Last year they had eight equity managers of any duration beyond a year. Seven of them had a cumulative record better than the S&P. All eight had a better record last year than the S&P. The net difference now between a median performance and the actual performance of the FMC fund over this period is $243 million. FMC attributes this to the mindset given to them about the selection of managers. Those managers are not the managers I would necessarily select but they have the common denominator of selecting securities based on value.

So these are nine records of "coin-flippers" from Graham-and-Doddsville. I haven't selected them with hindsight from among thousands. It's not like I am reciting to you the names of a bunch of lottery winners—people I had never heard of before they won the lottery. I selected these men years ago based upon their framework for investment decision-making. I knew what they had been taught and additionally I had some personal knowledge of their intellect, character, and temperament. It's very important to understand that this group has assumed far less risk than average; note their record in years when the general market was weak. While they differ greatly in style, these investors are, mentally, always *buying the business, not buying the stock.* A few of them sometimes buy whole businesses. Far more often they simply buy small pieces of businesses. Their attitude, whether buying all or a tiny piece of a business, is the same. Some of them hold portfolios with dozens of stocks; others concentrate on a handful. But all exploit the difference between the market price of a business and its intrinsic value.

I'm convinced that there is much inefficiency in the market. These Graham-and-Doddsville investors have successfully exploited gaps between price and value. When the price of a stock can be influenced by a "herd" on Wall Street with prices set at the margin by the most emotional person, or the greediest person, or the most depressed person, it is hard to argue that the market always prices rationally. In fact, market prices are frequently nonsensical.

I would like to say one important thing about risk and reward. Sometimes risk and reward are correlated in a positive fashion. If someone were to say to me, "I have here a six-shooter and I have slipped one cartridge into it. Why don't you just spin it and pull it once? If you survive, I will give you $1 million." I would decline—perhaps stating that $1 million is not enough. Then he might offer me $5 million to pull the trigger twice—now that would be a positive correlation between risk and reward!

The exact opposite is true with value investing. If you buy a dollar bill for 60 cents, it's riskier than if you buy a dollar bill for 40 cents, but the expectation of reward is greater in the latter case. The greater the potential for reward in the value portfolio, the less risk there is.

One quick example: The Washington Post Company in 1973 was selling for $80 million in the market. At the time, that day, you could have sold the assets to any one of ten buyers for not less than $400 million, probably appreciably more. The company owned the *Post, Newsweek,* plus several television stations in major markets. Those same properties are worth $2 billion now, so the person who would have paid $400 million would not have been crazy.

Now, if the stock had declined even further to a price that made the valuation $40 million instead of $80 million, its beta would have been greater. And to people who think beta measures risk, the cheaper price would have made it look riskier. This is truly Alice in Wonderland. I have never been able to figure out why it's riskier to buy $400 million worth of properties for $40 million than $80 million. And, as a matter of fact, if you buy a group of such securities and you know anything at all about business valuation, there is essentially no risk in buying $400 million for $80 million, particularly if you do it by buying ten $40 million piles for $8 million each. Since you don't have your hands on the $400 million, you want to be sure you are in with honest and reasonably competent people, but that's not a difficult job.

You also have to have the knowledge to enable you to make a very general estimate about the value of the underlying businesses. But you do not cut it close. That is what Ben Graham meant by having a margin of safety. You don't try and buy businesses worth $83 million for $80 million. You leave yourself an enormous margin. When you build a bridge, you insist it can carry 30,000 pounds, but you only drive 10,000-pound trucks across it. And that same principle works in investing.

In conclusion, some of the more commercially minded among

you may wonder why I am writing this article. Adding many converts to the value approach will perforce narrow the spreads between price and value. I can only tell you that the secret has been out for 50 years, ever since Ben Graham and Dave Dodd wrote *Security Analysis*, yet I have seen no trend toward value investing in the 35 years that I've practiced it. There seems to be some perverse human characteristic that likes to make easy things difficult. The academic world, if anything, has actually backed away from the teaching of value investing over the last 30 years. It's likely to continue that way. Ships will sail around the world but the Flat Earth Society will flourish. There will continue to be wide discrepancies between price and value in the marketplace, and those who read their Graham & Dodd will continue to prosper.

Tables 1–9 follow:

TABLE 1 Walter J. Schloss

Year	S&P Overall Gain, Including Dividends (%)	WJS Ltd Partners Overall Gain per year (%)	WJS Partnership Overall Gain per year (%)
1956	7.5	5.1	6.8
1957	–10.5	–4.7	–4.7
1958	42.1	42.1	54.6
1959	12.7	17.5	23.3
1960	–1.6	7.0	9.3
1961	26.4	21.6	28.8
1962	–10.2	8.3	11.1
1963	23.3	15.1	20.1
1964	16.5	17.1	22.8
1965	13.1	26.8	35.7
1966	–10.4	0.5	0.7
1967	26.8	25.8	34.4
1968	10.6	26.6	35.5

Standard & Poor's 28¼ year compounded gain	887.2%
WJS Limited Partners 28¼ year compounded gain	6,678.8%
WJS Partnership 28¼ year compounded gain	23,104.7%
Standard & Poor's 28¼ year annual compounded rate	8.4%
WJS Limited Partners 28¼ year annual compounded rate	16.1%
WJS Partnership 28¼ year annual compounded rate	21.3%

During the history of the Partnership it has owned over 800 issues and, at most times, has had at least 100 positions. Present assets under management approximate $45 million. The difference between returns of the partnership and returns of the limited partners is due to allocations to the general partner for management.

TABLE 1 Walter J. Schloss *(continued)*

Year	S&P Overall Gain, Including Dividends (%)	WJS Ltd Partners Overall Gain per year (%)	WJS Partnership Overall Gain per year (%)
1969	–7.5	–9.0	–9.0
1970	2.4	–8.2	–8.2
1971	14.9	25.5	28.3
1972	19.8	11.6	15.5
1973	–14.8	–8.0	–8.0
1974	–26.6	–6.2	–6.2
1975	36.9	42.7	52.2
1976	22.4	29.4	39.2
1977	–8.6	25.8	34.4
1978	7.0	36.6	48.8
1979	17.6	29.8	39.7
1980	32.1	23.3	31.1
1981	6.7	18.4	24.5
1982	20.2	24.1	32.1
1983	22.8	38.4	51.2
1984 1st Qtr.	2.3	0.8	1.1

TABLE 2 Tweedy, Browne Inc.

Period Ended (September 30)	Dow Jones* (%)	S & P 500* (%)	TBK Overall (%)	TBK Limited Partners (%)
1968 (9 mos.)	6.0	8.8	27.6	22.0
1969	–9.5	–6.2	12.7	10.0
1970	–2.5	–6.1	–1.3	–1.9
1971	20.7	20.4	20.9	16.1
1972	11.0	15.5	14.6	11.8
1973	2.9	1.0	8.3	7.5
1974	–31.8	–38.1	1.5	1.5
1975	36.9	37.8	28.8	22.0
1976	29.6	30.1	40.2	32.8
1977	–9.9	–4.0	23.4	18.7
1978	8.3	11.9	41.0	32.1
1979	7.9	12.7	25.5	20.5
1980	13.0	21.1	21.4	17.3
1981	–3.3	2.7	14.4	11.6
1982	12.5	10.1	10.2	8.2
1983	44.5	44.3	35.0	28.2
Total Return 15¾ years	191.8%	238.5%	1,661.2%	936.4%
Standard & Poor's 15¾ year annual compounded rate				7.0%
TBK Limited Partners 15¾ year annual compounded rate				16.0%
TBK Overall 15¾ year annual compounded rate				20.0%

* Includes dividends paid for both Standard & Poor's 500 Composite Index and Dow Jones Industrial Average.

TABLE 3 Buffett Partnership, Ltd.

Year	Overall Results From Dow (%)	Partnership Results (%)	Limited Partners' Results (%)
1957	–8.4	10.4	9.3
1958	38.5	40.9	32.2
1959	20.0	25.9	20.9
1960	–6.2	22.8	18.6
1961	22.4	45.9	35.9
1962	–7.6	13.9	11.9
1963	20.6	38.7	30.5
1964	18.7	27.8	22.3
1965	14.2	47.2	36.9
1966	–15.6	20.4	16.8
1967	19.0	35.9	28.4
1968	7.7	58.8	45.6
1969	–11.6	6.8	6.6
On a cumulative or compounded basis, the results are:			
1957	–8.4	10.4	9.3
1957–58	26.9	55.6	44.5
1957–59	52.3	95.9	74.7
1957–60	42.9	140.6	107.2
1957–61	74.9	251.0	181.6
1957–62	61.6	299.8	215.1
1957–63	94.9	454.5	311.2
1957–64	131.3	608.7	402.9
1957–65	164.1	943.2	588.5
1957–66	122.9	1156.0	704.2
1957–67	165.3	1606.9	932.6
1957–68	185.7	2610.6	1403.5
1957–69	152.6	2794.9	1502.7
Annual Compounded Rate	7.4	29.5	23.8

TABLE 4 Sequoia Fund, Inc.

	*Annual Percentage Change***	
Year	Sequoia Fund (%)	S&P 500 Index * (%)
1970 (from July 15)	12.1	20.6
1971	13.5	14.3
1972	3.7	18.9
1973	–24.0	–14.8
1974	–15.7	–26.4
1975	60.5	37.2
1976	72.3	23.6
1977	19.9	–7.4
1978	23.9	6.4
1979	12.1	18.2
1980	12.6	32.3
1981	21.5	–5.0
1982	31.2	21.4
1983	27.3	22.4
1984 (first quarter)	–1.6	–2.4
Entire Period	775.3%	270.0%
Compound Annual Return	17.2%	10.0%
Plus 1% Management Fee	1.0%	
Gross Investment Return	18.2%	10.0%

* Includes dividends (and capital gains distributions in the case of Sequoia Fund) treated as though reinvested.

** These figures differ slightly from the S&P figures in Table 1 because of a difference in calculation of reinvested dividends.

TABLE 5 Charles Munger

Year	Mass. Inv. Trust (%)	Investors Stock (%)	Lehman (%)	Tri–Cont. (%)	Dow (%)	Overall Partnership (%)	Limited Partners (%)
Yearly Results (1)							
1962	–9.8	–13.4	–14.4	–12.2	–7.6	30.1	20.1
1963	20.0	16.5	23.8	20.3	20.6	71.7	47.8
1964	15.9	14.3	13.6	13.3	18.7	49.7	33.1
1965	10.2	9.8	19.0	10.7	14.2	8.4	6.0
1966	–7.7	–9.9	–2.6	–6.9	–15.7	12.4	8.3
1967	20.0	22.8	28.0	25.4	19.0	56.2	37.5
1968	10.3	8.1	6.7	6.8	7.7	40.4	27.0
1969	–4.8	–7.9	–1.9	0.1	–11.6	28.3	21.3
1970	0.6	–4.1	–7.2	–1.0	8.7	–0.1	–0.1
1971	9.0	16.8	26.6	22.4	9.8	25.4	20.6
1972	11.0	15.2	23.7	21.4	18.2	8.3	7.3
1973	–12.5	–17.6	–14.3	–21.3	–23.1	–31.9	–31.9
1974	–25.5	–25.6	–30.3	–27.6	–13.1	–31.5	–31.5
1975	32.9	33.3	30.8	35.4	44.4	73.2	73.2

Compound Results (2)							
1962	–9.8	–13.4	–14.4	–12.2	–7.6	30.1	20.1
1962–3	8.2	0.9	6.0	5.6	11.5	123.4	77.5
1962–4	25.4	15.3	20.4	19.6	32.4	234.4	136.3
1962–5	38.2	26.6	43.3	32.4	51.2	262.5	150.5
1962–6	27.5	14.1	39.5	23.2	27.5	307.5	171.3
1962–7	53.0	40.1	78.5	54.5	51.8	536.5	273.0
1962–8	68.8	51.4	90.5	65.0	63.5	793.6	373.7
1962–9	60.7	39.4	86.9	65.2	44.5	1046.5	474.6
1962–70	61.7	33.7	73.4	63.5	57.1	1045.4	474.0
1962–71	76.3	56.2	119.5	100.1	72.5	1336.3	592.2
1962–72	95.7	79.9	171.5	142.9	103.9	1455.5	642.7
1962–73	71.2	48.2	132.7	91.2	77.2	959.3	405.8
1962–74	27.5	40.3	62.2	38.4	36.3	625.6	246.5
1962–75	69.4	47.0	112.2	87.4	96.8	1156.7	500.1
Average Annual Compounded Rate	3.8	2.8	5.5	4.6	5.0	19.8	13.7

TABLE 6 Pacific Partners, Ltd.

Year	S & P 500 Index (%)	Limited Partnership Results (%)	Overall Partnership Results (%)
1965	12.4	21.2	32.0
1966	–10.1	24.5	36.7
1967	23.9	120.1	180.1
1968	11.0	114.6	171.9
1969	–8.4	64.7	97.1
1970	3.9	–7.2	–7.2
1971	14.6	10.9	16.4
1972	18.9	12.8	17.1
1973	–14.8	–42.1	–42.1
1974	–26.4	–34.4	–34.4
1975	37.2	23.4	31.2
1976	23.6	127.8	127.8
1977	–7.4	20.3	27.1
1978	6.4	28.4	37.9
1979	18.2	36.1	48.2
1980	32.3	18.1	24.1
1981	–5.0	6.0	8.0
1982	21.4	24.0	32.0
1983	22.4	18.6	24.8

Standard & Poor's 19 year compounded gain	316.4%
Limited Partners 19 year compounded gain	5,530.2%
Overall Partnership 19 year compounded gain	22,200.0%
Standard & Poor's 19 year annual compounded rate	7.8%
Limited Partners 19 year annual compounded rate	23.6%
Overall Partnership 19 year annual compounded rate	32.9%

TABLE 7 Perlmeter Investments

Year	PIL Overall (%)	Limited Partner (%)
8/1–12/31/65	40.6	32.5
1966	6.4	5.1
1967	73.5	58.8
1968	65.0	52.0
1969	–13.8	–13.8
1970	–6.0	–6.0
1971	55.7	49.3
1972	23.6	18.9
1973	–28.1	–28.1
1974	–12.0	–12.0
1975	38.5	38.5
1/1–10/31/76	38.2	34.5
11/1/76–10/31/77	30.3	25.5
11/1/77–10/31/78	31.8	26.6
11/1/78–10/31/79	34.7	28.9
11/1/79–10/31/80	41.8	34.7
11/1/80–10/31/81	4.0	3.3
11/1/81–10/31/82	29.8	25.4
11/1/82–10/31/83	22.2	18.4

Total Partnership Percentage Gain 8/1/65 through 10/31/83	4277.2%
Limited Partners Percentage Gain 8/1/65 through 10/31/83	2309.5%
Annual Compound Rate of Gain Overall Partnership	23.0%
Annual Compound Rate of Gain Limited Partners	19.0%
Dow Jones Industrial Average 7/31/65 (Approximate)	882
Dow Jones Industrial Average 10/31/83 (Approximate)	1225
Approximate Compound Rate of Gain of DJI including dividends	7%

TABLE 8 The Washington Post Company, Master Trust, December 31, 1983

	Current Quarter		Year Ended		2 Years Ended*		3 Years Ended*		5 Years Ended*	
	% Ret.	Rank	% Ret.	Rank	% Ret.	Rank	% Ret.	Rank	% Ret.	Rank
All Investments										
Manager A	4.1	2	22.5	10	20.6	40	18.0	10	20.2	3
Manager B	3.2	4	34.1	1	33.0	1	28.2	1	22.6	1
Manager C	5.4	1	22.2	11	28.4	3	24.5	1	—	—
Master Trust (All Managers)	3.9	1	28.1	1	28.2	1	24.3	1	21.8	1
Common Stock										
Manager A	5.2	1	32.1	9	26.1	27	21.2	11	26.5	7
Manager B	3.6	5	52.9	1	46.2	1	37.8	1	29.3	3
Manager C	6.2	1	29.3	14	30.8	10	29.3	3	—	—
Master Trust (All Managers)	4.7	1	41.2	1	37.0	1	30.4	1	27.6	1
Bonds										
Manager A	2.7	8	17.0	1	26.6	1	19.0	1	12.2	2
Manager B	1.6	46	7.6	48	18.3	53	12.7	84	7.4	86
Manager C	3.2	4	10.4	9	24.0	3	18.9	1	—	—
Master Trust (All Managers)	2.2	11	9.7	14	21.1	14	15.2	24	9.3	30
Bonds & Cash Equivalents										
Manager A	2.5	15	12.0	5	16.1	64	15.5	21	12.9	9
Manager B	2.1	28	9.2	29	17.1	47	14.7	41	10.8	44
Manager C	3.1	6	10.2	17	22.0	2	21.6	1	—	—
Master Trust (All Managers)	2.4	14	10.2	17	17.8	20	16.2	2	12.5	9

* Annualized

Rank indicates the fund's performance against the A.C. Becker universe.

Rank is stated as a percentile: 1 = best performance, 100 = worst.

TABLE 9 FMC Corporation Pension Fund, Annual Rate of Return (Percent)

Period ending	1 Year	2 Years	3 Years	4 Years	5 Years	6 Years	7 Years	8 Years	9 Years
FMC (Bonds and Equities Combined)									
1983	23.0								*17.1
1982	22.8	13.6	16.0	16.6	15.5	12.3	13.9	16.3	
1981	5.4	13.0	15.3	13.8	10.5	12.6	15.4		
1980	21.0	19.7	16.8	11.7	14.0	17.3			
1979	18.4	14.7	8.7	12.3	16.5				
1978	11.2	4.2	10.4	16.1					
1977	–2.3	9.8	17.8						
1976	23.8	29.3							
1975	35.0							* 18.5 from equities only	
Becker large plan median									
1983	15.6								12.6
1982	21.4	11.2	13.9	13.9	12.5	9.7	10.9	12.3	
1981	1.2	10.8	11.9	10.3	7.7	8.9	10.9		
1980	20.9	NA	NA	NA	10.8	NA			
1979	13.7	NA	NA	NA	11.1				
1978	6.5	NA	NA	NA					
1977	–3.3	NA	NA						
1976	17.0	NA							
1975	24.1								

TABLE 9 FMC Corporation Pension Fund, Annual Rate of Return (Percent) *(continued)*

Period ending	1 Year	2 Years	3 Years	4 Years	5 Years	6 Years	7 Years	8 Years	9 Years
S&P 500									
1983	22.8								15.6
1982	21.5	7.3	15.1	16.0	14.0	10.2	12.0	14.9	
1981	–5.0	12.0	14.2	12.2	8.1	10.5	14.0		
1980	32.5	25.3	18.7	11.7	14.0	17.5			
1979	18.6	12.4	5.5	9.8	14.8				
1978	6.6	–0.8	6.8	13.7					
1977	7.7	6.9	16.1						
1976	23.7	30.3							
1975	37.2								

2. Important Rules Concerning Taxability of Investment Income and Security Transactions (in 1972)

Editor's note: Due to extensive changes in the rules governing such transactions, the following document is presented here for historical purposes only. When first written by Benjamin Graham in 1972, all the information therein was correct. However, intervening developments have rendered this document inaccurate for today's purposes. Following Graham's original Appendix 2 is a revised and updated version of "The Basics of Investment Taxation," which brings the reader up-to-date on the relevant rules.

Rule 1—Interest and Dividends

Interest and dividends are taxable as ordinary income except (a) income received from state, municipal, and similar obligations, which are free from Federal tax but may be subject to state tax, (b) dividends representing a return of capital, (c) certain dividends paid by investment companies (see below), and (d) the first $100 of ordinary domestic-corporation dividends.

Rule 2—Capital Gains and Losses

Short-term capital gains and losses are merged to obtain net short-term capital gain or loss. Long-term capital gains and losses are merged to obtain the net long-term capital gain or loss. If the net short-term capital gain exceeds the net long-term capital loss, 100 per cent of such excess shall be included in income. The maximum tax thereon is 25% up to $50,000 of such gains and 35% on the balance.

A net capital loss (the amount exceeding capital gains) is deductible from ordinary income to a maximum of $1,000 in the current year and in each of the next five years. Alternatively, unused losses may be applied at any time to offset capital gains. (Carry-overs of losses taken before 1970 are treated more liberally than later losses.)

Note Concerning "Regulated Investment Companies"

Most investment funds ("investment companies") take advantage of special provisions of the tax law, which enable them to be taxed substantially as partnerships. Thus if they make long-term security profits they can distribute these as "capital-gain dividends," which are reported by their shareholders in the same way as long-term gains. These carry a lower tax rate than ordinary dividends. Alternatively, such a company may elect to pay the 25% tax for the account of its shareholders and then retain the balance of the capital gains without distributing them as capital-gain dividends.

3. The Basics of Investment Taxation (Updated as of 2003)

Interest and Dividends

Interest and dividends are taxed at your ordinary-income tax rate except (a) interest received from municipal bonds, which is free from Federal income tax but may be subject to state tax, (b) dividends representing a return of capital, and (c) long-term capital-gain distributions paid by mutual funds (see below). Private-activity municipal bonds, even within a mutual fund, may subject you to the Federal alternative minimum tax.

Capital Gains and Losses

Short-term capital gains and losses are merged to obtain net short-term capital gain or loss. Long-term capital gains and losses are merged to determine your net long-term capital gain or loss. If your net short-term capital gain exceeds the net long-term capital loss, that excess is counted as ordinary income. If there is a net long-term capital gain, it is taxed at the favorable capital gains rate, generally 20%—which will fall to 18% for investments purchased after December 31, 2000, and held for more than five years.

A net capital loss is deductible from ordinary income to a maximum of $3,000 in the current year. Any capital losses in excess of $3,000 may be applied in later tax years to offset future capital gains.

Mutual Funds

As "regulated investment companies," nearly all mutual funds take advantage of special provisions of the tax law that exempt them from corporate income tax. After selling long-term holdings, mutual funds can distribute the profits as "capital-gain dividends," which their shareholders treat as long-term gains. These are taxed at a lower rate (generally 20%) than ordinary dividends (up to 39%). You should generally avoid making large new investments during the fourth quarter of each year, when these capital-gain distributions are usually distributed; otherwise you will incur tax for a gain earned by the fund before you even owned it.

4. The New Speculation in Common Stocks[1]

What I shall have to say will reflect the spending of many years in Wall Street, with their attendant varieties of experience. This has included the recurrent advent of new conditions, or a new atmosphere, which challenge the value of experience itself. It is true that one of the elements that distinguish economics, finance, and security analysis from other practical disciplines is the uncertain validity of past phenomena as a guide to the present and future. Yet we have no right to reject the lessons of the past until we have at least studied and understood them. My address today is an effort toward such understanding in a limited field—in particular, an endeavor to point out some contrasting relationships between the present and the past in our underlying attitudes toward investment and speculation in common stocks.

Let me start with a summary of my thesis. In the past the speculative elements of a common stock resided almost exclusively in the company itself; they were due to uncertainties, or fluctuating elements, or downright weaknesses in the industry, or the corporation's individual setup. These elements of speculation still exist, of course; but it may be said that they have been sensibly diminished by a number of long-term developments to which I shall refer. But in revenge a new and major element of speculation has been introduced into the common-stock arena from *outside* the companies. It comes from the attitude and viewpoint of the stock-buying public and their advisers—chiefly us security analysts. This attitude may be described in a phrase: primary emphasis upon future expectations.

Nothing will appear more logical and natural to this audience than the idea that a common stock should be valued and priced primarily on the basis of the company's expected future performance. Yet this simple-appearing concept carries with it a number of paradoxes and pitfalls. For one thing, it obliterates a good part of the older, well-established distinctions between investment and speculation. The dictionary says that "speculate" comes from the Latin "specula," a lookout. Thus it was the speculator who looked out and saw future developments coming before other people did. But today, if the investor is shrewd or well advised, he too must have his lookout on the future, or rather he mounts into a common lookout where he rubs elbows with the speculator.

Secondly, we find that, for the most part, companies with the best investment characteristics—i.e., the best credit rating—are the ones which are likely to attract the largest speculative interest in their common stocks, since everyone assumes they are guaranteed a brilliant future. Thirdly, the concept of future prospects, and particularly of continued growth in the future, invites the application of formulas out of higher mathematics to establish the present value of the favored issues. But the combination of precise formulas with highly imprecise assumptions can be used to establish, or rather to justify, practically any value one wishes, however high, for a really outstanding issue. But, paradoxically, that very fact on close examination will be seen to imply that no one value, or reasonably narrow range of values, can be counted on to establish and maintain itself for a given growth company; hence at times the market may conceivably value the growth component at a strikingly *low* figure.

Returning to my distinction between the older and newer speculative elements in common stock, we might characterize them by two outlandish but convenient words, viz.: endogenous and exogenous. Let me illustrate briefly the old-time speculative common stock, as distinguished from an investment stock, by some data relating to American Can and Pennsylvania Railroad in 1911–1913. (These appear in Benjamin Graham and David L. Dodd, *Security Analysis,* McGraw-Hill, 1940, pp. 2–3.)

In those three years the price range of "Pennsy" moved only between 53 and 65, or between 12.2 and 15 times its average earnings for the period. It showed steady profits, was paying a reliable $3 dividend, and investors were sure that it was backed by well over its par of $50 in tangible assets. By contrast, the price of American Can ranged between 9 and 47; its earnings between 7 cents and $8.86; the ratio of price to the three-year average earnings moved between 1.9 times and 10 times; it paid no dividend at all; and sophisticated investors were well aware that the $100 par value of the common represented nothing but undisclosed "water," since the preferred issue exceeded the tangible assets available for it. Thus American Can common was a representative speculative issue, because American Can Company was then a speculatively capitalized enterprise in a fluctuating and uncertain industry. Actually, American Can had a far more brilliant long-term future than Pennsylvania Railroad; but not only was this fact not suspected by investors or speculators in those days, but even if it had been it would probably have been put aside by the investors as basically irrelevant to investment policies and programs in the years 1911–1913.

Now, to expose you to the development through time of the importance of long-term prospects for investments. I should like to use as my example our most spectacular giant industrial enterprise—none other than International Business Machines, which last year entered the small group of companies with $1 billion of sales. May I introduce one or two autobiographical notes here, in order to inject a little of the personal touch into what otherwise would be an excursion into cold figures? In 1912 I had left college for a term to take charge of a research project for U.S. Express Company. We set out to find the effect on revenues of a proposed revolutionary new system of computing express rates. For this purpose we used the so-called Hollerith machines, leased out by the then Computing-Tabulating-Recording Company. They comprised card punches, card sorters, and tabulators—tools almost unknown to businessmen, then, and having their chief application in the Census Bureau. I entered Wall Street in 1914, and the next year the bonds and common stock of C.-T.-R. Company were listed on the New York Stock Exchange. Well, I had a kind of sentimental interest in that enterprise, and besides I considered myself a sort of technological expert on their products, being one of the few financial people who had seen and used them. So early in 1916 I went to the head of my firm, known as Mr. A. N., and pointed out to him that C.-T.-R. stock was selling in the middle 40s (for 105,000 shares); that it had earned $6.50 in 1915; that its book value—

including, to be sure, some nonsegregated intangibles—was $130; that it had started a $3 dividend; and that I thought rather highly of the company's products and prospects. Mr. A. N. looked at me pityingly. "Ben," said he, "do not mention that company to me again. I would not touch it with a ten-foot pole. [His favorite expression.] Its 6 per cent bonds are selling in the low 80s and they are no good. So how can the stock be any good? Everybody knows there is nothing behind it but water." (Glossary: In those days that was the ultimate of condemnation. It meant that the asset account of the balance sheet was fictitious. Many industrial companies—notably U.S. Steel—despite their $100 par, represented nothing but water, concealed in a written-up plant account. Since they had "nothing" to back them but earning power and future prospects, no self-respecting investor would give them a second thought.)

I returned to my statistician's cubbyhole, a chastened young man. Mr. A. N. was not only experienced and successful, but extremely shrewd as well. So much was I impressed by his sweeping condemnation of Computing-Tabulating-Recording that I never bought a share of it in my life, not even after its name was changed to International Business Machines in 1926.

Now let us take a look at the same company with its new name in 1926, a year of pretty high stock markets. At that time it first revealed the good-will item in its balance sheet, in the rather large sum of $13.6 million. A. N. had been right. Practically every dollar of the so-called equity behind the common in 1915 had been nothing but water. However, since that time the company had made an impressive record under the direction of T. L. Watson, Sr. Its net had risen from $691,000 to $3.7 million—over fivefold—a greater percentage gain than it was to make in any subsequent eleven-year period. It had built up a nice tangible equity for the common, and had split it 3.6 for one. It had established a $3 dividend rate for the new stock, while earnings were $6.39 thereon. You might have expected the 1926 stock market to have been pretty enthusiastic about a company with such a growth history and so strong a trade position. Let us see. The price range for that year was 31 low, 59 high. At the average of 45 it was selling at the same 7-times multiplier of earnings and the same 6.7 per cent dividend yield as it had done in 1915. At its low of 31 it was not far in excess of its tangible book value, and in that respect was far more conservatively priced than eleven years earlier.

These data illustrate, as well as any can, the persistence of the old-time investment viewpoint until the culminating years of the bull market of the 1920s. What has happened since then can be summarized by using ten-year intervals in the history of IBM. In 1936 net expanded to twice the 1926 figures, and the average multiplier rose from 7 to 17½. From 1936 to 1946 the gain was 2½ times, but the average multiplier in 1946 remained at 17½. Then the pace accelerated. The 1956 net was nearly 4 times that of 1946, and the average multiplier rose to 32½. Last year, with a further gain in net, the multiplier rose again to an average of 42, if we do not count the unconsolidated equity in the foreign subsidiary.

When we examine these recent price figures with care we see some interesting analogies and contrasts with those of forty years earlier. The one-time scandalous water, so prevalent in the balance sheets of industrial companies, has all been squeezed out—first by disclosure and then by writeoffs. But a different kind of water has been put back into the valuation by the stock market—by investors and speculators themselves. When IBM now sells at 7 times its book value, instead of 7 times earnings, the effect is practically the same as if it had no book value at all. Or the small book-value portion can be considered as a sort of minor preferred-stock component of the price, the rest representing exactly the same sort of commitment as the old-time speculator made when he bought Woolworth or U.S. Steel common entirely for their earning power and future prospects.

It is worth remarking, in passing, that in the thirty years which saw IBM transformed from a 7-times earnings to a 40-times earnings enterprise, many of what I have called the endogenous speculative aspects of our large industrial companies have tended to disappear, or at least to diminish greatly. Their financial positions are firm, their capital structures conservative: they are managed far more expertly, and even more honestly, than before. Furthermore, the requirements of complete disclosure have removed one of the important speculative elements of years ago—that derived from ignorance and mystery.

Another personal digression here. In my early years in the Street one of the favorite mystery stocks was Consolidated Gas of New York, now Consolidated Edison. It owned as a subsidiary the profitable New York Edison Company, but it reported only dividends received from this source, not its full earnings. The unreported Edison earnings supplied the mystery and the "hidden value." To my surprise I discovered that these hush-hush figures were actually on file each year with the Public Service Commission of the state. It was a simple matter to consult the records and to present the true earnings of Consolidated Gas in a magazine article. (Incidentally, the addition to profits was not spectacular.) One of my older friends said to me then: "Ben, you may think you are a great guy to supply those missing figures, but Wall Street is going to thank you for nothing. Consolidated Gas with the mystery is both more interesting and more valuable than ex-mystery. You youngsters who want to stick your noses into everything are going to ruin Wall Street."

It is true that the three M's which then supplied so much fuel to the speculative fires have now all but disappeared. These were Mystery, Manipulation, and (thin) Margins. But we security analysts have ourselves been creating valuation approaches which are so speculative in themselves as to pretty well take the place of those older speculative factors. Do we not have our own "3M's" now—none other than Minnesota Mining and Manufacturing Company—and does not this common stock illustrate perfectly the new speculation as contrasted with the old? Consider a few figures. When M. M. & M. common sold at 101 last year the market was valuing it at 44 times 1956 earnings, which happened to show no increase to speak of in 1957. The enterprise itself was valued at $1.7 billion, of which $200 million was covered by net assets, and a cool $1½ billion represented the market's appraisal of "good will." We do not know the process of calculation by which that valuation of good will was arrived at; we do know that a few months later the market revised this appraisal downward by some $450 million, or about 30 per cent. Obviously it is impossible to calculate accurately the intangible component of a splendid company such as this. It follows as a kind of mathematical law that the more important the good will or future earning-power factor the more uncertain becomes the true value of the enterprise, and therefore the more speculative inherently the common stock.

It may be well to recognize a vital difference that has developed in the valuation of these intangible factors, when we compare earlier times with today. A generation or more ago it was the standard rule, recognized both in average stock prices and in formal or legal valuations, that intangibles were to be appraised on a more conservative basis than tangibles. A good industrial company might be required to earn between 6 per cent and 8 per cent on its tangible assets, represented typically by bonds and preferred stock; but its excess earnings, or the intangible assets they gave rise to, would be valued on, say, a 15 per cent basis. (You will find approximately these ratios in the initial offering of Woolworth preferred and common stock in 1911, and in numerous others.) But what has happened since the 1920s? Essentially the exact reverse of these relationships may now be seen. A company must now typically earn about 10 per cent on its common equity to have it sell in the average market at full book value. But its excess earnings, above 10 per cent on capital, are usually valued more liberally, or at a higher multiplier, than the base earnings required to support the book value in the market. Thus a company earning 15 per cent on the equity may well sell at 13½ times earnings, or twice its net assets. This would mean that the first 10 per cent earned on capital is valued at only 10 times, but the next 5 per cent—what used to be called the "excess"—is actually valued at 20 times.

Now there is a logical reason for this reversal in valuation procedure, which is related to the newer emphasis on growth expectations. Companies that earn a high return on capital are given these liberal appraisals not only because of the good profitability itself, and the relative stability associated with it, but perhaps even more cogently because high earnings on capital generally go hand in hand with a good growth record and prospects. Thus what is really paid for nowadays in the case of highly profitable companies is not the good will in the old and restricted sense of an established name and a profitable business, but rather their assumed superior expectations of increased profits in the future.

This brings me to one or two additional mathematical aspects of the new attitude toward common-stock valuations, which I shall touch on merely in the form of brief suggestions. If, as many tests show, the earnings multiplier tends to increase with profitability—i.e., as the rate of return on book value increases—then the arithmetical consequence of this feature is that value tends to increase directly as the square of the earnings, but *inversely* the book value. Thus in an important and very real sense tangible assets have become a drag on average market value rather than a source thereof. Take a far from extreme illustration. If Company A earns $4 a share on a $20 book value, and Company B also $4 a share on $100 book value, Company A is almost certain to sell at a higher multiplier, and hence at higher price than Company B—say $60 for Company A shares and $35 for Company B shares. Thus it would not be inexact to declare that the $80 per share of greater assets for Company B are responsible for the $25 per share lower market price, since the earnings per share are assumed to be equal.

But more important than the foregoing is the general relationship between mathematics and the new approach to stock values. Given the three ingredients of (a) optimistic assumptions as to the rate of earnings growth, (b) a sufficiently long projection of this growth into the future, and (c) the miraculous workings of compound interest—lo! the security analyst is supplied with a new kind of philosopher's stone which can produce or justify any desired valuation for a really "good stock." I have commented in a recent article in the *Analysts' Journal* on the vogue of higher mathematics in bull markets, and quoted David Durand's exposition of the striking analogy between value calculations of growth stocks and the famous Petersburg Paradox, which has challenged and confused mathematicians for more than two hundred years. The point I want to make here is that there is a special paradox in the relationship between mathematics and investment attitudes on common stocks, which is this: Mathematics is ordinarily considered as producing precise and dependable results; but in the stock market the more elaborate and abstruse the mathematics the more uncertain and speculative are the conclusions we draw therefrom. In forty-four years of Wall Street experience and study I have never seen dependable calculations made about common-stock values, or related investment policies, that went beyond simple arithmetic or the most elementary algebra. Whenever calculus is brought in, or higher algebra, you could take it as a warning signal that the operator was trying to substitute theory for experience, and usually also to give to speculation the deceptive guise of investment.

The older ideas of common-stock investment may seem quite naïve to the sophisticated security analyst of today. The great emphasis was always on what we now call the defensive aspects of the company or issue—mainly the assurance that it would continue its dividend unreduced in bad times. Thus the strong railroads, which constituted the standard investment commons of fifty years ago, were actually regarded in very much the same way as the public-utility commons in recent years. If the past record indicated stability, the chief requirement was met; not too much effort was made to anticipate adverse changes of an underlying character in the future. But, conversely, especially favorable future prospects were regarded by shrewd investors as something to look for but not to pay for.

In effect this meant that the investor did not have to pay anything substantial for superior long-term prospects. He got these, virtually without extra cost, as a reward for his own superior intelligence and judgment in picking the best rather than the merely good companies. For common stocks with the same financial strength, past earnings record, and dividend stability all sold at about the same dividend yield.

This was indeed a shortsighted point of view, but it had the great advantage of making common-stock investment in the old days not only simple but also basically sound and highly profitable. Let me return for the last time to a personal note. Somewhere around 1920 our firm distributed a series of little pamphlets entitled *Lessons for Investors.* Of course it took a brash analyst in his middle twenties like myself to hit on so smug and presumptuous a title. But in one of the papers I made the casual statement that "if a common stock is a good investment it is also a good speculation." For, reasoned I, if a common stock was so sound that it carried very little risk of loss it must ordinarily be so good as to possess excellent chances for future gains. Now this was a perfectly true and even valuable discovery, but it was true only because nobody paid any attention to it. Some years later, when the public woke up to the historical merits of common stocks as long-term investments, they soon ceased to have any such merit, because the public's enthusiasm created price levels which deprived them of their built-in margin of safety, and thus drove them out of the investment class. Then, of course, the pendulum swung to the other extreme, and we soon saw one of the most respected authorities declaring (in 1931) that no common stock could *ever* be an investment.

When we view this long-range experience in perspective we find another set of paradoxes in the investor's changing attitude toward capital gains as contrasted with income. It seems a truism to say that the old-time common-stock investor was not much interested in capital gains. He bought almost entirely for safety and income, and let the speculator concern himself with price appreciation. Today we are likely to say that the more experienced and shrewd the investor, the less attention he pays to dividend returns, and the more heavily his interest centers on long-term appreciation. Yet one might argue, perversely, that precisely because the old-time investor did not concentrate on future capital appreciation he was virtually guaranteeing to himself that he would have it, at least in the field of industrial stocks. And, conversely, today's investor is so concerned with anticipating the future that he is already paying handsomely for it in advance. Thus what he has projected with so much study and care may actually happen and still not bring him any profit. If it should fail to materialize to the degree expected he may in fact be faced with a serious temporary and perhaps even permanent loss.

What *lessons*—again using the pretentious title of my 1920 pamphlet—can the analyst of 1958 learn from this linking of past with current attitudes? Not much of value, one is inclined to say. We can look back nostalgically to the good old days when we paid only for the present and could get the future for nothing—an "all this and Heaven too" combination. Shaking our heads sadly we mutter, "Those days are gone forever." Have not investors and security analysts eaten of the tree of knowledge of good and evil prospects? By so doing have they not permanently expelled themselves from that Eden where promising common stocks at reasonable prices could be plucked off the bushes? Are we doomed always to run the risk either of paying unreasonably high prices for good quality and prospects, or of getting poor quality and prospects when we pay what seems a reasonable price?

It certainly looks that way. Yet one cannot be sure even of that pessimistic dilemma. Recently, I did a little research in the long-term history of that towering enterprise, General Electric—stimulated by the arresting chart of fifty-nine years of earnings and dividends appearing in their recently published 1957 Report. These figures are not without their surprises for the knowledgeable analyst. For one thing they show that prior to 1947 the growth of G. E. was fairly modest and quite irregular. The 1946 earnings, per share adjusted, were only 30 per cent higher than in 1902—52 cents versus 40 cents—and in no year of this period were the 1902 earnings as much as doubled. Yet the price-earnings ratio rose from 9 times in 1910 and 1916 to 29 times in 1936 and again in 1946. One might say, of course, that the 1946 multiplier at least showed the well-known prescience of shrewd investors. We analysts were able to foresee then the really brilliant period of growth that was looming ahead in the next decade. Maybe so. But some of you remember that the next year, 1947, which established an impressive new high for G.E.'s per-share earnings, was marked also by an extraordinary fall in the price-earnings ratio. At its low of 32 (before the 3-for-1 split) G.E. actually sold again at only 9 times its current earnings and its average price for the year was only about 10 times earnings. Our crystal ball certainly clouded over in the short space of twelve months.

This striking reversal took place only eleven years ago. It casts some little doubt in my mind as to the complete dependability of the popular belief among analysts that prominent and promising companies will now always sell at high price-earnings ratios—that this is a fundamental fact of life for investors and they may as well accept and like it. I have no desire at all to be dogmatic on this point. All I can say is that it is not settled in my mind, and each of you must seek to settle it for yourself.

But in my concluding remarks I can say something definite about the structure of the market for various types of common stocks, in terms of their investment and speculative characteristics. In the old days the investment character of a common stock was more or less the same as, or proportionate with, that of the enterprise itself, as measured quite well by its credit rating. The lower the yield on its bonds or preferred, the more likely was the common to meet all the criteria for a satisfactory investment, and the smaller the element of speculation involved in its purchase. This relationship, between the speculative ranking of the common and the investment rating of the company, could be graphically expressed pretty much as a straight line descending from left to right. But nowadays I would describe the graph as U-shaped. At the left, where the company itself is speculative and its credit low, the common stock is of course highly speculative, just as it has always been in the past. At the right extremity, however, where the company has the highest credit rating because both its past record and future prospects are most impressive, we find that the stock market tends more or less continuously to introduce a highly speculative element into the common shares through the simple means of a price so high as to carry a fair degree of risk.

At this point I cannot forbear introducing a surprisingly relevant, if quite exaggerated, quotation on the subject which I found recently in one of Shakespeare's sonnets. It reads:

Have I not seen dwellers on form and favor
Lose all and more by paying too much rent?

Returning to my imaginary graph, it would be the center area where the speculative element in common-stock purchases would tend to reach its minimum. In this area we could find many well-established and strong companies, with a record of past growth corresponding to that of the national economy and with future prospects apparently of the same character. Such common stocks could be bought at most times, except in the upper ranges of a bull market, at moderate prices in relation to their indicated intrinsic values. As a matter of fact, because of the present tendency of investors and speculators alike to concentrate on more glamorous issues, I should hazard the statement that these middle-ground stocks tend to sell on the whole rather below their independently determinable values. They thus have a margin-of-safety factor supplied by the same market preferences and prejudices which tend to destroy the margin of safety in the more promising issues. Furthermore, in this wide array of companies there is plenty of room for penetrating analysis of the past record and for discriminating choice in the area of future prospects, to which can be added the higher assurance of safety conferred by diversification.

When Phaëthon insisted on driving the chariot of the Sun, his father, the experienced operator, gave the neophyte some advice which the latter failed to follow—to his cost. Ovid summed up Phoebus Apollo's counsel in three words:

Medius tutissimus ibis
You will go safest in the middle course

I think this principle holds good for investors and their security analyst advisers.

5. A Case History: Aetna Maintenance Co.

The first part of this history is reproduced from our 1965 edition, where it appeared under the title "A Horrible Example." The second part summarizes the later metamorphosis of the enterprise.

We think it might have a salutary effect on our readers' future attitude toward new common-stock offerings if we cited one "horrible example" here in some detail. It is taken from the first page of Standard & Poor's *Stock Guide,* and illustrates in extreme fashion the glaring weaknesses of the 1960–1962 flotations, the extraordinary overvaluations given them in the market, and the subsequent collapse.

In November 1961, 154,000 shares of Aetna Maintenance Co. common were sold to public at $9 and the price promptly advanced to $15. Before the financing the net assets per share were about $1.20, but they were increased to slightly over $3 per share by the money received for the new shares.

The sales and earnings prior to the financing were:

Year Ended	*Sales*	*Net for Common*	*Earned Per Share*
June 1961	$3,615,000	$187,000	$0.69
(June 1960)*	(1,527,000)	(25,000)	(0.09)
December 1959	2,215,000	48,000	0.17
December 1958	1,389,000	16,000	0.06
December 1957	1,083,000	21,000	0.07
December 1956	1,003,000	2,000	0.01

* For six months.

The corresponding figures after the financing were:

June 1963	$4,681,000	*$ 42,000* (def.)	*$0.11* (def.)
June 1962	4,234,000	149,000	0.36

In 1962 the price fell to 2⅔, and in 1964 it sold as low as ⅞. No dividends were paid during this period.

COMMENT: This was much too small a business for public participation. The stock was sold—and bought—on the basis of *one good year;* the results previously had been derisory. There was nothing in the nature of this highly competitive business to insure future stability. At the high price soon after issuance the heedless public was paying much more per dollar of earnings and assets than for most of our large and strong companies. This example is admittedly extreme, but it is far from unique; the instances of lesser, but inexcusable, overvaluations run into the hundreds.

Sequel 1965–1970

In 1965 new interests came into the company. The unprofitable building-maintenance business was sold out, and the company embarked in an entirely different venture: making electronic devices. The name was changed to Haydon Switch and Instrument Co. The earnings results have not been impressive. In the five years 1965–1969 the enterprise showed average earnings of only 8 cents per share of "old stock," with 34 cents earned in the best year, 1967. However, in true modern style, the company split the stock 2 for 1 in 1968. The market price also ran true to Wall Street form. It advanced from ⅞ in 1964 to the equivalent of 16½ in 1968 (after the split). The price now exceeded the record set in the enthusiastic days of 1961. This time the overvaluation was much worse than before. The stock was now selling at 52 times the earnings of its only good year, and some 200 times its average earnings. Also, the company was again to report a deficit in the very year that the new high price was established. The next year, 1969, the bid price fell to $1.

QUESTIONS: Did the idiots who paid $8+ for this stock in 1968 know anything at all about the company's previous history, its five-year earnings record, its asset value (very small)? Did they have any idea of how much—or rather how little—they were getting for their money? Did they care? Has anyone on Wall Street any responsibility at all for the regular recurrence of completely brainless, shockingly widespread, and inevitable catastrophic speculation in this kind of vehicle?

6. Tax Accounting for NVF's Acquisition of Sharon Steel Shares

1. NVF acquired 88% of Sharon stock in 1969, paying for each share $70 in NVF 5% bonds, due 1994, and warrants to buy 1½

shares of NVF at $22 per share. The initial market value of the bonds appears to have been only 43% of par, while the warrants were quoted at $10 per NVF share involved. This meant that the Sharon holders got only $30 worth of bonds but $15 worth of warrants for each share turned in, a total of $45 per share. (This was about the average price of Sharon in 1968, and also its closing price for the year.) The book value of Sharon was $60 per share. The difference between this book value and the market value of Sharon stock amounted to about $21 million on the 1,415,000 shares of Sharon acquired.

2. The accounting treatment was designed to accomplish three things: *(a)* To treat the issuance of the bonds as equivalent to a "sale" thereof at 43, giving the company an annual deduction from income for amortization of the huge bond discount of $54 million. (Actually it would be charging itself about 15% annual interest on the "proceeds" of the $99 million debenture issue.) *(b)* To offset this bond-discount charge by an approximately equal "profit," consisting of a credit to income of one-tenth of the difference between the cost price of 45 for the Sharon stock and its book value of 60. (This would correspond, in reverse fashion, to the required practice of *charging* income each year with a part of the price paid for acquisitions in *excess* of the book value of the assets acquired.) *(c)* The beauty of this arrangement would be that the company could save initially about $900,000 a year, or $1 per share, in income taxes from these two annual entries, because the amortization of bond discount could be deducted from taxable income but the amortization of "excess of equity over cost" did not have to be included in taxable income.

3. This accounting treatment is reflected in both the consolidated income account and the consolidated balance sheet of NVF for 1969, and pro forma for 1968. Since a good part of the cost of Sharon stock was to be treated as paid for by warrants, it was necessary to show the initial market value of the warrants as part of the common-stock capital figure. Thus in this case, as in no other that we know, the warrants were assigned a substantial value in the balance sheet, namely $22 million+ (but only in an explanatory note).

7. Technological Companies as Investments

In the Standard & Poor's services in mid-1971 there were listed about 200 companies with names beginning with Compu-, Data, Electro-, Scien-, Techno-. About half of these belonged to some part of the computer industry. All of them were traded in the market or had made applications to sell stock to the public.

A total of 46 such companies appeared in the S & P *Stock Guide* for September 1971. Of these, 26 were reporting deficits, only six were earning over $1 per share, and only five were paying dividends.

In the December 1968 *Stock Guide* there had appeared 45 companies with similar technological names. Tracing the sequel of this list, as shown in the September 1971 *Guide,* we find the following developments:

Total Companies	*Price Advanced*	*Price Declined Less Than Half*	*Price Declined More Than Half*	*Dropped from Stock Guide*
45	2	8	23	12

COMMENT: It is virtually certain that the many technological companies not included in the *Guide* in 1968 had a poorer subsequent record than those that were included; also that the 12 companies dropped from the list did worse than those that were retained. The harrowing results shown by these samples are no doubt reasonably indicative of the quality and price history of the entire group of "technology" issues. The phenomenal success of IBM and a few other companies was bound to produce a spate of public offerings of new issues in their fields, for which large losses were virtually guaranteed.

Endnotes

Introduction: What This Book Expects to Accomplish

1. "Letter stock" is stock not registered for sale with the Securities and Exchange Commission (SEC), and for which the buyer supplies a letter stating the purchase was for investment.
2. The foregoing are Moody's figures for AAA bonds and industrial stocks.

Chapter 1. Investment versus Speculation: Results to Be Expected by the Intelligent Investor

1. Benjamin Graham, David L. Dodd, Sidney Cottle, and Charles Tatham, McGraw-Hill, 4th. ed., 1962. A fascimile copy of the 1934 edition of *Security Analysis* was reissued in 1996 (McGraw-Hill).
2. This is quoted from *Investment and Speculation,* by Lawrence Chamberlain, published in 1931.
3. In a survey made by the Federal Reserve Board.
4. 1965 edition, p. 8.
5. We assume here a top tax bracket for the typical investor of 40% applicable to dividends and 20% applicable to capital gains.

Chapter 2. The Investor and Inflation

1. This was written before President Nixon's price-and-wage "freeze" in August 1971, followed by his "Phase 2" system of controls. These important developments would appear to confirm the views expressed above.
2. The rate earned on the Standard & Poor's index of 425 industrial stocks was about 11½% on asset value—due in part to the inclusion of the large and highly profitable IBM, which is not one of the DJIA 30 issues.

3. A chart issued by American Telephone & Telegraph in 1971 indicates that the rates charged for residential telephone services were somewhat less in 1970 than in 1960.
4. Reported in the *Wall Street Journal,* October, 1970.

Chapter 3. A Century of Stock-Market History: The Level of Stock Prices in Early 1972

1. Both Standard & Poor's and Dow Jones have separate averages for public utilities and transportation (chiefly railroad) companies. Since 1965 the New York Stock Exchange has computed an index representing the movement of all its listed common shares.
2. Made by the Center for Research in Security Prices of the University of Chicago, under a grant from the Charles E. Merrill Foundation.
3. This was first written in early 1971 with the DJIA at 940. The contrary view held generally on Wall Street was exemplified in a detailed study which reached a median valuation of 1520 for the DJIA in 1975. This would correspond to a discounted value of, say, 1200 in mid-1971. In March 1972 the DJIA was again at 940 after an intervening decline to 798. Again, Graham was right. The "detailed study" he mentions was too optimistic by an entire decade: The Dow Jones Industrial Average did not close above 1520 until December 13, 1985!

Chapter 4. General Portfolio Policy: The Defensive Investor

1. A higher tax-free yield, with sufficient safety, can be obtained from certain *Industrial Revenue Bonds,* a relative newcomer among financial inventions. They would be of interest particularly to the enterprising investor.

Chapter 5. The Defensive Investor and Common Stocks

1. *Practical Formulas for Successful Investing,* Wilfred Funk, Inc., 1953.
2. In current mathematical approaches to investment decisions, it has become standard practice to define "risk" in terms of average price variations or "volatility." See, for example, *An Introduction to Risk and Return,* by Richard A. Brealey, The M.I.T. Press, 1969. We find this use of the word "risk" more harmful than useful for sound investment decisions—because it places too much emphasis on market fluctuations.
3. All 30 companies in the DJIA met this standard in 1971.

Chapter 6. Portfolio Policy for the Enterprising Investor: Negative Approach

1. In 1970 the Milwaukee road reported a large deficit. It suspended interest payments on its income bonds, and the price of the 5% issue fell to 10.
2. For example: Cities Service $6 first preferred, not paying dividends, sold at as low as 15 in 1937 and at 27 in 1943, when the accumulations had reached $60 per share. In 1947 it was retired by exchange for $196.50 of 3% debentures for each share, and it sold as high as 186.
3. An elaborate statistical study carried on under the direction of the National Bureau of Economic Research indicates that such has actually been the case. Graham is referring to W. Braddock Hickman, *Corporate Bond Quality and Investor Experience* (Princeton University Press, 1958). Hickman's book later inspired Michael Milken of Drexel Burnham Lambert to offer massive high-yield financing to companies with less than sterling credit ratings, helping to ignite the leveraged-buyout and hostile takeover craze of the late 1980s.
4. A representative sample of 41 such issues taken from Standard & Poor's *Stock Guide* shows that five lost 90% or more of their high price, 30 lost more than half, and the entire group about two-thirds. The many not listed in the *Stock Guide* undoubtedly had a larger shrinkage on the whole.

Chapter 7. Portfolio Policy for the Enterprising Investor: The Positive Side

1. See, for example, Lucile Tomlinson, *Practical Formulas for Successful Investing;* and Sidney Cottle and W. T. Whitman, *Investment Timing: The Formula Approach,* both published in 1953.
2. A company with an ordinary record cannot, without confusing the term, be called a growth company or a "growth stock" merely because its proponent expects it to do better than the average in the future. It is just a "promising company." Graham is making a subtle but important point: If the definition of a growth stock is a company that will thrive in the future, then that's not a definition at all, but wishful thinking. It's like calling a sports team "the champions" before the season is over. This wishful thinking persists today; among mutual funds, "growth" portfolios describe their holdings as companies with "above-average growth

potential" or "favorable prospects for earnings growth." A better definition might be companies whose net earnings per share have increased by an annual average of at least 15% for at least five years running. (Meeting this definition in the past does not ensure that a company will meet it in the future.)

3. See Table 7-1.
4. Here are two age-old Wall Street proverbs that counsel such sales: "No tree grows to Heaven" and "A bull may make money, a bear may make money, but a hog never makes money."
5. Two studies are available. The first, made by H. G. Schneider, one of our students, covers the years 1917–1950 and was published in June 1951 in the *Journal of Finance.* The second was made by Drexel Firestone, members of the New York Stock Exchange, and covers the years 1933–1969. The data are given here by their kind permission.
6. See pp. 393–395, for three examples of special situations existing in 1971.

Chapter 8. The Investor and Market Fluctuations

1. Except, perhaps, in dollar-cost averaging plans begun at a reasonable price level.
2. But according to Robert M. Ross, authority on the Dow theory, the last two buy signals, shown in December 1966 and December 1970, were well below the preceding selling points.
3. The top three ratings for bonds and preferred stocks are Aaa, Aa, and A, used by Moody's, and AAA, AA, A by Standard & Poor's. There are others, going down to D.
4. This idea has already had some adoptions in Europe—e.g., by the state-owned Italian electric-energy concern on its "guaranteed floating rate loan notes," due 1980. In June 1971 it advertised in New York that the annual rate of interest paid thereon for the next six months would be 8⅛%.

   One such flexible arrangement was incorporated in The Toronto-Dominion Bank's "7%–8% debentures," due 1991, offered in June 1971. The bonds pay 7% to July 1976 and 8% thereafter, but the holder has the option to receive his principal in July 1976.

Chapter 9. Investing in Investment Funds

1. The sales charge is universally stated as a percentage of the selling price, which includes the charge, making it appear lower than if applied to net asset value. We consider this a sales gimmick unworthy of this respectable industry.
2. *The Money Managers,* by G. E. Kaplan and C. Welles, Random House, 1969.
3. See definition of "letter stock" on p. 579.
4. Title of a book first published in 1852. The volume described the "South Sea Bubble," the tulip mania, and other speculative binges of the past. It was reprinted by Bernard M. Baruch, perhaps the only continuously successful speculator of recent times, in 1932. *Comment:* That was locking the stable door after the horse was stolen. Charles Mackay's *Extraordinary Popular Delusions and the Madness of Crowds* (Metro Books, New York, 2002) was first published in 1841. Neither a light read nor always strictly accurate, it is an extensive look at how large numbers of people often believe very silly things–for instance, that iron can be transmuted into gold, that demons most often show up on Friday evenings, and that it is possible to get rich quick in the stock market. For a more factual account, consult Edward Chancellor's *Devil Take the Hindmost* (Farrar, Straus & Giroux, New York, 1999); for a lighter take, try Robert Menschel's *Markets, Mobs, and Mayhem: A Modern Look at the Madness of Crowds* (John Wiley & Sons, New York, 2002).

Chapter 10. The Investor and His Advisers

1. The examinations are given by the Institute of Chartered Financial Analysts, which is an arm of the Financial Analysts Federation. The latter now embraces constituent societies with over 50,000 members.
2. The NYSE had imposed some drastic rules of valuation (known as "haircuts") designed to minimize this danger, but apparently they did not help sufficiently.
3. New offerings may now be sold only by means of a prospectus prepared under the rules of the Securities and Exchange Commission. This document must disclose all the pertinent facts about the issue and issuer, and it is fully adequate to inform the *prudent investor* as to the exact nature of the security offered him. But the very copiousness

of the data required usually makes the prospectus of prohibitive length. It is generally agreed that only a small percentage of *individuals* buying new issues read the prospectus with thoroughness. Thus they are still acting mainly not on their own judgment but on that of the house selling them the security or on the recommendation of the individual salesman or account executive.

Chapter 11. Security Analysis for the Lay Investor: General Approach

1. Our textbook, *Security Analysis* by Benjamin Graham, David L. Dodd, Sidney Cottle, and Charles Tatham (McGraw-Hill, 4th ed., 1962), retains the title originally chosen in 1934, but it covers much of the scope of financial analysis.
2. With Charles McGolrick, Harper & Row, 1964, reissued by HarperBusiness, 1998.
3. These figures are from Salomon Bros., a large New York bond house.
4. At least not by the great body of security analysts and investors. Exceptional analysts, who can tell in advance what companies are likely to deserve intensive study and have the facilities and capability to make it, may have continued success with this work. For details of such an approach see Philip Fisher, *Common Stocks and Uncommon Profits,* Harper & Row, 1960.
5. On p. 295 we set forth a formula relating multipliers to the rate of expected growth.
6. Part of the fireworks in the price of Chrysler was undoubtedly inspired by two two-for-one stock splits taking place in the single year 1963—an unprecedented phenomenon for a major company. In the early 1980s, under Lee Iacocca, Chrysler did a three-peat, coming back from the brink of bankruptcy to become one of the best-performing stocks in America. However, identifying managers who can lead great corporate comebacks is not as easy as it seems. When Al Dunlap took over Sunbeam Corp. in 1996 after restructuring Scott Paper Co. (and driving its stock price up 225% in 18 months), Wall Street hailed him as little short of the Second Coming. Dunlap turned out to be a sham who used improper accounting and false financial statements to mislead Sunbeam's investors–including the revered money managers Michael Price and Michael Steinhardt, who had hired him. For a keen dissection of Dunlap's career, see John A. Byrne, *Chainsaw* (HarperCollins, New York, 1999).

7. Note that we do not suggest that this formula gives the "true value" of a growth stock, but only that it approximates the results of the more elaborate calculations in vogue.

Chapter 12. Things to Consider About Per-Share Earnings

1. Our recommended method of dealing with the warrant dilution is discussed below. We prefer to consider the market value of the warrants as an addition to the current market price of the common stock as a whole.

Chapter 13. A Comparison of Four Listed Companies

1. In March 1972, Emery sold at 64 times its 1971 earnings!

Chapter 14. Stock Selection for the Defensive Investor

1. Because of numerous stock splits, etc., through the years, the actual average price of the DJIA list was about $53 per share in early 1972.
2. In 1960 only two of the 29 industrial companies failed to show current assets equal to twice current liabilities, and only two failed to have net current assets exceeding their debt. By December 1970 the number in each category had grown from two to twelve.
3. But note that their combined market action from December 1970 to early 1972 was poorer than that of the DJIA. This demonstrates once again that no system or formula will guarantee superior market results. Our requirements "guarantee" only that the portfolio-buyer is getting his money's worth.
4. As a consequence we must exclude the majority of gas pipeline stocks, since these enterprises are heavily bonded. The justification for this setup is the underlying structure of purchase contracts which "guarantee" bond payments; but the considerations here may be too complicated for the needs of a defensive investor.

Chapter 15. Stock Selection for the Enterprising Investor

1. *Mutual Funds and Other Institutional Investors: A New Perspective*, I. Friend, M. Blume, and J. Crockett, McGraw-Hill, 1970. We should add that the 1966–1970 results of many of the funds we studied were

somewhat better than those of the Standard & Poor's 500-stock composite and considerably better than those of the DJIA.

2. Personal note: Many years before the stock-market pyrotechnics in that particular company the author was its "financial vice-president" at the princely salary of $3,000 per annum. It was then really in the fireworks business. In early 1929, Graham became a financial vice president of Unexcelled Manufacturing Co., the nation's largest producer of fireworks. Unexcelled later became a diversified chemical company and no longer exists in independent form.
3. The *Guide* does not show multipliers above 99. Most such would be mathematical oddities, caused by earnings just above the zero point.

Chapter 16. Convertible Issues and Warrants

1. This point is well illustrated by an offering of two issues of Ford Motor Finance Co. made simultaneously in November 1971. One was a 20-year nonconvertible bond, yielding 7½%. The other was a 25-year bond, subordinated to the first in order of claim and yielding only 4½%; but it was made convertible into Ford Motor stock, against its then price of 68½. To obtain the conversion privilege the buyer gave up 40% of income and accepted a junior-creditor position.
2. Note that in late 1971 Studebaker-Worthington common sold as low as 38 while the $5 preferred sold at or about 77. The spread had thus grown from 2 to 20 points during the year, illustrating once more the desirability of such switches and also the tendency of the stock market to neglect arithmetic. (Incidentally the small premium of the preferred over the common in December 1970 had already been made up by its higher dividend.)

Chapter 17. Four Extremely Instructive Case Histories

1. See, for example, the article "Six Flags at Half Mast," by Dr. A. J. Briloff, in *Barron's*, January 11, 1971.

Chapter 18. A Comparison of Eight Pairs of Companies

1. The reader will recall from p. 434 above that AAA Enterprises tried to enter this business, but quickly failed. Here Graham is making a pro-

found and paradoxical observation: The more money a company makes, the more likely it is to face new competition, since its high returns signal so clearly that easy money is to be had. The new competition, in turn, will lead to lower prices and smaller profits. This crucial point was overlooked by overenthusiastic Internet stock buyers, who believed that early winners would sustain their advantage indefinitely.

Chapter 19. Shareholders and Managements: Dividend Policy

1. Analytical studies have shown that in the typical case a dollar paid out in dividends had as much as four times the positive effect on market price as had a dollar of undistributed earnings. This point was well illustrated by the public-utility group for a number of years before 1950. The low-payout issues sold at low multipliers of earnings, and proved to be especially attractive buys because their dividends were later advanced. Since 1950 payout rates have been much more uniform for the industry.

Chapter 20. "Margin of Safety" as the Central Concept of Investment

1. This argument is supported by Paul Hallingby, Jr., "Speculative Opportunities in Stock-Purchase Warrants," *Analysts' Journal,* third quarter 1947.

Postscript

1. Veracity requires the admission that the deal almost fell through because the partners wanted assurance that the purchase price would be 100% covered by asset value. A future $300 million or more in market gain turned on, say, $50,000 of accounting items. By dumb luck they got what they insisted on.

Appendixes

1. Address of Benjamin Graham before the annual Convention of the National Federation of Financial Analysts Societies, May 1958.

Acknowledgments from Jason Zweig

My heartfelt gratitude goes to all who helped me update Graham's work, including: Edwin Tan of HarperCollins, whose vision and sparkling energy brought the project to light; Robert Safian, Denise Martin, and Eric Gelman of *Money* Magazine, who blessed this endeavor with their enthusiastic, patient, and unconditional support; my literary agent, the peerless John W. Wright; and the indefatigable Tara Kalwarski of *Money.* Superb ideas and critical readings came from Theodore Aronson, Kevin Johnson, Martha Ortiz, and the staff of Aronson + Johnson + Ortiz, L.P.; Peter L. Bernstein, president, Peter L. Bernstein Inc.; William Bernstein, Efficient Frontier Advisors; John C. Bogle, founder, the Vanguard Group; Charles D. Ellis, founding partner, Greenwich Associates; and Laurence B. Siegel, director of investment policy research, the Ford Foundation. I am also grateful to Warren Buffett; Nina Munk; the tireless staff of the Time Inc. Business Information Research Center; Martin Fridson, chief executive officer, FridsonVision LLC; Howard Schilit, president, Center for Financial Research & Analysis; Robert N. Veres, editor and publisher, *Inside Information;* Daniel J. Fuss, Loomis Sayles & Co.; F. Barry Nelson, Advent Capital Management; the staff of the Museum of American Financial History; Brian Mattes and Gus Sauter, the Vanguard Group; James Seidel, RIA Thomson; Camilla Altamura and Sean McLaughlin of Lipper Inc.; Alexa Auerbach of Ibbotson Associates; Annette Larson of Morningstar; Jason Bram of the Federal Reserve Bank of New York; and one fund manager who wishes to remain anonymous. Above all, I thank my wife and daughters, who bore the brunt of my months of round-the-clock work. Without their steadfast love and forbearance, nothing would have been possible.

Index